VARĀHAMIHIRA'S

BṚHAT SAṀHITĀ

बृहत्संहिता

with English Translation, Exhaustive Notes and Literary Comments

PART TWO

M. RAMAKRISHNA BHAT

MOTILAL BANARSIDASS PUBLISHERS
PRIVATE LIMITED • DELHI

First Edition : Delhi, 1982
Second Revised Edition: Delhi, 1987
Reprint : Delhi, 1993, 1997, 2003

ISBN: 81-208-1060-0 (Set)

Also available at:
MOTILAL BANARSIDASS
41 U.A. Bungalow Road, Jawahar Nagar, Delhi 110 007
8 Mahalaxmi Chamber, 22 Bhulabhai Desai Road, Mumbai 400 026
236, 9th Main III Block, Jayanagar, Bangalore 560 011
120 Royapettah High Road, Mylapore, Chennai 600 004
Sanas Plaza, 1302 Baji Rao Road, Pune 411 002
8 Camac Street, Kolkata 700 017
Ashok Rajpath, Patna 800 004
Chowk, Varanasi 221 001

Printed in India
BY JAINENDRA PRAKASH JAIN AT SHRI JAINENDRA PRESS,
A-45 NARAINA, PHASE-I, NEW DELHI 110 028
AND PUBLISHED BY NARENDRA PRAKASH JAIN FOR
MOTILAL BANARSIDASS PUBLISHERS PRIVATE LIMITED,
BUNGALOW ROAD, DELHI 110 007

PREFACE TO THE SECOND EDITION

Astrologers and lovers of Indian culture are found more and more attracted towards esoteric science handed down by ancient seers and sages, whose only aim was to help posterity that may thirst for knowledge or be anxious to get rid of its sufferings. Even in this dark age when man is generally actuated by base and selfish motives there are a few noble souls who adhere to the luminous path of *Dharma* or righteous conduct and are guided, nay inspired, by the ancient *Śāstras*, as the Lord declares in the Gītā.

The renowned works of the great *Varāhamihira*, whose *magnum opus*, the *Bṛhat Saṁhitā*, we had the good fortune of editing with English translation and notes in two volumes some time back, have great relevance even to the present scientific age. So we have great pleasure in bringing out this revised and enlarged second edition of the *Bṛhat Saṁhitā* Part II which contains an array of very interesting topics like Erotics, Iconography, Physiognomy, Preparation of Perfumes, Omens, Gemology, Zoology etc. which capture the imagination and rouse the curiosity of discerning lovers of literature. This volume is of special importance to those who fight for equality of women, inasmuch as it recognizes not only equality but superiority of woman to man. The Publishers of this work deserve the gratitude and praise of all lovers of Indian culture in general and astrology in particular for their abiding interest in propagating the ideas and ideals enshrined in ancient Indian texts.

M. R. Bhat

CONTENTS

PART II

		Page
Preface to the Second Edition		v
	Adhyāya—Chapter	
LVIII	प्रतिमालक्षणाध्याय:—Description of Idols	549
LIX	वनसम्प्रवेशाध्याय :—Entering Forest	564
LX	प्रतिमाप्रतिष्ठापनाध्याय:—Installation of Images	568
LXI	गोलक्षणम्—Features of Cows	574
LXII	श्वलक्षणम्—Characteristics of Dogs	580
LXIII	कुक्कुटलक्षणम्—Signs of Cocks	581
LXIV	कूर्मलक्षणम्—Characteristics of Tortoises	583
LXV	छागलक्षणम्—Signs of Goats	585
LXVI	अश्वलक्षणम्—Characteristics of Horses	588
LXVII	हस्तिलक्षणम्—Signs of Elephants	595
LXVIII	पुरुषलक्षणम्—Signs of Men	599
LXIX	पञ्चमहापुरुषलक्षणम्—Signs of the five great men	646
LXX	कन्यालक्षणम्—Characteristics of Maidens	660
LXXI	वस्त्रच्छेदलक्षणम्—Omens from Slits of Garments	676
LXXII	चामरलक्षणम्—Signs of Chowries	681
LXXIII	छत्रलक्षणम्—Signs of Umbrellas	684
LXXIV	स्त्रीप्रशंसाध्याय:—Praise of Women	686
LXXV	सौभाग्यकरणम्—Winning of Affection	693
LXXVI	कान्दर्पिकम्—Erotic Recipes	699
LXXVII	गन्धयुक्ति:—Preparation of perfumes	705
LXXVIII	पुंस्त्रीसमायोग:—Union of Man and Woman	719
LXXIX	शय्यासनलक्षणम्—Signs of Couches and Seats	729
LXXX	रत्नपरीक्षा—Examination of gems	737
LXXXI	मुक्तालक्षणम्—Signs of Pearls	742
LXXXII	पद्मरागलक्षणम्—Signs of Rubies	749
LXXXIII	मरकतलक्षणम्—Signs of Emeralds	752
LXXXIV	दीपलक्षणम्—Signs of Lamps	753
LXXXV	दन्तकाष्ठलक्षणम्—Token of Tooth Sticks	756
LXXXVI	शाकुनम्—Omens through Birds and Beasts	757
LXXXVII	अन्तरचक्रम्—The Circle of Quarters	785
LXXXVIII	विरुतम्—Cries of Birds and Beasts	795
LXXXIX	श्वचक्रम्—The Circle of Dogs	806

XC	शिवारुतम्—The cries of Jackals	814
XCI	मृगचेष्टितम्—Behaviour of Wild Animals	818
XCII	गवेङ्गितम्—Intention of Cows	819
XCIII	अश्वेङ्गितम्—Intention of Horses	820
XCIV	हस्तिचेष्टितम्—Attitude of Elephants	825
XCV	वायसविरुतम्—Cries of Crows	829
XCVI	शाकुनोत्तरम्—Further Omens	841
XCVII	पाकाध्यायः—Time of Fruition of Effects	861
XCVIII	नक्षत्रकर्मगुणाध्यायः—Functions and Properties of Asterisms	866
XCIX	तिथिकर्मगुणाध्यायः—Functions and Properties of Lunar Days	874
	Table of Asterisms, Lunar Days and Muhūrtas	879–882
C	करणगुणाध्यायः—Qualities of the Karaṇas	883
CI	नक्षत्रजातकाध्यायः—Effects of Birth in the Asterisms	888
CII	राशिविभागः—Division of the Zodiac	894
CIII	विवाहपटलम्—Planetary combinations at Marriage	896
CIV	ग्रहगोचराध्यायः—Transits of Planets	902
CV	रूपसत्रम्—Worship of the Stellar Deity	934
CVI	उपसंहाराध्यायः—Conclusion	939
CVII	शास्त्रानुक्रमणी—Table of Contents of the Work	942

APPENDIX

I(a)	Indian Planets Mentioned in the Bṛhat Saṁhitā	947
I(b)	Fauna Mentioned in the Text	956
II	Alberuni's Treatment of the Laghujātaka and Comets—A Critique	960
III	Fertilizers in Ancient India	967

INDEX of Verses and Prose Passages 975

Alphabetical Index of Important Words Occurring in the Text 1013

INDEX 1071

प्रतिमालक्षणाध्यायः ॥ ५८ ॥

Chapter LVIII — Description of Idols.

जालान्तरगे भानौ यदणुतरं दर्शनं रजो याति ।
तद् विन्द्यात् परमाणुं प्रथमं तद्धि प्रमाणानाम् ॥ १ ॥

The smallest particle of dust that comes to sight, when the sun passes through the interstice of a window, is to be understood as an *atom*. For, this is the smallest unit of all measurements.

[There is another definition of परमाणु:

जालान्तरगते रश्मौ यत्सूक्ष्मं दृश्यते रजः ।
तस्य त्रिंशत्तमो भागः परमाणुः स उच्यते ॥]

परमाणुरजो वालाग्रलिक्षयूकं यवोऽङ्गुलं चेति ।
अष्टगुणानि यथोत्तरमङ्गुलमेकं भवति संख्या ॥ २ ॥

An atom, a dust particle, a tip of the hair, a nit, a louse, a barley corn and a digit are in order eight times bigger than the preceding measure. One digit becomes an integer.

[The result may be tabulated as follows:

8 atoms	=	1 dust particle.
8 dust particles	=	1 tip of hair.
8 tips of hair	=	1 nit.
8 nits	=	1 louse.
8 lice	=	1 barley grain.
8 barley grains	=	1 digit.

The commentator quotes the following in support of this ;

जालान्तरगते भानौ यत्सूक्ष्मं दृश्यते रजः ।
प्रथमं तत्प्रमाणानां परमाणुं प्रचक्षते ॥
तस्माद्रजः कचाग्रं च लिक्षा यूका यवोऽङ्गुलम् ।
क्रमादष्टगुणं ज्ञेयं जिनसंख्याङ्गुलैः करः ॥]

देवागारद्वारस्याष्टांशोनस्य यस्तृतीयोंऽशः ।
तत्पिण्डिका प्रमाणं प्रतिमा तद्द्विगुणपरिमाणा ॥ ३ ॥

The height of the pedestal (of an idol) is a third of the height of the temple-door diminished by an eighth part. The idol will be twice as high as the pedestal.

[If the height of the temple-door is x cubits, the height of the pedestal would be = $\frac{7}{24}$ x cubits; and that of the idol = $\frac{7}{12}$ x cubits.]

Next he speaks of the measurements of the different parts of the idol.

स्वैरङ्गुलप्रमाणैर्द्वादश विस्तीर्णमायतं च मुखम् ।
नग्नजिता तु चतुर्दश दैर्घ्येण द्राविडं कथितम् ॥ ४ ॥

The face of an idol should be 12 digits long and broad, in terms of its own digit. According to Sage *Nagnajit*, however, its face should be 14 digits long and 12 digits broad, which is the measure prevalent in the Drāviḍa country.

['Its own digits' is explained by Utpala thus : Divide the total length of the stone or wooden piece which will cover the entire height of the idol from head to foot, into 108 equal parts. One of the parts would then be its own Aṅgula or digit.

Cf. नग्नजित्—

विस्तीर्णं द्वादश मुखं दैर्घ्येण च चतुर्दश ।
अङ्गुलानि तथा कार्यं तन्मानं द्राविडं स्मृतम् ॥]

नासाललाटचिबुकग्रीवाश्चतुरङ्गुलास्तथा कर्णौ ।
द्वे अङ्गुले च हनुनी चिबुकं च द्व्यङ्गुलं विततम् ॥५॥

The nose, forehead, chin and neck are four digits long; so are the ears. The jaws and the chin are two digits broad.

अष्टाङ्गुलं ललाटं विस्ताराद् द्व्यङ्गुलात् परे शङ्खौ ।
चतुरङ्गुलौ तु शङ्खौ कर्णौ तु द्व्यङ्गुलौ पृथुलौ ॥ ६ ॥

The forehead is eight digits in breadth. Two digits further off on both sides are the temples, being of four digits. The ears are two digits in breadth.

[According to Utpala the breadth of the temples is two digits and length four digits. I fear he has misinterpreted the expression, द्व्यङ्गुलात्परे, which means — *beyond two digits*. Otherwise the author would have used the expression, द्व्यङ्गुलौ परे शङ्खौ.]

कर्णोपान्तः कार्योऽर्धपञ्चमे भ्रूसमेन सूत्रेण ।
कर्णस्रोतः सुकुमारकं च नेत्रप्रबन्धसमम् ॥ ७ ॥

The tip of the ear should be $4\frac{1}{2}$ digits off the corner of the eye on a level with the brows. The ear-holes and the raised margin near it should lie at the same level as the corner of the eye and measure one digit.

[भ्रूसमेन is explained by the commentator thus: नेत्रमध्यगेन कर्णोपान्तः कार्यः, which means: The tip of the ear should be the meating point of a line that produces the arch of the brows, and the line that runs through the middle of the eye. We are beholden to the commentator for giving us the meaning of 'सुकुमारक'. He says further, नेत्रप्रबन्धशब्देन प्रदूषिकोच्यते.]

चतुरङ्गुलं वसिष्ठः कथयति नेत्रान्तकर्णयोर्विवरम् ।
अधरोऽङ्गुलप्रमाणस्तस्यार्धेनोत्तरोष्ठश्च ॥ ८ ॥

Sage Vasiṣṭha says that the distance between the corner of the eye and the ear should be four digits. The lower and the upper lip should be one digit and half a digit respectively in breadth.

[Cf. वसिष्ठ—

कर्णनेत्रान्तरं यच्च तद्विन्द्याच्चतुरङ्गुलम् ॥]

अर्धाङ्गुला तु गोच्छा वक्त्रं चतुरङ्गुलायतं कार्यम् ।
विपुलं तु सार्धमङ्गुलमव्यात्तं त्र्यङ्गुलं व्यात्तम् ॥ ९ ॥

The dimple above the lip should be made half a digit broad, The mouth should be four digits long and $1\frac{1}{2}$ digits broad, when closed, and three digits, when it is opened.

[Commenting on व्यात्तम् : Utpala says; विकसितं मर्त्यसिहादेस्त्र्यङ्गुलं विस्तीर्णं कार्यम् ।]

द्व्यङ्गुलतुल्यौ नासापुटौ च नासा पुटाग्रतो ज्ञेया ।
स्याद् द्व्यङ्गुलमुच्छ्रायश्चतुरङ्गुलमन्तरं चाक्ष्णोः ॥ १० ॥

The sides of the nose should measure two digits; the front part of the nose should be two digits in height and breadth. The space between the eyes is to be four digits.

द्व्यङ्गुलमितोऽक्षिकोशो द्वे नेत्रे तत्त्रिभागिका तारा ।
दृक्तारा पञ्चांशो नेत्र विकाशोऽङ्गुलं भवति ॥ ११ ॥

The socke' of the eye measures two digits; so does the eye. The pupil is one-third of the above i.e. $\frac{2}{3}$ digit; and the innermost circle of the pupil is $\frac{2}{9}$ digit. The width of the eye is one digit.

पर्यन्तात् पर्यन्तं दश भ्रुवोऽर्द्धाङ्गुलं भ्रुवोर्लेखा ।
भ्रूमध्यं द्वयङ्गुलकं भ्रूर्दैर्घ्येणाङ्गुलचतुष्कम् ॥ १२ ॥

The brows measure ten digits from end to end; the line of brows is ½ digit in width; the interval between the brows is two digits; and the length of each brow is four digits.

कार्या तु केशरेखा भ्रूबन्धसमाङ्गुलार्धविस्तीर्णा ।
नेत्रान्ते करवीरकमुपन्यसेदङ्गुलप्रमितम् ॥ १३ ॥

The line of hair should be made equal to the brows i.e. 10 digits, and half a digit thick. At the end of the eyes there should be the inner corner one digit in extent.

[The commentator explains : करवीरकं दूषिकेति प्रसिद्धम् which means the depression at the corner of the eye.]

द्वात्रिंशत्परिणाहाच्चतुर्दशायामतोऽङ्गुलानि शिरः ।
द्वादश तु चित्रकर्मणि दृश्यन्ते विंशतिरदृश्याः ॥ १४ ॥

The circumference of the head is 32 digits and its width 14 digits. In pictures, however, only 12 digits of the head are visible and the remaining 20 digits are not visible.

आस्यं सकेशनिचयं षोडश दैर्घ्येण नग्नजित्प्रोक्तम् ।
ग्रीवा दश विस्तीर्णा परिणाहाद्विंशतिः सैका ॥ १५ ॥

According to *Nagnajit* the face and the hair put together should measure 16 digits in length (i.e. 14 digits of face and 2 digits of hair-line). The neck is to be 10 digits in width and 21 digits in circumference.

[Cf. नग्नजित्—

द्वयङ्गुला केशरेखैवं मुखं स्यात् षोडशाङ्गुलम् ॥]

कण्ठाद् द्वादश हृदयं हृदयान्नाभी च तत्प्रमाणेन ।
नाभीमध्यान्मेढ्रान्तरं च तत्तुल्यमेवोक्तम् ॥ १६ ॥

The distance between the lower part of the neck and the heart is 12 digits; and the same between the heart and the navel. The distance between the centre of the navel and the male genital organ is the same as above.

[The commentator explains the second line thus:— नाभीमध्याद् मेढ्रान्तरं लिङ्गमध्यं च यावत्...। He has taken the word अन्तर in the sense of 'middle', but, it is better to take it in the sense of 'distance', though it has the first meaning also.

ऊरू चाङ्गुलमानैश्चतुर्युता विंशतिस्तथा जङ्घे ।
जानुकपिच्छे चतुरङ्गुले च पादौ च तत्तुल्यौ ॥ १७ ॥

The length of the thighs is to be 24 digits; the same is of the shanks. The knee caps are 4 digits and the feet too are of the same height.

द्वादशदीर्घौ षट् पृथुतया च पादौ त्रिकायताङ्गुष्ठौ ।
पञ्चाङ्गुलपरिणाहौ प्रदेशिनी त्र्यङ्गुलं दीर्घा ॥ १८ ॥

The feet are 12 digits long and 6 digits broad; the big toes are 3 digits in length and 5 digits in circumference; the second toe is 3 digits long.

[The commentator says that the length of the feet is measured from the heels to the roots of the big toes: पार्ष्णि प्रारभ्याङ्गुष्ठमूलं यावद् द्वादशाङ्गुलानि दीर्घौ कार्यौ ।]

अष्टांशाष्टांशोनाः शेषाङ्गुल्यः क्रमेण कर्तव्याः ।
सचतुर्थभागमङ्गुलमुत्सेधोऽङ्गुष्ठकस्योक्तः ॥ १९ ॥

The remaining three toes should be less by an eighth than the preceding one in order. The elevation of the big toe should be $1\frac{1}{4}$ digits; and that of the others less by an eighth than the preceding one in succession.

अङ्गुष्ठनखः कथितश्चतुर्थभागोनमङ्गुलं तज्ज्ञैः ।
शेषनखानामर्धाङ्गुलं क्रमात् किञ्चिदूनं वा ॥ २० ॥

Experts in sculpture have laid down that the nail of the big toe should be $\frac{3}{4}$ digit; and those of the other toes $\frac{1}{2}$ digit or a little lessened for each succeeding toe.

जङ्घाग्रे परिणाहश्चतुर्दशोक्तस्तु विस्तरात् पञ्च ।
मध्ये तु सप्त विपुला परिणाहात् त्रिगुणिताः सप्त ॥ २१ ॥

The circumference of the shanks at the end is to be 14 digits, and their breadth five digits; but in the middle they are 7 digits in width and 21 digits in circumference.

अष्टौ तु जानुमध्ये वैपुल्यं त्र्यष्टकं तु परिणाहः ।
विपुलौ चतुर्दशोरू मध्ये द्विगुणश्च तत्परिधिः ॥ २२ ॥

The width of the knee in the middle is 8 digits; its circumference, 24 digits. The thighs are 14 digits broad in the middle and their circumference is 28 digits.

कटिरष्टादश विपुला चत्वारिंशच्चतुर्युता परिधौ ।
अङ्गुलमेकं नाभी वेधेन तथा प्रमाणेन ॥ २३ ॥

The loins are 18 digits in breadth, and 44 digits in circumference. The navel is one digit both in depth and breadth.

चत्वारिंशद् द्वियुता नाभीमध्येन मध्यपरिणाहः ।
स्तनयोः षोडश चान्तरमूर्ध्वं कक्ष्ये षडङ्गुलिके ॥ २४ ॥

The circumference of the waist at the centre of the navel is 42 digits. The distance between the two paps is 16 digits. The armpits are to be at a height of 6 digits (in an oblique direction) from the paps.

अष्टावंसौ द्वादश बाहू कार्यौ तथा प्रबाहू च ।
बाहू षड्विस्तीर्णौ प्रतिबाहू त्वङ्गुलचतुष्कम ॥ २५ ॥

The extent of the shoulders should be 8 digits (from the side of the neck). The upper arms and fore-arms should measure 12 digits each in length; and 6 digits and 4 digits respectively in breadth.

षोडश बाहू मूले परिणाहाद् द्वादशाग्रहस्ते च ।
विस्तारेण करतलं षडङ्गुलं सप्त दैर्घ्येण ॥ २६ ॥

The circumference of the arms at the armpit is 16 digits, and at the wrist, 12 digits. The palm should be 6 digits in breadth and 7 digits in length.

पञ्चाङ्गुलानि मध्या प्रदेशिनी मध्यपर्वदलहीना ।
अनया तुल्या चानामिका कनिष्ठा तु पर्वोना ॥ २७ ॥

The middle finger should be 5 digits long; the fore-finger, half a joint shorter; the third finger (ring-finger), equal to the fore-finger; and the little finger, shorter by one joint.

पर्वद्वयमङ्गुष्ठः शेषाङ्गुल्यस्त्रिभिस्त्रिभिः कार्याः ।
नखपरिमाणं कार्यं सर्वासां पर्वणोऽर्धेन ॥ २८ ॥

The thumb should have two joints, while the remaining fingers, three each. The nail of each finger should measure a half of its joint.

वेशानुरूपभूषणवेषालङ्कारमूर्त्तिभिः कार्या ।
प्रतिमा लक्षणयुक्ता सन्निहिता वृद्धिदा भवति ॥ २६ ॥

An image should be made in such a way that its ornaments, dress, decorations and form conform to the traditions and practices of the country. If such an image, possessed of all good features, be installed in a place, it would bestow prosperity on the people that live in its presence.

[The principle enunciated here can be seen illustrated in the portraits and images of Indian Gods and heroes like Śrī Rāma and Hanumat that are prevalent in other countries such as Indonesia, Cambodia etc. We may remind ourselves, in this connection, of Bharata's rules regarding dress, speech etc. of dramatic characters belonging to different countries and stations: यद्देश्यं नीचपात्रं तु तद्देश्यं तस्य भाषितम् (साहित्यदर्पण VI. 465).

The rules given above occur also in the work of काश्यप—

द्वादशाङ्गुलकं वक्त्रं ललाटं चतुरङ्गुलम् ।
नासा ग्रीवा तु कर्तव्या तुल्या चैतत्प्रमाणतः ॥

शङ्खान्तरं ललाटस्य ज्ञेयमष्टाङ्गुलं पृथु ।
हनुद्वयं तु चिबुकमङ्गुलद्वितयं स्मृतम् ॥

चतुरङ्गुलिकौ कर्णौ भ्रुवावेव तथा स्मृते ।
द्व्यङ्गुलौ पृथुलौ कर्णौ भ्रूमध्यं तत्प्रमाणतः ॥

कर्णनेत्रान्तरं कुर्यात् तत्सार्धं चतुरङ्गुलम् ।
अधरोऽङ्गुलमानं तु तदर्धेनोत्तरं स्मृतम् ॥

चतुरङ्गुलकं वक्त्रं नासाग्रं द्व्यङ्गुलं स्मृतम् ।
नेत्रे द्व्यङ्गुलके दीर्घे तत्त्रिभागेन तारकः ॥

दृक्तारा पञ्चमांशेन दूषिकाङ्गुलसम्मिता ।
द्व्यङ्गुलं चाक्षिपुटकं तथा नासापुटौ स्मृतौ ॥

कर्णस्रोतोऽङ्गुलमितं सुकुमारं तथैव च ।
गोच्छा चाङ्गुलिका कार्या तत्समा केशरेखिका ॥

द्व्यङ्गुलौ तु स्मृतौ शङ्खावायतौ चतुरङ्गुलौ ।
चतुर्दशाङ्गुलः शीर्षो द्वात्रिंशत् परिणाहतः ॥

एकविंशत् स्मृता ग्रीवा विस्तारात्स्याद् दशाङ्गुला ।
कण्ठाच्चाहृदयं नाभीं मेढ्ं तद्द्वादशाङ्गुलम् ॥

ऊरू जङ्घे चतुर्विंशा जानुनी चतुरङ्गुले ।
द्वादशाङ्गुलिकौ पादौ विस्तारात्तु षडङ्गुलौ ॥
गुल्फादधोभागगतं चतुरङ्गुलमुन्नतम् ।
अङ्गुष्ठं त्र्यङ्गुलं दीर्घं पञ्चैव परिणाहतः ॥
शेषाः पादानुसारेण परिमाणं प्रकल्पयेत् ।
जङ्घाग्रे परिधिर्ज्ञेयो ह्यङ्गुलानि चतुर्दश ॥
ऊरू तद्द्विगुणौ प्रोक्तौ कटिस्तत्त्रिगुणा स्मृता ।
अङ्गुलं तु भवेन्नाभी वेधगाम्भीर्ययोरपि ॥
नाभीमध्ये परीणाहश्चत्वारिंशद्द्विसंयुतः ।
षोडश स्तनयोर्मध्यं कक्ष्ये ऊर्ध्वं षडङ्गुले ॥
अष्टाङ्गुलौ स्मृतौ स्कन्धौ बाहू विंशच्चतुर्युतौ ।
बाहू मूले षोडश स्याद्धस्ताग्रे द्वादश स्मृताः ॥
षडङ्गुलं हस्ततलं सप्त दैर्घ्येण च स्मृतम् ।
पञ्चाङ्गुला भवेन्मध्या तर्जन्यर्धाङ्गुलोनिता ॥
अनामिका च तत्तुल्या कनिष्ठा चाङ्गुलोनिता ।
सुरूपास्ताश्च कर्तव्या द्विपर्वाङ्गुष्ठिका स्मृता ॥
त्रिपर्वाङ्गुलयः शेषा नखाः पर्वार्धविस्तृताः ।
देशवेषयुतान् हस्तान् सौम्यरूपांश्च कारयेत् ॥
स्वरूपा लक्षणोपेता प्रतिमा वृद्धिदा भवेत् ॥]

दशरथतनयो रामो बलिश्च वैरोचनिः शतं विंशम् ।
द्वादशहान्या शेषाः प्रवरसमन्यूनपरिमाणाः ॥ ३० ॥

Both Śrī Rāma, son of king Daśaratha, and Bali, son of Virocana, should be made 120 digits high. The heights of other images, superior, medium and inferior ones, are less by 12 digits in succession, i.e. 108, 96 and 84 digits in order.

[The author means to say that the standard or main height of images is 108 digits and the rest are of medium and inferior height. Only two images are to be exceptions to this rule. So far measurements of different limbs have been given in terms of the standard image of 108 digits. When the height of an image is more or less than 108 digits, the measures of the limbs have to be increased or decreased as the case may be, proportionately.]

कार्योऽष्टभुजो भगवांश्चतुर्भुजो द्विभुज एव वा विष्णुः ।
श्रीवत्साङ्कितवक्षाः कौस्तुभमणिभूषितोरस्कः ॥ ३१ ॥

अतसीकुसुमश्यामः पीताम्बरनिवसनः प्रसन्नमुखः ।
कुण्डलकिरीटधारी पीनगलोरः स्थलांसभुजः ॥ ३२ ॥

खड्गगदाशरपाणिर्दक्षिणतः शान्तिदश्चतुर्थकरः ।
वामकरेषु च कार्मुकखेटकचक्राणि शङ्खश्च ॥ ३३ ॥

अथ च चतुर्भुजमिच्छति शान्तिद एको गदाधरश्चान्यः ।
दक्षिणपार्श्वे त्वेवं वामे शङ्खश्च चक्रं च ॥ ३४ ॥

द्विभुजस्य तु शान्तिकरो दक्षिणहस्तोऽपरश्च शङ्खधरः ।
एवं विष्णोः प्रतिमा कर्तव्या भूतिमिच्छद्भिः ॥ ३५ ॥

The image of Lord Nārāyaṇa must be made with eight, four or two arms. His breast must bear the *Śrivatsa* mark (a hairy circle) and be adorned with the *Kauśtubha* gem. He should be made as dark as the *Atasi* (*Linum usitatissimum*), clad in yellow robes, having a serene and gracious countenance, wearing a diadem and ear-rings, and possessed of plump neck, breast, shoulders and arms. Of the eight hands the four on the right side must have the sword, mace, arrow and the emblem of peace (the fingers being raised and the palm facing the devotees), and the four on the left side, the bow, buckler, discus and conch. In case He is desired with only four arms, the two hands on the right side will bear the emblem of peace and mace respectively; and on the left the conch and discus. If He is made with only two arms, then the right hand bestows peace and the left holds the conch. This is how the image of the Lord Viṣṇu is to be made for prosperity.

[The hairy circle on the breast of the Lord is known as *Śrivatsa*, His sword, mace, bow, discus and conch are named in order *Nandaka*, *Kaumodaki*, *Śārṅga*, *Sudarśana* and *Pāñcajanya*. The *Hand* of *Peace* is otherwise known as *Abhaya hasta*—the hand of protection, as the Lord assures His devotees 'Do not fear.']

बलदेवो हलपाणिर्मदविभ्रमलोचनश्च कर्तव्यः ।
बिभ्रत्कुण्डलमेकं शङ्खेन्दुमृणालगौरतनुः ॥ ३६ ॥

Baladeva (Śrīkṛṣṇa's elder brother) should be made having a plough in his hand, with his eyes rolling on account of intoxication, and wearing an ear-ring, his complexion being as white as conch, the Moon and lotus-stalk.

एकानंशा कार्या देवी बलदेवकृष्णयोर्मध्ये ।
कटिसंस्थितवामकरा सरोजमितरेण चोद्वहती ॥ ३७ ॥

कार्या चतुर्भुजा या वामकराभ्यां सपुस्तकं कमलम् ।
द्वाभ्यां दक्षिणपार्श्वे वरमर्थिष्वक्षसूत्रं च ॥ ३८ ॥

वामेऽथाष्टभुजायाः कमण्डलुश्चापमम्बुजं शास्त्रम् ।
वरशरदर्पणयुक्ताः सव्यभुजाः साक्षसूत्राश्च ॥ ३९ ॥

Goddess *Ekānaṁśā* should be placed between Baladeva and Śrī Kṛṣṇa, with her left hand placed on the hip and the other hand holding a lotus. If she is to be made with four arms, then her left hands should hold a book and a lotus, and her right hands, boon to the suppliants and a rosary. In case she is desired with eight arms, in the left hands she should have a water-pot, a bow, a lotus, and a book, and in the right ones, boon, an arrow, a mirror and a rosary.

[The वरदहस्त, hand of boons, and अभयहस्त, the hand of protection, are well-known gestures of hand in iconography. The *hand of boons* is the open palm with the fingers pointing downwards.]

शाम्बश्च गदाहस्तः प्रद्युम्नश्चापभृत् सुरूपश्च ।
अनयोः स्त्रियौ च कार्ये खेटकनिस्त्रिंशधारिण्यौ ॥ ४० ॥

Śāmba should be made with a mace in his hand; Pradymna, possessed of a charming personality, with a bow in his hand. Their wives also should be made with sword and shields in their hands.

[The commentator says that Śāmba has two arms. प्रद्युम्न means the God of Love.]

ब्रह्मा कमण्डलुकरश्चतुर्मुखः पङ्कजासनस्थश्च ।
स्कन्दः कुमाररूपः शक्तिधरो बर्हिकेतुश्च ॥ ४१ ॥

Brahman (creator) must have four faces, a water pot in his hand and be seated on a lotus. Skanda (or Kārttikeya) must have the appearance of a boy, hold a javelin in his hand and have a peacock for his ensign.

शुक्लश्चतुर्विषाणो द्विपो महेन्द्रस्य वज्रपाणित्वम् ।
तिर्यग् ललाटसंस्थं तृतीयमपि लोचनं चिह्नम् ॥ ४२ ॥

Indra should have a white, four tusked elephant, and the thunderbolt in his hand. He should have another mark as well viz. a third eye placed horizontally on the forehead.

[Indra, I think, is to be represented as being seated on the back of his Airāvata, the white elephant. Possibly, the transverse eye represents his thousand eyes.]

शम्भोः शिरसीन्दुकला वृषध्वजोऽक्षि च तृतीयमपि चोर्ध्वम् ।
शूलं धनुः पिनाकं वामार्धे वा गिरिसुतार्धम् ॥ ४३ ॥

A digit of the Moon should be represented on Lord Śiva's head; He should have his ensign viz. the bull; He has the third eye, vertical on the forehead; He has a trident in one hand and a bow called Pināka in the other. He may be represented as having Pārvatī for His left half.

[The अर्धनारीश्वर aspect of the Lord is very popular in sculpture. It is also highly significant in spiritual matters. It is this aspect that Kālidāsa pays homage to in his Raghuvaṁśa (I.1). In yoga both the इन्दुकला and the third eye have deep significance.]

पद्माङ्कितकरचरणः प्रसन्नमूर्तिः सुनीचकेशश्च ।
पद्मासनोपविष्टः पितेव जगतो भवति बुद्धः ॥ ४४ ॥

The Buddha should be represented seated on a lotus, as if he were the father of the world (creator), very forgiving, with hands and feet marked with lotuses, with a serene (compassionate) body and sparse hair.

[In the place of सुनीच there are two other readings सुनीत and सुनील. The first would mean, "well-trimmed" and the second "very dark."]

आजानुलम्बबाहुः श्रीवत्साङ्कः प्रशान्तमूर्तिश्च ।
दिग्वासास्तरुणो रूपवांश्च कार्योऽर्हतां देवः ॥ ४५ ॥

The God of the Jainas viz. Jina or Mahāvīra, should be represented naked, young, handsome and serene in appearance (i.e. self-controlled and free from attachment and aversion), with his arms reaching the knees and his breast bearing the *Śrivatsa* mark.

नासाललाटजङ्घोरुगण्डवक्षांसि चोन्नतानि रवेः ।
कुर्यादुदीच्यवेषं गूढं पादादुरो यावत् ॥ ४६ ॥

बिभ्राणः स्वकररुहे बाहुभ्यां पङ्कजे मुकुटधारी ।
कुण्डलभूषितवदनः प्रलम्बहारो वियद्गवृतः ॥ ४७ ॥

कमलोदरद्युतिमुखः कञ्चुकगुप्तः स्मितप्रसन्नमुखः ।
रत्नोज्ज्वलप्रभामण्डलश्च कर्तुः शुभकरोऽर्कः ॥ ४८ ॥

The Sun-God should be represented with elevated nose, forehead, shanks, thighs, cheeks and breast; He should be dressed in the northern style, covering the body from breast to foot. He holds two lotuses born of His hands, in His arms; wears a diadem; His face is beautified with ear-rings; He has a long pearl necklace and a girdle round the waist. His face is as lustrous as the interior of the lotus, His body is covered with an armour; face, pleasant with a smile, and has a halo of bright lustre of gems (or, a halo that is made very resplendent by gems on the crown). Such an image of the Sun will be beneficial to the maker (and to the worshipper).

[Next he mentions the good and evil consequences of different heights and flaws in the image of the Sun-God in particular and all images in general.

सौम्या तु हस्तमात्रा वसुदा हस्तद्वयोच्छ्रिता प्रतिमा ।
क्षेमसुभिक्षाय भवेत् त्रिचतुर्हस्तप्रमाणा या ॥ ४९ ॥

नृपभयमत्यङ्गायां हीनाङ्गायामकल्यता कर्तुः ।
शातोदर्यां क्षुद्भयमर्थविनाशः कृशाङ्गायाम् ॥ ५० ॥

मरणं तु सक्षतायां शस्त्रनिपातेन निर्दिशेत्कर्तुः ।
वामावनता पत्नीं दक्षिणविनता हिनस्त्यायुः ॥ ५१ ॥

अन्धत्वमूर्ध्वदृष्ट्या करोति चिन्तामधोमुखी दृष्टिः ।
सर्वप्रतिमास्वेवं शुभाशुभं भास्करोक्तसमम् ॥ ५२ ॥

An image of the Sun-God one cubit high is auspicious; one that is two cubits high bestows wealth; those of three and four cubits lead to happiness and abundant food respectively. If it be of larger limbs, there would be trouble from the king; if of shorter limbs, the maker would be afflicted with diseases; if of slender belly, danger of famine; if of thin limbs, loss of wealth; if there be injuries in it, the maker would be killed as a result of the fall of a weapon; if it be depressed on the left side, it would kill his wife; if on the right side, he would be deprived of his longevity if its eyes be turned upwards, he would lose his eye-sight; and they be bent downwards, it would cause worries to him. In this manner, all the good and bad effects mentioned for the image of the Sun-God will have to be applied to all images.

लिङ्गस्य वृत्तपरिधिं दैर्घ्येणासूत्र्य तत् त्रिधा विभजेत् ।
मूले तच्चतुरस्रं मध्ये त्वष्टाश्रि वृत्तमतः ॥ ५३ ॥

चतुरस्रमवनिखाते मध्यं कार्यं तु पिण्डिकाश्वभ्रे ।
दृश्योच्छ्रायेण समा समन्ततः पिण्डिका श्वभ्रात् ॥ ५४ ॥

Treat the circumference of (the round part of) the Emblem of Śiva (made of wood, stone or gem) as the height and divide it into three equal parts. The lowest part should be quadrilateral; that in the middle, octagonal; and the uppermost one, cylindrical. The quadrilateral part should be buried in the earth, the middle one, in the pit of the pedestal; and the pedestal around the pit must be equal in extent to the visible height of the Emblem.

कृशदीर्घं देशघ्नं पार्श्वविहीनं पुरस्य नाशाय ।
यस्य क्षतं भवेन्मस्तके विनाशाय तल्लिङ्गम् ॥ ५५ ॥

An Emblem of Śiva, being too thin or too tall, will destroy the country; being devoid of sides, it will ruin the town; and one with a wound on the head (i.e. top) will destroy the owner himself.

मातृगणः कर्तव्यः स्वनामदेवानुरूपकृतचिह्नः ।
रेवन्तोऽश्वारूढो मृगयाक्रीडादिपरिवारः ॥ ५६ ॥

The group of Divine Mothers should be represented with the characteristics peculiar to the Gods whose name they bear. Revanta (the Sun's son) should be shown seated on horse-back, with his attendants in hunting, sports etc.

[There are seven Mothers viz. ब्राह्मी, माहेश्वरी, कौमारी, वैष्णवी, वाराही, इन्द्राणी and चामुण्डा. Utpala, however, mentions some more viz. याम्य, वारुण्य:, कौबेर्य:, नारसिंह्य:, वैनायक्य: etc. The seven Mothers are mentioned in the सप्तशती. All these are the personified powers of the different deities. All the Mothers should be represented with charming breasts, slender waist and heavy hips, so that they may appear attractive.]

दण्डी यमो महिषगो हंसारूढश्च पाशभृद्वरुणः ।
नरवाहनः कुबेरो वामकिरीटी बृहत्कुक्षिः ॥ ५७ ॥

The God of death should be represented mounted on a buffalo, with a club in his hand; *Varuṇa*, on a swan, with a noose in his hand; and Kubera, the God of wealth, on a human being, with a pot-belly and a crown placed on the left side of the head.

[Some read खरवाहन: in the place of नरवाहन. Here the commentator gives a tip to sculptors: The author has, no doubt, laid down the rules for making images of Gods, but they should be suitably decorated and beautified according to the practices of the place, without, of course, offending the ruling regarding dimensions and characteristic features.

Cf. काश्यप—

एकदंष्ट्रो गजमुखश्चतुर्बाहुर्विनायकः ।
लम्बोदरः स्थूलदेहो नेत्रत्रयविभूषितः ।।
नवकुवलयकान्तिमक्षमालां कमलकमण्डलुदर्पणाक्षहस्ताम् ।
प्रणमत वरपीनपीठपद्मासनसुखितां परमेश्वरीं वितस्ताम् ।।
ब्रह्मा चतुर्मुखो दण्डी कृष्णाजिनकमण्डली ।
विष्णुश्चतुर्भुजः शार्ङ्गी शङ्खचक्रगदाधरः ।
श्रीवत्साङ्कः पीतवासा वनमालाविभूषितः ।।
नरसिंहः स्थूलदेहो रोमावर्तविभूषितः ।
उद्घाटितमुखः स्रग्वी वह्निकान्तिर्बृहद्भुजः ।।
वराहः सूकरमुखश्चतुर्बाहुविभूषितः ।
नीलाञ्जनचयप्रख्यो ध्यानशक्तः सुलोचनः ।।
ईश्वरो जटिलस्त्र्यक्षो वृषचन्द्राङ्कभूषितः ।
उरगेन्द्रोपवीती च कृत्तिवासाः पिनाकधृक् ।।
चण्डिकाष्टादशभुजा सर्वप्रहरणान्विता ।
त्र्यक्षा सिंहरथा धन्या महिषासुरसूदिनी ।।
मयूरवाहनः स्कन्दः शक्तिकुक्कुटधारकः ।
सुरूपदेहो विक्रान्तो देवः सेनापतिः शिशुः ।।
आदित्यस्तरुणः स्रग्वी कवची खड्गधृक् तथा ।
तेजस्वी पङ्कजकरः षड्वर्गश्च किरीटवान् ।।
ऐरावतश्चतुर्दन्तः श्वेतगात्रो महागजः ।
तदारूढो महेन्द्रस्तु वज्रहस्तो महाबलः ।।
तिर्यग्ललाटगं नेत्रं तृतीयं तस्य कारयेत् ।
नीललोहितवर्णा च शची तस्य समीपगा ।।
एवं देवगणाः सर्वे स्वायुधाभरणोज्ज्वलाः ।
कर्तव्याः स्वस्वरूपाश्च सम्पूर्णाः शुभलक्षणाः ।।
हस्तमात्रा भवेत् सौम्या द्विहस्तान्नधनप्रदा ।
सुभिक्षक्षेमदा पुण्या त्रिहस्ता तु चतुष्करा ।।
वैकल्यं कुरुते हीना कृशाङ्गी देहनाशिनी ।
मरणं सक्षतायां तु सुदीर्घा वित्तनाशिनी ।।
वामे नता हन्ति पत्नीं कर्तुर्दक्षिणभागगा ।
ऊर्ध्वदृष्टिर्नेत्ररोगं गोकर्णा स्यादधोमुखी ।।
सुरूपा सुप्रभागैव सर्वाभरणभूषिता ।
स्वायुधैश्च समायुक्ता कर्तव्या प्रतिमा शुभा ।।]

प्रमथाधिपो गजमुखः प्रलम्बजठरः कुठारधारी स्यात् ।
एकविषाणो बिभ्रन्मूलककन्दं सुनीलदलकन्दम् ॥ ५८ ॥

Lord Gaṇeśa, who is the lord of the *Pramatha* hosts of Śiva, has the face of an elephant, with a single tusk, a bulging belly, a hatchet in his hand and a radish bulb (*Raphanus sativus*) of very dark foliage and root.

[This verse does not occur in the Vārāṇaseya edition.]

प्रतिमाप्रतिष्ठापनाध्यायः ॥६०॥

Chapter LX—Installation of Images.

दिशि याम्यायां कुर्यादधिवासनमण्डपं बुधः प्राग्वा ।
तोरणचतुष्टययुतं शस्तद्रुमपल्लवच्छन्नम् ॥ १ ॥

पूर्वे भागे चित्राः स्रजः पताकाश्च मण्डपस्योक्ताः ।
आग्नेय्यां दिशि रक्ताः कृष्णाः स्युर्याम्यनैरृतयोः ॥ २ ॥

श्वेता दिश्यपरस्यां वायव्यायां तु पाण्डुरा एव ।
चित्राश्चोत्तरपार्श्वे पीताः पूर्वोत्तरे कार्याः ॥ ३ ॥

A learned man ought to construct in the south (north ?) or east the '*Platform for the Installation ceremony*' with four archways and covered with the sprouts of auspicious trees. For the eastern side of the platform variegated garlands and flags have been prescribed; for the south-eastern corner, red ones; for the southern and south-western sides, black ones; for the western side, white ones; for the north-western corner pale-white ones; for the northern side, multi-coloured ones; and for the north-eastern part, yellowish ones.

[In the first line सौम्यायां is another reading for याम्यायाम्.

The अधिवासनमण्डप is a temporary platform constructed for performing the preliminary ceremonies which include planting seeds in small earthen vessels. These ceremonies go on for a week or so until the seeds sprout up in all the vessels.]

आयुःश्रीबलजयदा दारुमयी मृण्मयी तथा प्रतिमा ।
लोकहिताय मणिमयी सौवर्णी पुष्टिदा भवति ॥ ४ ॥

रजतमयी कीर्तिकरी प्रजाविवृद्धिं करोति ताम्रमयी ।
भूलाभं तु महान्तं शैली प्रतिमाथवा लिङ्गम् ॥ ५ ॥

An image, made of wood or clay, confers longevity, prosperity, strength and victory; one made of precious stone leads to the weal of the world; one of gold bestows health or growth; one of silver, fame;

सुरदारुचन्दनशमीमधूकतरवः शुभा द्विजातीनाम् ।
क्षत्रस्यारिष्टाश्वत्थखदिरबिल्वा विवृद्धिकराः ॥ ५ ॥

वैश्यानां जीवकखदिरसिन्धुकस्यन्दनाश्च शुभफलदाः ।
तिन्दुककेसरसर्जार्जुनाम्रशालाश्च शूद्राणाम् ॥ ६ ॥

The deodar (*Cedrus deodara*) sandalwood (*Santalum album*), Śamī (*Prosopis spicigera*) and Madhūka (*Cynometra ramiflora*) are good for images to be installed by Brāhmaṇas; Ariṣṭa (*Xanthium strumarium*), Aśvattha (*Ficus religiosa*), Khadira (*Acacia catechu*) and Bilva (*Aegle marmelos*) bestow prosperity on the Kṣatriyas; Jīvaka, Khadira, Sindhuka and Syandana (Rathadru) are auspicious for Vaiśyas; and Tinduka, Kesara, Sarja, Arjuna, mango and Śāla are good for Śūdras.

[Cf. काश्यप—

सुरदारुः शमीवृक्षो मधूकश्चन्दनस्तथा ।
प्रतिष्ठार्थं ब्राह्मणानामेते प्रोक्ताः शुभावहाः ॥
अरिष्टाश्वत्थखदिरबिल्वाः क्षत्रियजातिषु ।
जीवकः खदिरश्चैव सिन्धुकः स्यन्दनस्तथा ॥
वैश्यानां शुभदाः प्रोक्तास्तिन्दुकः केसरस्तथा ।
सर्जार्जुनाम्रशालाश्च शूद्राणां शुभदाः स्मृताः ॥]

लिङ्गं वा प्रतिमा वा द्रुमवत् स्थाप्या यथादिशं यस्मात् ।
तस्माच्चिह्नयितव्या दिशो द्रुमस्योर्ध्वमथवाधः ॥ ७ ॥

Since an Emblem of Śiva or any image should be installed according to the directions of the tree, the different directions as well as the upper and lower parts should be marked on the tree.

[The different directions and tip and bottom of the tree should be marked, so that the idol may have the eastern part for its face, the western one for its back, the lower part for its feet and upper one for its head. If the image is made contrary to the directions of the tree, it will prove harmful to the maker as well as to the worshipper.

Cf. काश्यप—

वृक्षवत्प्रतिमा कार्या प्राग्भागाद्युपलक्षिता ।
पादाः पादेषु कर्तव्याः शीर्षमूर्ध्वे तु कारयेत् ॥]

परमान्नमोदकौदनदधिपललोल्लोपिकादिभिर्भक्ष्यैः ।
मद्यैः कुसुमैर्धूपैर्गन्धैश्च तरुं समभ्यर्च्य ॥ ८ ॥

सुरपितृपिशाचराक्षसभुजगासुरगणविनायकाद्यानाम् ।
कृत्वा रात्रौ पूजां वृक्षं संस्पृश्य च ब्रूयात् ॥ ९ ॥

After worshipping at night the tree with milk porridge, sweets, rice, curds, semi-ground sesamum seeds, eatables of various kinds, wine, flowers, incenses and perfumes, Gods, *manes*, goblins, demons, serpents, Asuras, Śiva's hosts, Gaṇeśa and others should be worshipped. Thereafter, touching the tree, one should recite the following hymn:

[Refer to XLIII. 17-18 for a similar idea. उल्लोपिका is some edible. Utpala satisfies himself and others by saying उल्लोपिका: प्रसिद्धा:.]

अर्चार्थममुकस्य त्वं देवस्य परिकल्पितः ।
नमस्ते वृक्ष पूजेयं विधिवत् सम्प्रगृह्यताम् ॥ १० ॥

यानीह भूतानि वसन्ति तानि बलिं गृहीत्वा विधिवत्प्रयुक्तम् ।
अन्यत्र वासं परिकल्पयन्तु क्षमन्तु तान्यद्य नमोऽस्तु तेभ्यः ॥ ११ ॥

'Oh Tree, thou hast been selected for the worship (through an image) of the particular Deity. Salutation to thee! This worship offered by me in accordance with the scriptural rules may kindly be accepted by thee. May all those beings that dwell in this tree accept the offerings made according to rules, and then depart to another tree for residing. May they pardon us now! We bow to them.'

वृक्षं प्रभाते सलिलेन सिक्त्वा पूर्वोत्तरस्यां दिशि सन्निकृत्य ।
मध्वाज्यदिग्धेन कुठारकेण प्रदक्षिणं शेषमतो निहन्यात् ॥ १२ ॥

In the morning the tree should be watered, and then cut on the north-eastern side with an axe whose blade has been smeared with honey and ghee. The remaining parts should be cut in a clockwise manner.

[The metre is उपजाति in this and the other two verses.]

पूर्वेण पूर्वोत्तरतोऽथवोदक् पतेद्यदा वृद्धिकरस्तदा स्यात् ।
आग्नेयकोणात्क्रमशोऽग्निदाहरुग्रोगरोगास्तुरगक्षयश्च ॥ १३ ॥

Should the tree fall on the east, norh-east or north, it would bring prosperity. On the other hand, if it should fall on the south-east, south, south-west, west and north-west, there would be outbreak of fires, disease, disease, disease and destruction of horses respectively (according to Sage Garga).

यन्नोक्तमस्मिन्वनसम्प्रवेशे निपातविच्छेदनवृक्षगर्भाः ।
इन्द्रध्वजे वास्तुनि च प्रदिष्टाः पूर्वं मया तेऽत्र तथैव योज्याः ॥ १४ ॥

Whatever has not been mentioned here in connection with the topic of 'Entering forest' viz. the fall of trees the cutting (XLIII 19-20) and interior of trees has already been explained by me in connection 'with Indra's Banner' and 'House-building' (LIII. 122-123). All those ideas have to be applied here too.

[There is practically nothing new in this chapter except the important principle about the directions of the image, given in verse 7.]

———

प्रतिमाप्रतिष्ठापनाध्यायः ॥६०॥

Chapter LX—Installation of Images.

दिशि याम्यायां कुर्यादधिवासनमण्डपं बुधः प्राग्वा ।
तोरणचतुष्टययुतं शस्तद्रुमपल्लवच्छन्नम् ॥ १ ॥

पूर्वे भागे चित्राः स्रजः पताकाश्च मण्डपस्योक्ताः ।
आग्नेय्यां दिशि रक्ताः कृष्णाः स्युर्याम्यनैर्ऋतयोः ॥ २ ॥

श्वेता दिश्यपरस्यां वायव्यायां तु पाण्डुरा एव ।
चित्राश्चोत्तरपार्श्वे पीताः पूर्वोत्तरे कार्याः ॥ ३ ॥

A learned man ought to construct in the south (north ?) or east the '*Platform for the Installation ceremony*' with four archways and covered with the sprouts of auspicious trees. For the eastern side of the platform variegated garlands and flags have been prescribed; for the south-eastern corner, red ones; for the southern and south-western sides, black ones; for the western side, white ones; for the north-western corner pale-white ones; for the northern side, multi-coloured ones; and for the north-eastern part, yellowish ones.

[In the first line सौम्यायां is another reading for याम्यायाम्.

The अधिवासनमण्डप is a temporary platform constructed for performing the preliminary ceremonies which include planting seeds in small earthen vessels. These ceremonies go on for a week or so until the seeds sprout up in all the vessels.]

आयुःश्रीबलजयदा दारुमयी मृण्मयी तथा प्रतिमा ।
लोकहिताय मणिमयी सौवर्णी पुष्टिदा भवति ॥ ४ ॥

रजतमयी कीर्तिकरी प्रजाविवृद्धिं करोति ताम्रमयी ।
भूलाभं तु महान्तं शैली प्रतिमाथवा लिङ्गम् ॥ ५ ॥

An image, made of wood or clay, confers longevity, prosperity, strength and victory; one made of precious stone leads to the weal of the world; one of gold bestows health or growth; one of silver, fame;

one of copper, increase or prosperity, of children; and an idol or Emblem of Śiva made of stone, influx of immense landed property.

[Cf. काश्यप—

यार्चा मृद्दारुसम्भूता सायुःश्रीबलदा मता ।
सौवर्णी पुष्टिदा ज्ञेया रत्नजा हितकारिणी ॥
राजती कीर्तिदा ज्ञेया ताम्रजा जनवर्धिनी ।
महत् करोति भूलाभं यार्चा पाषाणनिर्मिता ॥]

शङ्कूपहता प्रतिमा प्रधानपुरुषं कुलं च घातयति ।
श्वभ्रोपहता रोगानुपद्रवांश्च क्षयं कुरुते ॥ ६ ॥

An image being hurt by a wedge would destroy the chieftain and family; one being damaged by a hole would cause diseases, troubles and ruin.

[Cf. काश्यप—

यार्चा शङ्कूहता सा तु प्रधानकुलनाशिनी ।
छिद्रोपहता या तु बहुदोषकरी मता ॥]

मण्डपमध्ये स्थण्डिलमुपलिप्यास्तीर्य सिकतयाथ कुशैः ।
भद्रासनकृतशीर्षोपधानपादां न्यसेत्प्रतिमाम् ॥ ७ ॥

In the centre of the Platform the ground must be cleaned, and smeared with cow-dung. Then sand must be spread on that, and lastly sacred gran. The image should be placed there with its head resting on a throne and feet on a pillow.

[The अधिवासन rituals are described in this and the following eight verses. These are symbolical of the birth of divinity.]

प्लक्षाश्वत्थोदुम्बरशिरीषवटसम्भवैः कषायजलैः ।
मङ्गल्यसञ्ज्ञिताभिः सर्वौषधिभिः कुशाद्याभिः ॥ ८ ॥

द्विपवृषभोद्धतपर्वतवल्मीकसरित्समागमतटेषु ।
पद्मसरःसु च मृद्भिः सपञ्चगव्यैश्च तीर्थजलैः ॥ ९ ॥

पूर्वशिरस्कां स्नातां सुवर्णरत्नाम्बुभिश्च ससुगन्धैः ।
नानातूर्यनिनादैः पुण्याहैर्वेदनिर्घोषैः ॥ १० ॥

The image should be bathed with a decoction of the sprouts of Plakṣa (*Ficus arnottiana*) Aśvattha (*Ficus religiosa*), Udumbara (*Ficus racemosa*), Śirīṣa (*Albizzia lebbeck*) and banyan mixed with all kinds of herbs bearing auspicious names (such as Jayā, Jayantī and Jīvantī), with holy grass etc., with clay dug up by elephants and bulls, from mountains, ant-hills, river-banks at the confluences, and lotus-lakes, mixed with water from holy rivers, along with the five products of cows, and with scented waters containing gold and gems; and then it should be laid with its head pointing to the east, to the accompaniment of the sounds of various musical instruments and of the chantings of the Puṇyāha and other Vedic hymns.

[The commentator gives a long list of auspicious herbs viz. Jayā, Jayantī, Jīvantī, Jīvaputrī, Punarnavā (*Boerhaavia diffusa*), Viṣṇukrāntā, Abhayā, Viśvambharī, Mahāmodī, Sahadevī, Pūrṇakośā, Śatāvarī (*Asparagus racemosus*), Sahasravīryā and Lakṣmaṇā.

ऐन्द्र्यां दिशीन्द्रलिङ्गा मन्त्राः प्राग्दक्षिणेऽग्निलिङ्गाश्च ।
वक्तव्या द्विजमुख्यैः पूज्यास्ते दक्षिणाभिश्च ॥ ११ ॥

Learned Brāhmaṇas should chant in the east hymns in praise of Indra; and in the south-east, of the Fire-God. Those high priests ought to be honoured with monetary gifts.

[In the place of वक्तव्याः some read जप्तव्याः.]

यो देवः संस्थाप्यस्तन्मन्त्रैश्चानलं द्विजो जुहुयात् ।
अग्निनिमित्तानि मया प्रोक्तानीन्द्रध्वजोत्थाने ॥ १२ ॥

धूमाकुलोऽपसव्यो मुहुर्मुहुर्विस्फुलिङ्गकृन्न शुभः ।
होतुः स्मृतिलोपो वा प्रसर्पणं चाशुभं प्रोक्तम् ॥ १३ ॥

The Priest should worship the sacred fire with the hymns sacred to that God who is to be installed. The symptoms of the sacred fire have to be observed. These symptoms have already been explained by me in connection with the raising of 'Indra's Banner' (XLII. 32). If the fire is filled with excessive smoke, turned to the left, making murmuring sounds and sending out sparks continuously, it is not auspicious. The priest's loss of memory and moving forward are not considered to be auspicious.

[Utpala interprets प्रसर्पणं as पश्चाद् गमनम्. Then what would be the meaning of अपसर्पणम्? The author possibly means that any movement of the priest's body, forward, backward or sideways, is harmful.]

स्नातामभुक्तवस्त्रां स्वलङ्कृतां पूजितां कुसुमगन्धैः ।
प्रतिमां स्वास्तीर्णायां शय्यायां स्थापकः कुर्यात् ॥ १४ ॥

After the image has been bathed, clothed in new garments, tastefully decorated with ornaments, and worshipped with flowers and scents (like sandal paste), the priest who performs the installation should lay it on a well-spread couch.

सुप्तां सगीतनृत्यैर्जागरणैः सम्यगेवमधिवास्य ।
दैवज्ञसम्प्रदिष्टे काले संस्थापनं कुर्यात् ॥ १५ ॥

After the sleeping image has been porperly consecrated with the materials for waking up, accompanied by dance and songs, the installation should be done at the time prescribed by the astrologer i.e. in the northern solstice, bright fortnight etc.

अभ्यर्च्य कुसुमवस्त्रानुलेपनैः शङ्खतूर्यनिर्घोषैः ।
प्रादक्षिण्येन नयेदायतनस्य प्रयत्नेन ॥ १६ ॥

कृत्वा बलिं प्रभूतं सम्पूज्य ब्राह्मणांश्च सभ्यांश्च ।
दत्वा हिरण्यशकलं विनिक्षिपेत्पिण्डिकाश्वभ्रे ॥ १७ ॥

स्थापकदैवज्ञद्विजसभ्यस्थपतीन् विशेषतोऽभ्यर्च्य ।
कल्याणानां भागी भवतीह परत्र च स्वर्गी ॥ १८ ॥

Being worshipped with flowers, clothes and unguents, the image should be taken, to the accompaniment of the sounds of conchs and musical instruments, into the *sanctum sanctorum* with all precautions in a clock-wise procession. After making profuse offerings and worshipping Brāhmaṇas and members of the religious assembly, the image should be placed in the pit of the pedestal, in which a piece of gold has been deposited. Then the installer of the idol, astrologer, Brāhmaṇas, members of the assembly and the carpenter (sculptor) should be specially honoured. By doing this, one will be blessed with all glorious things on earth, and with heaven in the next world.

विष्णोर्भागवतान् मगांश्च सवितुः शम्भोः सभस्मद्विजान् ।
मातॄणामपि मण्डलक्रमविदो विप्रान् विदुर्ब्रह्मणः ।
शाक्यान्सर्वहितस्य शान्तमनसो नग्नाञ्जिनानां विदु-
र्ये यं देवमुपाश्रिताः स्वविधिना तैस्तस्य कार्या क्रिया ॥ १९ ॥

The priests who should install an idol of Lord Viṣṇu should be Bhāgavatas (i.e. devotees of the same Lord); of the Sun-God, the

Maga-Brāhmaṇas; of Lord Śiva, the Pāśupatas who are smeared with the holy ashes; of the Divine Mothers (Brāhmī etc.), those that are adepts in the methodology of the Maṇḍala-pūjā (circular worship); of Brahman (creator). Brāhmaṇas (well-versed in spiritual lore); of the Buddha, the All-benevolent, and of serene mind, the Śākyas (red-robed monks); and of the Jinas, naked (Digambara) Jain monks. The installation of the different Deities should be got performed by priests who are devoted to the respective Deities, according to the rules peculiar to each sect.

[It is interesting to note that our author is a devotee of the Sun-God and a scion of Sun-worshippers. For, his father was known as Ādityadāsa, servant of the Sun. Scholars like Sudhākara Dvivedi are of opinion that Varāhamihira's family originally belonged to the Magadha country. It is possible that that country was a great colony of the Maga priests. The derivation of that word would be: मगा धीयन्ते यस्मिन्निति मगधो देश:. Since they were the original worshippers of the Sun, a Maga priest alone was considered competent to perform the installation. Acccording to the भविष्य पुराण (CXVII-55) they are called Magadhas as they think of Maga (मगं ध्यायन्तीति). We cannot say if there is any connection between the Magas and the Magi. Perhaps the former became Magi in ancient Persia. It may also be argued that *Magadha* derived its name from a settlement of the Magi from Persia.

The procedure of worship in temples is governed by scriptures called Āgamas such as the *Pañcarātra*, *Pāśupata* and *Vaikhānasa*. Viṣṇu's worship is regulated by the *Pāñcarātra* school, Śiva's by the *Pāśupata* one, the Sun's by the Saura one, Buddha's by the *Pāramitā* method. Utpala says: वातुलतन्त्रोक्तेनान्यतन्त्रोक्तविधिना वाशम्भो:। The metre is शार्दूलविक्रीडित.]

उदगयने सितपक्षे शिशिरगभस्तौ च जीववर्गस्थे।
लग्ने स्थिरे स्थिरांशे सौम्यैर्धीधर्मकेन्द्रगतैः ॥ २० ॥

पापैरुपचयसंस्थैर्ध्रुवमृदुहरितिष्यवायुदेवेषु।
विकुजे दिनेऽनुकूले देवानां स्थापनं शस्तम् ॥ २१ ॥

The installation of Deities would be favourable and fortunate, if done in the northern solstice (i.e when the Sun is in any of the six Signs beginning with Capricorn), in the bright fortnight, when the Moon is situated in a Varga (part of the Zodiacal Sign) owned by Jupiter, when a fixed Sign and a fixed Navāṁśa rise when benefics

(Jupiter, Venus and Mercury) occupy the 5th, 9th and Kendras (1st, 4th, 7th and 10th) and malefics (the Sun, Mars and Saturn) *Upacaya* houses (3rd, 6th, 10th and 11th), and when the Moon is in any of the asterisms, viz. the three Uttaras, Rohiṇī, Mṛgaśīrṣa, Citrā, Anūrādhā, Revatī, Śravaṇa, Puṣya and Svātī, and on any convenient day except Tuesday.

[Generally six Vargas are considered in election astrology. They are the Rāśi, Horā, Drekkāṇa, Navāṁśa, Dvādaśāṁśa and Triṁśāṁśa. Among the fixed Signs only Taurus, Leo and Aquarius ascendants are recommended for this ceremony. The Taurus Navāṁśa of any Sign is also recommended. Suppose we are forced to elect Gemini, Cancer, Virgo, Libra, Sagittarius or Pisces for the ascendant. Then we have to go in for a fixed Navāṁśa therein. Saturday is not forbidden for this purpose. For, it is considered as the *fixed Day*. The word अनुकूले signifies that it should be such a day that it is ruled by a star which is favourable i.e. 2nd, 4th, 6th, 8th, or 9th, to the star of the owner of the house or temple]

सामान्यमिदं समासतो लोकानां हितदं मया कृतम् ।
अधिवासनसन्निवेशने सावित्रे पृथगेव विस्तरात् ॥ २२ ॥

I have thus expounded succinctly this subject in general terms for the benefit of mankind. However, in the work entitled *Sāvitra* the subjects of consecration and installation are explained in detail for each deity separately—or the consecration and installation of the Sun have been separately treated of extensively in that Śāstra revealed by the Sun-God.

[Our author refers here to an ancient work called *Sāvitra-śāstra* bearing on this subject. Utpala seems to be ignorant of it, as he is not sure of his own interpretation. The metre is वैतालीय.]

गोलक्षणम् ॥ ६१ ॥

Chapter LXI—Features of Cows.

[This topic is gathered by our author from the work wherein Sage Parāśara is said to have expounded the characteristics of cows to his disciple Bṛhadratha. Generally in classical texts on Āyurveda etc. the teacher expounds a particular science in response to the humble requests of his pupils. Utpala quotes in addition *Śālihotra* and a Gāthā in Prākṛt.]

पराशरः प्राह बृहद्रथाय गोलक्षणं यत् क्रियते ततोऽयम् ।
मया समासः शुभलक्षणास्ताः सर्वास्तथाऽप्यागमतोऽभिधास्ये ॥ १ ॥

This is a succinct account of the characteristics of cows that were taught by Sage Parāśara to his disciple *Bṛhadratha*. Although all types of cows are of auspicious signs, yet I shall delineate them on the authority of the Śāstra (Scientific work) written by the Sages.

[The metre is the usual उपजाति.]

सास्राविलरूक्षाक्ष्यो मूषकनयनाश्च न शुभदा गावः ।
प्रचलच्चिपिटविषाणाः करटाः खरसदृशवर्णाश्च ॥ २ ॥

दशसप्तचतुर्दन्त्यः प्रलम्बमुण्डानना विनतपृष्ठ्यः ।
ह्रस्वस्थूलग्रीवा यवमध्या दारितखुराश्च ॥ ३ ॥

श्यावातिदीर्घजिह्वा गुल्फैरतितनुभिरतिबृहद्भिर्वा ।
अतिककुदाः कृशदेहा नेष्टा हीनाधिकाङ्ग्यश्च ॥ ४ ॥

Cows with dirty and dry eyes, shedding tears, and resembling those of rats are not auspicious; nor are those that have flat, shaking horns, that are black and red in colour or have the colour of asses. So also are those that have ten, seven or four teeth, drooping hornless head depressed back, short and thick neck, middle resembling barley corn, broken hoofs, very long and blackish tongue, very small or very big ankle-joints, big hump, weak body and fewer or more limbs.

[Cf. पराशर—

साश्रुणी लोचने यासां रूक्षाल्पे च न ताः शुभाः ।
चलच्चिपिटशृङ्गाश्च करटाः खरसन्निभाः ॥
दशसप्तचतुर्दन्त्यो लम्बवक्त्रा न ताः शुभाः ।
विषाणवर्जिता ह्रस्वाः पृष्ठमध्यातिसन्नताः ॥
ह्रस्वस्थूलगला याश्च यवमध्याः शुभा न ताः ।
भिन्नपादा बृहद्गुल्फा याश्च स्युस्तनुगुल्फकाः ॥
श्यावातिदीर्घजिह्वाश्च महत्ककुदसंयुताः ।
याश्चातिकृशदेहाश्च हीना अवयवैश्च याः ॥
न ताः शुभप्रदा गावो भर्तुर्यूथस्य नाशनाः ॥

In the expression विनतपृष्ठ्यः the ङीप् is untenable according to Pāṇini IV. 1.54.]

वृषभोऽप्येवं स्थूलातिलम्बवृषणः शिराततक्रोडः ।
स्थूलशिराचितगण्डस्त्रिस्थानं मेहते यश्च ॥ ५ ॥

मार्जाराक्षः कपिलः करटो वा न शुभदो द्विजस्यैव ।
कृष्णोष्ठतालुजिह्वः श्वसनो यूथस्य घातकरः ॥ ६ ॥

A bull too possessing the above characteristics as well as large and hanging testicles, breast full of veins, and cheeks covered with thick veins, and one which urinates in three streams, brings no good luck. One tawny or dark-red, having cat's eyes is not good even for Brāhmaṇas. One with dark lips, palate and tongue and continually blowing, is destructive to the entire flock.

[Against the accepted meaning of the word क्रोड (chest) our commentator gives a strange meaning: पूर्वपादद्वयमध्यम which would mean the middle of the fore-legs.

In our previous edition we had adopted the meaning 'even to Brahmins' for द्विजस्यैव, which is followed here too. We cannot, however, account for the author's preference of एव to अपि. Does it mean: 'Such a bull is harmful only to a Brāhmaṇa and not to other's? Utpala does not make it clear. He says: तथाभूतो द्विजस्य ब्राह्मणस्यैव न शुभः । किन्त्वन्यवर्णानाम् । यतोऽनिष्टलक्षणसंयुक्तो द्विजस्य देय इति लोकस्थितिः । तस्यापि न शुभः ॥

All kinds of inauspicious things are to be made over to Brāhmaṇas. They can digest even poison with the power of Mantras.

The meaning of त्रिस्थान is not clear to Utpala. For, he says:

मूत्रपुरीषौ तुल्यकालं करोति । मक्षिभ्यां शिश्नेन च सिञ्चतीति केचित् । नित्यं गलदश्रुणी चक्षुषी भवत इत्यर्थः ।

For श्वसनः (breathing very much) he says त्रासयुक्तः which would mean, trembling or fearing.]

स्थूलशकृन्मणिशृङ्गः सितोदरः कृष्णसारवर्णश्च ।
गृहजातोऽपि त्याज्यो यूथविनाशावहो वृषभः ॥ ७ ॥

A bull that makes too much dung, has gem-like horns (or has too thick *glans penis* and big horns), while belly and colour of a spotted deer, should be abandoned, though born at home. For, it would otherwise bring ruin upon the entire flock.

श्यामकपुष्पचिताङ्गो भस्मारुणसन्निभो बिडालाक्षः ।
विप्राणामपि न शुभं करोति वृषभः परिगृहीतः ॥ ८ ॥

A bull whose body is full of dark spots resembling flowers, has gr' yish red-colour, and cat's eyes, does no good even to a Brāhmaṇa who accepts it as a gift.

[Bhaṭṭotpala says: श्यामकश्चासौ पुष्पचिताङ्गश्चेति केचित् । In that case we may have to take that the bull is black and the flower-like spots white. The Vāraṇaseya edition reads: श्यामकवर्णैः श्वेतैस्तिलकैः कुसुमाकारैश्चिताङ्गः । This is evidently wrong in respect of श्यामकवर्णैः.]

ये चोद्धरन्ति पादान् पङ्कादिव योजिताः कृशग्रीवाः ।
कातरनयना हीनाश्च पृष्ठतस्ते न भारसहाः ॥ ९ ॥

Those that have weak necks, tremulous eyes, stunted growth, and raise their feet as if from mire, while being yoked or engaged in carrying loads on their backs, would not be able to carry burdens.

[Cf. पराशर—

आपादक्षारकपिलाः कृष्णपुष्पचिताश्च ये ।
मार्जारकपिलाक्षाश्च दुर्बला यूथघातिनः ॥
पङ्कादिवार्ताः पादानुद्धरन्तो व्रजन्ति ये ।
अधूर्वहा भवन्त्येते भाराध्वनि विगर्हिताः ॥

In the first line of the second verse of Parāśara there are only 7 syllables instead of 8.]

Next the author enumerates auspicious traits.

मृदुसंहतताम्रोष्ठास्तनुस्फिजस्ताम्रतालुजिह्वाश्च ।
ह्रस्वतनूच्चश्रवणाः सुकुक्षयः स्पृष्टजङ्घाश्च ॥ १० ॥

आताम्रसंहतखुरा व्यूढोरस्का बृहत्ककुदयुक्ताः ।
स्निग्धश्लक्ष्णतनुत्वग्रोमाणस्ताम्रतनुशृङ्गाः ॥ ११ ॥

तनुभूस्पृग्वालधयो रक्तान्तविलोचना महोच्छ्वासाः ।
सिंहस्कन्धास्तन्वल्पकम्बलाः पूजिताः सुगमाः ॥ १२ ॥

Bulls that have soft, touching and red lips, small buttocks, palate and tongue red, ears short, small and raised, belly well-shaped, shanks touching each other, hoofs red and compact, breast strong and broad, hump large, skin and hair soft, smooth and thin, horns red and slender, tail thin and reaching the ground, corners of eyes red, breath long, shoulders similar to those of the lion, dewlap thin and small, and gait charming, are highly regarded.

[Many of the characteristics of bulls are applicable to cows as well. For example, the tail touching the ground is a mark of an excellent cow; so is the pot-like udder. For the good signs refer to the Raghuvaṁśa I 83-84.]

वामावर्तैर्वामे दक्षिणपार्श्वे च दक्षिणावर्तैः ।
शुभदा भवन्त्यनडुहो जङ्घाभिश्चैणकनिभाभिः ॥ १३ ॥

Bulls with hairy circles turning towards the left on the left side and with those turning towards the right on the right side are beneficial; even so are those whose shanks resemble those of antelopes.

[Utpala explains एणकनिभाभि: as परिपूर्णमांसाभिर्जङ्घाभि: with fleshy and full shanks. He also says: एणक: प्राणिविशेष: । अविरिति केचित् । If others took the meaning as *ram*, then their reading should be एडकनिभाभि:. The word अनडुह: is wrong, its correct form being अनड्वाह:.]

वैडूर्यमल्लिकाबुद्बुदेक्षणाः स्थूलनेत्रपक्ष्माणः ।
पार्ष्णिभिरस्फुटिताभिः शस्ताः सर्वे च भारसहाः ॥ १४ ॥

Bulls whose eyes have the hue of beryl, or are surrounded by white circles looking like jasmine wreaths, or resemble a water-bubble. whose eye-lashes are thick, and hind parts of hoofs unsplit, are all commendable and capable of carrying loads.

[Utpala explains the मल्लिकाक्ष type of horse and bull: दृङ्मण्डलबाह्ये मल्लिकाकुसुमसदृश्यो राज्यो यस्य भवन्ति स मल्लिकाक्ष:। एतल्लक्षणमश्वस्य पठ्यते । तथा च गाहा—

उज्जू अकिसणकन्ती तारन्ते ई समल्लिआकुसुमे ।
भाविज्जइ अच्छीइं जाणं ते मल्लिआअच्छा ॥

[ऋजुनी अकृष्णकान्तिनी तारान्ते समल्लिकाकुसुमे ।
भाव्येते अक्षिणी येषां ते मल्लिकाक्षाः ।।]

In the light of this Gāthā we have to emend slightly Utpala's interpretation: "Those are *Mallikākṣas* whose eyes are not crooked, have bright hue and possess jasmine flowers at the ends of the pupils."

Cf. also शालिहोत्र—

शुक्लराजिपरिक्षिप्ते यस्यान्तर्लोचने शुभे ।
मल्लिकाक्षो महाधन्यः स महाकृष्णतारकः ।।]

घ्राणोद्देशे सवलिर्मार्जारमुखः सितश्च दक्षिणतः ।
कमलोत्पललाक्षाभः सुवालधिर्वाजितुल्यजवः ।। १५ ।।

लम्बैर्वृषणैर्मेषोदरश्च संक्षिप्तवङ्क्षणक्रोडः ।
ज्ञेयो भाराध्वसहो जवेऽश्वतुल्यश्च शस्तफलः ।। १६ ।।

A bull that has wrinkles on its snout, a feline face, is white on the right side, or has the colour of lotus, lily or lac (white, black or red), has a fine tail, horse-like speed, hanging testicles, an ovine belly and narrow groins and breast is considered fit for both carrying heavy loads and travelling long distances, as well as equal to the horse in speed and of beneficial results.

[Cf. शालिहोत्र—

सक्थिजङ्घान्तरे पिण्डौ वङ्क्षणौ त्वभिनिर्दिशेत् ।
अग्रजङ्घान्तरं क्रोड उच्यते वङ्क्षणाग्रगः ।।]

सितवर्णः पिङ्गाक्षस्ताम्रविषाणेक्षणो महावक्त्रः ।
हंसो नाम शुभफलो यूथस्य विवर्धनः प्रोक्तः ।। १७ ।।

A bull which is white in colour, has tawny eyes, copper-coloured horns and eyes and a large mouth or face is termed *Haṁsa* (Swan) of auspicious results and is said to bring good luck and prosperity to the flock.

भूस्पृग्वालधिराताम्रविषाणो रक्तदृक्ककुद्मांश्च ।
कल्माषश्च स्वामिनमचिरात्कुरुते पतिं लक्ष्म्याः ।। १८ ।।

One whose tail touches the ground, whose horns and eyes are

red, hump prominent and colour a mixture of white, red and yellow, makes its owner a lord of wealth ere long.

यो वा सितैकचरणैर्यथेष्टवर्णश्च सोऽपि शुभफलकृत् ।
मिश्रफलोऽपि ग्राह्यो यदि नैकान्तप्रशस्तोऽस्ति ॥ १६ ॥

One that has completely white feet also produces auspicious results, whatever may be its bodily colour. When a bull of all auspicious features is not available, even one of partially auspicious marks should be acceptable.

[सितैकचरण: is another reading for सितैकचरणैः. That would mean — 'one with a single white foot'. Instead of नैकान्तप्रशस्त: some read नैकान्ते प्रशस्तः. Its meaning is explained by Bhaṭṭotpala in a peculiar manner:—मिश्रफलस्य शुभानामशुभानां च लक्षणानामन्तरं कृत्वा यद्येकान्तेऽशुभोऽन्तेऽवसाने नास्ति नातिरिच्यते. तदा शुभाशुभलक्षणोऽपि ग्राह्यः । This explanation which is far fetched should have been abandoned by him.

Cf. पराशर—

मृदुसंहतताम्रोष्ठास्तनुजिह्वास्तनुस्फिजः ।
वैदूर्यमधुवर्णैश्च जलबुद्बुदसन्निभैः ॥
रक्तस्निग्धैश्च नयनैस्तथा रक्तकनीनिकैः।
सिंहस्कन्धा महोरस्का दृढपुष्टाः ककुद्मिनः ॥
भूमौ कर्षति लाङ्गूलं प्रलम्बस्थूलवालधिः ।
पुरस्तादुन्नता नीचाः पृष्ठतः सुसमाहिताः ॥
वृत्ताङ्गाः स्थूलगात्राश्च विस्तीर्णजघनाश्च ये ।
स्पष्टताम्रतनुश्लक्ष्णैः शफैरविरलैर्दृढैः ॥
समुद्गवरसंस्थानैः समास्फुटितपार्ष्णिभिः ।
वृत्तस्थूलोद्धतग्रीवाः ककुदैश्च समुच्छ्रितैः ॥
एते भारसहा ज्ञेया धुरि याने च पूजिताः ।
आवर्तैर्दक्षिणावर्तैर्युक्ता दक्षिणतश्च ये ।'
वामावर्तैर्वामतश्च संयुक्तास्तेऽपि पूजिताः ।
प्रलम्बवृषणोऽत्यर्थं संक्षिप्तोदरवङ्क्षणः ॥
विस्तीर्णवक्षोजघनो भारे याने च पूजितः ।
स्निग्धपिङ्गेक्षणः श्वेतस्ताम्रशृङ्गो महानसः ॥
स तु गौः पद्मको नाम गोसहस्रप्रवर्धनः ॥

श्वलक्षणम् ॥ ६२ ॥

Chapter LXII—Characteristics of Dogs.

[The author does not state as to who his authority is. From Bhaṭṭotpala's quotation of *Garga's* verses it may be concluded that that Sage is the authority for Varāhamihira. The commentator does not quote any authority for the features of bitches given in the second verse.]

पादाः पञ्चनखास्त्रयोऽग्रचरणः षड्भिर्नखैर्दक्षिण-
स्ताम्रोष्ठाग्रनसो मृगेश्वरगतिर्जिघ्रन् भुवं याति च ।
लाङ्गूलं ससटं दृगृक्षसदृशी कर्णौ च लम्बौ मृदू
यस्य स्यात् स करोति पोष्टुरचिरात्पुष्टां श्रियं श्वा गृहे ॥ १ ॥

A dog whose three legs have five nails each and the right fore-foot six, whose lips and muzzle are red, whose gait resembles that of the lion, which moves forward smelling the earth, whose tail is shaggy, eyes like those of a bear and ears soft and hanging, will bring great opulence ere long to the house of its keeper.

[Cf. गर्ग—

त्रयः पादाः पञ्चनखा अग्रगो दक्षिणस्तथा ।
षण्नखस्ताम्रनासो यस्ताम्रोष्ठः सिंहविक्रमः ॥
महीं जिघ्रन् मुदा याति लाङ्गूलं जटिलं तथा ।
ऋक्षाभे चक्षुषी कर्णौ मृदू चातिप्रलम्बितौ ॥
स श्वा नृपस्य महतीं श्रियं यच्छति पोषितुः ॥

The metre is शार्दूलविक्रीडित.]

पादे पादे पञ्च पञ्चाग्रपादे वामे यस्याः षण्नखा मल्लिकाक्ष्याः ।
वक्रं पुच्छं पिङ्गलालम्बकर्णा या सा राष्ट्रं कुक्कुरी पाति पुष्टा ॥ २ ॥

A bitch which has five nails in each foot except the left fore-foot which has six nails, whose eyes have white, flower-like circles inside and which has a crooked tail, brown colour and hanging ears, would save the country, if she be properly nourished.

[The metre is शालिनी.]

कुक्कुटलक्षणम् ॥ ६३ ॥

Chapter LXIII—Signs of Cocks.

[Apart from horses and elephants, excellent bulls, dogs, cocks, tortoises and goats were kept by kings in ancient times. Some of these like cocks were used in sports and the rest for pleasure and fortune.]

कुक्कुटस्त्वृजुतनूरुहाङ्गुलिस्ताम्रवक्त्रनखचूलिकः सितः ।
रौति सुस्वरमुषात्यये च यो वृद्धिदः स नृपराष्ट्रवाजिनाम् ॥ १ ॥

A white cock whose feathers and talons are straight, face, nails and crest red, and which crows pleasantly at dawn, bestows prosperity on the king, country and horses.

[Cf. गर्ग—

श्वेतस्ताम्रनखः शुक्लस्ताम्राक्षस्त्वृजुवालधिः ।
अनावृताङ्गुलिः स्वङ्गस्ताम्रचूडः प्रशस्यते ॥
अत्यालापी यवग्रीवो दधिवर्णः शुभाननः ।
प्रशस्तास्यः स्थूलशिरा हारिद्रचरणो द्विजः ॥
अखञ्जास्ताम्रवक्त्राश्च स्निग्धवर्णाश्च पूजिताः ।
दीनाश्चैव विवर्णाश्च विस्वराश्च विगर्हिताः ॥

The metre is रथोद्धता.]

यवग्रीवो यो वा बदरसदृशो वापि विहगो
बृहन्मूर्धा वर्णैर्भवति बहुभिर्यश्च रुचिरः ।
स शस्तः सङ्ग्रामे मधुमधुपवर्णश्च जयकृ-
न्न शस्तो योऽतोऽन्यः कृशतनुरवः खञ्जचरणः ॥२ ॥

A cock whose neck resembles a barley corn, which resembles the ripe jujube fruit in colour (red), and has a big head, or which looks charming with many colours, is excellent for fighting. So does one endowed with the colour of honey or bee (black) confer victory. One that possesses contrary characteristics is not auspicious.

One that has an emaciated body, a feeble voice and lame legs also is not beneficial.

[Utpala remarks under यवग्रीव:—यवशिरा इति लोके प्रसिद्ध: । He says that the colour of honey is yellow. I do not think so. रुचिर: according to him means निर्मल: clean. The metre is शिखरिणी.]

कुक्कुटी च मृदुचारुभाषिणी स्निग्धमूर्तिरुचिराननेक्षणा ।
सा ददाति सुचिरं महीक्षितां श्रीयशोविजयवीर्यसम्पद: ॥ ३ ॥

A hen with a gentle and sweet voice, glossy body and beautiful face and eyes, brings abundant wealth, unique fame, victory and valour to kings for a long time.

[The metre is रथोद्धता.]

कूर्मलक्षणम् ॥ ६४ ॥

Chapter LXIV—Characteristics of Tortoises.

स्फटिकरजतवर्णो नीलराजीविचित्रः
कलशसदृशमूर्तिश्चारुवंशश्च कूर्मः ।
अरुणसमवपुर्वा सर्षपाकारचित्रः
सकलनृपमहत्त्वं मन्दिरस्थः करोति ॥ १ ॥

A tortoise which has the colour of crystal or silver, which is marked with blue lines, has a pot-like body, a beautiful back-bone, or has a red body and is bedecked with spots resembling white mustard seeds, bestows on one the over-lordship of all monarchs, when it is kept at home.

[Utpala says that the back-bone should not be too high. The present fashion of keeping tiny fishes etc. in glass cases at home is a survival of the ancient custom of kings and nobles.

The metre is मालिनी.]

अञ्जनभृङ्गश्यामतनुर्वा बिन्दुविचित्रोऽव्यङ्गशरीरः ।
सर्पशिरा वा स्थूलगलो यः सोऽपि नृपाणां राष्ट्रविवृद्ध्यै ॥ २ ॥

A tortoise whose body is as dark as collyrium or the bee, or is covered with spots, and which has a full-grown body (or free from defects), the head of a serpent or a broad neck, conduces to the prosperity of the realms of kings.

[The metre is चम्पकमाला.]

वैडूर्यत्विट् स्थूलकण्ठस्त्रिकोणो गूढच्छिद्रश्चारुवंशश्च शस्तः ।
क्रीडावाप्यां तोयपूर्णे मणौ वा कार्यः कूर्मो मङ्गलार्थं नरेन्द्रैः ॥ ३ ॥

A tortoise that has the lustre of beryl, a thick neck, a triangular body, hidden cavities, and a fine back-bone is praiseworthy. Such a tortoise should be kept by kings in pleasure-ponds or in pitchers (or jars) filled with water, for the sake of success and prosperity.

[Utpala goes off the mark when he construes तोयपूर्णे मणौ in the following words: 'मणौ वा कूपाद्योभावे तोयपूर्णे कार्यः' । This meaning is never intended by the author who has already given the first alternative viz. क्रीडावाप्याम्. The word simply means 'a jar' filled with water.

Cf. गर्ग, who gives more information:—

शङ्खदर्भप्रतीकाशश्छत्राभो रजतप्रभः ।
तथा वैदूर्यवर्णाभो यो भवेदष्टसर्षपः ॥
यश्च वा कोकिलाभासो राजीवाभश्च यो भवेत् ।
पीतकाञ्चनवर्णस्तु पुण्डरीकसमप्रभः ॥
गोधामुखं त्रिकोणं च तथा मण्डलवर्धनम् ।
स्त्रीपुत्रमतिदं विन्द्यात् कूर्मं राष्ट्रविवर्धनम् ॥

The metre is शालिनी.]

छागलक्षणम् ॥ ६५ ॥

Chapter LXV—Signs of Goats.

[The author mentions that his authority is Sage Garga who mentions four auspicious types of goats. The commentator also quotes relevant verses from the Mahābhārata.]

छागशुभाशुभलक्षणमभिधास्ये नवदशाष्टदन्तास्ते ।
धन्याः स्थाप्या वेश्मनि सन्त्याज्याः सप्तदन्ता ये ॥ १ ॥

I shall now expound the good and bad marks of goats: Those that possess eight, nine or ten teeth are blessed and deserve to be kept by one in one's residence, while those that have seven teeth ought to be discarded.

दक्षिणपार्श्वे मण्डलमसितं शुक्लस्य शुभफलं भवति ।
ऋष्यनिभकृष्णलोहितवर्णानां श्वेतमतिशुभदम् ॥ २ ॥

It is auspicious for a white goat to have a dark circle in the middle of the right side. Similarly, a goat that is blue like an elk, dark or red, with a white circle on the right side is highly beneficial.
[Ṛṣya is a variety of deer. It is also spelt as Ṛśya.]

स्तनवदवलम्बते यः कण्ठेऽजानां मणिः स विज्ञेयः ।
एकमणिः शुभफलकृद्धन्यतमा द्वित्रिमणयो ये ॥ ३ ॥

The object that hangs like a breast from the neck of goats is to be known as '*Maṇi*'. One with a single Maṇi is of auspicious results, and those that have two or three are exceedingly blessed.

मुण्डाः सर्वे शुभदाः सर्वसिताः सर्वकृष्णदेहाश्च ।
अर्धासिताः सितार्धा धन्याः कपिलार्धकृष्णाश्च ॥ ४ ॥

All the goats that have no horns, that are completely white or completely black, or are half-white or half-dark, or half-brown and half-black are auspicious and bring good luck.

विचरति यूथस्याग्रे प्रथमं चाम्भोऽवगाहते योऽजः ।
स शुभः सितमूर्धा वा मूर्धनि वा कृत्तिका यस्य ॥ ५ ॥

A goat that marches at the head of a flock, drinks the water first and has its head white or has six dark specks on the head is of good augury. (It is called *Kuṭṭaka*, according to Garga.)

[Though the word **अवगाहते** literally means, plunges or bathes, here what is meant is only touching or drinking. Utpala's explanation is in keeping with Garga's definition.

Cf. गर्ग—

यूथाग्रे यश्च चरति यश्चादौ स्पर्शयेज्जलम् ।
मूर्ध्नि षट् तिलका यस्य सोऽजो यूथविवर्धनः ॥]

सपृषतकण्ठशिरा वा तिलपिष्टनिभश्च ताम्रदृक् शस्तः ।
कृष्णचरणः सितो वा कृष्णो वा श्वेतचरणो यः ॥ ६ ॥

A goat with spotted neck or head, having the colour of pounded sesamum (a mixture of white and yellow) and red eyes is commendable. So is a white goat with black legs or a black one with white legs. (This type is called *Kutila.*)

[Cf. गर्ग—

श्वेतो यः कृष्णचरणः कृष्णः श्वेतशफोऽपि वा ।
पीतस्ताम्रेक्षणो मूर्ध्नि गले वा पृषतान्वितः ॥]

यः कृष्णाण्डः श्वेतो मध्ये कृष्णेन भवति पट्टेन ।
यो वा चरति सशब्दं मन्दं च स शोभनश्छागः ॥ ७ ॥

A white goat with dark testicles and a dark band (like a saddle) in the middle is auspicious. So is one that walks slowly with a jingling sound. (This variety is called Jaṭila.)

[Cf. गर्ग—

मन्दं सशब्दं चरति श्वेतः कृष्णाण्डसंयुतः ।
मध्ये कृष्णेन पट्टेन युक्तो यः सोऽपि वृद्धिदः ।]

ऋष्यशिरोरुहपादो यो वा प्राक् पाण्डुरोऽपरे नीलः ।
स भवति शुभकृच्छागः श्लोकश्चाप्यत्र गर्गोक्तः ॥ ८ ॥

A goat which has blue hair on the head, and blue feet, or

whose fore-part is white and hind part blue, brings good luck. (This type is called *Vāmana.*) The following is the verse taught by Sage Garga on the subject.

[We have already seen that Ṛṣya means a kind of deer, but Utpala says: ऋष्यः प्राणी स च लोके ऋक्ष इत्युच्यते । स च नीलवर्णो भवति । However, Ṛkṣa means a *bear.* If the author had meant it, he would have used the word ऋक्ष in the verse. Under verse 2 our commentator himself remarks: ऋष्यो मृगजातिः, स च नीलवर्णो भवति । To illustrate the use of 'ऋष्य' he quotes from Sage *Vyāsa*:

अश्वानृष्यसवर्णास्तु हंसवर्णैर्हयोत्तमैः ।
व्यामिश्रयद्रणे कर्णः पाण्डवाञ्छादयञ् शरैः ॥ (द्रोण-१३२-२७)
ते हया बह्वशोभन्त विमिश्रा वातरंहसः ।
सितासिता महावर्णा यथा व्योम्नि बलाहकाः ॥ (द्रोण-१३२-२६)

Cf. गर्गः—

ऋष्यमूर्धा नीलपादः प्राग्भागे यश्च पाण्डुरः ।
पश्चिमे नीलवर्णः स्यात् सोऽपि भर्तुर्विवृद्धिदः ॥]

कुट्टकः कुटिलश्चैव जटिलो वामनस्तथा ।
ते चत्वारः श्रियः पुत्रा नालक्ष्मीके वसन्ति ते ॥ ९ ॥

The four classes of goats *viz. Kuṭṭaka, Kuṭila, Jaṭila* and *Vāmana,* are the sons of the Goddess of Wealth. They do not dwell in a place of penury.

अथाप्रशस्ताः खरतुल्यनादाः प्रदीप्तपुच्छाः कुनखा विवर्णाः ।
निकृत्तकर्णा द्विपमस्तकाश्च भवन्ति ये चासिततालुजिह्वाः ॥ १० ॥

Now, the inauspicious ones are those that bleat like donkeys, that have crooked or erect tails, mis-shapen nails, inauspicious colours, cut ears, elephantine heads and dark palate and tongue.

[The metre is उपेन्द्रवज्रा.]

वर्णैः प्रशस्तैर्मणिभिः प्रयुक्ता मुण्डाश्च ये ताम्रविलोचनाश्च ।
ते पूजिता वेश्मनि मानवानां सौख्यानि कुर्वन्ति यशः श्रियं च ॥ ११ ॥

The goats that have commendable colours, Maṇis (that hang from the neck), heads without horns and red eyes are auspicious for a house, as they confer happiness, fame and prosperity on the people.

[At the end of the chapter the author once again emphasizes the good signs of goats.

The metre is इन्द्रवज्रा.]

अश्वलक्षणम् ॥ ६६ ॥

Chapter LXVI — Characteristics of Horses.

[This science of horses was a popular topic of study as it was very important for kings in maintaining their power. Śālihotra is considered a great authority on this subject. Śrīharsa makes use of his knowledge of this subject in the description of Nala's steed in Canto I of the *Naiṣadhiyacarita*. *Bhaṭṭotpala* quotes at length from some work which is meant for instruction of veterinary physicians in the study of the horse's limbs. He quotes also from *Parāśara* and *Vararuci*. The author, however, does not name any authority.

अविज्ञाय प्रदेशांस्तु भिषक् कर्मसु मुह्यति ।
प्रदेशोद्देशविज्ञानमतो यत्नेन वाजिनाम् ॥
वक्ष्यते तेष्वधीना हि सिद्धिः कर्मसु सर्वदा ।
जिह्वा कण्ठे निबद्धा हि गलनालं च तत् स्मृतम् ॥
सूनाधस्तात्तु जिह्वायास्तालु तस्यास्तथोपरि ।
पीठ्यो हनुनिबद्धा हि दंष्ट्रे तासामथाग्रजे ॥
ततो द्विजाव्यञ्जनिनस्तेषामुपरि चोत्तराः ।
अधस्ताद् द्विजदंष्ट्राणां मध्ये तु चिबुकं स्मृतम् ॥
दशनाच्छादनावोष्ठौ तयोः पार्श्वे च सृक्किणी ।
प्रपाणमुत्तरोष्ठस्य स्यादूर्ध्वं प्रोथमेव च ॥
नासापुटौ प्रोथपार्श्वे घोणा प्रोथाक्षिमध्यतः ।
नासावंशोऽभ्रुवो गल्लौ क्षीरिके च तथोपरि ॥
घोणाहन्वन्तरे गण्डौ तयोर्मध्येऽश्रुपातनम् ।
नेत्रे तथोपरि स्यातां तयोः प्रच्छादनं ततः ।
अभ्यन्तरं सितं कृष्णं दृष्टिमण्डलमेव च ।
कनीनिके चान्तकोणे तथापाङ्गौ च बाह्यतः ॥
वर्त्मोपरि च पक्ष्माणि अक्षिकूटे तथोपरि ।
भ्रुवौ तथोपरिष्टात्तु ललाटं भ्रूभ्रुवान्तरम् ॥
ध्रुवं ललाटोपरि च शिरः कर्णोत्तरं भवेत् ।
तदाश्रितो मस्तकश्च कर्णौ तस्यैव पार्श्वयोः ॥

कर्णमूले शष्कुली स्यात् कर्णशङ्खान्तरे कटः ॥
कटापाङ्गान्तरे शङ्खो घटी बाह्ये च शङ्खयोः ॥
चिबुकस्योपरि हनू गण्डावुपरि चैतयोः ।
हन्वोश्च गलनाड्योश्च निगालो मध्य उच्यते ॥
निगालाधो गलः कण्ठो वक्षः क्रोडोऽथ हृत् ततः
विधुर्मन्दविधुश्चैव कर्णस्याधः षडङ्गुले ॥
विध्वोरुभयतोऽधस्ताद् मध्ये कण्ठनिबन्धनम् ।
शिरोवाहान्तरे ग्रीवा जत्रुग्रीवान्तरे वहः ॥
स्कन्धस्य चोपरि ग्रीवा तस्याश्चोपरि केसरम् ।
वाहतो जत्रुतश्चोक्ताः काकसं ककुदं ततः ॥
आसनं चैव पृष्ठं च पृष्ठवंशस्ततः परम् ।
ककुदावस्थितावंसौ बाहू चांसनिबन्धनौ ॥
क्रोडाधस्तात्तथा बाहू बाह्वोर्बाह्ये षडङ्गुले ।
बाह्वोरभ्यन्तरे कक्ष्या पार्श्वतस्तौ च वक्षसः ॥
किणौ चाभ्यन्तरे विन्द्यादधस्ताज्जानुनी मते ।
जान्वोः कापालिके चाधो मन्विरं जानुपृष्ठतः ॥
जङ्घे च जानुनोऽधस्तात्पृष्ठतश्च कले मते ।
जङ्घाकलान्तरे ईषे परिहस्तस्तथाग्रतः ॥
पृष्ठतः परिहस्तस्य कूर्चौ तन्मध्यगौ किणौ ।
कूर्चाधस्तात् कुट्टिके च खुरसन्धिस्ततः खुरः ॥
पृष्ठतः पार्ष्णिशीर्षे च पार्ष्णी नखशिखातलम् ।
तलमध्ये तु मण्डूक्यौ क्षीरिके च तलान्तरे ॥
हृत्परो नाभिवंशश्च नाभेस्तु जठरं परम् ।
हृन्नाभिमूत्रकोशानां रोमराज्यन्तरे मता ॥
तदधो मेहनं कोशस्ततो मुष्कफलं ततः ।
अधस्तात्कटिसन्धेः स्यादूरुसन्धिस्तथोपरि ॥
सक्थिनी फलबन्धश्च ऊरुपाण्डुरिहोच्यते ।
ऊरोरूर्ध्वं पाण्डपिण्डौ वक्त्रसन्धी ततः स्थूरम् ॥
स्थूराधो मन्विरं प्रोक्तौ शङ्कू तन्मध्यगौ किणौ ।
स्थूराधस्तात्पूर्वमुक्त पृष्ठतश्च विभावयेत ॥
गात्रद्वयं शिरोग्रीवं पूर्वकायः स उच्यते ।
जघनं त्रिकपुच्छं च गात्रे द्वे चापि पश्चिमे ॥
प्रदेशा मध्यमा ये च सोऽन्तकायः प्रकीर्तितः ।
शरीराख्याश्च षट् प्रोक्ता मुखं गात्राणि वालधिः ॥
नखरोमाणि वालाश्च केशाश्चावयवाः स्मृताः ।

विन्यस्ता वक्त्रपुच्छान्तं मध्ये हीनाधिकं तथा ॥
अत्र नोक्तं तु यत्किञ्चिद्विन्द्यात् तदपि युक्तितः ।
इति प्रदेशा व्याख्याता वाजिनां देहसंश्रयाः ॥
तान् विज्ञाय भिषक् कर्म प्रयुञ्जन्नापराध्यति ॥]

दीर्घग्रीवाक्षिकूटस्त्रिकहृदयपृथुस्ताम्रताल्वोष्ठजिह्वः
सूक्ष्मत्वक्केशवालः सुशफगतिमुखो ह्रस्वकर्णोष्ठपुच्छः ।
जङ्घाजानूरुवृत्तः समसितदशनश्चारुसंस्थानरूपो
वाजी सर्वाङ्गशुद्धो भवति नरपतेः शत्रुनाशाय नित्यम् ॥ १ ॥

A horse which has a long neck and sockets of eyes, broad rump and heart, red palate, lips and tongue, fine skin, hair and tail, charming hoofs, gait and face, short ears, upper lip and root of the tail, round shanks, thighs and knees, white and uniform teeth, and a beautiful shape and appearance, is flawless in all limbs, and ever conduces to the destruction of the king's enemies.

[*Parāśara* gives the marks and measurements of three types of horses, ordinary, moderate and excellent:

जघन्यमध्यज्येष्ठानामश्वानामायतिर्भवेत् ।
अङ्गुलानां शतं ज्ञेयं विंशत्या दशभिस्त्रिभिः ॥
परिणाहाङ्गुलानि स्यात् सप्ततिः सप्तसप्ततिः ॥
एकाशीतिः समासेन त्रिविधः स्याद् यथाक्रमम् ॥
तथा षष्टिश्चतुष्षष्टिरष्टषष्टिः समुच्छ्रयः ।
द्विपञ्चसप्तकयुता विंशतिः स्यान्मुखायतिः ॥
श्मश्रुहीनं मुखं कान्तं प्रगल्भं तुङ्गनासिकम् ।
ह्रस्वप्रोथं तनुश्रोत्रं रक्तगम्भीरतालुकम् ॥
षडब्दमाद्वादशकं मृदुनासापुटं दृढम् ।
दीर्घोद्धतमुखग्रीवं ह्रस्वकुक्षिखुरं तथा ॥
विवशं चण्डवेगं च हंसमेघसमस्वनम् ।
हरितं शुकवर्णं वा श्वेतं कृष्णसमण्डलम् ॥
अश्वमीदृशमारोहेद्धस्तेन श्रवणेन वा ।
आश्विने नोदनाभिज्ञा वाहयेयुर्द्विजातयः ॥
तथा च वर्णेनैकेन स्निग्धवर्णो भवेद्यदि ।
स हन्याद्वर्णजान् दोषान् देहः सर्वत्र शस्यते ॥

Cf. also वररुचिः—

ज्ञानं त्रैलोक्यविद्भिर्मुनिभिरभिहितं लक्षणं यद्विशालं

दुर्ज्ञेयं तद्बहुत्वादपि विमलधिया किं पुनर्बुद्धिहीनैः ।
तस्मादेतत्समासात्स्फुटमधुरपदं श्रूयतामश्वसंस्थं
वर्णावर्तप्रभाङ्गस्वरगतिसहितैः सत्त्वगन्धैरुपेतम् ॥
रोमत्वक्केशवालैरसितहरिसितैस्तप्तहेमप्रभैश्च
कृष्णः शोणोपलक्षो हरिरिति कथिता मूलवर्णास्तुरङ्गाः ।
ते चान्योन्यानुषङ्गात्पवनवशगता यान्ति भूयो बहुत्वं
निर्देशस्तेषु वाच्यो विमलपटुधिया द्रव्यसत्त्वानुरूपः ॥

The metre is स्रग्धरा.]

अश्रुपातहनुगण्डहृद्गलप्रोथशङ्खकटिवस्तिजानुनि ।
मुष्कनाभिककुदे तथा गुदे सव्यकुक्षिचरणे तथाऽशुभाः ॥ २ ॥

Inauspicious are the hairy circles under the eyes, on the chin, cheeks, heart, throat-junction, nose, temple, hips, abdomen, knees, testicles, navel, shoulders, anus (or junction of neck and collar-bone), right side of the stomach and legs of horses.

[The author does not give the subject of अशुभाः. We have to get it आवर्ताः from Utpala's commentary. In the place of तथा, he says, some read अलुपे which means "अलुपं जत्रुगलसन्धिः"

Cf. वररुचिः—

शङ्खभ्रूगण्डनासाहनुकटिककुदक्रोडकक्षासनस्थै-
र्मन्याहृज्जानुकूर्चश्रवणगलगुदप्रोथकुक्ष्यश्रुपातैः ।
स्थूरास्फिक्काकसाधस्त्रिकवृषणवहस्कन्धनाभ्यूरुजातै-
रावर्तैरेवमेतैरशुभफलकरैर्वर्जनीयास्तुरङ्गाः ॥

[The metre of this and the following verse is रथोद्धता.]

ये प्रपाणगलकर्णसंस्थिताः पृष्ठमध्यनयनोपरि स्थिताः ।
ओष्ठसक्थिभुजकुक्षिपार्श्वगास्ते ललाटसहिताः सुशोभनाः ॥ ३ ॥

Auspicious are the hairy circles beneath the upper lip, on the throat, ears, middle of the back, above the eyes (near the brows), on the lips, haunches, fore-legs (above the hoofs), the left side of the belly, flanks and the fore-head (i.e. the space between the brows).

[The word गल appears in both the lists, auspicious and inauspicious. In the case of कुक्षि there is the adjective सव्य (right) in verse 2. So there is no difficulty. Our commentator tides over the difficulty by construing गल in verse 2 as the junction of the heart and the neck: गलो हृत्कण्ठसन्धिः । In the next verse is गलः taken to mean the neck "गलः कण्ठं निगालाधः ।"

Cf. वररुचि:

सक्थिप्रपाणश्रुवबाहुकण्ठकेशान्तवक्षःश्रवणोपरन्ध्रे ।
रन्ध्रे निगाले च ललाटदेशे ये रोमजास्ते श्रियमावहन्ति ॥
तथा च विशेषलक्षणानि—
बालार्काग्निप्रवालद्रुतकनकनिभा वह्निजैश्वर्यवृद्ध्यै
नीलाम्भोजाभ्रवर्णा भवति सलिलजा सर्वदुःखापहर्त्री ।
गम्भीरानेकवर्णा दिशति च तुरगे पार्थिवी सर्वकामान्
वायव्या रूक्षवर्णा त्वशुभफलकरी निन्दिता व्योमजा च ॥
इति कान्तिलक्षणम् ।
अथ स्वरलक्षणम्—
भेरीशङ्खाब्दसिंहद्विपपणववृषस्निग्धगम्भीरनादा
वीणापुंस्कोकिलानां मधुरपटुरवा वाजिनो राजवाहाः ।
काकोलूकोष्ट्रभासाः श्वखरवृषरवा रूक्षविच्छिन्नघोषा
अन्ये चेत्थंप्रकारास्त्वशुभफलकरा हानिशोकप्रदाश्च ॥

अथ गतिलक्षणम्—

त्वरितगतिविलासैर्विक्षिपन् पादमुच्चै-
र्व्रजति नकुलगामी कम्पयन् कं शिखाग्रम् ।
अथ विकटखुराग्रैर्दह्यमानां यथोर्वी
स्पृशति चरणपातैस्तैश्चिरं तस्य यातम् ॥
स्थिरपदवितताशो दूरमुन्नम्य वक्त्रं
व्रजति हि सुविलासैर्बर्हिवद् बर्हिगामी ।
सुगतमथ तुरङ्गं योऽधिरुह्यात् तदैव
स भवति सुखगामी शत्रुनाशं च कुर्यात् ॥
अजमहिषवराहश्वोष्ट्रमार्जारगामी
कपिवृषभशृगालैस्तुल्यगामी च योऽश्वः ।
स दिशति धननाशं शत्रुवृद्धिं च कुर्याद्
भवति च न सुखाय स्वामिनः शोकदाता ॥

अथ सत्त्वगन्धलक्षणमाह—

वर्णावर्तप्रभाङ्गस्वरगतिसहितः सत्त्वगन्धैरुपेतः
शौचाचाराभिजातिः स्मृतिविनयगुणैरन्वितो देवसत्त्वः ।
गन्धर्वैर्यातुधानैर्मुनिवरपतिभिस्तुल्यसत्त्वाः प्रशस्ता
ये चान्ये हीनसत्त्वास्त्वशुचिमलरता भीरवस्ते विवर्ज्याः ॥
मैरेयाम्भोजसर्पिःक्षितिमधुमदिराचन्दनोशीरलाजा-
कल्हाराशोकजातीवरतरुकुसुमैस्तुल्यगन्धाः प्रशस्ताः ।

ये चान्ये क्षारमूत्रक्षतजमलवसाबस्तिनिर्मोकगन्धाः
सन्त्याज्यास्तेऽपि नित्यं त्वशुभफलकरा ह्यानिशोकप्रदाश्च ॥
उरो विस्तीर्णं पृथु च जघनं नेत्रयुग्मं सुबद्धं
ग्रीवा वाच्या सुदीर्घा स भुजयुगलकं कण्ठपृष्ठं च ह्रस्वम् ।
स्वरो गम्भीरस्तनुरविरलं चेष्टितं चारु नित्यं
शोभा शारीरिकी स्याद्यदि च हि तुरगे दीर्घमायुः स जीवेत् ॥
व्यूढोरस्कध्रुवाङ्कस्तनपृथुजघना दीर्घरूक्षाक्षिघोषा
दुर्गन्धाः सर्वगात्रैस्तनुगतिविषमा लम्बकर्णोष्ठपुच्छाः ।
दुर्गन्धा दुष्टशीला विनिपतितमना भीरवो नष्टसंज्ञाः
सर्वाचारैश्च हीना यदि खलु तुरगाः सन्ति ह्रस्वायुषस्ते ॥]

तेषां प्रपाण एको ललाटकेशेषु च ध्रुवावर्त्ताः ।
रन्ध्रोपरन्ध्रमूर्धनि वक्षसि चेति स्मृतौ द्वौ द्वौ ॥ ४ ॥

Among the ten permanent hairy circles that horses have, there is one on the lower side of the upper lip, one in the hairs of the forehead, two between the belly and the navel, two just above that, two on the head and two on the breast.

[For the definition of रन्ध्र and उपरन्ध्र the commentator quotes the following line from some source :—

कुक्षिनाभ्यन्तरे रन्ध्रमुपरन्ध्रं तथोपरि ॥

Cf. also पराशर

दश ध्रुवावर्त्ताः । प्रपाणे एको ललाटे एक एव मूर्धनि द्वौ द्वौ वक्षसि रन्ध्रोपरन्ध्रयो द्वौ द्वाविति ॥

The hairy-circles on the प्रपाण and ललाट are said to be highly auspicious according to the previous verse, but here he says that they are among the ten permanent or necessary ones. This means that there may be some horses that are sub-normal.]

[In the next verse the author gives some clues, depending on the number of teeth, to enable us to find out the age of Lorses.]

षड्भिर्दन्तैः सिताभैर्भवति हयशिशुस्तैः कषायैर्द्विवर्षः
सन्दंशैर्मध्यमान्त्यैः पतितसमुदितैस्त्र्यब्धिपञ्चाब्दिकाश्वः ।
सन्दंशानुक्रमेण त्रिकपरिगणिताः कालिकाः पीतशुक्लाः
काचा मक्षीकशङ्खावटचलनमतो दन्तपातं च विद्धि ॥ ५ ॥

A colt of one year will have six white teeth, which become tawny when it is two years old; when it is three years, the incisors fall and reappear; when four years, the next teeth fall and reappear; when five years, the last teeth do likewise. The same three classes of teeth (*Sandaṁśa*, *Madhyama* and *Antya*) will after every subsequent period of three years become black, yellow, white, coloured like Kāca (a mineral), like a mineral substance looking like honey, conch shell, become hollow, shaky and at last fall down.

[Utpala gives a good deal of clarification here: Among the six teeth in each row the central two are called (*Sandaṁśa*, the two on their sides *Madhyama*, and the at the two extremities *Antya*. When the incisors get black spots on them, the horse is six years old. With the *central* ones having black spots it is seven and with the *Antyas* having the spots it is eight years. Similarly with the next characteristic viz. yellow colour, in the three sets of teeth 3 years elapse. Lastly when the Antyas fall, it is 32 years old.

Cf. वररुचि—

सन्दंशं मध्यमन्त्यं दशनयुगमधः सोत्तरं वर्षजाते
स्फीतं द्व्यब्दे कषायं पतितसमुदितं त्रिश्चतुष्पञ्चकेषु ।
त्रींस्त्रीनेकैकमब्दानसितहरिसिताकाचमाक्षीकशङ्खा-
च्छिद्रं चालं च्युतिश्च प्रभवति तुरगे लक्षणं वक्रजानाम् ।।

Cf. also पराशरमहर्षि—

अथ रेखा दीर्घा गम्भीरा अविच्छिन्नास्तिस्रः प्रोथे यस्य तस्यायुर्वर्षाणि त्रिंशत् । द्वाभ्यां विंशतिः । दशैकया च । दक्षिणेनाभिवृत्तया द्वादश । वंशाग्रमनुगतया अष्टादश । ह्रस्वजिह्मवक्रविच्छिन्नाव्यक्तरूक्षकबन्धकाकपादाकारया जघन्यमायुः ।।

Here the Sage gives some new clues viz. lines on the nose of the horse.

The metre is स्रग्धरा.]

हस्तिलक्षणम् ॥ ६७ ॥

Chapter LXVII—Signs of Elephants.

[This and the previous chapter have not been mentioned by the author in the table of contents at the end of the work. It is quite possible that some scholar might have introduced them before Bhaṭṭotpala's time in order to make the work appear complete in all respects. Here the commentator quotes from Parāśara and some definitions from some unknown work. Four classes of elephants and their definitions are given here. They are *Bhadra*, *Manda*, *Mṛga* and *Saṅkīrṇa*.]

मध्वाभदन्ताः सुविभक्तदेहा न चोपदिग्धा न कृशाः क्षमाश्च ।
गात्रैः समैश्चापसमानवंशा वराहतुल्यैर्जघनैश्च भद्राः ॥ १ ॥

Those elephants are called *Bhadras* whose tusks have the colour of honey, limbs are proportionately developed and distinct, which are not too stout, nor too lean, are fit for work (quite active), have equal limbs, backbone resembling a bow, and hips similar to those of boars (i.e. round).

[The metre is उपजाति here and in the 3rd verse; and it is इन्द्रवज्रा in 2, 4 and 5.]

वक्षोऽथ कक्षावलयः श्लथाश्च लम्बोदरस्त्वग्बृहती गलश्च ।
स्थूला च कुक्षिः सह पेचकेन सैंही च दृङ्मन्दमतङ्गजस्य ॥ २ ॥

The characteristics of the class designated as *Manda* are : a loose breast, loose folds on the waist (or loose waist and folds), a hanging belly, thick skin and neck, huge belly and root of the tail, and a leonine look.

मृगास्तु ह्रस्वाधरवालमेढ्रास्तन्वङ्घ्रिकण्ठद्विजहस्तकर्णाः ।
स्थूलेक्षणाश्चेति यथोक्तचिह्नैः सङ्कीर्णनागा व्यतिमिश्रचिह्नाः ॥ ३ ॥

Those that belong to the *Mṛga* class have short lip, tail-hair and penis, slender feet, neck, teeth, trunk and ears, and large eyes (or pupils). Those that belong to the *Saṅkīrṇa* class have the characteristics of the above three classes intermingled.

[According to the commentator some read ह्रस्वोदर instead of ह्रस्वाधर. In the first quarter there is a metrical flaw, as the conjunct consonant makes the preceding vowel गुरु but Piṅgala allows it.]

पञ्चोन्नतिः सप्त मृगस्य दैर्घ्यमष्टौ च हस्ताः परिणाहमानम् ।
एकद्विवृद्धावथ मन्दभद्रौ सङ्कीर्णनागोऽनियतप्रमाणः ॥ ४ ॥

The height of an elephant of the *Mṛga* class is 5 cubits; length, 7 cubits; and girth, 8 cubits. These numbers increased by one are those of the *Manda* class (i.e. 6, 8 and 9 cubits respectively); by two, of the *Bhadra* class (i.e. 7, 9 and 10 cubits). The *Saṅkīrṇa* has no fixed dimensions.

[The last class has the dimensions of some limbs of one class and of others of other classes. The length is measured from the root of the tail.

Cf. पराशर—

परिणाहो दशसमो नवायामः स उच्छ्रयः ।
सप्त ज्येष्ठप्रमाणस्य नागस्य समुदाहृतः ॥
ज्येष्ठात् सप्तमभागोनो मध्यमो मध्यमाद्गजः ।
अन्त्यः षड्भागहीनः स्यादतोऽन्यो न स पूजितः ॥
मुखादापेचकं दैर्घ्यं पृथु पार्श्वोदरान्तरम् ।
आनाह उच्छ्रयः पादा विज्ञेयो यावदासनम् ॥]

भद्रस्य वर्णो हरितो मदश्च मन्दस्य हारिद्रकसन्निकाशः ।
कृष्णो मदश्चाभिहितो मृगस्य सङ्कीर्णनागस्य मदो विमिश्रः ॥५॥

The colour of the *Bhadra* elephant is green; so is its ichor. That of the *Manda* class is yellow and its ichor too is yellow. That of the body and ichor of the *Mṛga* type is black, while that of the two of the *Saṅkīrṇa* type is of a mixed nature.

ताम्रोष्ठतालुवदनाः कलविङ्कनेत्राः
स्निग्धोन्नताग्रदशनाः पृथुलायतास्याः ।
चापोन्नतायतनिगूढनिमग्नवंशा-
स्तन्वेकरोमचितकूर्मसमानकुम्भाः ॥६॥
विस्तीर्णकर्णहनुनाभिललाटगुह्याः
कूर्मोन्नतद्विनवविंशतिभिर्नखैश्च ।

रेखात्रयोपचितवृत्तकराः सुवाला
धन्याः सुगन्धिमदपुष्करमारुताश्च ॥ ७ ॥

Blessed are the elephants that have red lower lip, palate and mouth; eyes like those of sparrows; glossy tusks that are raised at the lips; long and broad face; arched and long back-bone, lying deep and not protruding; the frontal globes resembling the back of tortoise, and covered with thin and scanty hair (each pore having a single hair); broad ears, jaws (chins), navel, forehead and penis; 18 or 20 nails that are convex like the tortoise; round trunk covered with three vertical lines; fine hairs and fragrant ichor and breath.

[About the nails *vide* पराशर—

विंशत्यष्टौ दश नखाः स्थिराः कूर्मसमाहिताः ।
गजानां पूजिताः पादा ये च स्युरकचाविलाः ॥

The metre of the two verses is वसन्ततिलका.]

दीर्घाङ्गुलिरक्तपुष्कराः सजलाम्भोदनिनादबृंहिणः ।
बृहदायतवृत्तकन्धराः धन्या भूमिपतेर्मतङ्गजाः ॥ ८ ॥

Elephants with long fingers and red tip of the trunk, with its trumpeting similar to the thunder of clouds, and with a long, broad and round neck, bring good fortune to a king.

[The fingers of elephants are nothing but fleshy projections on the tip of the trunk. The metre is वैतालीय.]

निर्मदाभ्यधिकहीननखाङ्गान् कुब्जवामनकमेषविषाणान् ।
दृश्यकोशफलपुष्करहीनाञ्श्यावनीलशबलासिततालून् ॥९॥

स्वल्पवक्त्ररुहमत्कुणषण्ढान् हस्तिनीं च गजलक्षणयुक्ताम् ।
गर्भिणीं च नृपतिः परदेशं प्रापयेदतिविरूपफलास्ते ॥ १० ॥

Elephants that are never intoxicated, that have too many too few nails and limbs, that are crooked or dwarfed, whose tusks resemble a ram's horns, whose testicles are prominent, which are devoid of the special lotus-shaped tip of the trunk (i.e. *Puṣkara*), whose palate is dusky, blue, variegated or black, which have tiny tusks or no tusks at all, or are impotent, are to be removed by the king to another country, as they produce very disastrous results. The same treatment should be given to a cow (elephant) which has the characteristics of a bull and to one that is pregnant.

[It has been laid down that an elephant should have at least 18 nails and not more than 20 ones. If an elephant had less than the minimum number or more than the maximum one, it would be inauspicious. A कुब्ज elephant is defined thus:—

सङ्‌क्षिप्तवक्षोजघनः पृष्ठमध्यसमुन्नतः ।
प्रमाणहीनस्तन्नाभिः स कुब्जो वारणाधमः ॥

वामन is defined thus:

आनाहायामसंयुक्तो योऽतिह्रस्वो भवेद्‌गजः ।
वामनः स समाख्यातो भर्तुर्नार्थयशःपदः ॥

The tip of the trunk is called *Puṣkara* as it is shaped like a lotus. The word वक्त्ररुह् is either tusk or the hair on the face, according to the commentator. I feel it is better to take it in the former sense. *Matkuṇa* is an elephant without tusks. It is defined thus:—

सर्वलक्षणसम्पूर्णो दन्तैस्तु परिवर्जितः ।
मत्कुणः स समाख्यातः सङ्ग्रामे प्राणघातकः ॥

The *Ṣaṇḍha* (impotent one) is defined thus:—

पादयोः सन्निकर्षः स्याद्यस्य नागस्य गच्छतः ।
स षण्ढोऽध्वनि युद्धे च लक्षणज्ञैर्न पूजितः ॥

A new type of elephants called *Vikaṭa*, not mentioned by the author, is brought to our notice by Utpala who quotes the relevant definition thus:—

अनन्त्याभ्यधिकं यस्य विस्तारेण स्तनान्तरम् ।
विकटः स च निर्दिष्टो दुर्गतिर्निन्दितो गजः ॥

Why should the king send such unwanted elephants elsewhere? According to the Dharmaśāstra elephants ought not to be killed except in battle. Here परदेश is not merely another country, but enemy's country, because the king would wish that his misfortune might overtake his enemy.

The metre is स्वागता].

पुरुषलक्षणम् ॥६८॥

Chapter LXVIII—Signs of Men.

[This is an important chapter dealing with the physiognomy of man. The origin of this science is traced to Lord Śiva, one of His numerous names being Samudra, and to a sage called *Samudra*. According to another view *Samudra* was Viṣṇu. Hence the popular name of this lore is *Sāmudrika-śāstra*. The human body is also called *Samudra* as it is imprinted with lines. (See note under 43 infra). There is a short treatise ascribed to *Prahlāda*, in Kannaḍa script. Our author was well versed in this science. He calls a physiognomist सामुद्रवित्. Our commentator too was a scholar in this branch of learning. For, he quotes profusely from the works of *Samudra*, *Garga* and some unnamed source. He quotes only one verse from *Parāśara*. In this connection we cannot but remember the remarkable knowledge of this science evinced by Hanumān in the Rāmāyaṇa (V. 35-8,9, 14-20,22).]

I Body.

उन्मानमानगतिसंहतिसारवर्ण-
स्नेहस्वरप्रकृतिसत्त्वमनूकमादौ ।
क्षेत्रं मृजां च विधिवत् कुशलोऽवलोक्य
सामुद्रविद्वदति यातमनागतं वा ॥ १ ॥

An adept in the science of physiognomy (features of human beings) carefully observes at first, according to the rules, the height, weight, gait, compactness (hardness), strength (based on the seven basic ingredients), complexion, glossiness, voice, natural character, courage, hereditary elements (those that suggest the particulars of one's previous life), parts of the body and natural lustre, and then explains the past and the future.

[This shows that the सामुद्रिकशास्त्र is very extensive and exhaustive containing every detail, internal and external of man. There are 13 items a physiognomist is expected to observe. All these points are explained by the author himself in the course of this chapter. According to Utpala सामुद्र seems to be a work. For, he says समुद्रे प्रोक्तं पुरुषलक्षणं सामुद्रम्. I think it is the name of a sage. Hence it should be

समुद्रेण प्रोक्तम्: Here he rebuts the view of some scholars who think that as *Varāhamihira* has stated in verse 114 *infra Prakṛti* and *Sattva* to be synonyms, the latter word is redundant. He asserts, "It is not redundant." For, *Sattva* is a quality of the mind. When that is present, one is not afraid of anything. Under no circumstance one gets despondency. Vide the following:—

एकाकिनि वनवासिनि अराजलक्ष्मणि अनीतिशास्त्रज्ञे
सत्त्वोच्छ्रिते मृगपतौ राज्येऽतिगिरः परिणमन्ति ॥

While delineating the marks of the five types of great men the Ācārya has mentioned (LXIX 4) सत्त्व and प्रकृति separately. This will be clear from verse 108 *infra*, which says that *Prakṛti* is the natural quality of the five elements etc. *Sattva* is derived from the Sun and Mars.

Next he takes up the reading adopted by some viz. प्रकृतयश्च ततो ह्यनुक्रम् in the second line and condemns it as grammatically untenable. For, प्रकृति being the object ought to be in the accusative. Sage कात्यायन is quoted here to distinguish between उन्मान and मान:—

ऊर्ध्वमानं किलोन्मानं मानं तु तुलया धृतम् ॥

For the height of best, moderate and ordinary types of men see verse 105 *infra*. Similarly for weight, gait, hardness, strength, colour, glossiness, voice, nature, prenatal existence, limbs and lustre *vide* verses 106, 115, 87, 100, 96, 87, 102, 101, 95, 108-114, 103, 89 and LXX. 24-26. *Mṛjā* is the lustre born of the five elements.

Cf. ऋषिपुत्र—

या च च्छाया प्रभा सैव षड्विधा सा प्रकीर्तिता ।
स्वच्छा स्निग्धा प्रसन्ना च कान्ता दीप्ता विदीपिनी ॥

The first two verses are in वसन्ततिलका metre.

Though human beings are generally described from head to foot. Varāha follows the convention established by समुद्र, गर्ग and other ancient authorities who have done it from the feet.]

अस्वेदनौ मृदुतलौ कमलोदराभौ
श्लिष्टाङ्गुली रुचिरताम्रनखौ सुपार्ष्णी ।
उष्णौ शिराविरहितौ सुनिगूढगुल्फौ
कूर्मोन्नतौ च चरणौ मनुजेश्वरस्य ॥ २ ॥

[The following are the characteristics of a King's feet: They do *not* perspire; their soles are soft; they possess the lustre of the interior of a lotus; their toes are joined together; they have beautiful red nails; their heels are fine; they are warm and devoid of veins; their ankle-joints are well hidden; and they arch like the back of a tortoise.

रुचिरपार्श्वनखौ is another reading in the second line. The commentator explains it as 'whose nails are beautiful on the sides.'

Cf. समुद्र—

पादैः समासैः सुस्निग्धैः सोष्णैः श्लिष्टैः सुशोभनैः ।
उन्नतैः स्वेदरहितैः शिराहीनैश्च पार्थिवः ॥

also गर्ग—

पद्मरक्तोत्पलनिभैस्तथा क्षतजसन्निभैः ॥
नृपाः पादतलैर्ज्ञेया ये चान्ये सुखभागिनः ॥

The following verses occur in the *Prahlāda-Sāmudrika* relating to the feet:—

आरक्तमृदुनीरन्ध्र ऋज्वङ्गुलिकराङ्घ्रकः ।
न स्विन्नपाणिपादश्च भाग्यवान् भवति ध्रुवम् ॥
कूर्मपृष्ठाग्रपदवान् किञ्चिदुष्णाङ्घ्रिरेव च ।
सद्बुद्धिस्सुन्दरो यश्च स भवेज्जनवन्दितः ॥]

शूर्पाकारविरूक्षपाण्डुरनखौ वक्रौ शिरासन्ततौ
संशुष्कौ विरलाङ्गुली च चरणौ दारिद्र्यदुःखप्रदौ ।
मार्गायोत्कटकौ कषायसदृशौ वंशस्य विच्छेददौ
ब्रह्मघ्नौ परिपक्वमृद्द्युतितलौ पीतावगम्यारतौ ॥३॥

Poverty and grief are produced by feet that have the shape of winnowing baskets, that are very rough, that have white nails, that are crooked or long, that are full of veins, that are very dry and have far-removed toes. Travelling is the effect of having the feet that are raised in the middle; destruction of family is the result of tawny feet; murder of Brāhmaṇas, of those whose soles have the colour of burnt earth; and cohabitation with forbidden women, of those that are yellow.

[Cf. समुद्र—

शूर्पाकारैस्तथा भग्नैर्वक्रैः शुष्कैः शिराततैः ।
सस्वेदैः पाण्डुरै रूक्षैश्चरणैरतिदुःखिताः ।।
उत्कटावध्वनि रतौ कषायौ कुलनाशनौ ।
ब्रह्मघ्नौ दग्धमृद्वर्णावानिपीतावगम्यदौ ।।

also *Prahlāda-Sāmudrika*:—

दीर्घपाच्छूर्पकर्णश्च रच्छिद्राङ्गुलिकस्तथा ।
दुर्बलश्शुष्कजघनो दुःखभाग्भवति ध्रुवम् ।।

The metre is शार्दूलविक्रीडित.]

प्रविरलतनुरोमवृत्तजङ्घा द्विरदकरप्रतिमैर्वरोरुभिश्च ।
उपचितसमजानवश्च भूपा धनरहिताः श्वशृगालतुल्यजङ्घाः ।।४।।

If the shanks are round with sparse and thin hair, the thighs, beautiful, resembling the elephant's trunk, and knees, well-developed i.e. fleshy, and even, the person concerned becomes a monarch; while shanks resembling those of a jackal or dog conduce to pennilessness.

[Cf. समुद्र—

जङ्घाभिरभिवृत्ताभिरैश्वर्यमभिनिर्दिशेत् ।
शृगालजङ्घा दुःखान्ताः श्वजङ्घा नित्यमध्वगाः ।।

also प्रह्लाद—

तूणीरसन्निभे जङ्घे बाहू करिकरोपमौ ।
नेत्रे च पद्मपत्राभे स पुमान् राजलक्षणः ।।

The metre is पुष्पिताग्रा.]

रोमैकैकं कूपके पार्थिवानां द्वे द्वे ज्ञेये पण्डितश्रोत्रियाणाम् ।
त्र्याद्यैर्निःस्वा मानवा दुःखभाजः केशाश्चैवं निन्दिताः पूजिताश्च ।।५।।

Kings have a single hair in a pore and scholars and Vedic experts, two in one. Three and more hairs in one pore make men penurious and miserable. In the same manner are the hairs on the head auspicious and inauspicious as the case may be.

[The word श्रोत्रिय means, according to both lexicon and *Pāṇini*, a Vedic scholar, but Utpala says, श्रोत्रियाणां नियमिनाम्. He quotes from some source the following:

रोमशाभिस्तु जङ्घाभिर्दुःखदारिद्र्यभागिनः ।
एकरोमा भवेद्राजा द्विरोमा च महायशाः ॥
त्रिरोमा बहुरोमा च नरो भाग्यविवर्जितः ॥

Cf. प्रह्लाद—

लोमकूपे तु लोमैकं भूपालो भवति ध्रुवम् ।
धनी लोमद्वये भूरिलोमा त्वथ च निर्धनः ॥

The metre is शालिनी.]

निर्मांसजानुर्म्रियते प्रवासे सौभाग्यमल्पैर्विकटैर्दरिद्राः ।
स्त्रीनिर्जिताश्चैव भवन्ति निम्नै राज्यं समांसैश्च महद्भिरायुः ॥६॥

A man with bony knees dies abroad; one with small knees becomes attractive (or fortunate); one with large and rugged ones, indigent; one with sunken ones, vanquished by women; one with fleshy ones, a king; and one with very thick ones, long-lived.

[The commentator interprets निम्नैः as स्वेदयुक्तैः i.e. perspiring.

Cf. समुद्र—

निर्मांसे जानुनी यस्य प्रवासे म्रियते तु सः ।
अल्पैर्भवति सौभाग्यं विकटैश्च दरिद्रता ॥
स्त्रीजितः स्यात् तथा निम्नैर्मांसयुक्तैर्नराधिपः ।
अतिस्थूलैश्चिरं कालं जीवेदैश्वर्यसंयुतः ॥

The metre is इन्द्रवज्रा.]

लिङ्गेऽल्पे धनवानपत्यरहितः स्थूलेऽपि हीनो धनै-
र्मेढ्रे वामनते सुतार्थरहितो वक्रेऽन्यथा पुत्रवान् ।
दारिद्र्यं विनते त्वधोऽल्पतनयो लिङ्गे शिरासन्तते
स्थूलग्रन्थियुते सुखी मृदु करोत्यन्तं प्रमेहादिभिः ॥७॥

A man with a small genital organ becomes rich, but issueless; one with a stout organ, poor; with one bent towards the left, devoid of issue and wealth; with one turned towards the right, blessed with sons; with one bent on the lower side, poor; with one full of veins, father of few children; with one having a thick knot, happy; and with a soft one, dies of gonorrhoea and the like.

The metre is शार्दूलविक्रीडित.]

कोशनिगूढैर्भूपा दीर्घैर्भग्नैश्च वित्तपरिहीनाः ।
ऋजुवृत्तशेफसो लघुशिरालशिश्नाश्च धनवन्तः ॥८॥

Men with the genital organ covered with sheath-like skin become kings; with a long and split one, indigent; and with a straight and round organ, as well as with one having slender veins, wealthy.

[Cf. समुद्र—

दक्षिणावर्त्तलिङ्गो यः स भवेत् पुत्रवान् नरः ।
वामावर्त्ते तथा कन्याः सुबह्व्यः सम्भवन्ति च ॥
स्थूलैः शिरालैः कठिनैर्नरो दारिद्र्यभाजनः ।
ऋजुभिर्वर्त्तुलैर्लिङ्गैः पुरुषाः सुखभागिनः ॥
यस्य पादोपविष्टस्य भूमिं स्पृशति मेहनम् ।
दुःखितः स तु विज्ञेयो नरो दारिद्र्यभाजनः ॥
स्थूलग्रन्थियुते लिङ्गे नरोऽतिसुखभाग्भवेत् ।
लिङ्गेन मृदुना मर्त्यो म्रियते कृच्छ्रपीडितः ॥

also प्रह्लाद—

लिङ्गह्रस्वे महाभोगी लिङ्गाधिक्ये दरिद्रता ।
सौख्यं बलकरं तस्य मुष्कप्राबल्यतो बलम् ॥]

जलमृत्युरेकवृषणो विषमैः स्त्रीचञ्चलः समैः क्षितिपः ।
ह्रस्वायुश्चोद्बद्धैः प्रलम्बवृषणस्य शतमायुः ॥९॥

A man with a single testicle will have a watery grave; with unequal ones, becomes addicted to concubinage; with equal ones, a king; with these raised high, short-lived; and with hanging ones, lives a hundred years.

[Cf. समुद्र—

एकाण्डो जलमृत्युः स्याद्विषमैः स्त्रीषु चञ्चलः ।
समाण्डो नरनाथश्च संलग्नैरल्पजीवितः ॥
प्रलम्बाण्डः समानां तु शतं जीवति मानवः ॥

also प्रह्लाद—

समाण्डत्वे सुखं चायुः ह्रस्वाण्डत्वे प्रभुर्भवेत् ।
वक्राण्डत्वे सेवकश्च चर्माण्डस्तु नपुंसकः ॥]

रक्तैराढ्या मणिभिर्निर्द्रव्याः पाण्डुरैश्च मलिनैश्च ।
सुखिनः सशब्दमूत्रा निःस्वा निःशब्दधाराश्च ॥१०॥

द्वित्रिचतुर्धाराभिः प्रदक्षिणावर्त्तवलितमूत्राभिः ।
पृथिवीपतयो ज्ञेया विकीर्णमूत्राश्च धनहीनाः ॥११॥

एकैव मूत्रधारा वलिता रूपप्रदा न सुतदात्री ।
स्निग्धोन्नतसममणयो धनवनितारत्नभोक्तारः ॥१२॥

मणिभिश्च मध्यनिम्नैः कन्यापितरो भवन्ति निःस्वाश्च ।
बहुपशुभाजो मध्योन्नतैश्च नात्युल्बणैर्धनिनः ॥१३॥

Men with a red tip of their generating organ become very rich; with a whitish or dark tip, penurious; those who urinate noisily become happy; without any sound, poor; with two, three or four streams of urine turning in a circular fashion from left to right, kings; with scattered urine, poverty-stricken; with a single stream turning in a circular manner, blessed with attractive features, but without sons (or blessed with charming children); with the tip glossy, raised and even, enjoyers of wealth, women and gems; with the tip depressed in the middle, fathers of girls and poor; with the tip raised in the middle, owners of large herds of cattle and the like; and with a very stout one, devoid of wealth.

[रूपप्रधानसुतदात्री is another reading in the second quarter of verse 12. Cf. the following quotation from some work (based on that of समुद्र) given by Utpala :—

रक्ताकृतिर्मणिर्यस्य समो मध्ये विराजते ।
पार्थिवः स तु विज्ञेयः समुद्रवचनं तथा ॥
सुपूर्णरजतप्रख्यैर्मणिमुक्तासमप्रभैः ।
प्रवालसदृशैः स्निग्धैर्मणिभिः पार्थिवो भवेत् ॥
पाण्डुरैर्मलिनै रूक्षैः श्यावैरल्पैश्च निर्धनः ।
मूत्रधारा पतेद् देहाद् दक्षिणावलिता यदि ॥
पार्थिवः स तु विज्ञेयः समुद्रवचनं यथा ।
द्विधारं च पतेन्मूत्रं स्निग्धं शब्दविवर्जितम् ॥
भोगवान् स तु विज्ञेयो गवाढ्यो नात्र संशयः ।
बहुधारे तथा रूक्षे सशब्दे पुरुषाधमः'।

Here the slight difference between our author and the authority quoted may be noted: 'निःस्वा निःशब्दधाराश्च' of our author and 'सशब्दे पुरुषाधमः' of the other.

See what प्रह्लाद says:—

सशब्दमूत्रोत्सर्गश्च मधुसन्निभशुक्लभाक् ।
धनवान्पुत्रवान्भूयाद्रेतोदौर्गन्ध्यतोऽन्यथा ॥]

परिशुष्कवस्तिशीर्षधनरहिता दुर्भगाश्च विज्ञेयाः ।
कुसुमसमगन्धशुक्रा विज्ञातव्या महीपालाः ॥ १४॥

मधुगन्धे बहुवित्ता मत्स्यसगन्धे बहून्यपत्यानि ।
तनुशुक्रः स्त्रीजनको मांससगन्धो महाभोगी ॥१५॥

मदिरागन्धे यज्वा क्षारसगन्धे च रेतसि दरिद्रः ।
शीघ्रं मैथुनगामी दीर्घायुरतोऽन्यथाल्पायुः ॥१६॥

Men with the upper part of the abdomen dry (i.e. without flesh) become indigent and disliked by the people (of repulsive appearance). With their semen having the smell of flowers, men become kings; having the smell of honey, very rich; of fish, fathers of many children; of flesh, enjoyers of all kinds of pleasures; of liquor, performers of sacrifices; and of salt, very poor. Those, whose semen is thin, beget only daughters; those who have too frequent sexual congress (or who experience orgasm too soon ?), live long, and those who have it rarely (or whose orgasm is very late ?) are short-lived.

[Cf. the unnamed authority:—

विस्तीर्णमांसला स्निग्धा वस्तिः पुंसां प्रशस्यते ।
निर्मांसा कर्कशा रूक्षा दुःखदारिद्र्यदा स्मृता ॥
गोमायोः सदृशी यस्य खरोष्ट्रमहिषस्य च ।
स भवेद् दुःखितो नित्यं धनहीनश्च मानवः ॥

पुष्पगन्धो भवेद्राजा बहुस्वा मधुगन्धिनः ।
मत्स्यगन्धः पुत्रवान्स्यात् स्त्रीप्रजास्तनुरेतसः ॥
मांसगन्धो महाभोगी याज्ञिको मदिरासमः ।
गन्धो येषां क्षारसमस्ते निःस्वा मनुजाः स्मृताः ॥

Cf. प्रह्लाद—

क्वचिद्रतिः क्वचिन्निद्रो भुङ्क्तेऽल्पं क्षिप्रमेव यः ।
चिरस्नायी दीर्घसक्षो (क्ष्यो?) भाग्यवान्भवति ध्रुवम् ॥]

निःस्वोऽतिस्थूलस्फिक् समांसलस्फिक् सुखान्वितो भवति ।
व्याघ्रान्तोऽध्यर्धस्फिग् मण्डूकस्फिग् नराधिपतिः ॥१७॥

A man with very stout buttocks becomes penurious; with fleshy or muscular ones, happy; with an extra half-buttock one each side, a killer of tigers (or a prey to tigers ?); and with frog-like ones, a king.

[व्याघ्रान्तः may be interpreted as व्याघ्राणामन्तः अन्तकः meaning killer of tigers; but Bhaṭṭotpala says: व्याघ्रः प्राणी तं मारयति i.e. he meets his end at the hands of a tiger. This may be explained thus: व्याघ्राद् अन्तः मरणं यस्य सः. We may make a compromise between these two meanings thus: He becomes a great hunter of tigers (kills many) and ultimately gets killed by one. Cf. the unnamed source:—

अतिस्थूलौ स्फिजौ यस्य निर्धनः स भवेन्नरः ।
समांसल स्फिक् सुखितो मण्डूकस्फिग् नराधिपः ॥
अध्यर्धस्फिग् नरो यस्तु व्याघ्रान्तः स तु कीर्तितः ॥]

सिंहकटिर्मनुजेन्द्रः कपिकरभकटिर्धनैः परित्यक्तः ।
समजठरा भोगयुता घटपिठरनिभोदरा निःस्वाः ॥ १८ ॥

A man with a waist similar to the lions becomes a king; with one like that of a monkey or camel, penniless; with an even belly (neither sunken nor raised), enjoyer of pleasures; and with a belly resembling a pot or a frying pan, utterly indigent.

[Cf. the same source:—

सिंहतुल्या कटिर्यस्य स नरेन्द्रो न संशयः ।
श्वशृगालखरोष्ट्राणां तुल्या यस्य स निर्धनः ॥
समोदरा भोगयुता विषमा निर्धनाः स्मृताः ॥

also प्रह्लाद—

कक्षकुक्षी च वक्षश्च घ्राणस्कन्धौ ललाटकम् ।
सर्वभूतेषु निर्दिष्टं तद्बुधिष्णु षडुन्नतम् ॥

The description of Śrī Rāma's body viz. षडुन्नतो नवतनुः—, agrees with this.]

अविकलपार्श्वा धनिनो निम्नैर्वक्रैश्च भोगसंन्त्यक्ताः ।
समकुक्षा भोगाढ्या निम्नाभिर्भोगपरिहीनाः ॥१९॥

उन्नतकुक्षाः क्षितिपाः कुटिलाः स्युर्मानवा विषमकुक्षाः ।
सर्पोदरा दरिद्रा भवन्ति बह्वाशिनश्चैव ॥२०॥

Men with fleshy sides become wealthy; with sunken and crooked ones, devoid of the pleasures of life; with an even stomach, blessed with all luxuries; with a sunken one, bereft of happiness; with a raised stomach, kings; with an uneven one, crafty; with a serpentine (very long and thin) one, penniless and gluttonous.

[Utpala explains कुक्षा thus: कुक्षाशब्देनोदरमध्यभाग उच्यते. Cf. the same source:—

पार्श्वैः समांसोपचितैर्धनिनो मानवाः स्मृताः ।
निम्नैर्वक्रैश्च विषमैर्नरा भोगविवर्जिताः ॥
समकुक्षा भोगयुक्ता निम्नाभिर्भोगवर्जिताः ।
नृपाश्चोन्नतकुक्षाः स्युर्विषमाभिर्दुराशयाः ॥
सर्पोदरा नरा निःस्वा स्मृता बह्वाशिनस्तथा ॥]

परिमण्डलोन्नताभिर्विस्तीर्णाभिश्च नाभिभिः सुखिनः ।
अल्पा त्वदृश्यनिम्ना नाभिः क्लेशावहा भवति ॥२१॥

वलिमध्यगता विषमा शूलाद् बाधां करोति नैस्व्यं च ।
शाठ्यं वामावर्ता करोति मेधां प्रदक्षिणतः ॥२२॥

Men become happy with a navel that is round, raised and broad; afflcted with troubles with one that is small, almost invisible and deep; poor and suffering from colic (or they die being impaled) with one that is uneven and surrounded by folds of skin; rogues with one that is turned from right to left; intelligent with one that circles from left to right; long-lived with one that is elongated at the sides; lords (opulent) with one that is elongated at the top; owners of cattle with one that is elongated at the lower end; and kings with one like the knob in the centre of a lotus.

[शूलाद् etc. is explained by the commentator as: 'शूलादभिन्नतनोस्तस्य मृत्युर्भवति' । He quotes a verse to explain the qualities of a rogue:

वचसा मनसा यश्च दृश्यतेऽकार्यतत्परः ।
कर्मणा विपरीतश्च स शठः सद्भिरिष्यते ॥

We may also take the following line :

मनस्यन्यद् वचस्यन्यत्कर्मण्यन्यद् दुरात्मनाम् ॥

The qualities of the intelligent are:—

शुश्रूषा श्रवणं चैव ग्रहणं धारणं तथा ।
ऊहापोहार्थविज्ञानं तत्त्वज्ञानं च धीगुणाः ॥

कर्णिका is explained thus: मध्येऽन्तः पद्मकर्णिकाकार उच्चभागो भवति । तत्सदृशी नाभिर्मध्योन्नता । Cf. the unnamed authority:—

वर्तुला विपुलात्युच्चा नाभिर्यदि नरेश्वरः ।
अल्पदृश्याः तथा निम्ना नाभिः क्लेशावहा भवेत् ॥
वलिमध्यगता या च सा शूलाद् वधकारिणी ।
वामावर्त्ता शाठ्यभावं धिषणां च प्रदक्षिणा ॥
पार्श्वयिता दीर्घजीवं धनयुक्तं तथोर्ध्वगा ।
अधो गोवाहुलं कुर्यान्नाभिर्भोगसमन्वितम् ॥
पद्मस्य कर्णिकातुल्या नाभिः कुर्यान्नरेश्वरम् ॥

also प्रह्लाद—

स्याद्वामावर्त्तनाभिस्तु दरिद्रो दक्षिणे धनी ।
वलिमध्ये तु नाभिश्चेन्निर्धनः पापकर्मभाक् ॥
उदरे वलिरेखा चेच्छस्त्रघातो भविष्यति ।
वलिद्वये स्त्रीविजयी त्रितये बहुभोगभाक् ॥
शूरश्चतुष्टये भूयात्फलमेवं पृथक् पृथक् ॥]

शस्त्रान्तं स्त्रीभोगिनमाचार्यं बहुसुतं यथासङ्ख्यम् ।
एकद्वित्रिचतुर्भिर्वलिभिर्विन्द्यान्नृपं त्ववलिम् ॥२४॥

विषमवलयो मनुष्या भवन्त्यगम्याभिगामिनः पापाः ।
ऋजुवलयः सुखभाजः परदारद्वेषिणश्चैव ॥२५॥

Persons with one, two, three, four and no folds at all on their belly become slain with weapons, enjoyers of many women, preceptors or teachers of men, fathers of many sons, and kings respectively. Those who have unequal folds become sinners and addicted to forbidden women; and those whose folds are straight enjoy happiness and hate other's wives (i.e. they remain pure in marital relations).

[About परदार Kālidāsa's statement is noteworthy:

वशिनां तु परपरिग्रहसंश्लेषपराङ्मुखी वृत्तिः ॥

Vide the unnamed authority:

एकवलिः शस्त्रमृत्युः स्त्रीभोगी द्विवलिः स्मृतः ।
त्रिभिराचार्य इत्याहुश्चतुर्भिः स्याद्बहुप्रजः ॥

अवलिस्तु नृपः प्रोक्तो यज्वा दानैकतत्परः ।
विषमा वलयो येषु ते चागम्याभिगामिनः ।।
ऋज्व्यस्तु वलयो येषु ते नराः सुखभागिनः ।।]

मांसलमृदुभिः पार्श्वैः प्रदक्षिणावर्तरोमभिर्भूपाः ।
विपरीतैर्निर्द्रव्याः सुखपरिहीनाः परप्रेष्याः ।।२६।।

With fleshy and tender sides having hairy circles going from left and right men become kings; whereas with these of contrary characteristics i.e. without flesh, rough and with hairy circles turning from right to left, they become indigent, devoid of happiness, and slaves of others.

[Utpala explains that पार्श्वं or side, is an area of 4 digits above the waist. Cf. the following:

मांसलैर्मृदुभिः पार्श्वैर्दक्षिणावर्तरोमभिः ।
नरा भूम्यधिपा ज्ञेया विपरीतैः सुदुःखिताः ।।

सुभगा भवन्त्यनुद्बद्धचूचुका निर्धना विषमदीर्घैः ।
पीनोपचितनिमग्नैः क्षितिपतयश्चूचुकैः सुखिनः ।।२७।।

People whose nipples are not raised become attractive and fortunate; while those whose nipples are unequal and long become poor. With stout (hard ?), muscular and sunken ones they become kings enjoying happiness.

[Cf. the above authority:—

चूचुकैश्चाप्यनुद्बद्धैः सुभगाः सुखभागिनः ।
निर्धना विषमैर्दीर्घैर्मग्नैर्मांसयुतैर्नृपाः ।।

also प्रह्लाद—

अदर्शने तु नाडीनां सुखभोजनमादिशेत् ।
उत्तुङ्गचूचुको भूयादनपत्यश्च दुःखभाक् ।।]

हृदयं समुन्नतं पृथु न वेपनं मांसलं च नृपतीनाम् ।
अधनानां विपरीतं खररोमचितं शिरालं च ।।२८।।

Only kings possess a heart that is raised, broad, muscular and not convulsive, while the penniless have one that has contrary features, and is full of veins and rough and thick hair.

[Cf. the same source:—

अचलं च पृथूच्चं च नृपाणां हृदयं स्मृतम् ।
विपरीतं शिरालं च रोमशं दुःखभागिनाम् ।।]

समवक्षसोऽर्थवन्तः पीनैः शूरा ह्यकिञ्चनास्तनुभिः ।
विषमं वक्षो येषां ते निःस्वाः शस्त्रनिधनाश्च ।।२६।।

People with an even chest (neither depressed nor raised) become wealthy; with a muscular one, heroes; with one deficient in flesh, penniless (or without manliness ?), and with an uneven one, indigent and meet their end by weapons.

[Cf. the same source:—

अर्थवान् समवक्षाः स्याद् दीर्घैः शूरा धनान्विताः ।
अल्पैश्च विकला दीना विषमैः शस्त्रमृत्यवः ।।

Utpala construes अकिञ्चनाः as 'अकिञ्चित्कराः पुरुषकारहीनाः'. This is quite opposed to the accepted meaning of the word. vide 'अकिञ्चनत्वं मखजं व्यनक्ति' of Kālidāsa.]

विषमैर्विषमो जत्रुभिरर्थविहीनोऽस्थिसन्धिपरिणद्धैः ।
उन्नतजत्रुर्भोगी निम्नैर्निःस्वोऽर्थवान् पीनैः ।।३०।।

One who has undulating (unequal ?) collar bones becomes cruel; with these having many bony knots or sharp joints, poor; with raised ones, enjoyer of pleasures; with sunken ones, penniless; and with stout ones, wealthy.

[We cannot understand Utpala's explanation:
'जत्रुः कुक्षयोः सन्धिः'. See what Kṣīrasvāmin says:—
'अंसवक्षसयोस्सन्धिरुद्भिन्नास्ति जत्रु" । (Amara II. 6-78).
Cf. the same source:—

जत्रुभिर्विषमैः क्रूरा दरिद्राः क्रूरसन्धिभिः ।
भोगी चोन्नतजत्रुः स्यान्निम्नै र्निःस्वोऽन्यथा धनी ।।

It is to be noted in this connection that according to Vālmīki, who says गूढजत्रुः about Śrī Rāma, the collar bone should not be prominent i.e. it should be hidden by muscles.]

चिपिटग्रीवो निःस्वः शुष्का सशिरा च यस्य वा ग्रीवा ।
महिषग्रीवः शूरः शस्त्रान्तो वृषसमग्रीवः ।।३१।।

कम्बुग्रीवो राजा प्रलम्बकण्ठः प्रभक्षणो भवति ।
पृष्ठमभग्नमरोमशमर्थवतामशुभदमतोऽन्यत् ॥३२॥

One is penniless with a neck that is flat, dry (without flesh) and full of veins; heroic with one like that of a buffalo; meets with one's end by weapons with a neck similar to a bull's; a king with one having three lines or folds (conch-like); and a glutton (spendthrift ?) with a hanging (or long) one. Men become wealthy, if their back is neither split nor filled with hair; and miserable if it is otherwise i.e. split and hairy.

[A conch-like neck is thus described:—

वलित्रयचितग्रीवः कम्बुग्रीवोऽभिधीयते ॥

Utpala construes प्रभक्षणः as प्रसञ्चयशीलः one who does not save anything, a spendthrift. *Vide* the following:

ग्रीवा च वर्तुला यस्य स नरो धनवान् स्मृतः ।
कम्बुग्रीवा नरा ये तु राजानस्ते न संशयः ॥
दीर्घग्रीवा नरा ये तु तेऽपि दुःखस्य भागिनः ।
वक्रग्रीवा नरा ये ते दाम्भिकाः पिशुनास्तथा ॥
निःस्वस्तु चिपिटग्रीवः शुष्कग्रीवस्तथैव च ।
शूरस्तु महिषग्रीवः शस्त्रान्तो वृषकन्धरः ॥
सुस्निग्धं मांसलं पृष्ठमभग्नं चाप्यरोमशम् ।
सधनानां विपर्यस्तं निर्धनानां प्रकीर्तितम् ॥

See प्रह्लाद—

ग्रीवा च जघनं पृष्ठमूलं जङ्घे तथैव च ।
ह्रस्वानि यस्य चत्वारि पूजामाप्नोति मानवः ॥]

अस्वेदनपीनोन्नतसुगन्धसमरोमसङ्कुलाः कक्षाः ।
विज्ञातव्या धनिनामतोऽन्यथार्थविहीनानाम् ॥३३॥

Men whose arm-pits do not perspire, and are plump (fleshy), raised, having good smell, even and hairy are to be understood as wealthy; otherwise (if they perspire, are without flesh, sunken, foul-smelling and bereft of hair), as penniless.

[*Vide* the following:—

निःस्वेदमांसलाः कक्षाः सुगन्धा रोमसङ्कुलाः ।
धनिनां तु विजानीयान्निर्धनानामतोऽन्यथा ॥]

निर्मांसौ रोमचितौ भग्नावल्पौ च निर्धनस्यांसौ ।
विपुलावव्युच्छिन्नौ सुश्लिष्टौ सौख्यवीर्यवताम् ॥३४॥

A poor man's shoulders are full of hair, split, small and without flesh, while those of the happy and the powerful are large, unsplit and compact (strong and sturdy).

[*Vide* the following:—

कदलीस्तम्भसङ्काशा अजस्कन्धाश्च ये नराः ।
राजानस्ते विजानीयुर्महाकोशा महाबलाः ॥
निर्मांसरोमबहुला निर्धनस्य प्रकीर्तिताः ॥]

करिकरसदृशौ वृत्तावाजान्ववलम्बिनौ समौ पीनौ ।
बाहू पृथिवीशानामधनानां रोमशौ ह्रस्वौ ॥३७॥

Kings have arms that resemble the trunks of elephants, that are round, equal, muscular and touching the knees; whereas the poor have hairy and short ones.

[*Vide* the following:—

उद्बद्धबाहुः पुरुषो वधबन्धमवाप्नुयात् ।
दीर्घबाहुर्भवेद्राजा समुद्रवचनं तथा ॥
प्रलम्बबाहुरैश्वर्यं प्राप्नुयाद् गुणसंयुतम् ।
ह्रस्वबाहुर्भवेद्दासः परप्रेष्यकरस्तथा ॥
वामावर्त्तभुजा ये तु ये तु दीर्घभुजा नराः ।
सम्पूर्णबाहवो ये तु राजानस्ते प्रकीर्त्तिताः ॥]

हस्ताङ्गुलयो दीर्घाश्चिरायुषामवलिताश्च सुभगानाम् ।
मेधाविनां च सूक्ष्माश्चिपिटाः परकर्मनिरतानाम् ॥३६॥

स्थूलाभिर्धनरहिता बहिर्नताभिश्च शस्त्रनिर्याणाः ।
कपिसदृशकरा धनिनो व्याघ्रोपमपाणयः पापाः ॥३७॥

Long fingers conduce to long life; those that are not crooked i.e. straight, to an attractive personality (or fortune); lean ones, to intellectual eminence; flat ones, to servitude; very thick ones, to poverty; and those that are bent backwards, to death by weapons. The rich have hands similar to those of monkeys; and sinners, of tigers.

[Here the author distinguishes six types of fingers and two of hands. In modern palmistry too these distinctions are seen. The commentator distinguishes मेधा, मति and प्रज्ञा by means of the following:

अतितानस्मृतिर्मेधा तत्कालग्राहिणी मतिः ।
शुभाशुभविचारज्ञा प्रज्ञा धीरैरुदाहृता ॥]

मणिबन्धनैर्निगूढैर्दृढैश्च सुश्लिष्टसन्धिभिर्नृपाः ।
हीनैर्हस्तच्छेदः श्लथैः सशब्दैश्च निर्द्रव्याः ॥३८॥

Wrists that are hidden, firm and of well-knit joints make men kings; deficient ones indicate severance of the hands; and loose and sounding ones, poverty.

पितृवित्तेन विहीना भवन्ति निम्नेन करतलेन नराः ।
संवृतनिम्नैर्धनिनः प्रोत्तानकराश्च दातारः ॥३९॥

विषमैर्विषमा निःस्वाश्च करतलैरीश्वरास्तु लाक्षाभैः ।
पीतैरगम्यवनिताभिगामिनो निर्धना रूक्षैः ॥४०॥

Men with sunken palms are without patrimony; with the palms having round depressions, wealthy; with raised ones, philanthropists; with rugged ones, cruel and poor; with those red like lac, very opulent; with yellowish ones, addicted to forbidden women; and with rough and dry ones, penniless.

[*Vide* प्रह्लाद—

पाणिपादतले रक्ते नेत्रान्ते च नखस्तथा ।
तालुजिह्वाधरोष्ठं च सप्तरक्तः श्रियः पदम्
यस्य हस्ततलं सम्यक् कठिनं स हि कर्मकृत् ॥]

तुषसदृशनखाः क्लीबाश्चिपिटैः स्फुटितैश्च वित्तसन्त्यक्ताः ।
कुनखविवर्णैः परतर्ककाश्च ताम्रैश्चमूपतयः ॥४१॥

Those whose nails resemble husk i.e. are rough and contain many lines, are impotent; with flat and split nails men become poor; with ugly and colourless ones, dependent on others; and with red ones, commanders of armies.

अङ्गुष्ठयवैराढ्याः सुतवन्तोऽङ्गुष्ठमूलजैश्च यवैः ।
दीर्घाङ्गुलिपर्वाणः सुभगाः दीर्घायुषश्चैव ॥४२॥

Wealthy are those that have the lines shaped like a barley corn in the middle of their thumb; blessed with sons, when the figure is at the root of the thumb; and amiable or fortunate and long-lived, if the knuckles are far-removed.

[*Vide* प्रह्लाद—

सूक्ष्माण्यङ्गुलिपर्वाणि केशदन्तनखत्वचः ।
दीर्घायुषो नरा येषां पञ्चसूक्ष्मत्वलक्षणम् ॥
अङ्गुष्ठस्थितपर्वान्तर्गोधूमयवरेखिकाः ।
सूचयन्त्यपि मृष्टान्नं धनधान्यादिसम्पदः ॥
पर्वान्तरालं सूक्ष्मं च पृथु पर्वं यदा भवेत् ।
संयोजने छिद्रदर्शी निर्धनो भविता नरः ॥]

स्निग्धा निम्ना रेखा धनिनां तद्व्यत्ययेन निःस्वानाम् ।
विरलाङ्गुलयो निःस्वा धनसञ्चयिनो घनाङ्गुलयः ॥४३॥

The wealthy possess glossy (clean) and deep lines on their palms; the poor, rough and not deep ones. The fingers of the poor are far removed from one another, while those of hoarders of wealth, thick.

[*Vide* प्रह्लाद—

रेखासमाकृतौ शस्तं वैकृते विकृतं फलम् ॥
रेखैव ह्यैश्वरी मुद्रा शरीरं हि समुद्रकम् ।
एतत्सामुद्रिकं शास्त्रं सङ्ग्रहेण समीरितम् ॥]

तिस्रो रेखा मणिबन्धनोत्थिताः करतलोपगा नृपतेः ।
मीनयुगाङ्कितपाणिर्नित्यं सत्रप्रदो भवति ॥४४॥

वज्राकारा धनिनां विद्याभाजां च मीनपुच्छनिभाः ।
शङ्खातपत्रशिबिकागजाश्वपद्मोपमा नृपतेः ॥४५॥

कलशमृणालपताकाङ्कुशोपमाभिर्भवन्ति निधिपालाः ।
दामनिभाभिश्चाढ्याः स्वस्तिकरूपाभिरैश्वर्यम् ॥४६॥

चक्रासिपरशुतोमरशक्तिधनुःकुन्तसन्निभा रेखाः ।
कुर्वन्ति चमूनाथं यज्वानमुलूखलाकाराः ४७॥

मकरध्वजकोष्ठागारसन्निभाभिर्महाधनोपेताः ।
वेदीनिभेन चैवाग्निहोत्रिणो ब्रह्मतीर्थेन ॥४८॥

वापीदेवकुलाद्यैर्धर्मं कुर्वन्ति च त्रिकोणाभिः ।
अङ्गुष्ठमूलरेखाः पुत्राः स्युर्दारिकाः सूक्ष्माः ॥४६॥

रेखाः प्रदेशिनिगताः शतायुषं कल्पनीयमूनाभिः ।
छिन्नाभिर्द्रुमपतनं बहुरेखारेखिणो निःस्वाः ॥५०॥

Three lines starting from the wrist and going towards the palm make one a king. One with a palm marked with a pair of fish performs sacrifice daily (or feeds the worthy); those who have the figure of the weapon *Vajra* become rich; of fish-tail, learned men; of conch, umbrella, palanquin, elephant, horse and lotus, kings; of a pitcher, lotus-stalk, flag and goad, very rich with buried treasures; of rope, wealthy; of *Svastika*, lords; of discus, sword, axe, lance, spike, bow and spear, commanders of armies; of mortar, sacrificers; of a crocodile, banner and store-room, blessed with immense wealth. Those whose root of the thumb is shaped like an altar, become worshippers of the sacred fire; men with the figures of a quadrangular tank, temple and the like (i.e. throne, Bilva tree and sacrificial post) as well as of a triangle, performers of religious and meritorious acts. Conspicuous and slender lines at the root of the thumb indicate sons and daughters respectively. Three lines touching the fore-finger make one live for 100 years; and for shorter ones proportionate reduction in the years will have to be made. If the lines are in the middle, the person will have a fall from a tree. Those who have either too many lines or no lines at all on their palms become utterly penniless.

[The *Vajra* weapon is shaped like dumb-bells. *Vide* the following:—

सुवर्तुलैर्निगूढैश्च मणिबन्धैः समन्विताः ।
दृढैश्च शब्दरहितै राजानस्ते प्रकीर्त्तिताः ॥
हीनैश्च छिन्नपाणिः स्यात् श्लथैर्दारिद्र्यभाजनः ।
निम्ने करतले यस्य पितृवित्तविवर्जितः ॥
निम्नेन संवृतेनैव वित्तवान् सौख्यसंयुतः ।
समुत्तानकरा ये च दातारस्ते न संशयः ॥
विषमैर्विषमा निःस्वा लाक्षाभैरीश्वराः करैः ।
अगम्यागामिनः पीतैर्नखैर्हस्तैश्च निर्धनाः ॥

शूर्पशुक्तौ तुषनखा नैकवर्णा महानखाः ।
स्फुटितार्धनखाश्चैव स्मृता द्रव्यविवर्जिताः ॥
निर्मलैर्लोहिताभैश्च नखैर्भवति पार्थिवः ।
पाण्डुरा विरला रूक्षा अङ्गुल्यः करसंस्थिताः ॥
येषां ते च नरा ज्ञेया दुःखदारिद्र्यभाजनाः ।
यस्य मीनसमा रेखाः कर्मसिद्धिस्तु तस्य वै ॥
धनवान् स तु विज्ञेयो बहुपुत्रश्च मानवः ।
तुला यस्य तु वेदिर्वा करमध्ये प्रदर्शिता ॥
वाणिज्यं सिद्ध्यते तस्य पुरुषस्य न संशयः ।
वेदी पाणितले यस्य द्विजस्य तु विशेषतः ॥
यज्ञयाजी भवेन्नित्यं बहुवित्तश्च मानवः ।
श्रीवत्समथवा पद्मं वज्रं चामरमेव वा ॥
यस्य हस्ते तु दृश्येत स भवेत्पृथिवीपतिः ।
शक्तितोमरखड्गाभा रेखाश्चापसमास्तथा ॥
यस्य हस्ते प्रदृश्यन्ते चमूनाथं च तं विदुः ।
वृक्षो वाप्यथवा शैलः करमध्ये तु दृश्यते ॥
अचलं प्राप्यते राज्यं मण्डले तु न संशयः ।
ध्वजं वाप्यथवा शृङ्गं (शङ्खं) दृश्यते करसंस्थितम् ॥
धनेशत्वं विजानीयात् समुद्रवचनं यथा ।
दक्षिणे तु कराङ्गुष्ठे यवो यस्य च दृश्यते ॥
सर्वविद्याप्रवक्तासौ भवतीति च निर्दिशेत् ।
यस्य पाणितले रेखा कनिष्ठामूलसम्भवा ॥
गता मध्ये प्रदेशिन्यां स जीवेच्छरदां शतम् ।
अङ्गुष्ठमूले या रेखाः पुत्रास्ते परिकीर्तिताः ॥
सूक्ष्माः कन्या विनिर्दिष्टाः समुद्रवचनं यथा ।
छिन्नाभिर्वृक्षपतनं प्रभूताभिरनीश्वराः ॥
अङ्गुष्ठमूलतीर्थेन यज्ञयाजी भवेन्नरः ॥

Vide प्रह्लाद—

मणिबन्धे त्रिरेखासु मणिभूषणभाग्भवेत् ।
साधारणो द्विरेखः स्यादेकरेखस्तु भिक्षुकः ॥
मणिबन्धे कङ्कणाख्याश्चतस्रो भोगलक्षणाः ।
राज्ञां तिस्रस्तु नारीषु कामिन्यां द्वितयं स्मृतम् ॥
अधः कनिष्ठिकादीनामङ्गुलीनामृजुद्वयम् ।
संसारिलक्षणं ब्रूते विपरीते विपर्ययः ॥

क्रीडाविद्या भोगपुण्यफलमन्त्यादि कीर्तितम् ।
सूक्ष्मद्विद्वयरेखाभ्यां तद्भङ्गे भङ्गसम्भवः ॥
गिरिर्गजोऽङ्कुशं शङ्खं कुण्डलं चन्द्रसूर्यकौ ।
योनिरान्दोलिका चैव कङ्कणं चापमस्तकम् ॥
नेत्रं च स्वस्तिकं शूलं किरीटं पानभाजनम् ।
कर्कटं (कङ्कटं ?) परशुश्चेति रेखा अङ्गुष्ठमूलगाः ॥
कुलिशाद्यास्तथा रेखा निर्दिष्टा हस्तमध्यगाः
रेखा अप्यनुरेखाश्च उपरेखाश्च सूक्ष्मगाः ॥
प्राणिकर्मानुसारेण देहजाः फलसूचकाः ।
विस्पष्टं परिदृश्यन्ते कर्मकृद्धस्तमध्यगाः ॥
किरीटं पुस्तकं वल्ली चित्रध्वजसमुद्भवाः ।
पाण्डित्यलक्षणा रेखा मस्तकं चौर्यलक्षणम् ॥
धनकृत्कलशं सर्पो वीणा गायनलक्षणा ।
जीवहिंसाकरः पाशः पानकृत्पानभाजनम् ॥
योन्यादिके तु दौर्भाग्यं यूपाद्ये यज्ञशीलता ।
त्रिशूलादौ भिक्षुकत्वं फलमुच्चावचं वदेत् ॥
पूर्णमायुः परीक्षेत पश्चाल्लक्षणमीरयेत् ।
आयुर्हीननराणां तु लक्षणैः किं प्रयोजनम् ॥
नवरन्ध्राणि हस्ताङ्घ्रिपृष्ठनाभिशिरोवपुः ।
कण्ठवक्षोदरोर्वादि सहरेखं परीक्षयेत् ॥
स्वरं दृष्टिं च शीलं च विज्ञाय फलमीरयेत् ॥

The following verses from the हरगौरीसामुद्रिक are interesting:—

यस्य मीनसमा रेखा कर्मसिद्धिश्च जायते ।
धनाढ्यस्तु स विज्ञेयो बहुपुत्रो न संशयः ॥
तुलाग्रामौ तथा रज्जुः करमध्ये च दृश्यते ।
तस्य वाणिज्यसिद्धिः स्यात्पुरुषस्य न संशयः ॥
शङ्खचक्रध्वजाकारो माषाकारश्च दृश्यते ।
सर्वविद्याप्रदानेन बुद्धिमान्स भवेन्नरः ॥
अङ्कुशं कुण्डलं चक्रं यस्य पाणितले भवेत् ।
तस्य राज्यं महच्छ्रेष्ठं सामुद्रवचनं तथा ॥
यस्य पाणावूर्ध्वरेखा कनिष्ठामूलसंस्थिता ।
स नरः परदेशेषु दीर्घमायुश्च विन्दति ॥
रेखैका मणिबन्धे तु राजभोगी भवेन्नरः ।
यदि द्वे स गुणी वक्ता धनवांश्च भविष्यति ॥

अनामिकापूर्वमूले कनिष्ठादिक्रमेण तु ।
आयुर्दशैव वर्षाणि सामुद्रवचनं तथा ॥
तर्जनीमूलपर्याप्तं कनिष्ठादिक्रमेण चेत् ।
आयुश्च विंशतेःषट्कं रक्तरेखा च दृश्यते ॥
यदा रेखान्तरैर्भिन्ना स्वयं भिन्ना च दृश्यते ।
तदा सम्यग् विजानीयाद् गण्डकालं विशेषतः ॥
सा निम्ना चेदधोभागे कनिष्ठादिक्रमेण तु ।
वृक्षादुन्नतदेशाद्वा वाहनात्पतनं भवेत् ॥

Vide also गर्गसामुद्रिक—

अङ्गुष्ठमूलगा रेखाः सन्तानं सूचयन्ति ताः ।
साङ्कुराश्च तथा नार्यः पुरुषाश्च जटाः स्मृताः ।
दीर्घा दीर्घायुषो ज्ञेया अल्पा अल्पायुषः स्मृताः ।
गर्भस्रावस्तु सूक्ष्मत्वे विच्छेदे बालघातकः ॥
तदभावे प्रजाभाव इति सन्तानलक्षणम् ।
दम्पत्यन्यतरालाभे तदभावोऽन्यथान्यथा ॥
कनिष्ठाङ्गुलिमूले तु रेखाः करतलान्तगाः ।
सहोदरान्सूचयन्ति पुत्रवत्तत्र निर्णयः ॥]

अतिकृशदीर्घैश्चिबुकैर्निर्द्रव्या मांसलैर्धनोपेताः ।
बिम्बोपमैरवक्रैरधरैर्भूपास्तनुभिरस्वाः ॥५१॥

प्रोष्ठैः स्फुटितविखण्डितविवर्णरूक्षैश्च धनपरित्यक्ताः ।
स्निग्धा घनाश्च दशनाः सुतीक्ष्णदंष्ट्राः समाश्च शुभाः ॥५२॥

Very lean and long chins suggest poverty; while fleshy ones, wealth; straight (not crooked) lower lips resembling the ripe *Bimba* fruit (*Coccina indica*) make men kings; while lean (without flesh) ones, indigent. The upper lips being split, cut, colourless and dry make men penurious. The teeth being glossy (clean), equal and close-knit and the canine ones very sharp and equal are auspicious.

[Cf. the following:—

निर्मांसैश्चिबुकैर्दीर्घैर्निर्द्रव्याश्चाशुवाचिनः ।
समांसलैर्धनोपेता बहुपुत्रसमावृताः ॥
रक्ताधरो नरपतिर्धनवान् कमलाधरः ।
स्थूलोष्ठा बहुलोमाश्च शुष्कैः क्षीणैश्च दुःखिताः ॥
उत्तरोष्ठैर्लोहितैश्च धनिनः सौख्यसंयुताः ।
खण्डैर्विवर्णैर्निर्द्रव्या रूक्षैर्दुःखसमन्विताः ॥

कुन्दकुड्मलसङ्काशैः प्राकारैर्दशनैर्नृपः ।
ऋक्षवानरदन्ताश्च नित्यं क्षुत्परिपीडिताः ॥
हस्तिदन्ताः खररदाः स्निग्धदन्ता गुणान्विताः ।
करालैर्विषमैर्दीर्घैर्दशनैर्दुःखजीविनः ॥
द्वात्रिंशद्दन्ता राजान एकोनश्चापि भोगवान् ।
त्रिंशद्दन्ता नरा ये ते सुखदुःखस्य भागिनः ॥
एकोनत्रिंशद्दशनाः पुरुषा दुःखजीविनः ।
अष्टाविंशद्रदा येषां तेऽतिदुःखस्य भाजनाः ॥

Vide प्रह्लाद—

चिबुके यस्य रोमाणि न वक्षसि न गण्डयोः ।
कुटिलं तं विजानीयात्समर्थं च खलं नरम् ॥
द्वात्रिंशद्दन्तवान्भोगी त्रिंशन्न्यूने तु निर्धनाः ।
कपटी रोमहीनश्च बहुरोमा तु बन्धभाक् ॥]

जिह्वा रक्ता दीर्घा श्लक्ष्णा सुसमा च भोगिनो ज्ञेया ।
श्वेता कृष्णा परुषा निर्द्रव्याणां तथा तालु ॥५३ ॥

Men who enjoy the pleasures of life have tongues that are reddish, long, tender and quite even, while the poor have them white or dark and rough. The same rules hold good in the case of the palate too i.e. it is beneficial if it is reddish, tender and even, while it is bad if it is white or black and rough.

[भोगिनां is another reading in the place of भोगिनः.

Cf. the following:—

कृष्णजिह्वा भवेद्यस्य समला यदि वा भवेत् ।
स पापवान् भवेन्मर्त्यः कृक्षा स्थूला तथा भवेत् ॥
श्वेतजिह्वा नरा ज्ञेयाः शौचाचारविवर्जिताः ।
पद्मपत्रसमा जिह्वा सूक्ष्मा दीर्घा सुशोभना ॥
न स्थूला नातिविस्तीर्णा येषां ते मनुजाधिपाः ।
निम्ना दीर्घा च ह्रस्वा च रक्ताग्रा रसना यदि ॥
सर्वविद्याप्रवक्ताऽसौ भवेन्नास्त्यत्र संशयः ।
कृष्णतालुर्नरो यस्तु स भवेत् कुलनाशनः ॥
विकृतं स्फुटितं यस्य तालु तस्य न शोभनम् ।
सिंहतालुर्नरपतिर्गजतालुस्तथैव च ॥
पद्मतालुर्भवेद्राजा श्वेततालुश्च निर्धनः ॥]

वक्त्रं सौम्यं संवृतममलं श्लक्ष्णं समं च भूपानाम् ।
विपरीतं क्लेशभुजां महामुखं दुर्भगाणां च ॥५४॥

The mouth being pleasant, round and closed, soft and even, makes men monarchs; being contrary (i.e. unpleasant, not closed, unclean, rough and uneven), miserable and penniless; and a very big mouth belongs to the unfortunate.

[Cf. the following:—

सौम्यं च संवृतं वक्त्रममलं यस्य देहिनः ।
महाराजो भवेन्नित्यं विपरीते तु निर्धनः ॥]

स्त्रीमुखमनपत्यानां शाठ्यवतां मण्डलं परिज्ञेयम् ।
दीर्घं निर्द्रव्याणां भीरुमुखाः पापकर्माणः ॥५५॥

चतुरस्रं धूर्त्तानां निम्नं वक्रं च तनयरहितानाम् ।
कृपणानामतिह्रस्वं सम्पूर्णं भोगिनां कान्तम् ॥५६॥

A feminine face belongs to those who are issueless; a round one, to rogues; a long one, to the poor; a timid one, to those who commit sinful acts; a quadrilateral one, to the treacherous; a sunken and crooked one, to the childless; a very small one, to misers; and a full, fleshy and attractive (bright) one, to those who enjoy pleasures.

[Cf. the following:—

स्त्रीमुखं निरपत्यानां मण्डलं शाठ्यसेविनाम् ।
दीर्घं मुखं च निःस्वानां भीरुवक्त्रा दुराशयाः ॥
चतुरस्रं तु धूर्त्तानां निम्नं सुतविवर्जितम् ।
कृपणानां तथा ह्रस्वं चिपिटं परजीविनाम् ॥
यन्मुखं मांसलं स्निग्धं सप्रभं प्रियदर्शनम् ।
वर्णाढ्यं सन्धिविश्लिष्टमजस्रं सुखभागिनाम् ॥]

अस्फुटिताग्रं स्निग्धं श्मश्रु शुभं मृदु च सन्नतं चैव ।
रक्तैः परुषैश्चौराः श्मश्रुभिरल्पैश्च विज्ञेयाः ॥५७॥

The moustaches and beard being smooth, soft, well-bent and having unsplit tips, are auspicious; being red, hard and short or sparse, they make men thieves.

[In the first line मृदु समुन्नतं चैव is another reading. *Vide* the following:—

स्निग्धमस्फुटिताग्रं च सन्नतं श्मश्रु चेष्यते ।
रक्तैरल्पैस्तथा रूक्षैः श्मश्रुभिस्तस्कराः स्मृताः ॥]

निर्मांसैः कर्णैः पापमृत्यवश्चपर्टैः सुबहुभोगाः ।
कृपणाश्च ह्रस्वकर्णाः शङ्कुश्रवणाश्चमूपतयः ॥५८॥
रोमशकर्णा दीर्घायुषश्च धनभागिनो विपुलकर्णाः ।
क्रूराः शिरावनद्धैर्व्यालम्बैर्मांसलैः सुखिनः ॥५९॥

With ears devoid of flesh men meet with tragic ends; with flat ones, become enjoyers of many pleasures; with short ones, miserly; with conical ones, commanders of armies; with hairy ones, long-lived ones; with broad ones, wealthy; with those filled with veins, cruel; with hanging and fleshy ones, happy.

[*Vide* the following:—

ह्रस्वकर्णा महाभोगा महाकर्णाश्च ये नराः ।
आवर्तकर्णा धनिनः स्निग्धकर्णास्तथैव च ॥
दीर्घायुषः शङ्कुकर्णाः स्फुटकर्णा महाधनाः ।
सुखान्विता दीर्घकर्णा लम्बकर्णास्तपस्विनः ॥
निर्मांसैः पापमरणाश्चर्पटैर्भोगिनो नराः ।
दीर्घायुषो लोमकर्णा धनिनो विपुलैः स्मृताः ॥
शिरावनद्धैर्विषमा मांसलैः सुखभागिनः ॥

Vide—प्रह्लाद—

कर्णरोमा तु दीर्घायुर्नाभिरोमा बहुप्रजः ।
विकलाङ्गोऽधिकाङ्गो वा दुःखी लक्षणवर्जितः ॥
महच्छिरो रोमहीनं विशालं च ललाटकम् ।
दीर्घकर्णं तुङ्गनासं शूरपण्डितलक्षणम् ॥]

भोगी त्वनिम्नगण्डो मन्त्री सम्पूर्णमांसगण्डो यः ।
सुखभाक् शुकसमनासश्चिरजीवी शुष्कनासश्च ॥६०॥

छिन्नानुरूपयागम्यगामिनो दीर्घया तु सौभाग्यम् ।
आकुञ्चितया चौरः स्त्रीमृत्युः स्याच्चिपिटनासः ॥६१॥

धनिनोऽग्रवक्रनासा दक्षिणविनताः प्रभक्षणाः क्रूराः ।
ऋज्वी स्वल्पच्छिद्रा सुपुटा नासा सभाग्यानाम् ॥६२॥

One becomes enjoyer of pleasures and luxuries with unsunken cheeks; a minister, with full and fleshy ones; happy, with a nose resembling the parrot's beak; long-lived, with a dry nose (without flesh); one comes to have sexual relations with forbidden women with one (nose) that appears cut; becomes attractive or fortunate with a long one; a thief, with a curved one; meets with death at the hands of a woman, with a flat one; becomes wealthy, with one crooked at the tip; cruel and gluttonous (improvident?), with one turned to the right; and highly fortunate, with a straight one with small nostrils and fine slopes.

[*Vide* the following:—

पुमान् सम्पूर्णगण्डो यः स मन्त्री समुदाहृतः ।
निम्नगण्डो भवेद्यस्तु स नरो भोगवान् स्मृतः ॥
शुकनासः सौख्यभागी शुष्कनासश्चिरायुषः ।
छिन्नानुरुपा येषां स्मान्नासा तेऽगम्यगामिनः ॥
दीर्घनासा भोगयुक्ता अग्रवक्रा धनान्विताः ।
क्रूरा दक्षिणवक्राश्च स्पष्टनासा नृपोत्तमाः ॥
स्त्रीमृत्यवश्चर्पटाभिः कुटिलाभिश्च तस्कराः ॥

Cf. प्रह्लाद—

भ्रूनसाहनुजानूनां दीर्घत्वे कण्ठजङ्घयोः ।
रसनाया मेहनस्य ह्रस्वत्वे भाग्यवान् भवेत् ॥]

धनिनां क्षुतं सकृद्द्वित्रिपिण्डितं ह्लावि सानुनादं च ।
दीर्घायुषां प्रमुक्तं विज्ञेयं संहतं चैव ॥६३॥

The sneezing of the wealthy is either only once, or twice or thrice and high-pitched and resonant; while that of the long-lived, prolonged and of the same pitch throughout.

[Bhaṭṭotpala refers to other commentators who interpret the verse thus: The rich sneeze but once; while the long-lived, twice or thrice in succession making it high-pitched, resonant, prolonged and of the same pitch throughout. He prefers the second interpretation in view of *Parāśara's* statement:

सकृत् क्षुतं भोगवतां द्विर्घनाय चिरायुषे ।
चतुः स्याद्रोगनाशाय परमस्मात् तदीशजाः ॥

Cf. also the following:—

आदिमध्यावसानेषु तुल्यो यः स च संहतः ॥
क्रोधहर्षव्याधिभयादिष्वविकृतः श्रोत्रपथं याति यः स स्निग्धः । यः

सर्वजनमनोऽभिप्रेतः स रक्तः ।]

पद्मदलाभैर्धनिनो रक्तान्तविलोचनाः श्रियो भाजः ।
मधुपिङ्गलैर्महार्घा मार्जारविलोचनैः पापाः ॥६४॥

हरिणाक्षा मण्डललोचनाश्च जिह्मैश्च लोचनैश्चौराः ।
क्रूराः केकरनेत्रा गजसदृशविलोचनाश्चमूपतयः ॥६५॥

ऐश्वर्यं गम्भीरैर्नीलोत्पलकान्तिभिश्च विद्वांसः ।
अतिकृष्णतारकाणामक्ष्णामुत्पाटनं भवति ॥६६॥

मन्त्रित्वं स्थूलदृशां श्यावाक्षाणां [च] भवति सौभाग्यम् ।
दीना दृग् निःस्वानां स्निग्धा विपुलार्थभोगवताम् ॥६७॥

People become wealthy with eyes similar to the petals of a lotus; very opulent and powerful, with those that have red corners; immensely rich, with those coloured tawny like honey; sinners, with feline eyes; thieves, with round and crooked ones as well as with those resembling the eyes of the deer; cruel, with squint eyes; commanders of armies, with elephantine ones; wealthy, with deep ones; learned, with those resembling blue lilies. The eyes whose pupils are extremely black will be pulled out. Broad and thick eyes make one a minister; green ones, lovely and fortunate; humble and abject ones, penniless; and glossy (clean) and large ones, enjoyer of vast wealth and pleasures of life.

[In the second quarter of the last verse there is one मात्रा missing. So I have put a च within brackets. This mistake must have been committed by the copyist. Utpala says:

केकरनेत्रा नीलाक्षाः. However, according to the accepted connotation of the word it should mean 'squint-eyed'. 'वलिरः केकरे' says Amara (II.6.49). Vide Kṣīrasvāmin's explanation: 'वलते चेष्टते वलिरं नेत्रं तद्योगाद् वलिरः। के मूर्ध्नि करोत्यक्षिणी चलत्तारकत्वात्केकरः।'

Vide the following:—

समे गोक्षीरवर्णाभे रक्तान्ते कृष्णतारके ।
प्रसन्ने च विशाले च स्निग्धे चैवायते शुभे ॥
अतसीपुष्पसङ्काशे भवेतां यस्य लोचने ।
भूपतिः स तु विज्ञेयः समुद्रवचनं यथा ॥
व्याघ्रचक्षुर्धनैर्युक्तः कर्कटाक्षः कलिप्रियः ।
बिडालहंसनेत्राश्च भवन्ति पुरुषाधमाः ॥

मयूरनकुलाक्षाश्च नरास्ते मध्यमाः स्मृताः ।
न श्रीस्त्यजति सर्वत्र पुरुषं मधुपिङ्गलम् ॥
आज्यपिङ्गलनेत्राश्च राजानो भोगसंयुताः ।
रोचनाहरितालाश्च गजपिङ्गा धनेश्वराः ॥
बलवन्तो गुणोपेताः पृथिव्यां चक्रवर्तिनः ।
तप्तहाटकवर्णाभे भवेतां तस्य लोचने ॥
भूपतिः स तु विज्ञेयः समुद्रवचनं यथा ॥
द्विमात्रस्पन्दिनो ये तु धनिनस्ते प्रकीर्तिताः ।
त्रिमात्रस्पन्दिनो ज्ञेयाः पुरुषाः सुखजीविनः ।
चतुर्मात्रनिमेषश्च धनवान् परिकीर्तितः ॥
दीर्घायुषो धर्मरताः पञ्चमात्रनिमेषिणः ॥

Śrī Rāma, according to Vālmīki, was रक्तान्तनयनः
Vide प्रह्लाद—

कुबेराक्षीसमाक्षश्च निष्ठुरो निर्धनस्तथा ।
बिडालतुल्यनेत्रस्तु पश्येन्निध्यञ्जनादिकम् ॥

[Kuberākṣī is *caesalpinia crista*, Kannaḍa—Gajjuga, Marathi—Gajaga.]

अभ्युन्नताभिरल्पायुषो विशालोन्नताभिरतिसुखिनः ।
विषमभ्रुवो दरिद्रा बालेन्दुनतभ्रुवः सधनाः ॥६८॥

दीर्घासंसक्ताभिर्धनिनः खण्डाभिरर्थपरिहीनाः ।
मध्यविनतभ्रुवो ये ते सक्ताः स्त्रीष्वगम्यासु ॥६९॥

Lofty brows lead to short life; large and lofty ones, to great happiness; unequal (or zigzag) ones, to poverty; bent ones resembling the crescent, to wealth; long and unconnected ones, to affluence; cut ones, to penury; and those that are bent in the middle, to addiction to forbidden women.

Vide the following:—

अभ्युन्नताभिः स्वल्पायुर्विशालाभिः सुखान्विताः ।
मध्योन्नतभ्रुवो ये च पापसक्ताश्च ते नराः ॥
बालेन्दुभ्रूसमाश्चाढ्या दरिद्रा विषमभ्रुवः ।
असंलग्नभ्रुवो ये तु धनिनस्ते नराः स्मृताः ।
खण्डाभिर्निर्धना ज्ञेया विषमाभिर्नराधमाः ॥

Vide प्रह्लाद—

नेत्रकर्णान्तरं सूक्ष्मं भ्रुवोः पर्यन्तरं महत् ।
तर्जनीतुलिता नासा कर्णौ मध्यमया समौ ॥

उन्नतविपुलैः शङ्खैर्धनिनो निम्नैः सुतार्थसन्त्यक्ताः ।
विषमललाटा विधना धनवन्तोऽर्धेन्दुसदृशेन ॥७०॥

शुक्तिविशालैराचार्यता शिरासन्ततैरधर्मरताः ।
उन्नतशिराभिराढ्याः स्वस्तिकवत् संस्थिताभिश्च ॥७१॥

निम्नललाटा वधबन्धभागिनः क्रूरकर्मनिरताश्च ।
अभ्युन्नतैश्चमूपाः कृपणाः स्युः संवृतललाटाः ॥७२॥

With broad and raised temples men become wealthy; with sunken ones, bereft of children and wealth. An uneven forehead leads to poverty; one resembling the half-Moon, to opulence; one large like a shell, to the position of preceptors of men; one full of veins, to addiction to unrighteous acts; one filled with raised veins as well as with those shaped like the *Svastika* figure, to great affluence; a depressed forehead, to imprisonment, foul death and cruel deeds; a raised one, to commandership of armies; and a round and small one, to miserliness.

Cf. the following:—

उन्नतैर्विपुलैः शङ्खैर्धनिनः सुखजीविनः ।
सुतार्थरहिता निम्नैर्मानुषा दुःखभागिनः ॥
ललाटेनार्धचन्द्रेण भवन्ति पृथिवीश्वराः ।
विपुलेन ललाटेन महाधनयुताः स्मृताः ॥
विषमेणाधमा ज्ञेयाः पापा मर्त्याः शिराततैः ।
निम्नेन तु ललाटेन क्रूरकर्मरता नराः ॥
अभ्युन्नतैश्चमूपाः स्युः संवृतैः कृपणाः स्मृताः ॥

रुदितमदीनमनश्रु स्निग्धं च शुभावहं मनुष्याणाम् ।
रूक्षं दीनं प्रचुराश्रु चैव न शुभप्रदं पुंसाम् ॥७३॥

Weeping which is soft, tearless and without wretchedness, is auspicious for men; whereas one that is rough, abject and accompanied with copious tears is disastrous to them.

Cf. the following:—

अदीनाश्वहृतं स्निग्धं रुदितं च शुभावहम् ।
रूक्षं दीनं बाष्पयुतं पुरुषाणामनिष्टदम् ॥

हसितं शुभदमकम्पं सनिमीलितलोचनं तु पापस्य ।
दुष्टस्य हसितमसकृत् सोन्मादस्यासकृत् प्रान्ते ॥७४॥

Laughter not accompanied by a convulsion of the body is auspicious; one accompanied by closed eyes belongs to a sinful man; a repeated one, to a wicked fellow; and a repetition at the end of one, to a madcap.

Cf. the following:—

हसितं कम्परहितं नृपाणामन्यथाऽशुभम् ।
असकृद्दोषयुक्तस्य मीलिताक्षस्य चाशुभम् ॥

In this connection it would be interesting to the readers to know what the rhetoricians say about हसित or laughter. The following extract from the साहित्यदर्पण (III. 247-49) explains it:—

ज्येष्ठानां स्मितहसिते मध्यानां विहसितावहसिते च ।
नीचानामपहसितं तथातिहसितं तदेष षड्भेदः ॥
ईषद्विकसितनयनं स्मितं स्यात्स्पन्दिताधरम् ।
किञ्चिल्लक्ष्यद्विजं तत्र हसितं कथितं बुधैः ॥
मधुरस्वरं विहसितं सांसशिरःकम्पमवहसितम् ।
अपहसितं सास्राक्षं विक्षिप्ताङ्गं च भवत्यतिहसितम् ॥

तिस्रो रेखाः शतजीविनां ललाटायताः स्थिता यदि ताः ।
चतसृभिरवनीशत्वं नवतिश्चायुः सपञ्चाब्दा ॥७५॥

विच्छिन्नाभिश्चागम्यगामिनो नवतिरप्यरेखेण ।
केशान्तोपगताभी रेखाभिरशीतिवर्षायुः ॥७६॥

पञ्चभिरायुः सप्ततिरेकाग्रावस्थिताभिरपि षष्टिः ।
बहुरेखेण शतार्धं चत्वारिंशच्च वक्राभिः ॥७७॥

भ्रूलग्नाभिस्त्रिंशद्विंशतिकश्चैव वामवक्राभिः ।
क्षुद्राभिः स्वल्पायुर्न्यूनाभिश्चान्तरे कल्प्यम् ॥७८॥

Three horizontal lines on the forehead indicate a life of hundred years; four such lines, kingship and a life of 95 years; cut lines or absence of lines, addiction to forbidden women and a life of 90 years; the lines touching the hair on both sides, a life of 80 years; five lines on the forehead indicate a life of 70 years; all the lines meeting at a point, a life of 60 years; many lines (i.e. six), a life of 50 years; crooked ones, one of 40 years; those touching the brows, one of 30 years; those bent towards the left, one of 20 years; slender and small ones, a short life; those short of the above number (i.e. one or two), a short life; and for any number in between the given ones, a life that is to be proportionately calculated.

Vide the following:—

रेखाः पञ्च ललाटे तु यस्यासौ धनवान् स्मृतः ।
शतं जीवति वर्षाणामैश्वर्यमधिगच्छति ॥
चतूरेखो ह्यशीतिस्तु त्रिभिः सप्ततिरेव च ।
षष्टिर्द्वाभ्यां तु रेखाभ्यां चत्वारिंशत्तथैकया ॥
अरेखेण ललाटेन भवन्ति निधिपालकाः ।
रेखाच्छेदैस्तु विज्ञेयाः पापकर्मरता नराः ॥
अल्पायुषस्तथाल्पासु व्याधियुक्ताश्च ते सदा ।
त्रिशूलं पट्टिशं वापि ललाटे यस्य दृश्यते ॥
ऐश्वर्यं तस्य विज्ञेयं सेनानां नायकश्च सः ॥

Vide प्रह्लाद—

यस्य फालतले रेखाः पञ्च पूर्णायुरुच्यते ।
विंशत्यब्दा तथैकैका सुरेखश्च धनी भवेत् ॥
ललाटरेखाबाहुल्ये दीर्घायुर्दृढगात्रवान् ।
पृष्ठावर्ते तु पञ्चाशत् पार्श्वावर्ते तु सप्ततिः ॥
ऊर्ध्वावर्ते तथाल्पायुः केशानां शिरसि ध्रुवम् ।
विंशत्यब्दोत्तरावर्ते क्षिप्रमेव मरिष्यति ॥
त्रिंशदब्दोत्तरावर्ते चिरजीवी भवेन्नरः ॥

परिमण्डलैर्गवाढ्याश्छत्राकारैः शिरोभिरवनीशाः ।
चिपिटैः पितृमातृघ्नाः करोटिशिरसां चिरान्मृत्युः ॥७९॥

घटमूर्धाध्वानरुचिर्द्विमस्तकः पापकृद्धनैस्त्यक्तः ।
निम्नं तु शिरो महतां बहुनिम्नमनर्थदं भवति ॥८०॥

Men with a round head become rich in cattle; with one resembling an umbrella, kings; with a flat one, murderers of parents; with one like a helmet or turban (lit. skull), long-lived; with a pot-like head, wanderers or tourists; with a double head, sinners and penniless; with a depressed head, illustrious; and with a too much depressed one, miserable.

Vide the following:—

उत्क्रान्तिदो निम्नशिरा अल्पोपहत एव च ।
छत्राकारशिरा राजा गवाढ्य: परिमण्डलै: ॥
विषमं तद्दरिद्राणां शिरो दीर्घं चिरायुषाम् ।
नागकुम्भशिरा राजा समं सर्वत्र भोगिन: ॥

एकैकभवै: स्निग्धै: कृष्णैराकुञ्चितैरभिन्नाग्रै: ।
मृदुभिर्न चातिबहुभि: केशै: सुखभाग्नरेन्द्रो वा ॥८१॥

बहुमूलविषमकपिला: स्थूलस्फुटिताग्रपरुषह्रस्वाश्च ।
अतिकुटिलाश्चातिघनाश्च मूर्धजा वित्तहीनानाम् ॥८२॥

One becomes a king or enjoyer of happiness, if the hairs on the head are single in each pore, glossy, dark, bent, with tips unsplit, soft, and not too thick (dense). One becomes penniless with the hair being many in a pore, of unequal length, brown, very thick, with tips split, rough, short, too crooked and too dense.

Vide the following:—

एकैकसम्भवा: स्निग्धा: कृष्णा नातिघना: कचा: ।
पूजिता विपरीताश्च निर्धनानां प्रकीर्तिता: ॥

In this connection Bhaṭṭotpala remarks:—**आचार्येणोक्तम्**—"सामुद्रविद्वदति यातमनागतं वेत्यतोऽत्रास्माभि: सामुद्राणि पुरुषलक्षणान्युदाहृतानि यावदाचार्यस्य तेभ्योऽप्यधिकमस्तीति ज्ञेयम्" इति ।

यद्यद्गात्रं रूक्षं मांसविहीनं शिरावनद्धं च ।
तत्तदनिष्टं प्रोक्तं विपरीतमत: शुभं सर्वम् ॥८३॥

Whatever limb of the body is rough, without flesh, and full of veins, it is considered to be inauspicious; and the opposite of these is beneficial.

त्रिषु विपुलो गम्भीरस्त्रिष्वेव षडुन्नतश्चतुर्ह्रस्व: ।
सप्तसु रक्तो राजा पञ्चसु दीर्घश्च सूक्ष्मश्च ॥८४॥

One becomes a monarch if one is broad in three limbs, deep in three, raised in six, short in four, red in seven, long in five and slender in five.

Cf. वाल्मीकिरामायण (V.-35-2-20):—

यानि रामस्य चिह्नानि लक्ष्मणस्य च वानर ।
कीदृशं तस्य संस्थानं रूपं रामस्य कीदृशम् ।
कथमूरू कथं बाहू लक्ष्मणस्य च शंस मे ।।
रामः कमलपत्त्राक्षः सर्वभूतमनोहरः ।
तेजसादित्यसङ्काशः क्षमया पृथिवीसमः ।।
विपुलांसो महाबाहुः कम्बुग्रीवः शुभाननः ।
गूढजत्रुः सुताम्राक्षो रामो देवि जनैः श्रुतः ।।
दुन्दुभिस्वननिर्घोषः स्निग्धवर्णः प्रतापवान् ।
समश्च सुविभक्ताङ्गो वर्णं श्यामं समाश्रितः ।।
त्रिस्थिरस्त्रिप्रलम्बश्च त्रिसमस्त्रिषु चोन्नतः ।
त्रिताम्रस्त्रिषु च स्निग्धो गम्भीरस्त्रिषु नित्यशः ।।
त्रिवलीवांस्त्र्यवनतश्चतुर्व्यङ्गस्त्रिशीर्षवान् ।
चतुष्कलश्चतुर्लेखश्चतुष्किष्कुश्चतुःसमः ।।
चतुर्दशसमद्वंद्वश्चतुर्दंष्ट्रश्चतुर्गतिः ।
महोष्ठहनुनासश्च पञ्चस्निग्धोऽष्टवंशवान् ।।
दशपद्मो दशबृहत्त्रिभिर्व्याप्तो द्विशुक्लवान् ।
षडुन्नतो नवतनुस्त्रिभिर्व्याप्नोति राघवः ।।

Cf. also प्रह्लाद—

पञ्चदीर्घं चतुर्ह्रस्वं पञ्चसूक्ष्मं षडुन्नतम् ।
सप्तरक्तं त्रिगम्भीरं त्रिविस्तीर्णं प्रशस्यते ।।

The five long limbs are (1) the space between the paps or nipples, (2) arms, (3) eyes, (4) nose and (5) jaws. The four short ones are, neck, top of the thighs, root of the back, and shanks. The five slender ones are—finger-joints, hair, teeth, nails and skin. The six raised ones are—arm-pits, belly, chest, nose, shoulders and fore-head. The seven red ones are—the palms, soles, corners of eyes, nails, palate, tongue and the lower lip. The three deep ones are—voice, courage and navel. Lastly the three broad ones are—the chest, face and fore-head.

Govindarāja quotes a number of authorities by name and otherwise. Some of the authors and works on this subject mentioned by him are: वररुचि, नन्दी, कात्यायन, गर्ग, मिहिर, नारद, ब्रह्मा, ब्राह्मपुराण, ब्रह्माण्ड, सामुद्रिक etc.

"ऊरुश्च मणिबन्धश्च मुष्टिश्च नृपतेः स्थिराः ।।"

"प्रलम्बा यस्य स धनी त्रयो भ्रूमुष्कबाहव:" इति सामुद्रिकोक्तेः ।
"केशाग्रं वृषणं जानु समं यस्य स भूपतिः ।" इत्युक्तेः ।
"नाभ्यन्तःकुक्षिवक्षोभिरुन्नतैः क्षितिपो भवेत् ॥"
"नेत्रान्तनखपाण्यङ्घ्रितलैस्ताम्रैस्त्रिभिः सुखी ॥"
"स्निग्धा भवन्ति वै येषां पादरेखाः शिरोरुहाः ।
तथा लिङ्गमणिस्तेषां महाभाग्यं विनिर्दिशेत् ॥"

बाह्ये तु — "स्वरे गतौ च नाभौ च गम्भीरस्त्रिषु शस्यते ॥"
"उन्नतकुक्षिः क्षितिपः परिमण्डलोन्नतनाभयः क्षितिपाः ।
हृदयं न वेपनं पृथु समोन्नतं मांसलं च नृपतीनाम् ॥"
"श्लिष्टाङ्गुली रुचिरताम्रनखौ सुपार्ष्णी
पादौ करावपि सुरक्तनखात्मरेखौ ॥"

वररुचिः — "ग्रीवा प्रजननं पृष्ठं ह्रस्वे जङ्घे च पूजिते ॥" इति ।
"आवर्त्तत्रययुक्तं यस्य शिरः क्षितिभृतामयं नाथः ॥"

नन्दी आह —

"मूलेऽङ्गुष्ठस्य रेखानां चतस्रस्तिस्र एव वा ।
एका द्वे वा यथायोगं वेदरेखा द्विजन्मनाम् ॥" इति ।

कात्यायनः —

"ललाटे यस्य दृश्यन्ते चतुस्त्रिद्व्येकरेखिकाः ।
शतद्वयं शतं षष्टिस्तस्यायुर्विंशतिः क्रमात् ॥" इति ।
"बाहुजानूरुगण्डानि चत्वार्यथ समानि च ॥"

अत्र गर्गः —

"स्थिरा त्रिरेखा सुभगोपपन्ना स्निग्धा सुमांसोपचिता सुवृत्ता ।
न चातिदीर्घा चतुरङ्गुला च ग्रीवा सुदीर्घा भवतीह धन्या ॥"

नारदः — "पादैः प्रस्वेदरहितैः शिराहीनश्च पार्थिवः ।
एकरोमा भवेद्राजा द्विरोमा पण्डितो भवेत् ॥
त्रिरोमा चतुरोमा च भवेद् भाग्यविवर्जितः ॥
समपादोपविष्टस्य गुल्फं स्पृशति मेहनम् ।
यस्येश्वरं तं जानीयात्सुखिनं चैव मानवम् ॥
निर्मांसः संहतो वस्तिर्येषां ते सुखभागिनः ॥
समवृत्तशिराश्चैव छत्राकारशिरास्तथा ।
एकच्छत्रां महीं भुङ्क्ते दीर्घमायुश्च विन्दति ॥
यस्य पादतले वज्रध्वजशङ्खाङ्कुशोपमाः ।
रेखाः सम्यक् प्रकाशन्ते मनुजेन्द्रं तमादिशेत् ॥" इति ।

ब्रह्मा —

पाणौ चतस्रो रेखाश्च यस्य तिष्ठन्त्यभङ्गुराः ।।" इति ।

ब्राह्मपुराणे —

"षण्णवत्यङ्गुलोत्सेधो यः पुमान्स दिवौकसः ।।"

ब्रह्माण्डे — "बाहुजानूरुगण्डाश्च चत्वार्यथ समानि च ।" इति ।

"भ्रुवौ नासापुटे नेत्रे कर्णावोष्ठौ च चूचुकौ ।।

कूर्परे मणिबन्धौ च जानुनी वृषणौ कटिः ।

करौ पादौ स्फिजौ यस्य समौ ज्ञेयः स भूपतिः ।।"

or

[स्कन्धौ गण्डौ तथा दन्ता ऊरू ज्ञेयौ च जत्रुणी ।।]

"स्निग्धा घनाश्च दशनाः सुतीक्ष्णदंष्ट्राः शुभाश्चतस्रः ।"

वररुचिः —

"चक्षुःस्नेहेन सौभाग्यं दन्तस्नेहेन भोजनम् ।

त्वचःस्नेहेन शयनं पादस्नेहेन वाहनम् ।।"

सामुद्रिकम् —

पृष्ठवंशः शरीरं च हस्तपादाङ्गुली करौ ।

नासिका चक्षुषी कर्णौ प्रजनो यस्य चायताः ।।"

मुखनेत्रास्यजिह्वोष्ठतालुस्तननखाः करौ ।

पादौ च दश पद्मानि पद्माकाराणि यस्य च ।।"

वररुचिः —

"उरः शिरो ललाटं च ग्रीवा बाह्वंसनाभयः ।

पादौ पृष्ठं श्रुती चैव विशालास्ते सुखप्रदाः ।।"

सामुद्रिकम् —

कक्षः कुक्षिश्च वक्षश्च घ्राणस्कन्धललाटिकाः ।

सर्वभूतेषु निर्दिष्टा उन्नतास्तु सुखप्रदाः ।।"

ब्राह्मे तु —

"शिरो ललाटे श्रवणे ग्रीवा वक्षश्च हृत्तथा ।

उदरं पाणिपादौ च पृष्ठं दश बृहन्ति च ।।"

नाभी स्वरः सत्त्वमिति प्रशस्तं गम्भीरमेतत् त्रितयं नराणाम् ।
उरो ललाटं वदनं च पुंसां विस्तीर्णमेतत् त्रितयं प्रशस्तम् ।।८५।।

वक्षोऽथ कक्षा नखनासिकास्यं कृकाटिका चेति षडुन्नतानि ।
ह्रस्वानि चत्वारि च लिङ्गपृष्ठं ग्रीवा च जङ्घे च हितप्रदानि ।।८६।।

नेत्रान्तपादकरताल्वधरोष्ठजिह्वा
रक्ता नखाश्च खलु सप्त सुखावहानि ।
सूक्ष्माणि पञ्च दशनाङ्गुलिपर्वकेशाः
साकं त्वचा कररुहा न च दुःखितानाम् ॥८७॥

हनुलोचनबाहुनासिकाः स्तनयोरन्तरमत्र पञ्चमम् ।
इति दीर्घमिदं तु पञ्चकं न भवत्येव नृणाममूभृताम् ॥८८॥

It is auspicious for men to have (a) the three viz. navel, voice and courage, deep; (b) the three viz. breast, forehead and mouth, broad; (c) the six viz. chest, arm-pits, nails, nose, face and the nape of the neck, raised; (d) the four viz. the genital organ, back, neck and shanks, short; (e) men become happy with the following seven viz. corners of eyes, feet, hands, palate, lower lip, tongue and nails, red; (f) very happy with the following five viz. teeth, finger knuckles, hair, skin and fingers, thin; and (g) monarch without doubt with the five viz. jaws (Hanu which is the part below the chin), eyes, arms, nose and the space between the paps, long.

Utpala says 'कक्षाशब्देन शरीरमध्यभाग उच्यते' । But the accepted meaning is बाहुमूलम्. For, says *Amara* (II. 6-79): "बाहुमूले उभे कक्षौ ।"

Vide गर्ग—

चतुर्दशसमो द्वन्द्वश्चतुःकृष्णश्चतुःसमः ।
दशपद्मो दशबृहत् त्रिशुक्लः शस्यते नरः ॥
पादौ गुल्फौ स्फिजौ पार्श्वे वृषणौ चक्षुषी स्तनौ ।
स्कन्धोष्ठौ वङ्क्षणे जङ्घे हस्तौ बाह्वंसकौ तथा ॥
चतुर्दशसमद्वन्द्वः समुद्रो नृपु शंसति ।
अक्षितारे भ्रुवौ श्मश्रुकेशाश्चैवासिताः शुभाः ॥
अङ्गुल्यो हृदयं नेत्रे दशनाश्च समा नृणाम् ।
चत्वारः सम्प्रशस्यन्ते सदैश्वर्यसुखावहाः ॥
जिह्वोष्ठतालु चास्यं च मुखं नेत्रे स्तनौ नखाः ।
हस्तौ पादौ च शस्यन्ते पद्माभा दश देहिनाम् ॥
पाणिपादमुरो ग्रीवा वृषणौ हृदयं शिरः ।
ललाटमुदरं पृष्ठं बृहन्तः पूजिता दश ॥
नेत्रे ताराविरहिते दशनाश्चलिताः शुभाः ।
एतच्च लक्षणं कृत्स्नं नराणां समुदाहृतम् ॥
पञ्चदीर्घश्चतुर्ह्रस्वः पञ्चसूक्ष्मः षडुन्नतः ।
पञ्चरक्तस्त्रिविस्तीर्णस्त्रिगम्भीरः प्रशस्यते ॥

बाहू नेत्रान्तरे चापि हनुनी वृषणौ तथा ।
स्तनयोरन्तरं चैव पञ्चदीर्घः प्रशस्यते ॥
ग्रीवा प्रजननं श्रोणिर्ह्रस्वे जङ्घे च पूजिते ।
तथेतरेषु सर्वेषु सर्वमेव प्रशस्यते ॥
सूक्ष्माण्यङ्गुलिपर्वाणि दन्ता रोमाणि च च्छविः ।
तथा नखाश्च सर्वे च पञ्चसूक्ष्मः प्रशस्यते ॥
कक्षाक्षिवक्षांसि तथा मुखं पृष्ठं कृकाटिका ।
सर्वभूतेषु निर्दिष्टः षडुत्सेधः प्रशस्यते ॥
पाणी पादौ तथा चास्यमुभे नेत्रे स्तनौ नखाः ।
पञ्च रक्तानि यस्याहुर्मनुजेन्द्रं तमादिशेत् ॥
उरो मुखं ललाटं च विविस्तीर्णः प्रशस्यते ।
सत्त्वं स्वरश्च नाभिश्च त्रिगम्भीरः प्रशस्यते ॥

The metres are उपजाति, वसन्ततिलका and वियोगिनी. Here ends the Section dealing with *Kṣetra* or physical part of man. Here I may be permitted to summarize some principles found in the प्रह्लाद सामुद्रिक :–

This science has three branches viz. palmistry, physiognomy and feminine features. The marks on the body are of three kinds, viz. natural, seasonal or temporal and casual. The lines are nothing but the writing of the Creator on the human body which can be read by experts. The whole body should be measured with a tape. If the height of the man is 7 cubits (of his own hand) or equal to the space between the finger-tips of his out-stretched arms, it is auspicious. If the navel comes to occupy exactly the middle of the whole body, it is beneficial. On the other hand, if the upper half be slightly more than the lower one, he would be a hero. If it be otherwise, he would be a fast runner. Find out the distance between the navel and the heart, or between the heart and the tip of the nose; the space between the paps should be equal to that. The circumference of the head should be double the previous measure. The space between the arms should be equal to the girth of the neck. The breadth of the forehead should be equal to the distance between the tip of the chin and the centre of the brows. The height of the forehead should be equal to the distance between the tip of the chin and the root of the nose. The eyes should stretch out as much as possible towards the ears, while the two brows, as far apart as possible. The nose is to be as long as the fore-finger; while the ears, as the middle finger. The circumference of the head should be equal to the waist-girth; the foot, equal to a cubit; the penis, to ten digits; a long penis leads to poverty. If the veins be strong, the person would be vigilant. With strong and sturdy bones one becomes very strong; with small teeth, blessed with food; and with a thin tongue, an orator. If the toe next to the big toe be longer than the latter, the man would be licentious. If the toes are crooked and separated, grief will be caused. With crooked nails one becomes a rogue. Yellowish, bluish (black) and lose nails lead to sinful activities, disease and poverty respectively. With long little toes one becomes a wealthy lord and a royal protege. With circular marks on the feet, sides, back and belly one becomes in order a wanderer, sleeps on the floor, bears loads, and eats sumptuous food always.

If the tip of the thumb touches the second (middle) knuckle of the fore-finger, the person will be proficient in fine arts or engineering, writing, military science and gymnastics. If the tip of the little finger touches the third (topmost) knuckle of the ring finger, he will be respected by the community, affluent and full of prowess. If there be three circular lines, one conch figure and one of a pot on the tips of the fingers (of one hand), he will be a king. Should there be a quadrangular figure between the knuckles of the little finger, the person would be a land-lord or one like a governor of a province. There should be four vertical lines on each of the other fingers, between the knuckles. If there is only one such line or no line at all, one becomes a recluse or undergoes great hardships, as the case may be. The figure of a conch or wheel at the tip of the little finger is good for finance, while that of a pitcher on the middle finger is beneficial. A wheel turning from left to right is highly auspicious on the remaining three finger-tips. The effects, good or bad, will be felt by a subject in the first 20 years, if the corresponding marks are found on the thumb. In this order we have to allot a period of 20 years to each of the fingers. The line that runs from the root of the thumb towards the root of the first finger is known as the Male line. It represents the man himself. The line next to it is his partner's. If these two lines are joined between the thumb and the first finger, the person will enjoy long conjugal happiness. If they are separated, the couple will remain away from each other. A cut or defect in a line indicates ill health or danger to life. The line that runs from the foot of the little finger to that of the fore-finger is called the Life line. The vertical line running from the wrist towards the root of the second finger is known as the Fortune (wealth) line. Man's left palm will indicate his wife's fortune, and *vice versa*. If the fortune line touches the root of the little finger, the person will go abroad and make his fortune there. If the vertical lines are three on each finger, one will become rich. If the total number of the lines on the four fingers is 13, one would be miserable. The effects of the total number being 14, 15, 16, 17, 18, 19, 20 and 21 are in order happiness and enjoyment of pleasures, stealing nature, gambling, committing sins, virtuous deeds, respectability and popularity, asceticism, and exceptional spiritual glory. The effects of wheels on the ten finger-tips, from 1 to 10, are; Enjoyment of pleasures, king's patronage, immense wealth, penury, addiction to pleasures, licentious nature, good fortune, disease, kingship, and proficiency in yoga. The effects of conch are : (i) happiness and enjoyment of pleasures; (ii) poverty; (iii) virtues; (iv) goodness; (v) poverty; (vi) valour; and (vi-x) royal splendour.

According to *Garga* the lines at the root of the thumb indicate issue; while those at the root of the little finger, brothers and sisters. The male and female lines (i.e. modern Life line and Head line) stand for mother and father respectively. The first six Signs beginning with Taurus represent 1) the testicle, 2) foot, 3) belly, 4) chest, 5) arms and 6) head — all on the right side; and the remaining six represent the same limbs on the left side. The first nine asterisms beginning with Aśvinī are to be assigned to the limbs beginning from the feet and ending with the hips; the second group of nine, to those from the hips to the neck; and the last one, to those from the neck to the locks. The planetary marks on the body or palm are 1) a circle for the Sun, 2) a square for the Moon, 3) a triangle for Mars, 4) an arrow for Mercury, 5) a long (sword ?) 6) a quadriletral figure, 7) a pentagon, 8) a bow and 9) a flag respectively. Find out the star and sign corresponding to the limb on which a planet's mark is discovered. The person must have been born at a time when that planet was posited in that star and Sign. If a planetary mark makes its appearance suddenly, it should be understood that the major period of that planet is prevailing at the time. To find out the natal ascendant of a person proceed thus :—

Take the total height of the person in digits and multiply it by the circumference of the head in digits. Divide the product by 12. The remainder gives the natal ascendant, beginning with Aries.

II Complexion

छाया शुभाशुभफलानि निवेदयन्ती
लक्ष्या मनुष्यपशुपक्षिषु लक्षणज्ञैः ।

तेजोगुणान् बहिरपि प्रविकाशयन्ती
दीपप्रभा स्फटिकरत्नघटस्थितेव ॥८९॥

Those that are proficient in this science ought to observe among men, beasts and birds the physical effulgence, which suggests both good and bad effects, and reveals out the virtues of the inner power, as does the flame of a lamp kept inside a crystal pot, the qualities of the burning fire inside.

The author here employs a fine simile which suggests that the soul inside men and others is an effulgent power and fire. So, the complexion is the light that comes out of the inner parts of the house viz. the heart, where burns the spiritual light of the Soul.

Cf. the बृहज्जातक (VIII-21) :—

छायां महाभूतकृतां च सर्वे निर्व्यञ्जयन्ति स्वदशामवाप्य।
क्ष्माम्ब्वग्निवाय्वम्बरजान्गुणांश्च नासास्यदृक्त्वक् श्रवणानुमेयान् ॥

The metre is वसन्ततिलका.

स्निग्धद्विजत्वग्नखरोमकेशाच्छाया सुगन्धा च महीसमुत्था।
तुष्ट्यर्थलाभाभ्युदयान् करोति धर्मस्य चाहन्यहनि प्रवृत्तिम् ॥९०॥

The physical lustre born of the element earth, makes the teeth, skin, nails and hair on the body and head glossy, produces fine smell, bestows contentment, wealth and progress in life, and causes engagement in religious and meritorious acts continuously.

The printed editions read केशा: in plural and Bhaṭṭotpala construes it as such : एते सर्वे एव स्निग्धा: सस्नेहा भवन्ति However, I feel that the author has taken the whole compound as an adjective qualifying the word छाया. In the last quarter प्रवृद्धिम् is another reading instead of प्रवृत्तिम् That would mean : Increase of meritorious activities. The metre is इन्द्रवज्रा.

स्निग्धा सिताच्छहरिता नयनाभिरामा
सौभाग्यमार्दवसुखाभ्युदयान् करोति।
सर्वार्थसिद्धिजननी जननीव चाप्या
छाया फलं तनुभृतां शुभमादधाति ॥९१॥

The lustre born of the element, water, is glossy, white, bright, clean, green, attractive to the eyes, gives amiable qualities, a tender nature, happiness and prosperity, and bestows all kinds of success and all-round good to human beings like a mother.

The elements are five in number, viz. Earth, Water, Fire, Wind and Ether. The human body has these elements as its constituents, which lend their special qualities to it. In this verse the author has employed very elegant and simple language containing a pleasing simile and alliteration. This simile is in tune with the Vedic statement : "आपो हि ष्ठा ··· उशतीरिव मातरः ··· आपो जनयथा च नः ।।" This proves the author's rich heritage of Vedic lore.

The commentator says : अच्छहरिता निर्मलनीलवर्णा. In Sanskrit black, blue and green are invariably interchanged. He explains नयनाभिरामा in a tortuous way : नयनाभ्यामाभिमुख्येन रमते यस्याम् He could have better said : नयनयोरभिरामा आभिमुख्येन रमयतीति । The metre is **वसन्ततिलका.**

चण्डाधृष्या पद्महेमाग्निवर्णा युक्ता तेजोविक्रमैः सप्रतापैः ।
आग्नेयीति प्राणिनां स्याज्जयाय क्षिप्रं सिद्धिं वाञ्छितार्थस्य धत्ते ।।६२।।

The lustre born of the element Fire, is irascible, irresistible, of the hue of lotus, gold or fire, endowed with brilliance, valour and vanquishing prowess, leads to victory of beings and confers immediate success of the desired object.

The metre is **शालिनी**.

मलिनपरुषकृष्णा पापगन्धानिलोत्था
जनयति वधबन्धव्याध्यनर्थार्थनाशान् ।
स्फटिकरावृशरूपा भाग्ययुक्तात्युदारा
निधिरिव गगनोत्था श्रेयसां स्वच्छवर्णा ।।६३।।

The lustre born of the element Air, is dusky, rough, dark, of foul smell, and causes murders, imprisonments, diseases, disasters (or loss of income) and loss of accumulated wealth. The lustre born of the element Ether, is of crystal hue, very generous, a bestower of good fortune, very clean and a treasure, as it were, of all good and desirable things.

Thus the author completes the delineation of the five kinds of lustre. Next he refers to another view, according to which there are ten varieties of lustre. The metre is **मालिनी**.

छायाः क्रमेण कुजलाग्न्यनिलाम्बरोत्थाः
केचिद्वदन्ति दश ताश्च यथानुपूर्व्या ।
सूर्याब्जनाभपुरुहूतयमोडुपानां
तुल्यास्तु लक्षणफलैरिति तत्समासः ।।६४।।

These are the five kinds of bodily lustre born of Earth, Water, Fire, Air and Ether respectively; but according to others (like Garga) there are five more, which are born, in order, of the Sun, Lord Nārāyaṇa, Indra, Yama (the God of Death) and the Moon. Since the latter five are similar to the others in characteristics and effects, the above five already mentioned are to be taken as containing all the varieties.

The commentator explains as to how the latter five varieties are equal to the former ones: The lustre belonging to Indra is similar to that of the Earth; that of the Moon, to that of the Water; that of the Sun, to that of Fire; that of Yama, to that of Air; and that of Nārāyaṇa, to that of Ether.

Cf. गर्ग—

भूम्यापोऽनलवाय्वभ्रसम्भूताः पञ्च कीर्त्तिताः ।
छायाभूविष्णुशक्रार्कचन्द्राणां च तथापराः ॥

Here it may be noted that Garga apparently names भू instead of Yama. We can get over the difficulty by combining छाया with भू which would mean Saturn or Yama.

The metre is वसन्ततिलका.

III Voice

करिवृषरथौघभेरीमृदङ्गसिंहाभ्रनिःस्वना भूपाः ।
गर्दभजर्जररूक्षस्वराश्च धनसौख्यसन्त्यक्ताः ॥६५॥

Persons become monarchs, if their voice is similar to the sound of elephants, bulls, a group of chariots (or chariots, streams), drums, tabors, lions or clouds. They become unhappy and poverty-stricken, if their voice is broken, rough or like that of a donkey.

The commentator, who is a great astrologer and scholar, does not bother about the genders of words : He uses वादित्र and अभ्र in masculine, though they are neuter according to the Amarakośa (I. 6-5 and I. 2-7). मन्द is another reading in the place of अभ्र making no difference in the meaning.

Vide Sage गर्ग—

गम्भीरो दुन्दुभिः स्निग्धो महांश्चैवानुनादवत् ।
इति स्वरगुणान्पञ्च समुद्रः प्राह तत्त्ववित् ॥
एभिरायुर्यशो विद्या मानं सौख्यं धनागमः ।
वाहनानि सुता नार्यो राज्यभोगागमास्तथा ॥
भिन्नो जर्जरितश्चैव मिमिणो गद्गदस्तथा ।
क्षामस्वरस्तथैवोक्ताः समुद्रेणाभिनन्दिताः ॥

स्वरैरेभिः कलिक्रोधलोभमोहतमोरजः ।
नैर्घृण्यमभिमानं च पारुष्यं शाठ्यमेव च ॥

IV Strength

सप्त भवन्ति च सारा मेदोमज्जात्वगस्थिशुक्राणि ।
रुधिरं मांसं चेति प्राणभृतां तत्समासफलम् ॥९६॥

Living beings have seven vital substances in their body, viz. fat, marrow, skin, bones, semen, blood and flesh. The following are their effects in brief :

In Āyurveda these are called *Dhātus* : रसासृङ्मांसमेदोऽस्थिमज्जाशुक्राणि धातवः । Sometimes three more are added to this list viz. केश, त्वच्, and स्नायु. The five elements, the Dhātus and the three humours viz. Vāta, Pitta and Kapha, are the basic principles that control the physical activities.

ताल्वोष्ठदन्तपालीजिह्वानेत्रान्तपायुकरचरणे ।
रक्ते तु रक्तसारा बहुसुखवनितार्थपुत्रयुताः ॥९७॥

If the palate, lips, jaws, tongue, corners of eyes, anus, hands and feet be red, men would have the vital substance of blood in abundance, and be blessed with all kinds of happiness, wealth and many wives and children.

In the printed editions including our own Bangalore edition the reading is चरणैः with रक्ते in the second line. This is evidently wrong. It must be either चरणैः रक्तैः or चरणे रक्ते. In the light of Utpala's explanation and Pāṇini's rule II.4-2 the latter reading should be preferred. The mistake must have been committed by scribes.

स्निग्धत्वक्का धनिनो मृदुभिः सुभगा विचक्षणास्तनुभिः ।
मज्जामेदःसाराः सुशरीराः पुत्रवित्तयुताः ॥९८॥

People with a glossy (not dry) skin become wealthy; with a soft one amiable or attractive; and with a thin one, scholars. Those that have fat and marrow in plenty come to have a handsome body and are blessed with sons and wealth.

स्थूलास्थिरस्थिसारो बलवान् विद्यान्तगः सुरूपश्च ।
बहुगुरुशुक्राः सुभगा विद्वांसो रूपवन्तश्च ॥९९॥

One who has thick bones is termed bone-strong and comes to have excellent physical strength, good features and sound bearing.

Fortunate, learned and handsome are those who have copious and thick semen.

[In the second line the author has unconsciously employed a pleasant pun on बहुगुरुशुक्राः which could also mean — 'Those who have strong Jupiter and Venus in their horoscopes.']

V. Joints

उपचितदेहो विद्वान् धनी सुरूपश्च मांससारो यः ।
सङ्घात इति च सुश्लिष्टसन्धिता सुखभुजो ज्ञेया ॥१००॥

One who has a well developed body is termed 'Flesh-strong', and possesses learning, wealth and handsome features.

'Cohesion' is the nature of those who have compact or strong joints. Men possessing such joints enjoy happiness in life.

VI. Gloss

स्नेहः पञ्चसु लक्ष्यो वाग्जिह्वादन्तनेत्रनखसंस्थः ।
सुतधनसौभाग्ययुताः स्निग्धैस्तैर्निर्धना रूक्षैः ॥१०१॥

Gloss is to be observed in five things, viz. speech, tongue, teeth, eyes and nails. If all these are glossy, men will be blessed with sons, wealth and attractive features; whereas if these are rough or dry, they will be poor.

VII. Colour

द्युतिमान्वर्णः स्निग्धः क्षितिपानां मध्यमः सुतार्थवताम् ।
रूक्षो धनहीनानां शुद्धः शुभदो न सङ्कीर्णः ॥१०२॥

A glossy and shining complexion belongs to kings; a medium one (i.e. neither too rough nor too glossy), to those that have wealth and children ; a rough one, to the poor ; a clean complexion is always auspicious ; and not so, a mixed one (i.e. in some parts glossy and in others rough).

VIII. Physiognomy

साध्यमनूकं वक्त्राद् गोवृषशार्दूलसिंहगरुडमुखाः ।
अप्रतिहतप्रतापा जितरिपवो मानवेन्द्राश्च ॥१०३॥

वानरमहिषवराहाजतुल्यवदनाः श्रुतार्थसुखभाजः ।
गर्दभकरभप्रतिमैर्मुखैः शरीरैश्च निःस्वसुखाः ॥१०४॥

The previous birth of a person is to be deduced from his face. Those whose face resembles that of a cow, bull, tiger, lion or eagle, had an excellent previous life, and will become in this life great kings of irresistible valour, vanquishing their enemies. Those whose face looks like that of a monkey, buffalo, boar or goat, had a moderate previous life, and will be blessed in this life with learning, wealth and happiness. Those whose face and body resemble those of a donkey or a camel, had a miserable previous existence, and will have in this birth neither wealth nor happiness.

[Here the author distinguishes three classes of animals viz. the upper, middle and lower class. The effects given for the present life of the three classes must be applied to their previous life as well.]

IX. Height

अष्टशतं षण्णवतिः परिमाणं चतुरशीतिरिति पुंसाम् ।
उत्तमसमहीनानामङ्गुलसङ्ख्या स्वमानेन ॥१०५॥

The height of the best type of men is 108 digits of themselves, that of the medium type, 96 digits, and that of the inferior one, 84 digits.

[Here the digit is not a standard measure, as it varies from person to person. If a person conforms to any of these measurement according to his own standard, he can be assigned to the concerned class.]

X. Weight

भारार्धतनुः सुखभाक् तुलितोऽतो दुःखभाग्भवत्यूनः ।
भारोऽतीवाढ्यानामध्यर्धः सर्वधरणीशः ॥१०६॥

A man who weighs half a Bhāra i.e. 100 Palas, will enjoy happiness; one weighing less than that will become miserable; persons weighing one Bhāra (i.e. 2000 Palas), immensely rich; and one weighing a Bhāra and a half (i.e. 3000 Palas), an emperor of the whole earth.

[Next the author discusses the age at which a man and woman should be weighed and measured.]

विंशतिवर्षा नारी पुरुषः खलु पञ्चविंशतिभिरब्दैः ।
अर्हति मानोन्मानं जीवितभागे चतुर्थे वा ॥१०७॥

The height and weight of a man and a woman ought to be taken at the age of 25 and 20 years respectively, or when they complete a fourth part of their span of life.

[Puruṣāyuṣa or man's span of life is considered a hundred years. If a person is supposed to live only 70 years according to his natal chart, then his height and weight must be taken towards the end of his 18th year.]

XI. Natural Character

भूजलशिख्यनिलाम्बरसुरनररक्षःपिशाचकतिरश्चाम् ।
सत्त्वेन भवति पुरुषो लक्षणमेतद्भवति तेषाम् ॥१०८॥

Man is constituted by the natural characteristics of Earth, Water, Fire, Air, Ether, Immortals, mortals, demons, devils and beasts. The following are their characteristics :

[The commentator refers to the reading तिर्यञ्चम् in the place of तिरश्चाम् and remarks that the older reading is correct and to be accepted.]

महीस्वभावः शुभपुष्पगन्धः सम्भोगवान् सुश्वसनः स्थिरश्च ।
तोयस्वभावो बहुतोयपायी प्रियाभिभाषी रसभाजनश्च ॥१०९॥

A man of earthy nature possesses the smell of fragrant flowers, enjoys pleasures, has a sweet breath, and is firm in character. One of watery nature drinks plenty of water, speaks sweetly and enjoys delicious and beautiful things.

[This verse may be read with advantage along with 90 and 91 *supra*, as there are some common features. No doubt, complexion, as I have already observed, is the outward manifestation of the inner qualities. Utpala here refers to another reading रसभोजनश्च in the place of रसभाजनश्च. He should have preferred that reading, inasmuch as that meaning befits the content more than the other, which is also grammatically wrong.

The metre is उपजाति.]

अग्निप्रकृत्या चपलोऽतितीक्ष्णश्चण्डः क्षुधालुर्बहुभोजनश्च ।
वायोः स्वभावेन चलः कृशश्च क्षिप्रं च कोपस्य वशं प्रयाति ॥११०॥

A man of fiery disposition is fickle-minded, very cruel, irascible, ever hungry and gluttonous. One of airy nature is unsteady in character, lean in body, and easily loses temper.

[This may be read with verses 92 and 93 *supra*.

The metre is इन्द्रवज्रा.]

खप्रकृतिर्निपुणो विवृतास्यः शब्दगतेः कुशलः सुशिराङ्गः ।
त्यागयुतः पुरुषो मृदुकोपः स्नेहरतश्च भवेत्सुरसत्त्वः ॥१११॥

A man born with the characteristic of ether becomes proficient in fine arts, open-mouthed (or has an expanded or large mouth), expert in grammar and speech (or the Śāstras), and possesses limbs that have beautiful veins. A man of divine nature is charitable, of soft temper, and devoted to friends.

[शब्द गतौ is another reading for शब्दगते:. Some scholar must have put it in the locative to make it sound in grammar. The metre is दोधक].

मर्त्यसत्त्वसंयुतो गीतभूषणप्रियः ।
संविभागशीलवान् नित्यमेव मानवः ॥११२॥

One endowed with a human nature is always fond of songs and ornaments, possesses a good character and shares his wealth with his fellowmen.

[The metre is समानिका].

तीक्ष्णप्रकोपः खलचेष्टितश्च पापश्च सत्त्वेन निशाचराणाम् ।
पिशाचसत्त्वश्चपलो मलाक्तो बहुप्रलापी च समुल्बणाङ्गः ॥११३॥

A man of demoniac nature is very hot-tempered, of wicked deeds, and sinful. One of devilish nature is fickle-minded, uncleanly, given to prattling and of a corpulent body.

[The metre is उपजाति.]

भीरुः क्षुधालुर्बहुभुक् च यः स्याज्ज्ञेयश्च सत्त्वेन नरस्तिरश्चाम् ।
एवं नराणां प्रकृतिः प्रदिष्टा यल्लक्षणज्ञाः प्रवदन्ति सत्त्वम् ॥११४॥

A man of bestial nature is cowardly, ever-hungry and gluttonous. Thus has been explained the nature of men which the scholars of characteristics call *Sattva*, inner mettle.

[Cf. गर्ग—

धन्यधन्यतरो वर्णो वर्णाद्धन्यतरः स्वरः ।
स्वराद्धन्यतरं सत्त्वं सर्वं सत्त्वे प्रतिष्ठितम् ॥

The metre is इन्द्रवज्रा.]

XII. Gait

शार्दूलहंससमदद्विपगोपतीनां
तुल्या भवन्ति गतिभिः शिखिनां च भूपाः ।
येषां च शब्दरहितं स्तिमितं च यातं
तेऽपीश्वरा द्रुतपरिप्लुतगा दरिद्राः ॥११५॥

Men become kings, if their gait resembles that of lions, swans, intoxicated-elephants, bulls or peacocks; rich, if their gait is slow and without any sound; and indigent, if their's is brisk and leaping.

[In the first line सिंह is another reading for हंस. The metre is वसन्ततिलका in this and the following verse.

श्रान्तस्य यानमशनं च बुभुक्षितस्य
पानं तृषापरिगतस्य भयेषु रक्षा ।
एतानि यस्य पुरुषस्य भवन्ति काले
धन्यं वदन्ति खलु तं नरलक्षणज्ञाः ॥११६॥

Those that are learned in the science of human characteristics call a man highly blessed and endowed with auspicious features, if he gets in time a conveyance, when he is fatigued; food, when hungry; drink, when thirsty; and protection, when in danger.

[This verse can serve as a good सुभाषित which has a universal appeal. There is a similar verse which describes the good fortunes of a worldly man:

अर्थागमो नित्यमरोगिता च प्रिया च भार्या प्रियवादिनी च ।
वश्यश्च पुत्रोऽर्थकरी च विद्या षड् जीवलोकस्य सुखानि राजन् ॥]

———

पञ्चमहापुरुषलक्षणम् ॥ ६९ ॥

Chapter LXIX—Signs of the Five Great Men

[This subject is dealt with in almost all astrological works. Though our author says 'मुनिमतानि निरीक्ष्य' the commentator does not quote any ancient sage except *Parāśara* in a solitary instance. Of course he quotes profusely from the सारावली which comes after our author. The chapter treats of the five classes of exalted men and their attendants.]

ताराग्रहैर्बलयुतैः स्वक्षेत्रस्वोच्चगैश्चतुष्टयगैः ।
पञ्च पुरुषाः प्रशस्ता जायन्ते तानहं वक्ष्ये ॥१॥

When the five non-luminaries viz. Mars, Mercury, Jupiter, Venus and Saturn, possessed of strength, occupy their own or exaltation Signs identical with kendras (1st, 4th, 7th, and 10th houses), five illustrious personages are born. I shall now describe them.

जीवेन भवति हंसः सौरेण शशः कुजेन रुचकश्च ।
भद्रो बुधेन बलिना मालव्यो दैत्यपूज्येन ॥ २ ॥

When Jupiter, Saturn, Mars, Mercury and Venus are strong, the five exalted men who come into existence are called in order *Haṁsa*, *Śaśa*, *Rucaka*, *Bhadra* and *Mālavya*.

[Cf. सारावली (XXXVII. 2)]:

स्वक्षेत्रे तु चतुष्टयेऽथ बलिभिः स्वोच्चे स्थितैर्वा ग्रहैः
शुक्राङ्गारकमन्दजीवशशिजैरेतैर्यथाप्रक्रमम् ।
मालव्यो रुचकः शशोऽथ कथितो हंसश्च भद्रस्तथा
सर्वेषामतिविस्तराद् मुनिमतात्सङ्क्षिप्यते लक्षणम् ॥

[Cf. also फलदीपिका VI. 1]

सत्त्वमहीनं सूर्याच्छारीरं मानसं च चन्द्रबलात् ।
यद्राशिभेदयुक्तावेतौ तल्लक्षणः स पुमान् ॥३॥

तद्धातुमहाभूतप्रकृतिद्युतिवर्णसत्त्वरूपाद्यैः ।
अबलरवीन्दुयुतैस्तैः सङ्कीर्णा लक्षणैः पुरुषाः ॥४॥

A person's excellent *Sattva*, inner strength, is derived from the Sun endowed with strength; physical lustre and mental strength (or qualities), from the Moon's strength. A person's characteristics depend upon the lords of the Zodiacal Signs and their sub-divisions (viz. Horā, Drekkāṇa. Navāṁśa, Dvādaśāṁśa and Triṁśāṁśa) in which these two luminaries are stationed (as well as upon the planets with which they are conjoined). Persons will be blessed with the particular physical constituent, great element, nature, lustre, colour, mettle, appearance etc. belonging to the planets owning the particular sub-divisions of Signs occupied by them. When both the luminaries are weak in respect of the Signs and sub-divisions, the characteristics would be of a mixed type.

[In the *Bṛhajjātaka* (II. 11) the author explains that muscles, bones, blood, skin, semen, fat and marrow belong in order to Saturn, the Sun, the Moon, Mercury, Venus, Jupiter and Mars. The colours of planets are given in the same work (II. 4) and appearance in II. 8. The five elements viz. Fire, Earth, Ether, Water and Air are presided over by Mars, Mercury, Jupiter, Venus and Saturn respectively (II. 6) The commentator tells us that the constituent, nature etc. of a person are to be deduced from the lords of the Rāśi and its subdivisions occupied by the stronger of the two luminaries.

Cf. सारावली (XXXVII. 28) :

बलरहितेन्दुरविभ्यां युक्तैर्भौमादिभिर्मिश्राः।
न भवन्ति भूमिपाला दशासु तेषां सुतार्थयुताः ॥

In the light of this statement the commentator says:—"एतेषामर्कचन्द्रबलवशाद्विशेषमाह।" The idea is that the *Mahāpuruṣayogas* become fully effective only when the luminaries are quite strong.]

भौमात्सत्त्वं गुरुता बुधात्सुरेज्यात्स्वरः सितात्स्नेहः।
वर्णः सौरादेषां गुणदोषैः साध्वसाधुत्वम् ॥५॥

People derive their valour from Mars; physical growth and weight from Mercury; voice from Jupiter; glossiness from Venus; and colour or complexion from Saturn. As a result of the merits and demerits (strength and weakness) of these planets, the above things (viz. valour etc.) become good and bad respectively.

[Cf. सारावली (XXXVII. 3):]

महीसुतात्सत्त्वमुदाहरन्ति गुरुत्वमिन्दोस्तनयाद् गुरोश्च।
स्वरः सितात् स्नेहमतोऽनुवर्णं बलाबलैः पूर्णलघूनि चैषाम् ॥

सङ्कीर्णाः स्युर्न नृपा दशासु तेषां भवन्ति सुखभाजः ।
रिपुगृहनीचोच्चच्युतसत्पापनिरीक्षणैर्भेदाः ॥६॥

Men who are born with mixed characteristics cannot hope to become Kings, but they will lead a happy life in the major periods (*Daśās*) of the Yoga-producing planets. These differences (between the *Excellent* and *Mixed* types) occur as a result of the concerned planets (among the five non-luminaries) being aspected by benefics occupying inimical Signs or debilitation ones or being fallen from exaltation, or by malefics, [or as a result of benefics in inimical houses etc. being aspected by malefics].

[According to Kalyāṇavarman the *Mixed* types are ushered into the world as a result of the Yoga-producing planet or planets from Mars onward being conjoined with the weak luminaries. In this verse our author states that the above conditions in addition, produce *Saṅkīrṇas*. The commentator construes the second line thus: रिपुगृहं शत्रुक्षेत्रम् । नीचगृहं प्रसिद्धम् । उच्चत्वं जातके प्रसिद्धम् । तस्माद्ये च्युताश्चलिता ग्रहास्तैरवलोकिता दृष्टाः सन्तः शुभग्रहाः··· । Grammatically this construction, I am afraid, is not sustainable. Later on he gives one of the correct alternatives. By straining the construction, no doubt, we could get the following meaning as well :— "As a result of both benefics and malefics aspecting the planets that are posited in inimical or debilitation Signs or fallen from exaltation, or vice versa."]

षण्णवतिरङ्गुलानां व्यायामो दीर्घता च हंसस्य ।
शशरुचकभद्रमालव्यसंज्ञितास्त्र्यङ्गुलविवृद्धया ॥७॥

The height and extent of the two arms outstretched (from one end to the other) of a man belonging to the *Haṁsa* clan are 96 digits; and those of *Śaśa*, *Rucaka*, *Bhadra* and *Mālavya* are 99, 102, 105 and 108 digits respectively.

[Cf. पराशर

उच्छ्रायः परिणाहस्तु यस्य तुल्यं शरीरिणः ।
स नरः पार्थिवो ज्ञेयो न्यग्रोधपरिमण्डलः ॥

The commentator adds that this rule is at variance with the author's statement under verses 18, 21 and 29 *infra*. I think that the author has given here the heights of the ideal types.

In verse 4 there is the word *Sattva* which stands for the three qualities viz. Sattva, Rajas and Tamas. These qualities are represented by (1) the Moon, Jupiter and the Sun, (2) Venus and Mercury, and (3) Mars and Saturn. The प्रकृति or nature of people is composed of these three qualities according to the strength of the concerned planets. In the next two verses the author discusses the virtues resulting from these qualities.]

यः सात्त्विकस्तस्य दया स्थिरत्वं सत्त्वार्जवं ब्राह्मणदेवभक्तिः ।
रजोऽधिकः काव्यकलाक्रतुस्त्रीसंसक्तचित्तः पुरुषोऽतिशूरः ॥८॥
तमोऽधिको वञ्चयिता परेषां मूर्खोऽलसः क्रोधपरोऽतिनिद्रः ।
मिश्रैर्गुणैः सत्त्वरजस्तमोभिर्मिश्रास्तु ते सप्त सह प्रभेदैः ॥९॥

A person who is endowed with the quality of goodness (*Sattva*) in abundance, becomes kind-hearted towards all beings, firm or steady in his attitude, courageous, straightforward and devoted to Brāhmaṇas and Gods; one in whom the quality of passion or intense activity (*Rajas*) predominates, is greatly interested in poetry or literature, fine arts, sacrifices and women (*sex*), and is very heroic; and one in whom the quality of darkness or ignorance (*Tamas*) is predominant, is deceitful, foolish, lazy, hot-tempered and addicted to sleeping. People of mixed characteristics are born as a result of the intermingling of these three qualities. With the varieties of the *Mixed* persons there are altogether 7 categories (i.e. four categories of the Mixed and three of unmixed nature).

[The word सत्त्वार्जवं is interpreted by Bhaṭṭotpala thus : सत्त्वानां प्राणिनामार्जवम् । He should have added सत्त्वानां विषये. Otherwise सत्त्वेषु आर्जवं would be preferable. Then it would mean : straightforwardness towards all beings. But that does not seem to be the meaning intended by the author. He must have used it in the sense of courage. I have a vague feeling that the author might have used the expression, सत्यार्जव in singular or dual.

For a clear description of the three qualities see the भगवद्गीता XIV 5-18. The last three of these verses are highly significant.

We get four categories of *Mixed* nature by mingling the three qualities : (1) Sattva and Rajas; (2) Rajas and Tamas; (3) Sattva and Tamas; and (4) all the three in one.

The metre is उपजाति.]

मालव्यो नागनासासमभुजयुगलो जानुसम्प्राप्तहस्तो
मांसैः पूर्णाङ्गसन्धिः समरुचिरतनुर्मध्यभागे कृशश्च ।
पञ्चाष्टौ चोर्ध्वमास्यं श्रुतिविवरमपि त्र्यङ्गुलोनं च तिर्य-
ग्दीप्ताक्षं सत्कपोलं समसितदशनं नातिमांसाधरोष्ठम् ॥१०॥

A person belonging to the Mâlavya type (caused by Venus) possesses arms that are long like the trunk of an elephant (or nose like the elephant's trunk and equal arms) and hands that touch the knees, limbs and joints (or joints of limbs) full of flesh, the body even (symmetrical), attractive and slender in the waist, the face 13 digits in height, the ear-holes 10 digits apart, shining eyes, fine-cheek, equal and white teeth, and not a very fleshy lower lip.

[The commentator notes another reading नागनास: instead of नागनासा. While explaining श्रुतिविवरमपि he states : चिबुकाच्छ्रवणविवरं यावत् त्र्यङ्गुलोनं तिर्यग् भवति, चिबुकमध्यात्कर्णविवरं यावत् तिर्यक्कृत्वा दशाङ्गुलानि भवन्तीत्यर्थः । This interpretation is not warranted by the text. For, the word तिर्यक् makes it clear that it is the horizontal distance of the ear-holes, and not the one between the centre of the chin and each ear-hole. The author uses ऊर्ध्वम् for the face and here तिर्यक्. Vide the फलदीपिका VI. 3 for a description of *Mālavya* :

पुष्टाङ्गो धृतिमान्धनी सुतवधूभाग्यान्वितो वर्धनो
मालव्ये सुखभुक् सुवाहनयशा विद्वान्प्रसन्नेन्द्रियः ॥

The metre is स्रग्धरा.]

मालवान्सभरुकच्छसुराष्ट्रान् लाटसिन्धुविषयप्रभृतींश्च ।
विक्रमार्जितधनोऽवति राजा पारियात्रनिलयान् कृतबुद्धिः ॥११॥

One belonging to the *Mālavya* type becomes a monarch of cultured mind, and rules over the Malwas, Broach, Surāṣṭra country, Lāṭas, Sindhu country and the regions of the Pāriyātra mountain, having amassed wealth by his prowess.

[These countries have been already mentioned in V. 68, VI. 10, XIV. 4, 11, 17, 19, XVI 6, 0, 17, 26 and 31 *supra*. Lāṭa is identified with the central and southern parts of Gujarat and is probably the same as Ptolemy's Larike which included Broach and Ujjain. Albiruni (I. 205) calls this Lārdesh. *Pāriyātra* is the western part of the Vindhya range west of Bhopal including the Aravali mountains.

The metre is स्वागता.

सप्ततिवर्षो मालव्योऽयं त्यक्ष्यति सम्यक् प्राणांस्तीर्थे ।
लक्षणमेतत्सम्यक् प्रोक्तं शेषनराणां चातो वक्ष्ये ॥१२॥

A person of this *Mālavya* class lives for 70 years and shuffles off his mortal coils in a sacred place through yoga or penance. Thus have I clearly explained the characteristics of this class, and now I shall proceed to define the remaining classes.

[In a musical verse, which has not been named in the texts on prosody, the author concludes the description of the *Mālavya* clan. The metre is called स्निग्धा by श्रीकृष्ण; see पिङ्गल footnote, p. 110.

Cf. सारावली (XXXVII. 29, 30).

न स्थूलौष्ठो न विषमवपुर्नातिरिक्ताङ्गसन्धि-
र्मध्यक्षामः शशधररुचिर्हंस्तिनासः सुगण्डः ।
सन्दीप्ताक्षः समसितरदो जानुदेशाप्तबाहु-
र्मालव्योऽयं विलसति नृपः सप्ततिर्वत्सराणाम् ॥
वक्त्रं त्रयोदशमितानि तथाङ्गुलानि
दैर्घ्येण कर्णविवराद् दश विस्तरेण ।
मालव्यसंज्ञमनुजः स भुनक्ति नूनं
लाटं समालवससिन्धुसपारियात्रम् ॥]

उपचितसमवृत्तलम्बबाहुर्भुजयुगलप्रमितः समुच्छ्रयोऽस्य ।
मृदुतनुधनरोमनद्धगण्डो भवति नरः खलु लक्षणेन भद्रः ॥१३॥

One who belongs to the *Bhadra* class (caused by Mercury) possesses well-developed, equal, round and long arms; height equal to the length of his out-stretched arms; and temples densely covered with tender and fine hair.

[The metre is पुष्पिताग्रा.]

त्वक्शुक्रसारः पृथुपीनवक्षाः सत्त्वाधिको व्याघ्रमुखः स्थिरश्च ।
क्षमान्वितो धर्मपरः कृतज्ञो गजेन्द्रगामी बहुशास्त्रवेत्ता ॥१४॥

प्राज्ञो वपुष्मान् सुललाटशङ्खः कलास्वभिज्ञो धृतिमान्सुकुक्षिः ।
सरोजगर्भद्युतिपाणिपादो योगी सुनासः समसंहतभ्रूः ॥१५॥

The person of *Bhadra* class has strong skin and semen, large and muscular breast, a lofty disposition, tigerlike face, steady mind, forbearance, attachment to meritorious activities, gratitude, gait like that of a lordly elephant, knowledge of many branches of learning, acute intelligence, a handsome personality, beautiful temples and forehead, proficiency in fine arts, courage, a fine belly, hands and feet with the lustre of the interior of lotus, love for contemplation (or meditation), a lovely nose and equal and well-knit brows.

[Sattva is explained variously by various scholars. It is a mental quality whereby a person does not get elated in prosperity, nor dejected in adversity. रजस्तमोभ्यामस्पृष्टं मनः सत्त्वमिहोच्यते is another definition. By शुक्रसार: is meant one who has copious and thick vitality.

The metre is उपजाति.]

नवाम्बुसिक्तावनिपत्रकुङ्कुमद्विपेन्द्रदानागुरुतुल्यगन्धता ।
शिरोरुहाश्चैकजकृष्णकुञ्चितास्तुरङ्गनागोपमगुह्यगूढता ॥१६॥

His person gives out the smell of the earth sprinkled with fresh rain, Laurus cassia, saffron, ichor of lordly elephants and *Aguru* (Commiphora roxburghii); his hairs are dark, curly and single in each pore; and his genital organ is hidden like that of a horse or elephant.

[The metre is वंशस्थ.]

हलमुसलगदासिशङ्खचक्रद्विपमकराब्जरथाङ्कितांघ्रिहस्तः ।
विभवमपि जनोऽस्य बोभुजीति क्षमति हि न स्वजनं स्वतन्त्रबुद्धिः ॥१७॥

His hands and feet are marked with the figures of ploughs, staves, maces, swords, (conch shells, wheels, elephants, crocodiles, lotuses and chariots. His wealth is fully enjoyed by the people. He has independent ideas and does not tolerate his kinsmen.

[The author uses the scholarly expression बोभुजीति, a frequentative. The word क्षमति is wrong as it is आत्मनेपदी.

The metre is पुष्पिताग्रा.

Cf. फलदीपिका VI. 2 :—

आयुष्मान् सकुशाग्रबुद्धिरमलो विद्वज्जनश्लाघितो
भूपो भद्रकयोगजोऽतिविभवश्चास्थानकोलाहलः ॥]

अङ्गुलानि नवतिश्च षडूनान्युच्छ्रयेण तुलयापि हि भारः ॥
मध्यदेशनृपतिर्यदि पुष्टास्त्र्यावयोऽस्य सकलावनिनाथः ॥१८॥

His height is 84 digits and weight a Bhāra (2000 Palas). He becomes the ruler of the middle country; but if his height and extent of outstretched arms be each 105 digits, he would be an emperor of the whole earth.

[In view of this statement of height, the commentator has said under verse 7 *supra* that there is a contradiction.

The metre is स्वागता.]

भुक्त्वा सम्यग्वसुधां शौर्येणोपार्जितामशीत्यब्दः ।
तीर्थे प्राणांस्त्यक्त्वा भद्रो देवालयं याति ॥१९॥

A person of the *Bhadra* class lives for 80 years, rules worthily over the country conquered by valour, and abandoning his mortal coil in a holy place ascends to the abode of the Gods.

[Cf. सारावली (XXXVII. 40-44) :—

शार्दूलप्रतिमाननो द्विपगतिः पीनोरुवक्षःस्थलो
लम्बापीनसुवृत्तबाहुयुगलस्तत्तुल्यमानोच्छ्रयः ।
कामी कोमलसूक्ष्मरोमनिकरैः संरुद्धगण्डः शठः
प्राज्ञः पङ्कजगर्भपाणिचरणः सत्त्वाधिको योगवित् ॥
शङ्खासिकुञ्जरगदाकुमुदेषुकेतु-
चक्राब्जलाङ्गलविचिह्नितपाणिपादः ।
पत्रागुरुद्विपमदप्रथमाम्बुसिक्त-
मृत्कुङ्कुमप्रतिमगन्धतनुः सुघोणः ॥
शास्त्रार्थविद्धृतियुतः समसंहतभ्रू-
र्नागोपमो भवति चापि निगूढगुह्यः ।
सत्कुक्षिधर्मनिरतः सुललाटशङ्खो
धीरः स्थिरस्त्वसितकुञ्चितकेशपाशः ॥
स्वतन्त्रः सर्वकार्येषु स्वजनं प्रति न क्षमः ।
भुज्यते विभवश्चास्य नित्यं बन्धुजनैः परैः ॥
भारस्तुलायास्तुलितो यदि स्यात् श्रीकान्यकुब्जाधिपतिस्तदासौ ।
यस्त्व्यादिपुष्टैः सहितैः स भद्रः सर्वत्र राजा शरदामशीतिम् ॥]

ईषद्दन्तुरकस्तनुद्विजनखः कोशेक्षणः शीघ्रगो
विद्याधातुवणिक्क्रियासु निरतः सम्पूर्णगण्डः शठः ।
सेनानीः प्रियमैथुनः परजनस्त्रीसक्तचित्तश्चलः
शूरो मातृहितो वनाचलनदीदुर्गेषु सक्तः शशः ॥२०॥

A person belonging to the *Śaśa* class (caused by Saturn) has slightly raised and small teeth, thin nails, large eye-balls, brisk gait, is attached to learning pertaining to minerals and metals, engaged in trade, of plump cheeks, and a rogue. He is a leader of armies, fond of sexual pleasures, addicted to others' wives, fickle-minded, heroic, devoted to his mother, and a lover of forests, mountains, rivers and fortresses (or, impenetrable areas).

[The metre is शार्दूलविक्रीडित.

Cf. फलदीपिका (VI. 4) :—

शस्तः सर्वजनैः सुभृत्यबलवान् ग्रामाधिपो वा नृपो
दुर्वृत्तः शशयोगजोऽन्यवनितावित्तान्वितः सौख्यवान् ॥]

दीर्घोऽङ्गुलानां शतमष्टहीनं साशङ्कचेष्टः पररन्ध्रविच्च ।
सारोऽस्य मज्जा निभृतप्रचारः शशो ह्यतो नातिगुरुः प्रविष्टः ॥२१॥

His height is 92 digits; he acts with apprehension, knows

others' weaknesses, has marrow as the dominant feature of his constitution, walks steadily (or quietly) and is not very corpulent.

[This and the following verses are in the उपजाति metre.]

मध्ये कृशः खेटकखड्गवीणापर्यङ्कमालामुरजानुरूपाः ।
शूलोपमाश्चोर्ध्वगताश्च रेखाः शशस्य पादोपगताः करे वा ॥२२॥

A person of the *Śaśa* class has a slender waist and vertical lines on the soles or palms resembling a shield, sword, lute, cot, garland, tabor and trident.

प्रात्यन्तिको माण्डलिकोऽथवायं स्फिक्स्रावशूलाभिभवार्तमूर्तिः ।
एवं शशः सप्ततिहायनोऽयं वैवस्वतस्यालयमभ्युपैति ॥२३॥

A person of this class becomes the lord of foresters or the governor of a province; his body will be afflicted with colic or a fistula in the buttocks; he will consequently go to Yama's abode at the age of 70 years.

[Cf. सारावली (XXXVII. 34-36):–

तनुद्विजः शीघ्रगतिः शशोऽयं शठोऽतिशूरो निभृतप्रचारः ।
वनाद्रिदुर्गेषु नदीषु सक्तः क्षयोदयी नातिलघुः प्रसिद्धः ॥
सेनानाथो बलिनिधिरतो दन्तुरश्चापि किञ्चि-
द्धातोर्वादे भवति निरतश्चञ्चलः कारणेषु ।
स्त्रीसंसक्तः परजनगृहे मातृभक्तः सुजङ्घो
मध्ये क्षामो बहुविधमती रन्ध्रवेदी परेषाम् ॥
पर्यङ्कशङ्खफरशास्त्रमृदङ्गमाला
वीणोपमा यदि करे चरणे च रेखाः ।
वर्षाणि सप्ततिमितानि करोति राज्यं
प्रात्यन्तिकः क्षितिपतिः कथितो मुनीन्द्रैः ॥

The metre is इन्द्रवज्रा.]

रक्तं पीनकपोलमुन्नतनसं वक्त्रं सुवर्णोपमं
वृत्तं चास्य शिरोऽक्षिणी मधुनिभे सर्वे च रक्ता नखाः ।
स्रग्दामाङ्कुशशङ्खमत्स्ययुगलक्रत्वङ्गकुम्भाम्बुजै-
श्चिह्नैर्हंसकलस्वनः सुचरणो हंसः प्रसन्नेन्द्रियः ॥ २४ ॥

A person belonging to the *Hamsa* class has a reddish face with fleshy cheeks, raised nose and a golden hue; his head is round; eyes are like honey in colour; all nails red; has the marks of a garland, goad, conch, a pair of fish, sacrificial appurtenance, pot and lotus. His voice is as sweet as that of a swan, feet beautiful, and limbs (organs of action) clean.

[Cf. फलदीपिका—(VI. 3)

हंसे सद्भिरभिष्टुतः क्षितिपतिः शङ्खाब्जमत्स्याङ्कुशै-
श्चिह्नैः पादकराङ्कितः शुभवपुर्मृष्टान्नभुग्धार्मिकः ॥

The metre is शार्दूलविक्रीडित.]

रतिरम्भसि शुक्रसारता द्विगुणा चाष्टशतैः पलैर्मितिः ।
परिमाणमथास्य षड्युता नवतिः सम्परिकीर्त्तिता बुधैः ॥ २५ ॥

A man of the *Haṁsa* class loves to sport in water; his semen is thick and copious; his weight is 1600 Palas; and his height and extent, as stated by the wise, are 96 digits.

[Here at least there is no difference in respect of height. See also verse 106 of LXVIII *supra*.

The metre is वियोगिनी.]

भुनक्ति हंसः खसशूरसेनान् गान्धारगङ्गायमुनान्तरालम् ।
शतं दशोनं शरदां नृपत्वं कृत्वा वनान्ते समुपैति मृत्युम् ॥ २६ ॥

This person of the *Haṁsa* type rules over the Khasas, Śūrasenas, Gāndhāras and the countries lying between the Ganges and the Jumna. He holds sway for 90 years and meets his end in a forest (penance-grove ?).

[The Khasas are a mountain tribe assigned to the East and North-east. The Śūrasenas belong to the central region.

The metre is उपजाति.

Cf. सारावली—

रक्ताभ्युन्नतनासिकः सुचरणो हंसः प्रसन्नेन्द्रियो
गौरः पीनकपोलरक्तकरजो हंसस्वरः श्लेष्मलः ।
शङ्खाब्जाङ्कुशदाममत्स्ययुगलैर्निस्त्रिंशमालाघटै-
श्चिह्नैः पादकराङ्कितो मधुनिभे नेत्रे च वृत्तं शिरः ॥
सलिलाशयेषु रमते स्त्रीषु न तृप्तिं प्रयाति कामार्तः ।
षोडशशतानि तुलितोऽङ्गुलानि दैर्घ्येण षण्णवतिः ॥
पातीह देशांश्च स शूरसेनान् गान्धारगङ्गायमुनान्तरालम् ।
जीवेन्नवघ्नीं दशवर्षसङ्ख्यां पश्चाद्वनान्ते समुपैति नाशम् ॥]

सुभ्रूकेशो रक्तश्यामः कम्बुग्रीवो व्यादीर्घास्यः ।
शूरः क्रूरः श्रेष्ठो मन्त्री चौरस्वामी व्यायामी च ॥ २७ ॥

A person belonging to the *Rucaka* type (caused by Mars) has fine brows and hair, dark and red complexion, conch-like neck and an oblong face. He is heroic, cruel, a leader among men, a minister, leader of a gang of thieves, and hard-working.

[Cf. मन्त्रेश्वर—

दीर्घास्यो बहुसाहसाप्तविभवः शूरोऽरिहन्ता बली
गर्विष्ठो रुचके प्रतीतगुणवान् सेनापतिर्जित्वरः ॥

The metre is विद्युन्माला.]

यन्मात्रमास्यं रुचकस्य दीर्घं मध्यप्रदेशे चतुरस्रता सा ।
तनुच्छविः शोणितमांससारो हन्ता द्विषां साहससिद्धकार्यः ॥ २८ ॥

The girth of the waist of a men of this class is equal to the length of his face. His complexion is good (or his skin is thin). He has blood and flesh as the strongest elements in his constitution. He destroys his enemies and accomplishes his objects through his adventurous spirit.

[The commentator takes छविः in the sense of skin. The metre is उपजाति in this and the following verse.]

खट्वाङ्गवीणावृषचापवज्रशक्तीन्द्रशूलाङ्कितपाणिपादः ।
भक्तो गुरुब्राह्मणदेवतानां शताङ्गुलः स्यात्तु सहस्रमानः ॥ २९ ॥

His hands and feet are marked with the figures of a club, lute, bull, bow, diamond (or thunderbolt) spear, Indra (hall) and trident. He is devoted to elders, Brāhmaṇas and Gods. His height and extent are 100 digits and weight 1000 Palas.

[It is not clear what is meant by the figure of *Indra*. *Indraka* also means an assembly room or hall. The commentator does not lend a helping hand either. According to the author's statement in verse 7 *supra* the height of *Rucaka* should be 102 digits. *Khaṭvāṅga* is a weapon of Lord Śiva. It resembles a club with a ball at the tip.]

मन्त्राभिचारकुशलः कृशजानुजङ्घो
विन्ध्यं ससह्यगिरिमुज्जयिनीं च भुक्त्वा ।
सम्प्राप्य सप्ततिसमा रुचको नरेन्द्रः
शस्त्रेण मृत्युमुपयात्यथवानलेन ॥ ३० ॥

He is proficient in spells and black magic; his knees and shanks are lean. He becomes a king and rules over the regions of the

Vindhyas, the Sahya mountain and Ujjain. He dies at the age of 70 years by weapons or fire.

[Cf. कल्याणवर्मा—

दीर्घास्यः स्वच्छकान्तिर्बहुरुचिचपलः साहसावाप्तकार्य-
श्चारुभ्रूर्नीलकेशः श्रमकरणरतो मन्त्रविच्चोरनाथः ।
रक्तश्यामोऽतिशूरो रिपुबलमथनः शङ्खकण्ठः प्रधानः
क्रूरो भक्तो नराणां द्विजगुरुनिरतः क्षाममज्जोऽनुजङ्घः ॥
खट्वाङ्गपाशवृषकार्मुकवज्रवीणाशक्त्यङ्कहस्तचरणश्च तथाङ्गुलिश्च ।
मन्त्राभिचारकुशलस्तुलया सहस्रं मध्यं च तस्य कथितं मुखदैर्घ्यतुल्यम् ॥
विन्ध्याचलमस्तगिरीन् भुक्त्वावन्तीं च सप्तितिं शरदाम् ।
शस्त्रानलकृतमृत्युः प्रयाति देवालयं रुचकः ॥

The metre is वसन्ततिलका.]

नृपानुचरलक्षणम् Kings' Attendants

पञ्चापरे वामनको जघन्यः कुब्जोऽथवा मण्डलकोऽथ साची ।
पूर्वोक्तभूपानुचरा भवन्ति सङ्कीर्णसञ्ज्ञाः शृणु लक्षणैस्तान् ॥ ३१ ॥

There are five other classes of men who are the attendants of the five above-named monarchs (Mālavya and others) viz. *Vāmanaka*, *Jaghanya*, *Kubja*, *Maṇḍalaka* and *Sācin*. Now listen to the characteristics of these types that are known as the '*Mixed* ones'.

[सामी is another reading for साची.

The metre is इन्द्रवज्रा.]

सम्पूर्णाङ्गो वामनो भग्नपृष्ठः किञ्चिच्चोरुमध्यकक्ष्यान्तरेषु ।
ख्यातो राज्ञां ह्येष भद्रानुजीवी स्फीतो राजा वासुदेवस्य भक्तः ॥ ३२ ॥

The person termed *Vāmanaka* possesses all the limbs well-developed except the thighs, waist and between the armpits, which are undeveloped. He is hunch-backed, a famous servant of the king of the *Bhadra* type, very rich, lordly and devoted to Lord Vāsudeva.

[The word भग्नपृष्ठः would mean, one of broken back. I feel that the author might have used the expression भुग्नपृष्ठः which gives better sense. The commentator interprets the second quarter as : ऊरुप्रदेशे मध्ये मध्यभागे कक्ष्यान्तरेषु किञ्चिदीषद्भग्न एव किञ्चिदसम्पूर्णाङ्गः । Though the sense may be the same grammatically this construction may not be right. For, the word *Bhagna* cannot be separated from the compound (though our author resorts to this forbidden device many a time), and the word *ūrū* is wrong inside a compound. I propose a better interpretation : ऊरू किञ्चिदेव भग्नौ । मध्यकक्ष्यान्तरेषु च किञ्चिदेव अपरिपूर्णो नरः ।

The metre is शालिनी.]

मालव्यसेवी तु जघन्यनामा खण्डेन्दुतुल्यश्रवणः सुसन्धिः ।
शुक्रेण सारः पिशुनः कविश्च रूक्षच्छविः स्थूलकराङ्गुलीकः ।। ३३ ।।

क्रूरो धनी स्थूलमतिः प्रतीतस्ताम्रच्छविः स्यात्परिहासशीलः ।
उरोऽङ्घ्रिहस्तेष्वसिशक्तिपाशपरश्वधाङ्कः स जघन्यनामा ।। ३४ ।।

The person called *Jaghanya* is a servant of the *Mālavya* king; he has crescent-like ears, good joints and thick and copious semen. He is a tale-bearer and a poet. His complexion is rough and fingers thick. He is cruel, wealthy, unintelligent, well-known, copper-coloured, of humorous disposition, and marked with the figures of a sword, spear, noose and axe on the chest, feet and hands.

[ताम्रच्छविर्दासनुचरः स नित्यम् is another reading in the third line. Utpala explains स्थूलमतिः as महाबुद्धिः which is wrong unless used in derision. He says पाशः सर्पः which is known as नागपाश. The expression शुक्रेण सारः in the text is grammatically untenable. It should have been शुक्रेण सारवान्, but it could have been changed to शुक्रोरुसारः or शुक्रस्वसारः, without spoiling the metre. The metre of the two is इन्द्रवज्रा and उपजाति respectively.]

कुब्जो नाम्ना यः स शुद्धो ह्यधस्तात् क्षीणः किञ्चित्पूर्वकाये नतश्च ।
हंसासेवी नास्तिकोऽर्थैरुपेतो विद्वाञ्शूरः सूचकः स्यात्कृतज्ञः ।। ३५ ।।

कलास्वभिज्ञः कलहप्रियश्च प्रभूतभृत्यः प्रमदाजितश्च ।
सम्पूज्य लोकं प्रजहात्यकस्मात्कुब्जोऽयमुक्तः सततोद्यतश्च ।। ३६ ।।

The one named *Kubja* (literally, hunch-backed) is well-developed in the lower limbs, but slightly weak and bent in the upper part of the body. He is the attendant of the *Haṁsa* class of kings, an atheist, wealthy, learned, brave, grateful and a tale-bearer. He is highly learned in fine arts, fond of quarrels, served by many servants, and vanquished by women. He honours the people and forsakes them suddenly. He is ever energetic.

[I do not know why Utpala construes अधस्तात् as अधोभागात् in the ablative. He should have used the locative instead. The verse is in शालिनी and the second in उपजाति metre.]

मण्डलकलक्षणमतो दचकानुचरोऽभिचारवित्कुशलः ।
कृत्यावेतालादिषु कर्मसु विद्यासु चानुरतः ।। ३७ ।।

वृद्धाकारः खरपरुषमूर्धजः शत्रुनाशने कुशलः ।
द्विजदेवयज्ञयोगप्रसक्तधीः स्त्रीजितो मतिमान् ।। ३८ ।।

Now listen to the characteristics of the *maṇḍalaka* person. He is the follower of the *Rucaka* class of kings, expert in black magic, clever, adept in witchcraft, creating magical women and ghosts, and in similar lores. He has the appearance of an old man with rough and hard hairs; he is capable of destroying his enemies; he is devoted to Brāhmaṇas, Gods, sacrifices and yoga (meditation); is controlled by women and intelligent.

[Abhicāra, Kṛtyā, Vetāla etc. are varieties of black magic. Through the first, one tries to harm his rivals etc., to exorcize an unwanted or troublesome spirit and to control others. Kṛtyā is a female spirit that rises from the fire as a result of spells and incantations, and for the purpose of destroying one's enemies. Vetāla or goblin is the raising of an abandoned dead body through spells. Similarly Yakṣas and Bhūtas are made to subserve human interests. In the last line दोह is another reading for योग.]

साचीति यः सोऽतिविरूपदेहः शशानुगामी खलु दुर्भगश्च ।
दाता महारम्भसमाप्तकार्यो गुणैः शशस्यैव भवेत् समानः ॥ ३९ ॥

A person called *Sācin* has a very ugly and deformed body; he is the follower of the *Śaśa* type of kings, is disliked by people, but charitably disposed. He undertakes great tasks and accomplishes them. He is similar to *Śaśa* in qualities.

[सामी is another reading for साची.
The metre is उपजाति.]

पुरुषलक्षणमुक्तमिदं मया मुनिमतानि निरीक्ष्य समासतः ।
इदमधीत्य नरो नृपसम्मतो भवति सर्वजनस्य च वल्लभः ॥ ४० ॥

Thus have I explained succinctly the characteristics of men, after studying the opinions of the Sages. By learning this, one could become the favourite of kings and a beloved of all the people.

[As remarked earlier, we are in the dark as to the authorities followed by Varāhamihira. It is possible that the works of ancient sages were lost before the time of Bhaṭṭotpala.

The metre is द्रुतविलम्बित.]

कन्यालक्षणम् ॥ ७० ॥

Chapter LXX—Characteristics of Maidens

This chapter forms a complementary to LXVIII. The commentator quotes समुद्र, गर्ग, पराशर and some unnamed authority, as before.

स्निग्धोन्नताग्रतनुताम्रनखौ कुमार्याः
पादौ समोपचितचारुनिगूढगुल्फौ ।
श्लिष्टाङ्गुली कमलकान्तितलौ च यस्या-
स्तामुद्वहेद्यदि भुवोऽधिपतित्वमिच्छेत् ॥ १ ॥

One wishing to become the lord of the earth must marry a maiden, the nails of whose feet are glossy, arched, pointed at the tip, and red, the ankle-joints, equal, well-developed (fleshy), beautiful and hidden; the toes, close-touching; and the soles, as lustrous as a lotus.

[Marriage is looked upon as a sacred link in the life of man in his journey towards perfection. A worthy and fortunate partner, therefore, would greatly help him in accomplishing his earthly ambitions as well as those of the other world. A knowledge of feminine physiognomy will stand one in good stead in the selection of a suitable bride. For, says प्रह्लाद:—

सुरूपा च सुशीला च दुर्लभा सत्कुलोद्भवा ॥
स्फुरच्चन्द्रमुखी नारी पद्मपत्रायतेक्षणा ।
अर्धेन्दुनिटिला वक्रभ्रूलताकुटिलालका ॥
चाम्पेयनासिका कुन्दरदना कोमलाङ्गिका ।
बिम्बोष्ठी कम्बुकण्ठी च कृशाङ्गी सूक्ष्ममध्यमा ॥
शातोदरी पृथुश्रोणी रम्भोरूर्भाग्यशालिनी ।
पद्मसन्निभपाण्यङ्घ्रिः सुशीला सुगुणान्विता ॥
सुगन्धा सत्कुलोत्पन्ना लज्जाविनयशालिनी ।
दयालुर्धर्मनिरता पातिव्रत्यपरायणा ॥
यत्र स्यादीदृशी नारी तत्र लक्ष्मीः प्रसीदति ।
आनन्दयति सा लोकं पितृभर्तृकुलद्वयम् ॥

The commentator seems to take नखौ, which actually qualifies

पादौ, in the sense of only the nails of the big toes and not of all the toes. Or he may be taking स्निग्ध, उन्नत, अग्रतनु and ताम्रनख joined in a कर्मधारय compound as adjectives qualifying the word पादौ. However, his analysis of अग्रतनु as अग्रे तनू ययो: is not happy, as there is no necessity for the adjectival compound.

The metre of verses 1-3, 5 and 7 is वसन्ततिलका.]

मत्स्याङ्कुशाब्जयववज्रहलासिचिह्ना-
    वस्वेदनौ मृदुतलौ चरणौ प्रशस्तौ ।
जङ्घे च रोमरहिते विशिरे सुवृत्ते
    जानुद्वयं सममनुल्बणसन्धिदेशम् ॥ २ ॥

ऊरू घनौ करिकरप्रतिमावरोमा-
    वश्वत्थपत्रसदृशं विपुलं च गुह्यम् ।
श्रोणीललाटमुरु कूर्मसमुन्नतं च
    गूढो मणिश्च विपुलां श्रियमादधाति ॥ ३ ॥

Laudable are the feet with tender, unsweating soles, accompanied by the marks of fish, goad, lotus, barley, thunderbolt, plough and sword. So are the shanks that are perfectly round and bereft of hair and veins. The knees should be equal or even and without very prominent joints. The thighs that are plump, hairless and similar to the trunks of elephants, the genital organ that is broad and of the shape of the Aśvattha (*Jicus religiosa*) leaf, the top of the thighs that is large and arched like the back of the tortoise, and the clitoris that is hidden confer immense wealth.

[Many of the ideas contained here could have been easily omitted by the author. The expression आरोमौ is wrong. It should have been अरोमाणौ. Here we can remember Kālidāsa's verse:—

नागेन्द्रहस्तास्त्वचि कर्कशत्वादेकान्तशैत्यात्कदलीविशेषाः ।
लब्ध्वापि लोके परिणाहि रूपं जातास्तदूर्वोरुपमानबाह्याः ॥

Kumāra. I.

Cf. समुद्र—

स्निग्धौ ताम्रनखौ धन्यौ कूर्मपृष्ठौ सुलोहितौ ।
निगूढगुल्फौ सुश्लिष्टौ घनाङ्गुलिसमन्वितौ ॥
मत्स्याङ्कुशयवाब्जेषुहलवज्रासिचिह्नितौ ।
सुस्पृशौ रोमरहितौ कुमार्याश्चरणौ शुभौ ॥
अतो विपर्यस्तगुणौ दुःखदारिद्र्यभागिनौ ।
यस्याः पादौ नतौ कन्यामुद्वहेन्न कदाचन ॥

जङ्घे तु रोमरहिते शिराहीने सुवर्तुले ।
सुश्लिष्टे जानुनी धन्ये शिरारोमविवर्जिते ॥
गजहस्तसमावूरू सम्पन्नौ सन्ततौ समौ ।
सुस्पर्शं कूर्मपृष्ठं वा विपुलं जघनं शुभम् ॥
मणिर्निगूढः सुश्लिष्टः स्फिजौ च विपुलौ शुभौ ।
नाभिदेशः सुगुप्तश्च यस्याः सा धनभागिनी ॥

Cf. also प्रह्लाद—

कनिष्ठिकाङ्गुलिः पादे गच्छन्त्या न स्पृशेद्ध्रुवम् ।
निम्नं पादतलं जारा निश्शब्दं भवति ध्रुवम् ॥
लम्बालका महामस्ता पृथुमध्या महोदरी ।
वामावर्त्ता च वैधव्यं दारिद्र्यं दुःखमाप्नुयात् ॥
विशालभगफाला च भर्तारं तत्कुलं तथा ।
अवमन्येत दुर्बुद्धिः स्थूलदन्ता तु निर्धना ॥
कट्यावर्ता सेवकस्त्री कण्ठावर्ता तु निष्प्रजा ।
फालावर्ता च विधवा जारिणी कलहप्रिया ॥
ग्रोष्ठचूचुककण्ठेषु कर्णयोर्भुजयोरपि ।
लोमानि न प्रकाशन्ते सा नारी भोगभागिनी ॥
प्लुतकेशा पतिं द्वेष्टि नाभिलोमा च जारसूः ।
लम्बस्तनी मृतापत्या विसुखा भगकेशिनी ॥]

विस्तीर्णमांसोपचितो नितम्बो गुरुश्च धत्ते रशनाकलापम् ।
नाभिर्गभीरा विपुलाङ्गनानां प्रदक्षिणावर्त्तगता च शस्ता ॥ ४ ॥

The hips that are broad, heavy and fleshy support (i.e. adorn) girdles and are auspicious; the navel that is deep, broad and with a whorl from left to right is praiseworthy in women.

[Vide the following:—

जघनं विपुलं यस्याः सुस्पर्शं रोमवर्जितम् ।
सुवर्णाभरणैर्युक्ता सा भवेद्राज्यभागिनी ॥
गम्भीरा विपुला नाभी दक्षिणावर्तमाश्रिता ।
शस्ता विपर्यये नेष्टा वामावर्ता विशेषतः ॥

Cf. प्रह्लाद—

नद्यावर्ताभनाभिश्च तनुरोमा सुरूपिणी ।
सुदन्ता सुमुखी भूयाद्राजपत्न्यतिकोमला ॥

The metre is उपजाति.]

मध्यं स्त्रियास्त्रिवलिनायमरोमशं च
वृत्तौ घनावविषमौ कठिनावुरस्यौ ।
रोमप्रवर्जितमुरो मृदु चाङ्गनानां
ग्रीवा च कम्बुनिचितार्थसुखानि दत्ते ॥ ५ ॥

The waist of a woman being possessed of three folds and devoid of hair; the bosoms, round, overlapping, equal and hard; the breast, tender and hairless; and the neck, adorned with three lines, bestow wealth and happiness.

[Here again we may remember the famous description of Pārvatī's body by the great poet Kālidāsa in his *Kumārasambhava* : एतावता नन्वनुमेयशोभि...; तस्याः प्रविष्टा नतनाभिरन्ध्रं...; मध्येन सा वेदि-विलग्नमध्या... अन्योन्यमुत्पीडयदुत्पलाक्ष्याः ... etc.

Vide the following :—

मध्यं वलित्रयचितं सुस्पर्शं रोमवर्जितम् ।
यस्याः सा राजमहिषी कन्या नास्त्यत्र संशयः ॥
स्तनौ सुवर्तुलौ धन्यौ सन्ततौ कठिनौ तथा ।
अरोमौ च शिराहीनौ पुत्रसौख्यधनप्रदौ ॥
वक्षो विलोम सुस्पर्शं विस्तीर्णं पतिसौख्यदम् ।
शिराततं च विषमं वैधव्यायासशोकदम् ॥

Cf. also गर्ग—

स्थिरा त्रिरेखा सुभगोपपन्ना स्निग्धा सुमांसोपचिता सुवृत्ता ।
न चातिदीर्घा चतुरङ्गुला च ग्रीवा च दीर्घा भवतीह धन्या ॥

Cf. प्रह्लाद—

समस्तनी च सौभाग्यं लभेच्छातोदरी सुखम् ।
स्थूलजङ्घा ह्रस्वफाला पुत्रपौत्रसुखं लभेत् ॥
तुङ्गकण्ठी तु निर्लज्जा ह्रस्वकण्ठी तु निर्धना ।
कम्बुकण्ठत्रिरेखाढ्या सुशीला कुलवर्धिनी ॥
कण्ठे वा पार्श्वयोर्वापि तिलकाकृतिचिह्निता ।
प्रथमप्रसवे पुत्रं प्राप्नुयान्नात्र संशयः ॥]

बन्धुजीवकुसुमोपमोऽधरो मांसलो रुचिरबिम्बरूपभृत् ।
कुन्दकुड्मलनिभाः समा द्विजा योषितां पतिसुखामितार्थदाः ॥ ६ ॥

The lower lip which is red like the *Bandhujiva* (*Pentapetes phoenicea*) flower, fleshy and shaped like a beautiful ripe Bimba (*coccinia indica*) fruit, and the teeth that are similar to the Kunda (*Jasminum multiflorum*) buds, bestow conjugal felicity and abundant wealth on women.

[Vide the following:

अधरो बिम्बसङ्काशो मांसलोऽस्फुटितस्तथा ।
यस्याः सा राजमहिषी कुमारी नात्र संशयः ।।

Cf. गर्ग—

तीक्ष्णाग्रवृत्ताः सुसमा दृढाश्च शुभा मृणालेन्दुसमानवर्णाः ।
निरन्तराः स्त्रीषु भवन्ति धन्या द्विजास्तथा ये रजतप्रकाशाः ।।

Cf. समुद्र—

द्वात्रिंशद्दशना यस्याः सर्वे गोक्षीरपाण्डुराः ।
सर्वे शिखरिणः स्निग्धा राजभार्या च सा भवेत् ।।

also प्रह्लाद—

स्थूलोष्ठी स्थूलदन्ता च वृत्ताक्षी वक्रनासिका ।
कक्षस्थनीलचिह्ना च भर्तुर्गृहविनाशिनी ।।

The metre is रथोद्धता here and in verse 9.]

दाक्षिण्ययुक्तमशठं परपुष्टहंस-
वल्गु प्रभाषितमदीनमनल्पसौख्यम् ।
नासा समा समपुटा रुचिरा प्रशस्ता
दृग्नीलनीरजदलद्युतिहारिणी च ।। ७ ।।

Women's speech being full of courtesy, free from roguery, sweet like the notes of the cuckoo or the swan, and not plaintive, confers on them unalloyed happiness. Laudable is the nose that is straight, charming and endowed with equal slopes. So are the eyes that take away the lustre of the petals of blue lily.

[The verse is noted for its happy alliteration and simile.

Cf. गर्ग—

हंसस्वना दुन्दुभिनेमिघोषा मेघस्वनाः शङ्खनिनादघोषाः ।
मयूरचक्रप्रतिमस्वनाश्च स्त्रियस्तथा कोकिलतुल्यशब्दाः ।।
कादम्बचक्राह्वयकिङ्किणीषु समस्वना याश्च भवन्ति नार्यः ।
सर्वाः प्रशस्ता धनपुत्रवत्यो भवन्ति धर्मानुरताः सदा ताः ।।

Vide the following :

स्पष्टा समा समपुटा नासा सौभाग्यदा मता ।।
नीलनीरजपत्राभा दृष्टिर्यस्या भवेत्सदा ।
सा राजमहिषी ज्ञेया ज्योतिःशास्त्रविशारदैः ।।

Pārvati's speech is described by the Poet as :

अप्यन्यपुष्टा प्रतिकूलशब्दा श्रोतुर्वितन्त्रीरिव ताड्यमाना ॥

also her glance as :

प्रवातनीलोत्पलनिर्विशेषमधीरविप्रेक्षितमायताक्ष्या ।
तया गृहीतं नु मृगाङ्गनाभ्यस्ततो गृहीतं नु मृगाङ्गनाभिः ॥

Cf. प्रह्लाद—

दरस्मेरमुखी नारी तरलाक्षी च जारिणी ।
प्रगल्भभाषिणी चैव लज्जानटनशालिनी ॥
पीतजिह्वा च वाचाला खरगन्धा च निन्दिता ।
सर्वत्रैव परित्याज्या पांसुला सा भवेद् ध्रुवम् ॥]

नो सङ्गते नातिपृथू न लम्बे शस्ते भ्रुवौ बालशशाङ्कवक्रे ।
अर्धेन्दुसंस्थानमरोमशं च शस्तं ललाटं न नतं न तुङ्गम् ॥ ८ ॥

Blessed are the brows that are neither joined together, nor very thick, nor hanging low, but arched like the crescent. So is the forehead which is neither depressed, nor raised, but is shaped like the half-Moon (semi-circular), and is devoid of hair.

[Vide the following :—

बालचन्द्रसमे वक्रे न लम्बे नातिसङ्गते ।
भ्रुवौ यस्याः कुमार्यास्तां महाराज्ञीं विनिर्दिशेत् ॥
नोन्नतं न च निम्नं वा शिरारोमविवर्जितम् ।
अर्धचन्द्राकृति सौम्यं ललाटं शस्यते स्त्रियाः ॥

It is strange and funny that one of the Sanskrit editions has given in the third line the reading शिरो रोमविवर्जितम्.

The metre is उपजाति.]

कर्णयुग्ममपि युक्तमांसलं शस्यते मृदु समाहितं समम् ।
स्निग्धनीलमृदुकुञ्चितैकजा मूर्धजाः सुखकराः समं शिरः ॥ ९ ॥

Praiseworthy are the ears that are sufficiently fleshy, soft, equal and close to the head (or compact). The hair being glossy, blue, soft, curled and single in each pore, confer happiness. So does the head which is even i.e. neither depressed, nor raised.

[At first sight the adjective युक्त in युक्तमांसल appears to be redundant, but actually it is a good adjunct in that it restricts the fleshy nature of the ears to proportionate limits. Vide the following :

नातिलम्बौ मृदू तुल्यौ संलग्नौ युक्तमांसलौ ।
कर्णौ यस्याः स्मृता सा तु राजभार्या न संशयः ॥

सुस्निग्धा नीलवर्णाश्च मृदवः कुञ्चिताः कचाः ।
शस्यन्ते योषितो नित्यं धनपुत्रप्रदा यतः ॥
नोन्नतं नाथवा निम्नं शिरः सौख्यप्रदं स्मृतम् ॥

Cf. प्रह्लाद—

मृदुकर्णा रत्नभूषां सौवर्णं कठिनश्रुतिः ।
कङ्कणं शुष्कहस्ता च व्यासोरो हारभूषणम् ॥]

भृङ्गारासनवाजिकुञ्जररथश्रीवृक्षयूपेषुभि-
र्मालाकुण्डलचामराङ्कुशयवैः शैलैर्ध्वजैस्तोरणैः ।
मत्स्यस्वस्तिकवेदिकाव्यजनकैः शङ्खातपत्राम्बुजैः
पादे पाणितलेऽथवा युवतयो गच्छन्ति राज्ञीपदम् ॥ १० ॥

Young women who have the marks of the following things on their soles or palms attain to the status of queens, viz. water-pot, seat, horse, elephant, chariot, Bilva tree (*Aegle marmelos*), sacrificial post, arrow, garland, ear-ring, chowry, goad, barley corn, mountain, banner, arch, fish, Svastika, altar, fan, conch, umbrella and lotus.

[The last line reminds us of Kālidāsa's line : यान्त्येवं गृहिणीपदं युवतयो वामाः कुलस्याधयः । (अभि. शाकु. IV)

The commentator tells us that the altar is a quadrilateral figure, narrow in the middle.

Cf. गर्ग—

मत्स्यः समुद्रो वसुधा धनं च ध्वजस्तथाद्रिर्दिनकृच्छशी च ।
शङ्खः पुरं चक्रमथासनं च यूपस्तथा व्यञ्जनतोरणं च ॥
छत्रं यवः पद्मथाङ्कुशं च सिंहोऽथवा स्वस्तिक एव वापी ।
कूर्मः पताका मकरः पुमांश्च दण्डः सरित् पूर्णघटो रथश्च ॥
पाणौ तथैतानि भवन्ति यासामेकं तथा द्वे च बहूनि वापि ।
अत्यन्तसौख्यं बहुपुत्रतां च स्त्रीणां तथा लक्षणमादिशेत ॥

Cf. समुद्र—

मत्स्यः पाणितले छत्रं कच्छपो वा ध्वजोऽपि वा ।
श्रीवत्सं कमलं शङ्खमासनं चामरं तथा ॥
अङ्कुशश्चैव माला च यस्या हस्ते तु दृश्यते ।
एकं सा जनयेत्पुत्रं राजानं पृथिवीपतिम् ॥
यस्याः पाणितले चास्ति कोष्ठागारः सतोरणः ।
अपि दासकुले जाता सा राजमहिषी भवेत् ॥

The metre is शार्दूलविक्रीडित.]

निगूढमणिबन्धनौ तरुणपद्मगर्भोपमौ
करौ नृपतियोषितस्तनुविकृष्टपर्वाङ्गुलौ ।
न निम्नमति नोन्नतं करतलं सुरेखान्वितं
करोत्यविधवां चिरं सुतसुखार्थसम्भोगिनीम् ॥ ११ ॥

A woman attains the status of a queen, when her wrist-joints are hidden, hands similar to the interior of a full-blown lotus, fingers slender, and knuckles far removed. One whose palm is neither sunken, nor raised, and is marked with fine lines (figures of auspicious objects), becomes an auspicious house-wife (i.e. she will not experience widowhood) and enjoys happiness, wealth and prosperity of children for a long time.

[Vide the following :

निगूढमणिबन्धौ तु पद्मगर्भसमप्रभौ ।
विकृष्टाङ्गुलिपर्वाणौ करौ नृपतियोषितः ॥
नोच्चं न निम्नं सुसमं सुरेखाभिः समन्वितम् ।
तलं यस्या भवेन्नार्याः सा राजमहिषी स्मृता ॥

The metre is पृथ्वी.]

मध्याङ्गुलिं या मणिबन्धनोत्था रेखा गता पाणितलेऽङ्गनायाः ।
ऊर्ध्वस्थिता पादतलेऽथवा या पुंसोऽथवा राज्यसुखाय सा स्यात् ॥ १२ ॥

A line rising from the wrist and touching the root of the middle finger (second finger) on the palm of a woman, or one running vertically from the heel to the root of the toes, would bestow the pleasures of kingship on her. This holds good in the case of a man as well.

[On the basis of Utpala's first interpretation, अथवा या रेखा पादतले चरणतले ऊर्ध्वस्थिता पुंसः पुरुषस्य. . . it might appear that the author wants us to take the two kinds of vertical lines on the palm and the sole separately with woman and man respectively; but immediately he states, "अथ चैवंविधा हस्त-तले पादतले वा भवति (स्त्रियाः पुंसो वा), सा राज्यसुखाय स्याद्," which leaves no doubt about the two lines being applicable to both men and women. A question may be asked here : Why did the author introduce suddenly *men's lines* when he is describing feminine characteristics? The reason is that he could not deal with the lines on the soles of men in LXVIII. I may venture to suggest another interpretation of पुंसः. . . The woman who has the line on her sole will herself become the ruler of a kingdom or her fortune will enable her husband to rule over it.

Cf. the following :

मणिबन्धनसम्भूता मध्याङ्गुलिसमाश्रिता ।
रेखा पाणितले यस्याः सा कन्या राज्यभागिनी ॥

This line on the palm is called the line of fortune in modern palmistry.

The metre is इन्द्रवज्रा in this as well as in 14, 23 and 24.]

कनिष्ठिकामूलभवा गता या प्रदेशिनी मध्यमिकान्तरालम् ।
करोति रेखा परमायुषः सा प्रमाणमूना तु तदूनमायुः ॥ १३ ॥

A line rising at the foot of the little finger and going to the space between the first and second fingers, bestows the maximum span of life, i.e. 120 years. If the line is shorter, proportionate reduction in the span will have to be made.

[According to the *Hara-gauri-sāmudrika*, if the life line (Indian, or heart line, western) touches the foot of the second finger, the span of life is 75 years; if it is a little shorter, 51 or 61 years; if it touches the foot of the third finger, 30 years. Vide the following :—

कनिष्ठामूलसम्भूता गता मध्यमिकान्तरम् ।
प्रदेशिन्याश्च सा रेखा यस्याः सा दीर्घजीविनी ॥

The metre in this and in verses 15 and 16 is उपेन्द्रवज्रा.]

अङ्गुष्ठमूले प्रसवस्य रेखाः पुत्रा बृहत्यः प्रमदास्तु तन्व्यः ।
अच्छिन्नमध्या बृहदायुषस्ताः स्वल्पायुषां छिन्नलघुप्रमाणाः ॥ १४ ॥

The lines at the foot of the thumb indicate the number of children one will have. Big ones represent sons, and slender ones daughters. If these lines are not cut in the middle, the children will live long; and if they are broken and short, they will have a short span of life.

[अच्छिन्नमूला is another reading for अच्छिन्नमध्याः—

Vide the following:

अङ्गुष्ठमूले या रेखाः स्थूलाः पुत्राश्च ते मताः ।
सूक्ष्मा दुहितरस्ताभ्यो विच्छिन्नाः स्वल्पजीविनः ॥
वामहस्ते तु नारीणां पुरुषाणां च दक्षिणे ।
चिह्नं निरूपयेद्धीमान् समुद्रवचनं यथा ॥]

इतीदमुक्तं शुभमङ्गनानामतो विपर्यस्तमनिष्टमुक्तम् ।
विशेषतोऽनिष्टफलानि यानि समासतस्तान्यनुकीर्तयामि ॥ १५ ॥

Thus have I described the auspicious features of women; and those that are contrary to the above, are said to be inauspicious. I shall now briefly enunciate those features that are especially of untoward effects.

कनिष्ठिका वा तदनन्तरा वा महीं न यस्याः स्पृशति स्त्रियाः स्यात् ।
गताथवाङ्गुष्ठमतीत्य यस्याः प्रदेशिनी सा कुलटाऽतिपापा ॥ १६ ॥

A woman whose little toe or the next one does not touch the ground, or whose fore-toe is longer than the big one, is the most sinful prostitute.

[Vide the following :—

कनिष्ठा पादयोर्यस्या भूमिं स्पृशति नाङ्गुलिः ।
न सा तिष्ठति कौमारी बन्धकीं तां विनिर्दिशेत् ॥
पादप्रदेशिनी यस्या अङ्गुष्ठादतिरिच्यते ।
कुमारी कुरुते जारं यौवनस्था तु किं पुनः ॥

Halāyudha has quoted the following verses bearing on feminine features :

यत्पादस्य कनिष्ठा न स्पृशति महीमनामिका वापि ।
सा सर्वधूर्तभोग्या भवेदवश्यं जघनचपला ॥
यस्याः पादाङ्गुष्ठं व्यतीत्य याति प्रदेशिनी दीर्घा ।
विपुले कुले प्रसूतापि सा ध्रुवं जघनचपला स्यात् ॥]

उद्बद्धाभ्यां पिण्डिकाभ्यां शिराले शुष्के जङ्घे लोमशे चातिमांसे ।
वामावर्त्तं निम्नमल्पं च गुह्यं कुम्भाकारं चोदरं दुःखितानाम् ॥ १७ ॥

Miserable are the women whose shanks are full of veins, dry (without flesh) or very fleshy, hairy and with calf-muscles raised high. So are those whose genital organ has hairy circles turned to the left, is sunken, and small; and whose belly is shaped like a pot.

[Vide the following :—

शुष्के जङ्घेऽतिमांसे वा रोमशे चोर्ध्वपिण्डिके ।
यस्याः सा दुःखिता नित्यं पुत्रवित्तविवर्जिता ॥
वामावर्त्तं भगं यस्या दीर्घं चुल्लीसमप्रभम् ।
निम्नं वा तेन दोषेण वेश्यास्त्रीत्वं च गच्छति ॥
लम्बोदरी च या कन्या दीर्घोदरसमन्विता ।
भग्नोदरी च दुःखार्ता दासीभावमवाप्नुयात् ॥

Cf. प्रह्लाद—

शुष्कावूरू तथा बाहू सरोमौ चेत्पतिं हरेत् ।
शुष्कयोनिश्च विरलद्विजा त्याज्या मनीषिभिः ॥

Vide *Halāyudhabhaṭṭa's* Mṛtasañjīvinī :—

मकरध्वजसद्मनि दृश्यते स्फुटं तिलकलाञ्छनं यस्याः ।
विपुलान्वयप्रजातापि जायते जघनचपलासौ ॥

The metre is शालिनी]

ह्रस्वयातिनिःस्वता दीर्घया कुलक्षयः ।
ग्रीवया पृथूत्थया योषितः प्रचण्डता ॥ १८ ॥

A woman whose neck is too short becomes utterly penniless; too long, cause of the extinction of the family; and too broad and flat, cruel.

[Vide the following :—

कुलक्षयकरी दीर्घा ग्रीवा ह्रस्वा च निर्धना ।
पृथूत्थया प्रचण्डत्वं ग्रीवया योषितो वदेत् ॥

The metre is समानिका in Prākṛt prosody]

नेत्रे यस्याः केकरे पिङ्गले वा सा दुःशीला श्यावलोलेक्षणा च ।
कूपौ यस्या गण्डयोश्च स्मितेषु निःसन्दिग्धं बन्धकीं तां वदन्ति ॥ १९ ॥

A woman whose eyes are squint or tawny or grey and fickle, is of wicked character; and one who shows dimples in her cheeks, while smiling, is declared an unchaste woman without doubt.

[Vide the following :—

पारावताक्षी या कन्या कातराक्षी तथापि या ।
उद्भ्रान्तचपलाक्षी च तां कन्यां वर्जयेद् बुधः ॥
यस्यास्तु हसमानाया जायन्ते गण्डकूपकाः ।
भर्तारं हन्ति सा क्षिप्रं नैकत्र रमते चिरम् ॥

Cf. पराशर—

यस्या हसन्त्या दृश्यन्ते कूपका गण्डयोर्द्वयोः ।
स्थूलकाकारगण्डा च विकृतास्या महाशना ॥
एकापि यस्या न महीं संस्पृशेच्चरणाङ्गुली ।
तलमध्यमधो यस्या अधमां तां विनिर्दिशेत् ॥

Vide हलायुध

चिबुके कपोलदेशेऽपि कूपिका दृश्यते स्मिते यस्याः ।
विपुलान्वयप्रजातापि जायते सा महाचपला ॥

यस्या विलोचने पिङ्गले भ्रुवौ सङ्गते मुखं दीर्घम् ।
विपुलोन्नताश्च दन्ताः कान्तासौ भवति मुखचपला ।।

Vide प्रह्लाद

मार्जारीस्वरसंयुक्ता निर्लज्जा रोषशालिनी ।
मृतप्रजा भवेन्नारी महच्चौर्यं करोति सा ।।
मार्जारनेत्री कुनखी नासान्तर्लोमसङ्कुला ।
मुग्धा च गड्डयुक्ताङ्गी अनेकोपपतींश्चरेत् ।।

The metre is शालिनी.]

प्रविलम्बिनि देवरं ललाटे श्वशुरं हन्त्युदरे स्फिजोः पतिं च ।
अतिरोमचयान्वितोत्तरोष्ठी न शुभा भर्तुरतीव या च दीर्घा ।। २० ।।

A woman with a hanging forehead kills her husband's brother; with a hanging belly, her father-in-law; with hanging buttocks, her own husband. A woman that is too tall, as well as one whose upper lip is covered with too much hair, is harmful to her husband.

[Vide the following :—

त्रीणि यस्याः प्रलम्बन्ते ललाटमुदरं स्फिजम् ।
त्रींश्च सा पुरुषान् हन्ति देवरं श्वशुरं पतिम् ।।
श्मश्रुयुक्ता च या कन्या याऽतिदीर्घा मलावृता ।
दासीभावमवाप्नोति देहदोषेण साऽङ्गना ।।

The metre is औपच्छन्दसिक.

Cf. प्रह्लाद—

दीर्घपृष्ठा भ्रातृहानिं वैशाल्ये बहुसोदरान् ।
लभते तनुमध्या च सुन्दरी बहुभूषणम् ।।]

स्तनौ सरोमौ मलिनोल्बणौ च क्लेशं दधाते विषमौ च कर्णौ ।
स्थूलाः कराला विषमाश्च दन्ताः क्लेशाय चौर्याय च कृष्णमांसाः ।। २१ ।।

Breasts that are hairy, dark (dirty) and too huge, as well as ears that are unequal, produce sufferings. Big, protruding and unequal teeth lead to misery; and black gums to thievishness.

[Vide the following :—

रोमयुक्तौ स्तनौ यस्या मलिनौ च शिराततौ ।
दुःखिता सा भवेन्नारी नित्यं प्रव्रजिता तथा ।।
शिरायुक्तौ न च समौ कर्णौ दारिद्र्यभाजनौ ।।

स्थूलाः कराला विषमाः कृष्णमांसा बहिर्गताः ।
दन्ता दुःखप्रदा ज्ञेया वैधव्यायासकारिणः ॥

The expression सरोमौ used by the author is not happy. It should have been सरोमाणौ. The metre of this and the following verse is उपजाति.]

क्रव्यादरूपैर्वृककाककङ्कसरीसृपोलूकसमानचिह्नैः ।
शुष्कैः शिरालैर्विषमैश्च हस्तैर्भवन्ति नार्यः सुखवित्तहीनाः ॥ २२ ॥

Women become unhappy and poor, if their hands are dry (without flesh), full of veins, unequal (or uneven) and marked with the figures of birds of prey (like the vulture), wolves, crows, herons, reptiles (worms ?) and owls.

[Vide the following :—

क्रव्यादसदृशैश्चिह्नैः काकोलूकसमप्रभैः ।
शुष्कैः करालैर्विषमैः करैर्दुःखान्विताः स्त्रियः ॥]

या तुङ्गरोष्ठेन समुन्नतेन रूक्षाग्रकेशी कलहप्रिया सा ।
प्रायो विरूपासु भवन्ति दोषा यत्राकृतिस्तत्र गुणा वसन्ति ॥ २३ ॥

A woman whose upper lip is very high, and the hair rough at the tips, is fond of quarrel. Generally, faults exist in those that are ugly or deformed; and virtues dwell in those that are possessed of a pleasing appearance or form.

[Here we find Varāhamihira in his true element as a poet *par excellence,* following in the footsteps of the master viz. Kālidāsa. This can be classed among the best *general statements* (*Arthāntaranyāsa*). The poets' verse (Kum. V. 36) has been quoted under a similar statement in II. 2 *supra.*

Vide the following :—

या तुङ्गरोष्ठेनोच्चेन केशाग्रं स्नेहवर्जितम् ।
यस्याः सा दुःखिता नित्यं भर्तुर्निधनकारिणी ॥]

पादौ सगुल्फौ प्रथमं प्रदिष्टौ जङ्घे द्वितीयं तु सजानुचक्रे ।
मेढ्रोरुमुष्कं च ततस्तृतीयं नाभिः कटिश्चैव चतुर्थमाहुः ॥ २४ ॥

उदरं कथयन्ति पञ्चमं हृदयं षष्ठमतः स्तनान्वितम् ।
अथ सप्तममंसजत्रुणी कथयन्त्यष्टममोष्ठकन्धरे ॥ २५ ॥

नवमं नयने च सभ्रुणी सललाटं दशमं शिरस्तथा ।
अशुभेष्वशुभं दशाफलं चरणाद्येषु शुभेषु शोभनम् ॥ २६ ॥

The feet with the ankle-joints are said to represent the *First Stage* of life; the shanks and the knees, the *Second*; the genital organ, thighs and testicles, the *Third*; the navel and the hips, the *Fourth*; the stomach, the *Fifth*; the heart and the breasts, the *Sixth*; the shoulders and the collar-bones, the *Seventh*; the lips and the neck, the *Eighth*; the eyes and the brows, the *Ninth*; and the head and the forehead, the *Tenth*. When the limbs, feet etc., are inauspicious (having bad shape and marks), the effects of the corresponding stages of life will be harmful; and they will be beneficial, when they are auspicious.

As the human span of life is said to be 120 years, each stage will have 12 years of life. If there are auspicious marks on the feet and ankles, the first period will be very happy. This rule has an exception: The duration of each stage will depend on the maximum expectation of life of the subject. For example, if the longevity is 70 years, each period should be taken to last for 7 years only. A limb is said to be inauspicious, if it is dry, without flesh and full of veins. This knowledge may be combined with what *Garga* says about the limbs and periods, quoted at the end of LXVIII, *supra*.

Halāyudha, the learned commentator of Piṅgala's Chandaś-śāstra, belonged to the 12th century A.D. and was a minister of king Lakṣmaṇasena of Bengal. The verses on feminine features, I presume, were composed by him, as he names the authority elsewhere. The following are his :—

अतिदारुणा द्विजिह्वा परस्य रन्ध्रानुचारिणी कुटिला ।
दूरात्परिहरणीया नारी नागीव मुखचपला ।।
धन्या त्रिषु नीचा कन्या तनुमध्या ।
श्रोणीस्तनगुर्वी उर्वीपतिभोग्या ।।

Vide प्रह्लाद—

सरोमोत्तुङ्गजङ्घा च फालोत्तानातिमूर्धजा ।
भुजोरुकेशयुक्ता च मस्तावर्ता पतिं हरेत् ।।
अत्यन्तनीलकेशा च शुष्कश्रोणी च दासताम् ।
विकटाङ्गुलिराप्नोति वैधव्यं चानपत्यताम् ।।
उष्णस्पर्शवती नारी रोदनं कुरुते मुहुः ।
अक्षमा कलहोद्युक्ता ज्येष्ठाऽलक्ष्मीसखी भवेत् ।।
कुमारीरसनीकाशस्वेदगन्धवती तथा ।
विलोमकेशी वक्राक्षी रिक्ता बहुसुताऽधवा ।।

[कुमारी—Aloe barbadensis]

कुन्दकुड्मलदन्ता स्त्री दरनीलालकालिका ।
निम्ननाभिश्च सुमुखी भर्तृसौभाग्यदायिनी ॥
दुःशीला कर्कशा चण्डी नित्यं कलहकारिणी ।
अतिभुङ्क्ते च या नारी सप्रजामपि तां त्यजेत् ॥
भीरुस्वप्नोन्मादवती रक्षोगणसमुद्भवा ।
शुष्काक्षिकुक्षिकण्ठा च प्रस्विन्नचरणा तथा ॥
दारिद्र्यं च दुराचारं वन्ध्यात्वं बहुमैथुनम् ।
लभते च स्तनस्थौल्ये बह्वाचारं च सन्ततिम् ।
[बाधां पैशाचिकीं लभेत्] ॥
प्रसन्नवक्त्रा मुग्धाक्षी दैवन्यस्तभरा तथा ।
कूर्मपृष्ठप्रपदिका तीर्थयात्राफलं भवेत् ॥
अभुक्तमूलसम्भूता वामोर्वन्तस्तिलद्वया ।
लभते नीचसंसर्गं गृहं त्यक्त्वा बहिर्व्रजेत् ॥
ह्रस्वत्वे दक्षिणाङ्गस्य भविता कीर्तिशालिनी ।
वामाङ्गस्य तु दुष्कीर्तिं प्राप्नुयात्पुंश्चली भवेत् ॥
वामाङ्घ्रिमध्यमाङ्गुल्यामधो रेखाद्वयं यदि ।
वाहनं लभते नारी गेहं च रुचिरं तथा ॥

The following verses of Vālmīki (VI. 48, 2-14) put in the mouth of Sītā refer to many feminine features that bring fortune or misfortune, as the case may be : "Lotuses on the soles of women make them queens of great emperors. These lotuses never fail in their effect. Thin hairs (on the head) that are black and of the same length, the brows not joined together, the shanks that are round and free from hair, close-knit teeth, the temporal bones, eyes, hands, feet, ankle-joints and thighs being narrow or full, fingers that are even, glossy and possessed of round nails, plump bosoms touching each other with their nipples sunk, a sunken navel tapering upwards, the sides and chest covered up, complexion similar to the lustre of gems, hair on the body being soft, the hands and feet having a nice colour, with full-fledged marks of barley, and the fingers and toes showing no holes in between, and lastly a gentle smile—all these make a woman the crowned queen of a mighty monarch." The relevant verses are :—

ऊचुर्लक्षणिनो ये मां पुत्रिणीं सधवां सदा ।
तेऽद्य सर्वे हते रामे ज्ञानिनोऽनृतवादिनः ॥
यज्वनो महिषीं ये मामूचुः पत्नीं च सत्रिणः ।
तेऽद्य सर्वे हते रामे ज्ञानिनोऽनृतवादिनः ॥

ऊचुः संश्रवणे ये मां द्विजाः कार्तान्तिकाः शुभाम् ।
तेऽद्य सर्वे हते रामे ज्ञानिनोऽनृतवादिनः ॥
वीरपार्थिवपत्नीत्वं ये धन्येति च मां विदुः ।
तेऽद्य सर्वे हते रामे ज्ञानिनोऽनृतवादिनः ॥
इमानि खलु पद्मानि पादयोर्यैः किल स्त्रियः ।
आधिराज्येऽभिषिच्यन्ते नरेन्द्रैः पतिभिः सह ॥
वैधव्यं यान्ति यैर्नार्योऽलक्षणैर्भाग्यदुर्लभाः ।
नात्मनस्तानि पश्यामि पश्यन्ती हतलक्षणा ॥
सत्यनामानि पद्मानि स्त्रीणामुक्तानि लक्षणैः ।
तान्यद्य निहते रामे वितथानि भवन्ति मे ॥
केशाः सूक्ष्माः समा नीला भ्रुवौ चासङ्गते मम ।
वृत्ते चारोमशे जङ्घे दन्ताश्चाविरला मम ॥
शङ्खे नेत्रे करौ पादौ गुल्फावूरू च मे चितौ ।
अनुवृत्तनखाः स्निग्धाः समाश्चाङ्गुलयो मम ॥
समौ चाविरलौ पीनौ ममेमौ मग्नचूचुकौ ।
मग्ना चोत्सङ्गिनी नाभिः पार्श्वोरस्काश्च मे चिताः ॥
मम वर्णो मणिनिभो मृदून्यङ्गरुहाणि च ।
प्रतिष्ठितां द्वादशभिर्मामूचुः शुभलक्षणाम् ॥
समग्रयवमच्छिद्रं पाणिपादं च वर्णवत् ।
मन्दस्मितेत्येव च मां कन्यालक्षणिनो विदुः ॥
आधिराज्येऽभिषेको मे ब्राह्मणैः पतिना सह ।
कृतान्तकुशलैरुक्तं तत्सर्वं वितथीकृतम् ॥

The metre of the last two verses of the text is वियोगिनी.]

———

वस्त्रच्छेदलक्षणम् ॥ ७१ ॥

Chapter LXXI – Omens from Slits of Garments

प्रभूतवस्त्रदाश्विनी भरण्यथापहारिणी ।
प्रदह्यतेऽग्निदैवते प्रजेश्वरेऽर्थसिद्धयः ॥ १ ॥

मृगे तु मूषकाद्भयं व्यसुत्वमेव शाङ्करे ।
पुनर्वसौ शुभागमस्तदग्रभे धनैर्युतिः ॥ २ ॥

भुजङ्गभे विलुप्यते मघासु मृत्युमादिशेत् ।
भगाह्वये नृपाद्भयं धनागमाय चोत्तरा ॥ ३ ॥

करेण कर्मसिद्धयः शुभागमस्तु चित्रया ।
शुभं च भोज्यमानिले द्विदैवते जनप्रियः ॥ ४ ॥

सुहृद्युतिश्च मित्रभे तदग्रभेऽम्बरक्षयः ।
जलप्लुतिश्च नैर्ऋते रुजो जलाधिदैवते ॥ ५ ॥

मिष्टमन्नमपि वैश्वदैवते वैष्णवे भवति नेत्ररोगता ।
धान्यलब्धिरपि वासवे विदुर्वारुणे विषकृतं महद् भयम् ॥ ६ ॥

भद्रपदासु भयं सलिलोत्थं तत्परतश्च भवेत्सुतलब्धिः ।
रत्नयुतिं कथयन्ति च पौष्णे योऽभिनवाम्बरमिच्छति भोक्तुम् ॥ ७ ॥

One who wishes to wear new clothes in the 27 constellations beginning with Aśvinī will experience the following results in order: (1) Acquisition of plenty of good clothes; (2) theft of clothes; (3) burning of the clothes; (4) achievement of objects (or wealth); (5) trouble from rats; (6) death; (7) arrival of auspicious things; (8) influx of wealth; (9) destruction of the clothes; (10) death; (11) trouble from the king; (12) acquisition of money; (13) accomplishment of undertakings; (14) auspicious functions; (15) good food; (16) popularity among the people; (17) meeting of friends; (18) loss of clothes; (19) loss of the same in water; (20) disease; (21) sumptuous feast; (22) eye-disease; (23) gain of corn; (24) great danger from poison; (25) danger through water; (26) birth of a son; and (27) acquisition of precious stones.

[The author has introduced here electional astrology in fine, alliterative verses. जलप्लुतिः may also mean the wearer's being carried away by floods.

The first five verses are in the प्रमाणिका metre, the next in रथोद्धता and the last and verse 14 in दोधक.]

भोक्तुं नवाम्बरं शस्तमृक्षेऽपि गुणवर्जिते ।
विवाहे राजसम्माने ब्राह्मणानां च सम्मते ॥ ८ ॥

It is advisable to wear new clothes even under an asterism that is devoid of good qualities, provided it is an occasion of marriage, reception of a king and one approved by worthy Brāhmaṇas.

[This exception is made in the case of shaving too. The metre is *Śloka.*]

In the following verses the author discusses the significance of tears, cuts and stains in the different parts of a cloth.

वस्त्रस्य कोणेषु वसन्ति देवा नराश्च पाशान्तदशान्तमध्ये ।
शेषास्त्रयश्चात्र निशाचरांशास्तथैव शय्यासनपादुकासु ॥ ९ ॥

In the four corners of a cloth (divided into 9 equal compartments as shown in the figure) dwell Gods; in the middle parts of the broad sides, men; and in the remaining three divisions, devils. The same rule applies to couches, seats and sandals.

[Figure showing the location of Gods, men and devils.

Gods	Devils	Gods
Men	Devils	Men
Gods	Devils	Gods

The commentator explains what is meant by the words पाशान्त and दशान्त, as वस्त्रस्य मूलम् i.e. the starting side of the cloth, and as अग्र' दशान्तः i.e. the tip. This explanation would be clear if we consider a Sāri (woman's cloth), which has a minor border at the पाशान्त and a more colourful one at the दशान्त. This rule should be applied to couches, seats and sandals as well. How are we to find out the lower and upper parts in a seat? The commentator says that they are to be determined from the position of the tree, whose plank is used in the making of the seat. In the case of the couch and sandals there is no difficulty about these parts.

Cf. गर्ग—

वस्त्रमुत्तरलोमं तु प्राग्देशं नवधा भवेत् (भजेत्?) ।
त्रिधा दशान्तपाशान्ते त्रिधा मध्यं पृथक् पृथक् ॥
चतुर्षु कोणेषु सुराः पाशान्ते मध्यमे नराः ।
दशान्ते च नरा भूयो मध्यभागे निशाचराः ॥
राक्षसान् विनिवृत्त्यैवं शय्यादिष्वप्ययं विधिः ॥

The metre is उपजाति.]

लिप्ते मषीगोमयकर्दमाद्यैश्छिन्ने प्रदग्धे स्फुटिते च विन्द्यात् ।
पुष्टं नवेऽल्पाल्पतरं च भुक्ते पापं शुभं चाधिकमुत्तरीये ॥ १० ॥

When a cloth is stained with sot (ink), cowdung, silt or any colour, when it is cut, singed or torn, one should know that the effects, whether good or bad, will be full, if the cloth is new; middling, if used for a short time; and almost nil, if it is old. These effects are greater in the case of upper clothes.

[This and the following three verses are in the इन्द्रवज्रा metre. In the following three verses the author discusses the good and bad effects of different types of stains, cuts etc.

रुग्राक्षसांशेष्वथवापि मृत्युः पुंजन्म तेजश्च मनुष्यभागे ।
भागेऽमराणामथ भोगवृद्धिः प्रान्तेषु सर्वत्र वदन्त्यनिष्टम् ॥ ११ ॥

A slit or stain in the divisions of *devils* bcdes disease or death to the wearer; the same in those of *men* presages birth of a son and brilliance or power; in those of *Gods*, increase of enjoyments; and in the borders it is invariably harmful, according to the sages.

[The author introduces a new element here viz. प्रान्त or edge, in addition to the nine divisions. Hence a stain or the like in a part of the edge on the four sides is supposed to be very bad.]

कङ्कप्लवोलूककपोतकाकक्रव्यादगोमायुखरोष्ट्रसर्पैः ।
छेदाकृतिर्दैवतभागगापि पुंसां भयं मृत्युसमं करोति ॥ १२ ॥

A slit in the form of a heron, Plava (the Kāraṇḍava duck?), owl, pigeon, crow, bird of prey, jackal, donkey, camel or snake, though appearing in a division belonging to *Gods*, causes a danger bordering on death to the wearers.

[The reader is aware that the marks of some of the inauspicious animals is an evil portent. Hence such slits or stains are inauspicious even in the divisions of *Gods*. Here the word *cheda* should be taken in the sense of other things as well, such as stains. The grammatical form सर्प: छेदाकृति: is faulty as it requires a word, तुल्या, to be supplied.]

छत्रध्वजस्वस्तिकवर्धमानश्रीवृक्षकुम्भाम्बुजतोरणाद्यैः ।
छेदाकृतिर्नैर्ऋतभागगापि पुंसां विधत्ते न चिरेण लक्ष्मीम् ॥ १३ ॥

A slit or stain in the shape of an umbrella, banner, Svastika, Vardhamāna, Bilva tree, water-pot, lotus, arch-way etc., though found in a division of *devils*, brings fortune ere long to men.

[*Svastika* and *Vardhamāna* are two kinds of auspicious diagrams (vide L. 2 *supra*). Other auspicious objects are the sacrificial ladle and pit, vase, elephant and horse. These shapes are beneficial even when they appear in the inauspicious divisions belonging to *devils*. They will be extremely beneficial in other parts. This shows that the poet has used the figure of speech, named अर्थापत्ति.]

विप्रमतादथ भूपतिदत्तं यच्च विवाहविधावभिलब्धम् ।
तेषु गुणै रहितेष्वपि भोक्तुं नूतनमम्बरमिष्टफलं स्यात् ॥ १४ ॥

A new cloth may be worn with advantage even under unfavourable stars, if it is worn with the permission of revered Brāhmaṇas, or if it is a gift from the king, or if it is presented on the occasion of a marriage.

[The idea is similar to the one contained in verse 8 *supra*. This verse is omitted in the recent *Vārāṇaseya* edition.

Sage *Parāśara* explains at length the effects of damages done to **sandals :—**

"अथाखुभक्षणे उपानच्छेदमुपदेक्ष्यामः । तत्र विंशतिश्छेदाः तेषां सप्त पूजिता विगर्हिताः शेषा भवन्ति । अङ्गुष्ठादिवैश्वानरदेशे प्रभक्षितेऽन्नपानस्त्रीलाभं विन्द्यात् । प्रदेशिन्या स्त्रीवस्त्रलाभम् । मध्यमया वधबन्धनम् । अनामिकया मातृमरणं स्वसृप्रव्रजनं च । कनिष्ठिकया पितृमरणं भ्रातुर्वा । नासातः स्त्रीलाभम् । अङ्गुष्ठाङ्गुलिमूले व्याधिभयम् । चूडायां वैमनस्यम् । ग्रीवायां शिरश्छेदनम् । स्थानबन्धेऽन्नपानधनप्राप्तिम् । कर्णिकाशकलभक्षणे सन्धिच्छेदभयं च । सकले कलहसम्प्रवृत्तिं च । पार्ष्णिबन्धेऽध्वगमनम् । पार्ष्णिस्थाने वाहनागमनम् । बाह्यपदपुटच्छेदावभक्षणात् सुहृद्भ्रातृविनाशं विन्द्यात् । मध्यमस्य विपुलमर्थागमम् । उत्तमस्य लाभम् । पदमध्ये शोकागमनम् । पार्श्वयोः पार्श्वरोगम्, सकलोपानद्भक्षणे मरणविद्रवायासा भवन्ति ।"

अपि च—

नवासु फलसामग्र्यमुपभुक्तासु मध्यमम् ।
शुभाशुभं विनिर्देश्यं जीर्णासु न भवेत्फलम् ॥
गुरुवृद्धद्विजाचार्यस्नानमङ्गलसेवनात् ।
अशुभानां च मर्त्यानां तस्माद् दोषात्प्रमुच्यते ॥

इत्युपानच्छेदलक्षणम् ॥

अथ वाससां शुभाशुभैष्यत्फलसूचकम् । अकस्मान्मषीकर्दमाञ्जनरुधिरगोमयैरुपरागस्तथाखुकीटगोजन्तुभिरवभक्षणं वा दूनं च काष्ठकण्टकैर्दाहो वा वह्निना भवति, तद्विज्ञानलक्षणफलमुपदेक्ष्यामः । यत्र प्राक्पाशं प्रत्यक्पाशं नवधा वस्त्रं विभजेत् त्रिवंशम् । अंशेषु तेषु क्रमात्फलनियमः । अर्थहानिः । अर्थागमः । धनक्षयः । स्त्रीविनाशः । पुत्रपीडा । दुहितृमरणम् । स्वशरीरव्याधिः । व्यसनागमश्चेति अष्टासु । नवमेऽध्वगमनमर्थागमः कर्मसिद्धयश्च । कुम्भादर्शकर्णशकलशस्त्रपदत्रिकूटेन्दुरुचकफलकगृहतोरणच्छत्रमेखलास्रगुपवेदीपद्मशङ्खश्रीवत्सस्वस्तिकमत्स्यवर्धमाननन्द्याकारैस्तु क्रमाद् विपुलोऽर्थागमः । कुक्षिरोगः । श्रोत्रपीडा । विरोधः । अध्वगमनम् । अनारोग्यम् । व्यसनम् । ऐश्वर्यम् । अभिषेकागमः । प्रार्थिताबन्धश्येनकेदारसूर्पसूचीपाशैश्च कङ्कालपीणिकाकारैर्मरणम् । द्विरदरथतुरगसदृशैः पशुपुत्रधनैश्वर्यावाप्तिः । हयगजभगतुलाचटकाकारैरुद्दारः प्राग्वत्कुटुम्बविनाशाय । पूर्वदक्षिणे नारीणाम् । दक्षिणे सुहृदाम् । दक्षिणापरे पशूनाम् । पश्चिमे प्रेष्याणाम् । पश्चिमोत्तरे ज्ञातेः । बन्धोश्चोत्तरे । पूर्वोत्तरे मध्यमस्य पूर्वे सर्वसम्पदाम् । अपि च—

विवर्णितं तु यद्वस्त्रं विनश्येच्छेदमङ्गुलम् ।
विवर्णितं तु यच्च स्यादनर्थाय विनिर्दिशेत् ॥
नवे वस्त्रे यथोक्तं स्यात् फलं जीर्णे तु नेष्यते ।
न रक्ते न पुनर्धौते न स्वयं दुग्धपाटिते ॥
विलक्षणं त्यजेद्वस्त्रं समच्छेदमसङ्कुलम् ।
विवर्णितं तु यद्वस्त्रं कुर्याद्देवद्विजार्चनम् ॥
जपहोमोपवासांश्चेत् तथा नाप्नोति किल्बिषम् ॥]

चामरलक्षणम् ॥ ७२ ॥

Chapter LXXII – Signs of Chowries

देवैश्चमर्यः किल बालहेतोः सृष्टा हिमक्ष्माधरकन्दरेषु ।
आपीतवर्णाश्च भवन्ति तासां कृष्णाश्च लाङ्गूलभवाः सिताश्च ॥ १ ॥

It is said that the camara deer were created in the Himalayan caves by the Gods for the sake of their hairs. The hairs growing on their tails are pale yellow, black and sometimes white.

[The commentator seems to suggest that the colour of the hair on the body of the camara deer is pale yellow or black, while that of the tail white also. It may also mean that on the tail there are clusters of hair of all the three colours.

In the second half of the verse the subject बाला: hair, is not mentioned, but understood. This verse and the following two and the last one are in the इन्द्रवज्रा metre, while the 4th is in उपजाति and the 5th in रथोद्धता.]

स्नेहो मृदुत्वं बहुबालता च वैशद्यमल्पास्थिनिबन्धनत्वम् ।
शौक्ल्यं च तासां गुणसम्प्रयुक्ता विद्धाल्पलुप्तानि न शोभनानि ॥ २ ॥

The excellences of the chowries are said to be glossiness, tenderness, density of the hair, brightness, being connected with a slender bone, and whiteness. Those that are pierced, small or broken off (bare) are inauspicious.

[The word वैशद्य is construed by Utpala as निर्मलता परस्परमश्लेषश्च meaning purity and being not joined together. The word तासां refers literally to the Camarīs, no doubt; but actually the author means the chowries or *cāmaras*, because he uses the neuter gender at the end viz. शोभनानि.]

अध्यर्धहस्तप्रमितोऽस्य दण्डो हस्तोऽथवाऽरत्निसमोऽथवाऽन्यः ।
काष्ठाच्छुभात् काञ्चनरूप्यगुप्ताद्रत्नैश्च सर्वश्च हिताय राज्ञाम् ॥ ३ ॥

The handle of the chowrie should measure one-cubit and a half, or one cubit, or at least one small cubit (which is equal to the length of the fore-arm with the fist closed). One made of auspicious wood, coated with gold or silver, and bedecked with all kinds of gems, would become beneficial to kings.

[Utpala says according to some, *Aratni* is a cubit upto the little finger.]

In the next verse the colours of the handle for different classes are given.

यष्ट्यातपत्राङ्कुशवेत्रचापवितानकुन्तध्वजचामराणाम् ।
व्यापीततन्त्रीमधुकृष्णवर्णा वर्णक्रमेणैव हिताय दण्डाः ॥ ४ ॥

The handles of clubs (sticks ?), umbrellas, goads, staffs (canes), bows, canopies, spears, banners and chowries of the four classes beginning with the Brāhmaṇa would be favourable to them, if their colours are yellow, red, the colour of honey, and dark respectively.

[Utpala says about the colours: तन्त्रीवर्णाः पीतलोहिताः क्षत्रियाणाम् । However sage *Garga* says it is *red*. Look at his careless expression: पीतवर्णं हिताय प्रशस्ताय । He ought to have said 'प्रशस्ताः'.

Cf. गर्ग—

विप्राणां पीतवर्णः स्यात् क्षत्रियाणां तु लोहितः ।
वैश्यानां पीतवर्णश्च शूद्राणामसितप्रभः ॥
दण्डः शुभप्रदो ज्ञेयो यष्टिश्छत्राङ्कुशादिषु ॥

मातृभूधनकुलक्षयावहा रोगमृत्युजननाश्च पर्वभिः ।
द्व्यादिभिर्द्विकविवर्धितैः क्रमाद् द्वादशान्तविरतैः समैः फलम् ॥ ५ ॥

The above-mentioned objects (viz. clubs, umbrellas etc.) with an even number of joints or knots i.e. two, four, six, eight, ten and twelve, cause loss of (1) mother, (2) lands, (3) wealth and (4) family, (5) disease, and (6) death respectively.

[According to the commentator the joints are of the handles. Of course in many cases, like the umbrella, the handle alone can have joints. In the case of *Kunta*, probably we may have to take the entire wooden body as its handle.]

यात्राप्रसिद्धिर्द्विषतां विनाशो लाभाः प्रभूताः वसुधागमश्च ।
वृद्धिः पशूनामभिवाञ्छिताप्तिस्त्र्याद्येष्वयुग्मेषु तदीश्वराणाम् ॥ ६ ॥

If the joints are odd, viz. three, five, seven, nine, eleven and thirteen, the beneficial effects accruing to the owners will be (1) success of the journey (or of the expedition), (2) destruction of enemies, (3) enormous gains, (4) acquisition of lands, (5) increase of cattle-wealth (or domestic animals), and (6) attainment of desired objects respectively.

[This shows that an odd number of joints is favourable. Beyond thirteen all odd numbers are good and even ones bad. Here the commentator suggests that the joints refer to the whole body of the objects, as he says दण्डादीनां स्वामिनां etc. which means यष्टयादीनां etc.]

छत्रलक्षणम् ॥ ७३ ॥

Chapter LXXIII – Signs of Umbrellas

निचितं तु हंसपक्षैः कृकवाकुमयूरसारसानां वा ।
दौकूल्येन नवेन तु समन्ततश्छादितं शुक्लम् ॥ १ ॥

मुक्ताफलैरुपचितं प्रलम्बमालाविलं स्फटिकमूलम् ।
षड्ढस्तशुद्धहैमं नवपर्वनगैकदण्डं तु ॥ २ ॥

दण्डार्धविस्तृतं तत् समावृतं रत्नभूषितमुदग्रम् ।
नृपतेस्तदातपत्रं कल्याणपरं विजयदं च ॥ ३ ॥

A white umbrella of the following description becomes excellent and brings all-round happiness (prosperity) and victory to a king : It should be filled (decorated) with the feathers of swans, cocks, peacocks or cranes; it should be covered all round with a fresh, white silken cloth. It must be adorned with pearls and have garland of pearls suspended all round from its edges; the bottom of its handle is made of crystal; the rod made of a single wooden piece, is to be six cubits in length, and covered with pure gold, having nine (or seven) joints. The diameter of the umbrella should be three cubits. Its joints should be well-knit all over and it should be adorned with gems.

[The expression नवपर्वनगैकदण्डं is explained by Utpala as consisting of a single rod having nine or seven joints. He takes नग to represent the number seven. Sage Garga is equally ambiguous. It could as well be interpreted thus : made of a single, excellent timber (i.e. auspicious tree), having nine joints: Here नग is to be taken in the sense of a tree.

Cf. गर्ग

हंसकुक्कुटपक्षैश्च मायूरैः सारसैस्तथा ।
निचितं पटसञ्छन्नं शुक्लं मुक्ताफलान्वितम् ॥
छत्रं स्फटिकमूलं यत् तत्र दण्डं तु षट्करम् ।
कारयेद्धेमसञ्छन्नं नवपर्वनगान्वितम् ॥
हस्तत्रितयविस्तीर्णं रत्नमालाभिरन्वितम् ।
तदातपत्रं नृपतेः कल्याणविजयावहम् ॥

युवराजनृपतिपत्न्योः सेनापतिदण्डनायकानां च ।
दण्डोऽर्धपञ्चहस्तः समपञ्चकृतोऽर्धविस्तारः ॥ ४ ॥

The rod of the umbrella belonging to a yuvarāja (heir-apparent) queen, commandant of the army and a general is 4½ cubits in height and 22 cubits in extent or diameter of the cloth.

The different subdivisions of an army are enumerated and defined in the *Mahābhārata* :

एको गजो रथश्चैको नराः पञ्च पदातयः ।
त्रयश्च तुरगास्तज्ज्ञैः पत्तिरित्यभिधीयते ।।

पत्तिस्त्रिगुणा सेनामुखम् । तन्त्रिगुणं गुल्मः । स त्रिगुणो गणः । स त्रिगुणो वाहिनी । सा त्रिगुणा पृतना । सा त्रिगुणा चमूः । सा त्रिगुणा अनीकिनी । दशानीकिनी अक्षौहिणी । (Kṣīrasvāmin under 81-82 Amara II. 8).

अन्येषामुष्णघ्नं प्रसादपट्टैर्विभूषितशिरस्कम् ।
व्यालम्बिरत्नमालं छत्रं कार्यं तु मायूरम् ॥ ५ ॥

The umbrella for other officers of state should be formed with peacock feathers so to ward off the Sun's heat, and having wreaths of gems hanging all round, its top being surmounted by a golden crown of the type intended for royal proteges.

For *Prasādapaṭṭa* see XL 3 *supra*. The author could have taken up this and the previous chapter as well as LXXIX soon after chapter L for better effect.

अन्येषां तु नराणां शीतातपवारणं तु चतुरस्रम् ।
समवृत्तदण्डयुक्तं छत्रं कार्यं तु विप्राणाम् ॥ ६ ॥

The umbrella of ordinary citizens should be of a square form, capable of warding off cold and heat. That of Brāhmaṇas should have a cylindrical rod.

Probably the author intends to convey the idea that the rod also should be square. In the case of Brāhmaṇas, however, the rod (and the umbrella?) should be cylindrical. From the text it cannot be made out that the umbrella of Vipras is to be circular. The commentator's explanation viz. 'विप्राणां ब्राह्मणानां समवृत्तं समन्ततः परिवर्तुलं दण्डयुक्तं छत्रं कार्यमिति' makes no sense, unless we combine परिवर्तुलं with the following word into a compound as परिवर्तुलदण्डयुक्तं. As we are not given the opinions of ancients, we have to leave this as a moot point.

———

स्त्रीप्रशंसाध्यायः ॥ ७४ ॥

Chapter LXXIV – Praise of Women

This and the following chapter could have been introduced more befittingly after LXX. Here the poet strays into the realm of pure epic poetry where erotics find full expression. This chapter can be ranked with the शृङ्गार शतक of भर्तृहरि, चौरपञ्चाशिका of बिल्हण etc. It was probably the author's intention to give something pleasing, as a relief, to the reader who must be tired as a result of studying many technical subjects in this work. After all the sentiment of Śṛṅgāra is the most delightful of all, परः प्रह्लादनो रसः

जये धरित्र्याः पुरमेव सारं पुरे गृहं सद्मनि चैकदेशः ।
तत्रापि शय्या शयने वरा स्त्री रत्नोज्ज्वला राज्यसुखस्य सारः ॥ १ ॥

Of the whole country that has been conquered the most essential part is the *one* city (i.e. the capital) ; in the city the most important part is a mansion; and in the mansion it is the bed-chamber that is the most desirable part; and even there the most beautiful thing is the couch, where on a charming damsel, bedecked with gems and gold ornaments, is the essence, the core of the happiness accruing from the rulership of a kingdom.

[This description of feminine excellence is on a par with what Bhartṛhari says, 'मधरमधु वधूनां भाग्यवन्तः पिबन्ति and Kālidāsa, किमिव हि मधुराणां मण्डनं नाकृतीनाम् and सृष्टिराद्येव धातुः. This verse contains the figure called सारालङ्कार. This and verse 6 are in उपजाति metre.]

रत्नानि विभूषयन्ति योषा भूष्यन्ते वनिता न रत्नकान्त्या ।
चेतो वनिता हरन्त्यरत्ना नो रत्नानि विनाङ्गनाङ्गसङ्गम् ॥ २ ॥

Damsels beautify gems and are not at all adorned (made more charming) by lustrous gems. For, they captivate the heart even without the aid of gems; but the gems do not, without their association with the limbs of charming maidens.

[The last quarter may also be interpreted thus : There are no gems (excellent things) apart from union with damsels *par excellence*. The figure of speech is called व्यतिरेकालङ्कार. Likewise says Kālidāsa :

आभरणस्याभरणं प्रसाधनविधेः प्रसाधनविशेषः ।
उपमानस्यापि सखे प्रत्युपमानं वपुस्तस्याः ॥

Cf. शक्तिभद्र—यस्य नैसर्गिकी शोभा तन्न संस्कारमर्हति
क: कलां शशिनो मार्ष्टि कौस्तुभः केन रज्यते ॥

The metre is मधुंविराट्, an *Ardhasamavṛtta.*]

आकारं विनिगूहतां रिपुबलं जेतुं समुत्तिष्ठतां
तन्त्रं चिन्तयतां कृताकृतशतव्यापारशाखाकुलम् ।
मन्त्रिप्रोक्तनिषेविणां क्षितिभुजामाशङ्किनां सर्वतो
दुःखाम्भोनिधिवर्त्तिनां सुखलवः कान्तासमालिङ्गनम् ॥ ३ ॥

The embrace of the beloved alone affords a bit of happiness to kings who have to suppress their feelings, who strive to vanquish the army of their enemies, who deeply ponder over the diplomatic procedure (viz. political expedients) which is replete with the ramifications of hundreds of steps that have been already taken as well as those not taken, who act upon the advice tendered by their ministers, who apprehend danger from every quarter (i.e. suspect everybody), and who are consequently plunged in the ocean of misery.

[This too is a fine example of good poetry. A good wife is considered by poets and scholars a safe boat to cross the ocean of worldly existence which is infested with the sharks and whales of all kinds of miseries and troubles. This is more so in the case of kings as 'uneasy lies the head that wears the crown.' Great kings like Śrīrāma are ranked among *Dhirodātta* heroes, who are अतिगम्भीर very dignified and unruffled. For this quality see रघुवंश I. 20 :–

तस्य संवृतमन्त्रस्य गूढाकारेङ्गितस्य च ।
फलानुमेयाः प्रारम्भाः संस्काराः प्राक्तना इव ॥

Or a verse quoted in Daśarūpaka as instance of Dhīrodātta :

आहूतस्याभिषेकाय विसृष्टस्य वनाय च ।
न मया लक्षितस्तस्य स्वल्पोऽप्याकारविभ्रमः ॥

Tantra consists of the application of the six Guṇas, Sandhi, Vigraha, Yāna, Āsana, Dvaidha and Āśraya. We are reminded of सर्वाकारकृतव्यथः कथमपि प्राप्नोमि नो निर्वृतिम् of the *Mudrārākṣasa.* Note also *Bhāravi's* dictum हिताश्न यः संशृणुते स किम्प्रभुः It is a fact that those who occupy very high positions are always afraid of everybody including their own sons and kinsmen. See what the great Śaṅkarācārya says : पुत्रादपि धनभाजां भीतिः सर्वत्रैषा विहिता नीतिः'

The metre is शार्दूलविक्रीडित.

श्रुतं दृष्टं स्पृष्टं स्मृतमपि नृणां ह्लादजननं
न रत्नं स्त्रीभ्योऽन्यत् क्वचिदपि कृतं लोकपतिना।
तदर्थं धर्मार्थौ सुतविषयसौख्यानि च ततो
गृहे लक्ष्म्यो मान्याः सततमबला मानविभवैः ॥ ४ ॥

Nowhere has the creator designed any gem other than women. For, this gem gives delight to men, when it is heard of, seen, touched or even remembered; for its sake are done meritorious deeds, and wealth amassed; and from that alone do men derive worldly pleasures and offspring. Such women are indeed the Goddesses of fortune living in mortal abodes. Hence they ought to be honoured always with respect and wealth.

[This idea is derived from Manu's statement, 'यत्र नार्यस्तु पूज्यन्ते रमन्ते तत्र देवताः'। We come across a similar idea in the *Mahābhārata* : 'पालिता निगृहीता च स्त्री श्रीर्भवति पार्थिव'।

The metre is शिखरिणी.]

येऽप्यङ्गनानां प्रवदन्ति दोषान् वैराग्यमार्गेण गुणान्विहाय।
ते दुर्जना मे मनसो वितर्कः सद्भाववाक्यानि न तानि तेषाम् ॥ ५ ॥

It is my conviction that those, who, as a result of their following the path of renunciation or dispassion, overlook the virtues of women and wax eloquent on their flaws, are indeed wicked and cynical. For, they do not mean what they say.

[This verse is in line with Kālidāsa's line

शिरीषपुष्पाधिकसौकुमार्यौ बाहू तदीयाविति मे वितर्कः।

It is true that people who aspire for spiritual progress shun women's company. There is a verse which depicts woman as a veritable demoness नारी प्रत्यक्षराक्षसी. Our author is of opinion that such expressions are the outcome of a defeatist mentality. For ascetics, no doubt, her company is repugnant as stated by the great poet : प्रत्यर्थिभूतामपि तां समाधेः and स्त्रीसन्निकर्षं परिहर्तुमिच्छन्. In the *Vikramorvaśiya* the same poet ridicules ascetics in relation to feminine beauty :

वेदाभ्यासजडः कथं नु विषयव्यावृत्तकौतूहलो
निर्मातुं प्रभवेन्मनोहरमिदं रूपं पुराणो मुनिः ॥

This verse as well as 17 and 20 are in the इन्द्रवज्रा metre.]

प्रब्रूत सत्यं कतरोऽङ्गनानां दोषोऽस्ति यो नाचरितो मनुष्यैः।
धार्ष्ट्येन पुम्भिः प्रमदा निरस्ता गुणाधिकास्ता मनुनात्र चोक्तम् ॥ ६ ॥

Please tell me the truth, what great fault is there in women that has not been committed already by men? Men have traduced women as impudent (*or*, men have outstripped women in impudence *or*, men have spurned women owing to their own obduracy). They are indeed superior to men in respect of merits. And the following are Manu's statements on this point.

सोमस्तासामदाच्छौचं गन्धर्वः शिक्षितां गिरम् ।
अग्निश्च सर्वभक्षित्वं तस्मान्निष्कसमाः स्त्रियः ॥ ७ ॥

The Moon gave them i.e. women, purity or cleanliness; *Gandharva*, cultured and sweet speech; and the Fire, the capacity to digest all sorts of food. Hence women are like unto pure gold.

[The following Mantra is the basis for Manu's statement:—

सोमः प्रथमो विविदे गन्धर्वो विविद उत्तरः ।
द्वितीयो अग्निष्टे पतिस्तृतीयस्ते मनुष्यजाः ॥

On the first night after marriage the bride is taken charge of by Soma, on the second by Gandharva and on the third by Agni. This verse of Manu suggests woman's intrinsic purity, sweet words and good digestion.]

ब्राह्मणाः पादतो मेध्या गावो मेध्याश्च पृष्ठतः ।
अजाश्वा मुखतो मेध्याः स्त्रियो मेध्यास्तु सर्वतः ॥ ८ ॥

Brāhmaṇas are pure through their feet; cows, through their back; goats and horses, through their mouth or face; and women are pure throughout the body.

[This shows the superiority of women over all other beings including Brāhmaṇas. It may be for this reason that the feet of Brāhmaṇas are worshipped. Hence the saying :

पुनन्तु मां ब्राह्मणपादपांसवः ।]

स्त्रियः पवित्रमतुलं नैता दुष्यन्ति कर्हिचित् ।
मासि मासि रजो ह्यासां दुष्कृतान्यपकर्षति ॥ ९ ॥

Being uniquely pure, women are never defiled. For, the menses remove their blemishes every month.

जामयो यानि गेहानि शपन्त्यप्रतिपूजिताः ।
तानि कृत्याहतानीव विनश्यन्ति समन्ततः ॥ १० ॥

Those houses (or families) that are cursed by respectable women (or daughters-in-law) as a result of their being not treated honourably, will utterly perish, as if destroyed by witch-craft.

जाया वा स्याज्जनित्री वा सम्भवः स्त्रीकृतो नृणाम् ।
हे कृतघ्नास्तयोर्निन्दां कुर्वतां वः कुतः शुभम् ॥ ११ ॥

Whether it is the wife or the mother, men are brought into existence only by women. What good can you expect, O ungrateful men, from censuring them ?

[Utpala quotes the Vedic authority for the word जायाः—"तज्जाया जाया भवति यदस्यां जायते पुनः" and "अङ्गादङ्गात्सम्भवसि हृदयादभिजायसे। आत्मा वै पुत्रनामासि त्वं जीव शरदां शतम् ।" This Vedic quotation proves that the wife is the vehicle for the re-emergence of oneself in the form of a son. It is for this reason that she is called *Jāyā*. Manu's idea is that man ought not to denigrate women, having sought their help to be their mothers for their reappearance in their own form and in that of their son. It would be an act of sheer perfidy.]

दम्पत्योर्व्युत्क्रमे दोषः समः शास्त्रे प्रतिष्ठितः ।
नरा न समवेक्षन्ते तेनात्र वरमङ्गनाः ॥ १२ ॥

It has been laid down in *Dharmaśāstras* (codes of conduct) that the offence of both husband and wife will be equal, if both go astray. But men pay no heed to their sins, (while women do). Hence women are superior in this respect.

[Vide the following rule :

न हीदृशमनायुष्यं यथान्यस्त्रीनिषेवणम् ॥]

बहिर्लोम्ना तु षण्मासात् वेष्टितः खरचर्मणा ।
दारातिक्रमणे भिक्षां देहीत्युक्त्वा विशुध्यति ॥ १३ ॥

A man guilty of going astray in matters sexual will be absolved of the sin by begging alms for six months, wearing a donkey's hide with its hair exposed.

न शतेनापि वर्षाणामपैति मदनाशयः ।
तत्राशक्त्या निवर्तन्ते नरा धैर्येण योषितः ॥ १४ ॥

Even after a hundred years men's sexual craving does not subside; but they refrain from the act because of their physical incapacity, whereas women do so by conviction and courage.

[Here Bhaṭṭotpala gives some queer expressions and unintelligible statements : योषितः पुनर्धैर्येण धृष्टत्वेनैनं निवर्तन्ते, (If it is धृष्टत्वेनैव it is correct). अनेन स्त्रीणामभिलाषशीलताप्राधान्यं प्रदर्शितं भवति । He should have stated ; स्त्रीणामिन्द्रियसंयमः प्रदर्शितो भवति ।]

अहो धाष्टर्यमसाधूनां निन्दतामनघाः स्त्रियः ।
मुष्णतामिव चौराणां तिष्ठ चौरेति जल्पताम् ॥ १५ ॥

How bold or impudent are the immoral fellows that slander blameless women ! They are like the thieves actually found stealing and yet crying—"Thief, stop !"

[The above statements of Manu, the Law-giver, amply proves his great regard for woman who was treated with respect in ancient times. He has given a fine simile which explains that man is the sinner and yet he blames woman. This is similar to a henpecked and cowardly man, who being beaten by the wife inside the house, shouts "Will you repeat the offence ?" in order to fool those that are standing outside.]

पुरुषश्चटुलानि कामिनीनां कुरुते यानि रहो न तानि पश्चात् ।
सुकृतज्ञतयाङ्गना गतासूनवगूह्य प्रविशन्ति सप्तजिह्वम् ॥ १६ ॥

A man does not resort to the same coaxing words and pleasing actions after he comes to know of their minor lapses, as he used to do before in privacy with his sweet-hearts; whereas the latter embrace their dead husbands out of gratitude for the good turns done unto them, and enter their funeral pyre.

[This too shows woman's superiority over man. In the days of Varāhamihira the *Sutee* custom was in vogue. However poet Bāṇa condemns it.

The metre is औपच्छन्दसिक]

स्त्रीरत्नभोगोऽस्ति नरस्य यस्य निःस्वोऽपि सम्प्रत्यवनीश्वरोऽसौ ।
राज्यस्य सारोऽशनमङ्गनाश्च तृष्णानलोद्दीपनदारु शेषम् ॥ १७ ॥

A man who enjoys the gem of a damsel is for the time being, (or, to me) a king, though he may be very poor. For, the quintessence of a kingdom consists of dainty food and damsels; and all else is only fuel for kindling the fire of greed.

[The other reading in the place of सम्प्रति is मां प्रति. However, the Vāraṇaseya edition has printed it as साम्प्रति. Being a Sahṛdaya and a poet the author is right in giving expression to the sentiment that is on a par with Vālmīki's: त्रैलोक्यराज्यं सकलं सीताया नाप्नुयात्कलाम् ।]

कामिनीं प्रथमयौवनान्वितां मन्दवल्गुमृदुपीडितस्वनाम् ।
उत्स्तनीं समवलम्ब्य या रतिः सा न धातृभवनेऽस्ति मे मतिः ॥ १८ ॥

It is my firm conviction that the erotic bliss that is derived from embracing a loving damsel in the prime of youth, with swelling bosoms, and murmuring sounds that are gentle, sweet, tender and suppressed, cannot be had even in the Creator's Heaven—*Brahmaloka.*

[Vedāntins say that the bliss of Brahman or self-knowledge is indescribable, but the poet, who rises here to the height of Śṛṅgāra-description, opines that Brahmānanda is nothing before this erotic experience. We have already seen Bhartṛhari's encomium. In this connection a verse attributed to the Paṇḍitarāja Jagannatha seems to be apt. That is :

यवनी नवनीतकोमलाङ्गी शयनीये यदि नीयते कदापि ।
अवनीतलमेव साधु मन्ये न वनी माघवनी विनोदहेतुः ॥

The metre is रथोद्धता in this and in the following verse.]

तत्र देवमुनिसिद्धचारणैर्मान्यमानपितृसेव्यसेवनात् ।
ब्रूत धातृभवनेऽस्ति किं सुखं यद्रहः समवलम्ब्य न स्त्रियम् ॥ १९ ॥

Tell me what pleasure is there in the world of Brahman other than the service of the *Manes* and other worshipful Beings rendered by the Gods, Sages, Siddhas and celestial bards, and which cannot be experienced by embracing a damsel in solitude.

[The commentator explains the second quarter thus : मान्यानां पूजनीयानां मानपितृणां पूजकानां सेव्यानां च सेवनाद् उपासनात्...। Is there a class of *manes* who are called *Mānapitaraḥ* ? I prefer to take it as मान्यमानाः पितरः]

आब्रह्मकीटान्तमिदं निबद्धं पुंस्त्रीप्रयोगेण जगत्समस्तम् ।
व्रीडात्र का यत्र चतुर्मुखत्वमीशोऽपि लोभाद्गमितो युवत्याः ॥ २० ॥

This entire universe, right from the creator (*Hiraṇyagarbha*) to the smallest worm, is born of the union of the male and female. So why should any body feel ashamed of it, when even the lord Śiva was forced to have four faces on account of His longing to have a look at a maiden ?

[The Purāṇic story relating to the Lord's assuming four faces is explained thus by the commentator :— Once the celestial courtesan *Tilottamā* was perambulating the Lord, on whose lap was seated Pārvatī. In order to enjoy the matchless beauty of the damsel He assumed four faces on all sides so that Pārvatī might not detect the Lord's longing for another damsel's beauty.

The moral that the author wants to emphasize is that sexual activities are not bad if they are channelized and kept within permitted bounds. That is why the Lord says in the Gītā:

धर्माविरुद्धो भूतेषु कामोऽस्मि भरतर्षभ ॥ (VII-II)]

सौभाग्यकरणम् ॥ ७५ ॥

Chapter LXXV – Winning of Affection

जात्यं मनोभवसुखं सुभगस्य सर्व-
मामासमात्रमितरस्य मनोवियोगात् ।
चित्तेन भावयति दूरगतापि यं स्त्री
गर्भं बिभर्त्ति सदृशं पुरुषस्य तस्य ॥ १ ॥

The man who captivates the heart of damsels enjoys all kinds of erotic pleasures of a high order, while one who is not attractive gets only sham pleasures because the woman's mind is not fixed on him. A woman develops a foetus similar to the man whom she intensely thinks of at the time of coitus, though she may be far off from him.

[The author expresses here a psychological problem: If the man is highly attractive, the woman in sexual union concentrates all her mental powers on him. Consequently the foetus takes all the features and qualities of the man. On the other hand, a woman might think of some other man, who is far away and who, in her eyes, is very handsome. The rule enunciated here is emphasized and insisted upon in the spiritual sphere. Vide the *Bhagavadgitā*—

यं यं वापि स्मरन्भावं त्यजत्यन्ते कलेवरम् ।
तं तमेवैति कौन्तेय सदा तद्भावभावितः ॥ (VIII. 6)

Our author expresses this idea in verse 4 below. This is analogous to the *Bhramarakiṭanyāya*. See also LXXVIII 14 *infra*.

The metre of this and verses 3 and 4 is वसन्ततिलका.]

भङ्क्त्वा काण्डं पादपस्योप्तमुर्व्यां बीजं वास्यां नान्यतामेति यद्वत् ।
एवं ह्यात्मा जायते स्त्रीषु भूयः कश्चित्तस्मिन् क्षेत्रयोगाद्विशेषः ॥ २ ॥

Just as a branch cut off from a tree or a seed planted in the soil does not change its nature i.e. does not grow into a different tree, even so is the soul-reborn in women. But as a result of the influence of the soil or mother, slight difference does occur in the fruit or child.

[This topic is discussed in the Mahābhārata, where Bhīṣma

says that the man is the seed and the woman the soil. So also : 'भस्त्रा माता पितुः पुत्रो येन जातः स एव सः ।' The poet employs good, elegant language and figures in these descriptions.

The metre is शालिनी.]

आत्मा सहैति मनसा मन इन्द्रियेण
स्वार्थेन चेन्द्रियमिति क्रम एष शीघ्रः ।
योगोऽयमेव मनसः किमगम्यमस्ति
यस्मिन्मनो व्रजति तत्र गतोऽयमात्मा ॥ ३ ॥

The soul combines with the mind, the mind with the senses, and the senses with their respective objects. This takes place in quick succession. The connection being such (i.e. so strong and intimate), is there anything unattainable for the mind ? And wither the mind goes, thither goes the soul too !

[In ordinary human beings the mind and soul appear to be inseparably bound together. Only yogins can find out and stop the evil activities of the mind. In the *Kaṭhopaniṣad* (III-3) *Yama* teaches the young *Naciketas*, "Know the Soul to be the master of the chariot; the mind the reins; the intellect the charioteer; and the objects the goal." Vide the Gītā III 40, 42 :—

इन्द्रियाणि मनो बुद्धिरस्याधिष्ठानमुच्यते ।
एतैर्विमोहयत्येष ज्ञानमावृत्य देहिनम् ॥
इन्द्रियाणि पराण्याहुरिन्द्रियेभ्यः परं मनः ।
मनसस्तु परा बुद्धिर्यो बुद्धेः परतस्तु सः ॥

Kālidāsa too expresses similar ideas when he says, "मनोरथानामगतिर्न विद्यते ।" Before him Sage Vālmīki had said, "मनो हि हेतुः सर्वेषामिन्द्रियाणां प्रवर्तने ।" The Indriyas are ten in number as stated below :

पायूपस्थं हस्तपादं वाक्तथैवात्र पञ्चमी ।
पञ्च कर्मेन्द्रियाण्याहुर्मनः षष्ठानि तानि तु ॥
श्रोत्रं त्वक्चक्षुषी जिह्वा नासिका चेति पञ्चमी ।
पञ्च बुद्धीन्द्रियाण्याहुर्मनः षष्ठानि तानि तु ॥]

आत्मायमात्मनि गतो हृदयेऽतिसूक्ष्मो
ग्राह्योऽचलेन मनसा सततामियोगात् ।
यो यं विचिन्तयति याति स तन्मयत्वं
यस्मादतः सुभगमेव गता युवत्यः ॥ ४ ॥

The soul which is extremely subtle is immersed in the Supreme

Soul in the region of the heart (Hṛtpuṇḍarīka—Heart-lotus). Such a soul should be comprehended or realized by a steadfast mind through constant practice. Since a person attains the nature of one whom he constantly thinks of, young women are mentally attached to their beloved ones.

[The author makes a highly significant statement which is well known in Vedāntic circles: In the *Kaṭhopaniṣad* it is stated thus :

"अङ्गुष्ठमात्रः पुरुषो मध्य आत्मनि तिष्ठति ।
ईशानो भूतभव्यस्य न ततो विजुगुप्सते । एतद् वै तत् ॥" (IV-12)

Vide the Gītā VIII 8-12. Advaitins maintain that the Ātman is to be realized by one's own self. This shows that our author was a subscriber to that school of philosophy. Kālidāsa too expresses a similar idea in "आत्मानमात्मन्यवलोकयन्तम्. The mystic seat of the soul is said to be *Daharākāśa* inside the heart. In the Upaniṣads there is an enchanting description of this seat :

पद्मकोशप्रतीकाशं हृदयं चाप्यधोमुखम् ।
अधो निष्ठ्या वितस्त्यान्ते नाभ्यामुपरि तिष्ठति ॥
ज्वालमालाकुलं भाति विश्वस्यायतनं महत् ।

The commentator interprets this verse appropriately thus :

अयमात्मा कर्मात्मा चिद्रूपो जीव आत्मनि परमात्मनि गतः स्वसत्तायां बोधरूपः स्थितः कर्ता ज्ञाता च सम्पन्नः । क्व ? हृदये । तथा च—

नाभेरूर्ध्वं वितस्ति च कण्ठाधस्तात् षडङ्गुलम् ।
हृदयं तद्विजानीयाद्विश्वस्यायतनं महत् ॥

Here too we can remember appropriately the भ्रमरकीटन्याय. The figure of speech is term काव्यलिङ्ग. The third line represents a general maxim in philosophy and psychology. 'ब्रह्मविद् ब्रह्मैव भवति' is a statement that corroborates our author's dictum.

Kālidāsa too echoes the same idea through the following statements :—

आशाबन्धः साहयति and

आशाबन्धः कुसुमसदृशं प्रायशो ह्यङ्गनानां
सद्यःपाति प्रणयिहृदयं विप्रयोगे रुणद्धि ॥ (मेघ०)]

दाक्षिण्यमेकं सुभगत्वहेतुर्विद्वेषणं तद्विपरीतचेष्टा ।
मन्त्रौषधाद्यैः कुहकप्रयोगैर्भवन्ति दोषा बहवो न शर्म ॥ ५ ॥

A favourable attitude or courtesy is the sole cause of winning the affection of the opposite sex; a contrary conduct produces aversion. Charms, potions and such other quack remedies produce only many harmful effects and not happiness.

[Many a time conjugal happiness is marred by the obduracy or non-adaptability of the partners. Here the author gives a piece of good advice to such people. There are some who administer certain drugs to the party that does not respond to the love of the other. Our author strictly forbids such artificial means of winning affection. This verse, 8 and 10 are in उपजाति metre.]

वाल्लभ्यमायाति विहाय मानं दौर्भाग्यमापादयतेऽभिमानः ।
कृच्छ्रेण संसाधयतेऽभिमानी कार्याण्ययत्नेन वदन् प्रियाणि ॥ ६ ॥

Man becomes the idol of woman by giving up arrogance; pride produces repulsion. A haughty person is able to accomplish his tasks with great difficulty, whereas one speaking sweetly does them easily.

[This verse is an excellent सुभाषित giving sound advice to the man of the world in his everyday life. People not knowing how to speak properly fail miserably in life in spite of their other qualities. That is why it is said : वचने का दरिद्रता.

Vide *Manu* :-

सत्यं ब्रूयात् प्रियं ब्रूयान्न ब्रूयात्सत्यमप्रियम् ।
प्रियं च नानृतं ब्रूयादेष धर्मः सनातनः ॥

Ācārya Daṇḍin puts this idea quite aptly thus!

गौर्गौः कामदुघा सम्यक् प्रयुक्ता स्मर्यते बुधैः ।
दुष्प्रयुक्ता पुनर्गोत्वं प्रयोक्तुः सैव शंसति ॥

The metre in this, 7 and 9 is इन्द्रवज्रा.]

तेजो न तद्यत् प्रियसाहसत्वं वाक्यं न चानिष्टमसत्प्रणीतम् ।
कार्यस्य गत्वान्तमनुद्धता ये तेजस्विनस्ते न विकत्थना ये ॥ ७ ॥

It is not valour to be fond of rash deeds; nor to speak harsh words that are generally uttered by the ignoble. Those who are not arrogant even after accomplishing their task are really valorous, and not those that are boastful.

[This reminds us of a famous verse that describes the qualities of a virtuous man : "One who is good to those that harm him is really virtuous." Similarly Bāṇa describes the evil qualities of rich people or upstarts (see Śukanāsopadeśa). This verse too can rank among the *Subhāṣitas* of Sanskrit language. The commentator's explanation of compounds looks some times rather funny. He explains प्रियसाहसत्वं as प्रियं यत्र वस्तुनि साहसत्वं न तत् तेजः शृंगारो भवति ।

In the first place the compound is wrongly explained and in the second, तेजः is construed as शृङ्गार which is utterly wrong. The correct method would be : प्रियं साहसं यस्य सः प्रियसाहसः, तस्य भावः प्रियसाहसत्वम्. It is our experience that astrologers are generally not strict about their language. The author says that great men never boast, but do their work quietly and even after success do not get elated.]

यः सार्वजन्यं सुभगत्वमिच्छेद् गुणान्स सर्वस्य वदेत्परोक्षम् ।
प्राप्नोति दोषानसतोऽप्यनेकान्परस्य यो दोषकथां करोति ॥ ८ ॥

One who wishes for universal love or popularity should express others' virtues behind their back, while one giving expression to others' faults comes to have many troubles, even though the faults may be real.

[Sometimes people pride themselves on exposing the wickedness of others. Here our author sounds a note of warning in that constant references to crimes and offences committed by bad characters tend to undermine the man's spiritual peace.

Utpala takes असतः in the ablative. It means 'troubles from the wicked'. It may also be taken as an adjective of दोषान्. In that case the meaning would be : The speaker gets many unmerited charges. असतो दुर्जनस्यापि परस्य is another construction. *Never speak ill of others, especially behind their back* is a golden precept which makes the author look like the sages who have laid down moral codes. The word सार्वजन्यं is grammatically unsound according to the Vārttika under Pāṇini V. 1-9. The correct form is सार्वजनिकम् or सर्वजनीनम्.

सर्वोपकारानुगतस्य लोकः सर्वोपकारानुगतो नरस्य ।
कृत्वोपकारं द्विषतां विपत्सु या कीर्तिरल्पेन न सा शुभेन ॥ ९ ॥

The whole world renders help to a man who is ever engaged in helping the people. The fame that is won by helping enemies in their distress cannot be acquired by a small measure of religious merit (Puṇya).

[This reminds us of Vyāsa's dictum :

श्लोकार्धेन प्रवक्ष्यामि यदुक्तं ग्रन्थकोटिभिः ।
परोपकारः पुण्याय पापाय परपीडनम् ॥]

तृणैरिवाग्निः सुतरां विवृद्धिमाच्छाद्यमानोऽपि गुणोऽभ्युपैति ।
स केवलं दुर्जनभावमेति हन्तुं गुणान्वाञ्छति यः परस्य ॥ १० ॥

The virtues of the good, though suppressed by the wicked, attain great eminence, just as fire blazes forth, though covered with straw. The person who tries (wishes) to destroy another's virtues gets his own wickedness proclaimed.

[All those who suffered in the past, such as Śrī Rāma, Yudhiṣṭhira etc., have become famous and worshippable, while Rāvaṇa, the Kauravas, Kaṁsa and other wicked men, become notorious for their evil deeds. A beautiful *simile* is employed in this verse. A similar idea is expressed in a verse meaning: 'Though fire is held topsy-turvy, its flames always shoot upwards'. Here the wicked are compared to the straw. Utpala mentions at the end of this chapter and the previous one that this chapter comes in the context of *discussion of the harem*, which is the topic of five chapters.]

कान्दर्पिकम् ॥ ७६ ॥

Chapter LXXVI – Erotic Recipes

रक्तेऽधिके स्त्री पुरुषस्तु शुक्रे नपुंसकं शोणितशुक्रसाम्ये ।
यस्मादतः शुक्रविवृद्धिदानि निषेवितव्यानि रसायनानि ॥ १ ॥

If at the time of sexual union the blood of the woman exceeds the sperm of man, the child will be female; if the sperm exceeds the woman's blood, it will be male; when both are equal, a hermaphrodite. For these reasons one ought to take tonics (or elixirs) that increase one's sperm.

[This idea is very ancient, being handed down by the writers on the Dharma-śāstra and Āyurveda. It boils down to this viz. the male sperm should contain more male elements than female ones for the birth of a male child. For, the ancients have accepted that the woman, possessing the ovum, is only the soil and it is the seed of man that germinates as the child. Sometimes it is wrongly interpreted that a female is born as a result of the woman's powerful blood. Actually both the principles are present in the male sperm.

The metre is उपजाति in this and in 4, 6, 7, 9 and 10.]

हर्म्यपृष्ठमुडुनाथरश्मयः सोत्पलं मधु मदालसा प्रिया ।
वल्लकी स्मरकथा रहः स्रजो वर्ग एव मदनस्य वागुरा ॥ २ ॥

Cupid's snare consists of the following group : viz. a terrace (of a mansion), the Moon's rays, wine with lily petals, a sweet-heart dull with intoxication, a lute, amatory talk, privacy and garlands.

[The following verse, which is almost a paraphrase of this, is given by the commentator of the *Vṛttaratnākara* as illustration of *Drutamadhyā* :

चन्दनमिन्दुमहश्च सुगन्धिर्मलयमरुन्मदिरा च मनोज्ञा ।
वामदृशां च वपुः सविलासं मनसिजपौष्टिकयोगविशेषः ॥

The commentator, Bhaṭṭotpala, makes the following remark on 'wine' : मद्यग्रहणमुपलक्षणार्थं शूद्रमधिकृत्यैतदुक्तम् । ब्राह्मणादेरन्यदभिमतं पानम् । I am afraid he is too solicitous for the interests of Brāhmaṇas. In fact, all these recipes are meant primarily for the king and his harem. It is well known that Kṣatriyas used to take wine in ancient times. Even Vālmīki states that Śrī Rāma, being separated from his beloved, has stopped drinking wine "न चैव मधु सेवते" The author seems to have preferred alliteration to grammatical correctness, in निषेवेत.

The metre is रथोद्धता.]

माक्षीकधातुमधुपारदलोहचूर्ण-
पथ्याशिलाजतुघृतानि समानि योऽद्यात् ।
सैकानि विंशतिरहानि जरान्वितोऽपि
सोऽशीतिकोऽपि रमयत्यबलां युवेव ॥ ३ ॥

A man, who though very old or an octogenarian eats for 21 days a mixture of equal quantities of pyrites, honey, mercury iron-dust, Harītakī (Terminalia chebula), bitumen, and ghee, will be able to please a damsel, as if he were a young man.

[About the proportion of the ingredients the commentator says: माक्षीकवर्जं सर्वाणि सममात्राणि । घृतमाक्षीकाभ्यां सममात्राभ्यां भावयित्वा गुलिका कार्या । The metre of this and of verse 12 is वसन्ततिलका.]

क्षीरं शृतं यः कपिकच्छुमूलैः पिबेत् क्षयं स्त्रीषु न सोऽभ्युपैति ।
माषान्पयः सर्पिषि वा विपक्वान् षड्ग्रासमात्रांश्च पयोऽनुपानम् ॥ ४ ॥

If one drinks milk boiled with the roots of Kapikacchu (*colocasia esculanta*), or eats only six morsels of black-gram (Phaseolus radiaters) boiled in milk and ghee (or in ghee prepared from milk itself), followed by a drink of milk, one will not be exhausted in sexual activities.

विदारिकायाः स्वरसेन चूर्णं मुहुर्मुहुर्भावितशोषितं च ।
शृतेन दुग्धेन सशर्करेण पिबेत् स यस्य प्रमदाः प्रभूताः ॥ ५ ॥

A man having numerous wives should take the powder of Vidārikā (*Solanum verbascifolium*) boiled seven times in its own juice and reduced (i.e. concentrated), and drink with it boiled milk mixed with sugar.

[The metre is उपेन्द्रवज्रा.]

धात्रीफलानां स्वरसेन चूर्णं सुभावितं क्षौद्रसिताज्ययुक्तम् ।
लीढ्वानु पीत्वा च पयोऽग्निशक्त्या कामं निकामं पुरुषो निषेवेत् ॥ ६ ॥

A man should boil well the powder of myrobalan (Emblica

officinalis) with its own juice and mix it with honey, sugar and ghee in equal quantities. He should lick this mixture (which is in liquid form) and drink milk according to his digestion. Then he will be able to enjoy sexual pleasures to his heart's content.

क्षीरेण बस्ताण्डयुजा शृतेन सम्प्लाव्य कामी बहुशस्तिलान् यः ।
सुशोषितानत्ति पयः पिबेच्च तस्याग्रतः किं चटकः करोति ॥ ७ ॥

A lustful man should boil milk with goat's testes and sesamum several (seven) times and thus concentrate it. He should eat and drink milk after that. He will then be able to put even the sparrow to shame by his exuberant virility.

[The last quarter is explained by Utpala thus:

बहुस्त्रीगमनम् अतीव स्त्रीषु बहुवारं शीघ्रगामी भवतीत्यर्थः ।

The sparrow is notorious for its sexual craving.]

माषसूपसहितेन सर्पिषा षष्टिकौदनमदन्ति ये नराः ।
क्षीरमप्यनुपिबन्ति तासु ते शर्वरीषु मदनेन शेरते ॥ ८ ॥

Men who eat boiled Ṣaṣṭika rice with ghee and black gram soup and then drink milk, sleep on those nights with the God of Love i.e. they indulge in sexual congress throughout the night.

[The Ṣaṣṭika rice is a variety that is harvested after 60 days. There are different varieties of rice, one of which, ripening in 90 days, is called *Navatika* in the west coast. This and verse 11 are in रथोद्धता metre.]

तिलाश्वगन्धाकपिकच्छुमूलैर्विदारिकाषष्टिकपिष्टयोगः ।
आजेन पिष्टः पयसा घृतेन पक्वं भवेच्छष्कुलिकातिवृष्या ॥ ९ ॥

Mix sesamum, Aśvagandhā (*withania somnifera*), roots of Kapi kacchu (*colocasia esculenta*) and Vidārikā (*Solanum verbascifolium*) with the paste of Ṣaṣṭika rice; then grind the mixture with goat's milk and fry this paste drawn into rings called Śaṣkulī (an eatable called *Cakkuli* in Kannaḍa and *Murukku* in Tamil). By eating this Śaṣkulī one will increase one's semen (i.e. it will be a good aphrodisiae).

क्षीरेण वा गोक्षुरकोपयोगं विदारिकाकन्दकभक्षणं वा ।
कुर्वंश्च सीदेद्यदि जीर्यतेऽस्य मन्दाग्निता चेद्विदमत्र चूर्णम् ॥ १० ॥

If a person suffers from old age, he should drink a decoction of the roots of either Gokṣura (*Tribulus terrestris*) or Vidārikā

(Solanum verbascifolium) boiled in milk. As a result of this tonic his sexual power will not be affected (in spite of his old age). If he suffers from weak digestion, he should take the following powder.

[The commentator supplies a word, कामुकत्वं- lust, in order to have a कर्ता, agent, for the verb जीर्यते. If a person loses his sexual craving, why should he resort to artificial methods for rousing it, unless he has youthful wives or is issueless? The fact is that even in old age men seldom lose कामुकत्व, but have no strength left for the act, as the author has already pointed out. Hence the straight course is to connect जीर्यते with the agent of कुर्वन् i.e. नरः or कश्चित्. अस्य should go with मन्दाग्निता.]

साजमोदलवणा हरीतकी शृङ्गवेरसहिता च पिप्पली ।
मद्यतक्रतरलोष्णवारिभिश्चूर्णपानमुदराग्निदीपनम् ॥ ११ ॥

A mixture of equal quantities of the powders of Ajamoda (Ajwan, *Trachyspermum ammi*), rock-salt, Harītakī (*Terminalia chebula*) ginger (*Zingiber officinale*) and Pippalī (*Piper longum*), being taken along with a drink of (or mixed with) liquor, butter-milk, rice gruel or hot water, improves digestion.

[Utpala says तरलं काञ्जिकम्, पय इति केचित्। But according to the Amarakośa II. 9-50 तरला, which is feminine, means only यवागूः i.e. rice gruel.]

अत्यम्लतिक्तलवणानि कटूनि वात्ति
यः क्षारशाकबहुलानि च भोजनानि ।
दृक्शुक्रवीर्यरहितः स करोत्यनेकान्
व्याजाञ्जरन्निव युवाप्यबलामवाप्य ॥ १२ ॥

One who eats things that are excessively sour, bitter, salt or pungent, and dishes consisting mostly of things mixed together and burnt (roasted) and leafy vegetables (or saline pot-herbs), will lose the power of sight, sperm and manhood, and on coming in contact with a damsel, will make several sham attempts, though he may be young, as if he were an aged man.

[Here the author gives a piece of sound advice to people, especially young men, on dieteties. It is a well known fact that food, by and large, conditions man's temperament or emotions. The food that is mentioned here is liked by the Rājasa type of men. Vide the Gītā.

कट्वम्ललवणात्युष्णतीक्ष्णरूक्षविदाहिनः ।
आहारा राजसस्येष्टा दुःखशोकामयप्रदाः ॥ (XVII ९)

In olden days leafy vegetables were not frequently used. 'शाकेन वर्धते व्याधि:' is an oft-quoted saying on the point. *Kṣāra* is explained by Utpala thus: 'द्रव्याणां संयोगं कृत्वा दग्ध्वा च क्षारं कारयेत् ।' This alkali is the Yavakṣāra which is explained by Kṣīrasvāmin as 'दग्ध्वा यवाङ्कुराञ्जन्यते यवक्षार: ।' Utpala quotes the following verse on the method of preparation and uses of the Kṣāra :—

क्षारो विषैंडगजचिर्भिटचव्यवह्नि-
व्योषं च संस्तरचितं लवणोपधानम् ।
दग्ध्वा विचूर्ण्य दधिमस्तुयुतं प्रयोज्यं
गुल्मोदरश्वयथुपाण्डुगदोद्भवेषु ॥]

———

गन्धयुक्तिः ॥ ७७ ॥

Chapter LXXVII—Preparation of Perfumes

The word *yukti* means, among others, combination and composition. Perfumes and scents are manufactured for the benefit of royal personages and inmates of harems. All these things show that the level of scientific and industrial enterprise was pretty high in ancient India. In fact civilization grows if peoples' desire increases for a happier living, which in turn finds new avenues of getting luxury goods. The commentator quotes the following verses from a *Nighaṇṭu* lexicon, to enable the student to understand the meanings of words used in the text :

अथात्र व्यवहारार्थं निघण्टुरभिलिख्यते ।
कस्तूरी मदनी नाभिर्मदो दर्पो मृगोद्भवा ॥

मृगदर्पो मृगमदो गन्धचेल्येकवाचकाः ।
स्फटिकेन्दुतुषाराख्यं कर्पूरं घनसारकम् ॥

काश्मीरं घुसृणं रक्तसंज्ञकं कुङ्कुमं विदुः ।
वानराख्यं चलाख्यं च तैलं सिह्लं तुरुष्ककम् ॥

कालीयं जोङ्गकं लोहं खलः कार्पासिकोऽगुरुः ।
हिमं शीताख्यमाहेयं मलयाख्यं च चन्दनम् ॥

सूक्ष्मैला बहुलाख्या च चन्द्रैला द्राविडी त्रुटिः ।
श्रीपुष्पं देवपुष्पं च लघुपुष्पं लवङ्गकम् ॥

कोलं कोलककक्कोले फलं जाती विदुर्बुधाः ।
उष्णं कटुफलं जातिं मालतीं जातिपत्रिकाम् ॥

फलं पत्रं तमालं च गन्धपत्रं च नेत्रकम् ।
भृङ्गाख्यं नेत्रराजं च वराङ्गं त्वक् तनुत्वचस् ॥

गणकाख्यं काञ्चनाख्यं केसरं नागकेसरम् ।
रसं गन्धरसं पिण्डरसं बोलं चलं विदुः ॥

पूतिकोशो बिडालाख्यश्चेलिस्तज्जातकाभिधः ।
लता लतानाभिनाम्नी रेणुः कुन्ती हरेणुका ॥

मेघाख्यं मुस्तमिच्छन्ति वक्राख्यं तगरं नतम् ।
करजाख्यं नखं शङ्खं तथा नखपदं स्मृतम् ॥

ज्वरक्षयोत्पलाख्यं च वाप्यं कुष्ठं गदोऽथ रुक् ।
मांसीं केशीं पिशाचीं च नलदं कमलं जटाम् ॥
श्यामा प्रियाख्या श्रीसंज्ञा प्रियङ्गुः फलिनी स्मृता ।
ग्रन्थिपर्णी ग्रन्थिपर्णं शुकं स्थौणेयकं विदुः ॥
ह्रीबेरं वारिसंज्ञं च ह्रीवारं बालकं स्मृतम् ।
रणं सेव्यं मृणालाख्यमुशीरमिह कथ्यते ।
रामो मृणालो रामञ्जो व्यामकं दवदग्धकम् ॥
प्रवालं विद्रुमाख्यं च वल्ली स्यान्नलिका नली ।
स्पृक्काऽसृग् ब्राह्मणी माला देवी च परिभाष्यते ॥
चक्राङ्गी कटुकी गन्धा जटिलोग्रा जया वचा ।
कचुं कर्चूरमुग्रं च गन्धमूलं च कीर्त्यते ॥
पुष्पा समन्तपुष्पा च शतपुष्पा शता मसिः ।
कुसुमालो भवेच्चण्डः स्तेनश्चौरोऽथ तस्करः ॥
आकृष्टं केशपलितं जरा स्थविरसंज्ञितम् ।
गिर्याख्यं गिरिजाख्यं च शैलेयं समुदाहृतम् ॥
दार्वी दारु निशाख्या च कालेयं पीतचन्दनम् ।
पीता हरिद्रा नक्ताख्या दारु तद्देवदारु यत् ॥
रक्ता समङ्गा मञ्जिष्ठा मधुकं मधुयष्टिका ।
धान्याकं धान्यकं धानीयकं कुस्तुम्बुरु स्मृतम् ॥
मरुं मरुवकं मूर्वी फणिज्जं सानवं तथा ।
सर्जा सर्जरसासंज्ञा राला चेह निगद्यते ॥
पुरं गुग्गुलु भद्रं च भद्राख्यं महिषाक्षकम् ।
रोहिषं पेशलं प्राहुः पर्यासं च कुठेरकम् ॥
क्षीरदध्याज्यसंज्ञश्च श्रीवासः श्रीश्च वासकः ।
जतु लाक्षा कृमिस्तज्जा धात्रीमामलकं विदुः ॥
हरीतक्यभया पथ्या विजया प्राणदाऽपि च ।
कलिर्विभीतकं चाक्षं त्रिफलं स्यादिदं त्रिकम् ॥
शुण्ठीमरीचपिप्पल्यस्त्र्यूषणं सर्वसंयुता ।
त्रिफला सत्रिजाता च त्रिवर्गं त्रितयं स्मृतम् ॥
त्वक् पत्रेला त्रिजातं स्याच्चतुर्जातं सकेसरम् ।
त्रिफला स्यात्तु कक्कोलकटुजातिफलैस्त्रिभिः ॥
घृतेन्दुकुङ्कुमैः पञ्चसुगन्धिः कोलपुष्पवत् ।
कोलोज्झितः सदर्पश्च देवराजः सदैव हि ॥
कर्पूरं कुङ्कुमं दर्पं त्रितयं स्यात् त्रिगन्धिकम् ।
लवङ्गफलकक्कोलकटुकर्पूरकुङ्कुमैः ॥

त्वग्लताजातिचूतोत्थरसैर्दंशसुगन्धिकः ।
तीक्ष्णं मरीचमिच्छन्ति चित्रकं वह्निसंज्ञितम् ॥
रोचना रुचिरा ज्ञेया शर्करा सिकता सिता ।
पुष्पासवः पुष्परसः सारघं मधु माक्षिकम् ॥
क्षौद्रं भ्रामरमित्याहुस्तन्मलं सिक्थकं विदुः ।
मदनं च मधूच्छिष्टं मधुसारं च पण्डिताः ॥
द्राक्षा फलोत्तमा बिल्वः श्रीफलः श्रीतरुस्तथा ।
लुङ्गं च मातुलुङ्गं च केशरी बीजपूरकम् ॥
सौभाञ्जनं सुभाञ्जं च शिग्रुवत्फलपल्लवाः ।
अजो वस्तो जरश्छागो मूत्रं स्रावस्तदम्बु वा ॥
त्वक्सहा सुरभिर्वञ्ची सुरभिश्च महातरुः ।
स्वर्णक्षीरी स्वर्णलता ज्योतिष्मत्यभिधीयते ॥
सुवीरं काचिकं वीरं तालुमालं च तालुकम् ।
सौभाग्यं टङ्कणं टङ्कं बाकुची मालतीभवम् ॥
निःसारं राक्षसं पद्मं कच्छं कतकजं फलम् ।
आम्रश्चूतश्च कामाङ्गः सहकारः स्मरप्रियः ॥
अक्षरं कोकिलाक्षश्च निघण्टुज्ञैरुदाहृतः ।

स्रग्गन्धधूपाम्बरभूषणाद्यं न शोभते शुक्लशिरोरुहस्य ।
यस्मादतो मूर्धजरागसेवां कुर्याद्यथैवाञ्जनभूषणानाम् ॥ १ ॥

As garlands, perfumes, incense, fine clothes, ornaments and the like do not shine in a man of grey hairs, one ought to use hair-dyes, just as one does collyrium for the eyes and ornaments.

[In the opinion of the author people with grey hair should add one item i.e. dyeing the hair, to their daily routine. One with grey hair need not wear fine clothes. This verse and 6 are in उपजाति metre.]

लौहे पात्रे तण्डुलान् कोद्रवाणां शुक्ते पक्वाँल्लोहचूर्णेन साकम् ।
पिष्टान्सूक्ष्मं मूर्ध्नि शुक्ताम्लकेशे दत्वा तिष्ठेद्वेष्टयित्वार्द्रपत्रैः ॥ २ ॥

याते द्वितीये प्रहरे विहाय दद्याच्छिरस्यामलकप्रलेपम् ।
सञ्छाद्य पत्रैः प्रहरद्वयेन प्रक्षालितं कार्ष्ण्यमुपैति शीर्षम् ॥ ३ ॥

Cook the grains of Kodrava (*Paspalum scrobiculatum*) in sour gruel or vinegar in an iron vessel; grind them well with iron dust and make a fine paste. After washing the hair with sour gruel (or vinegar) apply this paste to the head. Then, covering the head with green (juicy) leaves, remain for six hours. Thereafter remove the paste from the head and apply a paste of myrobalan (*Emblica officinalis*). Cover it again with green leaves and retain it for another six hours. On being washed, the hair will become black.

[In all the editions शुक्ल has been printed by mistake in the place of शुक्त. Kṣīrasvāmin quotes (under III. 3-83) the following verse from some Vaidyaka text.

यन्मूलादि शुचौ भाण्डे सक्षौद्रगुडकाञ्जिकम् ।
धान्यराशौ त्रिरात्रस्थं चुक्रं शुक्तं तदुच्यते ॥

The first is in शालिनी metre and verses 3, 4, 11, 22, 34 and 36 are in इन्द्रवज्रा metre.]

पश्चाच्छिरःस्नानसुगन्धतैलैर्लोहाम्लगन्धं शिरसोऽपनीय ।
हृद्यैश्च गन्धैर्विविधैश्च धूपैरन्तःपुरे राज्यसुखं निषेवेत् ॥ ४ ॥

After that one should remove the smell of the iron and vinegar by bathing the head and by the application of perfumed hair-oils, and then enjoy in the harem the pleasures of royalty along with pleasing perfumes and a variety of incense.

[Again the author uses निषेवेत् instead of निषेवेत. Here we have to admire Utpala's candid confession that he is not well-versed in this particular subject and its practical procedures :

अत्र द्रव्याणां सर्वेषां प्रायः काञ्जिकेन क्षालनं निर्मलेन केषाञ्चिज्जलेन केषाञ्चिद्गोमूत्रेण नखतिलतैलेनायसभाण्डे पचेत् । मृद्वग्निना पाकवेधगन्धधूपनानि लोकतो ज्ञेयानि । आचार्येण नोक्तानि । अस्माभिर्ग्रन्थविस्तरभयान्न प्रदर्शितानि : यतः सकलसंहिताऽस्माभिर्व्याख्यातुमारब्धा केवलमत्राक्षराणां व्याख्या क्रियते, न चास्माकमत्र तथाविधं प्रावीण्यम् । अतस्तज्ज्ञैर्लोकव्यवहारतः कार्यः प्रयोगनिश्चयः ॥]

Next the author speaks of royal head-bath.

त्वक्कुष्ठरेणुनलिकास्पृक्कारसतगरवालकैस्तुल्यैः ।
केसरपत्रविमिश्रैर्नरपतियोग्यं शिरःस्नानम् ॥ ५ ॥

A scented water fit for the washing of kings' head is prepared with equal quantities of woody cassia, costus (*Saussurea lappa*), Reṇukā (*Piper aurantiacum*), Nalikā (*Hibiscus* cannabinus), Spṛkkā). (*Bryonopsis* laciniosa ?), Rasa or Bola (Commiphora myrrha), Tagara (Valeriana Wallichii), Vālaka (*Aporosa lindieyana*), Nāgakesara (*Mesua* ferrea) and Patra (*Laurus cassia*).

मञ्जिष्ठया व्याघ्रनखेन शुक्त्या त्वचा सकुष्ठेन रसेन चूर्णः ।
तैलेन युक्तोऽर्कमयूखतप्तः करोति तच्चम्पकगन्धि तैलम् ॥ ६ ॥

A hair-oil having the perfume of the *campaka* flower (Michelia champaca) is made by mixing together equal quantities of the powders of Mañjiṣṭhā (*Rubia* cordifolia), *Vyāghranakha* (a tree or cuttle fish bone), *Nakha* (shell perfume), woody cassia, costus (*Saussurea lappa*) and *Bola* (*commiphora myrrha*) and the whole thing being mixed with the oil of *Sesamum indicum*, being heated by the Sun's rays.

[*Vyāghranakha* and *Śukti*, according to the commentator, are animal products. However, these names are found in the vegetable kingdom as well.]

तुल्यैः पत्रतुरुष्कवालतगरैर्गन्धः स्मरोद्दीपनः
सव्यामो बकुलोऽयमेव कटुकाहिङ्गुप्रधूपान्वितः ।
कुष्ठेनोत्पलगन्धिकः समलयः पूर्वो भवेच्चम्पको
जातीत्वक्सहितोऽतिमुक्तक इति ज्ञेयः सकुस्तुम्बुरुः ॥ ७ ॥

A scent called *Smaroddipana* (which aggravates passion) is prepared with equal quantities of Patra (*Laurus cassia*), juice of Turuṣka (*Tagetes erecta*), Vāla *Aporosa lindieyana*) and Tagara (*Valeriana wallichii*). The same ingredients along with *Vyāmaka*, being fumigated with Kaṭuka (*Picrorhiza kurroa*) and *Commiphora roxburghii* (i.e. Guggulu), yield a scent named *Bakula* i.e. similar to that of the flower of *Mimusops elengi*. The same with costus (*Saussurea lappa*) generates 'lotus-scent', and with Candana (*Santalum* album) 'Campaka-scent'. With Jātīphala (*Myristica fragrans*), woody cassia and coriander (*coriandrum sativum*) the above composition produces "Jasmine-scent'.

[*Hiṅgu* is taken by Utpala in the sense of Guggulu, which is preferable to 'asafoetida'. The word *Turuṣka*, whose synonym is *yāvana*, may throw some light on the history of incense in India. From ancient times traders from the West must have come to India to sell their materials of incense. Amarasiṁha too mentions this word in II. 6-128. The metre is शार्दूलविक्रीडित.]

शतपुष्पाकुन्दुरुकौ पादेनार्धेन नखतुरुष्कौ च ।
मलयप्रियङ्गुभागौ गन्धो धूप्यो गुडनखेन ॥ ८ ॥

Take one part of each of Śatapuṣpā (*Pimpinella anisum*),

Kunduruka (*Boswellia serrata*), Sandalwood and Priyaṅgu (*Aglaia* roxburghiana), and two of each of Nakha (shell perfume) and Turuṣka (*Tagetes erecta* ?), and fumigate the mixture with jaggery and Nakha. This becomes a good scent.

[Here the author does not give details of preparation. The commentator adds here a useful hint to the manufacturers: यत्र यत्र गन्धो धूप्यते तत्रादावेव हरीतक्या धूप्यः पश्चादुक्तद्रव्येणेत्यागमविदः प्राहुः । This shows his knowledge of the works on the subject.]

गुग्गुलुबालकलाक्षामुस्तानखशर्कराः क्रमाद्धूपः ।
अन्यो मांसीबालकतुरुष्कनखचन्दनैः पिण्डः ॥ ९ ॥

Guggulu, Vālaka, lac, Mustā bulbs (*cyperus rotundus*), Nakha and sugar in equal quantities constitute a compound perfume or incense. Another is made with Jaṭāmāṁsī (Nardostachys jatamansi), Vālaka, Turuṣka, Nakha and Candana.

[Here *Piṇḍa* means a compound incense. This word occurs in the *Amara* and is explained by Kṣīrasvāmin thus : पिण्डको द्रव्यान्तरैः सह पिण्डितः स्वरूपाच्च च्यवते ।]

हरीतकीशङ्खघनद्रवाम्बुभिर्गुडोत्पलैः शैलकमुस्तकान्वितैः ।
नवान्तपादादिविवर्धितैः क्रमाद्भवन्ति धूपा बहवो मनोहराः ॥ १० ॥

Many delightful perfumes are made from Harītakī (*Terminalia chebula*), Śaṅkha (Nakha), Ghana (*Cyperus rotundus* ?), Bola, Vālaka, jaggery, costus, benzoin and Mustaka bulbs by mixing them in proportions indicated by multiples of $\frac{1}{8}$th.

[Both *Ghana* and *Mustaka* mean one and the same thing. It may be that the author means घनसार, camphor, by घन. The third quarter is to be explained thus : There are nine ingredients mentioned here. You may take them in any order you like. In the first instance you take 1 part of Harītakī, 2 of Śaṅkha, 3 of Ghana, 4 of Bola, 5 of Vālaka, 6 of jaggery, 7 of costus, 8 of benzoin and 9 of Mustaka. This is one type of perfume. In this manner we can prepare 19 or 362880 varieties of perfumes. The commentator suggests another method of combination : Take the first five constituents mentioned in the verse and combine them in such a way that each succeeding thing is increased by one part i.e. a. 1 part, b. 2, c 3, d. 4 and e. 5 parts. This is one perfume. In the *second* you add 2 more ingredients of 6 and 7 parts respectively. In the *third* you add the last two of 8 and 9 parts respectively. Next you can have other combinations thus : Take 1 part of *a* and 2 of b. This becomes a new Dhūpa.

Next add to the above 3 parts of c. This is yet another variety. In this manner if you go on adding the ingredients, you will get 8 varieties of Dhūpa, according to this method.

The metre is वंशस्थ.]

भागैश्चतुर्भिः सितशैलमुस्ताः श्रीसर्जभागौ नखगुग्गुलू च ।
कर्पूरबोधो मधुपिण्डितोऽयं कोपच्छदो नाम नरेन्द्रधूपः ॥ ११ ॥

Four parts of each of sugar, benzoin and *Cyperus rotundus*, two parts of turpentine and resin (or *Shorea robusta*) as well as of Nakha and Guggulu, mixed with camphor powder and rolled into a ball with honey, make a royal perfume called *Kopacchada* or *Anger-lid* (which cools tempers).

[Our commentator has already revealed his knowledge of *Āgama* despite his modesty and here he quotes from a Prākṛta work, *Gandhavukti*, of one *Iśvara* :

ओल्लंमि ओल्लओ जो दिज्जइ वेह इति सो भणिओ ।
वोहो उण जो चुण्णो चुण्णविणि अच्छगन्धो सो ॥
आर्द्रे आर्द्रो यो दीयते वेध इति स भणितः ।
बोधः पुनर्यश्चूर्णश्चूर्णिते अच्छगन्धः सः ॥

The mixing together of two liquids is known as *Vedha* or *Piercing*, while that of two powders *Bodha* or *Expansion.*]

त्वगुशीरपत्रभागैः सूक्ष्मैलार्धेन संयुतैश्चूर्णः ।
पुटवासः प्रवरोऽयं मृगकर्पूरप्रबोधेन ॥ १२ ॥

Take equal quantities of woody cassia, Uśīra (*Vetiveria Zizanioides*) and Patra (*Laurus cassia*) and a half of the above of small cardamoms (*Elettaria cardamomum*) and pound them together into fine powder; which should be mixed (reinforced) with musk and camphor. This will make an excellent toilet powder (perfume for clothes).

[In the place of पुटवास some read पटवास. The former means अङ्गोद्धूलनम्. This shows that kings and other rich persons were using toilet powder and scents for their dress in ancient times.]

घनवालकशैलेयककर्पूरोशीरनागपुष्पाणि ।
व्याघ्रनखस्पृक्कागुरुमदनकनखतगरधान्यानि ॥ १३ ॥
कर्पूरचोलमलयैः स्वेच्छापरिवर्तितैश्चतुर्भिरतः ।
एकद्वित्रिचतुर्भिर्भागैर्गन्धार्णवो भवति ॥ १४ ॥

The *Gandhārṇava* (*Perfume-ocean*) is prepared from the following sixteen substances, if every four of them are permuted variously at will and that in one, two, three or four parts. The substances are

Cyperus rotundus, Aporosa lindieyana, benzoin, camphor Vetiveria zizanioides, Mesua ferrea, cuttle fish bone, Bryonopsis laciniosa. Aquilaria agallocha, Randia dumetorum, shell perfume, valeriana wallichii, coriander, Hedychium spicatum, Scirpus articulatus and Candana.

[Here altogether 96 varieties are obtained. Each set of four items has 24 permutations. Hence the four sets together will have $24 \times 4 = 96$ perfumes. The four sets are shown in the accompanying diagram below.

Ghana	Vâlaka	Śaibya	Karpūra
Uśīra	Nāgapuṣpa	Vyāghra-nakha	Spṛkkā
Aguru	Madanaka	Nakha	Tagara
Dhānya	Karcūra	Coraka	Candana

The commentator explains in detail how we get six varieties for each of the 4 ingredients with one part.]

अत्युल्बणगन्धत्वादेकांशो नित्यमेव धान्यानाम् ।
कर्पूरस्य तद्वनो नैतौ द्वितयादिभिर्देयौ ॥ १५ ॥

In no perfume should more than one part of coriander be used, as its smell is too strong. Camphor, being stronger still in smell, should be used in a still lesser proportion. These two, therefore, ought not to be mixed in two, three or four parts.

[After giving a general rule the author here makes an exception in respect of coriander and camphor which have very prominent smell of their own. In view of this proviso the total number of perfumes in the *Gandhārṇava* scheme will have to be suitably reduced.]

श्रीसर्जगुडनखैस्ते धूपयितव्याः क्रमान्न पिण्डस्थैः ।
बोधः कस्तूरिकया देयः कर्पूरसंयुतया ॥ १६ ॥

All the above-named products should be fumigated *separately*, and not in a mixture, with turpentine, resin, jaggery and shell perfume; and then they should be mixed with musk and camphor.

[Fumigation and *Bodha*, mixing, mentioned here constitute the final touches to the perfumes. If these are done, the products attain a high water-mark of excellence.]

अत्र सहस्रचतुष्टयमन्यानि च सप्ततिसहस्राणि ।
लक्षं शतानि सप्त विंशतियुक्तानि गन्धानाम् ॥ १७ ॥

The total number of perfumes resulting from the sixteen ingredients being mixed in all possible combinations is 174720 (i.e. 4000+70000+100000+720).

[Mathematics plays no insignificant role in almost all branches of Sanskrit learning. Our author was an astronomer, to boot. Either this verse is spurious, or it has been wrongly copied. For, there is a deficit of one Mātrā in the second quarter of the first line, and in the third quarter. They are rectified thus:—सप्तती-सहस्राणि। लक्षं सप्तशतानि च···।]

एकैकमेकभागं द्वित्रिचतुर्भागिकैर्युतं द्रव्यैः ।
षड्गन्धकरं तद्वद्द्वित्रिचतुर्भागिकं कुरुते ॥ १८ ॥

Each ingredient or substance taken in one part, being combined with three others in two, three and four parts successively, makes six varieties of scents. So do the others that are taken in two, three and four parts.

[This and the following two verses are in explanation of verses 13-14. Each one of the four substances in a set is to be taken as the starting point with its own part as one, while those of the remaining three will be fluctuating between two and four.]

द्रव्यचतुष्टययोगाद्गन्धचतुर्विंशतिर्यथैकस्य ।
एवं शेषाणामपि षण्णवतिः सर्वपिण्डोऽत्र ॥ १९ ॥

As in this manner four substances combined in different proportions produce 24 perfumes, even so the other tetrads. Hence the sum is 96.

षोडशके द्रव्यगणे चतुर्विकल्पेन भिद्यमानानाम् ।
अष्टादश जायन्ते शतानि सहितानि विंशत्या ॥ २० ॥

Out of the group of 16 substances, the number of perfumes that can be prepared by selecting any four at a time will be 1820.

[The method of arriving at the number 1820 is explained in verse 22 infra.]

षण्णवतिभेदभिन्नश्चतुर्विकल्पो गणो यतस्तस्मात् ।
षण्णवतिगुणः कार्यः सा सङ्ख्या भवति गन्धानाम् ॥ २१ ॥

Since this sum viz. 1820, is got by combining in four different ways the 96 variations, it should be multiplied by 96. The product will be the total of possible combinations of perfumes i.e. 174720.

[The commentator here makes a pertinent observation : एतद् गौणवृत्त्या न मुख्यया मुख्यवृत्त्या ४३६८० भवन्ति । यतश्चतुर्विकल्पो गणश्चतुर्विंशति-भेदभिन्नः । When 1820 is multiplied by 24 the product is 43680.]

पूर्वेण पूर्वेण गतेन युक्तं स्थानं विनान्त्यं प्रवदन्ति सङ्ख्याम् ।
इच्छाविकल्पैः क्रमशोऽभिनीय नीते निवृत्तिः पुनरन्यनीतिः ॥ २२ ॥

Write in a vertical column the numbers 1 to 16 upwards; in a second column by its side write 1, and then write above that the sum of the first two figures of the first column, viz. 3; add this result to the third number and write it above that; continue this process until you reach the penultimate number i.e. 15. Repeat this process in the third and fourth columns also, in each column the last number being neglected. The last number of the last column will give the number 1820.

[The ancient method of getting at the final number is explained by the commentator through the adjoining figure :

16			
15	120		
14	105	560	
13	91	455	1820
12	78	364	1365
11	66	286	1001
10	55	220	715
9	45	165	495
8	36	120	330
7	28	84	210
6	21	56	126
5	15	35	70
4	10	20	35
3	6	10	15
2	3	4	5
1	1	1	1

The numbers 1 to 16 in the first column represent in order the 16 substances mentioned in verses 13-14 *supra*. First, take the first three substances as constant and the fourth as variable. Then you can get 13 perfumes. Next, take substances 1, 3 and 4 as constant and one of the rest as variable. Then you will get 12 perfumes. Proceeding further in the same manner, you will get 11, 10, 9, 8, 7, 6, 5, 4, 3, 2, 1 varieties or 91 in all.

Next let us take 1, 2 and 4 as constant and one of the remaining as variable. Then we get 12 perfumes. By taking 1, 3 and 5 as constant, the number will be 11 and so on. The total will then be 78;

Similarly making 1, 2, 5; 1, 3, 6; 1, 4, 7 etc. as constant, we shall get 11, 10, 9, 8, 7, 6, 5, 4, 3, 2, 1 or a total of 66 varieties.

In this manner we shall get 91, 78, 66, 55, 45, 36, 28, 21, 15, 10, 6, 3, 1 or a grand total of 1820.

This is nothing but the number of combinations of 16 things taken 4 at a time (16c4) = 1820. Here, the commentator says that he has not given the processes of purification, cooking, *Vedha*, *Bodha* and fumigation etc. of the ingredients for fear of prolixity. We wish he had given some details of these too.]

द्वित्रीन्द्रियाष्टभागैरगुरुः पत्रं तुरुष्कशैलेयौ ।
विषयाष्टपक्षदहनाः प्रियङ्गुमुस्तारसाः केशः ॥ २३ ॥

स्पृक्कात्वक्तगराणां मांस्याश्च कृतैकसप्तषड्भागाः ।
सप्तर्तुवेदचन्द्रैर्मलयनखश्रीककुन्दुरुकाः ॥ २४ ॥

Take 2, 3, 5 and 8 parts respectively of Aguru, Patra, Turuṣka and Śaibya: 5, 8, 2 and 3 of Priyaṅgu, Mustā, Bola and Keśa (Vālaka) respectively; 4, 1, 7 and 6 in order of Spṛkkā, Tvak, Tagara and Māṁsī; and lastly 7, 6, 4 and 1 of Candana, Nakha, turpentine and Kunduruka.

[Put the substances in 4 rows of 4 each with their proportions as shown in the figure.]

Aguru 2	Patra 3	Turuṣka 5	Śaibya 8
Priyaṅgu 5	Mustā 8	Bola 2	Keśa 3
Spṛkkā 4	Tvak 1	Tagara 7	Māṁsī 6
Candana 7	Nakha 3	Śrīka 6	Kunduruka 1

षोडशके कच्छपुटे यथा तथा मिश्रिते चतुर्द्रव्ये ।
येऽत्राष्टादश भागास्तेऽस्मिन् गन्धादयो योगाः ॥ २५ ॥

नखतगरतुरुष्कयुता जातीकर्पूरमृगकृतोद्बोधाः ।
गुडनखधूप्या गन्धाः कर्तव्याः सर्वतोभद्राः ॥ २६ ॥

In a receptacle of 16 divisions in whatever manner (horizontally, vertically, diagonally etc.) you may mix four substances, you get 18 proportions for each of the various compounds of perfumes. Further, each of the compounds should be blended with Nakha, Tagara and Turuṣka, be mixed (re-inforced) with nutmeg, camphor and musk; and lastly be fumigated with jaggery and Nakha. In this manner are prepared scents called *Sarvatobhadra*—'Good for all purposes.'

[Here the rule is that you may choose four substances in any manner, provided their total proportions are 18. You get this number by combining the four corners, or four things in each corner, or the central four columns, or the four central ones on the four sides.]

जातीफलमृगकर्पूरबोधितैः ससहकारमधुसिक्तैः ।
बहवोऽत्र पारिजाताश्चतुर्भिरिच्छापरिगृहीतैः ॥ २७ ॥

Many perfumes for the mouth with the smell of Pārijāta (*Erythrina indica*) flower can be prepared from any tetrad among the above-mentioned 16 substances. They should, further, be re-inforced with nutmeg, musk and camphor, and sprinkled with mango-juice and honey.

[The commentator misreads at one place सिक्त : as सिक्थकै : (bees wax.]

सर्जरसश्रीवासक समन्विता येऽत्र सर्वधूपास्तैः ।
श्रीसर्जरसवियुक्तैः स्नानानि सवालकत्वग्भिः ॥ २८ ॥

In all perfumes into whose composition enter resin and turpentine, replace the latter two by Vālaka (*Aporosa lindieyana*) and woody cassia, and you will get perfumes for bathing.

रोध्रोशीरनतागुरुमुस्तापत्रप्रियङ्गुवनपथ्याः ।
नवकोष्ठात्कच्छपुटाद्द्रव्यत्रितयं समुद्धृत्य ॥ २९ ॥

चन्दनतुरुष्कभागौ शुक्त्यर्धं पादिका च शतपुष्पा ।
कटुहिङ्गुलगुडधूप्याः केसरगन्धाश्चतुरशीतिः ॥ ३० ॥

Make a receptacle of nine divisions and enter in them the following substances : Lodhra (*Symplocos* paniculata). Uśīra (*Vetiveria Zizanioides*), Nata (*Valeriana wallichii*). Aguru (*Aquilaria agallocha*) Mustā (*Cyperus rotundus*), Patra (*Laurus cassia*), Priyaṅgu (*Aglaia roxburghiana*). Vana (*Kyllinga* monocephala) and Harītakī (*Terminalia chebula*). Take any triad of substances from them and add to them one part of each of Candana and Turuṣka (*Tagetes* erecta ?) a half of Nakha (shell perfume) and a quarter of Śatapuṣpā (*Pimpinella anisum*), and fumigate the whole with Kaṭuka (*Picrorhiza kurroa*), Hiṅgula (black *Aquilaria agallocha*) and jaggery. In this way 84 varieties of perfumes of the fragrance of Bakula (*Mimusops elengi*) flowers are obtained.

[The two relevant diagrams are shown below :

Lodhra	Uśīra	Nata
Aguru	Mustā	Patra
Priyaṅgu	Vana	Pathyā

9		
8	36	
7	28	84
6	21	56
5	15	35
4	10	20
3	6	10
2	3	4
1	1	1

सप्ताहं गोमूत्रे हरीतकीचूर्णसंयुते क्षिप्त्वा ।
गन्धोदके च भूयो विनिक्षिपेद्दन्तकाष्ठानि ॥ ३१ ॥

एलात्वक्पत्राञ्जनमधुमरिचैर्नागपुष्पकुष्ठैश्च ।
गन्धाम्भः कर्तव्यं कश्चित्कालं स्थितान्यस्मिन् ॥ ३२ ॥

जातीफलपत्रैलाकर्पूरैः कृतयमैकशिखिभागैः ।
प्रवचूर्णितानि भानोर्मरीचिभिः शोषणीयानि ॥ ३३ ॥

Put tooth-sticks for a week in cow's urine mixed with the powder of Harītakī (*Terminalia chebula*), and then take them out and dip them again in a scented water prepared from equal quantities of small cardamoms, woody cassia, *Laurus cassia*, Añjana (Sauvīra-antimony?) honey, pepper, Nāgapuṣpa (Mesua ferrea) and costus, for half a night. Then powder them with a mixture of four parts of nutmeg, two of Patra, one of small cardamoms and three of camphor. This should then be dried in the sun.

[This is an excellent recipe for tooth-powder. Special sticks are prescribed for this. Vide LXXXV *infra*. As men use artificial food and bad artificial life, their dental health is affected and they are forced to use artificial teeth. I am sure, our author's prescription, if adhered to, would help in arresting tooth-decay among people]

वर्णप्रसादं वदनस्य कान्ति वैशद्यमास्यस्य सुगन्धितां च ।
संसेवितुः श्रोत्रसुखां च वाचं कुर्वन्ति काष्ठान्यसकृद्भवानाम् ॥ ३४ ॥

Tooth-sticks (that have been treated thus) impart brightness of complexion (or clarity of expression), facial lustre, cleanliness and fine smell of the mouth, and an agreeable voice, to persons who make use of them.

कामं प्रदीपयति रूपमभिव्यनक्ति
सौभाग्यमावहति वक्त्रसुगन्धिताञ्च ।
ऊर्जं करोति कफजांश्च निहन्ति रोगां-
स्ताम्बूलमेवमपरांश्च गुणान् करोति ॥ ३५ ॥

Betel stimulates love, reveals physical charm, enhances personal magnetism (i.e. makes one attractive), gives good smell to the mouth, strengthens the body, and dispels diseases arising from the vitiation of phlegm. It also bestows many other advantages.

[The word Ūrja, according to kṣīrasvāmin, is not Sānta. The commentator says that the other benefits are cleaning the throat, clearing the urine (?) and removing toxins. The metre of this and the last verse is वसन्ततिलका. This verse reminds us of Bhartṛhari's famous line :

किं किं न साधयति कल्पलतेव विद्या ।]

युक्तेन चूर्णेन करोति रागं रागक्षयं पूगफलातिरिक्तम् ।
चूर्णाधिकं वक्त्रविगन्धकारि पत्राधिकं साधु करोति गन्धम् ॥ ३६ ॥

Betel leaves used with a moderate dose of lime imparts red-colour (or love); an extra quantity of betel-nut spoils colour (or passion); excessive lime produces bad smell in the mouth; while an extra quantity of betel-leaf, pleasant smell.

[The author seems to have used the word Rāga in a double sense. The alliteration is quite pleasing.

In the next verse the author advises people when they should use more of leaves and when more of the betel-nut.]

पत्राधिकं निशि हितं सफलं दिवा च
प्रोक्तान्यथाकरणमस्य विडम्बनैव ।

कक्कोलपूगलवलीफलपारिजातै-
रामोदितं मदमुदा मुदितं करोति ॥ ३७ ॥

At night it is beneficial to have an over-dose of betel-leaf, while by day, of areca-nut. To change this order is a mere farce of betel-chewing. When betel-leaf is made fragrant by means of Kakkola (*Luffa echinata*), areca-nut, the fruit of Lavalī (*cicca acida*) and Jātīphala (*Myristica fragrans*), it makes one happy with the joy of amorous ardour.

[The author gives here a good tip to those who chew *pan* or Tāmbūla. Tobacco, no doubt, was not known in India at that time. Betel leaves were chewed with lime and betel-nut and swallowed. It helps digestion too. Caraka praises this habit. Even smoking of medicinal substances was permitted. The *Dhūmavarti* (Smoke wick), which was of various types, was considered a help for preserving health, provided it was used not more than thrice a day. Poet Bāṇa refers to it in the description of King Śūdraka. The commentator is wrong in identifying Lavalī fruit with Lavaṅgapuṣpa. Its fruit is astringent.]

पुंस्त्रीसमायोगः ॥ ७८ ॥

Chapter LXXVIII—Union of Man and Woman

शस्त्रेण वेणीविनिगूहितेन विदूरथं स्वा महीषी जघान ।
विषप्रदिग्धेन च नूपुरेण देवी विरक्ता किल काशिराजम् ॥ १ ॥

एवं विरक्ता जनयन्ति दोषान् प्राणच्छिदोऽन्यैरनुकीर्तितैः किम् ।
रक्ता विरक्ताः पुरुषैरतोऽर्थात् परीक्षितव्याः प्रमदाः प्रयत्नात् ॥ २ ॥

It is learnt that king Vidūratha was murdered by his own queen with a weapon concealed in her tresses, and that the king of Kāśī by his disaffected queen with her anklets smeared with poison. In this manner, women, when they are disgusted with one, bring about dangers amounting to death. What is the use of enumerating other troubles ? Hence, men ought to examine carefully whether the damsels are really attached to or disgusted with them.

[The two instances of feminine treachery are alluded to by *kāmandaka* and later by *Bāṇa* in the *Harṣacarita.* In ancient times kings used to have many queens in their harems. It may happen that at times some of the beautiful queens are agents of foreign powers for bringing about the king's downfall. This chapter deals mostly with erotics and the signs of real love and disaffection. This shows some affinity to dramatics. There are also some features found in astrology and Dharmaśāstra.

Vide कामन्दकि—

स्नातानुलिप्तः सुरभिः स्रग्वी रुचिरभूषणः ।
स्नातां स्वदत्तवसनां पश्येद् देवीं सभूषणाम् ॥
न हि देवीगृहं गच्छेदात्मीयात्सन्निवेशनात् ।
अत्यन्तवल्लभोऽपीह विस्रब्धः स्त्रीषु न व्रजेत् ॥
देवी गृहगतोद्भ्रान्ता भद्रसेनं ममार यत् ।
मातुः शय्यान्तरासीनं कारूपं चौरसं सुतम् ॥
लाजान् विषेण संयोज्य मधुनेति विलोभितम् ।
देवी तु काशीराजेन्द्रं निजघान रहोगतम् ॥

विषाक्तेन च सौवीरं मेखलामणिना नृपम् ।
नूपुरेण च वैवर्त्यं तद्रूपं दर्पणेन च ॥
वेण्यां शस्त्रं समादाय तथैव च विदूरथम् ॥

[The metre of these two verses and of 5 to 8 and 14 to 18 is उपजाति.]

स्नेहं मनोभवकृतं कथयन्ति भावा
नाभीभुजस्तनविभूषणदर्शनानि ।
वस्त्राभिसंयमनकेशविमोक्षणानि
भ्रूक्षेपकम्पितकटाक्षनिरीक्षणानि ॥ ३ ॥

Love arising from sexual desire is revealed by tell-tale blush etc., by exposing the navel, arms, bosoms and ornaments, by re-tying the garments, by loosening the locks, by twitches and tremblings of the brows, and by side-long glances.

[This shows that Varâhamihira, like Kālidāsa, was proficient in the *Kāmasūtra*.

Cf. कश्यप—

अनुरागस्थिता रक्ता विरक्ता वेशमानिनी ।
मनोदृष्टिनिबन्धेन हृदयेनाकुलीकृता ॥
आकारलिङ्गभेदैश्च ज्ञायते याऽनुरागिणी ।
विक्षिप्तमन्यचित्तत्वं गुरुगेहेऽप्यगोपनम् ॥
आह्लादनं च शब्देन यस्याः सा रागरञ्जिता ।
अतोऽपरा तु या नारी सा विरक्तेति कीर्तिता ॥

The metre is वसन्ततिलका]

उच्चैः ष्ठीवनमुत्कटप्रहसितं शय्यासनोत्सर्पणं
गात्रास्फोटनजृम्भणानि सुलभद्रव्याल्पसम्प्रार्थना ।
बालालिङ्गनचुम्बनान्यभिमुखे सख्याः समालोकनं
दृक्पाताश्च पराङ्मुखे गुणकथा कर्णस्य कण्डूयनम् ॥ ४ ॥

इमां च विन्द्यादनुरक्तचेष्टां प्रियाणि वक्ति स्वधनं ददाति ।
विलोक्य संहृष्यति वीतरोषा प्रमार्ष्टि दोषान् गुणकीर्तनेन ॥ ५ ॥

तन्मित्रपूजा तदरिद्विषत्वं कृतस्मृतिः प्रोषितदौर्मनस्यम् ।
स्तनोष्ठदानान्युपगूहनं च स्वेदोऽथ चुम्बाप्रथमाभियोगः ॥ ६ ॥

Other tokens of love are : A loud clearing of the throat and spitting, loud laughter in the presence of the lover, walking towards his seat or bed (or getting up from her seat or bed and walking towards him), producing sounds with limbs, yawning, asking for trivial and easily available things, embracing and kissing a child, looking significantly at a female friend, casting glances at him when he looks elsewhere, recounting his virtues, and scratching the ears. A damsel who speaks sweetly, spends her own money (for his sake), feels delighted on seeing him, forgets her anger, drowns his faults by extolling his virtues, honours his friends, hates his enemies, feels grateful to him for his good turns, feels miserable when he is away, offers her bosoms and lips, embraces him, perspires, and kisses him first, is also to be understood as one deeply attached through her actions.

[For similar ideas vide the साहित्यदर्पण III. 140-152.

Cf. काश्यप—

दृष्टिर्निक्षिपते तत्र मनसापि विचिन्तयेत् ।
मूलैर्न रक्षते सा तु चित्रं चित्रपटे यथा ॥
अकस्मात् पुरतो भूत्वा कश्चिदाश्लिषति भृशम् ।
ऊरू नितम्बे नाभी च भूषणानि पयोधरौ ॥
करजैरुत्किरेन्नाभिमनुरागेण रञ्जिताम् ।
जृम्भते ष्ठीवतेऽत्यर्थं वाग्दुष्टानि ददाति सा ॥
कुमारालिङ्गनं चैव दशनैरधरं दशेत् ।
एभिर्विकारैर्विज्ञेया मदनार्त्ता तु कन्यका ॥
दर्शनाद्हृष्यते या तु मित्रपक्षं च पूजयेत् ।
स्मितं पराङ्मुखं पश्येद् गुणांश्चैवानुकीर्तयेत् ॥

The metre of verse 4 and 12 is शार्दूलविक्रीडित.]

विरक्तचेष्टा भ्रुकुटीमुखत्वं पराङ्मुखत्वं कृतविस्मृतिश्च ।
असम्भ्रमो दुष्परितोषता च तद्द्विष्टमैत्री परुषं च वाक्यम् ॥ ७ ॥

स्पृष्ट्वाथवालोक्य धुनोति गात्रं करोति गर्वं न रुणद्धि यान्तम् ।
चुम्बाविरामे वदनं प्रमार्ष्टि पश्चात्समुत्तिष्ठति पूर्वसुप्ता ॥ ८ ॥

The following are the indications of the disaffection of a woman :—A frowning face, turning away the face (from the lover), forgetting the good turns done by him, indifference, not being pleased with anything offered, kindness towards his enemies, harsh words, shuddering on touching or seeing him, (or being touched she looks and shakes her limbs), assuming arrogance, not preventing him from going away, wiping off the mouth after being kissed, going to bed first and getting up last.

[Cf. कश्यप—

दष्ट्वा न दृश्यते मूढा स्पृष्ट्वा दुर्वचनं वदेत् ।
रतिकालावगूढा तु चुम्बिनी मार्जयेन्मुखम् ॥
सुप्ता विबुध्यते पश्चाच्छयने तु पराङ्मुखी ।
विरक्ता सा स्मृता नारी वर्जनीया प्रयत्नतः ॥

Here we find कश्यप and elsewhere काश्यप. I feel it is one and the same person. I think there is a reading स्पृष्टाथ in the place of स्पृष्ट्वाथ in verse 8.]

भिक्षुणिका प्रव्रजिता दासी धात्री कुमारिका रजिका ।
मालाकारी दुष्टाङ्गना सखी नापिती दूत्यः ॥ ९ ॥

कुलजनविनाशहेतुर्दूत्यो यस्मादतः प्रयत्नेन ।
ताभ्यः स्त्रियोऽभिरक्ष्या वंशयशोमानवृद्ध्यर्थम् ॥ १० ॥

Buddhist nuns, female ascetics, hand-maids, nurses, virgins, washer-women, flower-sellers, corrupt women, female companions and barbers' wives serve as go-betweens. As these are the causes of the ruin of respectable families, one should carefully protect women from them in order to enhance the reputation and honour of the family.

[It is well known that during the period of our author Buddhism was very popular in India, and so were their nuns. The word *Bhikṣuṇikā* is not, strictly speaking, a Sanskrit one; it is a Sanskritized Prākṛta word. The word रजिका is ungrammatical. In Alaṁkāra Sāstra the following Dūtīs are mentioned :

दूत्यः सखी नटी दासी धात्रेयी प्रतिवेशिनी ।
बाला प्रव्रजिता कारूः शिल्पिन्याद्याः स्वयं तथा ॥

Five kinds of *Kārus* (artisans) are mentioned viz. washer-man, carpenter, weaver, barber and cobbler. In this connection we can remind ourselves of what Arjuna says on कुलजनविनाश (I. 41-42).

अधर्माभिभवात्कृष्ण प्रदुष्यन्ति कुलस्त्रियः ।
स्त्रीषु दुष्टासु वार्ष्णेय जायते वर्णसङ्करः ॥
सङ्करो नरकायैव कुलघ्नानां कुलस्य च ।
पतन्ति पितरो ह्येषां लुप्तपिण्डोदकक्रियाः ॥]

रात्रौविहारजागररोगव्यपदेशपरगृहेक्षणिकाः ।
व्यसनोत्सवाश्च सङ्केतहेतवस्तेषु रक्ष्याश्च ॥ ११ ॥

Nocturnal recreation or walking, vigils, professing illness, staying in another's house, consultations with sooth-sayers, taking part in congregational mournings and festivals are occasions when women come in close contact with other men. Hence, they ought to be guarded on such occasions.

[Cf. काश्यप—

दुष्टसङ्गरता या तु सा क्षिप्रं नाशयेत् कुलम् ।
तीर्थयात्राटनं भेदे परवेश्मसमागमम् ॥
देवालये रात्र्यटनं परस्परनिवासिभिः ।
पितृवेश्मनिवासं च न श्रेयः स्वामिना विना ॥
घृतकुम्भोपमा नारी पुरुषवह्निवर्चसः ।
संश्लेषाद् द्रवते कुम्भस्तद्वत् स्त्री पुंसि भाविता ॥
निर्जने तु विविक्ताङ्गं या स्त्री पुरुषमीक्षते ।
तस्याः प्रस्विद्यते गुह्यमनुग्राह्येच्छयान्विता ॥]

आदौ नेच्छति नोज्झति स्मरकथां व्रीडाविमिश्रालसा
मध्ये ह्रीपरिवर्जिताभ्युपरमे लज्जाविनम्रानना ।
भावैर्नैकविधैः करोत्यभिनयं भूयश्च सा सादरा
बुद्ध्वा पुम्प्रकृतिं च यानुचरति ग्लानेतरैश्चेष्टितैः ॥ १२ ॥

A loving damsel would at first evince no desire, but would not give up amorous talk; in the beginning of the sexual act, she would be bashful and languid; in the middle, she would be free from bashfulness, and at the end, bashfully hang down her face. Then again she would show, during coitus, various graceful expressions of sentiment, and perceiving the disposition of her lover attentively adapt herself to him in movements indicative of weariness or enthusiasm, as the case may be.

[The description fully tallies with the nature of Śṛṅgāra heroines of Sanskrit dramas. *Bhāva* has been defined by *Viśvanātha* (III. 118) thus :—

निर्विकारात्मके चित्ते भावः प्रथमविक्रिया ।

Here the commentator quotes extensively from an Alaṁkāra work entitled *Bāhulaka* :—

लीला विलासो विच्छित्तिर्विभ्रमः किलकिञ्चितम् ।
मोट्टायितं कुट्टमितं बिब्बोको ललितं तथा ॥

विहृतं चेति विज्ञेया दश स्त्रीणां स्वभावजाः ।
तथा च—
वागङ्गालङ्करणैः श्लिष्टैः प्रीतिप्रयोजकैर्मधुरैः ।
इष्टजनस्यानुकृतिर्लीला ज्ञेया प्रयोगज्ञैः ।।
स्थानासनगमनानां हास्यभ्रूकर्मणां चैव ।
उत्पद्यते विशेषो यः श्लिष्टः स तु विलासः स्यात् ।।
मालाच्छादनभूषणविलेपनानादरन्यासः ।
स्वल्पोऽपि परां शोभां जनयेद् या सा तु विच्छित्तिः ।।
विविधानामर्थानां वागङ्गाहार्यसत्त्वयुक्तानाम् ।
मदरागहर्षजनितो व्यत्यासो विभ्रमः प्रोक्तः ।।
स्मितहसितरुचितभयपुलकरोषगर्वश्रमाभिलाषाणाम् ।
सङ्करकरणं हर्षादसकृत् किलकिञ्चितं ज्ञेयम् ।।
इष्टजनस्य कथायां हेलालीलादिदर्शनेनापि ।
तद्भावभावनकृतं तन्मोट्टायितमभिख्यातम् ।।
केशस्तनादिपीडनरागादतिहर्षसम्भ्रमोत्पन्नम् ।
कुट्टमितमनुवदन्ति हि सुखस्य दुःखोपचारेण ।।
इष्टानां भावानां प्राप्तावभिमानगर्भसम्भूतः ।
स्त्रीणामनादरकृतो बिब्बोको नाम विज्ञेयः ।।
हस्तपादादिविन्यासे भ्रूनेत्रौष्ठे प्रयोजिते ।
सौकुमार्यं भवेद् येन ललितं तत्प्रकीर्तितम् ।।
वाच्यानां प्रीतियुक्तानां प्राप्तानां यदभाषणम् ।
व्याजात् स्वभावतो वापि विहृतं नाम तद्भवेत् ।।

Viśvanātha enumerates 18 *Alaṁkāras* of women including the ten mentioned here. He distinguistes three kinds of these Alaṁkāras (ornaments) among the 28 *Sattvaja* ones, viz. 7 *Artless* or *Effortless* ones, 3 *Physical ones*, and 18 *Svabhāvaja* or *Natural* ones.]

स्त्रीणां गुणा यौवनरूपवेषदाक्षिण्यविज्ञानविलासपूर्वाः ।
स्त्रीरत्नसंज्ञा च गुणान्वितासु स्त्रीव्याधयोऽन्याश्चतुरस्य पुंसः ।। १३ ।।

The excellences of women are youth, beauty, charming dress, favourable attitude, knowledge of the arts of winning man's affection, graceful gait and the like. The best of those, possessed of the above excellences, are termed 'Gems of women', whereas others are only "Feminine Diseases for a cultured man".

[This verse should be read with LXXIV 4 and 17. In Bhāsa's *Svapnavāsavadatta* we come across such excellent qualities in the characters of Vāsavadattā and Padmāvatī. The epithet स्त्रीष्वाश्रयः is similar to Kālidāsa's line, "यान्त्येवं गृहिणीपदं युवतयो वामाः कुलस्याधयः" which must have been in the mind of Varāhamihira while writing this verse. Every group of things and beings has its gem according to the dictum : "जातौ जातौ यदुत्कृष्टं तद्रत्नमिति कथ्यते ।

Cf. also Sage व्यास

यस्य भार्या शुचिर्दक्षा मिष्टान्नप्रियवादिनी ।
आत्मगुप्ता भर्तृभक्ता सा श्रीरित्युच्यते बुधैः ॥
या च भार्या विरूपाक्षी कश्मला कलहप्रिया ।
उत्तरोत्तरवक्त्री च सा जरा न जरा जरा ॥
निर्विण्णे निर्विण्णा मुदिते मुदिता समाकुलाऽऽकुलिते ।
प्रतिबिम्बसमा कान्ता सङ्क्रुद्धे केवलं भीता ॥

The metre here and in 25 is इन्द्रवज्रा.]

न ग्राम्यवर्णैर्मलदिग्धकाया निन्द्याङ्गसम्बन्धिकथां च कुर्यात् ।
न चान्यकार्यस्मरणं रहःस्था मनो हि मूलं हरदग्धमूर्तेः ॥ १४ ॥

A woman ought not to discuss in vulgar language topics pertaining to the unseemly parts of the body, while she herself is unclean; nor should she while in the company of her lover in privacy, remember other duties or tasks. For, the mind is the root or birth place of Love whose body was burnt by Lord Śiva. [A woman whose body is unclean with rustic colours i.e. with dirt gathered from her household duties, should not talk of the private parts etc to her lover.

[The commentator interprets ग्राम्यवर्णैः as प्राकृतभाषिणीभिः or rustic women. I feel that that is not the intention of author. For, when she is physically unattractive on account of the dirt and dust on her body gathered during her domestic chores, a talk of private parts would rouse passion, but any activity of love at that time would be unnatural and mean. Love would be full and in the plenitude of its power when both mind and body are in harmony. That is why the woman is advised not to have any thought, except that of physical enjoyment, during sensual congress or when she is alone with her lover. This verse is a beautiful piece of art on account of the अर्थान्तरन्यास (general statement), which would remind one of the poet's famous line "मनो हि जन्मान्तरसङ्गतिज्ञम्"]

श्वासं मनुष्येण समं त्यजन्ती बाहूपधानस्तनवानवक्षा ।
सुगन्धकेशा सुसमीपरागा सुप्तेऽनुसुप्ता प्रथमं विबुद्धा ॥ १५ ॥

A woman who breathes in unison with her lover, is ready to make her arms a pillow for him, offers skilfully her breasts to him, has her locks finely scented, goes to sleep after he has fallen asleep and wakes up before he does, has sincere and abiding love for him.

[Utpala interprets सुसमीपरागा as शोभनं समीपे निकटे रागोऽनुरागो यस्याः । सुरतारम्भ एव जायते रागो यस्या इत्यर्थः ।

Cf. काश्यप

परस्परमनोरामै रमयित्वा मनः स्त्रियाः ।
गर्भं सम्भरते श्रेष्ठं सुभगं दीर्घजीवितम् ॥
दुर्मनःस्थौ विरक्तौ च भवेतां सङ्गमे यदि ।
तदा विरूपश्चाल्पायुर्मुक्ताङ्गो दुःखितो भवेत् ॥

Our author knew the psychological implications of the union of man and women. When the union is considered as a spiritual act, a veritable sacrifice, how abominable should humanity consider forced cohabitations and the like!]

दुष्टस्वभावाः परिवर्जनीया विमर्दकालेषु च न क्षमा याः ।
यासामसृग्वासितनीलपीतमाताम्रवर्णं च न ताः प्रशस्ताः ॥ १६ ॥

या स्वप्नशीला बहुरक्तपित्ता प्रवाहिनी वातकफातिरक्ता ।
महाशना स्वेदयुताङ्गदुष्टा या ह्रस्वकेशी पलितान्विता वा ॥ १७ ॥

मांसानि यस्याश्च चलन्ति नार्या महोदरा खिक्खिमिनी च या स्यात् ।
स्त्रीलक्षणे याः कथिताश्च पापास्ताभिर्न कुर्यात्सह कामधर्मम् ॥ १८ ॥

Those women that are wicked by nature and are impatient or incompetent during coitus, ought to be avoided. Inauspicious are those whose blood is dark, blue, yellow or slightly copper-red. Even so are those that are sleepy by nature, have too much blood and bile, have a dripping (or burning) organ, are of a rheumatic and phlegmatic constitution, gluttonous, sweaty, with deformed limbs, short-haired and with (prematurely) grey hair. Those whose muscles are flaccid, who have pot-bellies, and who produce some indistinet sounds always, as well as those who have been declared sinful in the chapter on the signs of damsels are to be shunned; and one ought not to have sexual relations with such women.

[प्रदाहिनी is another reading in the place of प्रवाहिनी in verse 17. The असृग् mentioned here is the menstrual one. प्रदाहिनी is explained thus : प्रकर्षेण यस्या गमने पुरुषस्य शिश्ने दाहो जायते । पुरतो दाहमुत्पादयति । For the inauspicious characteristics vide LXX. 16-23 *infra.*]

शशशोणितसङ्काशं लाक्षारससन्निकाशमथवा यत् ।
प्रक्षालितं विरज्यति यच्चासृक् तद्भवेच्छुद्धम् ।। १९ ।।

यच्छब्दवेदनावर्जितं त्र्यहात्सन्निवर्त्तते रक्तम् ।
तत्पुरुषसम्प्रयोगादविचारं गर्भतां याति ।। २० ।।

The menstrual blood is sound if it resembles hare's blood, or lac, and fades when it is washed. [That is fit for impregnation]. Such blood as is not accompanied by sound and pain, and ceasing to flow after three days, will undoubtedly develop into an embryo after union with man (i.e. with man's sperm).

न दिनत्रयं निषेव्यं स्नानं माल्यानुलेपनं स्त्रीभिः ।
स्नायाच्चतुर्थदिवसे शास्त्रोक्तेनोपदेशेन ।। २१ ।।

पुष्यस्नानौषधयो याः कथितास्ताभिरम्बुमिश्राभिः ।
स्नायात्तथात्र मन्त्रः स एव यस्तत्र निर्दिष्टः ।। २२ ।।

A woman in menses ought not to bathe, nor wear garlands, nor anoint her body (with scents, sandal paste etc.) for three days. She should bathe on the fourth day according to the rules prescribed in the Dharmaśāstras. She should use for her bath the herbs enumerated in the chapter on 'Royal Ablution' (XLVII. 39-42) mixed with water, and the same hymn mentioned there (55-70) will have to be recited on this occasion too.

युग्मासु किल मनुष्या निशासु नार्यो भवन्ति विषमासु ।
दीर्घायुषः सुरूपाः सुखिनश्च विकृष्टयुग्मासु ।। २३ ।।

They say that sexual union on even nights (after menses) produces male children, while on odd nights, female ones. On distant even nights, it leads to the birth of sons who will be long-lived, handsome and happy.

[According to the author the more distant the even night, the better it will be for the issue. The first four nights, no doubt, are forbidden for sexual union. The sixteenth is the last permitted night, as the remaining ones are termed the 'safe period'. These ideas are found in all the *Smṛti* texts.]

दक्षिणपार्श्वे पुरुषो वामे नारी यमावुभयसंस्थौ ।
यदुदरमध्योपगतं नपुंसकं तन्निबोद्धव्यम् ।। २४ ।।

A foetus situated on the right side of the womb will be a male; while one on the left side, a female. One situated on both the sides will be twins and one in the middle is to be understood as a eunuch.

केन्द्रत्रिकोणेषु शुभस्थितेषु लग्ने शशाङ्के च शुभैः समेते ।
पापैस्त्रिलाभारिगतैश्च यायात्पुञ्जन्मयोगेषु च सम्प्रयोगम् ॥ २५ ॥

A man should have sexual union with his wife, when the Kendras (angles) and Koṇas (trines) are occupied by benefics, when the ascendant and the Moon are conjoined with benefics, when malefics occupy the 3rd, 6th, and 11th houses (from the ascendant), and when there are planetary combinations ensuring the birth of a male child.

[For yogas for male birth vide *Bṛhajjātaka* IV. 11; also Phaladīpikā X. 10-11. See also this writer's "Fundamentals of Astrology" page 169.]

न नखदशनविक्षतानि कुर्यादृतुसमये पुरुषः स्त्रियाः कथञ्चित् ।
ऋतुरपि दश षट् च वासराणि प्रथमनिशात्रितयं न तत्र गम्यम् ॥ २६ ॥

A man ought not, on any account, to make any marks on his wife's body with his nails and tooth during her period of impregnation. Such a period lasts for sixteen days, of which the first three nights are unfit for union.

[The author here sounds a note of warning to passionate lovers The ṛtukāla consists of the first 16 nights of which the first three nights are utterly forbidden and even the fourth night is considered unfit for union. This is the last of the five chapters devoted to अन्तःपुरचिन्ता or 'discussion of matters relating to the harem', according to Utpala.

The metre is पुष्पिताग्रा.]

शय्यासनलक्षणम् ॥७९॥

Chapter LXXIX – Signs of Couches and Seats

सर्वस्य सर्वकालं यस्मादुपयोगमेति शास्त्रमिदम् ।
राज्ञां विशेषतोऽतः शयनासनलक्षणं वक्ष्ये ॥ १ ॥

Since this science dealing with the signs of couches and seats is useful for all persons at all times, especially for kings, I shall now expound it.

असनस्पन्दनचन्दनहरिद्रसुरदारुतिन्दुकीशालाः ।
काश्मर्यञ्जनपद्मकशाका वा शिंशपा च शुभाः ॥ २ ॥

The trees recommended for the construction of beds and seats are Asana (*Bridelia montana*), Spandana, Candana, Haridra (*coscinium* fenestratum), deodar (*cedrus deodara*), Tindukī (*Diospyros paniculata*), Śāla (*Shorea robusta*), Kāśmari (*Gmelina arborea*), Añjana (*Moringa oleifera*), Padmaka (*Prunus* cerasoides), Śāka (*Tectona grandis*) and Śiṁśapā (*Dalbergia sissoo*).

अशनिजलानिलहस्तिप्रपातिता मधुविहङ्गकृतनिलयाः ।
चैत्यश्मशानपथिजोर्ध्वशुष्कवल्लीनिबद्धाश्च ॥ ३ ॥

कण्टकिनो ये च स्युर्महानदीसङ्गमोद्भवा ये च ।
सुरभवनजाश्च न शुभा ये चापरयाम्यदिक्पतिताः ॥ ४ ॥

Inauspicious are the trees that have been pulled down by thunderbolts, water, storm and elephants; those in which bees and birds have built their abodes; those growing in sacred spots (or a towering tree in a cluster), burial grounds or roads; those that are withered at the top, and those that are entwined with creepers; so also are thorny trees; those growing at the confluence of great rivers, or near temples, and all those that have fallen in westernly or southernly direction.

प्रतिषिद्धवृक्षनिर्मितशयनासनसेवनात् कुलविनाशः ।
व्याधिभयव्ययकलहा भवन्त्यनर्था अनेकविधाः ॥ ५ ॥

[From the use of couches and seats made from forbidden (inauspicious) trees ensue the ruin of the family, diseases, danger, loss, quarrels and sorts of disasters.]

पूर्वच्छिन्नं यदि वा दारु भवेत्तत्परीक्ष्यमारम्भे ।
यद्यारोहेत्तस्मिन् कुमारकः पुत्रपशुदं तत् ॥ ६ ॥

Or if the timber had been cut formerly, then it should be examined carefully (if there be any signs of the forbidden variety) at the commencement of the work. Should a boy mount the timber, it would lead to the birth of sons and increase of cattle.

सितकुसुममत्तवारणदध्यक्षतपूर्णकुम्भरत्नानि ।
मङ्गल्यान्यन्यानि च दृष्ट्वारम्भे शुभं ज्ञेयम् ॥ ७ ॥

It should be taken as a good augury, if, at the beginning of the work, one happens to see white flowers, a rutting elephant, curds, coloured rice, full pot, gems and other auspicious articles.

In the following verses the author gives the dimensions of beds meant for kings.

कर्माङ्गुलं यवाष्टकमुदरासक्तं तुषैः परित्यक्तम् ।
अङ्गुलशतं नृपाणां महती शय्या जयाय कृता ॥ ८ ॥

A *Practical Digit* is the distance covered by eight husked barley grains touching one another in the middle. A great couch of kings measuring one hundred such digits would ensure victory.

नवतिः सैव षडूना द्वादशहीना त्रिषट्कहीना च ।
नृपपुत्रमन्त्रिबलपतिपुरोधसां स्युर्यथासङ्ख्यम् ॥ ९ ॥

The length of the couches of the royal prince, minister, commander-in-chief of the army and royal preceptor (as well as astrologer) should be in order 90 digits, 84, 78 and 72 digits.

अर्धमतोऽष्टांशोनं विष्कम्भो विश्वकर्मणा प्रोक्तः ।
आयामत्र्यंशसमः पादोच्छ्रायः सकुक्षिशिराः ॥ १० ॥

The width of a couch prescribed by *Viśvakarman* is $\frac{1}{8}$ less than half the length (i.e. $\frac{7}{16}$ of the total length). The height of the legs including the belly and top should be equal to third of the length of the couch.

[The length of a king's couch is 100 digits. So its width should be $100 \times \frac{7}{16}$ or $43\frac{3}{4}$ digits. The height of its legs would be $\frac{100}{3}$ or $33\frac{1}{3}$ digits. The same rule should be applied to the beds of others as well. Vide विश्वकर्मन्.

अन्योन्यमुदरासक्तं वितुषं तु यवाष्टकम् ।
कर्माङ्गुलमिति प्रोक्तं तेन मानेन कारयेत् ॥
नृपाणामङ्गुलशतं शय्या दीर्घा जयावहा ।
नवतिर्नृपपुत्रस्य सा षड्ूना तु मन्त्रिणः ॥
द्वादशोना बलेशस्य त्रिषट्कोना पुरोधसः ।
दैवज्ञमानमेवैतत् तुल्यत्वात्कारयेत्ततः ॥
दैर्घ्यमष्टमभागोनं विष्कम्भः परिकीर्तितः ।
आयामत्र्यंशतुल्यश्च पादोच्छ्रायः प्रकीर्तितः ॥
स कुक्ष्यशिरसो ज्ञेयः शय्यायाः शुभकारकः ।
ऊनाधिका च या शय्या सा ज्ञेया स्वामिनोऽशुभा ॥

There seems to be a mistake in the 7th line of Viśvakarman's text. For it says that the width is equal to the length reduced by an eighth part, while according to our author it is a half of the length diminished by an eighth part. The word कुक्ष्य seems to be a technical term, which Utpala does not explain. I feel that it is a protruding part at the bottom of the leg. For, the author says that the total height of the legs should be a third of the length.]

In the following verses the author mentions the special effects of the timber used.

यः सर्वः श्रीपर्ण्या पर्यङ्को निर्मितः स धनदाता ।
असनकृतो रोगहरस्तिन्दुकसारेण वित्तकरः ॥ ११ ॥

यः केवलशिंशपया विनिर्मितो बहुविधं स वृद्धिकरः ।
चन्दनमयो रिपुघ्नो धर्मयशोदीर्घजीवितकृत् ॥ १२ ॥

यः पद्मकपर्यङ्कः स दीर्घमायुः श्रियं श्रुतं वित्तम् ।
कुरुते शालेन कृतः कल्याणं शाकरचितश्च ॥ १३ ॥

केवलचन्दनरचितं काञ्चनगुप्तं विचित्ररत्नयुतम् ।
अध्यासन् पर्यङ्कं विबुधैरपि पूज्यते नृपतिः ॥ १४ ॥

A cot made wholly of Śrīparṇī (*Gmelina arborea*) bestows wealth; one of Asana (*Aridelia montana*) destroys diseases; one of the pith of Tinduka (*Diospyros paniculata*) leads to wealth; one made wholly of

Śiṁśapā (*Dalbergia sissoo*), to all-round prosperity; one sandal wood destroys enemies and bestows religious merit, fame and long life; one of Padmaka (*Prunus* cerasoides) gives long life, prosperity, learning and wealth; one of Śāla (*Shorea robusta*) or Śāka (*Tectona grandis*), happiness and prosperity. A king, reposing on a cot made entirely of sandal wood and covered with gold and bedecked with wonderful gems, will be honoured even by the Gods.

[It is a well-known fact that Sandal-wood is considered as the queen of timber endowed with many spiritual and medicinal properties. The author has committed a grammatical lapse in अध्यासन् He should have used मध्यासीन: Then he could have written the line as अध्यासीनो मञ्चं....Next he gives the effects of mixing up of the timber in the construction of cots and seats.]

अन्येन समायुक्ता न तिन्दुकी शिंशपा च शुभफलदा ।
न श्रीपर्णेन च देवदारुवृक्षो न चाप्यसनः ॥ १५ ॥

शुभदौ तु शालशाकौ परस्परं संयुतौ पृथक्चैव ।
तद्वत्पृथक् प्रशस्तौ सहितौ च हरिद्रककदम्बौ ॥ १६ ॥

सर्वः स्पन्दनरचितो न शुभः प्राणान् हिनस्ति चाम्बकृतः ।
असनोऽन्यदारुसहितः क्षिप्रं दोषान् करोति बहून् ॥ १७ ॥

अम्बस्पन्दनचन्दनवृक्षाणां स्पन्दनाच्छुभाः पादाः ।
फलतरुणा शयनासनमिष्टफलं भवति सर्वेण ॥ १८ ॥

A cot made of Tindukī or Śiṁśapā along with some other timber will not yield good results; so is one of Deodar or Asana along with Śrīparṇa. The Śāla and Śāka as well as Haridraka and Kadamba (*Anthocephalus indicus*) are good, whether used jointly or separately. A cot wholly made of Spandana or Amba tree (in Marathi. Ambāḍā?) is not auspicious, since it destroys life; one of Asana coupled with some other timber produces immediately all kinds of troubles. It is beneficial to have legs made of Spandana tree for cots made of Amba, Spandana and Candana. Cots and seats made of any fruit-tree will have favourable effects.

गजदन्तः सर्वेषां प्रोक्ततरूणां प्रशस्यते योगे ।
कार्योऽलङ्कारविधिर्गजदन्तेन प्रशस्तेन ॥ १९ ॥

Ivory is highly commended for use in the construction of cots and seats in combination with any of the approved timber. Hence decorations should be made with good ivory.

दन्तस्य मूलपरिधिं द्विरायतं प्रोज्झ्य कल्पयेच्छेषम् ।
अधिकमनूपचराणां न्यूनं गिरिचारिणां किञ्चित् ॥ २० ॥

Cut off the tusk leaving a length (from the bottom) equal to twice the circumference of the tusk at the bottom and use the remainder for decorative purposes. A little more of it will have to be left off in the case of elephants haunting marshy places, and a little less in the case of those haunting mountain-regions.

[Some editions read प्रोह्य in the place of प्रोज्झ्य. The reason why a littte less is to be cut off in the case of elephants living on mountains is given by Utpala thus : यतः पर्वतशिलास्तद्दन्तान् घर्षन्ति । There may be another reason as well, viz. in the marshy places the tusks are not very strong at the root, while in mountains they are hard right from the bottom.]

श्रीवृक्षवर्धमानच्छत्रध्वजचामरानुरूपेषु ।
छेदे दृष्टेष्वारोग्यविजयधनवृद्धिसौख्यानि ॥ २१ ॥

प्रहरणसदृशेषु जयो नन्द्यावर्ते प्रनष्टदेशाप्तिः ।
लोष्टे तु लब्धपूर्वस्य भवति देशस्य सम्प्राप्तिः ॥ २२ ॥

स्त्रीरूपे धननाशो भृङ्गारेऽभ्युत्थिते सुतोत्पत्तिः ।
कुम्भेन निधिप्राप्तिर्यात्राविघ्नं च दण्डेन ॥ २३ ॥

कृकलासकपिभुजङ्गेष्वसुभिक्षव्याधयो रिपुवशित्वम् ।
गृध्रोलूकध्वाङ्क्षश्येनाकारेषु जनमरकः ॥ २४ ॥

पाशेऽथवा कबन्धे नृपमृत्युर्जनविपत् स्रुते रक्ते ।
कृष्णे श्यावे रूक्षे दुर्गन्धे चाशुभं भवति ॥ २५ ॥

On cutting the tusk, if figures resembling a Bilva tree (*Aegle marmelos*), Vardhamāna emblem, umbrella, banner or chowries appear sound health, victory, increase of wealth and happiness are to be expected. A figure like a weapon causes victory; one like a spiral turning to the right, recovery of lost lands; one like a clod, complete possession of a country conquered before; one like a woman, loss of wealth; one like a vase, birth of a son; one like a pot, acquisition of a treasure; one like a rod, obstacle to a journey; those like chameleons, monkeys and serpents, famine, disease and imprisonment at the hands of an enemy; those like eagles, owls, crows and hawks, pestilence; one like a noose or a truncated body, bodes the king's death. If blood comes out from the cut, there will be calamity to the people; if the cut be dark, grey or rough and bad-smelling, there will be disaster.

[The author uses the word विघ्न in the neuter gender instead of the masculine.]

शुक्लः समः सुगन्धिः स्निग्धश्च शुभावहो भवेच्छेदः ।
अशुभशुभच्छेदा ये शयनेष्वपि ते तथा फलदाः ॥ २६ ॥

A cut that is white, even, fine-smelling and glossy, leads to good results. Just as auspicious and inauspicious cuts in ivory produce good and bad results, even so do they in the timber used for couches (and seats).

ईषायोगे दारु प्रदक्षिणाग्रं प्रशस्तमाचार्यैः ।
अपसव्यैकदिगग्रे भवति भयं भूतसञ्जनितम् ॥ २७ ॥

In fitting up the frame of the cot, the tips of the beams should be laid in a direction from left to right; so have the ancient sages declared. If they be laid contrariwise, or all the tips turned to the same direction, there would be danger from ghosts.

[Īṣā is a technical term. It is simply the frame consisting of two short and two long beams. The side beams are fixed into the two smaller ones. While fixing the side beams care should be taken to join the bottom of the head-side beam with the tip of the northern beam and the tip of the former with the bottom of the southern beam. In this arrangement the tip of the leg-side beam will face the north. Thus no two tips will be meeting each other. This is called *Pradakṣiṇāgra* (the tips being fixed in a clockwise manner). We must be beholden to the commentator for the very lucid explanation of the fitting of the frame.]

एकेनावाक्शिरसा भवति हि पादेन पादवैकल्यम् ।
द्वाभ्यां न जीर्यतेऽन्नं त्रिचतुर्भिः क्लेशवधबन्धाः ॥ २८ ॥

If one of the legs is put topsy-turvy, the owner will have one of his feet crippled; if two, he cannot digest his food; and if three or four, he will have misery, captivity and death.

[Here the topsy-turvy position refers to the timber from which the legs are made : The upper part of the tree should not occupy a lower position in the leg.]

सुषिरेऽथवा विवर्णे ग्रन्थौ पादस्य शीर्षगे व्याधिः ।
पादे कुम्भो यश्च ग्रन्थौ तस्मिन्नुदररोगः ॥ २९ ॥

कुम्भाधस्ताज्जङ्घा तत्र कृतो जङ्घयोः करोति भयम् ।
तस्याश्चाधारोऽधः क्षयकृद् द्रव्यस्य तत्र कृतः ॥ ३० ॥

खुरदेशे यो ग्रन्थिः खुरिणां पीडाकरः स निर्दिष्टः ।
ईषाशीर्षण्योश्च त्रिभागसंस्थो भवेन्न शुभः ॥ ३१ ॥

If there be a hollow or a discoloured knot in the upper part of the leg, the owner would have some cerebral ailment. If there be such a knot in its pot, he would have stomach trouble; if in the shank-like part below the pot, danger to his shanks; if in the support beneath that, loss of wealth; if in the hoof (lowest part), trouble to the hoofed animals. Inauspicious also is a knot occurring at a third of the length of the side-beams and cross beams.

[Here the leg is divided into five parts viz. *Śirṣa* or Head, *Kumbha* or Pot, *Jaṅghā* or shanks, *Ādhāra* or Support and *Khura* or Hoof. Though Śīrṣaṇī primarily means the head-side beams, the opposite beam also is to be included under the rule.]

निष्कुटमथ कोलाक्षं सूकरनयनं च वत्सनाभं च ।
कालकमन्यद्धुन्धुकमिति कथितश्छिद्रसङ्क्षेपः ॥ ३२ ॥

The different kinds of blemishes or holes in the wood may be summed up in the following list : *Niṣkuṭa* (cavity) *Kolākṣa* (Boar's Eye), *Sūkaranayana* (Hog's Eye) *Vatsanābha* (Calf's Navel), *Kālaka* (Dark Spot) and *Dhundhuka* (Cut Dark Spot).

घटवत् सुषिरं मध्ये च निष्कुटं छिद्रम् ।
निष्पावमाषमात्रं नीलं छिद्रं च कोलाक्षम् ॥ ३३ ॥

सूकरनयनं विषमं विवर्णमध्यर्धपर्वं दीर्घं च ।
वामावर्तं भिन्नं पर्वमितं वत्सनाभाख्यम् ॥ ३४ ॥

कालकसञ्ज्ञं कृष्णं धुन्धुकमिति यद् भवेद्विनिर्भिन्नम् ।
दारुसवर्णं छिद्रं न तथा पापं समुद्दिष्टम् ॥ ३५ ॥

The blemish or hole called *Niṣkuṭa* is like a pot, hollow in the middle and narrow at the mouth; the second viz. *Kolākṣa*, is blue like a grain of Niṣpāva (*Dolichos lablab*) or Māṣa (*Phascolus* radiatus i.e. black-gram) the third viz. *Sūkaranayana*, is uneven, discoloured and extending over one joint and a half; the fourth viz. *Vatsanābha*, is a spot running from left to right, broken and extending over one joint; the fifth viz. Kālaka, is a black spot; and the sixth viz. *Dhundhuka* is also dark, but cut. A blemish, having the same colour as the wood itself is not deemed so harmful.

निष्कुटसञ्ज्ञे द्रव्यक्षयस्तु कोलेक्षणे कुलध्वंसः ।
शस्त्रभयं सूकरके रोगभयं वत्सनाभाख्ये ॥ ३६ ॥

कालकधुन्धुकसञ्ज्ञं कीटैर्विद्धं च न शुभदं छिद्रम् ।
सर्वंग्रन्थिप्रचुरं सर्वत्र न शोभनं दारु ॥ ३७ ॥

The blemish named *Niṣkuṭa* causes loss of wealth; Kolākṣa, ruin of the family; *Sūkaranayana*, danger from weapons; *Vatsanābha*, threat of disease. The last two blemishes and a hole bored by insects are not beneficial. In general, timber that is full of knots is never good.

एकद्रुमेण धन्यं वृक्षद्वयनिर्मितं च धन्यतरम् ।
त्रिभिरात्मजवृद्धिकरं चतुर्भिरर्थं यशश्चाग्र्यम् ॥ ३८ ॥

पञ्चवनस्पतिरचिते पञ्चत्वं याति तत्र यः शेते ।
षट्सप्ताष्टतरूणां काष्ठैर्घटिते कुलविनाशः ॥ ३९ ॥

A cot or seat made from a single tree is blessed; more blessed is the one made from two kinds of trees; one of three kinds leads to the prosperity of one's children (or to birth of children and prosperity); one of four kinds, to wealth and exceptional fame. One made from five kinds of timber causes the death of the person who sleeps on it; and one of six, seven or eight kinds, the ruin of the family.

[Here 'single tree' means the same kind of timber. In this chapter neither the author nor the commentator names or quotes except in one place authority. Of course the former mentions once Viśvakarman and then refers to Ācāryas and says समुद्दिष्टम् and निर्दिष्टम् Varāhamihira must have had before him many works bearing on this subject.]

रत्नपरीक्षा ॥८०॥

Chapter LXXX—Examination of Gems

रत्नेन शुभेन शुभं भवति नृपाणामनिष्टमशुभेन ।
यस्मादतः परीक्ष्यं दैवं रत्नाश्रितं तज्ज्ञैः ॥ १ ॥

Since a jewel endowed with good characteristics ensures good luck to kings, and one with bad ones, disaster, connoisseurs ought to examine their fortune depending on jewels.

[It is well known that propitiation of evil planets is recommended by astrologers through appropriate gems, apart from worshipping the Deities presiding over the afflicted or afflicting planets. All gems are not found to be satisfactory owing to their having some defects. Hence proper examination and trial of jewels are very essential. In this connection, it may be remembered that planetary colours play an important role in man's life.]

द्विपहयवनितादीनां स्वगुणविशेषेण रत्नशब्दोऽस्ति ।
इह तूपलरत्नानामधिकारो वज्रपूर्वाणाम् ॥ २ ॥

The term 'Gem' is applied, generally, to elephants, horses, women and so on, on account of the excellence of their intrinsic merits; but here the context is that of precious stones such as diamonds.

[Every excellent representative of a class is designated as a 'Gem' in literature. Vide Amara, 'रत्नं स्वजातिश्रेष्ठेपि' Still here we are concerned with precious stones in particular, as they alone come under the *Adhikāra* (content). This word is met with in scientific literature such as Grammar, where there are *Adhikāra* aphorisms; which exercise sway over the entire delineated chapter or topic.]

रत्नानि बलाद्दैत्याद्दधीचितोऽन्ये वदन्ति जातानि ।
केचिद्भुवः स्वभावाद् वैचित्र्यं प्राहुरुपलानाम् ॥ ३ ॥

Gems, they say, were born of the bones of the demon Bala; while others state that they were born of Sage Dadhīci; yet others declare that the wonderful variety of gems is caused by the characteristic qualities of the earth.

[Utpala quotes here some Purāṇic verses :

सम्भूतानि बलाद्दैत्याद्रत्नानि विविधानि च ।
गतानि नानावर्णत्वमस्थिभ्यो भूमिसंश्रयात् ॥
रत्नानि दधीचिमुनेर्जातानि सहस्रशो लोके ।
अस्थिभ्यो भूमिवशाद् नानावर्णत्वमागतानि गुणैः ॥

Dadhīci is also spelt as Dadhīca. He offered his bones to the Gods who got them made into the *Vajrāyudha* by the celestial architect for Indra, who killed the mighty foe Vṛtra with it. Hence diamond is supposed to have originated from the Sage's bones. The last opinion is in agreement with the modern view to the effect that gems are the effect of great subterranean pressure. After all, they say, diamond is nothing but carbon. The commentator is right in his remark : उपला रत्नरूपत्वं प्राप्ताः कालान्तरेणेति प्राहुः ।]

वज्रेन्द्रनीलमरकतकर्केतरपद्मरागरुधिराख्याः ।
वैडूर्यपुलकविमलकराजमणिस्फटिकशशिकान्ताः ॥ ४ ॥

सौगन्धिकगोमेदकशङ्खमहानीलपुष्परागाख्याः ।
ब्रह्ममणिज्योतीरससस्यकमुक्ताप्रवालानि ॥ ५ ॥

The following are the gems :— Diamond, Sapphire, Emerald Agate, Ruby, Blood-stone, Beryl, Amethyst, Vimalaka, Royal gem (quartz?), Crystal, Moon-gem, Saugandhika, Opal, Conch, Azure stone, Topaz, Brahma-gem, Jyotīrasa, Sasyaka, Pearl and Coral.

[The commentator states that out of these 22 kinds of gems only four are most important. They are : diamond, pearl, ruby and emerald. The Ācārya accordingly treats of only these varieties.]

Next he describes the sources, deities etc. of diamonds.

वेणातटे विशुद्धं शिरीषकुसुमप्रभं च कौशलकम् ।
सौराष्ट्रकमाताम्रं कृष्णं सौर्पारकं वज्रम् ॥ ६ ॥

ईषत्ताम्रं हिमवति मतङ्गजं वल्लपुष्पसङ्काशम् ।
आपीतं च कलिङ्गे श्यामं पौण्ड्रेषु सम्भूतम् ॥ ७ ॥

Diamonds got from the banks of the Veṇā river are of the purest kind; those mined in Kosala have the lustre (whitish yellow) of the Śirīṣa flower (*Albizzia lebbeck*); those of Surāṣṭra, a reddish lustre; those of Saurpāra country are dark in colour; those of the Himalayan regions, slightly reddish (or copper coloured); those of Mataṅga country have the colour (pale white) of the Valla blossoms; those of Kaliṅga are yellowish; and those of Pauṇḍra, black.

[For Veṇā vide XVI. 9, XIV. 12 and IV. 26 supra. It is in the Southern Division and is the modern Wainganga, a tributary of the Godāvarī. For Puṇḍra or Pauṇḍra cf. V. 70, IX. 15, X. 14, XI. 27, XVI. 3 etc. The country corresponds to North Bengal and is identified with Mahasthan in Bogra district.]

ऐन्द्रं षडश्रि शुक्लं याम्यं सर्पास्यरूपमसितं च ।
कदलीकाण्डनिकाशं वैष्णवमिति सर्वसंस्थानम् ॥ ८ ॥

वारुणमबलागुह्योपमं भवेत् कर्णिकारपुष्पनिभम् ।
शृङ्गाटकसंस्थानं व्याघ्राक्षिनिभं च हौतभुजम् ॥ ९ ॥

वायव्यं च यवोपमशोककुसुमप्रभं समुद्दिष्टम् ।
स्रोतः खनिः प्रकीर्णकमित्याकरसम्भवस्त्रिविधः ॥ १० ॥

A white hexagonal diamond is presided over by Indra; a dark one of the shape of a snake's mouth by Yama; one with the colour (bluish yellow) of the plantain trunk (*Musa paradisiaca*), and of any shape, by Viṣṇu; one having the colour of the Karṇikāra flower (*Pterospermum acerifolium*) and shaped like the female genital organ (or clitoris), by Varuṇa; a triangular one of the colour of a tiger's eye (bluish red), by Fire; one having the shape of a barley corn and the hue of Aśoka flower (*Saraca indica*), by Vāyu (Wind). Diamonds have three different sources, viz. rivers, mines and other places where gems are found.

रक्तं पीतं च शुभं राजन्यानां सितं द्विजातीनाम् ।
शैरीषं वैश्यानां शूद्राणां शस्यतेऽसिनिभम् ॥ ११ ॥

Red and yellow diamonds are auspicious for Kṣatriyas; white ones, for Brāhmaṇas; those of the hue of Śirīṣa flower (whitish yellow), for Vaiśyas; and those of the colour (dark) of swords, for Śūdras.

सितसर्षपाष्टकं तण्डुलो भवेत्तण्डुलैस्तु विंशत्या ।
तुलितस्य द्वे लक्षे मूल्यं द्वि द्व्यूनिते चैतत् ॥ १२ ॥

पादत्र्यंशार्धोनं त्रिभागपञ्चांशषोडशांशाश्च ।
भागश्च पञ्चविंशः शतिकः साहस्रिकश्चेति ॥ १३ ॥

Eight seeds of white mustard are equal to one rice grain. The price of a diamond weighing 20 rice grains is two lakhs (Kārṣāpaṇas) one weighing 18 grains is worth a lakh and a half Kārṣāpaṇas (silver); one of 16 grains, $2\frac{2}{3}$ lakhs (or 133,333 $\frac{1}{3}$); one of 14 grains, one lakh; one of 12 grains, $\frac{2}{3}$ lakh (or (67,666 $\frac{2}{3}$); one of 10 grains, 40,000; one of eight grains, 12,500; one of six grains, 8,000; one of four grains, 2000; one of two grains 200 Kārṣāpaṇas of silver.

In these two verses the author gives a table of weights for weighing and assessing gems.

80 silver coins make one Paṇa and 20 Paṇas make one Kārṣāpaṇa. Cf. the following :

विशतिः श्वेतिकाः प्रोक्ता काकिण्येका विचक्षणैः ।
तच्चतुष्कं पण इति चतुर्थं तच्चतुष्टयम् ॥
चतुर्थकचतुष्कं तु पुराण इति कथ्यते ।
कार्षापणः स एवोक्तः क्वचित्तु पणविंशतिः ॥

This can be tabulated thus :

20 silver coins = 1 Kākiṇī,
4 Kākiṇīs = 1 Paṇa,
4 Paṇas = 1 Caturtha,
4 Caturthas = 1 Purāṇa or Kārṣāpaṇa.

Thus there are two values of Kārṣāpaṇa viz. 16 Paṇas and 20 Paṇas.]

सर्वद्रव्याभेद्यं लघ्वम्भसि तरति रश्मिवत् स्निग्धम् ।
तडिदनलशक्रचापोपमं च वज्रं हितायोक्तम् ॥ १४ ॥

A diamond is said to be beneficial to the owner, if it cannot be cut by any other substance, is light, cleaves through water like a ray of light, is glossy and similar in lustre to lightning, fire or the rain-bow.

[The commentator wrongly construes the words तरति and रश्मिवत्. The former means, according to him, *sinks*; and the latter, *full of rays*. तरति always means to float or to cross, and रश्मिवत् like a ray, because in the other sense the form would be रश्मिमत्.]

काकपदमक्षिकाकेशधातुयुक्तानि शर्करैर्विद्धम् ।
द्विगुणाश्रि दग्धकलुषत्रस्तविशीर्णानि न शुभानि ॥ १५ ॥

Inauspicious are the diamonds that show scratches like crows, claws. bees or hair, are mixed with coloured mineral substances or pierced by gravel, have double facets, are burnt, discoloured, lustreless or perforated.

यानि च बुद्बुददलिताग्रचिपिटवासीफलप्रदीर्घाणि ।
सर्वेषां चैतेषां मूल्याद् भागोऽष्टमो हानिः ॥ १६ ॥

So also are those that are covered with bubbles, split at the points, flattened, or oblong like the Vâsī fruit (sitsea chinensis ?). The price of all such is one-eighth less than that specified above (on the basis of the weight.)

वज्रं न किञ्चिदपि धारयितव्यमेके
पुत्रार्थिनीभिरबलाभिरुशन्ति तज्ज्ञाः ।
शृङ्गाटकत्रिपुटधान्यकवत् स्थितं य-
च्छ्रोणीनिभं च शुभदं तनयार्थिनीनाम् ॥ १७ ॥

Some authorities are of opinion that women wishing to beget sons should never wear diamonds; but (in our opinion) diamonds that are triangular, trigonal and like the coriander seed, or the buttocks, are productive of good results to damsels desiring male offspring.

[The commentator construes श्रोणीनिभं as स्त्र्यधररागसदृशम् cf. the following :

सुतार्थिनीभिर्धन्याभिर्न धार्यं वज्रसंज्ञकम् ।
यच्च शृङ्गाटकाकारं त्रिपुटं धान्यवत्स्थितम् ॥
श्रोणीनिभं सुवर्णं च स्निग्धं किरणसंयुतम् ।
तच्छस्तं धारणे स्त्रीणां पुत्रवृद्धिप्रदं स्मृतम् ॥

The metre is वसन्ततिलका.]

स्वजनविभवजीवितक्षयं जनयति वज्रमनिष्टलक्षणम् ।
अशनिविषभयारिनाशनं शुभमुपभोगकरं च भूभृताम् ॥ १८ ॥

A diamond with inauspicious characteristics causes the ruin of the wearer's kith and kin, wealth and life; whereas a good one destroys the enemies and danger from thunderbolt and poison. It especially confers a lot of enjoyments on kings.

[Some texts read उरुभोगकरम् instead of उपभोगकरम्.

The metre is अपरवक्त्र.]

मुक्तालक्षणम् ॥ ८१ ॥

Chapter LXXXI – Signs of Pearls

This and the following two chapters are only the subsections coming under the Adhikāra of 'Examination of Gems'.

द्विपभुजगशुक्तिशङ्खाभ्रवेणुतिमिसूकरप्रसूतानि ।
मुक्ताफलानि तेषां बहु साधु च शुक्तिजं भवति ॥ १ ॥

Pearls are got from (i) elephants, (ii) serpents, (iii) pearl-oysters, (iv) conch-shells, (v) clouds, (vi) bamboos, (vii) whales and (viii) hogs; but the best pearls are those that are got from pearl-oysters.

[Mallinātha quotes a similar verse

करीन्द्रजीमूतवराहशङ्खमत्स्याहिवेणूद्भवशुक्तिजानि ।
मुक्ताफलानि प्रथितानि लोके तेषां तु शुक्त्युद्भवमेव भूरि ॥

Kālidāsa refers to pearls being produced in the heads of lordly elephants on the Himalayas, in the following verse.

पदं तुषारस्रुतिधौतरक्तं यस्मिन्नदृष्ट्वापि हतद्विपानाम् ।
विन्दन्ति मार्गं नखरन्ध्रमुक्तैर्मुक्ताफलैः केसरिणां किराताः ॥]

सिंहलकपारलौकिकसौराष्ट्रकताम्रपर्णिपारशवाः ।
कौबेरपाण्ड्यवाटकहैमा इत्याकरास्त्वष्टौ ॥ २ ॥

There are eight sources of the best pearls, viz. (1) Siṁhalaka (Ceylon), (2) Paraloka (Travancore coast), (3) Surāṣṭra (Kathiawad peninsula), (4) Tāmraparṇī river (in the Madras State). (5) Pāraśava (Persia), (6) a Northern country, (7) Pāṇḍya-vāṭaka and (8) the Himalayas.

In ancient India Ceylon and the tiny islands around it were great pearl-producing centres. This is recorded by the Chinese pilgrim Fa-hien (399-414 A.D.). Paraloka is identified with Purali in Kerala. By Surāṣṭra is meant the Gulf of Cambay. The Pāṇḍya country lay in the southernmost part of the Indian peninsula.

बहुसंस्थानाः स्निग्धा हंसाभाः सिंहलाकराः स्थूलाः ।
ईषत्ताम्राः श्वेतास्तमोवियुक्ताश्च ताम्राख्याः ॥ ३ ॥

कृष्णाः श्वेताः पीताः सशर्कराः पारलौकिका विषमाः ।
न स्थूला नात्यल्पा नवनीतनिभाश्च सौराष्ट्राः ॥ ४ ॥

ज्योतिष्मत्यः शुभ्रा गुरवोऽतिमहागुणाश्च पारशवाः ।
लघु जर्जरं दधिनिभं बृहद्द्विसंस्थानमपि हैमम् ॥ ५ ॥

विषमं कृष्णश्वेतं लघु कौबेरं प्रमाणतेजोवत् ।
निम्बफलत्रिपुटधान्यकचूर्णाः स्युः पाण्ड्यवाटभवाः ॥ ६ ॥

The pearls got from Ceylon are multishaped, glossy, swan-white and large; those from the Tāmraparṇī river are white with a slight red tinge, and bright; those from Paraloka (Travancore area) are blackish, white or yellow, mingled with gravel and uneven; those from Surāṣṭra are neither too big nor too small, and with the lustre of butter; those from Persia are lustrous, clear, heavy and very valuable (of a very high calibre); those from the Himalayas are light, broken (discoloured ?), curd-like in appearance, large and double-shaped; those from the Northern country are rough (or uneven), black and white, light, of good size and brilliance; and those from Pāṇḍya-vāṭa are like the Neem fruit (*Azadirachta indica*) or coriander seed, trigonal and very tiny.

[The commentator says that जर्जर means विवर्णम्. About the pearl wealth of the Tāmraparṇī vide the Raghuvaṁśa IV :

ताम्रपर्णीसमेतस्य मुक्तासारं महोदधेः ।
ते निपत्य ददुस्तस्मै यशः स्वमिव सञ्चितम् ॥]

अतसीकुसुमश्यामं वैष्णवमैन्द्रं शशाङ्कसङ्काशम् ।
हरितालनिभं वारुणमसितं यमदैवतं भवति ॥ ७ ॥

परिणतदाडिमगुलिकागुञ्जाताम्रं च वायुदैवत्यम् ।
निर्धूमानलकमलप्रभं च विज्ञेयमाग्नेयम् ॥ ८ ॥

A pearl dark like the Atasī (*Linumusitatissimum*) flower is presided over by Viṣṇu; one like the Moon, by Indra; one having the hue yellow orpiment, by Varuṇa; a dark one, by Yama; one red like the seed of a ripe pomegranate (*Punica granatum*) or a Guñjā (*Abrus precatorius*), by Vāyu; and one having the brilliance of smokeless fire or the lustre of lotus (*Nelumbo nucifera*), by Fire.

माषकचतुष्टयधृतस्यैकस्य शताहता त्रिपञ्चाशत् ।
कार्षापणा निगदिता मूल्यं तेजोगुणयुतस्य ॥ ९ ॥

माषकदलहान्यातो द्वात्रिंशद्विंशतिस्त्रयोदश च ।
अष्टौ च शतानि शतत्रयं त्रिपञ्चाशता सहितम् ॥ १० ॥

पञ्चत्रिंशं शतमिति चत्वारः कृष्णला नवतिमूल्याः ।
सार्धास्तिस्रो गुञ्जाः सप्ततिमूल्यं धृतं रूपम् ॥ ११ ॥

गुञ्जात्रयस्य मूल्यं पञ्चाशद्रूपका गुणयुतस्य ।
रूपकपञ्चत्रिंशत्त्रयस्य गुञ्जार्धहीनस्य ॥ १२ ॥

The price fixed for a pearl of good lustre and quality, weighing four Māṣakas is 53,000 Kārṣāpaṇas Silver. The prices of pearls weighing 3½, 3, 2½, 2 and 1½ Māṣakas in order are 3200, 2000, 1300, 800 and 353 K. Silver. A pearl weighing one Māṣaka is worth 135 K.; one weighing four Guñjās or Rattis is worth 90 K.; one of 3½ Rattis, 70 K.; a good one of 3 Rattis, 50 silver pieces (Kārṣas); one of 2½ Rattis, 35 silver pieces.

[Five Guñjās (Rattis or Kṛṣṇalas) make one Māṣa. For the qualities of gems vide LXXXII. 3.]

पलदशभागो धरणं तद्यदि मुक्तास्त्रयोदश सुरूपाः ।
त्रिशती सपञ्चविंशा रूपकसङ्ख्याकृतं मूल्यम् ॥ १३ ॥

षोडशकस्य द्विशती विंशतिरूपस्य सप्ततिः सशता ।
यत्पञ्चविंशतिधृतं तस्य शतं त्रिशता सहितम् ॥ १४ ॥

त्रिंशत्सप्ततिमूल्यं चत्वारिंशच्छतार्धमूल्यं च ।
षष्टिः पञ्चोना वा धरणं पञ्चाष्टकं मूल्यम् ॥ १५ ॥

मुक्ताशीत्या त्रिंशच्छतस्य सा पञ्चरूपकविहीना ।
द्वित्रिचतुःपञ्चशता द्वादशषट्पञ्चकत्रितयम् ॥ १६ ॥

The 10th part of a pala is called one Dharaṇa. If thirteen good pearls together weigh one Dharaṇa, their price is fixed at 325 K. Silver. Sixteen pearls weighing a Dharaṇa are worth 200 K.; twenty pearls, 170 K.; twentyfive pearls, 130 K,; 30 pearls, 70 K,; 40 pearls, 50 K.; 60 or 55 pearls, 40 K.; 80 pearls, 30 K.; 100 pearls, 35 K.; 200, 300, 400 and 500 pearls weighing together one Dharaṇa are worth in order 12, 6, 5 and 4 silver pieces.

[Cf. the following :

पञ्चकृष्णलको माषस्ते सुवर्णस्तु षोडश ।
पलं सुवर्णाश्चत्वारः............... ॥

5 Guñjās = 1 Māṣa.
16 Māṣas = 1 Suvarṇa,
4 Suvarṇas = 1 Pala.
$\frac{1}{8}$ Pala = 1 Dharaṇa or Suvarṇa.]

पिक्कापिच्चार्घार्धा रवकः सिक्थं त्रयोदशाद्यानाम् ।
सञ्ज्ञाः परतो निगराश्चूर्णाश्चाशीतिपूर्वाणाम् ॥ १७ ॥

The term to denote a collection of 13 pearls which together weigh one Dharaṇa is *Pikkā*; a collection of 16 such pearls is known as *Piccā*; those of 20, 25, 30, 40, 55 and 80 and above are respectively *Arghā*, *Ardhā*, *Ravaka*, *Siktha*, *Nigara* and *Cūrṇa* (dust).

[It would be interesting to know the origin of these names.]

एतद्गुणयुक्तानां धरणधृतानां प्रकीर्तितं मूल्यम् ।
परिकल्प्यमन्तराले हीनगुणानां क्षयः कार्यः ॥ १८ ॥

कृष्णश्वेतकपीतकताम्राणामीषदपि च विषमाणाम् ।
त्र्यंशोनं विषमकपीतयोश्च षड्भागदलहीनम् ॥ १९ ॥

The above is the price fixed for the various collections of pearls of good quality weighing one *Dharaṇa*. The price of intermediate groups of pearls will have to be found out proportionately; but suitable reductions in the prices of inferior pearls should be made as shown below : The price of those that are slightly black, white, yellowish or copper-coloured or slightly uneven (rough), is that given above reduced by a third; whereas that of *utterly* rough and yellow pearls is less by a sixth and a half respectively.

ऐरावतकुलजानां पुष्यश्रवणेन्दुसूर्यदिवसेषु ।
ये चोत्तरायणभवा ग्रहणेऽर्केन्द्वोश्च भद्रेभाः ॥ २० ॥

तेषां किल जायन्ते मुक्ताः कुम्भेषु सरदकोशेषु ।
बहवो बृहत्प्रमाणा बहुसंस्थानाः प्रभायुक्ताः ॥ २१ ॥

नैषामर्घः कार्यो न च वेधोऽस्तीव ते प्रभायुक्ताः ।
सुतविजयारोग्यकरा महापवित्रा धृता राज्ञाम् ॥ २२ ॥

Those elephants that are born in the winter solstice (uttarāyaṇa) during an eclipse of the Sun or the Moon are named *Bhadra*. It is said that pearls are produced in the heads and in the sockets of the tusks of the elephants of Airâvata's family at the Moon's conjunction with the asterism Puṣya or Śravaṇa synchronous with a Sunday or Monday, as well as of the *Bhadra* class of elephants. These pearls are numerous, large, brilliant and of various shapes. These are beyond any estimate and should not be perforated, being too brilliant. When they are worn by kings, they prove highly sanctifying and bestow children, victory and sound health.

[The particle किल indicates that the author is only repeating the traditional account of pearls. He knows full well that ordinary mortals can have only the common variety of pearls got from pearl-oysters.]

दंष्ट्रामूले शशिकान्ति सप्रभं बहुगुणं च वाराहम् ।
तिमिजं मत्स्याक्षिनिभं बृहत् पवित्रं बहुगुणं च ॥ २३ ॥

Very valuable and lustrous like the Moon is the pearl born of the root of the boar's tusks; the pearl got from whales resembles a fish's eye, is large, pure and of great value.

वर्षोपलवज्जातं वायुस्कन्धाच्च सप्तमाद्भ्रष्टम् ।
ह्रियते किल खाद् दिव्यैस्तडित्प्रभं मेघसम्भूतम् ॥ २४ ॥

They say that pearl is produced in the clouds of the seventh layer of wind in the sky in the manner of hail-stones. It falls therefrom with the brilliance of lightning and is taken away (before it reaches the earth) by the denizens of heaven.

[This too is a traditional story. The seven layers of wind are आवहः, प्रवहः, संवहः, उद्वहः, विवहः, परिवहः and परावहः.]

तक्षकवासुकिकुलजाः कामगमा ये च पन्नगास्तेषाम् ।
स्निग्धा नीलद्युतयो भवन्ति मुक्ताः फणस्यान्ते ॥ २५ ॥

शस्तेऽवनिप्रदेशे रजतमये भाजने स्थिते च यदि ।
वर्षति देवोऽकस्मात्तज्ज्ञेयं नागसम्भूतम् ॥ २६ ॥

The serpents of the lineage of Takṣaka and Vâsuki and those that move at will, have bright, blue-tinged pearls on their hoods. If Indra suddenly rains on a blessed spot of the earth and into a silver vessel, it should be recognized as a pearl coming from the serpents.

अपहरति विषमलक्ष्मीं क्षपयति शत्रून् यशो विकासयति ।
भौजङ्गं नृपतीनां धृतमकृतार्घं विजयदं च ॥ २७ ॥

A pearl born of the serpents, being worn by kings, will prove invaluable to them, destroy their misfortune and enemies, enhance their reputation and bestow victory.

कर्पूरस्फटिकनिभं चिपिटं विषमं च वेणुजं ज्ञेयम् ।
शङ्खोद्भवं शशिनिभं वृत्तं भ्राजिष्णु रुचिरं च ॥ २८ ॥

A pearl is to be known to have sprung from bamboo, if it resembles camphor or crystal and is flat and uneven (or rough). The pearl born of conch shell is round, lustrous, beautiful and moon-like.

शङ्खतिमिवेणुवारणवराहभुजगाभ्रजान्यवेध्यानि ।
अमितगुणत्वाच्चैषामर्घः शास्त्रे न निर्दिष्टः ॥ २९ ॥

The pearls got from conch shells, whales, bamboos, elephants, boars, serpents and clouds ought not to be perforated (or cannot be easily recognized); and as they possess inestimable virtues or excellences, no price has been fixed for them by the authorities.

[The commentator takes the reading प्रवेद्यानि and interprets it as प्रवेदनीयानि.]

एतानि सर्वाणि महागुणानि सुतार्थसौभाग्ययशस्कराणि ।
रुक्शोकहन्तॄणि च पार्थिवानां मुक्ताफलानीप्सितकामदानि ॥ ३० ॥

All the above categories of pearls are extremely valuable, and bestow sons, wealth, popularity, renown on the wearers; and they are destroyers of disease and grief and bestowers of desired objects on kings.

[In the light of this verse, the verse 27 appears redundant. At times the author seems to be fond of prolixity. It is possible that such a flaw is a virtue in a *Saṁhitā*. In ईप्सितकामदानि two words are almost synonymous. The metre is उपजाति.]

In the following verses he describes various ornaments made of pearls.

सुरभूषणं लतानां सहस्रमष्टोत्तरं चतुर्हस्तम् ।
इन्द्रच्छन्दो नाम्ना विजयच्छन्दस्तदर्धेन ॥ ३१ ॥

शतमष्टयुतं हारो देवच्छन्दो ह्यशीतिरेकयुता ।
अष्टाष्टकोऽर्धहारो रश्मिकलापश्च नवषट्कः ॥ ३२ ॥

द्वात्रिंशता तु गुच्छो विंशत्या कीर्तितोऽर्धगुच्छाख्यः ।
षोडशभिर्माणवको द्वादशभिश्चार्धमाणवकः ॥ ३३ ॥

मन्दारसञ्ज्ञोऽष्टाभिः पञ्चलता हारफलकमित्युक्तम् ।
सप्तविंशतिमुक्ता हस्तो नक्षत्रमालेति ॥ ३४ ॥

अन्तरमणिसंयुक्ता मणिसोपानं सुवर्णगुलिकैर्वा ।
तरलकमणिमध्यं तद्विज्ञेयं चाटुकारमिति ॥ ३५ ॥

एकावली नाम यथेष्टसङ्ख्या हस्तप्रमाणा मणिविप्रयुक्ता ।
संयोजिता या मणिना तु मध्ये यष्टीति सा भूषणविद्भिरुक्ता ॥ ३६ ॥

A pearl-necklace consisting of 1008 strings and four cubits long, is used as an ornament for Gods and is termed *Inducchanda* (*or Moon's Pleasure*); one half of the above (i.e. 504 strings and 2 cubits long) is termed *Vijayacchanda* (or *Desire for Victory*); one of 108 strings and 2 cubits long is called *Hāra* (or *Necklace*); one of 81, *Devacchanda* (or *Gods' Pleasure*); one of 64 string, *Ardha-hāra* or *Half Necklace*); one of 54, *Raśmikalāpa* (or *Mass of Rays*); one of 32, *Guccha* (or *Bunch*); one of 20, *Ardha-guccha* (or *Half-bunch*); one of 16, *Māṇavaka* (or *Pupil*); one of 12, *Ardhamāṇavaka* (or *Semi-Pupil*); one of 8, *Mandāra*, one of 5 strings, *Hāraphalaka* (or Necklace-Slab). A necklace containing 27 pearls and of one cubit's length is called *Nakṣatramālā* (or *Wreath of Stars*); the same is called *Maṇisopāna* (or *Gem-stairs*) if it has other gems or gold beads inserted; it is called *Cāṭukāra* (or *Coaxer*), when it has a central gem set in gold. *Ekāvali* (or *Single-Stringed*) containing any number of pearls, measures one cubit and is devoid of other gems; but when it is adorned with a gem in the middle, it is designated as a *Yaṣṭi* (or *Stick*) by ornament-experts.

[Altogether 17 varieties of pearl-necklace are mentioned here, the bigger and heavier ones being meant for gods and Demi-gods as well as kings.

The author seems to prize pearls most of all the gems since he has devoted 36 verses to their praise. He has not paid so much attention to diamonds, though he has given them the pride of place. He has given only a single verse for emeralds.

The metre of the last verse is इन्द्रवज्रा.]

पद्मरागलक्षणम् ॥ ८२ ॥

Chapter LXXXII—Signs of Rubies

सौगन्धिककुरुविन्दस्फटिकेभ्यः पद्मरागसम्भूतिः ।
सौगन्धिकजा भ्रमराञ्जनाब्जजम्बूरसद्युतयः ॥ १ ॥

कुरुविन्दभवाः शबला मन्दद्युतयश्च धातुभिर्विद्धाः ।
स्फटिकभवा द्युतिमन्तो नानावर्णा विशुद्धाश्च ॥ २ ॥

Rubies are born of sulphur, Kuruvinda (black salt ?) and crystal. Those got out of sulphur exhibit the lustre of bees, antimony (or collyrium), lily, rose-apple (*Syzygium jambos*) or Rasa (*commiphora myrrha*). Those that are got from Kuruvinda are variegated (or grey), of pale lustre and mixed with mineral substances; those arising from crystal are lustrous, multi-coloured and pure.

[The commentator takes जम्बूरस as one word and explains it thus: जम्बूर्वृक्षविशेषः, तद्रससमकान्तयो लोहितवर्णाः. Would it not be better to construe it as lustre of the juice of Jambu fruits ? For, the author compares the gem to bees in colour.]

स्निग्धः प्रभानुलेपी स्वच्छोऽर्चिष्मान् गुरुः सुसंस्थानः ।
अन्तःप्रभोऽतिरागो मणिरत्नगुणाः समस्तानाम् ॥ ३ ॥

The general qualities of all excellent gems are smoothness, illumination with rays, purity, sparkle, heaviness, fine shape, brilliance within and bright redness.

[The word समस्तानां in this context should mean 'of all varieties of rubies', though it may also mean 'of all kinds of gems, diamonds and the like.' In that case 'अतिरागः' should be construed as 'of deep hue'. In the next verse the flaws of gems are mentioned.]

कलुषा मन्दद्युतयो लेखाकीर्णाः सधातवः खण्डाः ।
दुर्विद्धा न मनोज्ञाः सशर्कराश्चेति मणिदोषाः ॥ ४ ॥

Stones are defective, if they are impure, of dull lustre, full of scratches, mixed with mineral substances, broken, ill-perforated, not attractive, and mixed with gravel.

भ्रमरशिखिकण्ठवर्णो दीपशिखासप्रभो भुजङ्गानाम् ।
भवति मणिः किल मूर्धनि योऽनर्घेयः स विज्ञेयः ॥ ५ ॥

It is said that on the head of serpents there is a gem with the hue of a bee or peacock's neck, and shining like the flame of a lamp. Such a gem is to be known as of inestimable value.

[The author has used an expression, अनर्घेयः, of questionable grammatical soundness. Of course it has led to alliteration. He could have better put it as योऽनर्घोऽयं.]

यस्तं बिभर्ति मनुजाधिपतिर्न तस्य
दोषा भवन्ति विषरोगकृताः कदाचित् ।
राष्ट्रे च नित्यमभिवर्षति तस्य देवः
शत्रूंश्च नाशयति तस्य मणेः प्रभावात् ॥ ६ ॥

A king who wears such a serpent-gem will never have troubles arising from poison and diseases. Indra will always be pouring good rains in his realm, and as a result of the intrinsic power of the gem he will annihilate his enemies.

[The metre is वसन्ततिलका.]

षड्विंशतिः सहस्राण्येकस्य मणेः पलप्रमाणस्य ।
कर्षत्रयस्य विंशतिरुपदिष्टा पद्मरागस्य ॥ ७ ॥

अर्धपलस्य द्वादश कर्षस्यैकस्य षट्सहस्राणि ।
यच्चाष्टमाषकधृतं तस्य सहस्रत्रयं मूल्यम् ॥ ८ ॥

माषकचतुष्टयं दशशतक्रयं द्वौ तु पञ्चशतमूल्यौ ।
परिकल्प्यमन्तराले मूल्यं हीनाधिकगुणानाम् ॥ ९ ॥

वर्णन्यूनस्यार्धं तेजोहीनस्य मूल्यमष्टांशम् ।
अल्पगुणो बहुदोषो मूल्यात् प्राप्नोति विंशांशम् ॥ १० ॥

आधूम्रं व्रणबहुलं स्वल्पगुणं चाप्नुयाद्द्विशतभागम् ।
इति पद्मरागमूल्यं पूर्वाचार्यैः समुद्दिष्टम् ॥ ११ ॥

The price of a single ruby weighing a Pala (i.e. 4 Karṣas) has been fixed at 26,000 silver pieces or Kārṣāpaṇas; one of three Karṣas is worth 20,000 silver pieces; one of half a Pala or 2 Karṣas, 12,000 s.; one of one Karṣa, 6000 s.; one of eight Māṣas or Rattis, 3000 s.;

one of four Māṣas, 1000 s.; one of two Māṣas, 500 s. The price of rubies of intermediate weight must be calculated proportionately, and with due regard to their being of inferior or superior quality. A ruby deficient in colour will fetch half the usual price; one lacking brilliance, an eighth part; one with few good and many bad qualities with fetch only 1/20 of the standard price. A ruby somewhat dusky, with many holes (or scratches) and few good features will fetch 1/200 of its usual price. Thus have the prices of rubies been fixed by the ancient seers.

मरकतलक्षणम् ॥ ८३ ॥

Chapter LXXXIII – Signs of Emeralds

शुकवंशपत्रकदलीशिरीषकुसुमप्रभं गुणोपेतम् ।
सुरपितृकार्ये मरकतमतीव शुभदं नृणां विहितम् ॥ १ ॥

An emerald of the hue of parrots' wings, bamboo leaves, banana trunk (greyish yellow) or Śirīṣa (*Albizzia lebbeck*) blossom (whitish yellow) and of good qualities (such as smoothness, purity etc.), is highly beneficial to people when they wear it at ceremonies in honour of Gods and the *Manes.*

[For the Guṇas or qualities vide LXXXII 3 *supra.* This verse proves that gems have spiritual powers that can be utilized both for remedial and progressive purposes.

Thus these four chapters from LXXX onwards containing 66 verses in all constitute one theme viz. examination of gems. This might throw some light on the question of determination of the 100 Adhyāyas mentioned by the author.]

दीपलक्षणम् ॥ ८४ ॥

Chapter LXXXIV—Signs of Lamps

वामावर्त्तो मलिनकिरणः सस्फुलिङ्गोऽल्पमूर्त्तिः
क्षिप्रं नाशं व्रजति विमलस्नेहवर्त्यन्वितोऽपि ।
दीपः पापं कथयति फलं शब्दवान् वेपनश्च
व्याकीर्णार्चिर्विशलभमरुद् यश्च नाशं प्रयाति ॥ १ ॥

A lamp, whose flame moves from right to left, has dull rays, sputters sparks, is of little bulk, goes out quickly, although furnished with pure oil and wick, crackles, quivers, is diffused and gets extinguished without the agency of grasshoppers or the wind, forebodes evil consequences.

[The metre is मन्दाक्रान्ता.]

दीपः संहृतमूर्त्तिरायततनुर्निर्वेपनो दीप्तिमा-
न्निःशब्दो रुचिरः प्रदक्षिणगतिर्वैडूर्यहेमद्युतिः ।
लक्ष्मीं क्षिप्रमभिव्यनक्ति सुचिरं यश्चोद्यतं दीप्यते
शेषं लक्षणमग्निलक्षणसमं योज्यं यथायुक्तितः ॥ २ ॥

A light of compact (thick) form, long-sized, quiet (not shaky), brilliant, noiseless, beautiful, turned to the right, of the lustre of beryl or gold, and shining long and brilliant, heralds the immediate arrival of the Goddess of Wealth. The other symptoms are similar to those of fire and to be applied to lamps *mutatis mutandis*.

[This chapter seems to be redundant, or it could have been clubbed with XLIII. Vide verses 32, 33 and 35 therein.

[The metre is शार्दूलविक्रीडित.]

दन्तकाष्ठलक्षणम् ॥ ८५ ॥

Chapter LXXXV – Tokens of Tooth-sticks

वल्लीलतागुल्मतरुप्रभेदैः स्युर्दन्तकाष्ठानि सहस्रशो यैः ।
फलानि वाच्यान्यथ तत्प्रसङ्गो मा भूदतो वच्म्यथ कामिकानि ॥ १ ॥

Sticks for cleansing the teeth may be got from thousands of varieties of creepers, spreading plants, shrubs and trees, whose effects should be explained separately, but in order to avoid much prolixity, I shall delineate only those of favourable consequences.

This chapter being closely connected with the subject matter of "Dinacaryādhyāya" in Āyurveda is useful, inasmuch as it is relevant even to the present day society whose personal hygiene it caters for. The metre in this, 2 and 8 is उपजाति.]

अज्ञातपूर्वाणि न दन्तकाष्ठान्यद्यान्न पत्रैश्च समन्वितानि ।
न युग्मपर्वाणि न पाटितानि न चोर्ध्वशुष्काणि विना त्वचा च ॥ २ ॥

One ought not to use the following tooth-sticks : those that have not been tried so far; those that have leaves; those that have an even number of joints; those that are split; those that are withered at the top; and those that are without bark.

[The commentator explains the compound, अज्ञातपूर्वाणि, as a *Bahuvrihi*, which may suggest that the sticks were not merely unknown before, but their properties were not found out and classified.

Unknown twigs may harm the teeth. In this connection we can bear in mind the fact that monkeys that live in the midst of nature have no tooth-troubles.]

वैकङ्कतश्रीफलकाश्मरीषु ब्राह्मी द्युतिः क्षेमतरौ सुदाराः ।
वृद्धिर्वटेऽर्के प्रचुरं च तेजः पुत्रा मधूके सगुणाः प्रियत्वम् ॥ ३ ॥

Tooth-sticks belonging to the *Vikankata* (*Gymnosporia spinosa*), Bilva (*Aegle marmelos*) and Kāśmarī (*Gmelina arborea*) tend to spiritual splendour; those of the Kṣema tree (*Angelica* glauca?) bestow a good wife; of the banyan tree, prosperity; of the Arka (*calotropis gigantea*), great brilliance or power; and of Madhūka (*Cynometra ramiflora*), virtuous sons and popularity.

[All the sticks mentioned here are endowed with not only medicinal properties, but unseen esoteric powers. The metre of this and the following two verses is इन्द्रवज्रा. ककुभे is another reading for सगुणा: Kakubha is *Lagerstroemia speciosa.*]

लक्ष्मीः शिरीषे च तथा करञ्जे प्लक्षेऽर्थसिद्धिः समभीप्सिता स्यात् ।
मान्यत्वमायाति जनस्य जात्यां प्राधान्यमश्वत्थतरौ वदन्ति ॥ ४ ॥

Fortune is ensured by the use of the Śirīṣa (*Albizzia lebbeck*) and Karañja (*Pongamia pinnata*); gain of abundant wealth wished for, by that of the Plakṣa (*Ficus arnottiana*); honour and respect of the people by that of jāti stick (*jasminum officinale*); and prominence, it is said, by that of the Aśvattha stick (*Ficus religiosa*).

आरोग्यमायुर्बदरीबृहत्योरैश्वर्यवृद्धिः खदिरे सबिल्वे ।
द्रव्याणि चेष्टान्यतिमुक्तके स्युः प्राप्नोति तान्येव पुनः कदम्बे ॥ ५ ॥

Good health and long life can be attained by the use of Badarī (*Lizyphus jujuba*) and Bṛhatī (*Solanum xanthocarpum*) respectively; increase of wealth or power (or prosperity and profit), by Khadira (*Acacia catechu*) and Bilva; desired objects, by Atimuktaka (*Ougeinia dalbergioides*) and Kadamba (*Anthocephalus indicus*).

[Utpala notes another reading ऐश्वर्यलब्धि: for ऐश्वर्यवृद्धि: and explains it as ऐश्वर्यं for Khadira and लब्धि for Bilva. I feel that this reading must have been interpolated by some over-enthusiastic scholar before Utpala.]

नीपेऽर्थाप्तिः करवीरेऽन्नलब्धिर्भाण्डीरे स्यादन्नमेवं प्रभूतम् ।
शम्यां शत्रूनपहन्त्यर्जुने च श्यामायां च द्विषतामेव नाशः ॥ ६ ॥

A stick of the Nīpa tree (*Anthocephalus* indicus) confers wealth; one of Karavīra (*Nerium* indicum), plenty of good food; one of Bhāṇḍīra (Indian fig tree?), sumptuous feast. A Śamī *Prosopis spicigera*) stick would enable one to destroy one's enemies. So do those of Arjuna (*Terminalia arjuna*) and Śyāmā (*Echinochloa frumentacea*).

[The metre, coming under अर्धसमवृत्त, has been formed by combining वातोर्मी and शालिनी in the odd and even quarters respectively.]

शालेऽश्वकर्णे च वदन्ति गौरवं सभद्रदारावपि चाटरूषके ।
वाल्लभ्यमायाति जनस्य सर्वतः प्रियङ्ग्वपामार्गसजम्बुदाडिमैः ॥ ७ ॥

It is said that respectability results from the use of Śāla (*Shorea robusta*), Aśvakarṇa, deodar and Āṭarūṣaka (*Adhatoda* vasica). By using the twigs of the Priyaṅgu (*Aglaia roxburghiana*), Apāmārga *Achyranthes aspera*), jambū (*Syzygium jambos*) and pomegranate, one becomes the favourite of one and all.

[According to lexicon, Śāla, Aśvakarṇa and Sarjaka are synonymous. According to our author, however, they are different. The metre is इन्द्रवंशा.]

उदङ्मुखः प्राङ्मुख एव वाब्दं कामं यथेष्टं हृदये निवेश्य ।
अथावनिन्दंश्च सुखोपविष्टः प्रक्षाल्य जह्याच्च शुचिप्रदेशे ॥ ८ ॥

One should use a good tooth-stick, after cherishing in the heart one's desires for the coming year, sitting at ease, facing the north or the east without any resentment; and at the end wash it and leave it in a clean place.

अभिमुखपतितं प्रशान्तदिक्स्थं शुभमतिशोभनमूर्ध्वसंस्थितं यत् ।
अशुभकरमतोऽन्यथा प्रदिष्टं स्थितपतितं च करोति मृष्टमन्नम् ॥ ९ ॥

It is auspicious if the stick that has been used and thrown away, falls towards the user and in a *tranquil* (unscorched) direction; more auspicious, if it occupies a higher ground. One contrary to the above conditions is considered to be harmful; whereas one that falls down after standing erect for a while, brings sumptuous and tasty food.

[The utility of this chapter has already been stressed. The two points mentioned in the previous verse viz. one should sit down while cleaning the teeth, and throw the used stick, after being washed, in a clean place, are of great importance for public health and sanitation. We have to see if people observe these instructions.]

शाकुनम् ॥ ८६ ॥

Chapter LXXXVI—Omens through Birds and Beasts

SECTION I

[This subject of omens receives unusual attention of the author, in that he devotes eleven chapters to its various ramifications. According to him this is a very ancient discipline that has been handed down right from Indra, Bṛhaspati, Śukra and many Sages like Parāśara, Garga and Bhāradvāja. There was also a king of Avantī named Śrīdravyavardhana who wrote on this subject. We find in all branches of Sanskrit literature ample evidence for people's faith in omens, which are generally observed when a person goes on a journey. For, the author avers, the omens are indications of past deeds, good and bad, that are about to bear fruit. A true astrologer can never brush away these omens as superstitions. On the other hand, he advises his clients to do proper propitiation in order to ward off the evil consequences foreshadowed by bad omens. It is well known that astrology and Indian philosophy never teach pessimism or fatalism. Fate and free will are the two sides of the coin.]

यच्छक्रशुक्रवागीशकपिष्ठलगरुत्मताम् ।
मतेभ्यः प्राह ऋषभो भागुरेर्देवलस्य च ॥ १ ॥

भारद्वाजमतं दृष्ट्वा यच्च श्रीद्रव्यवर्धनः ।
आवन्तिकः प्राह नृपो महाराजाधिराजकः ॥ २ ॥

सप्तर्षीणां मतं यच्च संस्कृतं प्राकृतं च यत् ।
यानि चोक्तानि गर्गाद्यैर्यात्राकारैश्च भूरिभिः ॥ ३ ॥

तानि दृष्ट्वा चकारेमं सर्वशाकुनसङ्ग्रहम् ।
वराहमिहिरः प्रीत्या शिष्याणां ज्ञानमुत्तमम् ॥ ४ ॥

Out of love for his pupils did Varāhamihira write this science, the source of super knowledge, having abridged all the existing works on this Science of Omens, after reading the works of Ṛṣabha who incorporated in his work the teachings of Indra, Śukrācārya,

Bṛhaspati, sage Kapiṣṭhala and Garuḍa, of Bhāguri, of Devala, of the blessed king Dravyavardhana, ruler of Avanti, and born of the family of great emperors, who followed the work of Sage Bhāradvāja, of the Seven Sages, of Garga and other sages, of several authors on the subject of 'journey' and other works in Sanskrit and Prakrit.

[Dravyavardhana was, according to Dr. Mirashi, an Aulikara king (495-515 A.D.) who ruled from Ujjayinī. Varāhamihira uses the word Avanti in the sense of Ujjayinī. Here Utpala refers to our author as a Magadha Dvija. This suggests that his ancestors had lived in the Magadha country.

Śakuna and Portents are not identical.]

अन्यजन्मान्तरकृतं कर्म पुंसां शुभाशुभम् ।
यत्तस्य शकुनः पाकं निवेदयति गच्छताम् ॥ ५ ॥

When a person goes on a journey, an omen reveals the fruition of his deeds, good and bad, done in a previous birth.

[Belief in the transmigration of the soul is a fundamental principle of Hindu philosophy. It explains satisfactorily the multiple diversities of life and its conditions. It also urges man to do better things in order to get a higher and better life in the future existence.]

ग्रामारण्याम्बुभूव्योमद्युनिशोभयचारिणः ।
रुतयातेक्षितोक्तेषु ग्राह्याः पुंस्त्रीनपुंसकाः ॥ ६ ॥

Omens are of various kinds as those caused by beings that are rural, wild, aquatic, terrestrial, atmospheric, diurnal, nocturnal and diurnal-nocturnal. The sex of the creatures should be taken into consideration in respect of their cry, gait, look and utterance (which act as omens).

[For diurnal creatures etc. vide LXXXVIII. 1.3. Rural beings are men, horses, elephants and dogs; wild ones, lions, tigers, hogs, deer etc.; aquatic ones, swans and the like; terrestrial ones, porcupines, mongooses, serpents etc. The commentator explains that when there is a doubt about the sex of a distant omen (say, a bird), it is to be guessed from that of a person talking nearby.]

पृथग्जात्यनवस्थानादेषां व्यक्तिर्न लक्ष्यते ।
सामान्यलक्षणोद्देशे श्लोकावृषिकृताविमौ ॥ ७ ॥

Since it is very difficult to distinguish their sex owing to the multiplicity of their genera and the absence of a fixed habitat, Sage

Vṛddha Gaya has written the following two couplets explaining their general characteristics.

पीनोन्नतविकृष्टांसाः पृथुग्रीवाः सुवक्षसः ।
स्वल्पगम्भीरविरुताः पुमांसः स्थिरविक्रमाः ॥ ८ ॥

तनूरस्कशिरोग्रीवाः सूक्ष्मास्यपदविक्रमाः ।
प्रसक्तमृदुभाषिण्यः स्त्रियोऽस्तोऽन्यन्नपुंसकम् ॥ ९ ॥

"The male creatures have fleshy, high and large shoulders, broad necks, fine breast, small but deep sound and great valour; whereas the female ones have slender breast, head and neck, small face and feet, little courage and harmonious and melodious voice. Those that are possessed of characteristics different from these are eunuchs."

[The eunuch will possess the characteristics of both the male and female.]

ग्रामारण्यप्रचाराद्यं लोकादेवोपलक्षयेत् ।
सञ्चिक्षिप्सुरहं वच्मि यात्रामात्रप्रयोजनम् ॥ १० ॥

The creatures that live in villages, forests etc. are to be known only from traditional sources. Here I should like to delineate in brief only those omens that are relevant to journeys.

पथ्यात्मानं नृपं सैन्ये पुरे चोद्दिश्य देवताम् ।
सार्थे प्रधानं साम्ये स्याज्जातिविद्यावयोऽधिकम् ॥ ११ ॥

A man going on a journey ought to consider the omens, good or bad, as relating to his own person; in a marching army, to the sovereign; in a city, to the presiding Deity (or to the mayor); in an assembly (or caravan of merchants), to the leader. When there are many leaders of the same rank in an assembly, they refer to one who is seniormost by virtue of his birth, learning and age.

मुक्तप्राप्तैष्यदर्कासु फलं दिक्षु तथाविधम् ।
अङ्गारदीप्तधूमिन्यस्ताश्च शान्तास्ततोऽपराः ॥ १२ ॥

In the first watch (three-hour period) of the day beginning with sunrise the north-east is termed *Mukta-sūrya* i.e. one that has abandoned the Sun; the east, *Prāpta-Sūrya* or one that has attained the Sun; and the South-east, *Eṣyat-Sūrya* or one that is going to get the Sun; in the second watch of the day, the east, south-east and south respectively get these appellations; in the third watch, south-east, south and south-west; in the fourth watch, south, south-west and west; in the first watch of the night, south-west, west and north-west; in the second watch, west, north-west and north; in the third watch, north-west, north and north-east; and in the last (fourth) watch, north, north-east and east. The effects of omens in the respective directions are as signified by their names given above i.e. in the *Mukta-sūrya* quarter, the effect of the omen is already spent up; in the next quarter, it is to be experienced the same day; and in the next quarter, it is to be felt in the near future. The three quarters named above viz. *Mukta*, *Prāpta* and *Eṣya* (abandoned, prevailing and coming) are severally termed *Aṅgāra* (Charcoal), *Dīpta* (Burning) and *Dhūmini* (Smoking), and the remaining five quarters, *Śānta* (tranquil).

[The terms *Dīpta* and *Śānta* have already occurred in many previous chapters. The reader is requested to amend their meanings in the light of this verse.

The commentator condemns the explanation of some scholars who hold that the east is Prāpta-sūrya or Dīpta during the three-hour period made up of the last 1½ hours of the night and the first 1½ hours of the day. For, it goes against the rule enunciated by *Bhagavān Garga* in the following :—

उदये दीप्यते पूर्वा पूर्वाह्णे पूर्वदक्षिणा ।
मध्याह्ने दक्षिणा दीप्ताऽथापराह्णे तु नैरृंती ॥
पश्चिमास्तमये दीप्ता वायवी पूर्वरात्रिके ।
सौम्या तु मध्यरात्रे स्यादैशान्यपररात्रिके ॥
सम्प्राप्तानागतातीता दीप्यन्तेऽत्र सदा दिशः ।
व्याहरन्ते मृगास्तासु वेदयन्ति महद् भयम् ॥
ताश्च वृत्तमतीतायां दीप्तायां शंसते मृगः ।
अनागतायामाशादिदीप्तायां तद्दिने स्मृतम् ॥

Vide also the following :—

अङ्गारिणी दिग्रविविप्रमुक्ता यस्यां रविस्तिष्ठति सा प्रदीप्ता ।
प्रधूमिता यास्यति यां दिनेशः शेषाः प्रशान्ताः शुभदाश्च ताः स्युः ॥

तत्पञ्चमदिशां तुल्यं शुभं त्रैकाल्यमादिशेत् ।
परिशेषदिशोर्वाच्यं यथासन्नं शुभाशुभम् ॥ १३ ॥

Omens occurring in the 5th directions from these three viz. Aṅgāriṇī, Dīptā and Dhūminī, augur well equally for the past, present and future. The good or bad effects of omens occurring in the remaining two quarters will have to be judged from their proximity to the Śānta (tranquil) or one of the affected quarters (charcoal, Burning and Smoking).

[This idea can be made more explicit by means of the following diagram :

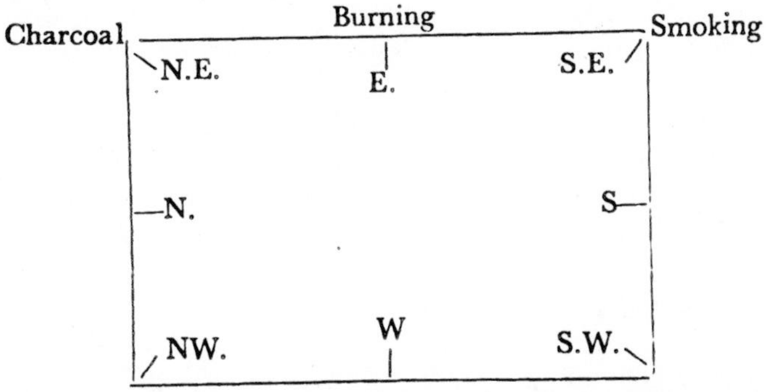

If you take this example meant for the first watch of the day, matters will become quite clear. Now what are the 5th ones for these three *affected* quarters ? They are S.W., W. and N.W. respectively. Now you know that all the five quarters other than the three *affected* ones are *Śānta* or Tranquil. Of these five the three mentioned happen to be the *fifth* ones; and the two remaining *Śānta* ones are the *Pariśeṣa* in the text. Starting with *Charcoal*, the 5th quarter is south-west. If a good omen occurs there, its good effect should be deemed to have already elapsed; and if a bad one happens, its bad effect, which is meagre, is past. Similarly a good omen occurring in the fifth from the *Burning* quarter i.e. west, will give its good effects the same day; and a bad omen there will produce slight evil effect the same day. A good omen in the fifth from the *Smoking* quarter i.e. north-west, will yield its good effects in the future, while a bad one, its *meagre* evil consequences in the future. What would be the effects, then, of good omens occurring in these three *affected* quarters? The beneficial effects of good omens there would be meagre, while the baneful ones of ill omens would be very great. Now look at the figure. Which are the remaining two quarters ? They are South and North. The former is between the *Smoking* quarter and the *Tranquil* one, while the latter is between the *Charcoal* and the *Tranquil*. Here you will have to see if the place of occurrence of the omen is nearer the *Affected* quarter or the *Tranquil* one. A good omen near the former will have very meagre wholesome effect, while near the latter in full measure. Similarly a bad omen near the former will yield disastrous results, while near the latter a little bad effect. Now to find out the time of fruition i.e. past, present and future, of the omen, you will have to find out the particular direction and the name of the quarter from which this is the 5th.

Now let us take *South* itself. It is 5th from the North. For the first watch of the day the results have been already given. Now we have to see at what time this North becomes one of the three *affected* quarters. From the second watch of the night onwards, it gets affected till the last watch, and gets the appellations *Smoking*, *Burning* and *Charcoal* respectively. Now apply the results mentioned already for omens occurring in or near the 5th, from any of these three. If there is a good omen near the 5th, from the *Smoking*, the evil effect in stone will be mild; if it is a bad one, the same will be very grave in the future. Cf. the following :—

यातमुक्तायां साम्प्रतं दीप्तायामेष्यं ज्ञेयं धूपितायामनिष्टम् ।
शान्तास्वेव दिक्षु तत्पञ्चमासु प्रत्यासन्नाशयैः शान्तदीप्तम् ॥]

शीघ्रमासन्ननिम्नस्थैश्चिरादुन्नतदूरगैः ।
स्थानवृद्ध्युपघाताच्च तद्वद् ब्रूयात्फलं पुनः ॥ १४ ॥

Omens occurring nearby and at a lower level bear fruit, good or bad, very soon; whereas those far off and at a higher place, in distant future. Moreover the predictions will have to be made suitably after a consideration of the growing or diminishing nature of the place on which the omen is perched.

[It is possible that the commentator has misread the word स्थानवृद्ध्युपघाताच्च as घातञ्च, as he says: "यत्र प्रत्यहं वृद्धिर्दृश्यते तत्रस्थोऽशुभः शकुने उपघातं करोति" Actually a bad omen seen on a growing thing e.g. a tree, will yield malefic effect which will not be excessive, similarly, a good omen there will produce excellent beneficial effects which would be increasing gradually. If a bad omen is sighted on a dying tree, the bad effects would be excessive; and if a good one, the beneficial ones, very meagre. Sage पराशर gives in the following verses two entirely different sets of *Dipta* and *Śānta* omens :–

श्लिष्टेषु तु भवेत् क्षिप्रं शुभं वा यदि वेतरत् ।
दूरस्थेषु तु सर्वेषु चिरात् सम्पद्यते फलम् ॥
दग्धवक्रातुरच्छिन्नशुष्ककण्टकिवृक्षगाः ।
अश्मनिम्नकपालास्थिसिकताकेशभस्मसु ॥

श्मशानाङ्गारवल्मीका ऊषराः पांसुमत्सराः ।
शीर्णंजीर्णाशुच्यशुभ्रदेशस्था दीप्तसंज्ञिताः ॥
मनोज्ञस्निग्धफलितक्षीरपुष्पतरुस्थिताः ।
समप्रशस्तभूमिष्ठाः शान्ताः स्युर्मृगपक्षिणः ॥]

क्षणतिथ्युडुवातार्कदैवदीप्तो यथोत्तरम् ।
क्रियादीप्तो गतिस्थानभावस्वरविचेष्टितैः ॥ १५ ॥

An omen is said to be *Devadipta* (Blasted by a divine agency) when it occurs in a malefic Muhūrta (a period of 48 minutes), lunar day and lunar mansion, when the wind blows foul and the Sun is in opposition; whereas it is *Kriyādipta* (Blasted by action), when it has untoward gait, position, disposition, sound and movements of limbs. In both the sets the power of each element is greater than its predecessor.

[A whole day consists of 30 Muhūrtas, 15 being in the day and 15 in the night. Among these some are good and the rest malefic. *Kṣaṇa-dipta* is an omen at a Muhūrta that belongs to a dreadful and fierce asterism. The lunar days are divided into five categories viz. Nandā, Bhadrā, Jayā, Riktā and Pūrṇā. Among these the 4th, 6th, 8th, 9th and 14th lunar days are termed *Diptā* or *Blasted.* An omen is said to be *Blasted* on these lunar days. So are the dreadful asterisms viz. Bharaṇī, Kṛttikā, Ardrā, Āśleṣā, Maghā, Pūrvaphalgunī, Viśākhā, Jyeṣṭhā and Mūla, called *Uḍudipta.* If the wind blows fierce, rough, strong and in the opposite direction, it is *Vātadipta.* The direction opposite to the Sun is *Arka-dipta.* The quarter that is *Vātadipta* as well as the one opposite to the Sun gets the same name. An omen that runs against lightning, meteor, the Sun and wind is termed *Gati-dipta* (*blasted-in-gait*). One becomes *blasted-in-position* while standing on a broken, cut, crooked, burnt, tattered or dirty support. One *blasted-in-disposition* is a lifeless or unconscious or partially conscious creature. One *blasted-in-voice* utters a word whose syllables are ill-pronounced and lengthened, the voice being feeble and broken. One *blasted-in-movement* is a bird that flaps its wings, shakes its beak, is about to fall down, cries hoarse and pecks at trees.

Cf. ऋषिपुत्र—

चतुर्थीषष्ठ्यष्टमीचतुर्दशीषु तिथिदीप्ताः । विष्ट्यां करणे करणदीप्ताः । मूलेन्द्रसर्प-रौद्रेन्द्राग्नेययाम्यपित्र्याग्नेयपूर्वासु नक्षत्रदीप्ताः । मुहूर्तेऽथैतेषामेव मुहूर्तदीप्ताः । विसंज्ञाः स्वल्पसंज्ञा भावदीप्ताः । खरपरुषभिन्नभैरवार्तोद्विजनीयविषमविप्लुताक्षरक्षामजर्जर-स्वराः स्वरदीप्ताः । अशनिहतपतितच्छिन्नभिन्नभग्नोन्मीलितार्धदलितोपमृष्टशुष्क-

व्याधितापत्राफलाक्षीरमलिनशीर्णविल्वगासारविरसकत्वाम्ललवणतिक्तक्वथितायतविषम-संश्रितसङ्घटितलतावितानावनतनिरोधान्याक्रान्तकटाग्निदग्धेषु तरुषु । प्राकारगोपुरा-ट्टालककुद्भूमिसंस्थाः स्थानदीप्ताः । ये शीर्णविषमनिम्नसङ्करकेशास्थिकपालवल्मीका-ङ्गारपलालविनष्टायुधाग्न्याधारकलहसर्पविद्युदुल्कार्कमारुतायुधाग्नीनुपधावन्ते ते गति-दीप्ताः । पक्षविपातोत्तुण्डविधूननैर्निपातपरोच्चावचभावकुट्टनैश्च चेष्टादीप्ताः । चण्डपरुषप्रतिलोममारुता वातदीप्ताः । अर्काभिमुखा दीप्तदिक्स्था रविदीप्ता इत्याह भगवान् इन्द्रः ॥]

दशधैवं प्रशान्तोऽपि सौम्यस्तृणफलाशनः ।
मांसामेध्याशने रौद्रो विमिश्रोऽन्नाशनः स्मृतः ॥ १६ ॥

In the same manner *Tranquil* omens too are of ten varieties i.e. five *Deva-śānta* (tranquil of a divine nature) and five *Kriyā-śānta* (tranquil in action). One eating grass or fruits is *Tranquil* and of beneficial effects, while one eating meat or ordure is Dreadful i.e. *blasted* and of untoward consequence. One eating cooked food is considered to be of a mixed kind i.e. *Tranquil cum—Blasted.*

[Cf. the following :

पिशिताशुचिभोजनः प्रदीप्तस्तृणफलभुक् च निसर्गतः प्रशान्तः ।
उभयः कथितस्तथान्नभोजी दिक्स्थानोदयकालतश्च चिन्त्यः ॥]

हर्म्यप्रासादमङ्गल्यमनोज्ञस्थानसंस्थिताः ।
श्रेष्ठा मधुरसक्षीरफलपुष्पद्रुमेषु च ॥ १७ ॥

Most excellent are the omens that are situated in mansions, temples (or palaces), auspicious abodes (such as are occupied by Gods, Brāhmaṇas and cows) and places that please the heart (by cool shade and fine carpet of grass), as well as those perched on trees which are laden with sweet fruits, which are milky, and which have flowers and fruits.

स्वकाले गिरितोयस्था बलिनो द्युनिशाचराः ।
क्लीबस्त्रीपुरुषा ज्ञेया बलिनः स्युर्यथोत्तरम् ॥ १८ ॥

Creatures that roam by day are strong during daytime on mountains (i.e. elevated places); so are those that roam at night, on water during night time. Among hermaphrodite, female and male omens, each is stronger than its predecessor.

[Cf. मनुधर्माः
गिरौ दिवा दिवाचारी निश्यनूपे निशाचराः ।
रोधवाक् शकुनो ज्ञेयो विभजेद् बलमन्यथा ॥

and the following :—

द्युनिशोभयचारिणः स्वकाले पुरवनमिश्रचराः स्वभूमिसंस्थाः ।
सफला विफला विपर्ययस्था गमनेच्छोः पुरपार्थिवाः शुभास्ते ॥]

जवजातिबलस्थानहर्षसत्त्वस्वरान्विताः ।
स्वभूमावनुलोमाश्च तदूनाः स्युर्विवर्जिताः ॥ १९ ॥

Creatures (omens) that possess superior speed, species, strength, position, jolly mood, courage and voice, and are in their respective haunts and periods, are strong, whereas those that are deficient in the above things, are weak.

[In case there are two omens occurring almost simultaneously, we are advised to heed the stronger of the two in respect of speed, strength and the like.]

In the following four verses the author discusses the strength of creatures in relation to the directions.

कुक्कुटेभपिरिल्यश्च शिखिवञ्जुलछिक्कराः ।
बलिनः सिंहनादश्च कूटपूरी च पूर्वतः ॥ २० ॥

The following are strong in the East: The cock, elephant, Pirilī (a bird), peacock, Vañjula, muskdeer (or civet cat?), Siṁhanāda (a bird) and Kūṭapūrī.

क्रोष्टुकोलूकहारीतकाककोकर्क्षपिङ्गलाः ।
कपोतरुदिताक्रन्दक्रूरशब्दाश्च याम्यतः ॥ २१ ॥

The following are strong in the South: The jackal, owl, Hārīta (a kind of pigeon), crow, ruddy goose, bear, Piṅgala (a kind of crane), dove, as well as weeping, crying and crual utterances.

गोशशक्रौञ्चलोमाशहंसोत्क्रोशकपिञ्जलाः ।
बिडालोत्सववादित्रगीतहासाश्च वारुणाः ॥ २२ ॥

The following are strong in the West: The cow, hare, curlew, jackal, swan, osprey, Tittiri bird (or cātaka), cat, as well as festivities, instrumental music, singing and laughter.

शतपत्रकुरङ्गाखुमृगैकशफकोकिलाः ।
चाषशल्यकपुण्याहघण्टाशङ्खरवा उदक् ॥ २३ ॥

The following are strong in the North: The woodpecker, deer, rat, antelope, horse or donkey, cuckoo, blue jay, porcupine, as well as the sound of chanting of benedictory Vedic hymns, of bells and of conch shells.

न ग्राम्योऽरण्यगो ग्राह्यो नारण्यो ग्रामसंस्थितः ।
दिवाचरो न शर्वर्यां न च नक्तञ्चरो दिवा ॥ २४ ॥

Rural creatures (omens) should not be taken into consideration when they are found in forests, nor the wild ones, in villages. Likewise, a diurnal creature should not be taken notice of if found at night and *vice versa.*

[This rule applies to both good omens and bad ones.]

द्वन्द्वरोगार्दितत्रस्ताः कलहामिषकाङ्क्षिणः ।
आपगान्तरिता मत्ता न ग्राह्याः शकुनाः क्वचित् ॥ २५ ॥

Omens that are in pair, sickly, frightened, anxious for fighting or eating meat, separated by a river and intoxicated (owing to the season) should on no account be taken into consideration.

[There is an exception to the omen in pair as far as cranes are concerned. See LXXXVIII. 37 *infra.* cf. the following:

द्वन्द्वादिरोगार्दितभीतमत्तवैरान्तयुद्धामिषकाङ्क्षिणश्च ।
सीमान्तनद्यन्तरिताश्च सर्वे न चिन्तनीयाः सदसत्फलेषु ॥]

रोहिताश्वाजवालेयाः कुरङ्गोष्ट्रमृगाः शशः ।
निष्फलाः शिशिरे ज्ञेया वसन्ते काककोकिलौ ॥ २६ ॥

The Rohita deer, horse, goat, donkey, deer, camel, antelope and hare are to be known as of no consequence in the winter season i.e. in the lunar months of Māgha and Phālguna; so are the crow and the cuckoo in the vernal season.

न तु भाद्रपदे ग्राह्याः सूकरश्ववृकादयः ।
शरद्यब्जादगोक्रौञ्चाः श्रावणे हस्तिचातकौ ॥ २७ ॥

The boar, dog, wolf and the like should not be considered in the month of Bhādrapada; likewise the swan, cow and curlew in autumn (Āśvina and Kārttika); and the elephant and the Cātaka bird in the month of Śrāvaṇa.

व्याघ्रर्क्षवानरद्वीपिमहिषाः सबिलेशयाः ।
हेमन्ते निष्फला ज्ञेया बालाः सर्वे विमानुषाः ॥ २८ ॥

Tigers, bears, monkeys, leopards, buffaloes, burrow-dwellers (mongoose, porcupines etc.) and all young animals are of no consequence in the dewy season (Mārgaśīrṣa and Pauṣa); but human children do have effect.

[Sage *Parāśara* describes the seasons and their effects on the sexual instincts of different animals in the following passage:
"अथ शकुनेषु कोकिलमयूरजीवजीवकप्रियपुत्रराजपुत्रीगोदापुत्रशतपत्रदात्यूहमदनसारिका-वर्षाभूकोयष्टिमहामुक्तकम (मू) षकदण्डिमाणवकवायसकुक्कुटबकोत्क्रोशशार्ङ्गप्लवकचित्र-कपोतपुष्परथोष्ट्ररथादीनां वसन्तो मदकाल:। शतपत्रोत्क्रोशभृङ्गराजमयूर-कोकिलबकबलाहकाप्लववाकधन्वनचातकसारङ्गाणां वर्षा:। चकोरकादम्बमदनशारिका-कीरपुष्करचातकहंसचक्रवाकसारसकुररक्रौञ्चकारण्डवभ्रमराणां शरत्। श्येनकुररक्रौञ्च-सारसादीनां हेमन्तशिशिरे। एवमादय: शकुनानां मदकालाश्च। मृगाणां पुनः पुरुषाणां च शिवाशशजम्बूकसृमरचमरवानरमार्जारनकुलगजगवयसिंहव्याघ्रकूर्मवराहादीनां प्राय: सर्वेषां मदकालश्च विशेषतश्च सारससृमरसिंहव्याघ्रादीनां ग्रीष्मे। हरिणगजवृषभादीनां प्रावृट्। वृषभरुरुमहिषगवयसृमरचमराणां शरत्। गोगवयवृषादीनां हेमन्त: शिशिर:" इति ॥]

In the following six verses the author divides the circle of quarters into 24+8=32 and allots persons following different professions to them.

ऐन्द्रानलदिशोर्मध्ये त्रिभागेषु व्यवस्थिता:।
कोशाध्यक्षानलाजीवितपोयुक्ता: प्रदक्षिणम्॥ २९॥

Divide the space between the East and South-east into three equal parts so as to have three points in between these two extremities and assign them from left to right in order to the Lord of the Exchequer, one that lives by the fire such as goldsmith, and hermit.

शिल्पी भिक्षुर्विवस्त्रा स्त्री याम्यानलदिगन्तरे।
परतश्चापि मातङ्गगोपधर्मसमाश्रया:॥ ३०॥

The three parts between the South-east and the South are occupied by an Artisan or Artist (such as painter, carpenter etc.), a Religious Mendicant, and a Nude Woman; and those between the South and the South-west, by an Elephant (or a Caṇḍāla), a cowherd and a Dhārmika (i.e. one engaged in religious deeds).

[The commentator takes मातङ्गगोपधर्मसमाश्रया: as मातङ्गसमाश्रय:, गोपसमाश्रय: and धर्मसमाश्रय: which mean — one who is riding an elephant, one that is dependent on a cowherd and one dependent on religion.]

नैर्ऋतीवारुणीमध्ये प्रमदासूतितस्कराः ।
शौण्डिकः शाकुनी हिंस्रो वायव्यापश्चिमान्तरे ॥ ३१ ॥

The three parts between the South-west and the West are assigned to a Proud Young Woman, Confinement (child birth), and a Thief; and those between the West and the North-west, to a Toddy-vendor or Distiller, a Fowler, and a Murderous Fellow.

[Utpala says शौण्डिको मधुपानसक्तः—a drunkard, कल्यपाल इति केचित् । According to Amara it means a distiller. "शुण्डा पानमदस्थानं सुरा वा पण्यमस्य शौण्डिकः" The meaning quoted by Utpala is preferable to his own interpretation. For, Kṣīrasvāmin says: सुराजीवी कल्यपालाख्यः । The word शाकुनी is grammatically wrong. It ought to have been शाकुनिकः by IV. 4-35 Pāṇini. Utpala too is wrong in construing this word as धीवरः fisherman.]

विषघातकगोस्वामिकुहकज्ञास्ततः परम् ।
धनवानीक्षणीकश्च मालाकारः परं ततः ॥ ३२ ॥

The three parts between North-west and North are occupied by Viṣaghātaka (one who murders by administering poison, or one that removes the effect of poison), Cattle-owner, and a Sorcerer or Magician; and those between the North and the North-east, by a wealthy person, an Astrologer (Diviner) and a Florist.

वैष्णवश्चरकश्चैव वाजिनां रक्षणे रतः ।
द्वात्रिंशदेवं भेदाः स्युः पूर्वदिग्भिः सहोदिताः ॥ ३३ ॥

The three parts between the North east and the East are occupied by a Devotee of Lord Viṣṇu, a Spy, and a Groom. In this manner there are altogether 32 divisions enumerated including the eight quarters beginning with the East.

राजा कुमारो नेता च दूतः श्रेष्ठी चरो द्विजः ।
गजाध्यक्षश्च पूर्वाद्याः क्षत्रियाद्याश्चतुर्दिशम् ॥ ३४ ॥

The owners of the eight quarters beginning with the East are (1) the King, (2) Prince, (3) Commander of the army, (4) Emissary, (5) Merchant, (6) Spy, (7) Brāhmaṇa and (8) Chief of the Elephant Corps respectively. Similarly, the four quarters East, South, West and North are owned by the Kṣatriyas, Vaiśyas, Śūdras and Brāhmaṇas in order.

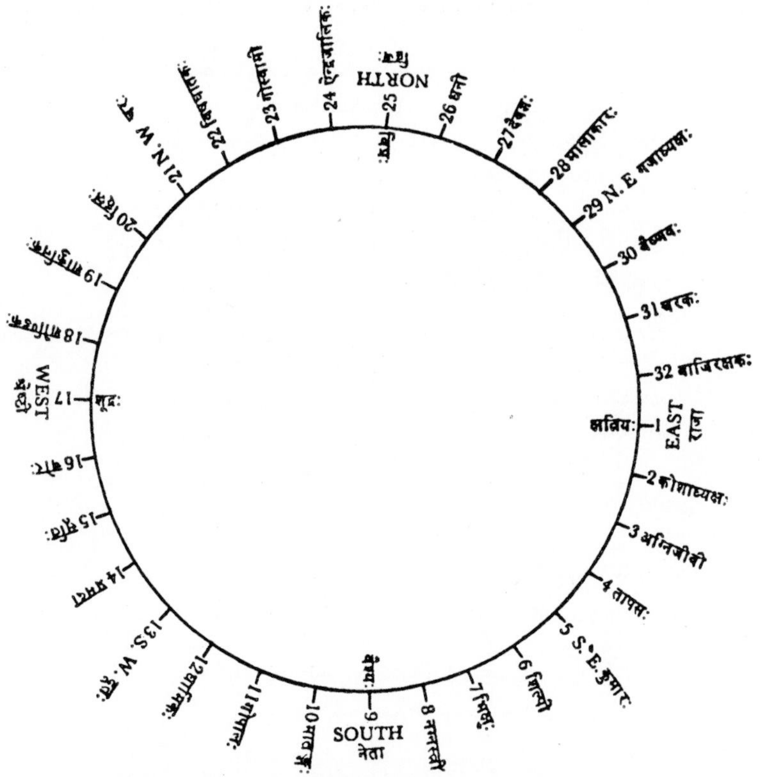

गच्छतस्तिष्ठतो वापि दिशि यस्यां व्यवस्थितः ।
विरौति शकुनो वाच्यस्तद्दिग्जेन समागमः ॥ ३५ ॥

If an omen (bird or beast) stands in a particular division of the quarters and cries, when a person is standing still in a place or is going on a journey, it should be predicted that he will meet the particular individual belonging to that division.

[In the cycle of quarters having 32 spokes or divisions, each point is allotted to a particular individual. For example, if an omen cries from the second point between the East and the South-east, the person will meet the same day a goldsmith or one that lives by fire. See the figure above].

भिन्नभैरवदीनार्तपरुषक्षामजर्जराः ।
स्वना नेष्टाः शुभाः शान्तहृष्टप्रकृतिपूरिताः ॥ ३६ ॥

Sounds that are broken, terrific, piteous, distressed, rough, feeble and gruff are inauspicious, whereas those that are serene, merry, natural and full are auspicious.

[Utpala interprets शान्त as शान्तदिक्स्थेनार्काभिमुखेन मधुरस्वरेण च पूरिताः, which does not appear to be intended by the author.

In the following three verses the author names the good and bad omens on the right and left sides.]

शिवा श्यामा रला छुच्छुः पिङ्गला गृहगोधिका ।
सूकरी परपुष्टा च पुन्नामानश्च वामतः ॥ ३७ ॥

The jackal, Śyāmā (pigeon?), Ralā (a bird otherwise known as kalahakārikā), a kind of rat (rabbit?), Piṅgalā (a kind of crane or owl), lizard, sow, cuckoo and those that have masculine names are auspicious omens when they are seen on the left side of a traveller.

[According to Apte's dictionary छुच्छुन्दरी means musk-rat. Cf. the following :—

छुच्छुन्दरी सूकरिका शिवा च श्यामा रला पिङ्गलिकाऽन्यपुष्टा ।
शस्ताः प्रयाणे गृहगोधिका च पुंसंज्ञिता ये च पतत्रिणः स्युः ॥]

स्त्रीसञ्ज्ञाः भासभषककपिश्रीकर्णधिक्कराः
शिखिश्रीकण्ठपिप्पीकरुरुश्येनाश्च दक्षिणाः ॥ ३८ ॥

Birds or beasts having feminine names, Bhāsa (a bird), Bhaṣaka (a bird named Karāyikā), monkey, Śrīkarṇa (a bird), Dhikkara (a kind of deer?), vulture, peacock, Śrīkaṇṭha, Pippīka, Ruru deer and hawk are beneficial if seen to the right of a traveller.

[Cf. पराशर—

"तेषां शिवागोधाकालकाराजपुत्रीभरद्वाजबलाकापोतकीसूकरिकापिप्पीकास्तुतक्षिप्रचला-पिण्डीकपिङ्गलाद्याः स्त्रीसञ्ज्ञाः शेषाः पुन्नामानः ॥"

Vide also :—

श्येनो रुरुः पूर्वकुटः कपिश्च श्रीकर्णधिक्कारकपिप्पिकाजाः ।
स्त्रीसंज्ञिता ये च शिखिद्विपौ च याने हिता दक्षिणभागसंस्थाः ॥

The commentator says that Dhikkāra is a kind of deer (Mṛgajāti) vide Lxxxviii 7 *infra*.]

क्ष्वेडास्फोटितपुण्याहगीतशङ्खाम्बुनिःस्वनाः ।
सतूर्याध्ययनाः पुंवत् स्त्रीववन्या गिरः शुभाः ॥ ३९ ॥

The sounds of clearing the throat, clapping (or striking the left arm with the right hand), Vedic benediction, songs, conch shells, water, instrumental music and Vedic chanting are auspicious to the left of a traveller. All other kinds of auspicious sounds are favourable to the right.

[Cf. the following :—

आक्ष्वेडितस्फोटितशङ्खतूर्यपुण्याहगीतध्वनिगीतशब्दाः ।
वामाः प्रशस्ताः शुभदा नराणामाक्रन्दितो दक्षिणतः परेषाम् ।।]

ग्रामौ मध्यमषड्जौ तु गान्धारश्चेति शोभनाः ।
षड्जमध्यमगान्धारा ऋषभश्च स्वरा हिताः ।। ४० ।।

The Madhyama (Ma), Ṣaḍja (Sa) and Gāndhāra (Ga) notes are auspicious; but the Ṣaḍja, Madhyama, Gāndhāra and Ṛṣabha (Ri) notes are practically auspicious for a journey.

[The Gāndhāra note is sung only by the Gods. The notes other than those mentioned above are not good for a journey. Cf. the following :—

गान्धारषड्जऋषभाः खलु मध्यमश्च याने स्वराः शुभकरा न तु येऽवशेषाः ।
ग्रामौ शुभावपि हि मध्यमषड्जसंज्ञौ गान्धारगीतमपि भद्रमुशन्ति देवाः ।।]

रुतकीर्तनदृष्टेषु भारद्वाजाजबर्हिणः ।
धन्या नकुलचाषौ च सरटः पापदोऽग्रतः ।। ४१ ।।

The skylark, goat, peacock, mongoose and the blue jay prove fortunate through their cries, the mention of their names, and their sight; whereas the sight of a chameleon in front is of harmful effect.

[The commentator says that the Cāṣa is known as Lāṭa, probably in the vernacular of his region. He says that Saraṭa is a bird and quotes another view that it means chameleon.]

जाहकाहिशशक्रोडगोधानां कीर्तनं शुभम् ।
रुतं सन्दर्शनं नेष्टं प्रतीपं वानरर्क्षयोः ।। ४२ ।।

The mention of the names of the chameleon, serpent, hare, boar and alligator is auspicious, while their sight and cry are not. In the case of the monkey and the bear, however, it is just the reverse.

[In the case of the monkey and the bear, their cry and sight are good, while the mention of their names is inauspicious. *Vide* the following :

भारद्वाज्यजवन्तिचाषनकुलाः सङ्कीर्तनाद् दर्शनात्
क्रोशन्तश्च शुभप्रदा न सरटो दृष्टः शिवाय क्वचित् ।
गोधासूकरजाहकाहिशशकाः पापा रुतालोकने
धन्यं कीर्तनमृक्षवानरकलं तद्व्यत्ययाच्छोभनम् ।।]

ओजाः प्रदक्षिणं शस्ता मृगाः सनकुलाण्डजाः ।
चाषः सनकुलो वामो भृगुराह्णापराह्णतः ।। ४३ ।।

An odd number of the deer, mongoose or birds moving from left to right of a traveller is auspicious, whereas the blue jay and mongoose are good in the afternoon when they move from right to left of a traveller, in the opinion of Sage Bhṛgu.

[According to Bhṛgu the blue jay and mongoose should prove auspicious if they move from left to right in the forenoon. So are the the dog and the jackal. Cf. भृगु "वामगौ चाषनकुलावपराह्णे शुभप्रदौ ।"]

छिक्करः कूटपूरी च पिरिली चाह्नि दक्षिणाः ।
अपसव्याः सदा शस्ता दंष्ट्रिणः सबिलेशयाः ।। ४४ ।।

The musk-rat (or a kind of deer) Kūṭapūrī (otherwise known as Karāyikā) and Pirilī (bird) are favourable in the daytime when they move from the left to the right of the traveller; whereas tusked animals such as boars, and burrow-dwellers, like the mongoose and porcupine, are always commendable when they move from the right to the left of the traveller.

[The commentator says that *Chikkara* which is otherwise known as Dhikkāra, means Śṛgālaḥ, a jackal, but under 20 *supra*. Chikkaro mṛgajātiḥ. Why should he make this difference? From 'ahni dakṣiṇāḥ' we can infer : 'Naktaṁ vāmāḥ'— At night they are favourable in the opposite direction. However, this will work under the restrictions laid down in verse 24 *supra*.]

श्रेष्ठे हयसिते प्राच्यां शवमांसे च दक्षिणे ।
कन्यका दधिनी पश्चादुदग्गोविप्रसाधवः ।। ४५ ।।

The horse and any white object are favourable in the east; a dead body and flesh, in the South; a virgin and curd, in the West; and a cow, a Brāhmaṇa and a pious man, in the North.

[Vide the following:

द्रव्याणि श्वेतानि तुरङ्गमश्च पूर्वेण याम्येन शवं समांसम् ।
पश्चात्कुमारी दधि चातिशस्तं सौम्येन गोब्राह्मणसाधवश्च ।।]

जालश्वचरणौ नेष्टौ प्राग्याम्यौ शस्त्रघातकौ ।
पश्चादासवषण्ढौ च खलासनहलान्युदक् ॥ ४६ ॥

Hunters with hounds and nets are not good in the east? (men armed with) weapons as well as butchers or killers in the south; (one carrying) liquor and a eunuch in the west; and a wicked fellow, (one carrying) a seat (or cot) and a plough in the north.

[In the light of the verse quoted below we have to interpret शस्त्र, आसन and हल as holders of the respective objects.

जालकरश्वकरौ न शुभौ प्राग् घातकशस्त्रकरौ यमदिक्स्थौ ।
षण्ढकमद्यकरावपि पश्चादासनशीरखलैः सहचोदक् ॥]

कर्मसङ्गमयुद्धेषु प्रवेशे नष्टमार्गणे ।
यानव्यस्तगता ग्राह्या विशेषश्चात्र वक्ष्यते ॥ ४७ ॥

On the occasions of starting an undertaking, meeting any person, a war, entering a new house etc. and searching for a lost article, the reverse of what has been laid down for journeys is to be taken. And the following are the special rules applicable to them.

[Those omens that are favourable on the right side of a person starting on a journey will be so if they are to his left on the five occasions mentioned in the text. Similarly, whatever is good in the front for a journey will be so if it is at the back. Likewise we have to take the opposite directions here. *Vide* the following:

नष्टावलोकनसमागमयुद्धकर्मवेश्मप्रवेशमनुजेश्वरदर्शनेषु ।
. . . . यानप्रतीपविधिना शुभदा भवन्ति ॥]

दिवा प्रस्थानवद्ग्राह्याः कुरङ्गरुरुवानराः ।
अह्नश्च प्रथमे भागे चाषवञ्जुलकुक्कुटाः ॥ ४८ ॥

पश्चिमे शर्वरीभागे नप्तृकोलूकपिङ्गलाः ।
सर्व एव विपर्यस्ता ग्राह्याः सार्थेषु योषिताम् ॥ ४९ ॥

The antelope, Ruru deer and monkey during the day are to be reckoned as for a journey. Similarly, are to be treated the blue jay, cock and Vañjula (otherwise known as Khadiracañcu) in the forenoon. In the latter half of the night, the Naptṛka (bird), owl and Piṅgala (a kind of crane) are to be considered as for a journey. For the bevies of women all the above-named omens should be taken in the reverse order both for journey and undertakings etc.

नृपसन्दर्शने ग्राह्यः प्रवेशेऽपि प्रयाणवत् ।
गिर्यरण्यप्रवेशेषु नदीनां चावगाहने ॥ ५० ॥
वामदक्षिणगौ शस्तौ यौ तु तावग्रपृष्ठगौ ।

For an interview with the King as well as for entering (a new house), the omens should be considered exactly as for a journey. For climbing mountains, entering forests and bathing in rivers the omens that are favourable to the left and right for a journey are good in front and behind respectively.

[The commentator takes 'Praveśa' as entering the royal palace. It would be better to interpret it as 'entering a new house'. He construes 'Avagāhane' as 'Uttaraṇe'—crossing. It should mean—getting into the river or bathing in it. Vide the following :

केचिज्जगुर्गमनवन्नृपदर्शनेषु......।]

क्रियादीप्तौ विनाशाय यातुः परिघसञ्ज्ञितौ ॥ ५१ ॥
तावेव तु यथाभागं प्रशान्तरुतचेष्टितौ ।
शकुनौ शकुनद्वारसञ्ज्ञितावर्थसिद्धये ॥ ५२ ॥

If there be two omens called *Parigha* which are *blasted in action* on both sides of a traveller, he would meet with his end. The same two omens situated in their appropriate quarters (right and left) and having pleasant cry and movements are called "Omen Gates" and lead to the acquisition of wealth or accomplishment of desired objects.

[Here two technical terms *Parigha* and *Śakuna-dvāra* are defined and their effects given. In the following verse another view is given regarding the latter.]

केचित्तु शकुनद्वारमिच्छन्त्युभयतः स्थितैः ।
शकुनैरेकजातीयैः शान्तचेष्टाविराविभिः ॥ ५३ ॥

Some hold that an 'Omen Gate' is brought about by birds or beasts of the same species, standing on both sides of a traveller and having *tranquil* movements and cries.

[For *Dipta* (blasted) and Śānta tranquil) see verse 15 and 16 *supra*. Vide नन्दि.

एकयोन्युद्भवैः शान्तैः शान्तचेष्टैर्व्यवस्थितैः ।
यथाभागगतैस्तैश्च शकुनद्वारमिष्यते ॥]

विसर्जयति यद्येक एकश्च प्रतिषेधति ।
सविरोधोऽशुभो यातुर्ग्राह्यो यो बलवत्तरः ॥ ५४ ॥

When one omen suggests success and another failure, the 'mutual contradiction' that is caused is harmful to a traveller. Or the stronger of the two omens is to be considered.

[How do we consider the relative strength of two omens? The answer is given in verse 19 *supra.*]

पूर्वं प्रावेशिको भूत्वा पुनः प्रास्थानिको भवेत् ।
सुखेन सिद्धिमाचष्टे प्रवेशे तद्विपर्ययात् ॥ ५५ ॥

Should an omen become at first favourable for entering and then for a journey, it would be an indication of the easy accomplishment of the traveller's object, while the reverse would be favourable for entering.

[It has been already laid down in verse 47 that for Praveśa (entry) etc. the favourable omens are the reverse for a journey. So what is good for a journey is not so for an entry. An omen, thus, may be unfavourable in the beginning and then favourable, at a journey. Then success is assured. Similarly, if at an entry the omen is unfavourable (i.e. good for journey) at first and then favourable (i.e. good for entry), then too success and prosperity can be achieved.]

विसर्ज्य शकुनः पूर्वं स एव निरुणद्धि चेत् ।
प्राह यातुररेर्मृत्युं डमरं रोगमेव वा ॥ ५६ ॥

If one and the same omen indicates first success of a journey and then forbids it (i.e. suggests failure), it forebodes the traveller's death at the hands of his enemy, an armed conflict or disease.

अपसव्यास्तु शकुना दीप्ता भयनिवेदिनः ।
आरम्भे शकुनो दीप्तो वर्षान्तस्तद्भयङ्करः ॥ ५७ ॥

Omens, situated in a Burning quarter and moving in the anti-clockwise manner, presage peril. An omen in a *Burning* direction at the commencement of an undertaking likewise indicates danger to it in the middle of the year.

तिथिवाय्वर्कभस्थानचेष्टादीप्ता यथाक्रमम् ।
धनसैन्यबलाङ्गेष्टकर्मणां स्युर्भयङ्कराः ॥ ५८ ॥

Omens that are *Blasted* in respect of the lunar day, wind, the

Sun, lunar mansion, position and movements, are harmful in order to wealth, army, strength, limb, desired object (or dear one) and work.

[In this list of *Dīptas* the first four belong to the *Devadīpta* group, while the last two to the *Kriyādīpta* one. It is also to be borne in mind that *Arkadīpta* and *Ceṣṭā-dīpta* are the most powerful elements in their respective groups. The commentator, while introducing the verse says: 'अधुना चेष्टादीप्तस्य लक्षणं तत्फलं चाह ।' In fact here the author gives only the results and not the definition, and that too of six elements and not of Ceṣṭā alone.]

जीमूतध्वनिदीप्तेषु भयं भवति मारुतात् ।
उभयोः सन्ध्ययोर्दीप्ताः शस्त्रोद्भवभयङ्कराः ॥ ५९ ॥

Omens situate in the *Burning* direction accompanied by peals of thunder presage peril from the wind (cyclone); while during the morning and evening twilights they reveal danger from weapons (clash of arms).

[The commentator construes *Jīmūtadhvani-dīpteṣu* as Megha-śabdena dīpteṣu—*blasted* by thunder, but thunder has not been included by the author in the list of *Devadīptas*. Otherwise he would have said 'Ubhābhyāṁ sandhyābhyāṁ dīptāḥ'. For, the twilights too are not included in the *Kṣaṇadīpta* kind.]

चितिकेशकपालेषु मृत्युबन्धवधप्रदाः ।
कण्टकीकाष्ठभस्मस्थाः कलहायासदुःखदाः ॥ ६० ॥

अप्रसिद्धिं भयं वापि निःसाराश्मव्यवस्थिताः ।
कुर्वन्ति शकुना दीप्ताः शान्ता याप्यफलास्तु ते ॥ ६१ ॥

Omens that are *blasted* and standing on funeral pyres, hair and skulls (or potsherds) cause in order death, imprisonment and murder; standing on thorns (or thorny trees), fire wood and ashes, quarrel, weariness (or troubles) and grief respectively; standing on hollow objects and stones, failure of the work undertaken and danger respectively. However, if these omens happen to be *tranquil*, their evil effects will be negligible.

प्रसिद्ध्यसिद्धिदौ ज्ञेयौ निर्हाराहारकारिणौ ।
स्थानाद्भुवन् व्रजेद्यात्रां शंसते त्वन्यथागमम् ॥ ६२ ॥

Omens that pass excreta or eat their food are to be understood to cause the failure or fulfilment of one's objects respectively. If an omen goes away from its place after crying, it indicates a journey; if it comes to its place crying, somebody's arrival.

कलहः स्वरदीप्तेषु स्थानदीप्तेषु विग्रहः ।
उच्चमादौ स्वरं कृत्वा नीचं पश्चाच्च दोषकृत् ॥ ६३ ॥

Omens having *blasted* voice and position indicate in order quarrel and battle. Those that cry aloud in the beginning and then produce a low sound cause trouble.

एकस्थाने रुवन् दीप्तः सप्ताहाद् ग्रामघातकः ।
पुरदेशनरेन्द्राणामृत्वयनवत्सरात् ॥ ६४ ॥

If a *blasted* omen stands crying in the same place (for a whole day), the concerned village will be destroyed in a week; the city, in two months; the country, in three months; and the king, in a year.

सर्वे दुर्भिक्षकर्तारः स्वजातिपिशिताशिनः ।
सर्पमूषकमार्जारपृथुलोमविवर्जिताः ॥ ६५ ॥

All creatures (i.e. omens) except snakes, rats, cats and fishes, eating the meat of their own species, cause famine.

It is natural for snakes, rats, cats and fishes to eat the meat of their own kind. Cf. the following :

विहाय सर्पाखुविडालमत्स्यान् स्वजातिमांसान्युपभुञ्जते वा ।
व्रजन्ति वा मैथुनमन्यजात्याम् . . . . ॥]

परयोनिषु गच्छन्तो मैथुनं देशनाशनाः ।
अन्यत्र वेसरोत्पत्तेर्नृणां चाजातिमैथुनात् ॥ ६६॥

Creatures mating members of another species bring about the ruin of the country, exception being made in the case of the birth of a mule, and of the sexual union of some human beings with members of sub-human species.

[The author refers to a human depravity here and the commentator illustrates it thus: 'यतो नरा वडवादिषु यान्ति'. It is reported that syphlis is the result of such human depravity.]

बन्धघातभयानि स्युः पादोरुमस्तकान्तिगैः ।
शष्पापःपिशितान्नार्द्रदोषवर्षक्षतग्रहाः ॥ ६७ ॥

An omen passing by a person's feet, thighs or head, he will

undergo imprisonment, beating or danger in order; if it is found eating tender grass, drinking water, eating meat or cooked food, there will be in order trouble, rain, wound or imprisonment.

[The commentator construes the word 'Graham' as 'संयोगं केनचिद् बन्धुना सह...' which is not warranted by the text. For, had the author intended that sense, he could have easily used 'क्षयागमा:' instead. See also verse 16 *supra.*]

क्रूरोग्रबोषदुष्टैश्च प्रधाननृपवृत्तकैः ।
चिरकालेन दीप्ताद्यास्वागमो विक्षु तन्नृणाम् ॥ ६८ ॥

If an omen stands in any of the eight quarters beginning with the *Diptā* (*Burning*), men will have meetings with cruel, hot-tempered (fierce), sinful and wicked persons, ministers, kings, rhapsodists and aged men respectively.

[Both the text and Utpala's commentary are vague. It is not clear why the author has preferred the expression चिरकालेन (which gives rise to a genuine doubt about its real import) to अतिवृद्धेन. The doubt is: why we should not take 'चिरकालेन आगम:', meaning—there will be meeting at a distant date.

The reader is already acquainted with the eight designations of the quarters viz. Dīptā, Dhūminī, Śāntā, Śāntā, Śāntā, Śāntā, Śāntā and Aṅgāriṇī. Here the first two Śāntā quarters represent rather bad persons. We have to find some explanation for this : In the first watch of the day the east, south-east etc. get these appellations. So the two moot quarters happen to be south and south-west which are presided over by Yama (God of death) and Nirṛti (Demon). This might be the reason for the above bad representation.

The commentator's explanation creates greater confusion : "तेन दीप्तायां दिशि स्थितः शकुनः कस्यचित्पुरुषस्य क्रूरेण हिंस्रेण संयुतस्यागमं करोति" —which means—"An omen situated in the *Burning* quarter brings about a man's meeting with one who holds a cruel beast." This interpretation is far-fetched. He construes वृत्तकेन as श्रावकेण. After giving this interpretation of some, he gives another given by other scholars : "There are four quarters, Dīptā, Dhūmitā, Śāntā and Aṅgāriṇī. The omen standing in these quarters causes meeting with one accompanied by a cruel man, by one that is guilty of the most heinous crime, by one who narrates the stories of great kings like Nahuṣa, and by one who has lived very long." At the end he says the latter interpretation is preferable. We do not understand in what way this interpretation is better than the first one. For, the author has consistently mentioned eight quarters in connection with *Aṅgāra* etc.]

सद्रव्यो बलवांश्च स्यात् सद्रव्यस्यागमो भवेत् ।
द्युतिमान् विनतप्रेक्षी सौम्यो दारुणवृत्तकृत् ॥ ६६ ॥

Should an omen be strong and accompanied by some substance (such as food), there would be the arrival of a person with something in his hand. Should it be brilliant, the person arriving would be a gentle person; and should it look down, he would be a perpetrator of dreadful deeds.

[Here too commentator's language is a bit confusing. He makes दारुणवृत्तकृत् as an adjective of शकुन and explains thus : If the omen being brilliant looks downward, though it may be auspicious, it will cause only untoward effects. We can also interpret the second half of the verse thus :—If the omen, though brilliant, looks down, then the person arriving, though of a gentle disposition, should have committed some dastardly sin. At the end the commentator adds "य आगच्छति सद्रव्यः पुमान् स उपद्रवं करोतीत्यर्थः ।"]

विदिक्स्थः शकुनो दीप्तो वामस्थेनानुवाशितः ।
स्त्रियाः सङ्ग्रहणं प्राह तद्दिगाख्यातयोनितः ॥ ७० ॥

If the cry of an omen stationed in a *Burning* intermediate quarter be followed by that of another to its left, it reveals a man's marital alliance with a woman of the class indicated by the direction.

[Here the marital alliance with a man or woman, as the case may be, is based on the classification found in the figure under verse 35 *supra*.]

शान्तः पञ्चमदीप्तेन विरुतो विजयावहः ।
विग्नरागमकारी वा दोषकृत्तद्विपर्यये ॥ ७१ ॥

If an omen standing in a *Tranquil* quarter is followed by another, crying and stationed in a quarter that is fifth from the Burning quarter at the time (i.e. facing the Sun), it will bestow victory, or will cause the arrival of the person assigned to that quarter. If it is otherwise i.e. the first omen being in a Burning quarter and the second crying in any quarter that is fifth from one of the Tranquil quarters, troubles will arise.

[Bhaṭṭotpala's explanation lands us in a difficulty: He says that the 5th from the Śānta should be Dīpta. The only *Dīpta* quarter fifth from a *Śānta* one, at one and the same period, is possible when the two are oppcsite to each other. Let us take, in the first watch of the day, the South as the *Tranquil* quarter where an omen is situated. Then the fifth from that would be the North, but it is not *Dipta* (Burning). Hence we have to interpret पञ्चमदीप्तेन as दीप्तात्पञ्चमेन i.e. the fifth from the *Burning* quarter. Similarly, in the reverse case we have to explain thus : दीप्तः शान्तात्पञ्चमेन i.e. The *burning* one being followed by another in a quarter that is fifth from one of the *Śānta* quarters.]

वामसव्यगतो मध्यः प्राह स्वपरयोर्भयम् ।
मरणं कथयन्त्येते सर्वे समविराविणः ॥ ७२ ॥

An omen standing between two others to its left and right with its cry being followed by them severally indicates danger from one's own kith and kin and from foes respectively. (If both the flanking omens cry together after it, then there will be trouble for both the parties.) All the three crying simultaneously portend death.

वृक्षाग्रमध्यमूलेषु गजाश्वरथिकागमः ।
दीर्घाब्जमुषिताग्रेषु नरनौशिबिकागमः ॥ ७३ ॥

An omen standing at the top, middle and foot of a tree indicates severally the arrival of a person riding an elephant, horse and chariot; one standing on a long object, a lotus or the like of it, and something whose top is chopped off, shows severally the arrival of a man carried by another man, by a ship, and by a sedan chair.

[The meaning of the second half is given on the basis of Utpala's commentary. It may also be taken as "the arrival of a man, a ship and a palanquin in order."]

शंकटेनोन्नतस्थे वा छायास्थे छत्रसंयुतः ।
एकत्रिपञ्चसप्ताहात् पूर्वाद्यास्वन्तरासु च ॥ ७४ ॥

An omen situated on a lofty height (such as mountain) indicates the arrival of a person in a carriage; one in the shade, of a person holding an umbrella. Whatever good or bad effects are indicated by the omens situated in the four quarters, east etc. or in the intermediate ones, south-east etc., will come to pass in order in one, three, five and seven days.

[The effect of an omen situated in the East or South-east will be experienced within 24 hours; in the South or South-west, in three days; in the West or North-west, in five days; and lastly in the North or North-east, in seven days.

So far all the verses of this chapter have been composed in the *Śloka* metre.]

सुरपतिहुतवहयमनिर्ऋतिवरुणपवनेन्दुशङ्कराः क्रमशः ।
प्राच्याद्यानां पतयो दिशः पुमांसोऽङ्गना विदिशः ॥ ७५ ॥

The lords of the eight quarters, East, South-east, South, South-west, West, North-west, North, and North-east are respectively Indra, Agni (fire God), Yama (God of death), Nirṛti (king of evil spirits), Varuṇa (Lord of waters), Vāyu (Wind God), the Moon and Śaṁkara. The four prime quarters are masculine, while the corners, feminine.

[This verse is of great utility to astrologers in that the lordships and sex of the quarters can be of help in finding out the name and sex of the person the querist is likely to meet the same day. His name may be a synonym of the particular lord; or he may be a worshipper of that Deity. This knowledge may also be put to use in horary astrology pertaining to lost or stolen articles, thieves, gain and loss, propitiation of Deities, and such other topics.

Cf. पराशर—

वर्णानां ब्राह्मणादीनामुत्तरादिदिशः स्मृताः ।
ऐशान्याद्याश्च विदिशस्ताः स्त्रीणां परिकीर्तिताः ॥

If a query is made or omen seen in a prime quarter, the querist should be thinking of a male or there will be a male birth.]

तरुतालो विदलाम्बरसलिलजशरचर्मपट्टलेखाः स्युः ।
द्वात्रिंशत्प्रविभक्ते दिक्चक्रे तेषु कार्याणि ॥ ७६ ॥

In the circle of quarters divided into 32 parts, if there be omens in the eight directions beginning with the east, the respective materials on which writing may exist will be a wooden board (bark or leaf), Palm-leaf, a worthless fragment of leaf, cloth, water-product (such as lotus-leaf), reed, leather and silk. The particular effects of the omens assigned to the different divisions will also be experienced.

[The effects of omens occurring in the 32 divisions are delineated in the following chapter. In the following verses the author discusses the places where the effects would be felt, colours of articles, signs of the quarters, things relating to the quarters and trees that may flourish there. There is also a special reference to omens relating to women.]

व्यायामशिखिनिकूजितकलहाम्भोनिगडमन्त्रगोशब्दाः ।
वर्णास्तु रक्तपीतककृष्णसिताः कोणगा मिश्राः ॥ ७७ ॥

If omens are found in the eight directions, their effects will be felt severally near a place of military exercise, near a fire-place, where some sound is heard, where a quarrel takes place, near water, where fetters and the like are kept, where Vedic hymns are chanted and where the lowing of cows is heard. The colours of things (that may be found or lost as a result of good and bad omens respectively) are red, yellow, black and white in order in the four prime quarters beginning with the east; but in the corners, they are mixed.

[In the south.east it is yellowish red; in south-west, dark-yellow; in the north-west, grey; and in north-east, pale-red. The use of this is : If an omen carries some article, the person will get some object of the colour assigned to the particular quarter. This knowledge may be utilized in cases of theft and missing articles, as well as of selection of colours of clothes, and devotion to deities owning the colours.]

चिह्नं ध्वजो दग्धमथ श्मशानं दरी जलं पर्वतयज्ञघोषाः ।
एतेषु संयोगभयानि विन्द्यादन्यानि वा स्थानविकल्पितानि ॥ ७८ ॥

The signs of the eight quarters beginning with the east are a banner, something burnt, burial ground, cave, water, mountain, sacrifice and hamlet of cowherds (or proclamation ?). Good or bad omens situated on these signs indicate a meeting with a good person or danger in order. Other things viz. good and effects presaged by omens, will take place in auspicious and inauspicious places.

[Utpala takes घोष in the sense of गह्वर, abyss or cavern. The metre is उपजाति.]

स्त्रीणां विकल्पा बृहती कुमारी व्यङ्गा विगन्धा त्वथ नीलवस्त्रा ।
कुस्त्री प्रदीर्घा विधवा च ताश्च संयोगचिन्तापरिवेदिकाः स्युः ॥ ७९ ॥

When the question pertains to women, omens appearing in the several quarters beginning with the east point to a buxom woman, a virgin, a woman of defective limbs, one that is stinking, one wearing blue clothes, a wicked woman, a tall one, and a widow respectively. These are useful in questions about meetings.

[Bhaṭṭotpala seems to have read two commentaries or two

schools of commentaries on this work. For, he says: एवं केचिद्व्याचक्षते। अन्ये चतस्रो दिश इच्छन्ति। According to the latter school only four intermediate quarters beginning with the north-east are to be taken here. The four types of women are in order (1) a buxom virgin, (2) a crippled and stinking woman, (3) a wicked woman in blue dress and (4) a tall widow. The metre is इन्द्रवज्रा]

पृच्छासु रूप्यकनकातुरभामिनीनां
मेषाख्ययानमखगोकुलसंश्रयासु।
न्यग्रोधरक्ततरुरोध्रककीचकाख्या-
श्चूतद्रुमाः खदिरबिल्वनगार्जुनाश्च ॥ ८० ॥

If at a query the querist or an omen stands in any of the eight quarters headed by the east, the question refers severally to silver, gold, a sick person, a charming damsel, a sheep, a vehicle (or journey), a sacrifice, or cow-shed. Similarly, the trees corresponding to these quarters are, in order, the banyan, a red tree, Lodhra (*Symploeos paniculata*), bamboo, mango, Khadira (*Acacia catechu*), Bilva (*Aegle marmelos*) and Arjuna (*Terminalia arjuna*).

[When there is a good omen in any of these quarters, one is likely to get the article belonging to it; otherwise one will lose it. Similarly, it indicates union or separation of persons as well as clues to theft etc. The second half of the verse gives us a clue as to which tree would flourish in each of the quarters. For the benefit of readers these characteristics of quarters are written in the adjoining table :

Description of Quarters

	East	South-east	South	South west	West	North-west	North	North-east
Lords	Indra	Fire	Yama	Nirṛti	Varuṇa	Wind	Moon	Śiva
Sex	Male	Fe-male	Male	Fe-male	Male	Fe-male	Male	Female
Writing material	Wood-en	Palm-leaf	Torn Leaf	Cloth	Lotus-leaf	Reed	Leath-er	Silk

Places of effect	where army exercise takes place	Fire-place	Full of sound	of quarrel	Water	where fetters are kept	where Vedic chanting is done	where there is lowing of cattle
Colours	Red	yellowish red	yellow	Dark yellow	Black	Grey	White	Pale red
Signs	Banner	Burnt thing	Burial ground	Cave	Water	Mountain	Sacrifice	Hamlet of cowherds
Substances etc.	Silver	Gold	Sick person	charming damsel	Sheep	Vehicle or journey	Sacrifice	Cowshed
Trees	Banyan	Red tree	Lodhra	Bamboo	Mango	Khadira	Bilva	Arjuna
Women	Buxom one	Virgin	of defective limbs	Stinking one	Blue-clothed	Bad one	Tall one	Widow

The commentator seems to have misread मेघाभ्य as मेषाढ्य and interpreted it as अज, goat.

The commentator says in his colophon "सर्वशाकुने मिश्रकं नाम . . ." which shows that this chapter treats of the general principles of omens and the following ones, of their special features. At the end of all these chapters he says सर्वशाकुने.

The metre is वसन्ततिलका.]

अन्तरचक्रम् ॥ ८७ ॥

Chapter LXXXVII – The Circle of Quarters
Section II

ऐन्द्र्यां दिशि शान्तायां विरुवन्नृपसंश्रितागमं वक्ति ।
शकुनः पूजालाभं मणिरत्नद्रव्यसम्प्राप्तिम् ॥ १ ॥

An omen crying in the east which happens to be *Tranquil* at the time, indicates the arrival of an officer of the king, the gaining of honour and the acquisition of excellent jewels and objects (like gold) from that quarter. [This applies to good omens. If it is moderate, the result will also be moderate. Should the omen be inauspicious, the effect would be very slightly beneficial.]

तदनन्तरदिशि कनकागमो भवेद्वाञ्छितार्थसिद्धिश्च ।
आयुधधनपूगफलागमस्तृतीये भवेद्भागे ॥ २ ॥

If the omen appears in the second division (i.e. of Koṣādhyakṣa) it indicates the gain of gold and the fulfilment of desired objects; if in the third division (of Agnijīvin), there will be the gain of weapons, wealth or betel nuts.

स्निग्धद्विजस्य सन्दर्शनं चतुर्थे तथाहिताग्नेश्च ।
कोणेऽनुजीविभिक्षुप्रदर्शनं कनकलोहाप्तिः ॥ ३ ॥

If it is in the fourth division, one will meet a Brāhmaṇa friend, and one who worships the sacred fire daily; if in the south-east corner (5th division), one will see one's servants or mendicants and get gold and iron (weapons).

याम्येनाद्ये नृपपुत्रदर्शनं सिद्धिरभिमतस्याप्तिः ।
परतः स्त्रीधर्माप्तिः सर्षपयवलब्धिरप्युक्ता ॥ ४ ॥

If it is in the first division of the South (6th), one will meet a prince, accomplish one's tasks and attain the desired object; if in the next division (7th), one will get a wife, acquire religious merit, mustard seeds and barley corn.

कोणाच्चतुर्थखण्डे लब्धिर्द्रव्यस्य पूर्वनष्टस्य ।
यद्वा तद्वा फलमपि यात्रायां प्राप्नुयाद्याता ॥ ५ ॥

If it is in the 4th division from the South-east corner (8th), one will recover one's lost property; and a traveller will reap whatever fruit has been laid down in respect of Journey.

यात्रासिद्धिः समयक्षिणेन शिखिमहिषकुक्कुटाप्तिश्च ।
याम्याद् द्वितीयभागे चारणसङ्गः शुभं प्रीतिः ॥ ६ ॥

If it is in the right South (9th), the purpose of one's journey will be achieved, and one will get peacocks, buffaloes and cocks; if in the second division therefrom (10th), one will come in contact with bards, actors, dancers and the like, enjoy auspicious things and have satisfaction.

ऊर्ध्वं सिद्धिः कैवर्तसङ्गमो मीनतित्तिराद्याप्तिः ।
प्रव्रजितदर्शनं तत्परे च पक्वान्नफललब्धिः ॥ ७ ॥

If it is in the next division (11th), one will come in contact with fishermen, come by fishes, Tittiris (francoline partridges) and the like (quails); if in the next (12th), one will see a recluse and get cooked food and fruits.

नैर्ऋत्यां स्त्रीलाभस्तुरगालङ्कारदूतलेखाप्तिः ।
परतोऽस्य चर्मतच्छिल्पिदर्शनं चर्ममयलब्धिः ॥ ८ ॥

If it is in the South-west (13th), one will get a wife, a horse, ornaments, messenger (or envoy) and letters; if in the next (14th) division, one will have the sight of hides and cobblers and win leathern articles (as presents or prize).

वानरभिक्षुश्रमणादलोकनं नैर्ऋतात्तृतीयांशे ।
फलकुसुमदन्तघटितागमश्च कोणाच्चतुर्थांशे ॥ ९ ॥

If it is in the 3rd division from the South-west corner (15th), one will see a monkey, an ascetic or a Buddhist monk; if in the next (16th), one will get fruits, flowers or ivory articles.

वारुण्यामर्णवजातरत्नवैदूर्यमणिमयप्राप्तिः ।
परतोऽतः शबरव्याधचौरसङ्गः पिशितलब्धिः ॥ १० ॥

If the omen is in the West (17th.), the man concerned will get marine products, gems, beryl or jewelled articles; if in the next division (18th), he will come in contact with foresters, hunters or thieves, and get meat.

परतोऽपि दर्शनं वातरोगिणां चन्दनागुरुप्राप्तिः ।
आयुधपुस्तकलब्धिस्तद्वृत्तिसमागमश्चोर्ध्वम् ॥ ११ ॥

If it is in the next division (19th), he meets persons suffering from rheumatism, and get sandal-wood or Aguru (*Aquilaria agallocha*); if in the next (20th), he will get weapons or books, and have contact with those living by them i.e. soldiers or weapon-makers, or authors, book-sellers or printers.

वायव्ये फेनकचामरौर्णिकाप्तिः समेति कायस्थः ।
मृन्मयलाभोऽन्यस्मिन् वैतालिकडिण्डिभाण्डानाम् ॥ १२ ॥

If it is in the North-west (21st), one will get an effervescent thing, chowries or blankets and meet a person of the writer-caste (born of Kṣatriya father and Śūdra mother); if in the next (22nd), he will get earthen vessels or drums and such other musical instruments, and meet bards.

[The commentator construes Vaitālika as a naked preceptor. He explains the other word of the compound thus: पटहमृदङ्गकरटाः समेता यत्र वाद्यन्ते तानि डिण्डिभाण्डानि ।]

वायव्याच्च तृतीये मित्रेण समागमो धनप्राप्तिः ।
वस्त्राश्वाप्तिरतः परमिष्टसुहृत्सम्प्रयोगश्च ॥ १३ ॥

If it is in the third division from the north-west (23rd), one will meet one's friend and get money; if in the next (24th), he will acquire clothes or a horse, and meet a beloved person or a friend.

दधितण्डुललाजानां लब्धिरुदग्दर्शनं च विप्रस्य ।
अर्थावाप्तिरनन्तरमुपगच्छति सार्थवाहश्च ॥ १४ ॥

If it occurs in the north (25th), the person concerned will obtain curds, rice or fried grains, and meet a Brāhmaṇa; if in the next (26th), he will come by wealth and meet a merchant.

वेश्यावटुदाससमागमः परे शुक्लपुष्पफललब्धिः ।
अत ऊर्ध्वं चित्रकरस्य दर्शनं चित्रवस्त्राप्तिः ॥ १५ ॥

If it is in the next division (27th), one will come in contact with a courtesan, a celibate, or a slave, and obtain white flowers and fruits; if in the next (28th), he will meet a painter and get clothes of varied colours or designs.

ऐशान्यां देवलकोपसङ्गमो धान्यरत्नपशुलब्धिः ।
प्राक् प्रथमे वस्त्राप्तिः समागमश्चापि बन्धक्या ॥ १६ ॥

If it is in the North-east (29th), one will come across a worshipper of a Deity, and get corn, gems or a cow; if in the next (30th) i.e. the first division of the east, he will get clothes and meet a harlot.

[Bhaṭṭotpala interprets *Devaloka* as *Bhojaka*. Does it mean 'one who eats at Śrāddhas etc.'?]

रजकेन समायोगो जलजद्रव्यागमश्च परतोऽतः ।
हस्त्युपजीविसमाजश्चास्माद्धनहस्तिलब्धिश्च ॥ १७ ॥

If it is in the next division (31st), one will meet a dyer and acquire aquatic products; if it is in the next (32nd), he will meet elephant-drivers and obtain wealth or an elephant.

[The commentator takes अस्माद् as referring to the meeting of elephant-drivers (समाजाद्). In fact, it means अस्मात्परतः in the next division.]

द्वात्रिंशत्प्रविभक्तं दिक्चक्रं वास्तुबन्धनेऽप्युक्तम् ।
अरनाभिस्थैरन्तः फलानि नवधा विकल्प्यानि ॥ १८ ॥

This cycle of Quarters divided into 32 parts is applicable to the construction of houses as well. On account of omens appearing inside in the eight spokes and the hub of the cycle, the effects are to be varied in nine ways.

[The Vārāṇaseya edition reads वास्तुवत् सनेम्युक्तम् in the place of वास्तुबन्धनेऽप्युक्तम्. The commentator interprets thus:
नेम्या सह कथितम् । नेमियुक्तस्यैतत् फलम् । यथा वास्तुबन्धने द्वात्रिंशद्भागप्रविभक्ते प्रतिदिशमष्टौ द्वाराणि विभक्तान्येवं दिक्चक्रमपि विभक्तम् ।]

नाभिस्थे बन्धुसुहृत्समागमस्तुष्टिरुत्तमा भवति ।
प्रागरक्तपट्टवस्त्रागमस्त्वरे नृपतिसंयोगः ॥ १९ ॥

When a *tranquil* omen appears at the hub of the cycle of quarters, the person concerned will meet relatives or friends, and have great mental satisfaction; when it is at the eastern spoke, he will obtain red silk or clothes and meet a king.

आग्नेये कौलिकतक्षपारिकर्माश्वसूतसंयोगः ।
लब्धिश्च तत्कृतानां द्रव्याणामश्वलब्धिर्वा ॥ २० ॥

When the *tranquil* omen is seen at the South-eastern spoke, he will meet a weaver, a carpenter, a labourer, a horse or a charioteer, and obtain articles made by them, or he will get a horse.

[The commentator explains पारिकर्मा as परिकर्म वेत्ति यः सः । गणितपरिकर्माणि जानाति यः One who is expert in mathematical calculations. केचित् कर्मज्ञा इत्याहुः ।]

नेमीभागं बुद्ध्वा नाभीभागं च दक्षिणे योऽरः ।
धार्मिकजनसंयोगस्तत्र भवेद्धर्मलाभश्च ॥ २१ ॥

Mark out the southern parts of the spoke both at the rim and the hub. When an omen is at either place, the person will come in contact with meritorious men and acquire religious merit.

उस्राक्रीडककापालिकागमो नैरृते समुद्दिष्टः ।
वृषभस्य चात्र लब्धिर्माषकुलत्थाद्यमशनं च ॥ २२ ॥

When the omen is at the South-western spoke, he will meet (or get) a cow, a sportsman or a Kāpālika recluse (follower of a Śaivite ascetic sect, and obtain a bull, black gram, horse-gram and the like (barley, wheat etc.) as well as food.

अपरस्यां दिशि योऽरस्तत्रासक्तिः कृषीवलैर्भवति ।
सामुद्रद्रव्यसुसारकाचफलमद्यलब्धिश्च ॥ २३ ॥

When it is at the Western spoke, he will meet farmers, and obtain marine articles, a gem named Susāra, glass, fruits or wine.

भारवहतक्षभिक्षुकसन्दर्शनमपि च वायुदिक्संस्थे ।
तिलककुसुमलब्धिः सनागपुन्नागकुसुमस्य ॥ २४ ॥

When the omen is at the North-western spoke, he will come across a load-bearer, a carpenter or a mendicant, and will get the flowers of the Tilaka (*Clerodendrum phlomoides*), Nāga (*Mesua ferrea*) and Punnāga (*Calophyllum inophyllum*) trees.

कौबेर्यां दिशि योऽरस्तत्रस्थो वित्तलाभमाख्याति ।
भागवतेन समागममाचष्टे पीतवस्त्रैश्च ॥ २५ ॥

When it is at the Northern spoke, it augurs gain of wealth and meeting with a devotee of Lord Viṣṇu and those clad in yellow robes (or getting yellow clothes).

ऐशाने व्रतयुक्ता वनिता सन्दर्शनं समुपयाति ।
लब्धिश्च परिज्ञेया कृष्णायःशस्त्रघण्टानाम् ॥ २६ ॥

When it is at the North-eastern spoke, a woman observing a religious vow will be met, and steel, weapons and gongs obtained.

[The author has thus given effects of omens appearing in the 8 spokes and the hub, which are common to house-construction. It is to be remembered that all the effects mentioned in this section refer only to *tranquil* omens.]

In the following two verses he applies these tranquil omens to 'Journeys'.

याम्येऽष्टांशे पश्चाद् द्विषट्त्रिसप्ताष्टमेषु मध्यफला ।
सौम्येन च द्वितीये शेषेष्वतिशोभना यात्रा ॥ २७ ॥

अभ्यन्तरे तु नाभ्यां शुभफलदा भवति षट्सु चारेषु ।
वायव्यानैर्ऋतयोररयोः क्लेशावहा यात्रा ॥ २८ ॥

If there be an omen in the southern point, in the 2nd, 3rd, 6th, 7th, and 8th of the west and in the 2nd of the north (of the cycle of 32 points), a journey would have only moderate good effects; while in the other points, splendid results. In the inner circle (of 8 spokes) of the hub, if the omen occurs in any of the six spokes, the journey will be blessed with beneficial results; while in the South-western and North-western spokes, it will be beset with troubles.

[Here the word Aṣṭāṁśa means one of the 8 points of the cycle of 32 points. The points yielding moderate results are the 9th, 18th, 19th, 22nd, 23rd, 24th, 26th, and the best are the rest. The second verse refers to the cycle of 8 spokes.]

In the following verses the bad effects of *blasted* omens are delineated.

शान्तासु दिक्षु फलमिदमुक्तं दीप्तास्वतोऽभिधास्यामि ।
ऐन्द्रयां भयं नरेन्द्रात् समागमश्चैव शत्रूणाम् ॥ २९ ॥

The effects so far enumerated refer only to 'Tranquil' quarters. I shall now explain those pertaining to the *Burning* ones. An omen occurring in the east which happens to be 'Burning' at the time, causes danger from the king, and contact with one's enemies.

तदनन्तरदिशि नाशः कनकस्य भयं सुवर्णकाराणाम् ।
अर्थक्षयस्तृतीये कलहः शस्त्रप्रकोपश्च ॥ ३० ॥

An omen in the next point will cause loss of gold, and threat to goldsmiths; in the 3rd loss of wealth, quarrel and clash of arms.

अग्निभयं च चतुर्थे भयमाग्नेये च भवति चौरेभ्यः ।
कोणादपि द्वितीये धनक्षयो नृपसुतविनाशः ॥ ३१ ॥

One in the 4th. division produces danger from fire; in the South-eastern corner (5th), danger from thieves; in the next division (6th), loss of wealth, and death of a prince.

प्रमदागर्भविनाशस्तृतीयभागे भवेच्चतुर्थे च ।
हैरण्यककारुकयोः प्रध्वंसः शस्त्रकोपश्च ॥ ३२ ॥

One in the third division from the south-east (7th) causes abortion of one's wife. In the next (8th), the destruction of goldsmiths (or gold vendors) and painters (sculptors etc.), and clash of arms.

अथ पञ्चमे नृपभयं मारीमृतदर्शनं च वक्तव्यम् ।
षष्ठे तु भयं ज्ञेयं गन्धर्वाणां सडोम्बानाम् ॥ ३३ ॥

An omen in the 5th 'Burning' division (9th from the starting point) produces danger from the king, pestilence and the sight of dead bodies; in the next (10th), danger from Gandharvas and acrobats (or, danger to musicians and acrobats).

[The compound मारीमृतदर्शनं should rather be interpreted thus: the sight of those that died of pestilence. The genitive of गन्धर्वाणां etc. suggests that the author has intended to convey the idea that such an omen causes trouble to singers and acrobats. Otherwise he would have used the ablative case without any metrical trouble.]

धीवरशाकुनिकानां सप्तमभागाद्भयं भवति दीप्ते ।
भोजनविघात उक्तो निर्ग्रन्थभयं च तत्परतः ॥ ३४ ॥

An omen in the 7th division from the corner (i.e. 11th) which is *Burning*, causes danger from fishermen and fowlers (or to them?); in the next (12th), destruction of food, and trouble from naked monks.

[The reading सप्तमभागाद् is evidently wrong and must have been introduced by scribes. For, the commentator repeats only सप्तमभागे in the locative.]

कलहो नैर्ऋतभागे रक्तस्रावोऽथ शस्त्रकोपश्च ।
अपराद्ये चर्मकृतं विनश्यते चर्मकारभयम् ॥ ३५ ॥

An omen in the South-western corner (13th) which happens to be *Burning*, causes quarrel, flow of blood and clash of arms (war); in the first division of the West (14th), destruction of leathern articles (like footwear) and danger to (or from?) cobblers.

[The author has committed a grammatical error by using the root णश् in आत्मनेपद, for the sake of metre.]

तदनन्तरे परिव्राट्श्रमणभयं तत्परे त्वनशनभयम् ।
वृष्टिभयं वारुण्ये श्वतस्कराणां भयं परतः ॥ ३६ ॥

An omen in the next division (15th) that is *Burning*, causes trouble to (or from?) ascetics and Buddhist monks; in the next (16th), threat of starvation; in the West (17th), danger from rain; in the next (18th), peril to (or from?) dogs and thieves.

[Does the commentator intend to convey the meaning that ascetics will have fear even from Buddhist monks? For, he explains thus : परिव्राजकस्य तपस्विनो भयं श्रमणाच्छाक्यभिक्षोश्च भयं भवति । This might not be the meaning intended by the author.]

वायुग्रस्तविनाशः परे परे शस्त्रपुस्तवार्त्तानाम् ।
कोणे पुस्तकनाशः परे विषस्तेन वायुभयम् ॥ ३७ ॥

An omen in the next division (19th) leads to destruction by storm; in the next (20th), to danger to those that live by weapons (soldiers and manufacturers of arms) and books (authors, sellers or printers); in the North-western corner (21st), to the loss of books; in the next (22nd), to danger from poison, thieves and wind.

परतो वित्तविनाशो मित्रैः सह विग्रहश्च विज्ञेयः ।
तस्यासन्नेऽश्ववधो भयमपि च पुरोधसः प्रोक्तम् ॥ ३८ ॥

An omen in the next *Burning* division (23rd) brings about loss of money, and strife with one's own friends; in the next (24th), death of one's horse (or death from a horse) and danger to (or from) the priest.

गोहरणशस्त्रघातावुदक्परे सार्थघातधननाशौ ।
आसन्ने च श्वभयं व्रात्यद्विजदासगणिकानाम् ॥ ३९ ॥

An omen in the north (25th) causes theft of one's cattle and blows from weapons; in the next (26th), slaughter of a caravan and loss of wealth; in the next (27th), trouble from dogs, and danger to the fallen twice-born, slaves and harlots.

[Vrātya is one belonging to any of the first three classes who has lost caste owing to the non-performance of the principal Saṁskāras, especially the Upanayana or investiture with the sacred thread and initiation into the sacred Gāyatrī Mantra. Vide Yājñavalkya I. 380.

सावित्रीपतिता व्रात्या व्रात्यस्तोमादृते क्रतोः ।

A Vrātya should undergo Prāyaścitta or atonement in order to get back his purity. According to others it means one who does not observe his religious duties. According to the commentator a Brāhmaṇa becomes Vrātya when his Upanayana takes place after his eighth year and before he completes his sixteenth year.]

ऐशानस्यासन्ने चित्राम्बरचित्रकृद्भयं प्रोक्तम् ।
ऐशाने त्वग्निभयं दूषणमप्युत्तमस्त्रीणाम् ॥ ४० ॥

An omen in the division (28th) previous to the North-east, causes trouble to one's coloured clothes and painters; one in the North-east (29th) peril from fire and corruption of noble women.

प्रोक्तस्यैवासन्ने दुःखोत्पत्तिः स्त्रिया विनाशश्च ।
भयमूर्ध्वं रजकानां विज्ञेयं काञ्छिकानां च ॥ ४१ ॥

An omen in the division next to the above (30th) produces grief and death of one's wife; one in the next (31st), danger to dyers or washermen and perfumers.

हस्त्यारोहभयं स्याद् द्विरदविनाशश्च मण्डलसमाप्तौ ।
अभ्यन्तरे तु दीप्ते पत्नीमरणं ध्रुवं पूर्वे ॥ ४२ ॥

An omen in the last (32nd) division of the circle causes trouble to (or, from) elephant drivers, and death of one's elephants (or, one's own death through an elephant). An omen stationed inside in the eastern spoke which is *Burning*, causes undoubtedly the death of the wife.

शस्त्रानलप्रकोपावाग्नेये वाजिमरणशिल्पिभयम् ।
याम्ये धर्मविनाशोऽपरेऽन्यवस्कन्दचोक्षवधाः ॥ ४३ ॥

अपरे तु कर्मिणां भयमथ कोणे चानिले खरोष्ट्रवधः ।
अत्रैव मनुष्याणां विसूचिकाविषभयं भवति ॥ ४४ ॥

उदगर्थविप्रपीडा विश्वैशान्यां तु चित्तसन्तापः ।
ग्रामीणगोपपीडा च तत्र नाभ्यां तथात्मवधः ॥ ४५ ॥

An omen appearing in the South-eastern spoke that is *Burning*, presages clash of arms and outbreak of fire as well as destruction of horses and danger to (or from) artists (sculptors, architects etc.); one in the Southern spoke will cause destruction of Dharma (meritorious deeds or religion); in the South-western spoke, fire-accidents, sudden attacks and killing of honest men; in the western spoke, danger to (or from) workers; in the North-western spoke, death of donkeys and camels, and danger to men from cholera and poison; one in the northern spoke, financial troubles and suffering of Brāhmaṇas; one in the North-eastern spoke, mental affliction, and trouble to (or, from) rustics and cowherds. An omen in the hub that is *Burning*, causes one's own death.

[Though the commentator has taken the words in the genitive in the text in the sense of the ablative, I feel strongly that the author's intention is to convey only the sense of the genitive. For example, in verse 41 रजकानां भयम् ought to mean danger to washermen, and *not*, danger from them. We have to remember one special feature here, which is, the effect of these *Burning* omens is applicable not merely to the observer but in many cases to entire classes of people. This is clear from the statement in the second half of verse 44. The commentator construes शिल्पिभयम् as शिल्पिभ्यो लेखपुस्तकचित्रकृद्भ्यो भयं भवति। He should have said—चित्रकृतां भयं भवति. The last compound in verse 43 can also be interpreted as: अग्न्यवस्कन्देन चोक्षाणां : i.e. destruction of Cokṣas by attacking with fire or by fire and attack. The Dictionary meaning of cokṣa is—Honest, clever, clean. But the commentator says: दुष्ट इति प्रसिद्धः— a notorious ruffian.]

विरुतम् ॥ ८८ ॥

Chapter LXXXVIII – Cries of Birds and Beasts
Section III

Here the author distinguishes animals that are diurnal, nocturnal etc., defines a new type of *Dipta* and gives the good and bad effects of different cries of various creatures as well as of their sight and flight. At the end he refers to a method of consulting the Piṅgala bird about the future.

श्यामाश्येनशशघ्नवञ्जुलशिखिश्रीकर्णचक्राह्वया-
श्चाषाण्डीरकखञ्जरीटकशुकध्वाङ्क्षाः कपोतास्त्रयः ।
भारद्वाजकुलालकुक्कुटखरा हारीतगृध्रौ कपिः
फेण्टः कुक्कुटपूर्णकूटचटकाः प्रोक्ता दिवासञ्चराः ॥ १ ॥

The following creatures are called *Diurnal*, those that roam by day : The Śyāmā (female cuckoo), hawk, the hare-killer (falcon), Vañjula bird, peacock, Śrīkarṇa, ruddy goose, blue jay, Aṇḍīraka, wagtail, parrot, crow, dove of three kinds (viz. grey, variegated and saffron-coloured), skylark, wild cock, donkey, Hārīta (a kind of pigeon), vulture, monkey, Pheṇṭa (a bird), cock, Pūrṇakūṭa (otherwise known as Karāyika) and sparrow.

[All except donkey and monkey are birds in this list.
The metre is शार्दूलविक्रीडित.]

लोमाशिका पिङ्गलछिप्पिकाख्यौ वल्गुल्युलूकौ शशकश्च रात्रौ ।
सर्वे स्वकालोत्क्रमचारिणः स्युर्देशस्य नाशाय नृपान्तका वा ॥ २ ॥

The hair-eater (jackal ?), Piṅgala (crane), chippikā (a bird), flying fox, owl and hare are nocturnal beings. If the creatures belonging to the two categories move contrary to their fixed periods, they lead to the destruction of the country or the king.

[Many of the names mentioned in the two lists are not found in Dictionaries. In the first quarter there is a metrical flaw, as पिङ्गलच्छिप्पिका is the correct form.

The metre is इन्द्रवज्रा.]

हयनरभुजगोष्ट्रद्वीपिसिंहर्क्षगोधा
वृकनकुलकुरङ्गश्वाजगोव्याघ्रहंसाः ।
पृषतमृगशृगालश्वाविदाख्यान्यपुष्टा
द्युनिशमपि बिडालः सारसः सूकरश्च ॥ ३ ॥

The horse, man, snake, camel, leopard, lion, bear, alligator, wolf, mongoose, deer, dog, goat, cow, tiger, swan, spotted antelope, stag, jackal, porcupine, cuckoo, cat, crane and boar are both diurnal and nocturnal.

[The metre is मालिनी.]

In the following five verses the author gives the synonyms of the names of some birds and beasts.

भषकूटपूरिकुरबककरायिकाः पूर्णकूटसञ्ज्ञाः स्युः ।
नामान्युलूकचेटयाः पिङ्गलिका पेचिका हक्का ॥ ४ ॥

कपोतकी च श्यामा वञ्जुलकः कीर्त्यते खदिरचञ्चुः ।
छुच्छुन्दरी नृपसुता वालेयो गर्दभः प्रोक्तः ॥ ५ ॥

स्रोतस्तडागभेद्यैकपुत्रकः कलहकारिका च रला ।
भृङ्गारवच्च विरुवति निशि भूमौ द्व्यङ्गुलशरीरा ॥ ६ ॥

दुर्बलिको भाण्डीकः प्राच्यानां दक्षिणः प्रशस्तोऽसौ ।
धिक्कारो मृगजातिः कृकवाकुः कुक्कुटः प्रोक्तः ॥ ७ ॥

गर्ताकुक्कुटकस्य प्रथितं तु कुलालकुक्कुटो नाम ।
गृहगोधिकेति सञ्ज्ञा विज्ञेया कुड्यमत्स्यस्य ॥ ८ ॥

दिव्यो धन्वन उक्तः क्रोडः स्यात् सूकरोऽथ गौरुस्रा ।
श्वा सारमेय उक्तो जात्या चटिका च सूकरिका ॥ ९ ॥

The synonyms of the bird Pūrṇakūṭa are Bhaṣa, Kūṭapūri, Kurabaka and Karāyika; those of Ulūkaceṭī (a small owl), Piṅgalikā, Pecikā and Hakkā; those of Potakī, Kapotakī and Śyāmā; Vañjulaka is also called Kadiracañcu; the Sugandhamūṣikā (musk-rat) is called Chucchundarī and Nṛpasutā; the donkey is known as Gardabha and Vāleya; the Ralā is called Srotobhedya (stream-cutter), Taḍāgabhedya (tank-breaker), Ekaputraka and Kalahakārikā (quarrelsome). This bird cries at night like a golden vase, and is two digits in height.

The Durbalika is also called Bhāṇḍika and is favourable to the eastern people, when situated to their right; Dhikkāra is a kind of deer; the cock is called Kṛkavāku and Kukkuṭa; the Gartākukkuṭa is known as Kulāla Kukkuṭa (wild cock); the lizard is called Gṛhagodhikā and Kuḍyamatsya (wall-fish); the Divya is known as Dhanvana; the boar is known as Kroḍa and Sūkara; the cow is called Go and Usrā; the dog is known as Svan and Śārameya; and by nature the female sparrow is called Caṭikā and Sūkarikā.

[Chikkara and Dhikkāra are the same. The commentator tells us that according to some Bhṛṅgāra means a bird of a particular species. In the dialect of Utpala the vase is called Dāṁdānī or Damanī. This will help scholars in fixing his native place. The author has strangely committed a metrical error in the first quarter of verse 5. He could have put it as :

श्यामा कपोतकी स्याद् ।]

एवं देशे देशे तद्विद्भ्यः समुपलभ्य नामानि ।
शकुनरुतज्ञानार्थं शास्त्रे सञ्चिन्त्य योज्यानि ॥ १० ॥

In this manner in every country one ought to ascertain the names of birds and beasts from those that are well acquainted with them, and apply them after proper analysis to the science bearing upon omens for understanding (the effects of) their cries.

[Our Bangalore edition reads सञ्चिन्त्य while the Vārāṇaseya one has सञ्चित्य (having collected); but the commentator explains it as 'विचार्य'. Hence the reading given above should be preferred.

Next the author defines a new variety of *Dipta* cry.]

वञ्जुलकरुतं तित्तिडिति दीप्तमथ किल्किलीति तत्पूर्णम् ।
श्येनशुकगृध्रकङ्काः प्रकृतेरन्यस्वरा दीप्ताः ॥ ११ ॥

The cry of the Vañjulaka resembling the sound "Tittiḍ' is called *Burning* i.e. malignant; but one like 'Kilkili', is *Full* i.e. auspicious. The hawk, parrot, vulture and heron having unnatural sounds are called *Burning*.

यानासनशय्यानिलयनं कपोतस्य सद्मविशनं वा ।
अशुभप्रदं नराणां जातिविभेदेन कालोऽन्यः ॥ १२ ॥

आपाण्डुरस्य वर्षाच्चित्रकपोतस्य चैव षण्मासात् ।
कुङ्कुमधूम्रस्य फलं सद्यः पाकं कपोतस्य ॥ १३ ॥

A dove sitting or building a nest on a vehicle (including horse), seat or bed, causes harm to the owners; and the time of its fruition is different for its different kinds. The grey variety of dove causes the evil consequences to be felt within a year; the variegated one, within six months; and the saffron-coloured one or the dark-red one, immediately i.e. the same day.

[The expression विभ्रनम् is ungrammatical used for metrical soundness.]

चिचिदिति शब्दः पूर्णः श्यामायाः शूलिशूलिति च धन्यः ।
चच्चेति च दीप्तः स्यात् स्वप्रियलाभाय चिक्चिगिति ॥ १४ ॥

The cry of the Śyāmā (female cuckoo ?), being like *Cicit* is *Full* and like *Śūliśūl* is lucky; but one like *Cacca*, is *Burning*; while one like *Cikcik* leads to the acquisition of one's cherished object or person.

हारीतस्य तु शब्दो गुग्गुः पूर्णोऽपरे प्रदीप्ताः स्युः ।
स्वरवैचित्र्यं सर्वं भारद्वाज्याः शुभं प्रोक्तम् ॥ १५ ॥

The *Guggu* sound of the Hārīta is *Full*, while others would be *Burning*; all the variations of sound of the Bhāradvāja (Skylark) are declared to be auspicious.

किष्किषिशब्दः पूर्णः करायिकायाः शुभः कहकहेति ।
क्षेमाय केवलं करकरेति न त्वर्थसिद्धिकरः ॥ १६ ॥

कोटुक्लीति क्षेम्यः स्वरः कटुक्लीति वृष्टये तस्याः ।
अफलः कोटिकिलीति च दीप्तः खलु गुंकृतः शब्दः ॥ १७ ॥

The *Kiṣkiṣi* sound of the Karāyikā is *Full* and 'Kaha-kaha', auspicious; while the *Kara-kara* sound is only for *status-quo* and not for fresh acquisition of wealth. Its own sound like *Koṭukli* confers sound health; *Kaṭukli* causes rain; *Koṭikili* is worthless; and the sound *Gum* is indeed *Burning*.

[It is really remarkable that the ancient Sages of India had observed minutely the different cries of birds and beasts as well as their psychological back-ground. We can also remember in this connection Kālidāsa's statement relating to good hunting, viz. सत्त्वानामपि लक्ष्यन्ते विकृतिमच्चित्तं भयक्रोधयोः. It is also known that many animals such as dogs have the instinctive power of scenting coming events. As such they are able to throw some hints about the coming danger and pleasure through their behaviour and cries.

If man is intelligent enough to read the lessons written on the pages of Nature, he can progress in life. Hence belief in omens and astrology cannot be dubbed as superstition.]

शस्तं वामे दर्शनं दिव्यकस्य सिद्धिर्ज्ञेया हस्तमात्रोच्छ्रितस्य ।
तस्मिन्नेव प्रोन्नतस्थे शरीराद् धात्री वश्यं सागरन्ताभ्युपैति ॥ १८ ॥

The sight of the Divyaka to the left is praiseworthy; when it is just one cubit above the ground in the same place, one's objects will be accomplished; when it is in the same place but at a higher level than the body of a traveller, the whole earth as far the oceans will come under his sway.

[Here the author uses the adjective वश्यं in the sense of वशं. The commentator accordingly interprets it as विधेयित्वं (meaning विधेयत्वम्). The last line of the verse could have been given without error thus:

Vide the following :—

वामे शस्तो धन्वनः सिद्धदाता प्रोत्तुङ्गश्चेद्धस्तमात्रं जयाय ।
आकायं चेदुन्नतो वामभागे पृथ्वीलाभं बन्धुनाशं करोति ॥

The metre is शालिनी.]

फणिनोऽभिमुखागमोऽरिसङ्गं कथयति बन्धुवधात्ययं च यातुः ।
अथवा समुपैति सव्यभागान्न स सिद्ध्यै कुशलो गमागमे च ॥ १९ ॥

A snake moving towards a traveller indicates an encounter with his enemies, and the death or ruin of his kinsmen. If it crawls from his right to his left, the object of his journey will not be achieved.

[The commentator takes the च in the second quarter in the sense of अथवा, *or.*

The metre of this verse is not named in any book on prosody. It can be called गाथा as it is a mixture of 2 quarters viz. 1st. and 3rd, similar to the odd lines of वियोगिनी with an extra long syllable at the end, the second quarter exactly like that of पुष्पिताग्रा, and the 4th resembling the even line of वियोगनी with an extra Guru. Otherwise we can call this an अर्धसम of the मात्रासमक metre, as both the halves have 34 Mātrās each.]

अब्जेषु मूर्धसु च वाजिगजोरगाणां
राज्यप्रदः कुशलकृच्छुचिशाद्वलेषु ।

भस्मास्थिकाष्ठतुषकेशतृणेषु दुःखं
वृष्टः करोति खलु खञ्जनकोऽब्दमेकम् ॥ २० ॥

The wagtail sun sitting on lotuses or on the heads of horses, elephants or snakes, bestows sovereignty; on clean sites or on green grassy tracts, happiness; while on ashes, bones, firewood, husks, hair or straw, it causes grief for a year without fail.

[The metre of this and 23, 25, 34 and 35 is वसन्ततिलका. The commentator construes शाद्वलेषु as दूर्वासु. But Amara says: शाद्वल: शादहरिते.]

किलिकिल्किलि तित्तिरिस्वनः शान्तः शस्तफलोऽन्यथापरः।
शशको निशि वामपार्श्वगो वाशञ्छस्तफलो निगद्यते ॥ २१ ॥

The 'Kilkili' sound of the Tittiri (francoline partridge) is *Tranquil* and of beneficial results; otherwise, it is *Burning* and harmful. A hare crying and running on the left side of a person at night is said to be of auspicious results.

[The author has taken liberty with grammar and made two changes in respect of वाश् viz. conjugation and the voice (Pada). The metre is a variety of वियोगिनी with the substitution of two Gurus for the first Sagaṇa in the even lines.]

किलिकिलिविरुतं कपेः प्रदीप्तं न शुभफलप्रदमुद्दिशन्ति यातुः।
शुभमपि कथयन्ति चुग्लुशब्दं कपिसदृशं च कुलालकुक्कुटस्य ॥ २२ ॥

The *Kilikili* sound of a monkey is said to be *Burning* and not conducive to good results to a traveller; but the *Cuglu* sound is spoken of as being auspicious. The cry of the wild cock is similar in effect to that of the monkey.

[The metre is पुष्पिताग्रा.]

पूर्णाननः कृमिपतङ्गपिपीलिकाद्यै-
श्चाषः प्रदक्षिणमुपैति नरस्य यस्य ।
खे स्वस्तिकं यदि करोत्यथवा यियासो-
स्तस्यार्थलाभमचिरात् सुमहत् करोति ॥ २३ ॥

If a blue jay with its mouth filled with worms, moths, ants and the like, flies from left to right of a person, who is about to start on a journey, or makes the Svastika figure in the sky by its flight, it bestows before long very great prosperity on him.

चाषस्य काकेन विरुध्यतश्चेत्पराजयो दक्षिणभागगस्य ।
वधः प्रयातस्य तदा नरस्य विपर्यये तस्य जयः प्रदिष्टः ॥ २४ ॥

When a blue jay fights with a crow and is defeated by the latter, the traveller to whose right the jay flies will meet with death; otherwise (when it is victorious and flies to the left), he will be successful.

[The commentator interprets दक्षिणभागगस्य as काकाद् दक्षिणभाग-गतस्य चाषस्य which means—the blue jay fighting with the crow is to the right of the latter.

Vide the following :

> पूर्णाननो यस्य करोति चाषः प्रदक्षिणं स्वस्तिकमेव वा खे ।
> लाभो महांस्तस्य पराभवाय काकेन भङ्गो विजयो जयस्य ॥

The metre of this, 26, 32, 40, 41, 45, 46 and 47 is उपजाति.]

> **केकेति पूर्णकुटवद्यदि वामपार्श्वे**
> **चाषः करोति विरुतं जयकृत्तदा स्यात् ।**
> **क्रेक्रेति तस्य विरुतं न शिवाय दीप्तं**
> **सन्दर्शनं शुभदमस्य सदैव यातुः ॥ २५ ॥**

When the blue jay flying to the left of a person cries as *Keka*, or does like the Pūrṇakuṭa (Karāyika, Kiṣkiṣi or Kaha-kaha), it bestows success; but its cry *Krekra* is *Burning* and is not conducive to happiness; its mere sight, however, is always favourable to a traveller.

> **अण्डीरकष्टीति रुतेन पूर्णष्टिट्टिट्टिशब्देन तु दीप्त उक्तः ।**
> **फेण्टः शुभो दक्षिणभागसंस्थो न वाशिते तस्य कृतो विशेषः ॥ २६ ॥**

The *Ṭi* cry of the Aṇḍīraka is said to be *Full* and auspicious, while the 'Ṭiṭṭiṭṭi' cry, *Burning* and harmful. The Phenṭa is auspicious when seen to the right of oneself; and no importance is attached to its cry.

> **श्रीकर्णरुतं तु दक्षिणे क्वक्वक्वेति शुभं प्रकीर्तितम् ।**
> **मध्यं खलु चिक्चिकीति यच्छेषं सर्वमुशन्ति निष्फलम् ॥ २७ ॥**

The *Kvakva* sound of the Śrīkarṇa flying to the right is said to be auspicious; the *Cikciki* one is moderate in effect, and all other sounds, they say, are without any good result.

[The metre here and in 30 is an अर्धसमवृत्त of the भद्रविराट् type with the final long syllable in each quarter dropped.]

दुर्बलेरपि चिरिल्विरिल्विति प्रोक्तमिष्टफलवं हि वामतः ।
वामतश्च यदि दक्षिणं व्रजेत्कार्यसिद्धिमचिरेण यच्छति ॥ २८ ॥

The sound *Cirilvirilu* of the Durbali (Bhāṇḍīka) too to the left is considered favourable in effect; if it flies from left to right, it leads ere long to the success of one's undertaking.

[The metre is रथोद्धता.]

चिक्चिकिवाशितमेव तु कृत्वा दक्षिणभागमुपैति च वामात् ।
क्षेमकृदेव न साधयतेऽर्थान् व्यत्ययगो वधबन्धभयाय ॥ २९ ॥

If the same bird viz. Durbalika, flies from left to right while crying like *Cikciki*, it helps only to maintain the *status quo* (or gives only sound health) and does not fulfil the desired objects. If it is otherwise i.e. flies from right to left, it causes fear of death or imprisonment (or death, imprisonment or danger).

[The words Artha and Kṣema here and in verse 16 *supra* mean *yoga-kṣema* used in the Gītā, when the first word means attainment of new objects and the second, maintaining what has been got already.

The metre is दोधक in this and in 37.]

क्रक्रेति च सारिका द्रुतं त्रेत्रे वाप्यभया विरौति या ।
सा वक्ति यियासतोऽचिराद् गात्रेभ्यः क्षतजस्य विस्रुतिम् ॥ ३० ॥

A Sārikā (mynah) crying quickly like *Krakra* or like *Tretre* fearlessly, indicates the flow of blood ere long from the limbs of a person starting on a journey.

फेण्टकस्य वामतश्चिरिल्विरिल्विति स्वनः ।
शोभनो निगद्यते प्रदीप्त उच्यतेऽपरः ॥ ३१ ॥

The *Cirilu-Irilu* sound of the Pheṇṭa to the left is declared to be auspicious; the contrary, *Burning*.

[This is a strange metre whose name is not found in works on prosody. It may be brought under गाथा as Piṅgala says "अत्रानुक्तं गाथा". It is an अर्धसमवृत्त formed with the odd quarters of समानिका and the even ones of the प्रमाणिका.]

श्रेष्ठं खरं स्थास्नुमुशन्ति वाममोङ्कारशब्देन हितं च यातुः ।
अतोऽपरं गर्दभनादितं यत्सर्वाश्रयं तत् प्रवदन्ति दीप्तम् ॥ ३२ ॥

A donkey standing still in a place to the left of a traveller is said to be beneficial; so is one producing the sound of *Om.* All other varieties of its braying, wherever it may stand, are called *Burning*.

आकाररावी समृगः कुरङ्ग ओकाररावी पृषतश्च पूर्णः ।
येऽन्ये स्वरास्ते कथिताः प्रदीप्ताः पूर्णाः शुभाः पापफलाः प्रदीप्ताः ॥ ३३ ॥

The stag and the deer producing the "Ā" sound, and the spotted antelope, the 'O' sound, are *Full*; all other sounds are declared *Burning*. Sounds that are *Full* are auspicious, while the *Burning* of evil consequences.

[The metre is इन्द्रवज्रा.]

भीता रुवन्ति कुकुकुक्विति ताम्रचूडा-
स्त्यक्त्वा रुतानि भयदान्यपराणि रात्रौ ।
स्वस्थैः स्वभावविरुतानि निशावसाने
ताराणि राष्ट्रपुरपार्थिववृद्धिदानि ॥ ३४ ॥

The cocks crow at night as *Kuku-kuku*, when they are frightened. All sounds except the above at night are harmful. The high-pitched and natural sounds produced by them at dawn, when they are free from illness, bestow prosperity on the realm, city and monarch.

नानाविधानि विरुतानि हि छिप्पिकाया-
स्तस्याः शुभाः कुलुकुलुर्न शुभास्तु शेषाः ।
यातुर्बिडालविरुतं न शुभं सदैव
गोस्तु क्षुतं मरणमेव करोति यातुः ॥ ३५ ॥

The Chippikā produces many sounds, but its *Kulu-kulu* sound alone is auspicious; and the rest are harmful. Never is the mewing of a cat favourable to a traveller. The sneezing of a cow certainly brings about the traveller's death.

[Even the cat's sight is considered unfavourable to a traveller, in society.]

हुं हुं गुग्लुगिति प्रियामभिलषन् क्रोशत्युलूको मुदा
पूर्णं स्याद् गुरुलु प्रदीप्तमपि च ज्ञेयं सदा किस्किसि ।
विज्ञेयः कलहो यदा बलबलं तस्याः सकृद्वाशितं
दोषायैव टटट्टटेति न शुभाः शेषाश्च दीप्ताःस्वराः ॥ ३६ ॥

When the owl wishes for mating, it cries joyously as *Huṁ-huṁ, Guglug.* Its *Gurulu* sound is *full,* while the *kiskisi* sound is always *Burning.* When it cries repeatedly as *Bala-bala,* it indicates quarrel; its *Ṭaṭaṭṭaṭa* sound leads only to sufferings; and the rest are *Burning* and harmful.

[Villagers forecast the fluctuation in the prices of some commodities from the cries of the owl.

The metre is शार्दूलविक्रीडित.]

सारसकूजितमिष्टफलं तद् यद्युगपद्विरुतं मिथुनस्य ।
एकरुतं न शुभं यदि वा स्यादेकरुते प्रतिरौति चिरेण ॥ ३७ ॥

The simultaneous cries of a pair of cranes are favourable in effect; but when one alone cries, or when the other responds to the first after a long interval, it is inauspicious.

[प्रविरौति is another reading for प्रतिरौति.]

चिरिल्विरिल्विति स्वनैः शुभं करोति पिङ्गला ।
अतोऽपरे तु ये स्वराः प्रदीप्तसञ्ज्ञितास्तु ते ॥ ३८ ॥

The Piṅgalā bird brings good luck with its cry, *Cirilu-irilu;* all other sounds of its cry are termed *Burning.*

[The metre is प्रमाणिका.]

इशिविरुतं गमनप्रतिषेधि कुशुकुशु चेत्कलहं प्रकरोति ।
अभिमतकार्यगतिं च यथा सा कथयति तं च विधिं कथयामि ॥ ३९ ॥

If the Piṅgalā produces an *Iśi* sound, then it is a hindrance to the journey i.e. the journey will not be successful; if a *Kuśu kuśu* sound, it leads to quarrel. I shall now explain the way in which the bird indicates the fulfilment of one's cherished objects.

[The metre is तामरस.]

दिनान्तसन्ध्यासमये निवासमागम्य तस्याः प्रयतश्च वृक्षम् ।
देवान् समभ्यर्च्य पितामहादीन् नवाम्बरस्तं च तरुं सुगन्धैः ॥ ४० ॥

एको निशीथेऽनलदिक्स्थितश्च दिव्येतरैस्तां शपथैर्नियोज्य ।
पृच्छेद्यथाचिन्तितमर्थमेवमनेन मन्त्रेण यथा शृणोति ॥ ४१ ॥

Being pure and clad in new clothes, one should approach in the evening the tree which is the abode of the Piṅgalā, and worship Brahman and other Gods as well as the tree with fine perfumes;

then one should stand alone to the south-east of the tree at midnight, convince her (the bird) by oaths, referring to both Gods and human beings, and consult her about the contemplated object in this manner with the following hymn so that she may hear it well.

विद्धि भद्रे मया यत् त्वमिममर्थं प्रचोदिता ।
कल्याणि सर्ववचसां वेदित्रि त्वं प्रकीर्त्यसे ॥ ४२ ॥

आपृच्छेऽद्य गमिष्यामि वेदितश्च पुनस्त्वहम् ।
प्रातरागम्य पृच्छे त्वामाग्नेयीं दिशमाश्रितः ॥ ४३ ॥

प्रचोदयाम्यहं यत् त्वां तन्मे व्याख्यातुमर्हसि ।
स्वचेष्टितेन कल्याणि यथा वेद्मि निराकुलम् ॥ ४४ ॥

"O auspicious one, kindly divine the object about which I am consulting thee. For, thou art praised as the knower of all languages. I shall take leave of thee, being informed of it by thee, but I shall come back in the morning and question thee, stationing myself in the south-eastern corner. I call upon thee to explain to me through thy activities the object I have in view, so that I may understand it without any ambiguity."

इत्येवमुक्ते तरुमूर्धगायाश्चिरिल्विरिल्वीति रुतेऽर्थसिद्धिः ।
अत्याकुलत्वं दिशिकारशब्दे कुचाकुचेत्येवमुदाहृते वा ॥ ४५ ॥
अवाक्प्रदानेऽपि हितार्थसिद्धिः पूर्वोक्तदिक्चक्रफलैरतोऽन्यत् ।
वाच्यं फलं चोत्तममध्यनीचशाखास्थितायां वरमध्यनीचम् ॥ ४६ ॥

If on being addressed in this manner she cries *Cirilvirilvi* from the top of the tree, there will be success in the undertaking; but if she cries *Diśikāra* or *Kucā-kucā*, there will be excessive mental suffering. When she does not cry at all, even then, there will be the accomplishment of the object. Other effects will have to be deduced from the 'Circle of Quarters' mentioned above (LXXXVII.) If she be perched on a high, middle or low branch, the effect will, in order, be very good, medium or bad.

[It is not clear if the 'कार' in दिशिकार is meant only to indicate the syllables दि and शि, as we use in connection with the sounds of the alphabet.]

दिङ्मण्डलेऽभ्यन्तरबाह्यभागे फलानि विन्द्याद् गृहगोधिकायाः ।
छुच्छुन्दरी चिच्चिडिति प्रदीप्ता पूर्णा तु सा तित्तिडिति स्वनेन ॥४७ ॥

The effect of the house-lizard will have to be deduced from its cry and position in the 'Circle of Quarters' whether in any of the spokes inside or of the 32 divisions. The musk-rat is malignant with the cry *Ciccid̤*, while it is *full* (auspicious) with *Tittiḍ*.

[The commentator explains some peculiarities of the cries and their effects: If the direction is *Tranquil* and the cry pleasant, the result will be excellent; if the cry is unpleasant, the effect will be moderate. On the other hand, if the direction is *Burning* and cry pleasing, the effect will be good; if the quarter is *Non-burning* but the cry *Burning* (harsh), it will be untoward. This also refers to Piṅgalā.]

श्वचक्रम् । ८९ ॥

Chapter LXXXIX—The Circle of Dogs
Section IV

नृतुरगकरिकुम्भपर्याणसक्षीरवृक्षेष्टकासञ्चयच्छत्रशय्यासनोलूखलानि ध्वजं चामरं शाद्वलं पुष्पितं वा प्रदेशं यदा श्वाऽवमूत्र्याग्रतो याति यातुस्तदा कार्यसिद्धिर्भवेदार्द्रके गोमये मिष्टभोज्यागमः शुष्कसम्मूत्रणे शुष्कमन्नं गुडो मोदकावाप्तिरेवाथवा ॥ १(क)

If a dog passes urine on a man, horse, elephant, pot, saddle, milky tree, heap of bricks, umbrella, bed, seat, mortar, banner, chowrie or a piece of ground covered with green grass or flowers, and goes ahead of a traveller, then he will be successful in his undertaking; if it urinates on wet cowdung, he will get a sumptuous meal; if on dry cow-dung, dry food, jaggery or sweets.

[This Daṇḍaka has no name given to it in the Vṛttaratnākara. It is a running prose passage where two Nagaṇas are followed by 31 Ragaṇas. This is one of the four quarters, the other quarters being given below.

Vide the following.

नरतुरगगजातपत्रकुम्भध्वजशयनासनपुष्पचामराणि ।
व्रजति यदि पुरोऽवमूत्र्य पक्षः (वा श्वा) क्षपयति शत्रुबलं तदा नरेन्द्रः ॥]

अथ विषतरुकण्टकीकाष्ठपाषाणशुष्कद्रुमास्थिश्मशानानि मूत्र्यावहत्याथवा यायिनोऽग्रेसरोऽनिष्टमाख्याति शय्याकुलालादिभाण्डान्यभुक्तान्यभिन्नानि वा मूत्रयन् कन्यकादोषकृद्-भुज्यमानानि चेद् दुष्टतां तद्गृहिण्यास्तथा स्यादुपानत्फलं गोस्तु सम्मूत्रणेऽवर्णजः सङ्करः ॥ १(ख)

Again, if the dog passes urine on or kicks a poisonous or thorny tree, fire-wood, stone, withered tree, bones or cremation ground, and goes ahead of a traveller, it indicates disasters to him; if it urinates on couches or vessels made by potters and the like that are unused and unbroken, virgins in his house will be spoiled; if on those that are being used, his wife's character will be soiled; the same refers to sandals also. If it passes urine on a cow, there will be an admixture of blood in his family by its contact with low-class people.

[Vide the following :

विषकण्टकशुष्कवृक्षलोष्टानवमूत्र्यास्थिचितेन याति चेच्छ्वा ।
न शुभोऽभिमुखं भषद्विधुन्वन् पुच्छाङ्गं विलिखन्नखे वसाश्च ॥

Both the author and the commentator have committed some grammatical errors: Instead of कण्टकि he has used कण्टकी; and अवमूत्र्य or सम्मूत्र्य, only मूत्र्य. The latter says: अभुक्ते उपानहावयमूत्रयन्. It should have been अभुक्तायाम् उपानहि.]

गमनमुखमुपानहं सम्प्रगृह्योपतिष्ठेद्यदा स्यात्तदा सिद्धये मांसपूर्णाननेऽर्थाप्तिरार्द्रेण चास्थ्ना शुभं साग्न्यलातेन शुष्केण चास्थ्ना गृहीतेन मृत्युः प्रशान्तोल्मुकेनाभिघातोऽथ पुंसः शिरोहस्तपादादिवक्त्रे भुवोऽभ्यागमो वस्त्रचीरादिभिर्व्यापदः केचिदाहुः सवस्त्रे शुभम् ॥ १ (ग)

When a dog comes towards a traveller with a slipper in its mouth, he will be successful in his undertakings; with meat, he will gain wealth; with a wet bone, prosperity or happiness; with a burning stick or dry bone, he will meet with his end; with an extinguished stick, he will get blows; with a human head, hand, foot or any other limb, he will get lands; with a cloth, tree-bark (or rags) or something like that, miseries; but according to some, good results will accrue, when it carries a cloth.

[Cf. पराशर—

गमने यातुर्वस्त्रगृहीतवक्त्रे सारमेये महानर्थलाभः ।]

प्रविशति तु गृहं सशुष्कास्थिवक्त्रे प्रधानस्य तस्मिन् वधः शृङ्खलाशीर्णवल्लीवरत्रादि वा बन्धनं चोपगृह्योपतिष्ठेद्यदा स्यात्तदा बन्धनं लेढि पादौ विधुन्वन् स्वकर्णावुपर्याक्रमं-श्चापि विघ्नाय यातुर्विरोधे विरोधस्तथा स्वाङ्गकण्डूयने स्यात् स्वपंश्चोर्ध्वपादः सदा दोषकृत् ॥ १ (घ)

When a dog enters a house with a dry bone in its mouth, the head of the family living in that house will die; when it comes towards a traveller with a chain, withered creeper, thong or some other means of tying, in its mouth, he will suffer imprisonment; when it licks his feet or shaking its ears, gets upon him, he will meet with obstacles; when it obstructs him, or scratches its own body, he will meet with hostility; when it sleeps with legs raised, there will be evil to him without doubt.

[Cf. गर्ग—

प्रस्थितस्य यदा श्वा वै मार्गं बद्ध्वा तु तिष्ठति ।
अवरुद्धं तदाध्वानं चौरैरिति विनिर्दिशेत् ॥]

सूर्योदयेऽर्काभिमुखो विरौति ग्रामस्य मध्ये यदि सारमेयः ।
एको यदा वा बहवः समेताः शंसन्ति देशाधिपमन्यमाशु ॥ २ ॥

If one or more dogs bark facing the Sun at sunrise from the middle of a village, it indicates an immediate change of the king.

[This verse, 6 and 19 are in the इन्द्रवज्रा metre; verses 3, 4, 5, 8, 14, 15, 16, 18 and 20 are in उपजाति.]

सूर्योन्मुखः श्वानलदिक्स्थितश्च चौरानलत्रासकरोऽचिरेण ।
मध्याह्नकालेऽनलमृत्युशंसी सशोणितः स्यात्कलहोऽपराह्णे ॥ ३ ॥

If a dog barks standing in the south-east corner and facing the Sun, there will ere long be danger from thieves and fire; if at mid-day, outbreak of fire and mortality (or death from fire); if in the afternoon, a sanguinary feud.

[Here in all the three periods, viz. forenoon, noon and afternoon, the dog should face the sun and stand in the S.E. corner.]

रुवन् दिनेशाभिमुखोऽस्तकाले कृषीवलानां भयमाशु वक्ते ।
प्रदोषकालेऽनिलदिङ्मुखश्च वक्ते भयं मारुततस्करोत्थम् ॥ ४ ॥

A dog barking at the Sun at sunset indicates immediate danger to agriculturists; one barking towards the north-west in the evening (i.e. after sunset), causes troubles from storm and thieves.

उदङ्मुखश्चापि निशार्धकाले विप्रव्यथां गोहरणं च शास्ति ।
निशावसाने शिवदिङ्मुखश्च कन्याभिदूषानलगर्भपातान् ॥ ५ ॥

A dog barking at the north at midnight portends trouble to Brāhmaṇas, and cattle-lifting; one facing the north-east towards the dawn, scandal about virgins, outbreak of fire and miscarriage of foetuses.

उच्चैःस्वराः स्युस्तृणकूटसंस्थाः प्रासादवेश्मोत्तमसंस्थिता वा ।
वर्षासु वृष्टिं कथयन्ति तीव्रामन्यत्र मृत्युं दहनं रुजश्च ॥ ६ ॥

If dogs standing on heaps of straw or on the tops of palaces (or temples) or mansions, bark very loud in the monsoon, it is an indication of severe rain; in other seasons, of death, fire and diseases.

प्रावृट्कालेऽवग्रहेऽम्भोऽवगाह्य प्रत्यावर्तं रेचकं श्चाप्यभीक्ष्णम् ।
आधुन्वन्तो वा पिबन्तश्च तोयं वृष्टिं कुर्वन्त्यन्तरे द्वादशाहात् ॥ ७ ॥

If during a drought in the rainy season dogs plunge in water, and then turning round and round shake off the water from their sides repeatedly, or stir or drink the water, there will be rain within 12 days.

[The commentator construes रेचकैः as पार्श्ववलितं कृत्वा पुनस्तदेव व्यत्ययेन करोति । This would mean turning round in the opposite direction. The metre is शालिनी in this as well as in 9, 10 and 11.]

द्वारे शिरोन्यस्य बहिःशरीरं रोरूयते श्वा गृहिणीं विलोक्य ।
रोगप्रदः स्यादथ मन्दिरान्तर्बहिर्मुखो वक्ति च बन्धकीं ताम् ॥ ८ ॥

If a dog barks looking at the lady of the house and placing its head on the threshold and body outside, there will be illness in the house; if, on the other hand, it stands inside the house and barks facing (her in) the yard outside, the lady is to be understood as an adulteress.

कुड्यमुत्किरति वेश्मनो यदा तत्र खानकभयं भवेत्तदा ।
गोष्ठमुत्किरति गोग्रहं वदेद्धान्यलब्धिमपि धान्यभूमिषु ॥ ९ ॥

If a dog scratches the wall of a house, there will be danger of its being burgled; when the ground in a cow-shed, cattle-lifting; when corn-fields or granaries, gain of corn.

[The metre is रथोद्धता.]

एकेनाक्ष्णा साश्रुणा दीनदृष्टिर्मन्दाहारो दुःखकृत्तद्गृहस्य ।
गोभिः साकं क्रीडमानः सुभिक्षं क्षेमारोग्यं चाभिधत्ते मुदं च ॥ १० ॥

A dog with tears in one eye, looking pitiable and eating very little, causes misery in the house; one sporting with cows indicates plenty of foodgrains, happiness, sound health and joy.

[All the editions read क्रीडमाणः which has two mistakes viz. the Śānac suffix and the cerebral nasal. It could be corrected thus:

गोभिः क्रीडन् साकमेवं ...]

वामं जिघ्रेज्जानु वित्तागमाय स्त्रीभिः साकं विग्रहो दक्षिणं चेत् ।
ऊरुं वामं चेन्द्रियार्थोपभोगः सव्यं जिघ्रेदिष्टमित्रैर्विरोधः ॥ ११ ॥

If a dog smells the left knee of a traveller, he will get money; if the right knee, he will have quarrels with women; if the left thigh, enjoyment of sexual pleasures; if the right thigh, dissensions with kinsmen and friends (or with very dear friends).

पादौ जिघ्रेद्यायिनश्चेदयात्रां प्राहार्थाप्तिं वाञ्छितां निश्चलस्य ।
स्थानस्थस्योपानहौ चेद्विजिघ्रेत् क्षिप्रं यात्रां सारमेयः करोति ॥ १२॥

If a dog smells the feet of a traveller, it forbids the journey; if those of a person standing still, it indicates the influx of the desired amount of wealth; if the slippers of one in his own place, an immediate journey.

उभयोरपि जिघ्रणे हि बाह्वोर्विज्ञेयो रिपुचौरसम्प्रयोगः ।
अथ भस्मनि गोपयीत भक्षान् मांसास्थीनि च शीघ्रमग्निकोपः ॥ १३ ॥

If it smells both the arms of a person, he will have a confrontation with his enemies and thieves; if it hides eatables, flesh or bones inside ashes, there will soon be an outbreak of fire.

[The expressions जिघ्रणम् and गोपयीत are incorrect. The correct forms are in order घ्राणम् and गोपाय्यात् or गुप्यात् ।

Cf. गर्ग—

यदा श्वा जिघ्रति भुजौ यातुर्द्वावपि निर्दिशेत् ।
रिपुचौरभयं घोरं तस्मिन्नुत्पातदर्शने ॥
आमिषं तु यदाऽऽगृह्य तृणैराच्छाद्य तिष्ठति ।
उत्पातं तादृशं दृष्ट्वा विन्द्यादग्निमुपस्थितम् ॥

The metre is औपच्छन्दसिक.]

ग्रामे भषित्वा च बहिः श्मशाने भषन्ति चेदुत्तमपुंविनाशः ।
यियासतश्चाभिमुखो विरौति यदा तदा श्वा निरुणद्धि यात्राम् ॥ १४॥

When dogs after barking in the village go out to the cemetery and bark there, a prominent person of the village will die. When a dog barks facing a person about to go on a journey, it forbids the journey.

उकारवर्णे विरुतेऽर्थसिद्धिरोकारवर्णेन च वामपार्श्वे ।
व्याक्षेपमौकाररुतेन विन्द्यान्निषेधकृत्सर्वरुतंश्च पश्चात् ॥ १५ ॥

When a dog howls producing the sound of "U" or 'O' to the left of a traveller, he will achieve success or get wealth; the sound of "Au" indicates distress; and all kinds of cries behind him forbid the journey.

[In उकार and ओकार the suffix कार comes in the sense of वर्ण. Hence उकारतुल्ये would have been better. The commentator does not connect वामपार्श्वे with the first sentence as well].

खं खेति चोच्चैश्च मुहुर्मुहुर्ये रुवन्ति दण्डैरिव ताड्यमानाः ।
श्वानोऽभिधावन्ति च मण्डलेन ते शून्यतां मृत्युभयं च कुर्युः ॥ १६ ॥

If dogs produce repeatedly the sound "Kham Khaṁ" in a loud voice, as if they were beaten with clubs, or run in a circular group towards a traveller, they indicate the futility of his journey and fear of death.

[According to the commentator this omen refers to the entire village or town. Hence the fourth line would mean:—"They foretell the devastation of the city and danger of death." However, the preposition अभि in अभिधावन्ति seems to refer to the traveller.]

प्रकाश्य दन्तान्यदि लेढि सृक्विणी तदाशनं मृष्टमुशन्ति तद्विदः ।
यदाननं लेढि पुनर्न सृक्विणी प्रवृत्तभोज्येऽपि तदान्नविघ्नकृत् ॥ १७ ॥

If a dog showing its teeth licks the corners of its mouth, the traveller will get a sumptuous feast, so opine those well-versed in the science; but if it licks its mouth (face) and not the corners of the mouth, there will be obstruction to his eating food, though he may have begun to eat it.

[प्रवृत्तभोज्येऽपि may also be interpreted as "Though one's food is ready." The metre is वंशस्थ.]

ग्रामस्य मध्ये यदि वा पुरस्य भषन्ति संहत्य मुहुर्मुहुर्ये ।
ते क्लेशमाख्यान्ति तदीश्वरस्य श्वारण्यसंस्थो मृगवद्विचिन्त्यः ॥ १८ ॥

If dogs bark repeatedly in a group in the middle of a village or town, its lord will have troubles; a wild dog shall be treated just like a deer.

[For omens connected with the deer refer to LXXXVI. 43 *supra.*]

वृक्षोपगे क्रोशति तोयपातः स्यादिन्द्रकीले सचिवस्य पीडा ।
वायोर्गृहे सस्यभयं गृहान्तः पीडा पुरस्यैव च गोपुरस्थे ॥ १९ ॥

भयं च शय्यासु तदीश्वराणां याने भषन्तो भयदाश्च पश्चात् ।
प्रयापसव्या जनसन्निवेशे भयं भषन्तः कथयन्त्यरीणाम ॥ २० ॥

If a dog barks standing near a tree, there will be rain; if near Indrakīla (cross bar of a door), the minister will suffer; if in the north-western corner inside a house, the crops will be endangered; if at the city gate, the city itself will have troubles; if on beds (or cots), their owners will be in peril. Dogs barking behind a traveller cause danger to him; those barking to the left of a group of men presage danger to them from their enemies.

[The commentator states in the colophon 'शाकुने' instead of 'सर्वशाकुने' which term he has used at the end of the previous three chapters. This suggests that this and the following chapters deal only with particular types of omens.]

शिवारुतम् ॥ ९० ॥

Chapter XC—On the Cries of Jackals.
Section V

श्वभिः शृगालाः सदृशाः फलेन विशेष एषां शिशिरे मदाप्तिः ।
हूहूरुतान्ते परतश्च टाटा पूर्णः स्वरोऽन्ये कथिताः प्रदीप्ताः ॥ १ ॥

Jackals are similar to dogs in effect, with the difference that the former get passion for mating in the Śiśira (i.e. last part of winter, in the months of Māgha and Phālguṇa). The sound 'Hūhū' at the end of their howling, and 'Ṭā-ṭā' thereafter are *full*; all other sounds are said to be *Burning*.

[The metre of this is उपजाति, of the next and of the 14 इन्द्रवज्रा. In winter the cries of jackals are of no consequence.]

लोमाशिकायाः खलु कक्कशब्दः पूर्णः स्वभावप्रभवः स तस्याः ।
येऽन्ये स्वरास्ते प्रकृतेरपेताः सर्वे च दीप्ता इति सम्प्रदिष्टाः ॥ २ ॥

The sound *Kakka* of the Lomāśikā (Hair-eating animal similar to the jackal) is *full*, as it is its natural cry. All other sounds being opposed to the natural one are termed *Burning*.

पूर्वोदीच्योः शिवा शस्ता शान्ता सर्वत्र पूजिता ।
धूमिताभिमुखी हन्ति स्वरदीप्ता दिगीश्वरान् ॥ ३ ॥

The jackal is commendable in the east and the north; one standing in a *Tranquil* quarter and having a pleasant sound is always highly favourable; one facing the *Smoking* quarter and having *Burning* (i.e. harsh) sound destroys the rulers of that direction.

[This and the following 9 verses are in the *Śloka* metre of the अनुष्टुभ् class.]

राजा कुमारो नेता च.........॥ ४ ॥ [This is a mere repetition of verse 34 of LXXXVI *supra*.]

सर्वविश्वशुभा दीप्ता विशेषेणाह्न्यशोभना ।
पुरे सैन्येऽपसव्या च कष्टा सूर्योन्मुखी शिवा ॥ ५ ॥

In all quarters, a *Burning* jackal is of evil consequences, especially in the day-time; one going from right to left of a town or army, and facing the Sun is harmful.

याहीत्यग्निभयं शास्ति टाटेति मृतवेदिका ।
धिग्धिगदुष्कृतिमाचष्टे सज्वाला देशनाशिनी ॥ ६ ॥

If its cry is like 'Yāhi', there will be danger from fire; if like 'Ṭāṭā', the news of somebody's death will be received; if like 'Dhig dhig', there will be great calamity; if it is flaming in the mouth, the country will be ruined.

[मृतिवेदिका is another reading for मृतवेदिका.]

नैव दारुणतामेके सज्वालायाः प्रचक्षते ।
अर्काद्यनलवत् तस्या वक्त्रं लालास्वभावतः ॥ ७ ॥

Some sages (such as Kāśyapa) do not attribute the dreadful nature to the flaming jackal. For, on account of the intrinsic nature of its Saliva, it mouth is fiery like the Sun and other luminaries.

[In the second line आक्रान्तानलवत् is another reading, referred to by Utpala, which appears to be more reasonable. It would mean: like a burning stick which when whirled round looks like a circle of fire.

Cf. काश्यप—

नैव दारुणता तस्याः सज्वालायाः स्वभावतः ।
लालायाः साग्निकं वक्त्रमतः सा शुभदा शिवा ॥]

अन्यप्रतिरुता याम्या सोद्बन्धमृतशंसिनी ।
वारुण्यनुरुता सैव शंसते सलिले मृतम् ॥ ८ ॥

The cry of a jackal stationed in the south being followed by another, indicates the death of a relative by hanging; but in the west, by drowning.

अक्षोभः श्रवणं चेष्टं धनप्राप्तिः प्रियागमः ।
क्षोभः प्रधानभेदश्च वाहनानां च सम्पदः ॥ ९ ॥

फलमासप्तमादेतदग्राह्यं परतो रुतम् ।
याम्यायां तद्विपर्यस्तं फलं षट्पञ्चमादृते ॥ १० ॥

When a jackal howls once, twice, thrice, four times, five times, six times or seven times, the effects will severally be freedom from distress, hearing good news, gain of wealth, arrival of a beloved person, turmoil, dissensions among the king's ministers (or breaking of a valuable article ?) or prosperity (increase) of vehicles. If it cries more times, it should be ignored; but if it cries in the south, the above effects of the frequency will be just the contrary, save for the fifth and the sixth. [The respective effects in the south will be – distress, hearing bad news, loss of wealth, separation from a beloved person, turmoil, dissensions and decay of vehicles.]

या रोमाञ्चं मनुष्याणां शकृन्मूत्रं च वाजिनाम् ।
रावात् त्रासं च जनयेत् सा शिवा न शिवप्रदा ॥ ११ ॥

A jackal that causes horripilation in men, horses to pass dung and urine, and frightens people through howl, leads to disastrous consequences.

मौनं गता प्रतिरुते नरद्विरदवाजिभिः ।
या शिवा सा शिवं सैन्ये पुरे वा सम्प्रयच्छति ॥ १२ ॥

When a jackal keeps quiet on its cry being re-echoed by men, elephants or horses, whether in a town or a military camp, prosperity will accrue to it therefrom.

भेभेति शिवा भयङ्करी भोभो व्यापदमादिशेच्च सा ।
मृतिबन्धनिवेदिनी फिफे हूहू चात्महिता शिवा स्वरे ॥ १३ ॥

If the jackal's cry sounds like 'Bhe-bhe', the effect will be dreadful; if like 'Bho-bho', there will be great misery; if like 'Phi-phe', death or imprisonment; and if like 'Hū-hū', benefit will accrue to the traveller.

[The expression भयङ्करी should have ended in आ according to grammatical rules. The commentator too commits a mistake here: the word रुवन्ती in शब्दं रुवन्ती should not have the nasal element. The metre is वैतालीय.]

शान्ता त्ववर्णात्परमारुवन्ती टाटामुदीर्णामिति वाश्यमाना ।
टे टे च पूर्वं परतश्च थे थे तस्याः स्वतुष्टिप्रभवं रुतं तत् ॥ १४ ॥

If a jackal stands in a *Tranquil* direction and having a pleasant voice produces the sound A first and then Ā or the harsh sound 'Ṭā-ṭā', or one like 'Ṭe-ṭe' first and then 'The-the', the result will be auspicious to the traveller [or because all such sounds are born of its heart's joy].

उच्चैर्घोरं वर्णमुच्चार्य पूर्वं पश्चात्क्रोशेत्क्रोष्टुकस्यानुरूपम् ।
या सा क्षेमं प्राह वित्तस्य चाप्तिं संयोगं वा प्रोषितेन प्रियेण ॥ १५ ॥

If a jackal cries at first producing some harsh sound in a very high pitch and then howls in its natural way, it indicates preservation and acquisition of wealth and union with a beloved person who had gone abroad.

[The metre is शालिनी.]

मृगचेष्टितम् ॥ ९१ ॥

Chapter XCI—Behaviour of Wild Animals
Section VI

सीमागता वन्यमृगा रुवन्तः स्थिता व्रजन्तोऽथ समापतन्तः ।
सम्प्रत्यतीतैष्यभयानि दीप्ताः कुर्वन्ति शून्यं परितो भ्रमन्तः ॥ १ ॥

Wild animals standing in a 'Burning' direction at the border of a town or village and crying indicate danger during the same day; those going away from the border in the same circumstance, danger that is over; and those coming towards it, danger that is impending. If they move around it, the town or village will be deserted.

[This and the following verse are in the उपजाति metre.]

ते ग्राम्यसत्त्वैरनुवाश्यमाना भयाय रोधाय भवन्ति वन्यैः ।
द्वाभ्यामपि प्रत्यनुवाशितास्ते वन्दिग्रहायै च मृगा रुवन्ति ॥ २ ॥

If the wild animals standing in a 'Burning' part of the border of a town cry and their cries are re-echoed by domestic rural animals, peril to the town is indicated; if by other wild animals, siege; and if by both domestic and wild animals, kidnapping of women.

[After giving the meaning of वन्दिग्रहा the commentator explains: तत्पुरं बलादेव शत्रुभिर्नीयत इत्यर्थः ।]

वन्ये सत्त्वे द्वारसंस्थे पुरस्य रोधो वाच्यः सम्प्रविष्टे विनाशः ।
सूते मृत्युः स्याद्भयं संस्थिते च गेहं याते बन्धनं सम्प्रविष्टम् ॥ ३ ॥

When a wild animal stands at the town-gate, the town will be besieged; when the animal enters it, it will be destroyed; when it brings forth a young one, there will be death; when it dies, danger; when it enters a house, its owner will be imprisoned.

[The metre is शालिनी.]

गवेङ्गितम् ॥ ९२ ॥

Chapter XCII—Intention of Cows
Section VII

गावो दीनाः पार्थिवस्याशिवाय पादैर्भूमिं कुट्टयन्त्यश्च रोगान् ।
मृत्युं कुर्वन्त्यश्रुपूर्णायताक्ष्यः पत्युर्भीतास्तस्करानारुवन्त्यः ॥ १ ॥

Cows looking pitiable indicate misery to the king (or its owner); burrowing the earth with their hoofs, diseases; with eyes filled with tears, owner's death; bellowing in panic, trouble from thieves.

[This and the last verse are in the शालिनी metre.]

अकारणे क्रोशति चेदनर्थो भयाय रात्रौ वृषभः शिवाय ।
भृशं निरुद्धा यदि मक्षिकाभिस्तदाशु वृष्टिं सरमात्मजैर्वा ॥ २ ॥

If a cow lows without any reason, there will be calamity; if at night, danger; but if a bull, happiness; if a cow is completely swarmed in front with flies, or obstructed by dogs, there will be rain in the near fature.

[The metre is उपेन्द्रवज्रा.]

आगच्छन्त्यो वेश्म बम्भारवेण संसेवन्त्यो गोष्ठवृद्ध्यै गवां गाः ।
आर्द्राङ्ग्यो वा हृष्टरोम्ण्यः प्रहृष्टा धन्या गावः स्युर्महिष्योऽपि चैवम् ॥ ३ ॥

If cows while returning home with the sweet cry of Bambhā, follow other cows (fondling them), there will be an increase of cattle wealth in the house; if they are wet in body, happy or have the hairs standing on ends, they bring fortune to their owner. All the above remarks apply to she-buffaloes as well.

[The author commits two errors in this verse, viz. संसेवन्त्यः for संसेवमानाः, and हृष्टरोम्ण्यः for हृष्टरोमाणः. Following the author Utpala too commits the mistake in निषेवन्त्यः. There is another reading viz. आगव्यूतेः instead of आगच्छन्त्यः, गव्यूति is a distance of about 4 miles.]

अश्वेङ्गितम् ॥ ९३ ॥

Chapter XCIII—Intention of Horses
Section VIII

उत्सर्गान्न शुभदमासनात्परस्थं वामे च ज्वलनमतोऽपरं प्रशस्तम् ।
सर्वाङ्गज्वलनमवृद्धिदं हयानां द्वे वर्षे वहनकणाश्च धूपनं वा ॥ १ ॥

It is a general rule that a flame behind and to the left of the saddle on a horse's back, is inauspicious; elsewhere it is favourable. Flaming all over the body of horses leads to loss; so do sparks or smoke on their body, for two years continuously.

[Such portents as mentioned here are mentioned in the Rāmāyaṇa and the Mahābhārata. The commentator remarks here: अश्वानामुत्पातवशेन ज्वालारूपमवयवेषु दृश्यते ।

Cf. the following

तत्रोत्सर्गेणासनपश्चिमभागाश्रये ज्वलनमेवम् ।
नेष्टमितरत्र शस्तं वामेतरपार्श्वयोस्तद्वत् ॥

The metre is प्रहर्षिणी.]

अन्तःपुरं नाशमुपैति मेढ्रे कोशः क्षयं यात्युदरे प्रदीप्ते ।
पायौ च पुच्छे च पराजयः स्याद्वक्त्रोत्तमाङ्गज्वलने जयश्च ॥ २ ॥

If the flame appears in the horse's penis, the king's harem will be ruined; in the stomach, his treasure; in the anus and the tail, the king will be defeated; in the face and head, he will be victorious.

[This verse is in इन्द्रवज्रा metre, 14 in उपेन्द्रवज्रा, and verses 3, 4, 10 and 11 in उपजाति.]

स्कन्धासनांसज्वलनं जयाय बन्धाय पादज्वलनं प्रदिष्टम् ।
ललाटवक्षोऽक्षिभुजे च धूमः पराभवाय ज्वलनं जयाय ॥ ३ ॥

The flaming of a horse's shoulders, back (where the saddle is put) or sides of the neck leads to the owner's victory; that of the hind legs, to his imprisonment; smoke on its forehead, breast, eyes or fore-legs, to defeat, while flame in them leads to victory.

[Though the two words स्कन्ध and अंस mean the same thing, the commentator explains the latter as ग्रीवापार्श्वगौ तदंसौ. But he says that पादाः शफाः—hoofs. I think that is not the meaning intended here in view of the word भुज in the next quarter. So पाद should mean, hind legs.]

नासापुटप्रोथशिरोऽश्रुपातनेत्रे च रात्रौ ज्वलनं जयाय ।

पलाशताम्रासितकर्बुराणां नित्यं शुकाभस्य सितस्य चेष्टम् ॥ ४ ॥

The flaming at night of the snout, middle of the nose, head, the lower part of the cheeks (where the tears fall) and eyes of horses that are green, reddish, dark or variegated (or grey?) leads to success; it is always i.e. both by day and night, auspicious with those that are white or have the hue of parrots.

[Vide the following :—

सममन्यत्पदकेसरपुच्छेषु ज्वलनदहनकणधूमाः ।
राष्ट्रभयशोकसम्भ्रमसपत्नवक्त्रापमर्दकराः ॥
प्राक्फलतुल्यं पृष्ठे जघने वालेषु चैव निर्दिष्टम् ।
अन्तःपुरप्रकोपो मेढ्ज्वलने सधूमे वा ॥
नित्यं च वालकिरणे दाहज्वाला स्फुलिङ्गानाम् ।
स्कन्धासनांसदेशे धूमाबन्धाय चरणेषु ॥
वक्षोऽक्षिललाटभुजे त्वश्वानां ह्रेषितं च वदनेभ्यः ।
ज्वालोत्पत्तिर्जयदा धूमोत्पत्तिस्त्वभावाय ॥
नासापुटाश्रुपातप्रोथशिरोलोचने च रजनीषु ।
विजयाय प्रज्वलनं ताम्रासितहरितशबलानाम् ॥
विजयाय सर्वदैव हि सुशुक्लशुकवर्णयोर्ज्वलनमेषु ।
एवं च यथासम्भवमन्येष्वपि वाहनेषु फलम् ॥]

प्रद्वेषो यवसाम्भसां प्रपतनं स्वेदो निमित्ताद्विना

कम्पो वा वदनाच्च रक्तपतनं धूमस्य वा सम्भवः ।

अस्वप्नश्च विरोधिनां निशि दिवा निद्रालसध्यानता

सादोऽधोमुखता विचेष्टितमिदं नेष्टं स्मृतं वाजिनाम् ॥ ५ ॥

Antipathy to grass and water, falling down, sweating, convulsion without any cause, falling of blood from or appearing of smoke in the mouth, keeping vigil at night through mutual hatred or quarrel, drowsiness and pensive mood by day, langour and down-cast face—none of these activities of horses is said to be auspicious.

[Cf. the following:—

निद्रानिरोधालसनीलनेत्राः प्रध्यानशून्यस्मृतयो दिनेषु ।

निशासु चान्योन्यविरोधनिद्रानष्टास्तुरङ्गा न शिवाय भर्तुः ॥

In the light of this quotation, the word विरोधिनां may also be taken as विरोधिता, meaning 'horses fighting with one another'.

The metre is शार्दूलविक्रीडित.]

आरोहणमन्यवाजिनां पर्याणादियुतस्य वाजिनः ।
उपवाह्यतुरङ्गमस्य वा कल्पस्यैव विपन्न शोभना ॥ ६ ॥

If a horse carrying a saddle and a rider gets upon another horse, or if the royal horse that is quite fit meets with some disaster, the result will not be favourable.

[The metre is वैतालीय.]

क्रौञ्चवद्रिपुवधाय ह्रेषितं ग्रीवया त्वचलया च सोन्मुखम् ।
स्निग्धमुच्चमनुनादि हृष्टवद्ग्रासरुद्धवदनैश्च वाजिभिः ॥ ७ ॥

If a horse neighs like a Krauñca bird (curlew or heron) or with its face raised and neck motionless, or has a pleasant, loud and resonant neigh, or neighs happily with its mouth filled with grass, the enemy will be killed.

[This and the following two verses are in रथोद्धता metre.]

पूर्णपात्रदधिविप्रदेवतागन्धपुष्पफलकाञ्चनादि वा ।
द्रव्यमिष्टमथवा परं भवेद्ध्रेषतां यदि समीपतो जयः ॥ ८ ॥

If in the vicinity of a neighing horse there is a full pot (filled with water or any other auspicious substances), curds, a Brāhmaṇa, a deity, perfumes, flowers, fruits, gold and the like, or some other desirable article, there will be victory.

भक्ष्यपानखलिनाभिनन्दिनः पत्युरौपयिकनन्दिनोऽथवा ।
सव्यपार्श्वगतदृष्टयोऽथवा वाञ्छितार्थफलदास्तुरङ्गमाः ॥ ६ ॥

Horses that willingly take to their fodder, drink and bit or other accoutrements, or cast glances at their right side, bestow all desired objects on their masters.

[The commentator takes पत्युः with औपयिकनन्दिनः and explains it as—liking whatever is used by the master. The following quotation, no doubt, uses the compound स्वाम्युपकरणाभिनन्दिता, which may be interpreted as Bhaṭṭotpala has done. However, it may also be construed as: liking its master and its equipments, Cf. the following:—

इष्टानिष्टव्यञ्जकमतः परं ह्रेषितं समवधार्यम् ।
तच्च चलितप्रसारितशिरोधरोद्भूतमिष्टफलम् ॥

ग्रासान्तर्वक्त्राणामुच्चैः स्निग्धानुनादि गम्भीरम् ।
द्विजपूर्णभाजनेष्टद्रव्यस्रग्गन्धसुरभूलैः ।।
खलिनान्नपानधर्मस्वाम्युपकरणाभिनन्दिता चैषाम् ।
सर्वार्थसिद्धये स्याद् दक्षिणपार्श्वे विलोकयताम् ।।]

वामैश्च पादैरभिताडयन्तो महीं प्रवासाय भवन्ति भर्तुः ।
सन्ध्यासु दीप्तामवलोकयन्तो ह्लेषन्ति चेद् बन्धपराजयाय ।। १० ।।

If horses stamp the earth with their left hoofs, their master will go abroad; if they neigh facing the 'Burning' quarter at any juncture (morning, evening, midday or midnight), he will suffer imprisonment or defeat.

प्रतीव ह्लेषन्ति किरन्ति बालान् निद्रारताश्च प्रवदन्ति यात्राम् ।
रोमत्यजो दीनखरस्वराश्च पांसून् ग्रसन्तश्च भयाय दृष्टाः ।। ११ ।।

If they neigh too much or too frequently, shake their tails or are sleepy, they indicate their master's journey; if they drop hair, have feeble or harsh sound, or eat the dust of the earth, they indicate danger to their master.

[According to Pāṇini ह्लेषन्ते and ग्रसमानाः would be correct. The conjunct consonant in ह्ले does not make the previous short syllable Guru, as Piṅgala has an exception in the case of प्र and ह्र. Cf. the following:—

सन्ध्यासु दीप्तदिङ्मुखसम्भ्रमगाढप्रनष्टनिद्राश्च ।
ह्लेषन्तो भयजनना वधबन्धपराजयकराश्च ।।
वक्रीकृतवालधयो दक्षिणपार्श्वानुशायिनो नेष्टाः ।
वामचरणैः क्षितितलं घ्नन्तो ज्ञेयाः प्रवासाय ।।]

समुद्गवद्दक्षिणपार्श्वशायिनः पदं समुत्क्षिप्य च दक्षिणं स्थिताः ।
जयाय शेषेष्वपि वाहनेष्विदं फलं यथासम्भवमादिशेद्बुधः ।। १२ ।।

If horses lie on their right side like a box, or stand on the ground with their right leg raised, they confer success on their masters. The same effects as given above will have to be applied by a wise man to other animals (such as elephants and camels) as well according to the circumstances.

[In the case of elephants, camels, etc. the appearance of smoke and sparks of fire is not applicable. The metre is वंशस्थ.]

आरोहति क्षितिपतौ विनयोपपन्नो
यात्रानुगोऽन्यतुरगं प्रतिह्रेषते च ।
वक्त्रेण वा स्पृशति दक्षिणमात्मपार्श्वं
योऽश्वः स भर्तुरचिरात्प्रचिनोति लक्ष्मीम् ॥ १३ ॥

The horse that is very obedient when the king mounts it, goes in or faces the direction to which the king is bound (or follows the party of sojourners), and reciprocates when others neigh, or touches its right side with its mouth, enhances ere long its master's wealth (and power).

[The metre is वसन्ततिलका.]

मुहुर्मुहुर्मूत्रशकृत् करोति न ताड्यमानोऽप्यनुलोमयायी ।
अकार्यभीतोऽश्रुविलोचनश्च शिवं न भर्तुस्तुरगोऽभिधत्ते ॥ १४ ॥

The horse that passes urine and dung too frequently, does not go along the proper direction in spite of being whipped, shows fright without any cause (such as vicinity of its enemies), and has tears in its eyes, does not betoken prosperity or happiness to its master.

[Here the word कार्य in अकार्यभीतः is used in the sense of कारण which is allowed in secondary expressions. The horse fears buffaloes, hogs, etc.]

उक्तमिदं हयचेष्टितमत ऊर्ध्वं दन्तिनां प्रवक्ष्यामि ।
तेषां तु दन्तकल्पनभङ्गम्लानादिचेष्टाभिः ॥ १५ ॥

Thus have I expounded the activities of horses. Hereafter I shall describe those of elephants. Their effects—good or bad—will have to be judged from the cutting, breaks, faded appearance, etc. of their tusks, and other features.

हस्तिचेष्टितम् ॥ ९४ ॥

Chapter XCIV—Attitude of Elephants
Section IX

दन्तस्य मूलपरिधिं द्विरायतं प्रोज्झ्य कल्पयेच्छेषम् ।
अधिकमनूपचराणां न्यूनं गिरिचारिणां किञ्चित् ॥ १ ॥

The elephant's tusk should be cut off at a height that is equal to twice its circumference at its root; but in the case of elephants roaming about marshy places a little more than the above should be left off, and in the case of those of mountains, a little less.

[This and the following five verses are mere repetitions of LXXIX 20-25 *supra*. Instead of श्रीवृक्ष, श्रीवत्स is the reading adopted here in verse 2. Cf. the following:

दन्तमूलपरिणाहदीर्घतां द्विः प्रमुच्य परतोऽपि कल्पयेत् ।
श्यावपूतिमलरक्तदर्शनं सर्पसत्त्वसदृशं च पापदम् ॥]

शुक्लः समः सुगन्धिः स्निग्धश्च शुभावहो भवेच्छेदः ।
गलनम्लानफलानि च दन्तस्य समानि भङ्गेन ॥ ७ ॥

If the cutting of the tusk be white, even glossy and of good smell, it would bestow prosperity. The effects of the dropping down, and the fading of colour of the tusk are similar to those of its breaking.

[Cf. the following:—

पार्थिवोपकरणोपमं यदा चिह्नमुद्वहति कल्पिते रदे ।
श्रीजयार्थबलवृद्धयस्तदा स्निग्धशुक्लरुचिराश्च शोभनाः ॥]

मूलमध्यदशनाग्रसंस्थिता देवदैत्यमनुजाः क्रमात्ततः ।
स्फीतमध्यपरिपेलवं फलं शीघ्रमध्यचिरकालसम्भवम् ॥ ८ ॥

The Gods, demons and human beings reside in the root, middle part and tip respectively of the elephant's tusk. The effects of omens in these parts will be in order great, moderate and slight, and will be felt in a short time (i.e. within a week), after some time (i.e. within a month), and after a long time (i.e. after a month) respectively.

[According to the commentators मनुजाः means देवविशेषाः. The metre of this and the following three verses is रथोद्धता]

दन्तभङ्गफलमत्र दक्षिणे भूपदेशबलविद्रवप्रदम् ।
वामतः सुतपुरोहितेभयान् हन्ति साटविकदारनायकान् ॥ ९ ॥

The effects of the right tusk breaking in these three parts (viz. root, middle and tip) are severally the fleeing of the king, the population and the army; of the left tusk, destruction of the prince, royal preceptor and the mahout, as well as of the army of mountaineers the king's consort and leading personages (commanders) respectively.

आदिशेदुभयभङ्गदर्शनात् पार्थिवस्य सकलं कुलक्षयम् ।
सौम्यलग्नतिथिभादिभिः शुभं वर्धतेऽशुभमतोऽन्यथा वदेत् ॥ १० ॥

If both the tusks are found to break, complete ruin of the royal family is to be predicted; but if the splitting occurs in a benefic ascendant (Taurus, Gemini, Cancer, Virgo, Libra, Sagittarius or Pisces), lunar day, asterism and the like, there will be an increase of prosperity and happiness; otherwise, there will be an increase of misery.

[Even Cancer would be a malefic ascendant, if the Moon be weak. The 15 days in a fortnight are divided into 5 groups, viz. Nandā, Bhadrā, Jayā, Riktā and Pūrṇā. According to Utpala all the lunar days except the Riktā ones are auspicious. This is not the whole truth, inasmuch as there are the Pakṣacchidras which are not considered to be auspicious. Benefic asterisms are those that are not termed Dreadful and Fierce. Even though the ascendant may technically be called malefic, yet it will give good results, provided it is occupied or aspected by benefics. Similarly, a benefic Lagna may be spoiled by the presence or aspect of malefics. In the case of mixed conditions, the results also will be mixed.]

क्षीरमृष्टफलपुष्पपादपेष्वापगातटविघट्टितेन वा ।
वाममध्यरदभङ्गखण्डने शत्रुनाशकृदतोऽन्यथा परम् ॥ ११ ॥

If the elephant be found to break or split the middle of its left tusk by striking against milky trees, or trees laden with sweet fruits or flowers, or against the banks of rivers, the destruction of the enemy is assured; otherwise (against thorny trees etc.) or at the breaking of the right tusk (or of the left one at the root or tip), there would be prosperity to the enemy.

[Elephants, and even bulls, indulge in a sport called *Vapra-kriḍā* in Sanskrit literature. This consists in the animal striking an embankment with its tusk.

Cf. वप्रक्रीडा परिणतगजप्रेक्षणीयं ददर्श । (Meghadūta).

स्खलितगतिरकस्मात् त्रस्तकर्णोऽतिदीनः
श्वसिति मृदु सुदीर्घं न्यस्तहस्तः पृथिव्याम् ।
द्रुतमुकुलितदृष्टिः स्वप्नशीलो विलोमो
भयकृदहितभक्षी नैकशोऽसृक्शकृत्कृत् ॥ १२ ॥

If the elephant has a stumbling gait, if its ears stop beating suddenly, if it appears very dejected, if it breathes soft and long, placing its trunk on the earth, if its eyes are full of tears or closed, if it is always sleepy, if it behaves in a refractory manner, if it eats something unwholesome, or if it passes blood (ichors?) and dung too frequently, it forebodes danger.

[Utpala construes द्रुत as चकित frightened or fleeting. The metre is मालिनी.]

वल्मीकस्थाणुगुल्मक्षुपतरुमथनस्वेच्छया हृष्टदृष्टि-
र्यायाद्यात्रानुलोमं त्वरितपदगतिर्वक्त्रमुन्नम्य चोच्चैः ।
कक्ष्यासन्नाहकाले जनयति च मुहुः शीकरं बृंहितं वा
तत्काले वा मदाप्तिर्जयकृदथ रदं वेष्टयन् दक्षिणं च ॥ १३ ॥

If the elephant breaks wantonly ant-hills, trunks of lopped trees, bushes, shrubs (or small trees) or trees, if it looks jolly, if it goes in the direction of the march, with quick steps, holding aloft its face, if at the time of its being accoutred it ejects spray or trumpets repeatedly, or if it gets intoxicated at the time, or if it takes its trunk around the right tusk, it confers victory.

[Utpala says क्षुपं शष्पम् meaning green grass. The metre is स्रग्धरा.]

प्रवेशनं वारिणि वारणस्य ग्राहेण नाशाय भवेन्नृपस्य ।
ग्राहं गृहीत्वोत्तरणं नृपस्य तोयात् स्थलं वृद्धिकरं नृभर्तुः ॥ १४ ॥

If an elephant is dragged into the water by a crocodile, the king will be destroyed; if, on the other hand, the elephant should drag the crocodile from the water to the bank, the king would be victorious (and prosperous).

[The word नृपस्य at the end of the third quarter must have been put instead of द्विपस्य by the scribes by mistake. For, there is another word meaning 'king' at the end of the verse. This verse contains happy alliteration.

The metre is उपजाति.]

वायसविरुतम् ॥ ९५ ॥

Chapter XCV – Cries of Crows
Section X

प्राच्यानां दक्षिणतः शुभदाः काकाः करायिका वामाः ।
विपरीतमन्यदेशेष्ववधिर्लोकप्रसिद्ध्यैव ॥ १ ॥

For the people of the eastern countries the sight of crows to their right and of the Karāyikā to their left, is favourable. This is to be reversed in other countries. The demarcation of countries is to be understood duly fiom convention.

[For the determination of the several countries refer to XIV *supra.*]

वैशाखे निरुपहते वृक्षे नीडः सुभिक्षशिवदाता ।
निन्दितकण्टकिशुष्केष्वसुभिक्षभयानि तद्देशे ॥ २ ॥

If a crow builds its nest in an unspoilt tree in the month of Vaiśākha (the second month of the lunar year), there will be plenty of food and happiness (as well as prosperity); if in a condemned, thorny or dry tree, there will be danger of famine in that country.

नीडे प्राक्शाखायां शरदि भवेत्प्रथमवृष्टिरपरस्याम् ।
याम्योत्तरयोर्मध्यात्प्रधानवृष्टिस्तरोरुपरि ॥ ३ ॥

शिखिदिशि मण्डलवृष्टिर्नैर्ऋत्यां शारदस्य निष्पत्तिः ।
परिशेषयोः सुभिक्षं मूषकसम्पच्च वायव्ये ॥ ४ ॥

If the crow's nest be in an eastern branch of a tree, there would be good rain in the autumnal season (i.e. in the month of Āśvina and Kārttika); if it be on a western branch, it would be in the rainy season itself; if it be on a southern or northern branch, it would be between the two seasons, rainy and autumnal (i.e. in the months of Bhādrapada and Āśvina); if it be on the top of the tree, there would be copious rain in all the four months viz., Śrāvaṇa, Bhādrapada, Āśvina and Kārttika; if it be in the south-eastern branch, there would be sporadic rain; if in the south-western one, autumnal crops would flourish; if in the other two corners, there would be plenty of foodgrains, but in the north-western branch, rats would multiply enormously.

शरदर्भगुल्मवल्लीधान्यप्रासादगेहनिम्नेषु ।
शून्यो भवति स देशश्चौरानावृष्टिरोगार्त्तः ॥ ५ ॥

If the crow builds its nest on reeds (*Jypha elephantina*), holy gran (*Desmostachya bipinnata*), bushes, creepers, corn, temples, house or in pits, the country will be denuded being afflicted with robbers, drought and disease.

[Cf. यात्रा—

शस्तो नीडस्तु वैशाखे पादपे निरुपद्रवे ।
देशोत्थानं तु वल्मीकचैत्यधान्यगृहादिषु ॥]

द्वित्रिचतुःशावत्वं सुभिक्षदं पञ्चभिर्नृपान्यत्वम् ।
अण्डावकिरणमेकाण्डताऽप्रसूतिश्च न शिवाय ॥ ६ ॥

A crow with two, three or four fledgelings confers abundant food; with five, brings about a change of rulers; one throwing away the eggs, or laying a single egg or no egg at all, is not at all auspicious.

चौरकवर्णैश्चौराश्चित्रैर्मृत्युः सितैस्तु वह्निभयम् ।
विकलैर्दुर्भिक्षभयं काकानां निर्दिशेच्छिशुभिः ॥ ७ ॥

If the fledglings of the crow are of the colour of Coraka (*curcuma latifolia*), there will be trouble from robbers; if of variegated colours, there will be death; if white, there will be danger from fire; of crippled (deficient in limbs), fear of famine.

[Cf. the following:

काकानां स्रवणे द्वित्रिचतुःशावाः शुभावहाः ।
चोरचित्रकश्वेताश्च वर्णाश्चौराग्निमृत्युदाः ॥
अण्डावकिरणैर्ध्वाङ्क्ष्या दुर्भिक्षमरकावुभौ ।
शावानां विकलत्वे वा निःशावत्वे कृतौ तथा ॥

अनिमित्तसंहतैर्ग्राममध्यगैः क्षुद्भयं प्रविरुवद्भिः ।
रोधश्चक्राकारैरभिघातो वर्गवर्गस्थैः ॥ ८ ॥

If crows congregate without any cause in the middle of a village and caw aloud, there will be danger of famine; if they fly in a circular group, the village will be besieged; if they appear in several groups, there will be disaster.

[Cf. the following:—

अकार्यसंहतैर्भेदो रोधश्चक्राकृतिस्थितैः ।
वर्गगैश्चाभिघातः स्याद् रिपुवृद्धिश्च निर्भयैः ॥]

अभयाश्च तुण्डपक्षैश्चरणविघातैर्जनानभिभवन्तः ।
कुर्वन्ति शत्रुवृद्धिं निशि विचरन्तो जनविनाशम् ॥ ९ ॥

If the crows attack people fearlessly with their beaks, wings or kicks, there will be increase of enemies; if they fly at night, destruction of the people is indicated.

सव्येन खे भ्रमद्भिः स्वभयं विपरीतमण्डलैश्च परात् ।
अत्याकुलं भ्रमद्भिर्वातोद्भ्रामो भवति काकैः ॥ १० ॥

If crows fly in clockwise fashion, the person concerned will have trouble from his own kinsmen; if in the anti-clockwise manner, from enemies; if in a very disorderly fashion, there will be a whirlwind.

[Second line is explained by Utpala in a peculiar manner: अत्याकुलं सोद्यमं . . . वातोद्भ्रामो भवत्यनवस्थितिरित्यर्थः It may be that the commentator has not been reported properly. Cf. the following:

पुरसैन्योपरि व्योम्नि व्याकुलैरनिलाद्भयम् ।
सव्यमण्डलगैः स्वोत्थमपसव्यैः पराद्भयम् ॥]

ऊर्ध्वमुखाश्चलपक्षाः पथि भयदाः क्षुद्भयाय धान्यमुषः ।
सेनाङ्गस्था युद्धं परिमोषं चान्यभृतपक्षाः ॥ ११ ॥

If crows raise their beaks and flap their wings, a traveller will experience danger on his way; if they steal corn, there will be famine, if they are perched on something belonging to the army, a battle; if they have wings similar (very dark) to those of the cuckoo, robbery.

[Cf. the following:—

युद्धं सेनाङ्गसंस्थेषु मोषकृत् स्वविलेखने ।
चरन्निशि विनाशाय दुर्भिक्षं चान्नमोषकृत् ॥]

भस्मास्थिकेशपत्राणि विन्यसन् पतिवधाय शय्यायाम् ।
मणिकुसुमाद्यवहनने सुतस्य जन्मान्यथाङ्गनायाश्च ॥ १२ ॥

If it throws ashes, bones, hair or leaves on a bed, the owner will meet with his end; if it strikes the bed with a gem, flower or something like that (e.g. fruit), a son will be born to him; if with something else, a daughter.

[Cf. the following:—

तृणभस्मास्थिकेशाश्च शयने स्वामिमृत्युदाः ॥

The commentator explains अन्यथा तृणकाष्ठादिनावहननं करोति . . ., but in the light of the line quoted above, तृण—grass being a bad omen cannot be an indication for the birth of a daughter. I feel that it should be something like लता, creeper that is green.]

पूर्णाननेऽर्थलाभः सिकताधान्यार्द्रमृत्कुसुमपूर्वैः ।
भयदो जनसंवासाद्यदि भाण्डान्यपनयेत्काकः ॥ १३ ॥

When the crow's beak is filled with sand, corn, wet clay, flower or the like, there will be gain of wealth; when it takes away vessels or treasures (valuables) from a place where dwell many people, there is danger in store.

वाहनशस्त्रोपानच्छत्रच्छायाङ्गकुट्टने मरणम् ।
तत्पूजायां पूजा विष्ठाकरणेऽन्नसम्प्राप्तिः ॥ १४ ॥

If the crow strikes a vehicle, weapon, slipper, shade of the umbrella or man himself, the person concerned will die; if it worships (with flowers etc.) any of these, he will get honour; if it passes excreta on it, he will get food.

[Cf. the following :—

उपानच्छस्त्रयानाङ्गच्छत्रच्छायावकुट्टने ।
मृत्युं तत्स्वामिनो ब्रूयात्पूजा स्यात्तत्प्रपूजने ॥]

यद्द्रव्यमुपनयेत्तस्य लब्धिरपहरति चेत्प्रणाशः स्यात् ।
पीतद्रव्यैः कनकं वस्त्रं कार्पासिकैः सितैं रूप्यम् ॥ १५ ॥

A person will gain or lose the same article as has been brought near or taken away from him. If the article brought or taken away be yellow in colour, it will be gold; if cotton, clothes; if white, silver.

[Cf. the following:—

हरेदुपनयेद् वापि यद् द्रव्यं वायसोऽग्रतः ।
तन्नाशलब्धी विज्ञेये हेम पीते विनिर्दिशेत् ॥]

सक्षीरार्जुनवञ्जुलकूलद्वयपुलिनगा रुवन्तश्च ।
प्रावृषि वृष्टिं दुर्दिनमनृतौ स्नाताश्च पांसुजलैः ॥ १६ ॥

If in the rainy season the crow caws sitting on a milky tree, the Arjuna (*Terminalia arjuna*), the Vañjula (*calamus rotang*) or on both the sand banks of rivers, there will be good rains; in other seasons, merely the sky will be overcast. Similarly, if it bathes in dust or water in the rainy season, there will be rain; in others, only a cloudy sky.

[According to rural Indian tradition the sight of a bathing crow is very inauspicious.]

दारुणनादस्तरुकोटरोपगो वायसो महाभयदः ।
सलिलमवलोक्य विरुवन् वृष्टिकरोऽब्दानुरावी च ॥ १७ ॥

If the crow caws frightfully from the interior of a tree-hollow, there will be great danger; if it caws looking at water, or after the thunder of clouds, there will be rain.

दीप्तोद्विग्नो विटपे विकुट्टयन् वह्निकृद्विधुतपक्षः ।
रक्तद्रव्यं दग्धं तृणकाष्ठं वा गृहे विदधत् ॥ १८ ॥

If it strikes its beak in pain against a branch, standing in the 'Burning' quarter and shaking its wings, there is danger from fire; if it brings into a house a red substance, something burnt, grass or wood, the same effect will follow.

[The commentator takes दग्ध as an adjective to तृणकाष्ठम्. Cf. the following:—

रक्तद्रव्यं प्रदग्धं च धान्यं गेहेऽग्निदः स्मृतः ॥]

ऐन्द्र्याद्विदिगवलोकी सूर्याभिमुखो रुवन् गृहे गृहिणः ।
राजभयचोरबन्धनकलहाः स्युः पशुभयं चेति ॥ १९ ॥

If the crow facing the Sun caws from a house, looking at the east, south, west or north, the owner will have trouble from the king, thieves, imprisonment or quarrel in order; if at any intermediate quarter, his domestic animals will be in trouble (or his life will be endangered by his domestic animals).

शान्तामैन्द्रीमवलोकयन् रुयाद्राजपुरुषमित्राप्तिः ।
भवति च सुवर्णलब्धिः शाल्यन्नगुडाशनाप्तिश्च ॥ २० ॥

If the crow caws looking at the east that is 'Tranquil', the person will be meeting king's officers and friends, acquiring gold and eating food consisting of rice and sweet pudding.

आग्नेय्यामनलाजीविकयुवतिप्रवरधातुलाभश्च ।
याम्ये माषकुलुत्थाभोज्यं गान्धर्विकैर्योगः ॥ २१ ॥

When it caws looking at the south-east that is 'Tranquil', one would gain (through) goldsmiths (those that live by fire), young damsels and costly minerals; if at the south, one would eat food prepared from black-gram and horse-gram, and come in contact with musicians.

[The word कुलुत्था is used here instead of कुलत्थ, the final long vowel being necessitated by the metre. Since the author uses the locative of आग्नेयी, it may also be construed that the crow stands in the S. E. and looks at the 'Tranquil' quarter.]

नैर्ऋत्यां दूताश्वोपकरणदधितैलपललभोज्याप्तिः ।
वारुण्यां मांससुरासवधान्यसमुद्ररत्नाप्तिः ॥ २२ ॥

If the crow caws looking at the 'Tranquil' south-west, one will get messengers, horses, implements (or equipments of horses), curds, oils, flesh and food; if at the west, flesh, toddy, spirituous liquor, corn and oceanic gems.

[Here too the alternative meaning may be given. According to the commentator पलल means अर्धपीडितास्तिलाः—half-crushed sesamum seeds.]

मारुत्यां शस्त्रायुधसरोजवल्लीफलाशनाप्तिश्च ।
सौम्यायां परमान्नाशनं तुरङ्गाम्बरप्राप्तिः ॥ २३ ॥

If it caws looking at the 'Tranquil north-west, one will get weapons, lotuses, fruits of creepers, and food; if at the north, milk porridge, horses and clothes.

[It is not clear why the author has used two words meaning 'weapon', unless he wants to distinguish between ordinary and sophisticated weapons.]

ऐशान्यां सम्प्राप्तिर्घृतपूर्णानां भवेदनडुहश्च ।
एवं फलं गृहपतेर्गृहपृष्ठसमाश्रिते भवति ॥ २४ ॥

If it caws looking at the 'Tranquil' north-east, one will eat edibles prepared in ghee, and get bulls. Thus the effects mentioned above accrue to the owner of the house, on whose roof the crow sits and caws.

गमने कर्णसमश्चेत् क्षेमाय न कार्यसिद्धये भवति ।
अभिमुखमुपैति यातुर्विरुवन् विनिवर्त्तयेद्यात्राम् ॥ २५ ॥

A crow flying at a height equal to that of a traveller's ear, leads to his health, but not to success in his work; one coming towards him cawing obstructs the journey.

[Utpala interprets कर्णसमः as कर्णप्रदेशे यातुर्गच्छति. The crow should fly without cawing in the same direction and at the height of the traveller's ear. Vide the following:—

यातुः कर्णसमो ध्वाङ्क्षः क्षेमे नार्थप्रसाधकः ॥]

वामे वाशित्वादौ दक्षिणपार्श्वेऽनुवाशते यातुः ।
अर्थापहारकारी तद्विपरीतोऽर्थसिद्धिकरः ॥ २६ ॥

If a crow caws at first to the left and then to the right of a traveller, his wealth will be stolen; if it is in the opposite direction, he will get wealth.

यदि वाम एव विरुवन् मुहुर्मुहुर्यायिनोऽनुलोमगतिः ।
अर्थस्य भवति सिद्ध्यै प्राच्यानां दक्षिणश्चैवम् ॥ २७ ॥

If a crow caws repeatedly to the left of a traveller and flies in the same direction, his wealth will increase; this will be the effect, if it caws to the right of the people of the eastern countries.

वामः प्रतिलोमगतिर्विरुवन् गमनस्य विघ्नकृद्भवति ।
तत्रस्थस्यैव फलं कथयति तद्वाञ्छितं गमने ॥ २८ ॥

If a crow caws to the left of a traveller and flies in the opposite direction, his journey will be hindered. The success or otherwise of the object of a person's journey is indicated by the crow before he sets out.

दक्षिणविरुतं कृत्वा वामे विरुयाद्यथेप्सितावाप्तिः ।
प्रतिवाश्य पुरो यायाद् द्रुतमत्यर्थागमो भवति ॥ २९ ॥

If the crow caws at first to the right and then to the left of a person, he will get the desired objects; if it cries and flies fast in front of him, he will gain quickly abundant wealth.

[Vide the following:—

वामपार्श्वस्थिताद्याति दक्षिणाद्वापि वामगः ॥]

प्रतिवाश्य पृष्ठतो दक्षिणेन यायाद् द्रुतं क्षतजकारी ।
एकचरणोऽर्कमीक्षन् विरुवंश्च पुरो रुधिरहेतुः ॥ ३० ॥

If it caws first behind him and then flies fast to his right, or if it caws in front looking at the Sun and standing on one leg alone, he will soon bleed.

[ईक्षन् is wrong for ईक्षमाणः ।]

दृष्ट्वार्कमेकपादस्तुण्डेन लिखेद्यदा स्वपिच्छानि ।
पुरतो जनस्य महतो वधमभिधत्ते तदा बलिभुक् ॥ ३१ ॥

If it scratches with its beak its own feathers, looking at the Sun and standing in front on one leg, then a great massacre of men is indicated.

सस्योपेते क्षेत्रे विरुवति शान्ते ससस्यभूलब्धिः ।
आकुलचेष्टो विरुवन् सीमान्ते क्लेशकृद्यातुः ॥ ३२ ॥

If the crow caws standing in a 'Tranquil' quarter of a corn-field, the person concerned will get lands consisting of corn-fields; if it caws behaving in a disorderly manner in the border of a village, the traveller will have troubles.

सुस्निग्धपत्रपल्लवकुसुमफलानम्रसुरभिमधुरेषु ।
सक्षीराव्रणसंस्थितमनोज्ञवृक्षेषु चार्थसिद्धिकरः ॥ ३३ ॥

The crow sitting on a tree with soft (glossy) leaves, sprouts, flowers and fruits, on a sweet-smelling tree, one with sweet fruits, a milky one, one without holes, or an attractive tree, brings wealth or success.

निष्पन्नसस्यशाद्वलभवनप्रासादहर्म्यहरितेषु ।
धन्योच्छ्रयमङ्गल्येषु चैव विरुवन् धनागमदः ॥ ३४ ॥

A crow cawing from a place full of crops and green grass, from a house, temple, mansion or something green, or from a blessed, lofty or auspicious place, causes influx of wealth.

गोपुच्छस्थे वल्मीकगेऽथवा दर्शनं भुजङ्गस्य ।
सद्यो ज्वरो महिषगे विरुवति गुल्मे फलं स्वल्पम् ॥ ३५ ॥

If a crow caws sitting on the tail of a cow or on an anthill, one will have the sight of a snake; if on a buffalo, one will be suffering from fever the same day; if on a bush, the effect is negligible.

कार्यस्य व्याघातस्तृणकूटे वामगेऽम्बुसंस्थे वा ।
ऊर्ध्वाग्निप्लुष्टेऽशनिहते च काके वधो भवति ॥ ३६ ॥

When the crow caws sitting on a heap of straw or on water to the left of a person, his work will be spoiled by obstacles; when it is perched on tree whose top is burnt by fire or struck by lightning, death will ensue.

कण्टकमिश्रे सौम्ये सिद्धिः कार्यस्य भवति कलहश्च ।
कण्टकिनि भवति कलहो वल्लीपरिवेष्टिते बन्धः ॥ ३७ ॥

If it sits on an auspicious but thorny tree, there will be success of the undertaking and quarrel too; if on a thorny tree, there will be quarrel; if on a tree entwined with creepers, imprisonment.

छिन्नाग्रेऽङ्गच्छेदः कलहः शुष्कद्रुमस्थिते ध्वाङ्क्षे ।
पुरतश्च पृष्ठतो वा गोमयसंस्थे धनप्राप्तिः ॥ ३८ ॥

If it sits on a tree whose top is chopped off, one will be deprived of a limb; if on a withered tree, there will be quarrel; if on cowdung in front of or behind a person, he will get money.

मृतपुरुषाङ्गावयवस्थितोऽभिविरुवन् करोति मृत्युभयम् ।
भञ्जन्नस्थि च चञ्च्वा यदि विरुवत्यस्थिभङ्गाय ॥ ३९ ॥

If it caws sitting on a limb of a dead body in front, there will be fear of death; if it breaks a bone with its beak and caws, the traveller's bone will be fractured.

रज्ज्वस्थिकाष्ठकण्टकिनिःसारशिरोरुहानने रुवति ।
भुजगगवदंष्ट्रितस्करशस्त्राग्निभयान्यनुक्रमशः ॥ ४० ॥

If the crow caws holding in its mouth a rope, bone, stick, thorn, rubbish and hair, the effects in order are danger from serpents, diseases, tusked animals, thieves, weapons and fire.

[Vide the following:—

काष्ठरज्ज्वस्थिनिःसारकेशकण्टकिभृद्रुवन् ।
व्यालाहिव्याधिशस्त्राग्नितस्करेभ्यो भयङ्करः ॥]

सितकुसुमाशुचिमांसाननेऽर्थसिद्धिर्यथेप्सिता यातुः ।
पक्षौ धुन्वन्नूर्ध्वानने विघ्नं मुहुः क्वणति ॥ ४१ ॥

If it caws holding in its beak a white flower, dirt or flesh, the tourist will achieve his desired objects; if it caws frequently shaking its wings and raising its face, his journey will be hindered.

यदि शृङ्खलां वरत्रां वल्लीं वाऽऽदाय वाशते बन्धः ।
पाषाणस्थे च भयं क्लिष्टापूर्वाध्विकयुतिश्च ॥ ४२ ॥

If a crow caws holding a chain, strap or creeper, the traveller will get imprisonment; if it stands on a stone, he will have danger and contact with a suffering stranger who is a wayfarer.

[The word आध्विक is not correct. The author could have used अध्वग without changing the metre, the other correct form being आध्वनिक.]

अन्योन्यभक्षसङ्क्रामिताननने तुष्टिरुत्तमा भवति ।
विज्ञेयः स्त्रीलाभो दम्पत्योर्विरुवतोर्युगपत् ॥ ४३ ॥

If two crows put some food into the mouth of each other, the traveller will have the greatest satisfaction. If a male and a female crow caw simultaneously, he will get a damsel.

प्रमदाशिरउपगतपूर्णकुम्भसंस्थेऽङ्गनार्थसम्प्राप्तिः ।
घटकुट्टने सुतविपद्घटोपहदनेऽन्नसम्प्राप्तिः ॥ ४४ ॥

If a crow sits on a full pot on the head of a damsel, the traveller will win the hand of a woman and wealth; if it strikes the pot, there will be danger to his son's life; if it passes excreta on the pot, he will get food.

स्कन्धावारादीनां निवेशसमये रुवंश्चलत्पक्षः ।
सूचयतेऽन्यत्स्थानं निश्चलपक्षस्तु भयमात्राम् ॥ ४५ ॥

If a crow caws beating its wings at the time of encampment or making a halting place, change of place is indicated; if it does not shake its wings, there will be only fear.

[Vide पराशर—

सेनानिविष्टः सार्थे वा वासो हृष्टो न वाशते ।
तस्य देशप्रयातस्य भयमत्रोपजायते ॥]

प्रविशद्भिः सैन्यादीन् सगृध्रकङ्कैर्विनामिषं ध्वाङ्क्षैः ।
प्रविरुद्भिस्तैः प्रीतिर्द्विषतां युद्धं विरुद्धैश्च ॥ ४६ ॥

If crows enter an army, town or village along with vultures and herons, without carrying meat and without fighting among themselves, one will make peace with one's enemies; if they fight, there will be war with the enemies.

बन्धः सूकरसंस्थे पङ्काक्ते सूकरे द्विकेऽर्थाप्तिः ।
क्षेमं खरोष्ट्रसंस्थे केचित्प्राहुर्वधं तु खरे ।। ४७ ।।

If two crows are seen standing on a hog, there will be imprisonment; if on a hog covered with silt, gain of wealth; if on a donkey or camel, happiness; but according to some, there will be death, if it is on the donkey.

[Vide the foll owing:—

वधबन्धकरः क्रोशन् खरसूकरपृष्ठगः ।
पङ्कदिग्धशरीरस्य वराहस्योपरिस्थितः ।।
वायसः शस्यते यातुस्तूष्णींभूतो रुवन्नपि ।।]

वाहनलाभोऽश्वगते विरुवत्यनुयायिनि क्षतजपातः ।
अन्येऽप्यनुव्रजन्तो यातारं काकवद्विहगाः ।। ४८ ।।

If a crow caws sitting on the back of a horse, one will get vehicles; if it caws following a traveller, his blood will be spilt. Other birds that follow a traveller also produce the same effects as the crow.

[Vide काश्यप—

उलूककङ्कप्लवगा गृध्रश्येनादयश्च ये ।
मांसाशिनश्च विहगास्तुल्या वायसचेष्टितैः ।।]

द्वात्रिंशत्प्रविभक्ते दिक्चक्रे यद्यथा समुद्दिष्टम् ।
तत्तथैव विधेयं गुणदोषफलं यियासूनाम् ।। ४९ ।।

Whatever good or bad effects have been predicted of other omens in 32 parts of the 'Cycle of Quarters' are to be applied to the crow as well in the case of those that wish to undertake a journey.

[The commentator explains how the 'Cycle of Quarters' is to be applied to the crow: If a crow caws in the east that is 'Tranquil' and if its cry is not harsh or behaviour not inauspicious, then the traveller will get the great blessings of the gods he worships; if its behaviour is inauspicious, the effect will be moderate; if the east is 'Burning' and its behaviour cruel, the traveller will have trouble from the king.

का इति काकस्य रुतं स्वनिलयसंस्थस्य निष्फलं प्रोक्तम् ।
कव इति चात्मप्रीत्यै केति रुते स्निग्धमित्राप्तिः ॥ ५० ॥

करेति कलहं कुरुकुरु च हर्षमथ कटकटेति दधिभक्तम् ।
के के विरुतं कु कु वा धनलाभं यायिनः प्राह ॥ ५१ ॥

If the crow sitting in its nest caws as *Kā*, there is no effect (good or bad) at all; if as *Kava*, one will get the greatest joy; if as *Ka*, one will meet one's bosom friend; if as *Kara*, one will have quarrel; if as *Kuru Kuru*, joy; if as *Kaṭa Kaṭa*, curded rice; if as *Ke ke* or *Ku ku*, the traveller will get wealth.

[In the second verse कलहं should have preceded करेति.]

खरे खरे पथिकागममाह कखाखेति यायिनो मृत्युम् ।
गमनप्रतिषेधिकमा कखला सद्योऽभिवर्षाय ॥ ५२ ॥

If the crow produces the sound, *Khare Khare*, it indicates the arrival of a traveller (guest); if *Ka-khā-khā*, the traveller's death; if *Ā*, the journey is forbidden; if *Ka-Kha-lā*, immediate rainfall is indicated.

[In this verse also the author has spoiled the metre by introducing जगण in the first place. He could have put it thus: पथिकागममाह खरे खरे कखाखेति यायिनो मृत्युम् ।]

काकेति विघातः काकटीति चाहारदूषणं प्राह ।
प्रीत्यास्पदं कवकवेति बन्धमेवं कगाकुरिति ॥ ५३ ॥

If the crow produces the sound *Kā kā*, there will be ruin (or hindrance?); if *Kākaṭi*, the food will be vitiated or poisoned; if *Kava-kava*, one will make friends with somebody; if *Kagāku*, one will get imprisoned.

[The commentator draws our attention to a reading viz. प्रीत्या स्वदम्पती कवकव, and rejects it on the authority of गर्ग as given below:—

रुते कवकवेति स्यात् प्रस्थिते वायसस्य तु ।
अपूर्वप्रीतये तच्च धनलाभाय निर्दिशेत् ॥
एवं कगाकु इति रुते बन्धोबंन्धनं भवति ॥]

करगौ विरुते वर्षं गुडव त् त्रासाय वडिति वस्त्राप्तिः ।
कलयेति च संयोगः शूद्रस्य ब्राह्मणैः साकम् ॥ ५४ ॥

If the crow cries as *Karagau*, there will be rain; if as Guḍa, fear; if as Vaḍ, gain of clothes; if as *Kalaya*, Śūdras will come in contact with Brāhmaṇas.

कडिति फलाप्तिः फलदाहिदर्शनं टड्डिति प्रहाराः स्युः ।
स्त्रीलाभः स्त्रीति रुते गडिति गवां पुडिति पुष्पाणाम् ॥ ५५ ॥

If the crow caws as *Kaḍ*, there will be the attainment of one's desired objects as well as the sight of such surpents as bestow good results; if as *Taḍ*, one will receive blow; if as *Strī*, one will get a damsel; if as *gaḍ*, cows; if as *puḍ*, flowers.

[The commentator interprets फलदाहिदर्शनं in many ways: 'फलाप्तिः सदाप्तिः फलदा ततोऽपि विशिष्टतरं फलं लभ्यते। तथाहिदर्शनं भवति।' It may also be construed thus: फलं द्यतीति फलदं शुभफलभञ्जकम् अहिदर्शनम्—sight of a snake which spoils the good effects. Or it may be dissolved as फलं दहतीति फलदाही. तस्य दर्शनम्—sight of some person or thing which burns the good effects.]

युद्धाय टाकुटाक्विति गुहु वह्निभयं कटेकट कलहः ।
टाकुलि चिण्टिचि केकेकेति पुरं चेति दोषाय ॥ ५६ ॥

If it produces the sound *Ṭāku-ṭāku*, there will be a fight; if *Guhu*, danger from fire; if *Kaṭe-kaṭe*, quarrel. The sounds *Ṭākuli*, *Ciṇṭici*, *Ke-Ke-Ke* and *Pura*, all lead to harmful results.

काकद्वयस्यापि समानमेतत्फलं यदुक्तं रुतचेष्टिताद्यैः ।
पतत्रिणोऽन्येऽपि यथैव काको वन्याः श्ववच्चोपरिदंष्ट्रिणो ये ॥ ५७ ॥

Whatever effects have been assigned to the cry, movements etc. of a single crow, equally apply to those of two crows also. Other birds (not mentioned here) too are to be treated on a par with the crow; and wild animals that have tusks above (like boars) are likened to the dogs.

[Vide पराशर—

शकुनाः पुंसनामानो वायसेन प्रकीर्तिताः ।
तथैव स्त्रीसनामानः पिपील्याः परिकीर्तिताः ॥

The metre of this verse and 61 is उपजाति, while that of 59 उपेन्द्रवज्रा.]

स्थलसलिलचराणां व्यत्ययो मेघकाले
प्रचुरसलिलवृष्टयै शेषकाले भयाय ।
मधु भवननिलीनं तत्करोत्याशु शून्यं
मरणमपि च नीला मक्षिका मूर्ध्नि लीना ॥ ५८ ॥

When terrestrial and aquatic animals change their places i.e. move in water and on land respectively in the rainy season, there will be heavy rains; but in other seasons, it indicates danger; bees building their honey-comb inside a house, will make it empty soon; blue flies clinging to the head bring about death.

[The metre is मालिनी.]

विनिक्षिपन्त्यः सलिलेऽण्डकानि पिपीलिका वृष्टिनिरोधमाहुः ।
तरुं स्थलं वापि नयन्ति निम्नाद्यदा तदा ताः कथयन्ति वृष्टिम् ॥ ५९ ॥

Ants laying eggs on water bespeak drought; if they carry their eggs from a pit either to a tree or an elevated ground, they indicate rain.

कार्यं तु मूलशकुनेऽन्तरजे तदह्नि
विन्द्यात्फलं नियतमेवमिमे विचिन्त्याः ।
प्रारम्भयानसमयेषु तथा प्रवेशे
प्राह्यं क्षुतं न शुभदं क्वचिदप्युशन्ति ॥ ६० ॥

The effect of an undertaking (or journey) is to be judged from the initial omen; the effect of one occurring in the middle (i.e. later) will be felt on the same day. In this manner all these omens mentioned so far must needs be taken into account at the commencement of any work and at the time of journeys, as well as of entering a new house; but sneezing should be paid special attention to, as nowhere is it admitted as a beneficial omen.

[The metre is वसन्ततिलका.]

शुभं दशापाकमविघ्नसिद्धिं मूलाभिरक्षामथवा सहायान् ।
दुष्टस्य संसिद्धिमनामयत्वं वदन्ति ते मानयितुर्नृपस्य ॥ ६१ ॥

Good omens indicate the maturing of a Daśā (major period of a planet) in a beneficial manner, accomplishment of the objects without obstacles, preservation of the hereditary kingdom (or wealth), getting allies, easy subjugation of unyielding enemies, and enjoyment of sound health, to a king who has faith in them.

[This is said with reference to those who have belief in astrology and omens which form a part of Indian culture. Unbelievers may say, 'we do not believe in them', but like the Sun's light the Lord's command applies equally to all, and संशयात्मा विनश्यति—the unbeliever suffers. The word मानयिता in the text has exactly the same significance as मानना in Hindi.]

क्रोशादूर्ध्वं शकुनविरुतं निष्फलं प्राहुरेके
तत्रानिष्टे प्रथमशकुने मानयेत् पञ्च षट् च ।
प्राणायामान्नृपतिरशुभे षोडशैव द्वितीये
प्रत्यागच्छेत् स्वभवनमतो यद्यनिष्टस्तृतीयः ॥ ६२ ॥

According to some authorities (such as Sage Kāśyapa) the cries of omens heard after one has gone a Krośa (about 2 miles) have no effect at all. If the first omen within that distance is untoward, the king should do eleven Prāṇāyāmas; if the second too proves evil, he should do 16 Prāṇāyāmas, and if the third too persists in being inauspicious, he should return home.

[Vide काश्यप—

क्रोशादनन्तरं यत् स्याच्छुभं वा यदि वाऽशुभम् ।
निष्फलं तच्च विज्ञेयं शकुनानां विचेष्टितम् ॥

A Prāṇāyāma is defined thus:

सव्याहृतिं सप्रणवां गायत्रीं शिरसा सह ।
त्रिः पठेदायतप्राणः प्राणायामः स उच्यते ॥

Vyāhṛtis are seven in number. The Gāyatrīśiras is आपो ज्योती रसोऽमृतं ब्रह्म भूर्भुवः स्वरोम् । A Prāṇāyāma consists of three parts: Pūraka, filling in, Kumbhaka, retention and Recaka, evacuation. The metre is मन्दाक्रान्ता.]

शाकुनोत्तरम् ॥ ९६ ॥

Chapter XCVI – Further Omens
Section XI

दिग्देशचेष्टास्वरवासरर्क्षमुहूर्तहोराकरणोदयांशान् ।
चरस्थिरोन्मिश्रबलाबलं च बुद्ध्वा फलानि प्रवदेद्रुतज्ञः ॥ १ ॥

One well versed in the science of the cries of birds and beasts ought to declare the effects of omens only after taking into consideration the relative strength of the omens as well as of the particular quarter (east etc. as well as *Charcoal*, *burning* etc.), place (good and bad), movements, sound (*Burning* and *Tranquil*), weekday, asterism (Dhruva, Mṛdu, Dāruṇa, Kṣipra, Ugra, Cara or Sādhāraṇa), Muhūrta (a period of 48 minutes), Horā (distance of 15° or Kālahorā), Karaṇa (Bava etc.), Ascendant, its subdivision (such as decanate, Navāṁśa, Dvādaśāṁśa or Triṁśāṁśa) and its being a movable, fixed or dual sign.

[The metre of this, 7, 8 and 15 is उपजाति and of 4 and 17 उपेन्द्रवज्रा and of 5, 6, 9, 10, 11 and 16 इन्द्रवज्रा.]

द्विविधं कथयन्ति संस्थितानामागामिस्थिरसञ्ज्ञितं च कार्यम् ।
नृपदूतचरान्यदेशजातान्यभिघातः स्वजनादि चागमाख्यम् ॥ २ ॥

In the case of persons who are not on the move, there are two kinds of the effects of omens viz. the stable (past and present) and the unstable or the future. To the latter category belong those relating to the king, envoy, spy, foreign countries, attack or troubles, and kinsmen.

[The metre is औपच्छन्दसिक.]

उद्बद्धसङ्ग्रहणभोजनचौरवह्नि-
वर्षोत्सवात्मजवधाः कलहो भयं च ।
वर्गः स्थिरोऽयमुदयेन्दुयुते स्थिरर्क्षे
विन्द्यात् स्थिरं चरगृहे च चरं यदुक्तम् ॥ ३ ॥

The effects of omens pertaining to imprisonment (hanging ?), acquisition (or meeting), meals, thieves, fire, rain, festivities, sons, death, quarrels and fears belong to the *Stable* category, provided the Ascendant and the sign occupied by the Moon at the time are fixed signs; if they are movable ones, they will come under the *unstable* category.

[Here the commentator gives widely divergent meanings of some words: उद्बद्धम् means, according to him, संलग्नं तत्रैव संस्थितं गमागमवर्जितम्, meaning stuck or not moving. But it should mean, confined or hanged. He adds, एष वर्गो यदि स्थिरस्थानेषूत्पन्नः स्थिरस्थानस्थितेन शकुनेन सूचितस्तदा स्थिरसंज्ञः If these things are indicated by an omen standing on a stable or stationary object or place, then we must think that they are past ones; otherwise they will take place in the future. He says if the incident is stable, it is either past or will take place the same day.

[The metre is वसन्ततिलका.]

स्थिरप्रदेशोपलमन्दिरेषु सुरालये भूजलसन्निधौ च ।
स्थिराणि कार्याणि चराणि यानि चलप्रदेशादिषु चागमाय ॥ ४ ॥

The effects (good or bad) are called *Stable*, when the omens occur in a firm place, on a stone, in a house, a temple, on the earth and water; and *unstable* or *Future*, when they are moving objects (like carts or animals).

[भूजलसन्निधौ should ordinarily mean in the presence or vicinity of the earth and water. What is intended by the author seems to be 'on the earth and on water'.]

प्राप्योदयर्क्षक्षणदिग्जलेषु पक्षावसानेषु च ये प्रदीप्ताः ।
सर्वेऽपि ते वृष्टिकरा रुवन्तः शान्तोऽपि वृष्टिं कुरुतेऽम्बुचारी ॥ ५ ॥

All omens crying and situated in an Ascendant that happens to be a watery sign (Cancer, Capricorn or Pisces), in a watery asterism (Pūrvāṣāḍhā or Śatabhiṣak), in a watery Muhūrta (having the name of water or presided over by Varuṇa), and in a place where there is water, that occur at the end of the fortnights, that are *Blasted* (by Gods or by action), produce rain. Under the above circumstances, even a *Tranquil* omen that is aquatic causes rain.

आग्नेयदिग्लग्नमुहूर्तदेशेष्वर्कप्रदीप्तोऽग्निभयाय रौति ।
विष्ट्यां यमर्क्षोदयकण्टकेषु निष्पत्रवल्लीषु च दोषकृत्स्यात् ॥ ६ ॥

An omen *blasted* by the Sun crying and situated in the south-east, in a fiery Ascendant (Aries, Leo, Scorpio, Capricorn or

Aquarius), in a fiery Muhūrta, in the asterism Kṛttikā, and in a place where fire is kept, causes danger from fire; similarly, harmful is one occurring in the Viṣṭi karaṇa'* in a star presided over by Yama. (i.e. Bharaṇī), in a sign of Saturn happening to be the Ascendant and in thorny trees, and on creepers without leaves.

ग्राम्यः प्रदीप्तः स्वरचेष्टिताभ्यामुग्रो रुवन् कण्टकिनि स्थितश्च ।
भौमर्क्षलग्ने यदि नैर्ऋतीं च स्थितोऽभितश्चेत्कलहाय दृष्टः ॥ ७ ॥

A rural omen that is *blasted* by voice or action, that is crying fiercely, that is sitting on a thorny tree in the south-west, in the Ascendant owned by Mars (Aries or Scorpio), and facing a person, causes quarrels, when seen.

[Since the author has used नैर्ऋतीम् in the accusative, it may be taken along with अभितः, which would mean—facing the south-west. Otherwise why should he have not used the expression नैर्ऋते? The word अभितः may also be taken in the sense of 'on either side'.]

लग्नेऽथवेन्दोर्भृगुभांशसंस्थे विदिक्स्थितोऽधोवदनश्च रौति ।
दीप्तः स चेत्सङ्ग्रहणं करोति योन्या तया या विदिशि प्रदिष्टा ॥ ८ ॥

Or, when the omen cries with its face hung down, standing in an intermediate quarter and in the Navāṁśa of Venus (i.e. Libra) in the Ascendant of Cancer (which is presided over by the Moon), and being *blasted* (in place or sound), the person will get a woman of the type assigned to the particular corner (vide LXXXVI. 79).

[योन्योऽनुयायाद्दिशि सम्प्रदिष्टः is anothor reading. This would mean: He will meet somebody that is assigned to that quarter (where the omen is situated) and that happens to go along the same path. It appears that there is another reading viz. इन्दौ in the place of इन्दोः which is not noticed by the commentator. If such a reading be accepted, the meaning would be: When the Ascendant or the Moon occupies at the time a sign or Aṁśa owned by Venus, or when the Moon is in the Ascendant in an Aṁśa of Venus.]

पुंराशिलग्ने विषमे तिथौ च दिक्स्थः प्रदीप्तः शकुनो नराख्यः ।
वाच्यं तदा सङ्ग्रहणं नराणां मिश्रे भवेत् षण्ढकसम्प्रयोगः ॥ ९ ॥

An omen that is *Blasted* and posited in a male (odd) Ascendant, in an odd Tithi (lunar day) and in a cardinal direction is

*For a detailed account of the Karaṇas refer to the author's 'Fundamentals of Astrology' p. 185.

termed *Masculine*. In this case one will come in contact with men; if it is mixed i.e. in a male sign and in an even Tithi or *vice versa* or if the male omen is situated in an intermediate (female) quarter or *vice versa*, he will meet eunuchs.

एवं रवेः क्षेत्रनवांशलग्ने लग्ने स्थिते वा स्वयमेव सूर्ये ।
दीप्तोऽभिधत्ते शकुनो विरौति पुंसः प्रधानस्य हि कारणं तत् ॥ १० ॥

Similarly, if an omen that is *blasted*, cries, when the Ascendant or its Navāṁśa is owned by the Sun or when the Sun himself occupies the Ascendant, the arrival of an eminent personage is indicated.

[The word एवम् indicates that the conditions mentioned in the previous verse are to be repeated here.]

प्रारभ्यमाणेषु च सर्वकार्येष्वर्कान्विताद्भाद्गणयेद्विलग्नम् ।
सम्पद्विपच्चेति यथाक्रमेण सम्पद्विपच्चेति तथैव वाच्या ॥ ११ ॥

At the commencement of all works, count the distance in signs from the one occupied by the Sun to the Ascendant in the manner of 'Weal' and 'Woe' in order. Accordingly, prosperity or adversity of nndertakings will have to be predicted.

[If the Ascendant is an odd number from the Sign occupied by the Sun, the result will be auspicious; if even, harmful. In the next two verses the description of persons one is likely to meet is given.]

काणेनाक्ष्णा दक्षिणेनैति सूर्ये चन्द्रे लग्नाद् द्वादशे चेतरेण ।
लग्नस्थेऽर्के पापदृष्टेऽन्ध एव कुब्जः स्वर्क्षे श्रोत्रहीनो जडो वा ॥ १२ ॥

क्रूरः षष्ठ क्रूरदृष्टो विलग्नाद् यस्मिन् राशौ तद्गृहाङ्गे व्रणोऽस्य ।
एवं प्रोक्तं यन्मया जन्मकाले चिह्नं रूपं तत्तदस्मिन् विचिन्त्यम् ॥ १३ ॥

If the Sun occupies the 12th house from the Ascendant at the time, the person whom one will meet will be blind of the right eye; if the Moon be there, he will be blind of the left eye; if the Sun be in the Ascendant itself and be aspected by malefic, he will be completely blind. If the Sun in the above condition be in his own Sign, the person will be hunch-backed, deaf or an imbecile. If the 6th house from the Ascendant be occupied and aspected by malefics, the person will have an ulcer in the limb indicated by that sign. In this way, whatever marks or forms (or colours) have been expounded by me in connection with the time of births will have to be adopted here too.

[This is a clear reference to the Bṛhajjātaka which was evidently written before this work. In that work I.4 he explains the various limbs of the Time-Being beginning with the head. Here the first Sign, Aries, represents the head. Cf. also "त्रिकोणगे ज्ञे विबलैस्तथापरैर्मुखाङ्घ्रिहस्तैर्द्विगुणैस्तदा भवेत्" (IV. 17). Vide the following also. (IV·18-20):—

सौम्यर्क्षांशे रविजरुधिरौ चेत्सदन्तोऽत्र जातः
कुब्जः स्वर्क्षे शशिनि तनुगे मन्दमाहेयदृष्टे ।
पङ्गुर्मीने यमशशिकुजैर्वीक्षिते लग्नसंस्थे
सन्धौ पापे शशिनि च जडः स्यान्न चेत्सौम्यदृष्टिः ॥
सौरशशाङ्कदिवाकरदृष्टे वामनको मकरान्त्यविलग्ने ।
धीनवमोदयगैश्च दृकाणैः पापयुतैरभुजाङ्घ्रिशिराः स्यात् ॥
रविशशियुते सिंहे लग्ने कुजार्किनिरीक्षिते
नयनरहितः सौम्यासौम्यैः सबुद्बुदलोचनः ।
व्ययगृहगतश्चन्द्रो वामं हिनस्त्यपरं रवि-
रशुभगदिता योगा याप्या भवन्ति शुभेक्षिताः ॥

Here the the commentator remarks thus : अथागतस्याख्या न ज्ञानमाचार्यः करोति । तच्चाल्पबहुलं स्वल्पग्रन्थं मृदुबुद्धीनामगम्यमतोऽस्माभिस्तदेव **बोधियात्रायां यवनेश्वरकृतश्चाक्षरकोशो** व्याख्यायते । Then he comments on all the 32 verses of the Akṣarakośa of Yavaneśvara.]

अतः परं लोकनिरूपितानि द्रव्येषु नानाक्षरसङ्ग्रहाणि ।
इष्टप्रणीतानि विभाजितानि नामानि केन्द्रक्रमशः प्रवक्ष्ये ॥ १ ॥

Hereafter (after ascertaining the nature of the query) I shall explain in the order of the Kendras (angles) the names that are held by the objects of the world viz. minerals, vegetables and animals, with multifarious distinctions made at will and composed of various syllables.

[इष्टप्रणीतानि is interpreted by Utpala thus: इष्टैराप्तैर्नारायणार्कवसिष्ठपराशरमयप्रभृतिभिः प्रणीतानि So far Yavaneśvara has been treating of the method of guessing the exact object of the query.]

लग्नाम्बुसंस्थास्तनभःस्थितेषु क्षेत्रेषु ये लग्नगता गृहांशाः ।
तेभ्योऽक्षराण्यात्मगृहाश्रयाणि विन्द्याद्ग्रहाणां स्वगणक्रमेण ॥ २ ॥

The syllables belonging to the signs in accordance with the respective classes of sounds assigned to the planets will have to be gathered from the Navāṁśas of the signs signifying the Ascendant, the 4th, the 7th and the 10th houses.

कवर्गपूर्वान् कुजशुक्रचान्द्रिजीवार्कजानां प्रवदन्ति वर्गान् ।
यकारपूर्वाः शशिनो निरुक्ता वर्णास्त्वकारप्रभवा रवेः स्युः ॥ ३ ॥

The guttural, palatal, lingual, dental and labial class of consonants belong severally to Mars, Venus, Mercury, Jupiter and Saturn; the eight letters beginning with *ya* belong to the Moon; and the vowels to the Sun.

द्रेष्काणवद्ध्या प्रवदन्ति नाम त्रिपञ्चसप्ताक्षरमोजराशौ ।
युग्मे तु विन्द्याद् द्विचतुष्कषट्कं नामाक्षराणि गृहदृष्टिवद्ध्या ॥ ४ ॥

The number of letters constituting a name is to be deduced from the decanate that is rising. In an odd sign, the numbers will be three, five and seven respectively for the first, second and third decanates; and in an even sign, they will in order be 2, 4 and 6. They are also ascertained from the strength of the aspect of planets.

[There are four kinds of aspects viz. the *quarter* on the 3rd and 10th, the *half* on the 5th and the 9th; the *three-fourths* on the 4th and the 8th and the *full* aspect on the 7th house. Saturn, Jupiter and Mars exercise their *full* aspects even when they are $\frac{1}{2}$, $\frac{1}{4}$ and $\frac{3}{4}$ respectively.]

वर्गोत्तमे द्व्यक्षरकं चरांशे स्थिरर्क्षभागे चतुरक्षरं तत् ।
ओजेषु चैभ्यो विषमाक्षराणि स्युर्द्विस्वभावेषु तु राशिवच्च ॥ ५ ॥

If the Vargottama Navāṁśa of a Sign be signified by an even and a movable one, the name would consist of two syllables; if by an even and at the same time a fixed sign, four syllables. If the Vargottama Navāṁśa be an odd as well as a movable sign, there would be three letters; if it be a fixed as well as odd sign, five letters. If the Lagna be a dual sign, the name will consist of as many letters as correspond to the nature (odd or even) of the Sign.

[If Cancer or Capricorn be the Vargottamāṁśa rising at the time of query, it is both even and movable Rāśi (2 letters). The Vargottamāṁśa of Taurus, Leo, Scorpio and Aquarius is fixed, but of Taurus and Scorpio even (4 letters) and of Leo and Aquarius odd (5 letters). When the said Aṁśa is movable in an odd sign, the name will have three letters; if it is a fixed one in the same sign, five letters. Among the dual signs, if the Vargottama is an odd Aṁśa (in Gemini and Sagittarius), it will have three and seven letters respectively. On the other hand, if it is an even Aṁśa (in Virgo and Pisces), the name will consist of four and six letters respectively. Vide the following:—

त्रिपञ्चसप्ताक्षरमोजराशौ युग्मे तु विन्द्याद् द्विचतुष्कषट्कम् ॥

The result of this may be shown in the following diagram:

Odd Sign			Even Sign		
Movable Aṁśa	Fixed Aṁśa	Dual Aṁśa	Movable	Fixed	Dual
3 letters	5 letters	7 letters	2 letters	4 letters	6 letters]

द्विमूर्तिसञ्ज्ञे तु वदेद् द्विनाम सौम्येक्षिते द्विप्रकृतौ च राशौ ।
यावान् गणः स्वोदयगोंऽशकानां तावान् ग्रहः सङ्ग्रहकेऽक्षराणाम् ॥ ६ ॥

In the case of a dual Sign, two names will have to be predicted; when it is aspected by benefics, then too the same result. The particular Navāṁśa rising at the time gives the number of letters constituting the name.

[सौम्येक्षिते is construed as 'when seen by Mercury', by the commentator.]

संयोगमादौ बहुलेषु विन्द्यात् कूटेषु संयोगपरं वदन्ति ।
स्वोच्चांशके द्विष्कृतमृक्षयोगाद् गुर्वक्षरं तद्भवनांशके स्यात् ॥ ७ ॥

If the rising sign be odd, the name would begin with a conjunct consonant; if even, with a letter followed by a conjunct consonant. When the planet (contributing a letter to the name) is posited in his highest exaltation, the letter is repeated according to the nature of the particular sign (odd or even); a name will have a strong syllable (Guru) in the particular place signified by the Navāṁśa rising at the time.

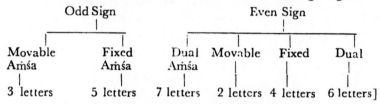

[The examples for the odd sign are Śrīdhara, Kṣīra, Smara etc.; those for the even sign Padma, Dharma, Vatsa etc. In a four-syllabled name it is like Vasudatta, Vasugupta etc. If the ascendant is an odd sign and if its lord is in his highest exaltation (vide Bṛhajjātaka I.13), then the letter in the odd place will be repeated, e.g. Darada, Dāmodara etc.; and if it is even, or in the even place, e.g. Devadeva, Dharādhara; in a two-syllabled name it will be like Kappa, Yappa, Valla etc. In an odd Sign the Guru syllable will be in the odd place, as in Kapittha, Aśvattha etc.; and in an even sign, in the even place, as in Khukkha, Ghaggha, Śuddha (in two-syllabled names), and Śuddhodana etc. (in four-syllabled ones).]

मात्राबियुक् स्याद् ग्रहयुक् त्रिकोणे द्रेष्काणपर्यायवदक्षरेषु ।
नभोबलेषूर्ध्वमधोऽम्बुजेषु ज्ञेयो विसर्गोऽस्तबलान्वितेषु ॥ ८॥

When the 5th or 9th house is occupied by planets, there will be an extra syllabic instant in the letter signified by the decanate. When the 10th house is strong, there will be the upper sign of a long syllable; when the 4th, lower sign; when the 7th, a Visarga.

[Vide the following:—

मनुष्यरूपा बलिनो विलग्नाश्चतुष्पदाश्चाक्षरमध्यसंस्थाः ।
जलोद्भवाख्या बलिनो जलस्थाः कीटोऽस्तगो व्योगतले द्विमूर्ताः ॥

also the बृहज्जातक I. 17—

कण्टककेन्द्रचतुष्टयसञ्ज्ञाः सप्तमलग्नचतुर्थखभानाम् ।
तेषु यथा विहितेषु बलाढ्याः कीटनराम्बुचराः पशवश्च ॥]

शीर्षोदयेषूर्ध्वमुशन्ति मात्रामधश्च पृष्ठोदयशब्दितेषु ।
तिर्यक् च विन्द्यादुभयोदये तां दीर्घेषु दीर्घामितरेषु चान्याम् ॥ ९॥

When a Śīrṣodaya (that rises with head foremost) Sign is rising, the syllabic instant will be upwards; when it is a Pṛṣṭhodaya (that rises with the hind part first), it will be downwards. In the case of a dual sign rising (Pisces which rises both ways), it is across; when it is a long sign, there is a long syllable; when it is medium or short, it will be short.

[Vide the following:—

शीर्षोदया मानुषसर्वरूपाः ससिंहकीटा यवनैर्निरुक्ताः ।
मत्स्यद्वयं तूभयतः प्रवृत्तं पृष्ठेन शेषास्तु सदोदयन्ति ॥

also बृ. जा. I.10—

गोजाश्विकर्किमिथुनाः समृगा निशाख्याः
पृष्ठोदया विमिथुनाः कथितास्त एव ।
शीर्षोदया दिनबलाश्च भवन्ति शेषा
लग्नं समेत्युभयतः पृथुरोमयुग्मम् ॥

The upper Mātrās are, we are told, *O* and *Au*; the lower ones, *U* and *Ū*; and the transverse, *E* and *Ai*. The commentator says that the long (Dīrgha) ones are *Ā*, *Ī*, *Ū*, *E*, *Ai*, *O* and *Au*. In that case there would be overlapping of all the varieties. Hence it is necessary to demarcate their spheres.

The signs Leo, Virgo, Libra and Scorpio are said to be long; Gemini, Cancer, Sagittarius and Capricorn, medium; and Aries, Taurus, Aquarius and Pisces, short.*

Vide the following:—

आद्यन्तराश्योरुदयप्रमाणं द्वौ द्वौ मुहूर्तौ नियतं प्रदिष्टम् ।
क्रमोत्क्रमाभ्यामतिपञ्चमं स्याच्चक्रार्धयोर्विद्ध्युदयप्रमाणम् ॥
एवं प्रमाणानि गृहाणि बुद्ध्या ह्रस्वानि मध्यानि तथायतानि ।
चक्राङ्गभेदैः सदृशीकृतानि मार्गप्रमाणान्यपि कल्पयन्ति ॥]

प्राग्लग्नतोयास्तनभःस्थितेषु भेष्वंशकेभ्योऽक्षरसङ्ग्रहः स्यात् ।
क्रूरोऽक्षरं हन्ति चतुष्टयस्थो दृष्ट्यापि मात्रां च त्रिकोणगो वा ॥ १० ॥

The letters of a name are derived from the Navāṁśas of the signs that are the 1st, 4th, 7th, and 10th houses. A malefic situated in a Kendra (angle) destroys a syllable, while in a Koṇa (triangular one), he destroys a Mātrā (syllabic instant). The same result takes place even by his aspect.

शुभग्रहस्तूर्जितवीर्यभागी स्थानांशतुल्याक्षरदः स चोक्तः ।
पश्यन् स्थितः केन्द्रत्रिकोणयोर्वा स्वोच्चेऽपि वर्णद्वयमात्मभागे ॥ ११ ॥

A strong benefic is said to contribute as many syllables as the Navāṁśas travelled by him; or when he is posited in a Kendra, Koṇa, exaltation or own Navāṁśa and aspects the Lagna, he gives two letters.

क्षेत्रेश्वरे क्षीणबलेंऽशके च मात्राक्षरं नाशमुपैति तज्जम् ।
असम्भवेऽप्युद्भवमेति तस्मिन् वर्गाद्यमुच्चांशयुजीशदृष्टे ॥ १२ ॥

When the lord of the Ascendant as also its Navāṁśa are weak, the syllabic instant as well as the syllable caused by that is destroyed. Still, in its stead, the first letter of the particular class comes into being, provided the said lord is posited in the Navāṁśa that is owned by his exaltation sign and the Navāṁśa sign aspected by its own lord (or, and aspected by the lord of that sign or Navāṁśa sign ?).

*For a different classification vide the "Fundamentals of Astrology" p. 10.

[The first part of the second half is interpreted in a confusing manner by Utpala. For, he says:
तस्मिन्नेव क्षीणेश्वरे क्षीणबलांशके चासम्भवे तस्य मात्राक्षरस्य नाश उद्भवमेत्युद्भूतिं लभते। This would mean—'When it is not possible to have either a weak lord or Aṁśa, the Mātrā and letter contributed by him and by it get lost'. This meaning is not at all convincing.]

केन्द्रे यथास्थानबलप्रकर्षं क्षेत्रस्य तत्क्षेत्रपतेश्च बुद्ध्वा ।
कार्योऽक्षराणामनुपूर्वयोगो मात्रादिसंयोगविकल्पना च ॥ १३ ॥

The order of the letters as well as the joining of the Mātrās (upper, lower and transverse), conjunct consonants at the beginning or the end should be fixed only after ascertaining fully the extent of the positional strength of the Kendra houses and their lords.

[Among the four lords of Kendras the strongest will give the first letter. It is not clear why the commentator interprets wrongly स्थानबल as स्थानं च बलं च, which would show that there are two different sources of strength viz. position and strength. Later he says
स्थानबलेन प्रथमो लभ्यते, दृष्टिबलेन द्वितीयादयः ।
I feel that the strength of aspect is not intended here.]

तत्राबिराश्यादिचतुर्विलग्नमाद्यंशकाविक्रमपर्ययेण ।
ग्रहांशकेभ्यः स्वगणाक्षराणामन्वर्थने प्राप्तिरियं विधार्या ॥ १४ ॥

In reconstructing a name the following method is to be adopted: Take the four Kendras beginning with the first sign (i.e. Aries, Cancer, Libra and Capricorn) and their Navāṁśas in regular order for the first; then take the letters of the classes belonging to the respective planets owing to their position in the Navāṁśas identical with the above ones.

[In the following 15 verses Yavaneśvara gives the letters for the different Kendras when the nine Navāṁśas rise. At the end of the section a table is provided to facilitate the readers' memory.]

मेषे ककारो हिबुके यकारस्तुले चकारो मकरे पकारः ।
मेषे छकारो हिबुकेऽप्यकारस्तुले खकारो मकरे फकारः ॥ १५ ॥

When the first Navāṁśa of Aries is rising, the letter is *Ka*; for Cancer the 4th house, *Ya*; for Libra the 7th, *Ca*; for Capricorn the 10th, *Pa*; similarly for the second Navāṁśas of these four signs, the letters are in order *Cha*, *A*, *Kha* and *Pha*.

[It has been explained that the letters are to be deduced from the Navāṁśas of the four Kendras, 1, 4, 7 and 10, on the basis of the planets that own the Aṁśas. When Aries happens to be the rising sign and when its first Navāṁśa is in question, we have to consider the lords of all the four initial Navāṁśas of Aries, Cancer, Libra and Capricorn. These are owned by Mars, the Moon, Venus and Saturn respectively. Since they are the first Aṁśas, we have to take the first letters of the classes belonging to the planets, viz. क, य, च and प. In the case of the second Navāṁśas of the same four signs, the letters will be for the same reason the second letters of the respective classes. In Aries the second Aṁśa belongs to Venus, so the second letter of चवर्ग i.e. छ, should be taken. There is one exception to this rule i.e. if a certain class of letters comes in for the first time, then irrespective of its place we have to take only the first letter of that class.]

मेषे टकारो हिबुके ठकारस्तुले तकारो मकरे थकारः ।
मेषे तु रेफो हिबुके जकारस्तुले बकारो मकरे गकारः ॥ १६ ॥

When the third Navāṁśa of Aries is rising, the letter for it is *Ṭa*; for the fourth i.e. Cancer, it is *Ṭha*; for the seventh i.e. Libra, *Ta*; for Makara (Capricorn), Tha. For the 4th Navāṁśas of Meṣa, Karka, Tulā and Makara, the letters are in order *Ra*, *Ja*, *Ba* and *Ga*.

[Though the Aṁśa is the 3rd, still the letter taken is the first of Mercury's class Ṭa, since it is the first occasion that the planet gets, a chance. Look at the 4th Aṁśa; it gets the letter *Ra* which is not the 4th in the Moon's यवर्ग, but only the second, because this is the second chance that she gets in this scheme.]

आकारमाद्येऽश्वुगते घकारमस्ते भकारं मकरे झकारम् ।
लग्ने डकारं हिबुके दकारमस्ते धकारं मकरे ढकारम् ॥ १७ ॥

17. When the 5th Navāṁśa of Aries is rising, the letters for the four houses are *Ā*, *Gha*, *Bha* and *Jha* respectively; similarly for the sixth Navāṁśas of these four houses, the letters are in order *Ḍa*, *Da*, *Dha* and *Ḍha*.

लग्ने ञकारो हिबुके मकारस्तुले ङकारो मकरे लकारः ।
लग्ने ककारो हिबुके पकारस्तुले चकारो मकरे इकारः ॥ १८ ॥

When the 7th Navāṁśa of Aries is rising, the letters for

the four Kendras are Ña, *Ma*, *Ṅa* and *La* respectively; for the 8th Navāṁśa, they are in order *Ka*, *Pa*, *Ca* and *I*.

लग्ने नकारो हिबुके तकारस्तुले णकारो मकरे टकारः ।
इत्येतदुक्तं चरसञ्ज्ञकस्य वक्ष्ये स्थिराख्यस्य चतुष्टयस्य ॥ १९ ॥

When the 9th Navāṁśa of Aries is rising, the letters for the four Kendras are *Na*, *Ta*, *Ṇa* and *Ṭa* respectively. Thus have I explained the letters for the Kendras that are movable signs. Now I shall explain the same for those that are fixed signs.

वृषे फकारो हिबुके खकारः कीटे वकारो नृघटे छकारः ।
आद्यांशकेभ्यो मतिमान् विदध्यादनुक्रमेण स्थिरसंज्ञकेषु ॥ २० ॥

When the first Navāṁśa of Taurus is rising, the letters for the four Kendras are *Pha*, *Kha*, *Va* and *Cha* respectively. In this manner, the letters for the initial Navāṁśas of the fixed signs are to be deduced in reguler order by a wise man.

लग्ने बकारो हिबुके जकार ईकारमस्तेऽम्बरगे गकारः ।
वृषे थकारो हिबुके टकारः कीटे डकारो नृघटे दकारः ॥ २१ ॥

21. When the second Navāṁśa of Taurus is rising, the letters for the four Kendras are *Ba*, *J*, *Ī* and *Ga* respectively; for the third Aṁśas of these, they are in order *Tha*, *Ṭa*, *Da* and *Da*.

वृषे घकारो हिबुके शकारः कीटे झकारो नृघटे भकारः ।
लग्ने ञकारो हिबुके उकारः कीटे ङकारो नृघटे मकारः ॥ २२ ॥

22. When the fourth Navāṁśa of Vṛṣabha is rising, the letters for the four Kendras are in order *Gha*, *Śa*, *Jha* and *Bha*; for the 5th Aṁśa, they are in order Ña, *U*, *Ṅa* and *Ma*.

लग्ने ढकारोऽथ जले णकारश्चास्ते धकारोऽम्बरगे नकारः ।
वृषे षकारो हिबुके चकारः कीटे पकारो नृघटे ककारः ॥ २३ ॥

When the 6th Navāṁśa of Taurus is rising, the letters for the four Kendras are *Ḍha*, *Ṇa*, *Dha* and *Na* respectively; for the 7th Aṁśa, they are in order *Ṣa*, *Ca*, *Pa* and *Ka*.

ऊकारमाहुर्वृषभे जले खमस्ते फकारो नृघटे छकारः ।
अन्त्ये वृषे टं तमुशन्ति सिंहे थं सप्तमे ठं प्रवदन्ति कुम्भे ॥ २४ ॥

When the 8th Navāṁśa of Taurus is rising, the letters for the four Kendras are in order *Ū*, *Kha*, *Pha* and *Cha*; for the 9th Aṁśa they are *Ṭa*, *Ta*, *Tha* and *Ṭha* respectively.

द्विमूर्तिसंज्ञे मिथुने जकारः षष्ठे बकारः प्रथमांशके स्यात् ।
धनुर्धरेऽस्तोपगते गकारो मीनद्वये चाम्बरगे सकारः ॥ २५ ॥

When the first Navāṁśa of Gemini, a dual sign, is rising, the letters for the four Kendras will be in order *Ja*, *Ba*, *Ga* and *Sa*.

लग्ने घकारो हिबुके भकारश्चास्ते झकारोऽम्बरमध्यगे ई ।
लग्ने दकारो हिबुके धकारमस्ते डकारं विबुरम्बरे ढम् ॥ २६ ॥

When the second Navāṁśa of Gemini is rising, the letters for the four Kendras are in order *Gha*, *Bha*, *Jha* and *Ī*; for the third Aṁśa they are *Da*, *Dha*, *Ḍa* and *Ḍha* respectively.

लग्ने मकारो हिबुके ङकारश्चास्ते हकारोऽम्बरगे ञकारः ।
लग्ने पकारो जलगे चकार ऐकारमस्तेऽम्बरगे ककारः ॥ २७ ॥

When the 4th Aṁśa of Gemini is rising, the letters for the four Kendras are *Ma*, *Ṅa*, *Ha* and Ñ*a* respectively; for the 5th Navāṁśa, they are in order *Pa*, *Ca*, *Ai* and *Ka*.

प्राग्लग्नगे नं जलगे णमाहुरस्तं गते टं नभसि स्थिते तम् ।
प्राग्लग्नगे खं जलगे यमाहुरस्तं गते छं नभसि स्थिते फम् ॥ २८ ॥

When the 6th Navāṁśa of Gemini is rising, the letters for the four Kendras are *Na*, *Ṇa*, *Ṭa* and *Ta* respectively; for the 7th Navāṁśa, they are in order *Kha*, *Ya*, *Cha* and *Pha*.

लग्ने जमोकारमथाम्बुसंस्थे गमस्तसंस्थे विबुरम्बरे बम् ।
ठं लग्नगेऽन्त्ये हिबुकाश्रिते डं थमस्तगे दं नभसि स्थिते वं ॥ २९ ॥

When the 8th Navāṁśa of Gemini is rising, the letters for the four Kendras are in order *Ja*, *O*, *Ga* and *Ba*; and for the 9th Aṁśa they are *Ṭha*, *Ḍa*, *Tha* and *Da* respectively.

एवं विकल्पोऽक्षरसङ्ग्रहोऽयं नाम्नां निरुद्दिष्टविधान उक्तः ।
सर्वेषु लग्नेषु च केचिदेवमिच्छन्ति पूर्वोक्तविधानवत्तु ॥ ३० ॥

In this manner the given method of gathering the letters

constituting names has been explained. Some sages have thus opined as given above for all the signs rising at the time of query.

[From the reference made to केचित् by Yavaneśvara it appears that this system of reconstructing a name was very ancient and was derived from the works of ancient sages of India.]

केन्द्राणि वा केन्द्रगतांशकैः स्वैः पृथक्पृथक् सङ्गुणितानि कृत्वा ।
त्रिकृद्विभक्तं विदुरक्षरं तत् क्षेत्रेश्वरस्यांशपरिक्रमस्वम् ॥ ३१ ॥

Or, multiply separately the several Kendra Signs by their corresponding rising Navāṁśas (according to their ownership) and divide the result by 9. The remainder will reveal the letter required belonging to the Navāṁśa of the planet.

[In each set of Kendras there are 4 Signs. In working out this problem we have to take the number of the signs, e.g. in the first set take 1, 4, 7 and 10; in the second set 2, 5, 8 and 11; and in the third set 3, 6, 9 and 12. Now multiply the number representing the sign of each Kendra by the number of its Navāṁśas (i.e. the no. of planets owning its 9 Aṁśas) and divide the product by 9; the remainder gives a particular Navāṁśa from whose lord the letter is to be deduced.

Let us take Aries to be rising; then multiply 1 by the number 6, because 6 planets own its 9 parts, and divide by 9. Thus we get $\frac{1 \times 6}{9}$ Here the remainder is 6. This means it is the 6th Navāṁśa of Aries, which belongs to Mercury. So the letter must belong to टवर्ग. If the Navāṁśa rising is the first, then it will be टकार itself. In this manner the letters will have to be ascertained.

The following table gives the results of this section for easy reference:—

मेष	वृषभ	मिथुन	कर्कटक	सिंह	कन्या	तुला	वृश्चिक	धनु	मकर	कुम्भ	मीन
क	फ	ज	य	ख	व	च	व	ग	प	छ	स
छ	व	घ	अ	ज	भ	ख	ई	झ	फ	ग	ई
ट	भ	द	ठ	ट	ध	त	ड	ड	थ	द	ढ
र	घ	म	ज	श	ङ	ब	झ	ह	ग	भ	ञ
आ	ञ		घ	उ	च	भ	ङ	ऐ	ङ	म	क

ड	ढ	न	द	ण	ण	ध	ध	ट		न	त
ञ	ष	ख	म	च	य	ङ	प	छ	ल	क	फ
क	ऊ	ज	प	ख	ओ	च	फ	ग	इ	छ	ब
न	ट	ठ	त	त	ड	ण	थ	थ	ट	ठ	द

सञ्चिन्तितप्रार्थितनिर्गतेषु नष्टक्षतस्त्रीरतिभोजनेषु ।
स्वप्नर्क्षचिन्तापुरुषादिवर्गेष्वेतेषु नामान्युपलक्षयेत ।। ३२ ।।

One ought to find out the names in connection with queries relating to (1) things thought of, (2) things wished for, (3) departures, (4) lost articles, (5) damaged things, (6) women, (7) sports or sexual act, (8) food, (9) dreams, (10) stars, (11) worries and (12) groups of men and others from the four Kendras in order.

[The commentator takes स्त्रीरति as one word and says उत्तमादिस्त्रिया सह रमणम्, but later when he wants to have 12 subjects for the sake of bringing them under the three groups of four Kendra houses he separates them. He says that the names of 1, 5 and 9 should be deduced from the Ascendant; those of 2, 6 and 10 from the 4th Kendra; those of 3, 7 and 11 from the 7th Kendra; and those of 4, 8 and 12 from the 10th Kendra.

The commentator closes this section of Akṣarakośa with the following verse:

रचिताक्षरकोशस्य टीका शिष्यहितावहा ।
भट्टोत्पलेन सुस्पष्टा श्लोकैः खाङ्गाश्विसम्मितैः ।।]

द्व्यक्षरं चरगृहांशकोदये नाम चास्य चतुरक्षरं स्थिरे ।
नामयुग्ममपि च द्विमूर्तिषु त्र्यक्षरं भवति चास्य पञ्चभिः ।। १४ ।।

If at the time of a query or somebody's arrival the rising sign and or Navāṁśa is movable, the name of the person concerned will consist of two syllables; if it is fixed, of four syllables; if it is a dual sign (or Aṁśa), he will have a double name, of which the first will have 3 syllables and the second 5.

[The metre is रथोद्धता.]

काद्यास्तु वर्गाः कुजशुक्रसौम्यजीवार्कजानां क्रमशः प्रविष्टाः ।
वर्णाष्टकं यादि च शीतरश्मे रवेरकारात्क्रमशः स्वराः स्युः ॥ १५ ॥

नामानि चाग्न्यम्बुकुमारविष्णुशक्रेन्द्रपत्नीचतुराननानाम् ।
तुल्यानि सूर्यात्क्रमशो विचिन्त्य द्वित्र्यादिवर्णैर्घटयेत्स्वबुद्ध्या ॥ १६ ॥

The guttural, palatal, lingual, dental and labial classes respectively belong to Mars, Venus, Mercury, Jupiter and Saturn; the eight letters beginning with *Ya*, to the Moon; and the vowels beginning with *A*, to the Sun. For the planets beginning with the Sun (owning the rising sign or Navāṁśa) the names will be synonymous with those of Fire, Water, Subrahmaṇya (or Kārttikeya), Viṣṇu, Indra, Śacī and Brahman respectively; and they will have to be reconstructed as consisting of two, three, four or five syllables, with one's own intelligence.

[The method of reconstructing names has been explained in the *Akṣarakośa*. If the concerned planet is in Vargottamāṁśa, own house, own decanate, Navāṁśa, exaltation or is retrograde, then the letter will have to be doubled or trebled as in the case of the calculation of the span of life. A malefic, not posited in Vargottama etc., will destroy the letter contributed by him. In the reconstruction of a name one should start with Lagna Kendra and take up the other Kendras viz. 4th, 7th and 10th in order. It may also be started with the letter contributed by the strongest of the planets owning the Aṁśas of the Kendras. According to other scholars, referred to by Utpala, for every 150' traversed by the Sun in the sign occupied there should be one syllable belonging to his class in regular order; for every 225' traversed by the Moon; and for every 200', by other planets. When the Sun happens to be the lord of the Ascendant or its Aṁśa (when he is stronger of the two), the person's name will be synonymous with Agni (Fire). He adds: बलिनो ग्रहस्याक्षरमुत्तरम् । मध्यबलस्य मध्यगतम् । बलहीनस्याधो योज्यम् ।

These verses are in उपजाति and इन्द्रवज्रा respectively. The following is in उपेन्द्रवज्रा metre.]

वयांसि तेषां स्तनपानबाल्यव्रतस्थिता यौवनमध्यवृद्धाः ।
अतीव वृद्धा इति चन्द्रभौमज्ञशुक्रजीवार्कशनैश्चराणाम् ॥ १७ ॥

The ages of persons will have to be deduced from the planets, the Moon, Mars, Mercury, Venus, Jupiter, the Sun and Saturn, as those of a sucking baby (upto 2 years), a child (upto 6 years), a

Brahmacārin (religious student upto 16 years), a youth (upto 30 years), a middle-aged person (upto 50 years), an old man (upto 80 years) and a very old man (upto 100 years) respectively.

[As the big section of omens closes with this chapter the commentator composes a verse at the end, meaning that he has constructed this boat of explanation to enable students to cross the 'ocean of omens' made by the Teacher Varāhamihira.]

पाकाध्यायः ॥ ९७ ॥

Chapter XCVII—Time of Fruition of Effects

पक्षाद्भानोः सोमस्य मासिकोऽङ्गारकस्य वक्रोक्तः ।
आदर्शनाच्च पाको बुधस्य जीवस्य वर्षेण ॥ १ ॥

षड्भिः सितस्य मासैरब्देन शनेः सुरद्विषोऽब्दार्धात् ।
वर्षात् सूर्यग्रहणे सद्यः स्यात् त्वाष्ट्रकीलकयोः ॥ २ ॥

त्रिभिरेव धूमकेतोर्मासैः श्वेतस्य सप्तरात्रान्ते ।
सप्ताहात् परिवेषेन्द्रचापसन्ध्याभ्रसूचीनाम् ॥ ३ ॥

The effects, good or bad, accruing from the transit of the Sun will come to pass within a fortnight; of the Moon, within one month; of Mars, within the period taken for his retrograde motion (vide VI *supra*); of Mercury, before he gets eclipsed; of Jupiter, within a year; of Venus, within 6 months; of Saturn, within a year; of Rāhu (i.e. lunar eclipse), within 6 months; of solar eclipse, within 1 year; of Tvāṣṭra and Tāmasakīlaka, the same day; of Dhūmaketu (dusky comet), within 3 months; of Śvetaketu (white comet), within one week; of halos, rainbows, twilight and shapes of clouds within a week.

[The commentator reads वक्रोक्ताः as वक्त्रोक्ताः and explains it as the time prescribed for the various kinds of वक्त्र mentioned in VI *supra*, but he forgets that no time-limit has been given there for the fruition of effects. Moreover, उष्णवक्त्र, अश्रुमुख, व्यालामुख etc. are different types of the planet's retrograde motion. Hence the reading वक्रोक्त: alone is correct, and it means that the period of fruition of its effect is the same as his retrograde motion i.e. before Mars becomes direct again.]

शीतोष्णविपर्यासः फलपुष्पमकालजं दिशां दाहः ।
स्थिरचरयोरन्यत्वं प्रसूतिविकृतिश्च षण्मासात् ॥ ४ ॥

The effects of the bad omens caused by the reversal of the nature of hot and cold things (or seasons), appearance of flowers and fruits out of season, burning of quarters, reversal of the states of moving and stationary objects and abnormal births, will come to pass within six months.

अक्रियमाणककरणं भूकम्पोऽनुत्सवो दुरिष्टं च ।
शोषश्चाशोष्याणां स्रोतोऽन्यत्वं च वर्षार्धात् ॥ ५ ॥

Things being done without an agent, earthquake, stoppage of festivities, terrible calamities, withering or drying of never-drying things, and streams flowing upwards (or tanks drying or increasing), will have their effects felt within six months.

[The commentator explains अक्रियमाणकरणम् as अप्राप्तचारस्य करणम्... अथवा यन्न कदाचित् कृतमकस्मात् क्रियते । The expression स्रोतोऽन्यत्वम् may also be construed as 'changing of the course of rivers'.]

स्तम्भकुसूलार्चानां जल्पितरुदितप्रकम्पितस्वेदाः ।
मासत्रयेण कलहेन्द्रचापनिर्घातपाकाश्च ॥ ६ ॥

The effects of the speaking, weeping, quaking and sweating of pillars, granaries and images as well as those of quarrels, rainbows and portentous thunder will be felt within three months.

[In verse 3 above the effect of rainbow is stated to be felt within a week. Here it is extended upto three months. The idea is that the effect should be felt latest in three months.]

कीटाखुमक्षिकोरगबाहुल्यं मृगविहङ्गविरुतं च ।
लोष्टस्य चाप्सु तरणं त्रिभिरेव विपच्यते मासैः ॥ ७ ॥

The effects of the increase of pests viz. insects, rats, flies and snakes, of the cries of beasts and birds, and of the floating of clods of earth in water, will be felt undoubtedly within three months.

[तरणं, according to our commentator, means मज्जनं *sinking*, not प्लवनं *floating*.]

प्रसवः शुनामरण्ये वन्यानां ग्रामसम्प्रवेशश्च ।
मधुनिलयतोरणेन्द्रध्वजाश्च वर्षात् समधिकाद्वा ॥ ८ ॥

The effects of bitches bringing forth their young ones in the forest, the entry of wild animals into the village, bee-hives, arches and Indra's Banner will be felt in a year or a little more.

गोमायुगृध्रसङ्घा दशाह्निकाः सद्य एव तूर्यरवः ।
आक्रुष्टं पक्षफलं वल्मीको विवरणं च भुवः ॥ ९ ॥

Groups of jackals and vultures make their effects felt within ten days; the sound of musical instruments (when no sound appears, being struck or when sound is heard even when it is not struck), the same day; imprecations, sudden appearance of anthills in a house, and bursting of the earth, in a fortnight.

अहुताशप्रज्वलनं घृततैलवसादिवर्षणं चापि ।
सद्यः परिपच्यन्ते मासेऽध्यर्धे च जनवादः ॥ १० ॥

The effects of flames appearing without the existence of fire, the shower of ghee, oil, fat and the like (i.e. blood, flesh, food, drink, flowers, fruits, leaves, mud and stones), come to pass the same day; and those of the utterances of people, in a month and a half.

छत्रचितियूपहुतवहबीजानां सप्तभिर्भवति पक्षैः ।
छत्रस्य तोरणस्य च केचिन्मासात्फलं प्राहुः ॥ ११ ॥

The effects of (omens connected with) royal umbrellas, sacrificial altars, sacrificial posts, fire and seeds will be felt in three months and a half; but, according to some, the effects of umbrellas and arches will be felt in a month.

[Vide Sage गर्ग—

चितियूपहुताशेषु फलं पक्षैस्तु सप्तभिः ।
आतपत्रफलं मासात् तोरणस्यैवमस्त्विति ॥]

अत्यन्तविरुद्धानां स्नेहः शब्दश्च वियति भूतानाम् ।
मार्जारनकुलयोर्मूषकेण सङ्गश्च मासेन ॥ १२ ॥

The effects of friendship between deadly enemies, sounds of animals in the sky, and sexual union of the cat or the mongoose with the rat will come to pass in a month.

गन्धर्वपुरं मासाद्रसवैकृत्यं हिरण्यविकृतिश्च ।
ध्वजवेश्म पांसुधूमाकुला दिशश्चापि मासफलाः ॥ १३ ॥

The effects of aerial cities, sudden change of taste of articles, dis-colouration of gold, breaking of flags, some unnatural happenings in houses, and the quarters filled with dust or smoke will be felt in a month.

[Hereafter he explains the effects of omens or portents relating to asterisms.]

नवकैकाष्टदशैककषट्त्रिकत्रिकसंख्यमासपाकानि ।
नक्षत्राण्यश्विनिपूर्वकाणि सद्यःफलाश्लेषा ॥ १४ ॥

The eight asterisms beginning with Aśvinī (when their yogatārā is afflicted) make their effects felt in nine, one, eight, ten, one, six, three and three months respectively and Āśleṣā, the same day.

[This verse suffers from metrical defect, as the third Gaṇa contains a Jagaṇa and the conjunct consonant त्रि has been treated as a simple one. The line can be rectified as follows:

नवकैकाप्टदशैककषट्त्रित्रिकसंख्यमासपाकानि ।]

पित्र्यान्मासः षट् षट् त्रयोऽर्द्धमष्टौ च त्रिषडेकैकाः ।
मासचतुष्केऽषाढे सद्यःपाकाभिजित्तारा ॥ १५ ॥

The twelve asterisms beginning with Maghā (when afflicted) make their effects felt in one month, six months, six months, three months, half a month, eight months, three months, six months, one month, one month, four months and four months respectively; and Abhijit, the same day.

[This verse too contains a metrical flaw in the second quarter. This makes one suspect the genuineness of such verses. It is possible that the manuscript was illegible or damaged in this part of the work and some astrologer without sufficient knowledge of prosody might have completed the verses. The correct form would be:—

त्रयोऽर्द्धमष्टौ त्रयः षडेकैकाः ॥]

सप्ताष्टावध्यर्धं त्रयस्त्रयः पञ्च चैव मासाः स्युः ।
श्रवणादीनां पाको नक्षत्राणां यथासङ्ख्यम् ॥ १६ ॥

The asterisms beginning with Śravaṇa make their effects felt in seven, eight, one and a half, three and five months respectively.

[The portents whose times of fruition have not been mentioned here are enumerated in XXXII 23, 30. When abnormal occurrences are sighted, their evil effects can be warded off through proper propitiatory rites. The author answers the question, "What would happen if propitiations were not done?" in the following verse.]

निगदितसमये न दृश्यते चेदधिकतरं द्विगुणे प्रपच्यते तत् ।
यदि न कनकरत्नगोप्रदानैरुपशमितं विधिवद् द्विजैश्च शान्त्या ॥ १७ ॥

If the effects of the portents and evil omens mentioned above do not come to pass at the prescribed time, they will do so with redoubled vigour at double the time, if they are not warded off by expiatory ceremonies performed according to the Śāstraic rules by Brāhmaṇas, along with gifts of gold, gems and cows.

[Indian tradition believes in propitiatory rites and is an indication that man is not utterly helpless in the hands of a cruel Fate. He can try to improve his position by means of Vedic recitations, charities and the like. The metre is पुष्पिताग्रा.]

नक्षत्रकर्मगुणाध्यायः ॥ ९८ ॥

Chapter XCVIII—Functions and Properties of the Asterisms

शिखिगुणरसेन्द्रियानलशशिविषयगुणर्तुपञ्चवसुपक्षाः ।
विषयैकचन्द्रभूतार्णवाग्निरुद्राश्विवसुवहनाः ॥ १ ॥

भूतशतपक्षवसवो द्वात्रिंशच्चेति तारकामानम् ।
क्रमशोऽश्विन्यादीनां कालस्ताराप्रमाणेन ॥ २ ॥

नक्षत्रजमुद्वाहे फलमब्दैस्तारकामितैः सदसत् ।
दिवसैर्ज्वरस्य नाशो व्याधेरन्यस्य वा वाच्यः ॥ ३ ॥

The number of stars constituting the constellations from Aśvinī are 3, 3, 6, 5, 3, 1, 5, 3, 6, 5, 8, 2, 5, 1, 1, 5, 4, 3, 11, 2, 8, 3, 5, 100, 2, 8 and 32 respectively. The periods also of these constellations are represented by the number of stars. The effect, good or bad, of an asterism at a marriage will come to pass in as many years as there are stars in it. A fever or some other ailment will disappear in so many days.

[In verse 2 भूतशर is another reading. Its meaning would be 5 and 5. The star Mṛgaśiras is highly praised for marriage. It consists of three stars. So the beneficial effects of a marriage should be realized in 3 years. Similarly, the bad effects of forbidden stars, e.g. Ārdrā, will be felt in one year. If a person falls ill on a day ruled by Viśākhā, he should be free from it in 5 days.

In the next two verses the presiding deities of the constellations are given.]

अश्वियमदहनकमलजशशिशूलभृददितिजीवफणिपितरः ।
योन्यर्यमदिनकृत्त्वष्टृपवनशक्राग्निमित्राश्च ॥ ४ ॥

शक्रो निर्ऋतिस्तोयं विश्वे ब्रह्मा हरिर्वसुर्वरुणः ।
अजपादोऽहिर्बुध्न्यः पूषा चेतीश्वरा भानाम् ॥ ५ ॥

The presiding deities of the 28 asterisms beginning with Aśvinī are the Divine Physicians, the God of Death, Fire, the Creator, the

Moon, Rudra, Aditi, Jupiter, Serpent, the *Manes*, Bhaga, Aryaman, Savitṛ, Tvaṣṭṛ, the Wind, Indra-Agni, Mitra, Indra, Nirṛti, Water, Viśve-devas, Brahman, Viṣṇu, Vasu, Varuṇa, Ajaikapāt, Ahirbudhnya, and Pūṣan respectively.

त्रीण्युत्तराणि तेभ्यो रोहिण्यश्च ध्रुवाणि तैः कुर्यात् ।
अभिषेकशान्तितरुनगरधर्मबीजध्रुवारम्भान् ॥ ६ ॥

Among these 28 constellations the four viz. the three Uttaras and Rohiṇī are called *Dhruva* or Fixed. Coronations, expiatory rituals, planting of trees, laying the foundation of towns, commencement of meritorious deeds, sowing seeds and other permanent things should be undertaken when the Moon passes through these asterisms.

[Vide पराशर—

चत्वारो हि चतुष्का ध्रुवो मृदुर्दारुणस्तथा क्षिप्रः ।
उग्राणि पञ्च पञ्च च चराणि साधारणे द्वे च ॥

चत्वारि खलु नक्षत्रेषु ध्रुवाणि भवन्ति । प्राजापत्यं त्रीण्युत्तराणि । तेषु पुरनगरग्रामकाननोपवनभवनानि । वेशनतरुकुसुमबीजवपनस्थिरनिधिनिधानकृषिधनगोऽश्वमित्रसङ्ग्रहणस्नपनालङ्करणपत्न्युद्वहनचरणाभिगमननृपतिनायकाभिषेकमन्त्रेज्याव्रतनियमायुष्यपौष्टिकशान्तिकधान्यान्यन्यानि स्थिराणि कारयेत् । ऋणधनप्रयोगपथगमनमद्यवैरक्षौराणि च वर्जयेत्]

मूलशिवशक्रभुजगाधिपानि तीक्ष्णानि तेषु सिध्यन्ति ।
अभिघातमन्त्रवेतालबन्धवधभेदसम्बन्धाः ॥ ७ ॥

The following asterisms are called *Tikṣṇa* (Dāruṇa—dreadful): Mūla, Ārdrā, Jyeṣṭhā and Āśleṣā. These are good for success in attacks, incantations, raising of goblins, imprisonment of others, murders, separation of friends and alliance with kings and the like.

[Vide पराशर—

चत्वारि नक्षत्रेषु दारुणानि भवन्ति । आर्द्राश्लेषा ज्येष्ठा मूलमित्येतेष्वरिनगरस्कन्धावारावरोधनमथ नरेन्द्राभिघातयुद्धकलहकूटसाहसोपघानभेदवञ्चनविवादचौर्यानृतशपथकितवच्छलनपणयन्त्रायुधग्रहणकरणदर्शनाभिचारगदवियोगवधभृत्यनिग्रहचतुष्पददमनभटनियोगान् । विशेषतो मूले मूलकर्म । रुद्रर्क्षेषु पीडनवपनधान्यतरुकुसुमबीजवेश्मप्रवेशस्थिरनिधिनियोगांश्च कारयेत् । सर्वेषु च सर्वं दारुणं कर्म ॥]

उग्राणि पूर्वभरणीपित्र्याण्युत्सादनाशशाठ्येषु ।
योज्यानि बन्धविषदहनशस्त्रघातादिषु च सिद्ध्यै ॥ ८ ॥

The following five asterisms are termed *Ugra* or Fierce:—the three Pūrvas (Pūrvaphalgunī, Pūrvāṣāḍhā and Pūrvābhadrapadā), Bharaṇī and Maghā. They are to be used with success in ruining enemies, destruction, deceit, imprisoning, poisoning, arson, striking with weapons and murders and the like.

[Vide पराशर—

पञ्च नक्षत्रेषूग्राणि भवन्ति। मघा भरणी त्रीणि पूर्वाणीति। एषु भटचौरगुल्मपुरुषदूतकारशौल्क्यशाठिकक्षुद्रान् स्थापयेत्। तथा निभृतनियमनप्रणिधिसम्प्रयोगवैरोत्थानकलहकोलाहलसम्प्रहारवञ्चनविवादान्यद्रव्यहरणान्यदारगमनद्यूताभिसारबिलप्रवर्तनयुद्धयोद्धायुधग्रहणकरणदर्शनारम्भाणि । नगरग्रामजनपदपुराभिघातयन्त्रोपकरणदुर्गक्रियाणां परायिकप्रयोगान्। युद्धसङ्ग्रामाभियोगेषु प्रथममरयोऽभिहन्तव्या इत्यादिषु विषप्रयोगानलविसर्गाभिचारं कारयेत्। विशेषतः पित्र्येऽपितृपिण्डसम्प्रदानकोष्ठागारविविधाकारनिधानानि। भाग्ये सौभाग्यकस्यावरणानि आप्ये जलवाहसुरासवकूपनदीवाहकुल्याखननानि सर्वेषु। सर्वमुग्रं च ॥]

लघु हस्ताश्विनपुष्याः पण्यरतिज्ञानभूषणकलासु।
शिल्पौषधयानादिषु सिद्धिकराणि प्रदिष्टानि ॥ ९ ॥

The asterisms Hasta, Aśvinī, and Puṣya (Abhijit too) are termed *Kṣipra* or Swift. They are beneficial in trade, sensual sports, education, decorations (or making ornaments), fine arts, skilled labour (like carpentery, smithy etc.), medical treatment, journey and the like (taking or giving loan etc).

[Vide पराशर—

चत्वारि नक्षत्राणि क्षिप्राणि भवन्ति। हस्तः पुष्योऽभिजिदश्विनमित्येतेषु विविधपण्यविक्रयधनप्रयोगगोऽश्वाश्वतरखरकरभदमनस्कन्धावारबलसार्थनिर्याणदूतचरसम्प्रेषणाध्वगमनयजनयाजनाध्ययनाध्यापनशिल्पारम्भध्वजपताकातपत्रवालव्यजनसमुच्छ्रयस्नपनगजग्रहणारोहणभैषज्यरक्षोघ्नगदगदौषधग्रहणधारणानि सर्वाण्येव चात्र क्षिप्राणि कर्माणि कारयेत् ॥]

मृदुवर्गोऽनूराधाचित्रापौष्णैन्दवानि मित्रार्थे।
सुरतविधिवस्त्रभूषणमङ्गलगीतेषु च हितानि ॥ १० ॥

The four asterisms, Anurādhā, Citrā, Revatī and Mṛgaśiras, are known to belong to the class of *Mṛdu* or Tender ones. They are used with advantage in making friends, sexual union, use of garments and ornaments, performance of auspicious ceremonies (like marriage, Upanayana and Cūḍākaraṇa) and singing.

Vide पराशर—

चत्वारि नक्षत्रेषु मृदूनि भवन्ति । मृगशिरश्चित्रानूराधा रेवतीत्येतेषूपनयनचूडाकरणगोदानादिव्रतनियमजप्यस्वस्त्ययनवहनवपनविस्मापनकौतुकमङ्गलयज्ञवाहनाध्ययनाध्यापनकन्यावरणपाणिग्रहणधनप्रयोगान् गुरुनरेन्द्राणां वाद्यगीतनृत्ताभिनयालापहास्योद्यानहर्षपरिवर्धनान्यारभेत । मणिरजतालङ्कारास्वरधारणकरणसङ्ग्रहणविक्रयशिल्पप्रयोगगमनप्रयोगसुहृत्सम्बन्धिबान्धवसम्बन्धान्यायुष्यपौष्टिकधर्मार्थकामयुक्तानि सर्वाण्येव चात्र नयनाञ्जनसौभाग्यविचित्रचित्राणि विशेषतः सर्वेषु सर्वाणि मृदूनि कर्माणि कारयेत् ।।]

हौतभुजं सविशाखं मृदुतीक्ष्णं तद्विमिश्रफलकारि ।
श्रवणत्रयमादित्यानिले च चरकर्मणि हितानि ।। ११ ।।

The two asterisms Kṛttikā and Viśākhā are known as *Mṛdu-tīkṣṇa* or Tender-Dreadful (or Sādhāraṇa) and yield mixed results. The five asterisms Śravaṇa, Dhaniṣṭhā, Śatabhiṣak, Punarvasu and Svāti are termed *Cara* or Temporary and are beneficial for emphemeral things.

[Vide पराशर—

द्वे नक्षत्रे साधारणे भवतः। कृत्तिका विशाखेति। तयोर्मृदूनि दारुणानि कर्माणि कुर्यात्। धातूत्पादनावर्तनभाण्डागारविपणिपण्योपकरणानि । यज्ञेष्टिदहनोपतापनेक्षुघृतविपाचनं वृषभोत्सर्गपशुसङ्कुलनदमनान्यारभेत । सर्वप्रहरणानि कारयेत् ग्रामशिबिरपुरव्रजननगरव्युत्पथबन्धम् । विशाखायां विशेषेणेक्षुवृक्षबीजलताकुसुमानि वापयेत् ।।

पञ्च नक्षत्राणि चराणि भवन्ति—स्वातिः पुनर्वसुः श्रवणं धनिष्ठा शतभिषगिति । एतेषु कुञ्जरमृगमहिषतुरगखरकरभगवां समावहनानि । विशेषेण पुनर्वसौ पुनर्भूगमनं विटकरणम् । वारुणे सुरासवसन्धानसरःसरित्सेत्वौषधविधानानि । सर्वेषु विशेषेण सर्वं चरकर्म कुर्यात् ।।

Here the commentator shows his knowledge of Pāṇini's grammar by quoting two Sūtras viz. IV.3-120 and VII.2.117 to explain the formation of हौतभुजम्.]

हस्तत्रयं मृगशिराः श्रवणत्रयं च
पूषाश्विशक्रगुरुभानि पुनर्वसुश्च ।
क्षौरे तु कर्मणि हितान्युदये क्षणे वा
युक्तानि चोडुपतिना शुभतारया च ।। १२ ।।

The asterisms recommended for shave are Hasta, Citrā, Svāti, Mṛgaśiras, Śravaṇa, Dhaniṣṭhā, Śatabhiṣak, Revatī, Aśvinī, Jyeṣṭhā, Punarvasu and Puṣya. It is to be had when these asterisms rise, or when the Muhūrtas bearing the names of the deities presiding over the asterisms are current, when the Moon is auspscious i.e. passing through the 1st, 3rd, 6th, 7th, 10th or 11th with respect to the Janma-rāśi (sign occupied by the natal Moon) and when the asterism is favourable to the person concerned i.e. the 2nd, 4th, 6th or 8th from his natal one.

[There are five conditions mentioned here, viz. the asterism ruling the day, the ascendant, the Muhūrta, Candrānukūlya and Tārānukūlya. Of these four are essential, the second and third being interchangeable. If one cannot get the proper Muhūrta, one can have any of these stars on the ascendant. For example Aśvinī is one of the stars permitted for shave. Now Aśvinī will be on the ascendant when 13°-20' of Aries rise. To get at an appropriate Muhūrta proceed thus: There are 15 Muhūrtas in the daytime and an equal number in the night. Each Muhūrta has a name, as shown in the verse quoted below. If this name and that of the deity owning an asterism are the same or synonymous, the Muhūrta is beneficial. The deity of Hasta is Sūrya and the third Muhūrta of the day is called Mitra meaning the Sun. So one can opt for this Muhūrta. For the names of the Muhūrtas refer to यात्रा—

Cf. in the notes the verse शिवभुजग...under XLIII. 12 *supra* with the difference in the reading viz चन्द्रादिति there, and इन्द्रदिति here. The source was not mentioned there. This and the following verse are in वसन्ततिलका metre.]

न स्नातमात्रगमनोन्मुखभूषिताना-
मभ्यक्तभुक्तरणकालनिरासनानाम् ।
सन्ध्यानिशाशनिकुजार्कतिथौ च रिक्ते
क्षौरं हितं न नवमेऽह्नि न चापि विष्टयाम् ॥ १३ ॥

It is not advisable to have a shave soon after bath, just before starting on a journey, after decorating oneself, anointing oneself with oil for bath, eating food, at the time of war, without a seat, at a twilight (morning or evening), at night, on Saturdays, Tuesdays and Sundays, in Riktā lunar days (i.e. 4th, 9th, 14th), on a day that is 9th from that of the previous shave, and in the Viṣṭi Karaṇa.

[In the last line in the place of न नवमेऽह्नि there is the reading, न च नवेऽह्नि, which is interpreted as 'not on the 1st day of the fortnight'. Some explain the term नवमेऽह्नि thus: 'Though the ninth lunar day has been already debarred owing to its being a Riktā Tithi, its re-statement is intended to show its complete rejection, while the 4th and 14th are not so bad'. The commentator rejects these explanations and accepts only the one given above. See what व्यासमहर्षि says:

चतुर्थीं चैव षष्ठीं च अष्टमीं च चतुर्दशीम् ।
तथा पञ्चदशीं चैव ब्रह्मचारी भवेत्सदा ॥
श्मश्रुकर्मशिरोऽभ्यङ्गमञ्जनं दन्तधावनम् ।
पर्वस्वेतानि यः कुर्याल्लक्ष्मीस्तत्र न तिष्ठति ॥

Vide तन्त्रान्तरोक्तम्—

क्षौरं न निशि न भुंक्ते न पक्षसन्धौ न जन्मनक्षत्रे ।
न प्रसवनोपवासे न देवपितृकार्ययोरन्तः ॥

Vide पराशर—

प्रतिपत्षष्ठ्योर्विवाहक्षेत्रासववास्तुबीजवपनमित्रधनसङ्ग्रहाभिषेकसत्रादिस्थिरमिष्टमनिष्टमध्वाध्यापनमध्ययनं क्षुरकर्मेति ॥

सन्ध्यायामशुभे चन्द्रे विष्टयां सोमदिनोदये ।
क्षुरकर्म कृतं विन्द्यादनायुष्यकरं नृणाम् ॥

The following verses are quoted by Utpala with the statement, आचार्येण प्रदेशान्तरेण प्रदर्शितम्—

राज्ञः कार्यं पञ्चमे पञ्चमेऽह्नि क्षौरर्क्षे वा श्मश्रु तस्योदये तु ।
त्यक्ता तारा सप्तमी च त्रिपूर्वा यात्राकाले नैव कार्यं न युद्धे ॥
मासादूर्ध्वमनायुष्यमधः पक्षान्न सम्पदः ।
पञ्चमे पञ्चमे वापि राज्ञः क्षौरं प्रशस्यते ॥

These verses are taken from the योगयात्रा, according to IAIB.

He adds: तथा च वैदिकैः पठ्यते—

'पञ्चमकं दशमकं वा प्रत्यायुष्यम्' आयुष्यं क्षौरपर्यायः प्रति प्रति आयुष्यं प्रत्यायुष्यम् । पञ्चमे पञ्चमे दिवसे कर्तव्यम् । क्षौरदिवसात् पञ्चमे दिवसे यदि क्षौरं न कृतं ततस्तस्मात्प्रथमदिवसाद् दशमे दिवसे क्षौरं कर्तव्यम् । न नवमदिवसे । अस्मिन्नेवार्थे स्पष्टतरः श्लोकः—

क्षौरं राज्ञः सदा शस्तं पञ्चमे पञ्चमे दिने ।
क्षौराहान्नवमे त्वह्नि नेष्टमात्ययिकेष्वपि ॥

He quotes the following verse, possibly from the योगयात्रा, as he says तन्त्रान्तर, to prove that the 9th day after arrival is forbidden for departure:

निगमान्नवमे त्वह्नि प्रवेशं चात्र वर्जयेत् ।
शुभनक्षत्रयोगेऽपि प्रवेशाद्वापि निर्गमम् ॥]

नृपाज्ञया ब्राह्मणसम्मते च विवाहकाले मृतसूतके च ।
बद्धस्य मोक्षे क्रतुदीक्षणासु सर्वेषु शस्तं क्षुरकर्म भेषु ॥ १४ ॥

Shaving is approved under all asterisms, if there is a royal command, advice of Brāhmaṇas, the occasion of a marriage, pollution caused by death, release from prison, and consecration for a sacrifice.

[This verse is in उपजाति metre, while verse 16 is in इन्द्रवज्रा.]

हस्तो मूलं श्रवणा पुनर्वसुर्मृगशिरस्तथा पुष्यः ।
पुंसञ्ज्ञितेषु कार्येष्वेतानि शुभानि धिष्ण्यानि ॥ १५ ॥

The asterisms Hasta, Mūla, Śravaṇa, Punarvasu, Mṛgaśīrṣa and Puṣya are auspicious for all *masculine* sacraments or works.

['Marriage' is a masculine sacrament, but Punarvasu is not one of the prescribed stars for that. This verse is not found in some editions. Hence it may be an interpolation, since Utpala's commentary is not found. Moreover the same idea is repeated in the next verse.]

सावित्रपौष्णानिलमैत्रतिष्यत्वाष्ट्रे तथा चोडुगणाधिपर्क्षे ।
संस्कारदीक्षाव्रतमेखलादि कुर्याद्गुरौ शुक्रबुधेन्दुयुक्ते ॥ १६ ॥

Sacraments (like the naming ritual), consecrations (for sacrifices), vows, upanayana (initiation of a twice-born boy into religious studentship) and such other things (like the tonsure ceremony) should be performed on a Thursday, Friday, Wednesday or Monday, when the Moon is in conjunction with Hasta, Revatī, Svāti, Anurādhā, Puṣya Citrā or Mṛgaśīrṣa.

[Bhaṭṭotpala comes to our help in explaining गुरौ etc. Otherwise it should mean—'When Jupiter is conjoined with Venus, Mercury or the Moon'.

शुद्धैर्द्वादशकेन्द्रनैधनगृहैः पापैस्त्रिषष्ठायगै-
र्लग्ने केन्द्रगतेऽथवा सुरगुरौ दैत्येन्द्रपूज्येऽपि वा ।
सर्वारम्भफलप्रसिद्धिरुदये राशौ च कर्तुः शुभे
संग्राम्यस्थिरभोदये च भवनं कार्यं प्रवेशोऽपि वा ॥ १७ ॥

All undertakings will be crowned with success, if the 12th, 8th and the Kendra houses (i.e. 4th 7th and 10th, as well as the elected ascendant) are uncontaminated (i.e. not occupied by malefics), the malefics occupy the 3rd, 6th or the 11th house (from the

Lagna), and Jupiter or Venus, the ascendant or any other Kendra. A house should be constructed or entered when the rising Sign and the one occupied by the Moon are favourable to the owner (i.e. when they do not happen to be the 12th or 8th from his natal ascendant and Moon) and when the ascendant happens to be a rural and fixed sign.

[The rural signs are Aries, Taurus, Gemini, Virgo, Libra, Sagittarius and Aquarius. Of these only two viz. Taurus and Aquarius, are fixed signs. But Aquarius is not good as the ascendant.

Vide यवनेश्वर—

लग्नेषु जीवेँन्दवभार्गवेषु पश्यत्सु चैँतेषु गृहर्क्षमंशम् ।
राशावथो वा विचरे गृहस्थे गृहांशयोर्वा भृगुनन्दनेन्द्वोः ।।
जलाशये वा गृहमागतेंऽशे गृहे स्वनाथाश्रितलक्षिते वा ।
चन्द्रे शुभस्थे च शुभानि विन्द्याद् वास्तुप्रवेशादिनिवेशनानि ।।

The metre is शार्दूलविक्रीडित.]

तिथिकर्मगुणाध्यायः ॥ ९९ ॥

Chapter XCIX—Functions and Properties of Lunar Days

कमलजविधातृहरियमशशाङ्कषड्वक्त्रवसुभुजगाः ।
धर्मेशसवितृमन्मथकलयो विश्वे च तिथिपतयः ॥ १ ॥

पितरोऽमावास्यायां सञ्ज्ञासदृशाश्च तैः क्रियाः कार्याः ।
नन्दा भद्रा विजया रिक्ता पूर्णा च तास्त्रिविधाः ॥ २ ॥

यत्कार्यं नक्षत्रे तद्दैवत्यासु तिथिषु तत्कार्यम् ।
करणमुहूर्त्तेष्वपि तत् सिद्धिकरं देवतासदृशम् ॥ ३ ॥

The lords of the lunar days are in their order: (1) Brahman, (2) Vidhātṛ. (3) Viṣṇu, (4) Yama, (5) the Moon, (6) Subrahmaṇya (Kārttikeya), (7) Indra, (8) the Vasus, (9) Serpent, (10) Dharma, (11) Rudra, (12) Āditya (the Sun), (13) Manmatha (Cupid), (14) Kali and (15) Viśve-devas; those of the New Moon are the *Manes*. Functions appropriate to the presiding deities must be performed on their respective Tithis. These are further divided into five classes of three days each: 1, 6 and 11. *Nandas*; 2, 7 and 12-*Bhadras*; 3, 8 and 13-*Jayas*; 4, 9 and 14-*Riktās*; and 5, 10 and 15 *Pūrṇas*. Works that are prescribed for the several asterisms should be done on the lunar days that are owned by the same deities. In the same manner, they should be done with reference to the Karaṇas and Muhūrtas by the identity of the presiding deities for ensuring success.

[Since Brahman presides over the first lunar day, all Brahminic ceremonies such as marriage may be performed that day; on the second, laying of foundations for houses etc.; on the 3rd tonsure etc.; on the 4th, things for harming enemies etc. may be undertaken; on the 5th, emetics, tonics ete. may be taken; on the 6th, getting new friends coronation etc. may be done; on the 7th, construction of vehicles, journeys etc; on the 8th, taking up of arms, fortification etc.; on the 9th, ruining and killing enemies; on the 10th, meritorious deeds, worship of Brāhmaṇas, etc.; on the 11th, things that are permanent, ephemeral, and tender; on the 12th, installation of the sacred fire, etc.; on the 13th, forming friendship, enjoyment of sensual pleasures etc.; on the 14th, administration of poison, mercury, etc.; on the 15th, propitiation of the *Manes*, etc. In the following extract sage पराशर gives separate names for all the 15 Tithis and the rituals to be performed:

तिथयस्तु नन्दा भद्रा जया रिक्ता पूर्णा मासा मित्रा महाबलोग्रसेना सुधन्वा सुनन्दा यमा जयोग्रा सिद्धिरिति । तासु कर्माणि प्रतिपत्षष्ठ्योर्विवाहक्षेत्रासववास्तुबीजवपनमित्रधनसङ्ग्रहाभिषेकसत्रादि स्थिरमिष्टमनिष्टमध्वाध्यापनमध्ययनं क्षुरकर्मेति: । द्वितीयासप्तमीत्रयोदशीषु पत्युद्वहनभवनशयनशकटयानक्रियाध्वगमनाम्बरालङ्कारधारणशिल्पभैषज्यस्वस्त्ययनपौष्टिकव्रतायुष्याणि । विशेषतो मित्रायां मित्रकर्मनृपतिशासनसन्धानानि । तृतीयायां वलकरणदमनानि । प्रतिपदि द्वितीयायां चतुर्थ्यामपि विषमथनदमनबन्धनानि चारभेदकवाटाभियोगाग्निविषसम्प्रयोगक्रियोग्रोग्रसेनयोश्च । पञ्चमीदशम्येकादशीषु भवनशयनस्वस्त्ययनौषधपौष्टिकसुभगाध्वगमनकेदारव्यवहारभूषणकन्यावरणोद्वहनस्थिरचरसौम्यमृदुकर्माणि । एकादश्यां स्त्रीभृत्यनिग्रहा विशेषेण । अष्टम्यां बलोपकरणदर्शनायुधग्रहणदुर्गोपकरणावरणपरिखाभिखननकेदारव्यवहारभूषणकन्यावरणोद्वहनस्थिरचरसौम्यगुप्तिकरणानि । द्वादश्यां स्थिरचरकर्माग्न्याधानयज्ञोपनयननिधिनिधानपाणिग्रहणानि । पञ्चदश्यां पितृयज्ञदेवगोगुरुबल्युपवासेष्टिक्रिया: प्रशस्यन्ते । अपि च ब्रह्मामरमन्त्रिजनार्दनयमसोमकुमारमुनिवसुपिशाचीधर्मरुद्ररविकामरुद्रपितरस्तिथिदेवा: ॥

Since Rohiṇī star and Pratipad (I lunar day) are presided over by Brahman, all the works that are allowed under the star can be performed on the Tithi too. Similarly, it is with regard to the star Abhijit and the second lunar day; Śravaṇa and the 3rd day; Bharaṇī and the 4th; Mṛgaśīrṣa and the 5th; Kṛttikā and the 6th; Jyeṣṭhā and the 7th; Hasta and the 12th; Pūrvaphalgunī and the 13th; Āśleṣā and the 14th, Uttarāṣāḍhā and the 15th; and Maghā and the New Moon. Vide *Garga*:—

नन्दा प्रतिपदित्युक्ता प्रशस्ता ध्रुवकर्मसु ।
ज्ञानस्य च समारम्भे प्रवासे च विगर्हिता ॥
नाद्यादत्र तप: कुर्यात् पुष्टिसौभाग्यमेव च ।
जन्म चात्रोत्तमं विन्द्यात्स्वयम्भूर्देवता यत: ॥
भद्रेत्युक्ता द्वितीया तु शिल्पिव्यायामिनां हिता ।
आरम्भे भेषजानां च प्रवासे च प्रवासिनाम् ॥
ग्रावाहांश्च विवाहांश्च वास्तुक्षेत्रगृहाणि च ।
पुष्टिकर्मकरश्रेष्ठा देवता च बृहस्पति: ॥
बलेत्युक्ता तृतीया तु बलसम्पच्च कारयेत् ।
गोऽश्वकुञ्जरभृत्यानां दमनं मानसानि च ॥

कुर्यादासवकर्माणि बीजान्यपि च वापयेत् ।
बलकर्मारभेतैव विष्णुं विन्द्याच्च दैवतम् ॥

रिक्ता प्रोक्ता चतुर्थी च क्षुद्रकर्म प्रयोजयेत् ।
गोग्रहं दारुणं कुर्यात् कूटशास्त्रं समारभेत् ॥

अत्र सम्मारणं कुर्यादभिघाताश्रयाणि च ।
ध्रुवसेनावधं कुर्याद्यमं विन्द्याच्च दैवतम् ॥

पूर्णा च पञ्चमी प्रोक्ता प्रशस्ता ध्रुवकर्मणि ।
नवान्नाग्रयणानां च शयनासनवेश्मनाम् ॥

जन्मक्षेत्रविभूषार्था व्यवहारौषधक्रिया ।
प्रशान्तं पौष्टिकं कर्म सोमं विन्द्याच्च दैवतम् ॥

षष्ठी मासा तिथिर्नाम प्रशस्ता ध्रुवकर्मसु ।
क्षेत्रारम्भं गृहं कुर्याद् देवतायतनानि च ॥

कारयेत् सङ्क्रमद्वारगोपुराद्यालयानि च ।
आधानं च न कर्तव्यं कुमारश्चात्र दैवतम् ॥

सप्तमी मित्रनामा तु मित्रकार्याध्रुवाणि च ।
कुर्याद्राज्ञो ध्वजं छत्रमासनं शयनानि च ॥

रत्नानि मणिमुक्तादिवस्त्राण्याभरणानि च ।
कारयेद् भूषणाद्यांश्च देवाः सप्तर्षयस्तथा ॥

महाबलाष्टमी चैव कुर्याद् बालनिदर्शनम् ॥
अधिकारान् प्रयुञ्जीत यन्त्राकारधनूंषि च ॥

कुर्याच्च नगरे गुप्ति सुरङ्गान् परिखास्तथा ।
हस्त्यश्वांश्च प्रयुञ्जीत वसवश्चात्र दैवतम् ॥

उग्रसेना तु नवमी बन्धने वधबन्धने ।
अमित्रदमनार्थे च हिता शत्रुवधाय च ॥

अध्वानं च न गच्छेत प्रोष्यं न प्रविशेद् गृहम् ।
संहरेत विषादीनि रुद्राणी चात्र दैवतम् ।

सुधन्वा दशमीं प्राह ध्रुवं विन्द्याद्यशस्करम् ।
कूपान् खनेन्नदीश्चैव कूपं पुष्करणीयुतम् ॥

आरामान् नगरीश्चैव क्षेत्राणि च गृहाणि च ।
पुण्यशालां सभां कुर्याद्धर्मं विन्द्याच्च दैवतम् ॥

सुनन्दैकादशीमाह ध्रुवं विन्द्यान्महानसम् ।
निवेशनगरग्रामयज्ञविप्रसभास्तथा ॥

स्त्रीषु चोग्रं प्रवर्तेत दासकर्मकरेषु च ।
गूढार्थं न प्रयुञ्जीत कामशत्रुश्च देवता ॥

द्वादशीं तु यमामाह ध्रुवं विन्द्याद्यशस्करम् ।
मङ्गल्यान्यत्र कुर्वीत चूडोपनयनानि च ॥
कोष्ठागाराणि कुर्वीत निधानं च निधापयेत् ।
ऋणं चात्र न गृह्णीयादादित्यश्चात्र देवता ॥
जया त्रयोदशीमाह कर्तव्यं कर्म शोभनम् ।
वस्त्रमाल्यमलङ्कारविप्राण्याभरणानि च ॥
सौभाग्यकरणं स्त्रीणां कन्यावरणमेव च ।
मुण्डनं युग्मवसनं कामं विन्द्याच्च देवताम् ॥
उग्रां चतुर्दशीं विन्द्याद्दारुणान्यत्र कारयेत् ।
बन्धनं रोधनं चैव घातनं च विशेषतः ॥
पूर्वाभिहननं चैव दारुणं वधघातनम् ।
ग्रामसेनावधं कुर्याद् विन्द्याद्रुद्रोऽत्र दैवतम् ॥
अमावस्या तु सिद्धार्था पितृयज्ञोऽत्र शस्यते ।
देवकार्याणि कुर्वीत गोकुलं तु निवेशयेत् ॥
पुरोहिताय वरणं कुर्याद् यज्ञक्रियां तथा ।
बलिं चैवोपहारांश्च पितरश्चात्र देवता ॥
कल्याणी पौर्णमासी तु देवकर्माधिकारिणी ।
विप्रकार्येऽग्निकार्ये च गवां घोषे निवेशयेत् ॥
राज्ञः पुरोहितं कुर्याद् यज्ञानि विविधानि च ।
शुभं कर्म च कर्तव्यं सोमं विन्द्याच्च देवताम् ॥

As asterisms and lunar days are treated on a par with each other on account of their common rulership, even so are the lunar mansions and the Karaṇas: Jyeṣṭhā and Bava Karaṇa; Rohiṇī and Bālava; Anurādhā and Kaulava; Uttaraphalgunī and Taitila; Jyeṣṭhā and Gara; Śravaṇa and Vaṇij; Bharaṇī and Viṣṭi; Āśleṣā and Śakuni; Rohiṇī and Catuṣpād; Āśleṣā and Nāga; Svāti and Kiṁstughna.

[Vide पराशर—

शकुनौ शकुनिग्रहणप्रहरणभृत्ययोद्वयुद्धोपकरणक्रियाः सर्वमुग्रं कुर्यात् । चतुष्पदे नृपतिविजयाभिषेकपितृदेवधर्मक्रियाचतुष्पददानानि । नागे सलिलोपकरणावेशनप्रवेशागदगदौषधधारणानि । किंस्तुघ्ने सुरगुरुतीर्थव्रतदीक्षाभिगमनस्नपनानि । बवे मणिकनकरजतालङ्कारवास्तुक्रियाभिप्रयाणासवकुसुमगन्धाधिकाराणि । बालवे व्रतोपवासनियमसत्रयज्ञद्विजगुरुसेवनानि । कौलवे पुरक्षेत्रलेख्यगन्धगान्धर्वपितृदेवधर्मक्रियाः । तैतिले निष्कर्मसाहसद्यूतयुद्धाभिषेकमङ्गलव्रतदीक्षागृहप्रवेशाः । गरे दारूद्यानवनाधिकारिकोपभोगा वैवाहिकादिकरणानि । वणिजि वणिक्प्रयोगाध्ययनशिल्पसम्बन्धार्थाभिवादावनबलिकर्मविधिभिर्यद्यारभ्यते क्रिया काचित् । विष्ट्यां न किमपि समृद्धिमेति बीजमिव यथोषरप्राप्तम् ॥

The pairs of asterisms and Muhūrtas having common rulers are the following:—Ārdrā and Śiva; Āśleṣā and Bhujaga; Anurādhā and Mitra; Maghā and Pitṛ; Dhaniṣṭhā and Vasu; Pūrvāṣāḍhā and Jala; Uttarāṣāḍhā and Viśva; Abhijit and Virañci; Rohiṇī and Brahman: Viśākhā and Indrāgni; Mūla and Nairṛta; Śatabhiṣaj and Vāruṇa; Uttaraphalgunī and Aryaman; P. Phalgunī and Bhāgya; P. Bhādra and Ajaikapāda; U. Bhādra and Ahirbudhnya; Revatī and Pūṣan; Aśvinī and Dasra; Bharaṇī and Antaka (Yama); Kṛttikā and Āgneya; Mṛgaśiras and Indu; Punarvasu and Aditi; Puṣya and Guru; Śravaṇa and Hari; Hasta and Ravi; Citrā and Tvaṣṭṛ; and Svāti and Anila.

Vide the following:—

नक्षत्रतत्क्षणानां परिघातादीश्वरैः समं चिन्त्यम् ।
फलमपि तदेव दृष्टं गर्गाद्यपराशरश्लोकैः ॥
अहोरात्रं च सम्पूर्णं चन्द्रनक्षत्रयोजितम् ।
तन्नक्षत्रमुहूर्ताश्च समकर्मगुणाः स्मृताः ॥

Cf. पराशर—

रौद्रमितमैत्रसाधनसारभटात्मसहवैश्वदेवाभिजिद्रोहिणीन्द्रबलजयपित्र्यभाग्यवरुणनैर्ऋताग्नेययाम्यगन्धर्वध्यानपदराक्षसेन्द्राग्नेयप्राजापत्याश्विनेन्द्रब्रह्मगुरुसावित्र्यवैष्णवपौष्णाः । तेषां यत्समानदैवतनक्षत्रं तन्नक्षत्रवत् कर्माण्यारभेत । विशेषोपदेशमुपदेश्या(क्ष्या ?)मः— तत्र श्वेतमैत्रात्मसहरोहिणीषु रोहिणीव सर्वसाधनम् । इष्टिव्रताधानाध्ययननि । सारभटे ऽभिचारवधवादान् । अभिजिति सर्वकर्माणि । बले नृपतिबलसमारम्भाः । जयेऽन्नप्रमाणम् । गन्धर्वे गान्धर्वरतिविवाहाः । ध्यानपदेऽभिषेकभूषणमङ्गल्यानि । सन्ध्ययोस्तु पूर्वाऽग्निदेवता पश्चिमा रौद्री तयोर्न किञ्चित्कर्मारम्भो नान्यत्र नियमात् प्रयतमुपतिष्ठन्नोपासीत । पश्चिमायां विशेषतश्चाग्नौ न प्रविशन्नाश्नीयान्न मैथुनमभिगच्छेत् ॥

The reader may note here that some of the names of the Muhūrtas in Parāśara's list are different from those given by our author. The words Paścimā and Agni in Parāśara's text may better be taken in the sense of the evening and morning Sandhyā respectively. (See the table giving details of asterisms, Tithis, Karaṇas, Muhūrtas and the rituals or undertakings prescribed under them.)]

TABLE OF ASTERISMS, LUNAR DAYS AND MUHURTAS

Asterisms	*Presiding Deities*	*Number of Stars*	*Limbs of Stellar Deity*	*Nature*	*Tithis*	*Suitable Works*	*Corresponding Karaṇas*	*Corresponding Mmuhūrtas*
Aśvinī	Divine Physicians	3	Knees	Swift		Trade, fine arts, etc.		Dasra (night) 5th
Bharaṇī	Gold of Death	3	Head	Fierce	4th	Destruction, Deceit ete.	Viṣṭi	Yama (night) 6th
Kṛttikā	Fire	6	Hips	Tender, Sharp, Mixed	6th	Mixed type of work		Āgneya (night) 7th
Rohiṇī	Creator	5	Shanks	Fixed	1st	Coronation, Sowing of Seeds & other permanent things	Bālava & Catuṣpāt	Brahman (day) 8th, (night) 8th
Mṛgaśiras	Moon	3	Eyes	Tender	5th	Sex, making friends, ornaments, marriage etc.		Indu (night) 9th
Ārdrā	Rudra	1	Hair	Sharp	11th	Attacks, Incantations, murders, separation of friends		Śiva 1st (day & night)

Asterisms	*Presiding Deities*	*Number of Stars*	*Limbs of Stellar Deity*	*Nature*	*Tithis*	*Suitable Works*	*Corresponding Karaṇas*	*Corresponding Muhūrtas*
Punar-vasu	Aditi	5	Fingers	Movable or Temporary		Temporary works		Aditi (night) 10th
Puṣya	Jupiter	3	Mouth	Swift		Trade, Sex, fine arts etc.		Guru (night) 11th
Āśleṣā	Serpent	6	Nails	Sharp	9th & 11th	Incantations, Attacks etc.	Śakuni & Nāga	Serpent 2nd (day)
Maghā	Manes	5	Nose	Fierce	New Moon	Destruction, Deceit etc.		Manes 4th (day)
Pūrva-Phalgunī	Bhaga	8	Privities	Do.	13th	Do.		Bhāgya (day) 15th
Uttara-Phalgunī	Aryaman	2	Do.	Fixed	10th	Coronation, Sowing of seeds & other perma-nent things	Taitila	Aryaman (day) 14th
Hastā	Savitṛ	5	Hands	Swift	12th	Trade, sex, fine arts etc.		Ravi (night) 13th
Citrā	Tvaṣṭṛ	1	Fore-head	Tender		Marriage, ornaments, sex etc.		Tvaṣṭṛ (night) 14th
Svātī	Wind	1	Teeth	Temporary		Temporary work	Kiṁstu-ghna	Anila (night) 15th

Asterisms	*Presiding Deities*	*Number of Stars*	*Limbr of Stellar Deity*	*Nature*	*Tithis*	*Suitable Works*	*Corresponding Karaṇas*	*Corresponding Muhūrtas*
Viśākhā	Indra-Agni	5	Arms	Tender-Sharp		Mixed type of work		Indrāgnī (day) 11th
Anurādhā	Mitra	4	Breast	Tender		Sex, making friends, ornaments, marriage etc.	Kaulava	Mitra (day) 3rd
Jyeṣṭhā	Indra	3	Neck	Sharp	7th	Incantations, attacks etc.	Bava & Gara	Indra (day) 10th
Mūla	Nirṛti	1!	Feet	Sharp		Do.		Nairṛta (day) 12th
Purvā-ṣāḍhā	Water	2	Thigh	Fierce		Destruction, deceit etc.		Water (day) 6th
Uttarā-ṣāḍhā	Viśve-Devas	8	Do.	Fixed	15th	Coronation, Sowing of seeds & other permanent works		Viśva (day) 7th
Abhijit	Brahman			Swift	2nd	Trade, fine arts, sex etc.		Viriñci (day) 9th
Śravaṇa	Viṣṇu	3	Ears	Temporary	3rd	Temporary works	Vaṇij	Hari (night) 12th
Dhaniṣṭhā	Vasu	5	Back	Do.	8th	Do.		Vasu (day) 5th

Asterisms	*Presiding Deities*	*Nvmber of Stars*	*Limbs of Stellar Deity*	*Nature*	*Tithis*	*Suitable Works*	*Corresponding Karaṇas*	*Corresponding Muhūrtas*
Śata-bhiṣaj	Varuṇa	100	Laughter	Temporary		Temporary works		Vāruṇa (day) 13th
P. Bhādra	Ajaikapāt	2	Sides	Fierce	9th	Destruction, deceit etc.		Ajaikapāda (night) 2nd
U.Bhādra	Ahir-budhnya	8	Do.	Fixed	11th	Coronation, sowing of seeds & other perma-nent work		Ahirbudhnya (night) 3rd
Revatī	Pūṣan	32	Stomach	Tender		Sex, making friends, orna-ments, marriage etc.		Pūṣan (night) 4th

करणगुणाध्यायः ॥ १०० ॥

Chapter C—Qualities of the Karaṇas

बवबालवकौलवतैतिलाख्यगरवणिजविष्टिसंज्ञानाम् ।
पतयः स्युरिन्द्रकमलजमित्रार्यमभूश्रियः सयमाः ॥ १ ॥

The lords of the seven movable Karaṇas, viz. Bava, Bālava, Kaulava, Taitila, Gara, Vaṇija and Viṣṭi, are Indra, Brahman, Mitra, Aryaman, Bhū (Earth), Śrī (Goddess of Wealth) and Yama (Death) respectively.

कृष्णचतुर्दश्यर्धाद् ध्रुवाणि शकुनिश्चतुष्पदं नागम् ।
किंस्तुघ्नमिति च तेषां कलिवृषफणिमारुताः पतयः ॥ २ ॥

The fixed or Dhruva Karaṇas, viz. Śakuni, Catuṣpada, Nāga and Kiṁstughna, begin from the latter half of the 14th day of the dark fortnight and are presided over by Kali, Vṛṣa, Phaṇin (Serpent) and Māruta (Wind) respectively.

[The fixed Karaṇas appear only once in a lunar month. A Karaṇa is equal to half a Tithi. So there must be 60 Karaṇas in a month. But the fixed ones are assigned to the latter half of the dark 14th day, the two halves of the new moon and the first half of the first lunar day of the bright fortnight. Hence 56 Karanas remain to be filled with the 7 Karaṇas repeated 8 times. Bava prevails in the latter half of the bright Pratipad; Bālava and Kaulava in the two halves of the second; Taitila and Gara in the two parts of the third Tithi; Vaṇij and Viṣṭi in those of the fourth. In this manner these seven movable Karaṇas have to be repeated in both the fortnights, without touching the provinces of the four fixed Karaṇas.]

कुर्याद्बवे शुभचरस्थिरपौष्टिकानि
धर्मक्रियाद्विजहितानि च बालवाख्ये ।
सम्प्रीतिमित्रवरणानि च कौलवे स्युः
सौभाग्यसंश्रयगृहाणि च तैतिलाख्ये ॥ ३ ॥

कृषिबीजगृहाश्रयजानि गरे वणिजि ध्रुवकार्यवणिग्युतयः ।
न हि विष्टिकृतं विदधाति शुभं परिघातविषादिषु सिद्धिकरम् ॥ ४ ॥

One should do in Bava Karaṇa auspicious, temporary, permanent and things that increase one's health and strength; in Bālava, religious or meritorious acts, and things that are beneficial to Brāhmaṇas; in Kaulava, things based on love, choosing friends as well as selecting a bride; in Taitila, things leading to popularity, taking shelter, and affairs connected with a house; in Gara, cultivation of lands, sowing seeds and construction of houses and the like; in Vaṇij, lasting things, trading and association. Nothing done in Viṣṭi leads to beneficial results, but attacking enemies, administering poison and such other things do succeed.

[The metres of the two verses are वसन्ततिलका and तोटक respectively.]

कार्यं पौष्टिकमौषधादि शकुनौ मूलानि मन्त्रस्तथा
गोकार्याणि चतुष्पदे द्विजपितॄनुद्दिश्य राज्यानि च ।
नागे स्थावरदारुणानि हरणं दौर्भाग्यकर्माण्यतः
किंस्तुघ्ने शुभमिष्टिपुष्टिकरणं मङ्गल्यसिद्धिक्रियाः ॥ ५ ॥

In Śakuni, tonics, medicines, herbs (roots) and spells become fruitful; in Catuṣpada, things relating to cattle, Brāhmaṇas, *manes* and countries (political affairs); in Nāga, things pertaining to immovable objects, cruel acts, taking things by force as well as hateful activities; in Kiṁstughna, meritorious acts, sacrifices, nutritive things, auspicious ceremonies like marriage and those that promote the above things.

[Vide गर्ग—

आद्यं तु शकुनिर्नाम रात्रौ कृष्णचतुर्दशी ।
आदानग्रहणे चैवमिष्टमत्र पलायनम् ॥
योधानां शकुनानां च ग्रहणं पोषणं तथा ।
चिकित्सा चैव युद्धं च सर्वमेतत् प्रशस्यते ॥
ततश्चतुष्पदं नाम कृष्णपञ्चदशी दिवा ।
चतुष्पदानां सर्वेषां कर्मारम्भेषु शस्यते ॥
पितॄंश्च पूजयेदेव प्रेतकार्यं च कारयेत् ।
नष्टं दृष्टिपथाल्लब्धं ब्रूयादत्र न संशयः ॥
नागं तु करणं रात्रौ कृष्णपञ्चदशी भवेत् ।
तत्रावमर्दसाध्यानि प्रसह्य हरणानि च ॥
भेदनानि च कर्माणि मूलानि च फलानि च ।
कर्माणि चोदनीयानि सर्वाण्येव प्रकल्पयेत् ॥
अतः परं प्रवक्ष्यामि किंस्तुघ्नं करणं ध्रुवम् ।
तत्तु शुक्लप्रतिपदि दिवसे प्रतिपद्यते ॥

तस्मिन् दिव्यानि कार्याणि वैश्वदेवमथानलम् ।
प्राजापत्यं च यत्कर्म सर्वमत्र प्रयोजयेत् ॥
इत्येतानि निबद्धानि ध्रुवाणि करणानि च ।
अतः परं प्रवक्ष्यामि बवान्यन्यानि सप्त वै ॥
बवं च बालवं चैव कौलवं तैतिलं तथा ।
गराख्यं वणिजं चैव विष्टिर्ज्ञेया तु सप्तमी ॥
बवे तु ध्रुवकर्माणि क्षिप्राण्यपि च कारयेत् ।
निर्याणे च प्रवेशे च तद्धि सर्वार्थसाधकम् ॥
बालवं ब्राह्मणानां तु सर्वारम्भेषु शस्यते ।
अनारम्भोऽत्र वर्णानां शेषाणामिति निश्चयः ॥
मित्रयुक्तं च यत्कर्म यच्च स्यात् सिद्धिकारणम् ।
स्थावराणि च सर्वाणि कौलवे सम्प्रयोजयेत् ॥
तैतिलेन च कर्तव्यं राजद्वारिकमेव यत् ।
अलङ्कारांश्च विविधान् सर्वाधिकरणानि च ॥
गरादिना च कर्तव्यं कर्म गृहसमुद्भवम् ।
कृषि प्रवेशं वस्तूनां ग्रहणं क्षेत्रकर्मणाम् ॥
सर्वकार्याणि वणिजि विवादोत्थानि कारयेत् ।
पण्यविक्रयणं चैव शस्त्रारम्भं च कारयेत् ॥
विष्टिर्नामेह करणं येन कर्म न कारयेत् ।
यत्नेनापि कृतं कर्म भवत्यल्पफलोदयम् ॥

The metre is शार्दूलविक्रीडित; so is that of 7 and 8. In the next verse the author gives auspicious planetary positions for boring the ear-lobes.]

लाभे तृतीये च शुभैः समेते पापैर्विहीने शुभराशिलग्ने ।
वेध्यौ च कर्णावमरेज्यलग्ने पुष्येन्दुचित्राहरिपौष्णभेषु ॥ ६ ॥

When benefics are posited in the 11th and the 3rd houses, when an auspicious sign (owned by benefic) is rising and is free from malefics, and Jupiter is in the Ascendant, the boring of the ear-lobes may be done, provided the Moon is posited in any one of the following asterisms: Puṣya, Mṛgaśiras, Citrā, Śravaṇa and Revatī.

[The auspicious signs are Taurus, Gemini, Virgo, Libra, Sagittarius, Pisces and Cancer (when the Moon is waxing). The metre is इन्द्रवज्रा.]

रोहिण्युत्तररेवतीमृगशिरोमूलानुराधामघा-
हस्तस्वातिषु षष्ठतौलिमिथुनेषूद्यत्सु पाणिग्रहः ।

सप्ताष्टान्त्यबहिःशुभैरुडुपतावेकादशद्वित्रिग
क्रूरैस्त्र्यायषडष्टगैर्न तु भृगौ षष्ठे कुजे चाष्टमे ॥ ७॥

दम्पत्योर्द्विनवाष्टराशिरहिते चारानुकूले रवौ
चन्द्रे चार्ककुजार्किशुक्रवियुते मध्येऽथवा पापयोः ।
त्यक्त्वा च व्यतिपातवैधृतिदिनं विष्टिं च रिक्तां तिथिं
क्रूराहायनपौषचैत्रविरहे लग्नांशके मानुषे ॥ ८ ॥

Marriage may be solemnized in any of the asterisms, Rohiṇī, the three Uttarās, Revatī, Mṛgaśiras, Mūla, Anurādhā, Maghā, Hasta and Svāti, when Gemini, Virgo or Libra is rising, when benefics are posited in houses other than the 7th, 8th, and 12th, when the Moon is in the 2nd, 3rd or 11th house from the ascendant, when the malefics are in the 3rd, 6th, 8th and 11th houses, when Venus is not in the 6th, and Mars not in the 8th. It should also be noted that the natal signs (Janma-rāśis) of the bride and the bride-groom are not 2nd and 12th, 5th and 9th, or 6th and 8th from the elected Moon's sign (i.e. they may be in opposition, 3rd and 11th the same Rāśi, or 4th and 10th), that the Sun for the bride-groom and the Moon for the bride are favourable in their transit, that the Moon is not in conjunction with the Sun, Mars, Saturn or Venus (she may be conjoined with Jupiter or Mercury or both), that she is not hemmed in between malefics, that the day chosen is free from Vyatipāta and Vaidhṛti yoga, Viṣṭi Karaṇa and Riktā Tithi; that the day is presided over by a benefic planet, that the season chosen is the northern solstice, that the month is any one but Caitra and Pauṣa, (even in the southern solstice the months of Kārttika and Mārgaśīrṣa are acceptable), and that the rising Navāṁśa is owned by a biped sign (Gemini, Virgo or Libra).

[Vide the following:—

हस्तोत्तरास्वातिमघानुराधाप्राजेशपौष्णैन्दवनैर्ऋतेषु ।
उद्वाहसौभाग्यसुखानि कन्या प्राप्नोति शेषैः सुतभर्तृशोकम् ॥
कन्यातुलावन्मिथुनेषु साध्वी शेषेष्वसाध्वी धनवर्जिता च ।
अन्येषु भेषु द्विपदांश इष्टः कन्यादिलंग्नेषु न चान्त्यभागः ॥
सौम्यान् व्ययास्तनिधनेष्वरिभे च शुक्रं
हित्वा स्थितस्त्रिधनलाभगतः शशाङ्कः ।
पापास्त्रिषड्निधनलाभगता विवाहे
हित्वाष्टमं क्षितिजमिष्टफलानि दद्युः ॥
त्रिकोणषष्ठाष्टधनव्ययेषु पापप्रदानं शुभमन्यभेषु ।

गोचरशुद्धाविन्दुं कन्याया यत्नतः शुभं वीक्ष्य ॥
तिग्मकिरणं च पुंसां शेषैरबलैरपि विवाहः ।
नान्यैः समेतः शुभकृच्छशाङ्कः केषाञ्चिदिष्टो बुधजीवयुक्तः ॥
मध्ये पापग्रहयोः पाणिग्रहणे शशी न सौख्यकरः ।
तस्माद्यत्नाच्चन्द्रः कन्यायाः सुस्थितो देयः ॥
न वै धृतिदिनं कुर्याद् व्यतीपातयुतेऽह्नि ।
रिक्तासु च न कर्तव्यं न विष्टिदिवसे तथा ॥
आग्नेयग्रहवासरेषु कलहः प्रीतिस्तु सत्सूत्तमा ।
केचित्स्थैर्यमुशन्ति सौरदिवसे चन्द्रे ससापत्न्यकम् ॥
उत्तरां भजमानेन काष्ठां वै सप्तसप्तिना ।
चतुर्णामपि वर्णानां विवाहः श्रेष्ठ उच्यते ॥
माघफाल्गुनवैशाखा ऐन्द्रसौम्यानलास्तथा ।
षडेते पूजिता मासाश्चातुर्वर्ण्येऽपि नित्यशः ॥
एषूढा सुभगा साध्वी पुत्रिणी धर्मवत्सला ।
धनिनी देवभक्ता च यथासङ्ख्यं प्रकीर्तिता ॥
आषाढचैत्रपौषाश्च नभस्यः श्रावणस्तथा ।
कुत्सिताः सर्ववर्णानां विवाहेषु मनीषिभिः ॥
आषाढे नष्टशौचा तु खला सन्तानवर्जिता ।
वैशाखे सर्वसामान्या चैत्रे चातृप्तमैथुना ॥
पौषे भर्तृविहीना स्यान्नभस्येऽपि च दुर्भगा ।
एवमाश्वयुजोढा तु श्रावणे तु मृतप्रजा ॥
द्विपदभवनं प्राप्तो योंऽशः शुभोऽन्यगृहोदये ।
द्विपदभवनेष्वप्यन्यांशा भवन्त्यशुभावहाः ॥
विलग्नांशः स्वनाथेन यद्युद्वाहे न दृश्यते ।
पुंविनाशस्ततोऽस्तांशो यद्येवं योषितस्ततः ॥]

———

नक्षत्रजातकाध्यायः ॥ १०१ ॥

Chapter CI—Effects of Birth In the Asterisms

This chapter is a mere repetition of XVI of the Bṛhad Jātaka.

प्रियभूषणः सुरूपः सुभगो दक्षोऽश्विनीषु मतिमांश्च ।
कृतनिश्चयसत्यारुग्दक्षः सुखितश्च भरणीषु ॥ १ ॥

One born under the asterism Aśvinī will be fond of ornaments, lovely in appearance, attractive or liked by all, efficient and intelligent. The asterism Bharaṇī makes one carry out one's determination, truthful, free from ill health, efficient and happy.

[The intellect has got eight functions as enunciated below:—

शुश्रूषा श्रवणं चैव ग्रहणं धारणं तथा ।
ऊहापोहार्थविज्ञानं तत्त्वज्ञानं च धीगुणाः ॥

Vide पराशर also:—

विज्ञानवानरोगो भिषक् प्रदातार्थभृत्यवनितेशः ।
दक्षः क्षितिपतिसेवी जातः स्यादाश्विने शूरः ॥
धीरः क्रूरोऽनृतवाक् परवित्तहरो नरश्चपलबुद्धिः ।
बहुशत्रुपुत्रभृत्यो याम्ये प्रियमांसमद्यश्च ॥

Thus, we see that the effects of both Aśvinī and Bharaṇī are quite good according to our author; but, according to Parāśara, Bharaṇī makes one cruel, untruthful, fickle-minded, a thief etc.]

बहुभुक्परदाररतस्तेजस्वी कृत्तिकासु विख्यातः ।
रोहिण्यां सत्यशुचिः प्रियंवदः स्थिरमतिः सुरूपश्च ॥ २ ॥

Birth under the asterism Kṛttikā makes one a glutton, addicted to others' wives, brilliant and famous. The person born under Rohiṇī will be truthful, pure, sweet-tongued, with a steady mind, and lovely in appearance.

[Sage पराशर gives a good certificate in the following verse to one born under Kṛttikā. The effects of Rohiṇī are a little better here:

धर्ममतिर्बहुवित्तः स्वाध्यायाभिजनरूपसम्पन्नः ।
अकृपणमतिः शशियुते जातः स्यादग्निदैवत्ये ॥
सुतधनपशुमान् विद्वान् दाता धीरोऽल्पवाक् स्थिरमतिश्च ।
वृषभगतिस्तेजस्वी प्राजापत्ये नरो जातः ॥]

चपलश्चतुरो भीरुः पटुरुत्साही धनी मृगे भोगी ।
शठगर्वितः कृतघ्नो हिंस्रः पापश्च रौद्रर्क्षे ॥ ३ ॥

One born under the star Mṛgaśīrṣa becomes fickle, clever, timid, eloquent, industrious, wealthy and endowed with sensual pleasures. The asterism Ārdrā makes one perfidious, haughty, (irascible), ungrateful, cruel and sinful.

[The Vārāṇaseya edition reads the second line as—शठगर्वितचण्डकृतघ्नहिंस्रपापश्च रौद्रर्क्षे ।

Vide पराशर—

प्रतिशीलरूपदृष्टः सौम्यमतिः सोद्यमः श्रुतिरहस्यः ।
चपलमतिः सुविनीतो जातः स्यादिन्दुदैवत्ये ॥
रौद्रः क्रूरः क्रोधी परदारार्थापहारशीलश्च ।
वाग्निष्ठुरोऽतिधीरो जातः स्याद् रुद्रदैवत्ये ॥]

दान्तः सुखी सुशीलो दुर्मेधा रोगभाक् पिपासुश्च ।
अल्पेन च सन्तुष्टः पुनर्वसौ जायते मनुजः ॥ ४ ॥

One born under the star Punarvasu will be self-controlled, happy, of good character, dull-witted, ailing, very thirsty and easily satisfied.

[Vide पराशर—

क्षयवृद्धिभावनायां यशांसि विदिशो भवन्ति कृच्छ्राणि ।
व्याधिबहुलो बहुसुतः पुनर्वसौ जायते मनुजः ॥]

शान्तात्मा सुभगः पण्डितो धनी धर्मसंश्रितः पुष्ये ।
शठसर्वभक्षपापः कृतघ्नधूर्तश्च भौजङ्गे ॥ ५ ॥

One born under the star Puṣya will possess a tranquil mind, amiable features, learning, affluence and attachment to meritorious deeds. The asterism Āśleṣā makes one insincere, inclined to eat everything, sinful, ungrateful and deceitful.

[Vide पराशर—

द्युतिकान्तिसत्त्वयुक्तो बहुश्रुतो दारदासधनचेष्टः ।
विपुलकुलवंशकर्ता वक्ता पुष्ये नरो जातः ॥

स्वल्पगतिर्जिह्माक्षः क्रूरः क्रोधी नरः सदामर्षः ।
दाता हन्ता भोक्ता सार्पे जातो बहुव्यसनः ।।]

बहुभृत्यधनो भोगी सुरपितृभक्तो महोद्यमः पित्र्ये ।
प्रियवाग्दाता द्युतिमानटनो नृपसेवको भाग्ये ।। ६ ।।

A person whose birth takes place under the star Maghā will be very rich and will have many servants, will enjoy pleasures, worship the Gods and the *manes*, and be very industrious. The star Pūrvaphalgunī makes one sweet-tongued, liberal in gifts, bright in appearance, fond of wandering, and a servant of the king.

[Cf. पराशर—

पितृभक्तः क्रोधवशो मात्रा पितृयज्ञसत्रयाजी च ।
द्विचतुष्पदमित्राढ्यो बह्वरिमित्रो नरः पित्र्ये ।।
बहुभाग्योऽल्पापत्यः सुभगः प्रियदर्शनो नरोऽल्पधनः ।
नातिप्रबुद्धबुद्धिः परभाग्यविभुर्भवति भाग्ये ।।]

सुभगो विद्याप्तधनो भोगी सुखभाग्द्वितीयफाल्गुन्याम् ।
उत्साही धृष्टः पानपोऽघृणी तस्करो हस्ते ।। ७ ।।

The person born under the star Uttaraphalgunī will be very popular, will earn money by his learning, will be voluptuous and happy. The star Hasta makes one industrious, impudent, fond of drinking, merciless and thievish.

[Cf. पराशर—

हयगजरथप्रयायी दाता भोक्ता विहाररतिशीलः ।
मृदुवाग्गीतरतिः स्यादार्यम्णे मानवो विद्वान् ।।
उपचितकरचरणभुजो बहुविधधनधान्यताग्रणीः सेर्ष्यः ।
धर्मार्थकामभागी हस्ते सुतवान् नरो जातः ।।]

चित्राम्बरमाल्यधरः सुलोचनाङ्गश्च भवति चित्रायाम् ।
दान्तो वणिक् कृपालुः प्रियवाग्धर्माश्रितः स्वातौ ।। ८ ।।

Under the asterism Citrā one comes to have colourful garments and flower-garlands as well as beautiful eyes and limbs. The star Svāti makes one self-controlled, clever in trade, kind-hearted, virtuous and of pleasant speech.

[Instead of कृपालुः, तृषालुः is another reading.]

Cf. पराशर—

वेदार्थशास्त्रकुशलः पशुमानत्यन्तशिल्पकर्मा च ।
चित्राक्षश्चित्रायां सुभगश्च नरस्त्रिपुत्रश्च ।।
बहुजनभर्ता वक्ता त्रिवर्गभोक्ता प्रियो महोत्साहः ।
वामाचारोऽल्परिपुः स्वातौ जातः कुलाग्र्यश्च ।।

ईर्ष्युर्लुब्धो द्युतिमान्वचनपटुः कलहकृद्विशाखासु ।
प्राढ्यो विदेशवासी क्षुधालुरटनोऽनुराधासु ।। ९ ।।

One born under Viśākhā becomes jealous, greedy, bright in appearance, clever in speech, and quarrelsome. The person born under Anurādhā becomes very wealthy, dwells in foreign lands, is unable to endure hunger and wanders from place to place.

[Cf. पराशर—

श्रीमानिज्याभिरतः प्राज्ञोऽनुपसाधुकृत् कृतार्थपतिः ।
तीक्ष्णोऽभिमानयुक्तश्चैन्द्राग्नौ ख्यातकीर्तिश्च ।।
स्थिरमित्रस्तेजस्वी सुतवानत्यन्तसौख्यभागी च ।
ज्ञातिष्वग्र्योऽर्थपरो जातः स्यान्मित्रदैवत्ये ।।

This sage gives only good effects for Anurādhā.]

ज्येष्ठासु न बहुमित्रः सन्तुष्टो धर्मकृत्प्रचुरकोपः ।
मूले मानी धनवान् सुखी न हिंस्रः स्थिरो भोगी ।। १० ।।

One born in the star Jyeṣṭhā will not have many friends, will be contented, interested in meritorious deeds and exceedingly irritable. Under Mūla one becomes proud, wealthy, happy, of a gentle nature, firm-minded and luxurious in his living.

[Cf. पराशर—

ज्ञातिषु गुणेषु राजसु पूजां प्राप्नोति नाशयति शत्रून् ।
तेजोऽधिकोऽर्थभागी जातः स्यादिन्द्रदैवत्ये ।।
धनधान्याढ्यो दाता परवित्तहरो नरः कलहशीलः ।
क्रूरः परोपतापी मूले मूलोपजीवी च ।।]

इष्टानन्दकलत्रो मानी दृढसौहृदश्च जलदैवे ।
वैश्वे विनीतधार्मिकबहुमित्रकृतज्ञसुभगश्च ।। ११ ।।

The person born under Pūrvāṣāḍhā will have an amiable and jolly wife, will be proud and firm in friendship. The star Uttarāṣāḍhā will make one modest, virtuous, have many friends, grateful and attractive.

[वीरो is another reading for मानी.

Cf. पराशर—

सलिलपथकर्मसिद्धः क्लेशसहिष्णुः परस्य दारेच्छुः ।
नित्यमकल्यशरीरः प्रियमद्यः पूर्वषाढासु ॥
यानोद्यानवनरतिः प्रवाससुरतीर्थसाधुसेवी च ।
बहुशिल्पार्थः प्रियवाक् जातः स्याद्वैश्वदेवे च ॥]

श्रीमाञ्छ्रवणे श्रुतवानुदारदारो धनान्वितः ख्यातः ।
दाताऽऽढ्यशूरगीतप्रियो धनिष्ठासु धनलुब्धः ॥ १२ ॥

One born under the asterism Śravaṇa becomes learned, has a generous wife, and is possessed of wealth and fame. Star Dhaniṣṭhā makes one charitable, heroic, wealthy, greedy for money, and fond of music.

[The alliteration in the first line is pleasing. Utpala gives two explanations of उदारदारः, उदारेषु दारः and the other, the correct one. It is not clear as to what he means by the first explanation.

Cf. पराशर—

ज्ञातिश्रेष्ठो धनवान्दानरुचिर्भवति दक्षिणो दक्षः ।
नित्यमरोगशरीरः श्रवणे हतशत्रुपक्षश्च ॥
धनधान्यसञ्चयानामीशः स्याद्भूपतिसत्कृतो यज्वा ।
अक्लेशभाग् जितरिपुः श्रविष्ठयाभीष्टता(दा ?)रश्च ॥]

स्फुटवाग्व्यसनी रिपुहा साहसिकः शतभिषक्षु दुर्ग्राह्यः ।
भद्रपदासूद्विग्नः स्त्रीजितधनपटुरदाता च ॥ १३ ॥

One born in the star Śatabhiṣaj speaks clearly (or frankly), is unfortunate (or has some vice), conquers his enemies, is daring and hard to be won over. Under the star Pūrvabhadrapadā one will be unhappy, henpecked, wealthy and clever, but a miser.

[Vide पराशर—

परदारमद्यसेवी क्लेशसहो वारुणे नरो धीरः ।
स्थिरसञ्चयः स्थिरसुहृद्भिषक्क्रियापण्डितो रोगी ॥
दारुणकर्मा क्रोधी निशाचरस्तीक्ष्णविक्रमश्चपलः ।
विषमः प्रसह्य हन्ता प्राक्प्रोष्ठपदे भवति जातः ॥

The commentator interprets स्फुटवाक् as निष्ठुरभाषी—one who speaks harshly.]

वक्ता सुखी प्रजावान् जितशत्रुर्धार्मिको द्वितीयासु ।
सम्पूर्णाङ्गः सुभगः शूरः शुचिरर्थवान् पौष्णे ॥ १४ ॥

The person born under the asterism Uttarābhādra will be a good speaker, happy, blessed with children, will vanquish his enemies and be virtuous. The star Revatī makes one have a symmetrical body (a perfect body), attractive, heroic, pure and wealthy.

[Vide पराशर—

नृपसत्कृतो बहुसुतः प्रदानशीलो जले सततभीरुः ।
इज्याध्ययनरतिः स्यादाहिर्बुध्न्ये नरो जातः ॥
सर्वार्थभुक् प्रदाता प्रवासनिरतो विशुद्धकुलशीलः ।
गोमाननल्पपुत्रः पौष्णे विद्वान् नरो जातः ॥]

राशिविभागः ॥ १०२ ॥

Chapter CII—Division of the Zodiac into Signs

[This chapter appears to be an interpolation done before our commentator, since the author does not include it in his table of contents at the end of this work. Some scholar must have added this chapter on the rudiments of astrology in order to make this work complete in all aspects of the Science.]

अश्विन्योऽथ भरण्यो बहुलापादश्च कीर्त्यते मेषः ।
वृषभो बहुलाशेषं रोहिण्योऽर्धं च मृगशिरसः ॥ १ ॥

The Sign Aries comprises the whole (all the four quarters of) asterisms of Aśvinī and Bharaṇī and the first quarter of Kṛttikā; Sign Taurus, the remaining three quarters of Kṛttikā, the whole of Rohiṇī and the first half of Mṛgaśīrṣa.

[In the Bṛhad Jātaka our author states:

मेषाश्विप्रथमा नवर्क्षचरणाश्चक्रस्थिता राशयः । (I.4)]

मृगशिरसोऽर्धं रौद्रं पुनर्वसोरंशकत्रयं मिथुनः ।
पादश्च पुनर्वसुतस्तिष्यः श्लेषा च कर्कटकः ॥ २ ॥

Sign Gemini is constituted by the latter half of Mṛgaśiras, the whole of Ārdrā and the first three quarters of Punarvasu; sign Cancer, by the last quarter of Punarvasu, the whole of Puṣya and Āśleṣā.

सिंहोऽथ मघा पूर्वा च फल्गुनी पाद उत्तरायाश्च ।
तत्परिशेषं हस्तश्चित्रार्धं च कन्याख्यः ॥ ३ ॥

The Sign Leo consists of the whole of Maghā and Pūrvaphalgunī and the first quarter of Uttaraphalgunī; Sign Virgo, of the remaining three quarters of Uttaraphalgunī, the whole of Hasta, and the first half of Citrā.

तौलिनि चित्रान्त्यार्धं स्वातिः पादत्रयं विशाखायाः ।
अलिनि विशाखापादस्तथानुराधान्विता ज्येष्ठा ॥ ४ ॥

The Sign Libra comprises the latter half of Citrā, the whole of Svāti and the initial three quarters of Viśākhā; sign Scorpio, the last quarter of Viśākhā and the whole of Anurādhā and Jyeṣṭhā.

मूलमषाढा पूर्वा प्रथमश्चाप्युत्तरांशको धन्वी ।
मकरस्तत्परिशेषं श्रवणः पूर्वं धनिष्ठार्धम् ॥ ५ ॥

Sign Sagittarius consists of the whole of Mūla and Pūrvāṣāḍhā and the first quarter of Uttarāṣāḍhā; sign Capricorn, of the remaining three quarters of Uttarāṣāḍhā, the whole of Śravaṇa, and the first half of Dhaniṣṭhā.

कुम्भोऽन्त्यधनिष्ठार्धं शतभिषगंशत्रयं च पूर्वायाः ।
भद्रपदायाः शेषं तथोत्तरा रेवती च झषः ॥ ६ ॥

Sign Aquarius comprises the latter half of Dhaniṣṭhā, the whole of Śatabhiṣaj, and the first three quarters of Pūrvābhādra; sign Pisces, the last quarter of Pūrvābhādra, and the whole of Uttarābhādra and Revatī.

अश्विनीपित्र्यमूलाद्या मेषसिंहहयादयः ।
विषमर्क्षाण्निवर्तन्ते पादवृद्ध्या यथोत्तरम् ॥ ७ ॥

The signs Aries, Leo and Sagittarius commence with the beginning of Aśvinī, Maghā and Mūla respectively and the following odd asterisms (3rd, 5th, 7th and 9th) retire from each sign with one or more quarters in an increasing order.

[The 3rd star is Kṛttikā and so it closes Aries with its first quarter. Mṛgaśiras is the 5th in order. So it retires with two quarters; Punarvasu, being the 7th retires with three quarters, and lastly the 9th, Āśleṣā, with its fourth quarter. The metre is *Śloka.*]

विवाहपटलम् ॥ १०३ ॥

(विन्ध्यवासिकृतम्)

Chapter CIII—Planetary Combinations at Marriage

(Written by Vindhyavāsin)

[This chapter is patently by another author named above. The commentator could have, however, added this chapter at the end of Chapter C, where he comments upon विवाहपटल of two verses, with the remark: "इदानीं संक्षेपेणावसरप्राप्तं विवाहपटलमाह ।" For, what is treated of in this chapter is nothing but an elaboration of the matter contained in those two verses. The reason for this must be that before our commentator, others must have seen this work with the inclusion of this Vivāhapaṭala as a separate chapter, since he notices a variant reading in verse 8 *infra.*]

मूर्तौ करोति दिनकृद्विधवां कुजश्च
राहुर्विपन्नतनयां रविजो दरिद्राम् ।
शुक्रः शशाङ्कतनयश्च गुरुश्च साध्वी-
मायुःक्षयं प्रकुरुतेऽथ विभावरीशः ॥ १ ॥

If the Sun or Mars occupy the ascendant at a marriage, the girl would become a widow; if Rāhu, she would lose her children; if Saturn, she would become penniless; if Venus, Mercury or Jupiter, she would be blessed with an ideal character; and if the Moon, her life would be cut short.

[All the verses in this chapter, except the last one which is in स्रग्धरा metre, are in the वसन्ततिलका metre.]

कुर्वन्ति भास्करशनैश्चरराहुभौमा
दारिद्र्यदुःखमतुलं नियतं द्वितीये ।
वित्तेश्वरीमविधवां गुरुशुक्रसौम्या
नारीं प्रभूततनयां कुरुते शशाङ्कः ॥ २ ॥

The Sun, Saturn, Rāhu or Mars occupying the 2nd house from the ascendant cause undoubtedly indescribable miseries arising from poverty; while Jupiter, Venus or Mercury therein make the girl abundantly rich and have a long-lived husband. The Moon in that position confers many children on her.

सूर्येन्दुभौमगुरुशुक्रबुधास्तृतीये
कुर्युः सदा बहुसुतां धनभागिनीं च ।
व्यक्तां दिवाकरसुतः सुभगां करोति
मृत्युं ददाति नियमात् खलु सैंहिकेयः ॥ ३ ॥

The Sun, Moon, Mars, Mercury, Jupiter or Venus in the 3rd house from the ascendant make her always wealthy and blessed with many children; Saturn makes her famous, and attractive to her husband; while Rāhu invariably causes death.

स्वल्पं पयः स्रवति सूर्यसुते चतुर्थे
दौर्भाग्यमुष्णकिरणः कुरुते शशी च ।
राहुः सपत्नमपि च क्षितिजोऽल्पवित्तं
दद्याद्भृगुः सुरगुरुश्च बुधश्च सौख्यम् ॥ ४ ॥

Saturn occupying the 4th house causes scarcity of breast-milk in the bride; the Sun or the Moon in that position makes her unfortunate (i. e. disliked by the husband); Rāhu creates enemies (or a co-wife); Mars causes poverty; Venus, Jupiter or Mercury bestow happiness.

नष्टात्मजां रविकुजौ खलु पञ्चमस्थौ
चन्द्रात्मजो बहुसुतां गुरुभार्गवौ च ।
राहुर्ददाति मरणं शनिरुग्ररोगं
कन्याविनाशमचिरात्कुरुते शशाङ्कः ॥ ५ ॥

The Sun and Mars (singly or together) in the 5th house from the Lagna will certainly destroy her issue; Mercury, Jupiter and Venus bestow many children; Rāhu causes death; Saturn, a fell disease; the Moon brings about the girl's death before long.

षष्ठाश्रिताः शनिदिवाकरराहुजीवाः
कुर्युः कुजश्च सुभगां श्वशुरेषु भक्ताम् ।
चन्द्रः करोति विधवामुशना दरिद्रा-
मृद्धां शशाङ्कतनयः कलहप्रियां च ॥ ६ ॥

Saturn, the Sun, Rāhu, Jupiter and Mars occupying the 6th house make the bride beloved of her husband, and devoted to the elders (such as the father-in-law and mother-in-law); the Moon makes her a widow; Venus, penurious; and Mercury, wealthy, but fond of quarrels.

[In the 6th house five planets are beneficial, while the Moon is definitely bad, Mercury being partly favourable.]

सौरारजीवबुधराहुरवीन्दुशुक्राः
कुर्युः प्रसह्य खलु सप्तमराशिसंस्थाः ।
वैधव्यबन्धनवधक्षयमर्थनाश-
व्याधिप्रवासमरणानि यथाक्रमेण ॥ ७ ॥

Saturn, Mars, Jupiter, Mercury, Rāhu, the Sun, the Moon and Venus occupying the 7th house, cause perforce widowhood, imprisonment, destruction, decay, loss of wealth, disease, absence from home and death respectively.

[It is a well-known rule to be observed in electional astrology relating to marriage that the 7th house from the ascendant at the time of marriage must be free from planets. That is why no good effect has been given here for any planet.]

स्थानेऽष्टमे गुरुबुधौ नियतं वियोगं
मृत्युं शशी भृगुसुतश्च तथैव राहुः ।
सूर्यः करोत्यविधवां सरुजां महीजः
सूर्यात्मजो धनवतीं पतिवल्लभां च ॥ ८ ॥

Jupiter and Mercury in the 8th house cause separation between the husband and wife for certain; the Moon, Venus and Rāhu cause death; the Sun makes her predecease her husband; Mars, sickly; Saturn, wealthy and beloved of her husband.

[According to this only two planets namely the Sun and Saturn, are beneficial in the 8th house. The commentator speaks of a different reading in the third line viz. सुभगां instead of सरुजाम्.]

धर्मे स्थिता भृगुदिवाकरभूमिपुत्रा
जीवश्च धर्मनिरतां शशिजस्त्वरोगाम् ।
राहुश्च सूर्यतनयश्च करोति वन्ध्यां
कन्याप्रसूतिमटनां कुरुते शशाङ्कः ॥ ९ ॥

Venus, the Sun, Mars and Jupiter posited in the 9th house make the girl devoted to virtue or religion; Mercury gives her good health; Rāhu and Saturn make her barren; and the Moon gives her daughters and a wandering habit.

राहुर्नभःस्थलगतो विधवां करोति
पापे रतां दिनकरश्च शनैश्चरश्च ।
मृत्युं कुजोऽर्थरहितां कुलटां च चन्द्रः
शेषा ग्रहा धनवतीं सुभगां च कुर्युः ॥ १० ॥

Rāhu occupying the 10th house from the ascendant at marriage makes a girl a widow; the Sun and Saturn therein lead her to sinful activities; Mars causes death; the Moon makes her indigent and unchaste; and the others viz. Mercury, Jupiter and Venus, wealthy and beloved of the husband.

आये रविर्बहुसुतां सधनां शशाङ्कः
पुत्रान्वितां क्षितिसुतो रविजो धनाढ्याम् ।
आयुष्मतीं सुरगुरुः शशिजः समृद्धां
राहुः करोत्यविधवां भृगुरर्थयुक्ताम् ॥ ११ ॥

The Sun situated in this 11th house bestows many sons; the Moon, wealth; Mars, sons; Saturn, much wealth; Jupiter, long life; Mercury, great prosperity; Rāhu, long life on the husband; and Venus, riches.

अन्ते गुरुर्धनवतीं दिनकृद्दरिद्रां
चन्द्रो धनव्ययकरीं कुलटां च राहुः ।
साध्वीं भृगुः शशिसुतो बहुपुत्रपौत्रीं
पानप्रसक्तहृदयां रविजः कुजश्च ॥ १२ ॥

Jupiter in the 12th house confers wealth on the bride; the Sun leads to poverty; the Moon makes her a spend-thrift; Rāhu, immoral; Venus, devoted to her husband; Mercury bestows many children and grand children; Saturn and Mars make her an addict to drink.

गोपैर्यष्ट्या हतानां खुरपुटदलिता या तु धूलिर्दिनान्ते
सोद्वाहे सुन्दरीणां विपुलधनसुतारोग्यसौभाग्यकर्त्री
तस्मिन्काले न चर्क्षं न च तिथिकरणं नैव लग्नं न योगः
ख्यातः पुंसां सुखार्थं शमयति दुरितान्युत्थितं गोरजस्तु ॥ १३ ॥

The dust that is raised in the evening by the pointed hoofs of the cows beaten with sticks by the cow-herds, is favourable for the marriage of charming girls. It bestows abundant wealth, sons, sound health and husband's affection. It is not at all necessary at this time to consider the asterism, the lunar day, karaṇa, yoga and ascendant. For, the dust raised by cows is noted for giving happiness to men, as it wards off all sins.

[The results of this section can be put in a table for ready reference as shown below:

Planets Houses	Sun	Moon	Mars	Murcury	Jupiter	Venus	Saturn	Rāhu
I	Widow	Short Life	Widow	Chastity	Chastity	Chastity	Poverty	Loss of children
II	Suffering due to poverty	Many children	Suffering due to poverty	Riches & auspiciousness	Riches & auspiciousness	Riches & auspiciousness	Suffering due to poverty	Suffering due to poverty
III	Many sons & wealth	Many sons & wealth	Many sons & wealth	Many sons & wealth	Many sons & wealth	Many sons & wealth	Famous & beloved of husband	Death
IV	Unfortunate	Unfortunate	Poverty	Happiness	Happiness	Happiness	Little milk in breasts	Enemies
V	Loss of children	Death soon	Loss of children	Many children	Many sons	Many children	fell disease	Death

VI	Attractive & respectful to elders	Widow	Attractive & respectful to elders	Rich & quarrelsome	Attractive & respectful to elders	Poor	Attractive & respectful to elders	Attractive & respectful to elders
VII	Disease	Going away from home	Imprisonment	Decay	Death	Death	Widowhood	Sons of wealth
VIII	Long lived husband	Death	Sickly	Separation	Separation	Death	Rich & beloved of husband	Death
IX	Virtuous	Birth of only daughters & wandering	Virtuous	Healthy	Virtuous	Virtuous	Barren	Barren
X	Sinful	Poor & immoral	Death	Rich & attractive	Rich & attractive	Rich & attractive	Sinful	Widowhood
XI	Many sons	Rich	Many children	Rich	Long life	Wealthy	Rich	Long-lived husband
XII	Poor	Spendthrift	Drunkard	Many children & grand children	Rich	Chaste	Drunkard	Immoral

ग्रहगोचराध्यायः ॥ १०४ ॥

Chapter CIV—Transits of Planets

The aim of the author is to include in his work all branches of learning, though his main object is to teach astrological and allied principles. So he wants to illustrate many of the metres while expounding the effects of planetary transits. Being a great scholar endowed with a creative genius, he uses many figures of speech and introduces cleverly the names of metres, he employs, through pun. Primarily Sanskrit metres are classified under two heads viz. Vṛtta and Jāti. The former is based on groups of three syllables called Akṣara gaṇas, while the latter, upon groups of four Mātrās or syllabic instants. There are 8 Akṣaragaṇas viz. Ma, Ya, Ra, Sa, Ta, Ja, Bha and Na. They are shown below:

मगणः =	— — — ;	आदित्यः	तगणः =	— — ∪ ;	विघ्नेश
यगणः =	∪ — — ;	पिनाकः	जगणः =	∪ — ∪ ;	पुरारि
रगणः =	— ∪ — ;	शङ्करः	भगणः =	— ∪∪ ;	भूसुर
सगणः =	∪ ∪ — ;	सततम्	नगणः =	∪ ∪ ∪ ;	गिरिश

Here (—) stands for a long syllable, while (∪) for a short one. These Gaṇas have their own presiding deities viz. the Earth, Water, Fire, Wind, Sky, Sun, Moon and Heaven. According to Piṅgala, Antaka or Death takes the place of Wind, and Serpent instead of Heaven. Their effects in order are: Prosperity, growth, death, journey, emptiness, disease, fame and joy. The following verse gives the mutual relationship of the Gaṇas:

मनौ सखायौ कथितौ भयौ भृत्यावुदीरितौ ।
उदासीनौ तजौ प्रोक्तौ सरौ शत्रू मताविह ॥

The Jāti type of metre is based on syllabic instants. Here a Gaṇa has four syllabic instants. Among the Akṣaragaṇas there are only three viz. सगण, जगण and भगण, which have four Mātrās. In addition to these we can have नगण and one लघु. Our author is fond of the आर्या metre belonging to the Jāti group. In the ordinary variety of this Āryā, the first and third quarters must have three groups of four Mātrās each; the second, 4 groups with a long syllable (which has two Mātrās) at the end. The fourth quarter has 15 Mātrās, distributed among four Gaṇas followed by a long syllable. In this, the third Gaṇa is represented by only one Mātrā of a short syllable. It is a rule that the odd groups ought not to have Jagaṇa (∪—∪) and the sixth (i.e. the 3rd in the second quarter) ought to have Jagaṇa or a Nagaṇa and a Laghu (∪∪∪∪). The author names here several varieties of the Āryā viz. मुखचपला, जघनचपला, पथ्या, विपुला, वक्त्र, वतालीय, औपच्छन्दसिक, Daṇḍakas viz. चण्डवृष्टिप्रयात, वर्णकदण्डक, समुद्रदण्डक, and 47 Vṛttas.

प्रायेण सूत्रेण विनाकृतानि प्रकाशरन्ध्राणि चिरन्तनानि ।
रत्नानि शास्त्राणि च योजितानि नवैर्गुणैर्भूषयितुं क्षमाणि ॥ १ ॥

Generally ancient gems and Śāstras (scientific works) which are without strings (i.e. unstrung) and a metrical form (respectively), whose bores are quite visible and faults apparent (as a result of obsolete words), become fit to be worn as ornaments and to be held in high esteem, when they are joined together with new strings and excellent ideas couched in fine metres (respectively).

[Here the author uses pun (Śleṣa) and Samuccayālaṁkāra. The metre is उपजाति.]

प्रायेण गोचरो व्यवहार्योऽतस्तत्फलानि वक्ष्यामि ।
नानावृत्तैरार्या मुखचपलत्वं क्षमध्वं नः ॥ २ ॥

Generally, the transit of planets comes within the purview of our daily experience. Hence I shall expound its effects, O noble scholars, in varied metres. Kindly excuse my volubility.

[Here he has introduced the name of the metre मुखचपला with pun, as it also means 'talkative'. In society people speak about their good and bad prospects accruing from the transit of the planets with reference to their natal Moon. Hence it is a very useful subject in which even ordinary persons are unusually interested. Now to understand मुखचपला type of आर्या, we have to know first what is चपला. In both the halves there should be जगण in the second and fourth places, being surrounded (i. e. preceded and followed) by Gurus or long syllables. It is arranged thus:

∪∪—, ∪—∪, — —, ∪—∪, — —, ∪—∪, — —, Long,
∪∪—, ∪—∪, — —, ∪—∪, — —, ∪, — —, Long,,

Here the Jagaṇas in II and IV places are flanked by (—)s, in both halves. Hence the name. If the first half alone follows this rule, it is called मुखचपला. Let us put the example in symbols :

— —, ∪— ∪, —∪ ∪, — —, — —, ∪— ∪, — —, Long,
— —, — —, — —, ∪∪ ∪∪, — —, ∪, — —, Long,,

The author has not followed in the first half the rules of चपला strictly, as the IV Gaṇa is not preceded by a long syllable, though it is followed by one. It is no जगण either. Here, since the first half alone is of the चपला variety and the second of the ordinary आर्या, it is termed चपला in the मुख or opening.]

माण्डव्यगिरं श्रुत्वा न मदीया रोचतेऽथवा नैवम् ।
साध्वी तथा न पुंसां प्रिया यथा स्याज्जघनचपला ॥ ३ ॥

Or, my statements on this subject will surely be liked by the learned who have heard those of Māṇḍavya. For, men do not love their devout and chaste wives so much as they do courtesans.

[It is inferred that Rāṭa and Māṇḍavya were the joint authors of some sacred works. They are mentioned in Piṅgala's work. Māṇḍavya is mentioned in the Baudhāyana-sūtra, Āśvalāyana-sūtra and the Mahābhārata (Ādi. 107). The commentator quotes two verses of Māṇḍavya which contain a bombastic style and appear to be modern:

सर्वेऽप्याकाशवासाः स्फटिकबिसलताशङ्खकार्पासभासा-
स्ते लग्नं वर्द्धयन्तो नरपतितिलकं तं समुत्पादयन्ति ।
यत्सेनोत्तालवाजिव्रजखुरजरजोव्याप्तमालोक्य बिम्बं
मुच्यन्ते प्रेयसीभिर्दुरनुभवनिशाशङ्कया चक्रवाकाः ॥
कोर्पैरन्यत्र मुक्ताविचकिलधवलो रोहिणीप्राणनाथः
सर्वैः संवीक्ष्यमाणः खवलयनिलयैस्तं समुत्पादयेद्धि ।
नीतं यस्य प्रगाढैर्धनमलिनमपि श्वेतिमानं यशोभि-
र्बिभ्राणा शम्भुशङ्कां मधुमथनमहो मन्दमालिङ्गति श्रीः ॥

The metre जघनचपला is so called because it is like the चपला only in the second half, the first half being like the ordinary Āryā. So this is the converse of मुखचपला. In this verse the author shows his humility in that he says that though his statements are not picturesque like a courtesan, yet being factual they would be liked by scholars.]

सूर्यः षट्त्रिदशस्थितस्त्रिदशषट्सप्ताद्यगश्चन्द्रमा
जीवः सप्तनवद्विपञ्चमगतो वक्रार्कजौ षट्त्रिगौ ।

सौम्यः षड्द्विचतुर्दशाष्टमगतः सर्वेऽप्युपान्ते शुभाः
शुक्रः सप्तमषड्दशर्क्षसहितः शार्दूलवत् त्रासकृत् ॥ ४ ॥

The Sun is beneficial in transit in the 3rd, 6th, and 10th places from a person's natal Moon; the Moon in the 1st, 3rd, 6th, 7th and 10th houses; Jupiter in the 2nd, 5th, 7th and 9th houses; Mars and Saturn in the 3rd and 6th; Mercury in the 2nd, 4th, 6th, 8th and 10th; all planets are beneficial in the 11th place. Venus causes fear (unfavourable effects) like the tiger, when he moves in the 6th, 7th, and 10th places; (in others he is auspicious).

[Sometimes the effects of good transits are not experienced by people, as they are hindered by those of Vedha (obstruction) produced by other planets. For an explanation of Vedha see this author's 'Fundamentals of Astrology' page 236. The metre of this verse is शार्दूलविक्रीडित which is defined thus: सूर्याश्वैर्मसजाः स्तताः सगुरवः शार्दूलविक्रीडितम् ।]

In the following three verses the author explains in detail the transit effects of the Sun in the 12 houses from the natal Moon.

जन्मन्यायासबोऽर्कः क्षपयति विभवान् कोष्ठरोगाध्ववाता
वित्तभ्रंशं द्वितीये दिशति च न सुखं वञ्चनां दृग्रुजं च ।
स्थानप्राप्तिं तृतीये धननिचयमुदा कल्यकृच्चारिहर्ता
रोगान्वत्ते चतुर्थे जनयति च मुहुः स्रग्धरा भोगविघ्नम् ॥ ५ ॥

The Sun passing through the sign of the natal Moon causes fatigue, reduces wealth, brings about diseases of the bowels, wealth and wearisome journeys. He causes, in the 2nd house, loss of wealth, and happiness, eye-disease and deceit. In the 3rd house, acquisition of a new position, advent of much wealth, happiness, sound health and destruction of enemies will be the result. In the 4th house, the Sun causes diseases, and constant impediments to the native in the enjoyment of conjugal happiness.

[In the second line in the place of दिशति, मनसि is another reading. This verse is in the स्रग्धरा metre which is defined as:

म्रभ्नैर्यानां त्रयेण त्रिमुनियतियुता स्रग्धरा कीर्तितेयम् ।]

पीडाः स्युः पञ्चमस्थे सवितरि बहुशो रोगारिजनिताः
षष्ठेऽर्को हन्ति रोगान्क्षपयति च रिपून् शोकांश्च नुदति ।
अध्वानं सप्तमस्थो जठरगदभयं दैन्यं च कुरुते
रुक्त्रासौ चाष्टमस्थे भवति सुवदना न स्वापि वनिता ॥ ६ ॥

When the Sun passes in transit through the 5th house, there will be innumerable troubles caused by illness and enemies; through the 6th, he removes illness, enemies and grief; through the 7th, he causes wearisome travelling, diseases of the stomach, and humiliation; through the 8th, the person will suffer from illness and fright; and consequently his own wife will speak harshly to him.

[This verse is in the सुवदना metre which is defined as :
ज्ञेया सप्ताश्वषड्भिर्मरभनययुतौ भ्लौ गः सुवदना ।]

रवावापद्दैन्यं रुगिति नवमे वित्तचेष्टाविरोधो
जयं प्राप्नोत्युग्रं दशमगृहगे कर्मसिद्धिं क्रमेण ।
जयस्थानं मानं विभवमपि चैकादशे रोगनाशं
सुवृत्तानां चेष्टा भवति सफला द्वादशे नेतरेषाम् ॥ ७ ॥

The Sun in the 9th house causes danger, poverty (or humiliation), disease and impediments to acquisition of wealth and undertakings; in the 10th house, a mighty task will be completed successfully, and all the projects will be carried to success. In the 11th house, the native will attain an illustrious position, honour, wealth and freedom from disease. When the Sun passes through the 12th house, the activities of only those of an ideal character will be successful and not of others.

[Cf. the following regarding good results accruing to the virtuous:—

मङ्गलाचारयुक्तानां नित्यं च प्रयतात्मनाम् ।
जपतां जुह्वतां चैव विनिपातो विनश्यते ॥

Vide the फलदीपिका XXVI. 50.

Vide also यवनेश्वर—

हृद्रोगशोकाध्वविवाहदैन्यक्रोधक्षयव्याधिभयार्तिदोषान् ।
स्थाने शशाङ्कस्य रविः करोति व्यर्थश्रमोद्वेगमपि द्वितीये ॥
तृतीयसंस्थो धनमानधर्मस्थानासनप्रीतिसुखप्रदोऽर्कः ।
चतुर्थगस्तु क्षतजप्रवृत्तिज्वरामयो भेदविवादकारी ॥
नृपावमर्दात्मजबन्धुशोकव्याधिप्रदः पञ्चमसंस्थितोऽर्कः ।
आरोग्यसौख्यारिविनाशहर्षख्यातिक्रियासिद्धिकरश्च षष्ठः ॥
जामित्रसंस्थो रुधिरप्रवृत्तिज्वरक्लमाजीर्णविषाध्वकारी ।
सूर्योऽष्टमे स्त्रीसुतबन्धुदुःखव्याधिप्रदोपद्रवमृत्युकृत्स्यात् ॥
दैन्यस्थितिभ्रंशगुरुस्वबन्धुप्रद्वेषकृत् स्यान्नवमाश्रितोऽर्कः ।
मेषूरणस्थो द्विचतुष्पदस्त्रीहिरण्यरौप्याम्बरलाभकर्ता ॥

एकादशे स्थानयशःप्रहर्षमिष्टाशनारोग्यसुखप्रदोऽर्कः
स्थाने निरुक्तं शशिनो विधिज्ञैः क्रियाफलाधातकृदन्त्यराशौ ॥

The metre of the verse is सुवृत्ता which is defined thus : यमौ न्सौ रौ गश्चेद् द्विरसमुनिभिः स्याद्विरामैः सुवृत्ता ।

It is also known as मेघविस्फूर्जिता, according to the Vṛttaratnākara, which defines it thus:

रसर्त्वश्वैर्य्मौ न्सौ ररगुरुयुतौ मेघविस्फूर्जिता ।]

शशी जन्मन्यन्नप्रवरचयनाच्छादनकरो
द्वितीये मानार्थान् ग्लपयति सविघ्नश्च भवति ।
तृतीये वस्त्रस्त्रीधनविजयसौख्यानि लभते
चतुर्थेऽविश्वासः शिखरिणि भुजङ्गेन सदृशः ॥८॥

When the Moon passes through the natal sign, one gets excellent food, couches and clothes; through the second house, one loses honour and wealth, and experiences obstacles; through the 3rd, one gets garments, damsels (or conjugal falicity), wealth, success and happiness; through the 4th house, one loses trust in others. as in a mountain infested with snakes.

[The poet introduces a simile combined with pun. The metre is शिखरिणी which is defined thus:

रसै रुद्रैश्छिन्ना यमनसभला गः शिखरिणी ।]

दैन्यं व्याधिं शुचमपि शशी पञ्चमे मार्गविघ्नं
षष्ठे वित्तं जनयति सुखं शत्रुरोगक्षयं च ।
यानं मानं शयनमशनं सप्तमे वित्तलाभं
मन्दाक्रान्ते फणिनि हिमगौ चाष्टमे भीर्न कस्य ॥९॥

The Moon passing through the 5th house brings about humiliation, illness, grief and obstruction to journey; through the 6th, confers wealth and happiness, and destroys enemies and diseases; through the 7th, confers vehicles, honour, couches, food and money. Whoever is not frightened when the Moon is in the 8th house, as when a snake is accidentally trodden upon ?

[Here too he uses pun and Samuccayālaṁkāra. The metre is मन्दाक्रान्ता which is defined thus:

मन्दाक्रान्ता जलधिषडगैर्म्भौ नतौ ताद्गुरू चेत् ।]

नवमगृहगो बन्धोद्वेगश्रमोदररोगकृद्
दशमभवने चाज्ञाकर्मप्रसिद्धिकरः शशी ।

उपचयसुहृत्संयोगार्थप्रमोदमुपान्त्यगो
वृषभचरितान्दोषानन्त्ये करोति च सव्ययान् ।।१०।।

The Moon in the 9th house causes imprisonment, agony, weariness and stomach diseases; in the 10th, she confers a position of authority and accomplishment of one's objects; in the 11th, prosperity, association with friends, riches and joy; in the 12th, causes expenses and blemishes caused by one's own foolishness, as in the case of a bull (which spoils both its hoofs and horns by striking the earth etc).

[The metre is called वृषभचरित or हरिणी, which is defined thus : वृषभचरितं न्सौ म्रौ स्लौ गो रसोदधिसप्तकैः । or रसयुगहयैर्न्सौ म्रौ स्लौ गो यदा हरिणी तदा ।

Vide यवनेश्वर—

स्वस्थानगो भोजनगन्धमाल्यनारीसुहृद्वस्त्ररतिप्रदः स्यात् ।
चन्द्रो द्वितीयर्क्षगतस्तु तस्माद् बहुव्ययायासविवादकारी ।।
तृतीयगो वस्त्रहिरण्ययोषित्सुहृद्यशोभोजनदो हिमांशुः ।
स्वबन्धुपीडाधननाशजानि कुर्वीत दुःखानि चतुर्थसंस्थः ।।
धनक्षयाजीर्णरुगध्वदैन्यविक्षोभकृत् पञ्चमगः शशाङ्कः ।
शत्रुक्षयारोग्यसुखार्थसिद्धि स्निग्धागमप्रीतिकरश्च षष्ठः ।।
जामित्रगः स्त्रीजनबन्धुशय्याहिरण्यभोज्याम्बरदः शशाङ्कः ।
क्षुद्व्याधिचिन्ताकलहार्थनाशो मृत्युक्षयोपद्रवदोऽष्टमस्थः ।।
धनक्षयारिव्ययमानभङ्गरोगादिकारी नवमः शशाङ्कः ।
मेषूरणस्थो बहुमानहर्षचेष्टाफलौदार्यविरोधकारी ।।
एकादशः स्निग्धविवाहशय्यास्त्रीभोजनप्राप्तिसुखार्थकारी ।
निशाकरो द्वादशगस्तु दैन्यमालस्यमीर्ष्यापचयं च कुर्यात् ।।]

कुजेऽभिघातः प्रथमे द्वितीये नरेन्द्रपीडाकलहारिदोषैः ।
भृशं च पित्तानलचौररोगैरुपेन्द्रवज्रप्रतिमोऽपि यः स्यात ।।११।।

Mars passing through the natal sign causes bodily affliction; through the second sign, trouble from the king and enemies, quarrels, excessive biliousness, fire accidents, robbery and disease, though the person may be like Upendra (Viṣṇu) or the thunderbolt.

[The person may be as great as Indra's younger brother or his chief weapon. The metre is called उपेन्द्रवज्रा, defined thus:

उपेन्द्रवज्रा तु जतौ जगौ गः ।]

तृतीयगश्चौरकुमारकेभ्यो भौमः सकाशात्फलमादधाति ।
प्रदीप्तिमाज्ञां धनमौर्णिकानि धात्वाकराढ्यानि किलापराणि ।।१२।।

Mars in the 3rd confers benefits through thieves and urchins, energy, authority, wealth, woollen articles, mineral wealth and the like.

[This verse is in the उपजाति metre which is a combination of the इन्द्रवज्रा and उपेन्द्रवज्रा. In this the first Gaṇa of the feet may be both जगण and तगण.]

भवति धरणिजे चतुर्थगे ज्वरजठरगदासृगुद्भवः ।
कुपुरुषजनिताच्च सङ्गमात्प्रसभमपि करोति चाशुभम् ।।१३।।

Mars in the 4th causes fever, stomach ailments and bleeding as well as great harm through the association with the wicked.

[The metre is called प्रसभ which is defined thus: प्रसभमपि ननौ रलौ गरुः । In the Vṛttaratnākara it is called सुभद्रिका or चन्द्रिका.]

रिपुगदकोपभयानि पञ्चमे तनयकृताश्च शुचो महीसुते ।
द्युतिरपि नास्य चिरं भवेत् स्थिरा शिरसि कपेरिव मालती यथा ।।१४।।

Mars in the 5th causes enmity, anger, illness, fear, grief on account of children, and a quick loss of energy like the tossing of a jasmine wreath from the head of a monkey.

[The metre is called मालती which is defined thus:
भवति नजावथ मालती जरौ ।]

रिपुभयकलहैर्विवर्जितः सकनकविद्रुमताम्रकागमः ।
रिपुभवनगते महीसुते किमपरवक्त्रविकारमीक्षते ।।१५।।

When Mars passes through the 6th house, one will be free from danger from enemies, (or from enemies and fear) as well as quarrels; one will also get gold, corals and copper, so that one may hold one's head aloft (i.e. one need not look for signs of others' pleasure and pain).

[The metre is called अपरवक्त्र which is defined as : अयुजि ननरला गुरुः समे तदपरवक्त्रमिदं नजौ जरौ । This is an अर्धसमवृत्त where the odd feet have 11 syllables, while the even ones 12.]

कलत्रकलहाक्षिरुग्जठररोगकृत्सप्तमे
क्षरत्क्षतजरूक्षितः क्षपितवित्तमानोऽष्टमे ।
कुजे नवमसंस्थिते परिभवार्थनाशादिभि-
र्विलम्बितगतिर्भवत्यबलदेहधातुक्लमैः ।।१६।।

Mars in the 7th house causes quarrels with one's wife, eye-disease and stomach-ailment; in the 8th, makes the native weak through bleeding, and lose wealth and honour; in the 9th house, suffer insults, loss of wealth and impeded gait owing to the loss of bodily fluids and consequent weakness.

[The Dhātus are mentioned in the following line:

वसाऽसृग्मांसमेदोऽस्थिमज्जाशुक्राणि धातवः ।

The metre is called विलम्बितगति which is defined thus: विलम्बितगतिर्जसौ जसयलैर्गयुक्तैर्भवेत् । The same is called पृथ्वी in the V. Ratnākara.]

दशमगृहगते समं महीजे विविधधनाप्तिरुपान्त्यगे जयश्च ।
जनपदमुपरि स्थितश्च भुङ्क्ते वनमिव षट्चरणः सुपुष्पिताग्रम् ॥१७॥

Mars in the 10th house produces neutral effects; in the 11th, confers various types of riches as well as success, and enables one to exercise power and authority over the country, just as the bee has free movements and enjoyment in a forest of abundant flowers.

[The metre is called पुष्पिताग्रा of the अर्धसमवृत्त group and is defined thus : अयुजि नयुगरेफतो यकारो युजि च नजौ जरगाश्च पुष्पिताग्रा ।]

नानाव्ययैर्द्वादशगे महीसुते सन्ताप्यतेऽनर्थशतैश्च मानवः ।
स्त्रीकोपपित्तैश्च सनेत्रवेदनैर्योऽपीन्द्रवंशाभिजनेन गर्वितः ॥१८॥

Mars in the 12th house tortures a person with expenditure on various counts, innumerable disasters, wrath of women (or wife), bilious affections and eye-trouble, though he may be proud of his being a scion of Indra.

[The metre is called इन्द्रवंशा which is defined thus: 'स्यादिन्द्रवंशा ततजैरसंयुतैः ।' This is just like वंशस्थ with the difference that here we have a long initial syllable instead of the short one.

Vide यवनेश्वर—

नृपानलव्यालविषाग्निशस्त्रव्याध्यर्थनाशी क्षयभङ्गकारी ।
भौमः शशिस्थानगतो द्वितीये त्वनर्थसूयामिषवञ्चनाकृत् ॥
ऐश्वर्यमानद्युतिहर्षकारी तृतीयसंस्थोऽन्नसुवर्णदश्च ।
चतुर्थगस्तूदररुग्जरासृक्प्रवृत्तिनिर्वेदकरो धराजः ॥
मृतार्थनाशक्षतवैरमोषव्याधिप्रदः पञ्चमराशिसंस्थः ।
षष्ठे कुजेऽरिक्षयमानहर्षप्रख्यापनारोग्यसमृद्धिकारी ॥
जामित्रसंस्थो धनमित्रनाशक्लेशोदराक्ष्यामयरोगकृत्स्यात् ।
भौमेऽष्टमे रुग्विषशत्रुशस्त्रक्षतक्षयोपद्रवदैन्यकारी ॥

शस्त्रक्षताक्षेमसुवर्णनाशखेदाध्वकारी नवमो महीजः ।
मेषूरणे व्याध्यरिशस्त्रचौरव्रणार्तिकृत् सिद्धिकरश्च पश्चात् ॥
मानात्मजाज्ञाक्षितिताम्रहेमद्युतिप्रदो रुद्रपदेऽरिजिच्च ।
स्त्रीविग्रहोद्वेजनपादरोगस्वप्नावभङ्गश्रमदः कुजोऽन्त्ये ॥]

दुष्टवाक्यपिशुनाहितभेदैर्बन्धनैः सकलहैश्च हृतस्वः ।
जन्मगे शशिसुते पथि गच्छन् स्वागतेऽपि कुशलं न शृणोति ॥१९॥

When Mercury passes through the first sign in transit, a man will be deprived of his wealth by wicked persons (using foul language), tale-bearers, enemies, duplicity, imprisonment and quarrels, and he will not hear even a kind word of welcome in his travels.

[The metre is स्वागता whose definition is—

स्वागतेति रनभाद् गुरुयुग्मम् ।]

परिभवो धनगते धनलब्धिः सहजगे शशिसुते सुहृदाप्तिः ।
नृपतिशत्रुभयशङ्कितचित्तो द्रुतपदं व्रजति दुश्चरितैः स्वैः ॥२०॥

When Mercury passes through the 2nd house, one will suffer humiliation, but acquire wealth; when he travels through the 3rd, one will have new friends, will be afraid of the king and enemies and will run away as a result of his own wicked deeds.

[The metre is द्रुतपद which is defined thus:

द्रुतपदं नभजयैः कथितं तत् ।]

चतुर्थगे स्वजनकुटुम्बवृद्धयो धनागमो भवति च शीतरश्मिजे ।
सुतस्थिते तनयकलत्रविग्रहो निषेवते न च रुचिरामपि स्त्रियम् ॥२१॥

During Mercury's transit through the 4th house the person's kinsmen and family will prosper, and he will gain wealth; through the 5th house, the native will have quarrels with his wife and sons and will not be able to enjoy even his charming wife.

[The metre is रुचिरा, defined thus:

जभौ सजौ गिति रुचिरा चतुर्ग्रहैः ।]

सौभाग्यं विजयमथोन्नतिं च षष्ठे वैवर्ण्यं कलहमतीव सप्तमे ज्ञः ।
मृत्युस्थे जयसुतवस्त्रवित्तलाभा नैपुण्यं भवति मतिप्रहर्षणीयम् ॥२२॥

During Mercury's transit through the 6th house the person concerned gets popularity, victory and rise; through the 7th sign, he loses his lustre and has frequent quarrels; through the 8th, he will have gains, success, children, clothes, money and skill that brings joy to his heart.

[The metre is प्रहर्षणीय defined thus:

म्नौ ज्रौ गस्त्रिदशयतिः प्रहर्षणीयम् ।]

विघ्नकरो नवमः शशिपुत्रः कर्मगतो रिपुहा धनदश्च ।
सप्रमदं शयनं च विधत्ते तद्गृहदोऽस्य कथां स्तरणं च ॥२३॥

When Mercury passes through the 9th house, he creates obstacles to all undertakings; through the 10th house, destroys the enemies and bestows wealth, a beautiful damsel on a couch, her house property, sweet words and sheets.

[In the place of कथां स्तरणं there is another reading viz. कुथास्तरणं which means—the rug that is spread on the elephant's back. The metre is दोधक, defined thus:— 'दोधकवृत्तमिदं भभभाद्गु: ।' The name of the metre is cleverly introduced in the verse by means of verbal pun or Mudrālaṅkāra.]

धनसुतसुखयोषिन्मित्रवाहाप्तितुष्टि-
स्तुहिनकिरणपुत्रे लाभगे मृष्टवाक्यः ।
रिपुपरिभवरोगैः पीडितो द्वादशस्थे
न सहति परिभोक्तुं मालिनीयोगसौख्यम् ॥२४॥

When Mercury passes in transit through the 11th house, the native will be jubilant with the attainment of wealth, sons, happiness, wife, friends and vehicles; he will also speak sweetly and pleasantly; when his transit takes place through the 12th house, the person will be troubled by enemies, insults and diseases, and consequently he will not be able to enjoy the pleasure of union with his bedecked beloved.

[Here for the sake of metre the author has forsaken the grammatical rule regarding the root Sah which is Ātmanepadin. He could have put it thus : प्रभवति न हि भोक्तुं . . . The metre is मालिनी, defined thus : ननमययुतेयं मालिनी भोगिलोकैः ।

Vide यवनेश्वर—

स्थाने शशाङ्कस्य शशाङ्कसूनुः सौभाग्यविद्यामतिमानहर्ता ।
द्वितीयसंस्थस्त्वपवादशोकस्वैरक्रियामन्वतिदैन्यकारी ॥
तृतीयगो बन्धुविरोधरोधव्यापत्तिकर्ता द्रविणस्य सौम्यः ।
चतुर्थगो मानगुणप्रशंसाप्रमोदयोषिद्धनलाभकारी ॥

नैष्ठान्यमुद्वेगमनर्थचर्यां कुर्याद्बुधः पञ्चमगोऽरतं च ।
षष्ठे विवृद्धिं मनसः प्रहर्षमुत्साहलाभोपचयं करोति ॥
जामित्रगश्चान्द्रिरनिष्टमार्गसन्तापदैन्याद्रुचिरोधकारी ।
स्यादष्टमस्थो विविधोपकारी बुद्धिप्रसादस्थितिसौख्यकर्ता ॥
भङ्गापवादाध्वपरिश्रमान्तरायापकारी नवमर्क्षसंस्थः ।
क्रियाप्रसिद्धिं दशमेऽर्थलाभं विस्रब्धमानं च बुधो ददाति ॥
एकादशे मानचतुष्पदस्त्रीचिन्तार्थसौभाग्यविनोदकर्ता ।
बुधोऽन्त्यराशौ विचरंश्च कुर्यादुद्वेजनं कार्यपरिश्रमं च ॥]

जीवे जन्मन्यपगतधनधीः स्थानभ्रष्टो बहुकलहयुतः ।
प्राप्यार्थेऽर्थान् व्यरिरपि कुरुते कान्तास्याब्जे भ्रमरविलसितम् ॥२५॥

When Jupiter in transit is in the natal sign, the person will lose his wealth, intellectual clarity and position; he will also have quarrels frequently; when he moves through the 2nd house, the person will obtain wealth and be free from enemies and will sport with the mouth of his beloved as does a bee with the lotus.

[The metre is भ्रमरविलसित defined thus:

म्भौ न्लौ गः स्याद् भ्रमरविलसितम् । or मो गो नौ गो भ्रमरविलसितम् ।]

स्थानभ्रंशात् कार्यविघाताच्च तृतीयेऽ-
नेकैः क्लेशैर्बन्धुजनोत्थैश्च चतुर्थे ।
जीवे शान्तिं पीडितचित्तश्च स विन्दे-
न्नैव ग्रामे नापि वने मत्तमयूरे ॥२६॥

When Jupiter passes through the 3rd house, the native will be troubled by loss of position, and by the ruination of his undertakings; when through the 4th house, he will be afflicted by all kinds of worries caused by his kith and kin, and consequently he will get peace of mind neither in the village (i.e. at home), nor in the forest abounding in intoxicated peacocks.

[The metre is मत्तमयूर, defined thus:

वेदै रन्ध्रैर्म्तौ यशगा मत्तमयूरम् ।]

जनयति च तनयभवनमुपगतः
परिजनशुभसुतकरितुरगवृषान् ।
सकनकपुरगृहयुवतिवसनकृ-
न्मणिगुणनिकरकृदपि विबुधगुरुः ॥२७॥

Jupiter moving through the 5th house bestows servants, meritorious acts (or auspicious rituals), sons, elephants, horses, bulls, gold, houses in town, marriage with a young woman, garments, gems and a number of virtues such as learning and valour.

[The metre is called मणिगुणनिकर, defined as:

वसुमुनियतिरिति मणिगुणनिकरः. The V. Ratnākara, however, calls it मणिगणकिरण.]

न सखीवदनं तिलकोज्ज्वलं न च वनं शिखिकोकिलनादितम् ।
हरिणप्लुतशावविचित्रितं रिपुगते मनसः सुखदं गुरौ ॥२८॥

When Jupiter passes through the 6th house, even the wife's face bright (attractive) with the Tilaka will not please a person's heart; nor will the forest that resounds with the notes of pea-cocks and cuckoos and looks wonderful by the frisking of the fawns.

[Here the word सखी should not be taken in its narrow sense of 'female-companion' but in that of 'one's life-partner'. The expression suggests that even the most intimate, affectionate persons become enemies and good things appear distasteful. The metre is हरिणप्लुत, defined as—

सयुगात् सलघू विषमे गुरुर्युजि नभौ च भरौ हरिणप्लुता ।]

त्रिदशगुरुः शयनं रतिभोगं धनमशनं कुसुमान्युपवाह्यम् ।
जनयति सप्तमराशिमुपेतो ललितपदां च गिरं धिषणां च ॥२९॥

Jupiter in the 7th house confers fine couches, erotic pleasures, wealth, tasty food, flowers, vehicles, elegant speech and intellectual eminence.

[The metre is called ललितपद, defined as—'ललितपदं नजयैर्भवतीह', but this does not include the second जगण. Hence it should be emended as—'ललितपदं नजजैः सयकारैः'. This is called तामरस in the V. Ratnākara—"इति वद तामरसं नजजाद्यः ।"]

बन्धं व्याधिं चाष्टमे शोकमुग्रं मार्गक्लेशान् मृत्युतुल्यांश्च रोगान् ।
नैपुण्याज्ञापुत्रकर्मार्थसिद्धिं धर्मे जीवः शालिनीनां च लाभम् ॥३०॥

Jupiter in the 8th house causes imprisonment, disease, intense f, hardships on a journey, and ailments almost amounting to ı. In the 9th he confers skill in work, authority, sons, success lertakings, wealth and fertile lands.

[Bhaṭṭotpala gives another meaning also of the expression शालिनीनाम् । 'अथवा स्वगुणैर्याः स्त्रियः शालन्ते श्लाघन्ते (शोभन्ते ?) तासां लाभं करोति', which means—'Getting or marrying virtuous or illustrious women.' The metre is called शालिनी, defined as—

मात्तौ गौ चेच्छालिनी वेदलोकैः ।]

स्थानकल्यधनहा दशर्क्षगस्तत्प्रदो भवति लाभगो गुरुः ।
द्वादशेऽध्वनि विलोमदुःखभाग् याति यद्यपि नरो रथोद्धतः ॥३१॥

Jupiter in the 10th destroys one's position, health and wealth; in the 11th, he bestows the above things; in the 12th, he gives grief arising from the person's swerving from the right path, though he may be rich enough to drive in a chariot.

[The metre is रथोद्धता defined as—

रान्नराविह रथोद्धता लगौ ।

Vide यवनेश्वर—

मोहार्थनाशस्थितिमानभङ्गग्रामाध्वरुग्जातिविरोधवैरान् ।
गुरुः शशिस्थानगतः करोति स्थानात्मजाज्ञाधनदो द्वितीये ।
गुरुस्तृतीये स्वजनार्थनाशक्रियावधाध्वश्रमवञ्चनाकृत् ।
विमानसेष्टापचयापवादबन्धुक्षयोद्वेगकरश्चतुर्थे ॥
भृत्याम्बरस्थानसुवर्णमानपुत्रप्रदः पञ्चमगोऽरिजिच्च ।
षष्ठे गुरुर्बन्धुविवादवैरत्रासप्रचेष्टाफलहानिकारी ॥
जामित्रगः स्त्रीवसनान्नपानसौमुख्यसुस्फीतकलाध्वकर्ता ।
जीवोऽष्टमस्थो वधभङ्गबन्धव्याधिश्रमानर्थविवादकारी ॥
करोति जीवो नवमे सुतस्त्रीभूस्थानमानार्थसमृद्धिमग्र्याम् ।
मेषूरणस्थोऽक्षिरुगिष्टहानिश्लेष्मामयायाससुतान्तकारी ॥
एकादशे भूभवनात्मजस्त्रीहिरण्यधान्याम्बरवाहनानाम् ।
दाता गुरुर्द्वादशगोऽथ चन्द्राद् विदेशचर्याश्रमशोककारी ॥]

प्रथमगृहोपगो भृगुसुतः स्मरोपकरणैः
सुरभिमनोज्ञगन्धकुसुमाम्बरैरुपचयम् ।
शयनगृहासनाशनयुतस्य चानुकुरुते
समदविलासिनीमुखसरोजषट्चरणताम् ॥३२॥

When Venus in transit travels through the first house (viz. the natal lunar sign) he confers on a person all kinds of erotic requisites (couch, ornaments, dress, scents, music and dance), fragrant and attractive perfumes, flowers and garments, couches, houses, seats and tasty dishes. Consequently, the person will act the part of a bee on the lotus of the face of an intoxicated (or proud) young beloved.

[The expression अनुकुरुते in the text is misleading, as it would mean 'imitates' whereas he intends to convey the sense of making or conferring. The metre is विलासिनी which is defined as:—

भवति विलासिनी यदि नजौ भजौ भलगुरू ।

This is found neither in the Piṅgalacchandas nor in the Vṛtta-ratnākara, which points to the possibility of the existence of some other ancient work on prosody that was studied by our author.]

शुक्रे द्वितीयगृहगे प्रसवार्थधान्य-
भूपालसन्नतकुटुम्बहितान्यवाप्य ।
संसेवते कुसुमरत्नविभूषितश्च
कामं वसन्ततिलकद्युतिमूर्धजोऽपि ॥३३॥

Venus passing through the second house bestows children, wealth, corn, royal favour, family prosperity, flowers and gems for ornaments. Consequently, the person though grown old with grey hair (as white as the Tilaka—clerodendrum phlomoides flowers in the spring), enjoys sexual pleasures.

[The commentator interprets भूपालसन्नत as—

भूपालो राजा सन्नतः सम्यग् नतः प्रह्वो भवति, राजवाल्लभ्यम् ।

If this were the meaning, he should have explained it as भूपालस्य सन्नतं सम्मानः, भावे क्तः । He says further on : वसन्ततिलको वृक्षः, but the tree is named only तिलक and the compound means वसन्ते तिलकः Tilaka in the spring. For, it blossoms in that season. Vide Kālidāsa :

मुखे मधुश्रीस्तिलकं प्रकाश्य ।
रागेण बालारुणकोमलेन चूतप्रवालोष्ठमलञ्चकार ॥

The metre is the well known वसन्ततिलका, defined as :—

उक्ता वसन्ततिलका तभजा जगौ गः ।]

आज्ञार्थमानास्पदभूतिवस्त्रशत्रुक्षयान् दैत्यगुरुस्तृतीये ।
दत्ते चतुर्थश्च सुहृत्समाजं रुद्रेन्द्रवज्रप्रतिमां च शक्तिम् ॥३४॥

When Venus travels in the 3rd house, the person gets authority, wealth, honour, position, prosperity, clothes and destruction of enemies. When he is in the 4th, the person associates with friends, and gets power and strength similar to that of Rudra, Indra and the thunderbolt.

[The metre is called इन्द्रवज्रा defined thus:]

स्यादिन्द्रवज्रा यदि तौ जगौ गः ।

जनयति शुक्रः पञ्चमसंस्थो गुरुपरितोषं बन्धुजनाप्तिम् ।
सुतधनलब्धि मित्रसहायानवसितत्वं चारिबलेषु ॥३५॥

Venus in the 5th house leads to the favours of elders and teachers, meeting with one's relations (or getting new ones), attainment of wealth, friends and companions, birth of sons and demoralization in the army of the enemy.

[The commentator makes use of a term, सार्थिनः to explain the word सहायान्. No doubt, the word सार्थ meaning a group, is in vogue in the Sanskrit language, but not its adjectival form. It is to be found out whether this usage was due to the influence of Utpala's regional or mother tongue. The metre is called अनवसिता which is defined as: अनवसिता न्यौ भ्गौ गुरुरन्ते ।]

षष्ठो भृगुः परिभवरोगतापदः स्त्रीहेतुकं जनयति सप्तमोऽशुभम् ।
यातोऽष्टमं भवनपरिच्छदप्रदो लक्ष्मीवतीमुपनयति स्त्रियं च सः ॥३६॥

When Venus travels in the 6th house, the native will suffer humiliation, disease, and mental torment; when in the 7th, some disaster pertaining to or caused by women; when in the 8th, he gets houses, attendants and a rich woman as his partner.

[The metre is लक्ष्मी whose definition is—

लक्ष्मीरियं तभसजगैरुदाहृता ।]

नवमे तु धर्मवनितासुखभाग् भृगुजेऽर्थवस्त्रनिचयश्च भवेत् ।
दशमेऽवमानकलहान् नियमात्प्रमिताक्षराण्यपि वदन् लभते ॥३७॥

When Venus passes through the 9th house, the subject performs religious acts, gets women (or marries), happiness, wealth and clothes; when through the 10th, he suffers insults and quarrels invariably, although he speaks very few words.

[The metre is प्रमिताक्षरा, defined thus :

प्रमिताक्षरा सजससैरुदिता ।]

उपान्त्यगो भृगोः सुतः सुहृद्धनान्नगन्धदः ।
धनाम्बरागमोऽन्त्यगः स्थिरस्तु नाम्बरागमः ॥३८॥

When Venus passes through the 11th house, the person gets friends, wealth, food and perfumes; when through the 12th, he gets wealth and garments, but loses some of the latter.

[The metre is स्थिर defined as—लगौ स्थिरः प्रकीर्तितः। However, it is called प्रमाणिका in the Vṛttaratnākara.

Vide यवनेश्वर—

हिरण्यनारीरयतार्थविद्यासुताम्बरस्थानचतुष्पदानाम् ।
लाभं शशिस्थानमुपेत्य शुक्रः कुर्याद् द्वितीये तु वराङ्गनाप्तिम् ॥
मित्रान्नवस्त्रात्मजमानहर्षस्थानाङ्गनारोग्यकरस्तृतीये ।
शुक्रश्चतुर्थे धनपत्निपुत्रमित्रेष्टभाज्याम्बरगन्धदः स्यात् ॥
सुहृत्सुतोद्भूतिगुणप्रवृत्तिख्यातिप्रदः पञ्चमगोऽर्थदश्च ।
षष्ठे भृगुर्दैन्यविवादरोगद्वेषोद्भवान् मानवधांश्च कुर्यात् ॥
जामित्रसंस्थो भृगुजस्तृषाध्वस्त्रीहेतुकोद्वेगकुमित्रदः स्यात् ।
स्त्रीसौख्यविख्यापनमानहर्षप्रियागमाच्छादनदोऽष्टमस्थः ॥
सुहृद्गुरुस्त्रीधनधर्मविद्यायशोगुणाप्ति नवमर्क्षसंस्थः ।
करोति शुक्रो दशमे सबन्धुसम्प्रीतिचेष्टाफलमानविघ्नान् ॥
एकादशे स्त्रीशयनान्नपानभूषारतिस्वेदगृहार्थकारी ।
भृग्वात्मजो द्वादशगस्तु चन्द्राद् भोग्यप्रदो वस्त्रविनाशकृच्च ॥]

प्रथमे रविजे विषवह्निहतः स्वजनैर्वियुतः कृतबन्धुवधः ।
परदेशमुपेत्य सुहृद्भवनो विमुखार्थसुतोऽटकदीनमुखः ॥३९॥

When Saturn in transit travels through the first house i.e. the natal sign, the subject will be troubled by poison and fire, separated from his kith and kin, will kill one of his relatives, will wander in foreign countries, will have neither friends, nor a house to live in, will be hateful in appearance, poor, without children, a wanderer and pale in face.

[The metre is तोटक, defined thus: 'वद तोटकमब्धि-सकारयुतम् ।'

Vide फलदीपिका about Saturn's transit effect in the 1st, 8th and 12th places:

द्वादशाष्टमजन्मस्थाः शन्यर्काङ्गारका गुरुः ।
कुर्वन्ति प्राणसन्देहं स्थानभ्रंशं धनक्षयम् ॥ (XXVI. 33)]

चारवशाद् द्वितीयगृहगे दिनकरतनये
रूपसुखापवर्जिततनुर्विगतमदबलः ।
अन्यगुणैः कृतं वसुचयं तदपि खलु भव-
त्यम्भ्विव वंशपत्रपतितं न बहु न च चिरम् ॥४०॥

When Saturn passes through the 2nd house in his transit, the person will be bereft of good appearance, happiness, pride and vitality; even if he should earn much wealth through other channels, it would not be sufficient, nor stable like the water that has fallen on a bamboo leaf.

[The metre is called वंशपत्रपतित, defined thus:

दिङ्मुनि वंशपत्रपतितं भरनभनलगैः ।]

सूर्यसुते तृतीयगृहगे धनानि लभते
वासपरिच्छदोष्ट्रमहिषाश्वकुञ्जरखरान् ।
सद्मविभूतिसौख्यममितं गदच्युपरमं
भीरुरपि प्रशास्त्यधिरिपूंश्च वीरललितैः ॥४१॥

When Saturn passes through the 3rd house, one will get money, slaves, attendants, camels, buffaloes, horses, elephants, donkeys, houses, wealth, sound health and freedom from ailments; and even if he is a coward, he will curb his mighty enemies through his heroic efforts.

[The metre is said to be ललिता as defined in—'स्याद्भरना रनौ च गुरुनाम सा च ललिता ।' However, according to Pingala, it is called धीरललिता defined as : सङ्कुलिता भरौ नरनगाश्च धीरललिता । Our author too must have a name similar to this in his mind.]

चतुर्थं गृहं सूर्यपुत्रेऽभ्युपेते सुहृद्वित्तभार्यादिभिर्विप्रयुक्तः ।
भवत्यस्य सर्वत्र चासाधु दुष्टं भुजङ्गप्रयातानुकारं च चित्तम् ॥४२॥

When Saturn moves through the fourth house, the native will be separated from his friends, wealth, wife and others; and everywhere his mind will be wicked, sinful and crooked like the serpent's crawling.

[The metre is called भुजङ्गप्रयात, defined thus:

भुजङ्गप्रयातं चतुर्भिर्यकारैः ।]

सुतधनपरिहीणः पञ्चमस्थे प्रचुरकलहयुक्तश्चार्कपुत्रे ।
विनिहतरिपुरोगः षष्ठयाते पिबति च वनितास्यं श्रीपुटोष्ठम् ॥४३॥

When Saturn passes through the fifth house, one will be without wealth and sons, and be involved in serious quarrels; when through the sixth house, he will overcome both his enemies and diseases, and will kiss the mouth of his beloved having charming close lips.

[The metre is पुटा, defined as : 'वसुजलधिविरामौ नौ पुटा म्यौ ।' It is clear that this metre is nothing but a tail-less form of *Mālinī*.]

गच्छत्यध्वानं सप्तमे चाष्टमे च हीनः स्त्रीपुत्रैः सूर्यजे दीनचेष्टः ।
तद्वद्धर्मस्थे वैरहृद्रोगबन्धैर्धर्मोऽप्युच्छिद्येताङ्गरवदेवीप्रभावः ॥४४॥

When Saturn passes through the 7th house, the person will wander away from home; when through the 8th, he will be without wife and children, and will engage himself in mean activities; when through the 9th, he will suffer similar troubles, and his religious duties such as worshipping the sacred fire, will have a break through hatred, heart-disease and imprisonment.

We may also interpret the first half thus: Saturn in the 7th and 8th makes one wander away, lose the company of his wife and children, and engaged in ignoble or servile activities.

[The metre is called वैश्वदेवी, defined thus:

पञ्चाश्वैश्छिन्ना वैश्वदेवी ममौ यौ ।]

कर्मप्राप्तिर्दशमेऽर्थक्षयश्च विद्याकीर्त्योः परिहानिश्च सौरे ।
तैक्ष्ण्यं लाभे परयोषार्थलाभश्चान्त्ये प्राप्नोत्यपि शोकोर्मिमालाम् ।।४५।।

When Saturn travels through the tenth house, the subject will get some work (or job), but will suffer loss of wealth, learning and fame; when through the 11th, he will become aggressive, and attached to others' wives and get others' wealth; when through the 12th house, he will be plunged in a series of the waves of miseries.

[The metre is ऊर्मिमाला, defined thus:

'म्भौ तो गौ चेत् कथिता सोर्मिमाला' । However, the Vṛttaratnākara calls it वातोर्मी and defines it as 'वातोर्मीयं गदिता म्भौ तगौ गः ।'

Cf. also यवनेश्वर—

बन्धाध्वशस्त्रानिलरुग्विषार्तिविडम्बनस्त्रीसुतवित्तनाशम् ।
स्थाने विधत्ते शशिनोऽर्कपुत्रस्ततो व्ययायासकरो द्वितीये ।।
तृतीयगोऽरिक्षयमानहर्षसौभाग्यबह्वागमदोऽर्कसूनुः ।
चतुर्थगो बन्धुवधावमानच्छायाविघाताध्वभयार्तिकारी ।।
स्थितिक्रियारम्भसुतार्थनाशस्वबन्धुविद्वेषविवादकारी ।
शनैश्चरः पञ्चमगोऽथ षष्ठे शत्रुक्षयामोदसुतार्थदाता ।।
छायाविघातश्रमगुह्यरोगस्त्रीमित्रनाशाध्वकृदर्कसूनुः ।
जामित्रसंस्थोऽष्टमगोऽथ शोकक्षुद्बन्धुभृत्यव्यसनार्तिकारी ।।
व्याध्यध्ववैरश्रमवित्तनाशक्षुत्क्लेशदः स्यान्नवमर्क्षसंस्थः ।
ऐश्वर्यचेष्टाफलसञ्चयघ्नो मेषूरणे व्याध्यपकीर्तिकृच्च ।।
यशःपरस्त्रीधनभृत्यलाभक्रियासमृद्धिस्थितिमानदस्तु ।
एकादशे द्वादशगस्तु चेष्टानैपुण्यकीर्तिद्युतिमानहर्ता ।।]

अपि कालमपेक्ष्य च पात्रं शुभकृद्विदधात्यनुरूपम् ।
न मघौ बहु कं कुडवे वा विसृजत्यपि मेघवितानः ।।४६।।

A planet that bestows by nature beneficial results yields its effects in conformity with the Daśā period through which the person is passing and with his merits. For, the cloudy canopy does not release sufficient water even to fill the Kuḍava measure in the spring season.

[The author here refers to two factors for the effects to be full viz. the period or the conditions must be good, and the person also must be deserving owing to his good conduct. In the simile we find that the Daśā is compared to the spring season, and the person deserving to the Kuḍava measure. It is well known that the spring is not the time for the rains, nor the Kuḍava a proper recipient. The metre is मेघवितान, though the commentator names it mere वितान. It is defined in the V. R. thus:

त्रिसगा अपि मेघवितानम् ।]

रक्तैः पुष्पैर्गन्धैस्ताम्रैः कनकवृषबकुलकुसुमैर्दिवाकरभूसुतौ
भक्त्या पूज्याविन्दुर्धेन्वा सितकुसुमरजतमधुरैः सितश्च मदप्रदैः ।
कृष्णद्रव्यैः सौरिः सौम्यो मणिरजततिलककुसुमैर्गुरुः परिपीतकैः
प्रीतैः पीडा न स्यादुच्चाद्यदि पतति विशति यदि वा भुजङ्गविजृम्भितम् ॥४७॥

The Sun and Mars should be devoutly worshipped with red flowers, copper-coloured perfumes, gold, bulls and the Bakula (*Mimusops elengi*) flowers; the Moon, with cows, white flowers, silver and sweet substances; Venus, with aphrodisiacs (and white substances); Saturn, with black substances; Mercury, with gems, silver and the Tilaka (*Clerodendrum phlomoides*) flowers; Jupiter, with yellow articles. When these planets are propitiated, there will be no trouble to the person, even if he falls down from a great height or enters the midst of sporting snakes.

[This proves that our author firmly believes in the efficacy of propitiatory rites to turn the threatened evil happenings into benefits or at least into harmless things. The metre of the verse having 26 syllables is called भुजङ्गविजृम्भितम्, defined thus:

'वस्वीशाश्वच्छेदोपेतं ममतनयुगनरसलगैर्भुजङ्गविजृम्भितम् ।]

शमयोद्गतामशुभदृष्टिमपि विबुधविप्रपूजया ।
शान्तिजपनियमदानदमैः सुजनाभिभाषणसमागमैस्तथा ॥४८॥

Ward off the evil effects of malefic aspects by the worship of Gods and Brāhmaṇas, by propitiatory ceremonies (like Grahayajñas),

Japa (repetition of sacred Mantras), observances (of celibacy, fasts etc.), gifts, self-control and speaking to and associating oneself with the virtuous.

[The metre is an अर्धसमवृत्त known as उद्गता which is defined in the प्राकृतपिङ्गलसूत्र II. 322 thus:

प्रथमे सजौ यदि सलौ च नसजगुरुकाण्यनन्तरे ।
यद्यथ च भनभगाः स्युरथो सजसा जगौ भवतीयमुद्गता ॥]

रविभौमौ पूर्वार्धे शशिसौरौ कथयतोऽन्त्यगौ राशेः ।
सवसल्लक्षणमार्यागीत्युपगीत्योर्यथासङ्ख्यम् ॥४६॥

The Sun and Mars produce the effects of their transit, good or bad, in the first half of the sign traversed by them, while the Moon and Saturn, in the latter half. The Gīti and Upagīti types of the Āryā metre follow respectively the first half and the second half of the ordinary Āryā in both the halves.

[The Gīti type of Āryā has 18 Mātrās in both the second and fourth quarters; while the Upagīti, 15 Mātrās in both. They are defined thus:

आर्याप्रथमदलोक्तं यदि कथमपि लक्षणं भवेदुभयोः ।
दलयोः कृतयतिशोभां तां गीतिं गीतवान् भुजङ्गेशः ॥
आर्याद्वितीयकेऽर्धे यद्गदितं लक्षणं तत्स्यात् ।
यद्युभयोरपि दलयोरुपगीतिं तां मुनिर्ब्रूते ॥

See also Bṛhad Jātaka XXIII. 6.]

आदौ यादृक् सौम्यः पश्चादपि तादृशो भवति ।
उपगीतेर्मात्राणां गणवत् सत्सम्प्रयोगो वा ॥५०॥

Mercury causes the same effects, good and bad, at the end of a sign as in its beginning i.e. he gives the same effects throughout a sign, just as the number of groups of syllabic instants is the same in both the halves of the Upagīti, or as friendship with the virtuous.

[Vide "शशितनयः फलदस्तु सर्वकालम्" । (बृ. जा.)

The metre is उपगीति.]

आर्याणामपि कुरुते विनाशमन्तर्गुरुर्विषमसंस्थः ।
गण इव षष्ठे दृष्टः स सर्वलघुतां जनं नयति ॥५१॥

Jupiter (as well as Venus) passing through the middle of odd (or unfavourable) houses, produces disasters even to the righteous, and through the 6th house, reduces the person to abject slavery or degradation, just as all varieties of the Āryā are spoiled by the presence of the Jagaṇa in the odd places (or, just as the Gaṇa-deities ruin even great monarchs, when they are not propitiated properly at the commencement of an expedition), but it should find a place in the 6th group, or it should consist of four short syllables.

[Vide Bṛ. Jā:—"गुरुमृगुजौ भवनस्य मध्ययातौ ।"
In the यात्रा it has been stated: "अनर्चितास्ते नृपतिं सवाहनं विनाशयन्ति . . . " in connection with the sacrifice for the Gaṇa-devatās. In this verse the author lays down a rule for the use of Jagaṇa in the Āryā.]

अशुभनिरीक्षितः शुभफलो बलिना बलवा-
नशुभफलप्रदश्च शुभदृग्विषयोपगतः ।
अशुभशुभावपि स्वफलयोर्व्रजतः समता-
मिदमपि गीतकं च खलु नर्कुटकं च यथा ॥५२॥

When a strong planet yielding good results is aspected by another strong planet causing evil consequences, or when a strong malefic is aspected by a strong benefic, his benefic or malefic effects will be neutralized, just as the (Prākṛta) Gītaka and the (Sanskrit) Narkuṭaka are equal in all respects.

[The metre is नर्कुटक defined thus:—'हयदशभिर्नजौ भजजला सगु नर्कुटकम् ।' It is called कुटक in the V.R. The Gītaka is illustrated in the following:

महुरअसोअपण्णपणओज्जलसोह अआ
मणहरवाणिसद्दपरिपन्थिअकोइलआ ।
महुरसघुण्णमाणणअणद्धणिरिक्खणिआ
मइ सअणाण पुण्णरहिआण मुहेकखणिआ ॥]

नीचेऽरिभेऽस्ते चारिदृष्टस्य सर्वं वृथा यत् परिकीर्तितम् ।
पुरतोऽन्धस्येव कामिन्याः सविलासकटाक्षनिरीक्षणम् ॥५३॥

All the good effects enumerated above will be nullified, when the planet under consideration is in depression, in an inimical house, is eclipsed, or is aspected by an enemy, just as the amorous sidelong glances of a loving damsel are futile on a blind man.

[Vide यवनेश्वर—

द्विड्वेश्मगा नीचगृहस्थिता वा दुर्मार्गगाः सूर्यमनुप्रविष्टाः ।
उक्तानि निघ्नन्ति शुभानि चैते फलान्यनिष्टान्यभिवर्धयन्ति ॥

This is a विषमवृत्त where all the four quarters are dissimilar. It is called विलास and defined thus :

तो मो यगौ यस्याद्यपादे स्यात्तौ ज्गौ तथा यत्र च दृश्यते ।
तदनु स्तौ मश्चतुर्थे स्यात् सससा ल्गु विलासमुदाहृतम् ॥]

सूर्यसुतोऽर्कफलसमश्चन्द्रसुतश्छन्दतः समनुयाति यथा ।
स्कन्धकमार्यागीतिर्वैतालीयं च मागधी गाथाऽऽर्याम् ॥५४॥

Saturn gives the same effects as the Sun does in transit, while Mercury resembles in effect the planet he conjoins with, just as the (Prākṛta) Skandhaka follows the (Sanskrit) Gīti; Māgadhī, Vaitālīya, and Gāthā, Āryā in metrical form.

[We can give another interpretation in respect of Mercury's transit effects: Mercury follows in effect the Moon. The word *Chandataḥ* means 'at will or without any fixed rules'. The Prākṛta metre Skandhaka is the same as the Sanskrit Āryā Gīti. It is defined thus:

गुर्वन्ताष्टमगणभागार्या पूर्वार्घसदृशशकलद्वितया ।
आर्यैरार्यागीतिर्गीता सङ्गीतगीतिभिर्गीतविधौ ॥

Vaitāliya is defined thus:

षड्विषमेऽष्टौ समे कलाः षट् च समे स्युर्नो निरन्तराः ।
न समात्र पराश्रिता कला वैतालीयेऽन्ते रलौ गुरुः ॥]

सौरोऽर्करश्मियोगात् सविकारो लब्धवृद्धिरधिकतरम् ।
पित्तवदाचरति नृणां पथ्यकृतां न तु तथाऽऽर्याणाम् ॥५५॥

When Saturn gets eclipsed by the Sun's rays, his power to do harm to human beings increases greatly, except in the case of those noble persons who act righteously, just as bile being greatly vitiated (made powerful) by men basking in the Sun, troubles them, leaving out those careful men who have a regulated diet.

[The metre is पथ्या, defined thus:

त्रिष्वंशकेषु पादो दलयोराद्येषु दृश्यते यस्याः ।
पथ्येति नाम तस्याः प्रकीर्तित नागराजेन ॥

This is an ordinary Āryā where the first and third quarters have each three groups unlike the *Vipulā* variety.]

यादृशेन ग्रहेणेन्दुर्युक्तस्तादृग्भवेत्सोऽपि ।
मनोवृत्तिसमायोगाद्विकार इव वक्त्रस्य ॥५६॥

The nature of the Moon varies according to the planet she conjoins with, just as the facial expression does according to the mental frame.

[It has been already explained that the Moon is the mind of the Kāla-puruṣa. The mind takes the form of the object which it thinks of. The face too is the index of the mind.

The metre is वक्त्र, which is defined thus:

रौ यदा गौ तु वक्त्रं स्याद् भ्रौ गावन्यत्र दृश्येते ।
तृतीये चरणे यसौ गौ जसौ गुरुरथो गः स्यात् ॥

The V.R. gives it thus :

वक्त्रं नाद्यान्नसौ स्यातामब्धेर्योऽनुष्टुभि ख्यातम् ।]

पञ्चमं लघु सर्वेषु सप्तमं द्विचतुर्थयोः ।
यद्वच्छ्लोकाक्षरं तद्वल्लघुतां याति दुःस्थितैः ॥५७॥

When planets are ill-placed, the subject is humiliated, just as the 5th syllable in all the quarters and the 7th in the second and fourth feet are short in the Śloka metre.

[This metre was made prominent and popular by the pronouncement of Sage Vālmīki, who says:

पादबद्धोऽक्षरसमस्तन्त्रीलयसमन्वितः ।
शोकार्तस्य प्रवृत्तो मे श्लोको भवतु नान्यथा ॥

Kālidāsa too says thus :

निषादविद्धाण्डजदर्शनोत्थः श्लोकत्वमापद्यत यस्य शोकः । (रघु. XIV)

The metre is called *Śloka*, a variety of the अनुष्टुभ् group.]

प्रकृत्यापि लघुर्यश्च वृत्तबाह्यो व्यवस्थितः ।
स याति गुरुतां लोके यदा स्युः सुस्थिता ग्रहाः ॥५८॥

A person, though low-born and of reprehensible conduct, becomes respectable in the world, when the planets are well-placed in transit, just as a short syllable occurring at the end of a foot comes to be treated as long.

[It is a rule in metrics that the final syllable, if short, may, according to necessity, be treated as long or Guru. The rule states 'वान्ते पादान्ते . . . '. This verse too is in the Śloka metre.]

प्रारब्धमसुस्थितैर्ग्रहैर्यत् कर्मात्मविवृद्धये बुधैः ।
विनिहन्ति तदेव कर्म तान् वैतालीयमिवायथाकृतम् ॥५९॥

Any work done by the wise for achieving prosperity, better health and the like, at a time when the planets are situated in unfavourable positions, will itself destroy them, just as the ceremony of raising a goblin, done improperly, destroys the doer himself.

[The metre is वैतालीय, defined thus:

षड् विषमेऽष्टौ समे कलाः षट् च समे स्युर्नो निरन्तराः ।
न समात्र पराश्रिता कला वैतालीयेऽन्ते रलौ गुरुः ।।

This is a peculiar type of metre where both the Akṣara Gaṇas and Mātrās operate. In other words it is an admixture of the both Jāti and Vṛtta. Here in the odd quarters there should be 14 Mātrās i.e. 6 Mātrās followed by Ragaṇa, a short and a long syllable, and in each of the even ones, 16 Mātrās, i.e. 8 Mātrās followed by the same Ragaṇa, Laghu and Guru. There is however a condition viz. in he even feet there should not be six contiguous short syllables. Moreover, the Mātrās in the even places should not be combined with the following Mātrā i.e. the 2nd, 4th, and 6th should not form Sandhi with the 3rd, 5th and 7th Mātrās respectively.]

सौस्थित्यमवेक्ष्य यो ग्रहेभ्यः काले प्रक्रमणं करोति राजा ।
अणुनापि स पौरुषेण वृत्तस्यौपच्छन्दसिकस्य याति पारम् ।।६०।।

A king, though possessing a small army or very little prowess, starting on an expedition at the proper time, in view of the favourable positions of the planets (as explained in XVI. 40 *supra*), achieves the supreme position that is the fruit of actions eulogized or laid down in the scriptures.

[The metre is called औपच्छन्दसिक, defined thus:

पर्यन्ते यौ तथैव शेषमौपच्छन्दसिकं सुधीभिरुक्तम् ।

This is nothing but the वैतालीय with the addition of a long syllable at the end of each quarter, which makes a Yagaṇa with the Laghu and Guru, existing already.

Here the commentator refers to a work on यात्रा by सिद्धार्थ and quotes the following:

स्वराशिं वा स्ववर्गं वा त्रिवर्गजगृहाणि वा ।
स्वोच्चं वा भवनं यातो विचरन् प्राकृतीं गतिम् ।।
वपुष्मान् वर्णवान् भास्वान् बलैः सर्वैः समन्वितः ।
बलिभिः कारकैर्मित्रैर्ग्रहैः समवलोकितः ।।
दिवि भौमान्तरिक्षैश्च यश्चोत्पातैरपीडितः ।
स्वजन्मस्थं च वर्गं च मार्गं चोपगतः शुभः ।।
योऽनुकूलो विजेता वा स ज्ञेयः सुस्थितो ग्रहः ।
यथोक्तविपरीतो यो विज्ञातव्यः स दुःस्थितः ।।

मानमाज्ञायशोवित्तं सुस्थितैः प्रवसन् ग्रहैः ।
विन्दते दुःस्थितैस्त्वेतैस्तद्विपर्ययमश्नुते ।।

Vide नन्दी–

दैवोपहता यात्रा कथञ्चिदपि भवति यातुश्चेत् ।
क्षितिपस्यानुपकारा सर्वस्य विनाशनीया स्यात् ।।
तस्मादतिसामर्थ्ये प्रवर्तमानेऽपि दैवहीनेन ।
यात्रोद्यमो न कार्यः स्वसुखोदयमिच्छता राज्ञा ।।

Vide also Varāhamihira's tips for यात्रा–

यात्राऽजसिंहतुरगोपगता वरिष्ठा मध्या शनैश्चरबुधोशनसां गृहेषु ।
भानौ कुलीरशशिवृश्चिकगेऽतिदीर्घा शस्ता तु देवलमतेऽध्वनि पृष्ठतो वा ।।
यात्रा नृपस्य शरदीष्टफला मघौ च छिद्रे रिपोर्न नियमोऽत्र च केचिदाहुः ।
छिद्रेऽप्यरेर्भवति दैवयुतस्य सिद्धिः सामान्यमामिषमिदं प्रतिभूमिपानाम् ।।]

Next the author switches over to Daṇḍakas in order to explain the different activities to be performed on the different weekdays. Here each Daṇḍaka is treated as a foot.

उपचयभवनोपयातस्य भानोर्दिने कारयेद्धेमताम्राश्वकाष्ठास्थिचर्मौर्णिकाद्रिद्रुमत्वग्-नखव्यालचौरायुधीयाटवीक्रूरराजोपसेवाभिषेकौषधक्षौमपण्याद्विगोपालकान्तारवैद्याश्म-कूटावदाताभिविख्यातशूराहवश्लाध्ययाय्यग्निकर्माणि सिद्ध्यन्ति लग्नस्थिते वा रवौ ।

On the day presided over by the Sun who passes through the 3rd, 6th, 10th or 11th house from the natal Moon, or is posited in the ascendant at the time, work connected with the following things may be undertaken to achieve success: Gold, copper, horse, wood, bones, skin, woollen articles, mountain, tree, the perfume Tvac (cassia bark), shell (*unguis odoratus*), serpent, thief, weapons, forest, cruel deeds, service of kings, coronation of kings, medicine, silk, trade (or jungle products), cowherd, desert physician, stone, fraud, spotless ones, famous ones, heroes, those famous for fighting, marchers and fire.

[The commentator notes two variant readings viz. ऊर्मिका and वन्यादि instead of और्णिका and पण्यादि respectively 'ऊर्मिका जलधिवेला'—says he.

Vide the समाससंहिता –

नृपाग्निपशुकर्माणि युद्धकार्याणि यानि च ।
सूर्यस्य दिवसे प्राज्ञस्तानि सर्वाणि कारयेत् ।।

Vide यवनेश्वर—

नृपप्रतिष्ठायुधयुद्धयोधहेमाग्निगोमूत्रभिषक्प्रयोगान् ।
रवेर्दिने वन्यमृगार्दनादि प्रशस्यते द्विड्भयकृच्च कर्म ।।

Vide गर्ग—

क्रौर्यं शाठ्यं नृपाद्भेदं शत्रूणां चैव बन्धनम् ।
अध्वानं च विवाहं च निधिकार्यं च कारयेत् ॥
तनुशुद्धिसिराकर्म वडवाश्वविमोचनम् ।
सर्वमेतद् यथोद्दिष्टं कारयेद् रविवासरे ।]

शिशिरकिरणवासरे तस्य वाप्युद्गमे केन्द्रसंस्थेऽथवा भूषणं शङ्खमुक्ताब्जरूप्याम्बुयज्ञेक्षुभोज्याङ्गनाक्षीरसुस्निग्धवृक्षक्षुपानूपधान्यद्रवद्रव्यविप्राश्वगीतक्रियाशृङ्गिकृष्यादिसेनाधिपाक्रन्दभूपालसौभाग्यनक्तञ्चरश्लैष्मिकद्रव्यमातुल्यपुष्पाम्बरारम्भसिद्धिर्भवेत् ॥

On a day presided over by the Moon or when she is the ascendant or when Sign Cancer is rising or when she is posited in one of the Kendras (angles), work relating to the following things will be successful:–Ornaments, conch-shells, pearls, lotus and the like, silver, water, sacrifice, sugar-cane, eatables, women, milk, milky trees, grass, marshy place, corn, liquids, Brāhmaṇas, path (or travel), singing, horned animals, agriculture etc., commander of an army, a king who attacks another from behind, kings, popularity, nocturnal beings (or evil spirits), medicines for phlegmatic troubles, maternal uncle, flowers and clothes.

[Vide the समाससंहिता–

जलस्त्रीराजकर्माणि मृदून्यन्यानि यानि च ।
तानि चन्द्रदिने कुर्यात् शुक्लपक्षे विशेषतः ॥

Vide also यवनेश्वर–

स्त्रीसङ्गमालङ्करणाम्बरत्नप्रतिक्रियाहर्षसुखाश्रयांश्च ।
कुर्वीत चन्द्रस्य दिने प्रदानयज्ञोत्सवान् रत्नरसार्जनं च ॥

Cf. also गर्ग—

उपभोगं तथा शय्यां नवमिश्रं गृहं चरेत् ।
पचेद् घृतं च तैलं च सम्बन्धं चात्र कारयेत् ॥
क्षुरकर्म तथा दानं गवां वेश्मप्रवेशनम् ।
नृपसन्दर्शनं विन्द्यात् कुर्याच्चैव निवेशनम् ॥
सर्वमेतद्यथोद्दिष्टं कुर्याच्चन्द्रदिने शुभे ॥]

क्षितितनयदिने प्रसिद्ध्यन्ति धात्वाकरादीनि सर्वाणि कार्याणि चामीकराग्निप्रवालायुधक्रौर्यचौर्याभिघाताटवीदुर्गसेनाधिकारास्तथा रक्तपुष्पद्रुमा रक्तमन्यच्च तिक्तं कटुद्रव्यकूटाहिपाशार्जितस्वाः कुमारा भिषक्छाक्यभिक्षुक्षपावृत्तिकोशेशशाठ्यानि सिद्ध्यन्ति दम्भास्तथा ॥

On the day presided over by Mars, the following things become fruitful:– All activities connected with mines, ores etc. (their preparation etc.) gold, fire, corals, weapons, cruel deeds, theft, hitting (or attacking), forests, command of an army, trees with red flowers, other red substances, bitter and pungent things, earning wealth by fraud and snake-charm, boys, physicians, Buddhist monks, nocturnal activities, lord of the exchequer, roguery and snobbery.

[In the place of कोशेश some read कौशेय, meaning silk.

Vide the समाससंहिता –

दुर्गग्रहणकर्माणि हेमकर्माणि यानि च ।
तथा च पशुकर्माणि कुर्याद् भौमदिने नरः ।

Cf. यवनेश्वर–

वधावरोधावृतडिम्बभेदाः स्तेयादिशस्त्रादिविषप्रयोगाः ।
दिने कुजस्य ध्वजिनीनिवेशाः कार्याः सुवर्णाजपशुक्रियाश्च ॥

Vide गर्ग–

आयुधं कारयेत् प्राज्ञः पापकर्म तथैव च ।
बन्धनाद्यानि कर्माणि लुण्ठनं तु क्षयादिकम् ॥
षण्मुखस्यात्र कर्तव्या पूजा च शिखिकुक्कुटैः ।
पूजयेदनलं चात्र यन्त्रकार्यं समारभेत् ॥
मन्त्रकर्म विवाहं च दिने भौमस्य वर्जयेत् ॥]

हरितमणिमहीसुगन्धीनि वस्त्राणि साधारणं नाटकं शास्त्रविज्ञानकाव्यानि सर्वाः कलायुक्तयो मन्त्रधातुक्रियावादनैपुण्यपुण्यव्रतायोगदूतास्तथाऽऽयुष्यमायानृतस्नान-ह्रस्वाणि दीर्घाणि मध्यानि च च्छन्दतश्चण्डवृष्टिप्रयातानुकारीणि कार्याणि सिध्यन्ति सौम्यस्य लग्नेऽह्नि वा ॥६१॥

On a day presided over by Mercury or when Mercury is on the ascendant, all work undertaken in connection with the following things will be crowned with success: Green substances, gems, lands, perfumes, garments, things that are both harsh and mild, drama, Śāstra, science (metaphysics), poetry, all fine arts, preparation of compounds, mixtures etc., achieving control over a Mantra, alchemy, arguments, skill, meritorious deeds, observance of vows, messengers, elixirs (that prolong life), feigned talk, falsehood, bath, things done in a short, moderate and long interval to captivate other's hearts, (or short, medium and long articles?) like the foot-prints on the earth during a heavy rain.

[The स्नान, bath, mentioned here may be taken to mean the

'royal ablution' known as पुष्यस्नान, as well. When there is heavy rain, the footprints on the earth, soaked by rain, appear in various shapes, some short, some medium and some others long. The metre too is called चण्डवृष्टिप्रयात, which is defined thus:

प्रथमक इह दण्डकश्चण्डवृष्टिप्रयातो भवेन्नद्वयेनाथ रैः सप्तभिः ।
प्रतिपदमिह रेफवृद्धाः स्युरर्णार्णवव्यालजीमूतलीलाकरोद्दामशङ्खादयः ॥

The prototype of this Daṇḍaka has in each foot two Nagaṇas followed by 7 Ragaṇas. The Agnipurāṇa (334-30) says that we get अर्ण, अर्णव, व्याल, जीमूत etc. types of Daṇḍaka with 8, 9, 10, 11 etc. Ragaṇas at the end. Our author, who has used 32 Ragaṇas in each foot, has not tried to split the hair and given different names. In his view all the varieties where Ragaṇas are employed after 6 short syllables in the beginning, should be brought under the single name of चण्डवृष्टिप्रयात. There are many other types of Daṇḍakas where instead of Ragaṇa, we have Yagaṇa. It is then called प्रचित. There are also varieties where Jagaṇa takes the place of Ragaṇa. According to रात and माण्डव्य this Daṇḍaka in the text is सुवर्ण. For they say :— सुवर्णश्च-ण्डवेगश्च प्लवो जीमूत एव च । बलाहको भुजङ्गश्च समुद्रश्चेति दण्डकाः ॥

Vide the समाससंहिता—

स्वाध्यायशिल्पव्यायामकलाकर्मरतानि च ।
तानि सौम्यदिने कुर्याद् यदि पापैर्न सङ्गतः ॥

Cf. also यवनेश्वर—

स्वाध्यायसेवालिपिलेख्यशिल्पव्यायामनैपुण्यकलाविशेषाः ।
इष्टिक्रियाः काञ्चनधातुयुक्तिवाग्युक्तिसन्धिप्रभृता बुधेऽह्नि ॥

Cf. also गर्ग—

बन्धयोधवधं सर्वं व्यायामं च विशेषतः ।
नृपसेवा च यात्रा च तथैव क्रयविक्रयौ ॥
वीरांश्च योजयेत्प्राज्ञो बद्धान्पाशांश्च मोचयेत् ।
एवं मित्रं च शिष्यं च बन्धुभिः सह सङ्गमम् ॥
आश्रमे च तथा भूमौ केदारे वपने तथा ।
शिक्षेत रूपकर्माणि दिने चन्द्रसुतस्य च ॥]

सुरगुरुदिवसे कनकं रजतं तुरगाः करिणो वृषभा भिषगौषधयः
द्विजपितृसुरकार्यपुरःस्थितधर्मनिवारणचामरभूषणभूपतयः ।
विबुधभवनधर्मसमाश्रयमङ्गलशास्त्रमनोज्ञबलप्रवसत्यगिरः
व्रतहवनधनानि च सिद्धिकराणि तथा रुचिराणि च वर्णदण्डकवत् ॥६२॥

On the day presided over by Jupiter, all things pertaining to the following may be done with advantage:— Gold, silver, horses, elephants, bulls, physicians, medicines (or herbs), propitiation of Brāhmaṇas, the *manes* and Gods, leaders (infantry), umbrellas, chowries, ornaments, kings, temples (or installation of deities and construction of houses), performance of religious acts, auspicious ceremonies, Śāstras (scriptures), attractive things, tonics (or nutritious food), truthful speech, observance of vows, sacrifices, wealth, beautiful and excellent things, like a stick with good colours.

The metre too is called वर्णकदण्डक, having four feet, each foot having 2 Nagaṇas in the beginning followed by 7 Bhagaṇas and a long syllable coming at the end. This is not mentioned in the available texts on prosody. That is why Bhaṭṭotpala does not quote any definition, but only scans the line.

Vide the समाससंहिता—

शान्तिपौष्टिककर्माणि तथा ज्ञानाश्रितानि च ।
तानि कृत्स्नं विधेयानि दिने देवगुरोः शुभे ॥

also यवनेश्वर—

दिने गुरोर्धार्मिकपौष्टिकेज्याबाध्याभिधेयक्रतुमुण्डनादि ।
क्रियाश्रिता धर्मसुवर्णवस्त्रदेहाश्रयाश्चाश्वरथाश्रयाश्च ॥

also गर्ग—

यज्ञं च विविधं कुर्यात्तपांसि च विशेषतः ।
यज्ञे यज्ञे तपस्तेपे छादयेत् कारयेद् गृहम् ॥
आरभेद् भारतं चेदं ज्यौतिषं च विशेषतः ।
ग्राहयेन्नववस्त्राणि यातां दद्यान्नृपस्य च ॥
आदिशेच्च व्रतं पुत्रे बीजान् सर्वांश्च वापयेत् ॥
योजयेच्छकटं चात्र दिने देवगुरोः शुभे ॥

भृगुसुतदिवसे चित्रवस्त्रवृष्यवेश्यकामिनीविलाससहासयौवनोपभोगरम्यभूमयः, स्फटिकरजतमन्मथोपचारवाहनेक्षुशारदप्रकारगोवणिक्कृषीवलौषधाम्बुजानि च ।

On a day owned by Venus, things connected with the following may be done successfully:— Painting, clothes, aphrodisiacs, courtezans, loving damsels, sports, augh, enjoyment of youth, places of attraction (like gardens), ,rystals, silver, indulging in amorous activities, vehicles. sugarcane, autumnal crops, cattle, trade, agriculture, medicines, and lotus and the like.

This is only the first half of a Daṇḍaka, the latter half being given in the next passage.

Vide the समाससंहिता—

कलागन्धर्वकर्माणि रत्नकर्माणि यानि च ।
तानि कार्याणि दिवसे सदा दैत्यगुरोः शुभे ।।

also यवनेश्वर—

गान्धर्वविद्यामणिरत्नगन्धगोभूमिशय्याम्बरभूषणानाम् ।
स्त्रीपण्यकोशोत्सवनन्दनानां क्रियाविधिः शुक्रदिने प्रशस्तः ।।

Cf. गर्ग—

गजमश्वं प्रयुञ्जीत कर्णबन्धे नियोजयेत् ।
पिबेत्सुरां च मद्यं च प्रचरेत्कुसुमाम्बरम् ।।
गन्धांश्च विविधानद्यात् कामयेच्च वराङ्गनाः ।
द्यूते च सहसा प्रीतिं तिलं तैलं च योजयेत् ।।
मङ्गलं स्थापयेदेव रोपयेच्चैव पादपान् ।
सर्वमेतद्यथोद्दिष्टं कुर्याच्छुक्रदिने शुभे ।।

सवितृसुतदिने च कारयेन्माहिष्यजोष्ट्रकृष्णलोहदासवृद्धनीचकर्मपक्षिचौरपाशिकान् च्युतविनयविशीर्णभाण्डहस्त्यपेक्षविघ्नकारणानि चान्यथा न साधयेत्समुद्रगोऽप्यपां कणम् ।।६३।।

On the day presided over by Saturn, one should do work relating to the following things for achieving success:— She-buffaloes, goats, camels, iron, slaves, old persons, lowborn persons, birds (like vultures), thieves. hunters, the mannerless, broken pots, elephant-catching and obstructionist activities. Otherwise (in other activities), one will not get even a drop of water in the ocean.

The metre is called समुद्रदण्डक which has न न र ज र ज र ज र ज र ल गु i.e. letters with two Nagaṇas in the beginning followed by 4 groups of Ra-Jagaṇas and Ragaṇa, a short and a long syllable.

Vide the समाससंहिता—

शस्त्राणि पाशकर्माणि पशुकर्माणि यानि च ।
तानि सौरदिने कुर्याल्लोहकर्माणि यानि च ।।
संवत्सरे तथा मासे होरायामुदये तथा ।
उक्तानि यानि कर्माणि तथा कुर्याद् ग्रहस्य च ।।

Cf. यवनेश्वर—

विषाश्मशस्त्रत्रपुसीसलोहप्राकारबन्धावृतमारणानि ।
सर्वं च पापात्मकमर्कजाह्नि कार्पासवप्रव्रजितानि चेष्टम् ।।

also गर्ग –

नियोगान् विविधान् कुर्याद्विश्म चापि प्रवेशयेत् ।
कर्म चौर्यं मृतिं चैवाश्वरथेष्वश्वयोजनम् ॥
हस्त्यपेक्षा विघ्नकर्म द्रव्यं दम्भाश्रितं तथा ।
वर्जयेच्चैव यात्रां च दिने सूर्यसुतस्य च ॥]

विपुलामपि बुद्ध्वा छन्दोविचितिं भवति कार्यमेतावत् ।
श्रुतिसुखवृत्तसङ्ग्रहमिममाह वराहमिहिरोऽतः ॥६४॥

Although one knows the extensive ramifications of the science of prosody, one cannot do more than what has been shown (i.e. cannot employ all the varieties of metres). Hence Varāhamihira has given here the essence of metres that are pleasant to hear.

[This is in विपुला, a kind of Aryā defined thus:

उल्लङ्घ्य गणत्रयमादिमं शकलयोर्द्वयोर्भवति पादः ।
यस्यास्तां पिङ्गलनागो विपुलामिति समाख्याति ॥

The main characteristic of this metre is that the first quarter goes beyond three Gaṇas i.e. the third Gaṇa breaks in the middle of a word. In our example the third Gaṇa is made up of द्ध्वा of बुद्ध्वा and छन् of छन्दो. When this kind of breaking is done in the first half, it is called आदिविपुला, when in the second half, अन्तविपुला; and when in both the halves, उभयविपुला. See छन्दःशास्त्र of पिङ्गल footnotes, page 51. Halāyudha says that there will be 80 varieties of the Āryā by the combinations of पथ्या, the 3 kinds of विपुला, the three of चपला and the four of गीति. Bhaṭṭotpala, echoing the author's statement to the effect that he has summarized metrics in a pleasing manner, remarks:

बहुभिराचार्यैश्छन्दोलक्षणमुक्तं तच्च दुर्विज्ञेयमश्रव्यं च । वराहमिहिरेण पुनः श्रव्यं सुखबोधं व्यापकं संक्षिप्तमुक्तमिति ।

Feeling this chapter to be of unusual importance the commentator closes his विवृति with the following verse:

वराहमिहिरीयेऽस्मिञ्छन्दसां सारसङ्ग्रहे ।
उत्पलो गोचरे टीकां चक्रे शिष्यहितावहाम् ॥]

— ——

रूपसत्रम् ॥१०५॥

Chapter CV — Worship of the Stellar Deity

पादौ मूलं जङ्घे च रोहिणी जानुनी तथाश्विन्यः ।
ऊरू चाषाढद्वयमथ गुह्यं फल्गुनीद्वितयम् ॥१॥

कटिरपि च कृत्तिका पार्श्वयोश्च यमला भवन्ति भद्रपदाः ।
कुक्षिस्था रेवत्यो विज्ञेयमुरोऽनुराधा च ॥२॥

पृष्ठं विद्धि धनिष्ठां भुजौ विशाखा स्मृतौ करौ हस्तः ।
अङ्गुल्यश्च पुनर्वसुराश्लेषासञ्ज्ञिताश्च नखाः ॥३॥

ग्रीवा ज्येष्ठा श्रवणं श्रवणौ पुष्यो मुखं द्विजाः स्वातिः ।
हसितं शतभिषगथ नासिका मघा मृगशिरो नेत्रे ॥४॥

चित्रा ललाटसंस्था शिरो भरण्यः शिरोरुहाश्चार्द्रा ।
नक्षत्रपुरुषकोऽयं कर्तव्यो रूपमिच्छद्भिः ॥५॥

The feet of the Stellar Deity are represented by the asterism Mūla; the shanks, by Rohiṇī; the knees, by Aśvinī; the thighs, by the two (Pūrva and Uttara) Āṣāḍhās; the privities, by the two (Pūrva and Uttara) Phalgunīs; the hips, by Kṛttikā; the sides, by the two (Pūrva and Uttara) Bhadrapadās; the stomach, by Revatī; the breast, by Anurādhā; the back, by Dhaniṣṭhā; the arms, by Viśākhā; the hands, by Hasta; the fingers, by Punarvasu; the nails, by Āśleṣā; the neck, by Jyeṣṭhā; the ears, by Śravaṇa; the mouth, by Puṣya; the teeth, by Svāti; laughter, by Śatabhiṣaj; the nose, by Maghā; the eyes, by Mṛgaśiras; the forehead, by Citrā; the head, by Bharaṇī; and the hair, by Ārdrā. In this manner, the form of the Stellar Deity has to be constituted by those who wish for good physical features.

[It is well known that the 12 signs of the zodiac represent the various limbs of the Kālapuruṣa. Likewise the 27 asterisms are distributed among the limbs of the Nakṣatra-puruṣa. It is an accepted principle in Sanskrit literature that description of heavenly beings should start with the feet and go upwards. The exact meaning of रूपसत्र is 'the sacrifice of the form'.]

चैत्रस्य बहुलपक्षे ह्यष्टम्यां मूलसंयुते चन्द्रे ।
हृयुपवासः कर्तव्यो विष्णुं सम्पूज्य धिष्ण्यं च ॥६॥

One should worship Lord Viṣṇu and the Stellar Deity and then observe fast on the 8th day of the dark fortnight in the month of Caitra, when the Moon passes through the asterism Mūla, synchronizing with Monday.

[The fast and worship should be gone through in the order of the limbs of the Nakṣatra-puruṣa i.e. after Mūla, it should be done on a day ruled by the asterism Rohiṇī, and then by Aśvinī and so on, until the last asterism viz. Ārdrā, is reached.

Cf. गर्गे—

अष्टम्यां मधुमासस्य कृष्णपक्षे तु नैर्ऋते ।
नक्षत्रे चन्द्रवारे तु मुहूर्त्ते तु गुणान्विते ॥
प्रारभेद्रूपसत्राख्यं व्रतं धर्मात्मकः पुमान् ।
येन पूर्णेन मनुजो रूपशोभामवाप्नुयात् ॥]

दद्याद् व्रते समाप्ते घृतपूर्णं भाजनं सुवर्णयुतम् ।
विप्राय कालविदुषे सरत्नवस्त्रं स्वशक्त्या च ॥७॥

When this observance has been completed, the performer should make a gift of a vessel filled with ghee, along with gold, gems and clothes, according to his means, to a Brāhmaṇa, well versed in astrology.

अन्नैः क्षीरघृतोत्कटैः सह गुडैर्विप्रान् समभ्यर्चयेद्
दद्यात्तेषु सुवर्णवस्त्ररजतं लावण्यमिच्छन्नरः ।
पादर्क्षात्प्रभृति क्रमादुपवसन्नङ्गर्क्षनामस्वपि
कुर्यात्केशवपूजनं स्वविधिना धिष्ण्यस्य पूजां तथा ॥८॥

A person wishing for attractive features should worship and feed Brāhmaṇas with dishes prepared in milk and ghee, mixed with jaggery; he should also present them with gold, silver and clothes. Then he should fast regularly on the days when the Moon passes through the several asterisms beginning with Mūla and representing the various limbs of the Stellar Person, and also worship, in accordance with the rules of the Pañcarātra system of worship, Lord Hari, and the Stellar Deity.

[There are many systems of worship, the chief of which are the Pañcarātra, Vaikhānasa and Pāśupata. The metre is शार्दूलविक्रीडित.]

प्रलम्बबाहुः पृथुपीनवक्षाः क्षपाकरास्यः सितचारुदन्तः ।
गजेन्द्रगामी कमलायताक्षः स्त्रीचित्तहारी स्मरतुल्यमूर्तिः ॥ ९ ॥

A man who performs this worship of the Stellar Deity will have (in the next birth) long arms (touching the knees), broad and muscular breast, moon-like face, white and beautiful teeth, the gait of lordly elephant, long eyes resembling the lotus, a personality that captivates the hearts of damsels, and a body verily like that of Cupid.

[The metre is उपजाति.]

शारदमलपूर्णचन्द्रद्युतिसदृशमुखी सरोजदलनेत्रा ।
रुचिरदशना सुकर्णा भ्रमरोदरसन्निभैः केशैः ॥१०॥

पुंस्कोकिलसमवाणी ताम्रोष्ठी पद्मपत्रकरचरणा ।
स्तनभारानतमध्या प्रदक्षिणावर्तया नाभ्या ॥११॥

कदलीकाण्डनिभोरुः सुश्रोणी वरकुकुन्दरा सुभगा ।
सुश्लिष्टाङ्गुलिपादा भवति प्रमदा मनुष्यश्च ॥१२॥

A woman who performs this worship will be born with a face as bright and lustrous as the autumnal full Moon, eyes like the petals of lotus, beautiful (and sparkling) teeth, fine ears, hair resembling the belly of the bees, a voice as sweet as that of an intoxicated cuckoo, red lips, hands and feet as tender and charming as lotus-petals, a slender waist bending under the weight of the bosoms, a navel with turns from left to right, thighs similar to banana trunks, fine buttock and excellent loins. She will win the love of her husband, and have well-knit toes. These results accrue, *pari passu*, to men as well.

I think that verses 9 to 12 form one unit, and the subject of verse 9 is given at the end of verse 12. Hence it is not necessary to construe मनुष्यश्च as 'the woman may also be born a man'. Here the author like Kālidāsa, has heaped together all the available standards of comparison. Vide LXX and notes *supra*. कुकुन्दुर is जघनकूप the cavity of the loins just above the hips. Vide 'नितम्बरू(कू)पकौ यौ तु तौ कुकुन्दरसञ्ज्ञितौ ।']

यावन्नक्षत्रमाला विचरति गगने भूषयन्तीह भासा
तावन्नक्षत्रभूतो विचरति सह तैर्ब्रह्मणोऽह्नोऽवशेषम् ।

कल्पादौ चक्रवर्ती भवति हि मतिमांस्तत्क्षयाच्चापि भूयः

संसारे जायमानो भवति नरपतिर्ब्राह्मणो वा धनाढ्यः ॥१३॥

Such a person, man or woman, (as has performed this worship) will become a star and move with the stars in the firmament, as long as the rows of stars move in the sky and illumine the world, till the end of the Creator's day i.e. Kalpa. And when the universe is re-created, the person will become a wise monarch; and will be reborn in the world as a king or a rich Brāhmaṇa.

[With this the topic of 'the sacrifice to the form of the Stellar Deity' is concluded. The following verses give names of months. The metre of this verse is स्रग्धरा.]

मृगशीर्षाद्याः केशवनारायणमाधवाः सगोविन्दाः ।

विष्णुमधुसूदनाख्यौ त्रिविक्रमो वामनश्चैव ॥१४॥

श्रीधरनामा तस्मात् सहृषीकेशश्च पद्मनाभश्च ।

दामोदर इत्येते मासाः प्रोक्ता यथासङ्ख्यम् ॥१५॥

The twelve lunar months beginning with Mārgaśīrṣa are said to be presided over by Keśava, Nārāyaṇa, Mādhava. Govinda, Viṣṇu, Madhusūdana, Trivikrama, Vāmana, Śrīdhara, Hṛṣīkeśa, Padmanābha and Dāmodara respectively.

[These are the twelve famous names of Lord Hari. Here the counting of months is done, not from Caitra, but from Mārgaśīrṣa, which has some historical importance. At one time the year must have started with that month. That is probably the reason for the Lord's statement in the Gītā, 'मासानां मार्गशीर्षोऽहम्'. In the last line in the place of मासा प्रोक्ताः some read as मासेशाः स्युः.]

मासनामसमुपोषितो नरो द्वादशीषु विधिवत्प्रकीर्तयन् ।

केशवं समभिपूज्य तत्पदं याति यत्र न हि जन्मजं भयम् ॥१६॥

One who fasts (on the 11th days) of the several months and worships Lord Keśava according to rules, repeating the respective names on the 12th days, attains His world i.e. Viṣṇu-loka, where there is absolutely no fear of rebirth (as he attains emancipation or oneness with the Lord).

[Though the text may be interpreted that the fasting is to be done on the 12th day (Dvādaśī) of every month, yet in the light of the rules laid down in the Dharma-Śāstra, fasting is allowed only on the Ekādaśī day and Pāraṇā (breakfast), the next day after the worship of the Lord. For the glory of Viṣṇupada see Ṛgveda I. 154-6.

The metre is रथोद्धता.]

उपसंहाराध्यायः ॥१०६॥

Chapter CVI – Conclusion

ज्योतिःशास्त्रसमुद्रं प्रमथ्य मतिमन्दराद्रिणाऽथ मया ।
लोकस्यालोककरः शास्त्रशशाङ्कः समुत्क्षिप्तः ॥१॥

Having churned the ocean of astrology with the Mandara mountain of my intelligence, I have taken out the Moon of Science (this work) that affords light (enlightenment) to the world (people).

[According to the Purāṇas the Gods and demons churned the milk-ocean for the sake of ambrosia. Before that many things such as Kāmadhenu, Kalpa-vṛkṣa, Kaustubha gem, the Moon etc. were brought out. Even the Goddess of wealth was one of the products. Vāsukī, King of Serpents, was made the rope and mount Mandara, the churning rod. This idea is behind the metaphor employed here by the author. He suggests that this work represents the essence of the entire astrological lore, which is a fact. For, there is nothing of astrology or astronomy which does not find a place here. In fact it has been made a veritable encyclopaedia, containing many subjects like botany, zoology, water-divination, meteorology, gemology, perfumery, palmistry etc.]

पूर्वाचार्यग्रन्था नोत्सृष्टाः कुर्वता मया शास्त्रम् ।
तानवलोक्येदं च प्रयतध्वं कामतः सुजनाः ॥२॥

I have not discarded the works of ancient seers while writing this scientific work. Hence, O ye good men, you may by all means compare mine with theirs, and accept which ever you like.

[The suggestion is that the readers may find our author's work more acceptable than those of the ancient sages, as this is composed succinctly, lucidly and in a charming manner. Here we are reminded of Kālidāsa's words to the following effect :

पुराणमित्येव न साधु सर्वं न चापि काव्यं नवमित्यवद्यम् ।
सन्तः परीक्ष्यान्यतरद्भजन्ते मूढः परप्रत्ययनेयबुद्धिः ॥ (मालवि.)]

अथवा कृशमपि सुजनः प्रथयति दोषार्णवाद्गुणं दृष्ट्वा ।
नीचस्तद्विपरीतः प्रकृतिरियं साध्वसाधूनाम् ॥३॥

Or, good men, on finding some excellence, though slender, in an ocean of faults, proclaim it, while the mean-minded do contrariwise (i.e. finding a minor flaw in an ocean of excellences, proclaim the fault alone). This is the nature of the good and the wicked.

दुर्जनहुताशतप्तं काव्यसुवर्णं विशुद्धिमायाति ।
श्रावयितव्यं तस्माद्दुष्टजनस्य प्रयत्नेन ॥४॥

The gold of poetry being heated by the fire of wicked men gets purified. Hence, it should be read to the wicked by all means.

[A fine satire on the carping criticism of wicked men is found here. Generally great poets praise good critics and condemn the bad ones. The metaphor employed by the author is very striking. This metaphor has been suggested by the famous verse of Kālidāsa in the Raghu-I.10 :

तं सन्तः श्रोतुमर्हन्ति सदसद्व्यक्तिहेतवः ।
हेम्नः संलक्ष्यते ह्यग्नौ विशुद्धिः श्यामिकापि वा ॥]

The famous Karṇāṭaka Saint composer, Purandaradāsa says in one of his songs: 'There ought to be traducers. Without them the glory of the virtuous would not gain celebrity. For example, the paddy grain would be worthless without its slender thorn'.]

ग्रन्थस्य यत्प्रचरतोऽस्य विनाशमेति
लेख्याद् बहुश्रुतमुखाधिगमक्रमेण ।
यद्वा मया कुकृतमल्पमिहाकृतं वा
कार्यं तदत्र विदुषा परिहृत्य रागम् ॥५॥

Whatever matter of this work gets lost or altered in the course of its circulation by the fault of scribes or of students receiving oral instruction from the learned, may kindly be supplied or set right by scholars avoiding jealousy; so too, whatever I have ill-done, done niggardly, or not done at all.

[The author shows his humility and appeals to the learned not to misjudge him. The metre is वसन्ततिलका.]

दिनकरमुनिगुरुचरणप्रणिपातकृतप्रसादमतिनेदम् ।
शास्त्रमुपसङ्गृहीतं नमोऽस्तु पूर्वप्रणेतृभ्यः ॥६॥

With my intellectual power blessed by the Divine Sun (and other planets), the Sages (like Vasiṣṭha) and my preceptor (i.e. my own father Ādityadāsa), as a result of my having made obeisance to their feet, I have only summarized (or given the essence of) this science. Hence I offer salutations to the ancient authors.

शास्त्रानुक्रमणी ॥१०७॥

Chapter CVII—Table of Contents of this Work

According to Utpala great scholars append a table of contents to their works in order to save them from the flaws introduced by scribes and manuscripts.

शास्त्रोपनयः पूर्वं सांवत्सरसूत्रमर्कचारश्च ।
शशिराहुभौमबुधगुरुसितमन्दशिखिग्रहाणां च ॥१॥

The first chapter in this work treats of 'introduction of the science'; the next, of the 'rules for astrologers'; the next, of the 'transit of the Sun'; the next (4th) of the Moon, 5th of Rāhu, 6th of Mars, 7th of Mercury, 8th of Jupiter, 9th of Venus, 10th of Saturn and 11th of the Ketus.

चारश्चागस्त्यमुनेः सप्तर्षीणां च कूर्मयोगश्च ।
नक्षत्राणां व्यूहो ग्रहभक्तिर्ग्रहविमर्दश्च ॥२॥

The 12th chapter deals with the transit of Agastya or Canopus; the 13th with that of the Great Bear (Seven Sages); the 14th with the division of the country on the basis of the stars; the 15th with the Nakṣatra-vyūha (allotment of objects to the asterisms); the 16th with Grahabhakti (Planetary Dominions); the 17th with planetary conflicts.

ग्रहशशियोगः सम्यग्ग्रहवर्षफलं ग्रहाणां च ।
शृङ्गाटसंस्थितानां मेघानां गर्भलक्षणं चैव ॥३॥

The 18th chapter deals with the conjunction of the Moon with the planets; the 19th with the years presided over by the planets and their effects; the 20th with the planetary triangle; and the 21st with the pregnancy of clouds.

धारणवर्षणरोहिणिवाय्वाषाढभद्रपदयोगाः ।
क्षणवृष्टिः कुसुमलताः सन्ध्याचिह्नं दिशां दाहः ॥४॥

The 22nd chapter is on the retention of foetus; the 23rd on the quantity of rainfall; the 24th on the Moon's conjunction with Rohiṇī; the 25th on her conjunction with Svāti; the 26th on her conjunction with Āṣāḍhā; the 27th on Bhādrapadayoga; the 28th on immediate rain; the 29th on flowers and creepers; the 30th on the signs at twilight; and the 31st on the glow at the horizon.

[In our text we have वातचक्र or 'wind circle' instead of the *Bhadra padayoga*. It is quite possible that the original chapter being lost some one must have put this in its stead.]

भूकम्पोल्कापरिवेषलक्षणं शक्रचापखपुरं च ।
प्रतिसूर्यो निर्घातः सस्यद्रव्यार्घकाण्डं च ॥५॥

The next i.e. 32nd chapter deals with earthquakes; the 33rd with meteors; the 34th with halos; the 35th with rainbows; the 36th with aerial city; the 37th with mock Suns; (the 38th with haze); the 39th with portentous thunder; the 40th with the growth of crops; the 41st with the classification of substances; and the 42nd with fluctuation of prices.

[In this list chapter 38 on रजोलक्षण is not found. Hence it is evidently an interpolation.]

इन्द्रध्वजनीराजनखञ्जनकोत्पातबार्हिचित्रं च ।
पुष्याभिषेकपट्टप्रमाणमसिलक्षणं वास्तु ॥६॥

The next i.e. 43rd chapter, deals with the glories of Indra's banner; the 44th with lustration ceremony; the 45th with wagtails; the 46th with portentous phenomena; the 47th with Mayūracitraka (motley miscellany); the 48th with royal ablutions; the 49th with royal crowns: the 50th with swords; (the 51st and 52nd with Aṅgavidyā and Piṭakalakṣaṇa respectively); and 53rd with architecture.

उदकार्गलमारामिकममरालयलक्षणं कुलिशलेपः ।
प्रतिमा वनप्रवेशः सुरभवनानां प्रतिष्ठा च ॥७॥

The next chapter viz. 54th, deals with the exploration of water-springs; the 55th with the treatment of trees; the 56th with the description of temples; the 57th with adamantine glue; the 58th with idols; the 59th with entry into the forest; and the 60th with installation of idols.

चिह्नं गवामथ शुनां कुक्कुटकूर्माजपुरुषचिह्नं च ।
पञ्चमनुष्यविभागः स्त्रीचिह्नं वस्त्रविच्छेदः ॥८॥

The next chapter viz. 61st, treats of the signs of cows; the 62nd of dogs; the 63rd of cocks; the 64th of tortoises; the 65th of goats; (the 66th and 67th treat of the Signs of horses and elephants respectively); the 68th of men; the 69th of the five kinds of great men; the 70th of maidens; and the 71st of slits of garments.

चामरदण्डपरीक्षा स्त्रीस्तोत्रं चापि सुभगकरणं च ।
कान्दर्पिकानुलेपनपुंस्त्रीकाध्यायशयनविधिः ॥९॥

The 72nd chapter treats of chowries; the 73rd of umbrellas; the 74th of praise of women; the 75th of winning of affection; the 76th of erotic remedies; the 77th of perfumes; the 78th of sexual union; and the 79th of couches.

वज्रपरीक्षामौक्तिकलक्षणमथ पद्मरागमरकतयोः ।
दीपस्य लक्षणं दन्तधावनं शाकुनं मिश्रम् ॥१०॥

The next chapter viz. 80th treats of gems (diamonds); the 81st of pearls; the 82nd of rubies; the 83rd of emeralds; the 84th of lamps; the 85th of tooth-sticks; and the 86th of omens through birds and beasts.

अन्तरचक्रं विरुतं श्वचेष्टितं विरुतमथ शिवायाश्च ।
चरितं मृगाश्वकरिणां वायसविद्योत्तरं च ततः ॥११॥

The next chapter, 87th treats of the circle of the quarters; the 88th of cries of birds and beasts; the 89th of the circle of dogs; the 90th of the cries of jackals; the 91st of the movements of wild animals; (the 92nd of the intention of cows); the 93rd of horses; the 94th of elephants; the 95th of the cries of crows; and the 96th of further omens.

पाको नक्षत्रगुणास्तिथिकरणगुणाः सधिष्ण्यजन्मगुणाः ।
गोचरमथ ग्रहाणां कथितो नक्षत्रपुरुषश्च ॥१२॥

The next chapter viz. 97th treats of the time of fruition of effects; the 98th of the functions and qualities of the asterisms; the 99th of the functions and properties of lunar days; and the 100th of the qualities of the Karaṇas; and the 101st of the effects of birth in the several asterisms; (the 102nd and 103rd treat of the division of the zodiac and marriage respectively) ; the 104th of the transits of planets; and the last i.e. 105th, of the worship of the Stellar Deity.

[According to the author there are only 100 chapters in his work upto this point, but we have counted 105 chapters. It has been already pointed out that the following chapters are spurious viz. (1) XXVII on the Wind circle; (2) XXXVIII on 'Haze'; (3) LI on Prediction through limbs; (4) LII on Pimples; (5) CII on the division of the zodiac; and (6) CIII on marriage. Then what about one chapter by which the total number becomes short ? The author mentions in the place of Vātacakra, Bhadra-padayoga, which is missing here. If you add this one to the 99 chapters, we arrive at the author's total of 100 chapters. According to this line of reasoning of the other chapters viz. LXVI, LXVII and XCII, the first two may be explained as being included in the author's list by interpreting अज in verse 8 as अजादि i.e. signs of goats and other domestic animals, or taking कूर्मज as कूर्मादि. Another reason why we should take these two chapters as genuine is that while dealing with omens the author mentions 'चरितं मृगाश्वकरिणाम्', which can lead us to believe that he could not have omitted to deal with their characteristics. Similarly, since he has listed 'गोलक्षणं' as one of the chapters (LXI), 'गवेङ्गित' (XCII) too can claim to be a genuine chapter. Though Bhaṭṭotpala claims CII (राशिविभाग) to be genuine, I feel otherwise. For, the expression 'सधिष्ण्यजन्मगुणाः' can by no stretch of imagination be interpreted to include or suggest 'राशिविभाग.']

शतमिदमध्यायानामनुपरिपाटिक्रमादनुक्रान्तम् ।
अत्र श्लोकसहस्राण्यावद्धान्यूनचत्वारि ॥१३॥

Thus have the above one hundred chapters been listed in regular order and verses equivalent to 3900 ones of the Śloka metre have been composed in this work.

[The commentator says that the number 3900 does not include the verses of chapters XXVII, LI, LII, LXVI and LXVII. This is not correct. For, Utpala himself has admitted the first three chapters of this group to be spurious. He says that with the verses of these chapters the total number of Ślokas comes to 4000. However, the original work of Varāhamihira could not have contained more than 3900 verses in the 100 chapters.]

अत्रैवान्तर्भूतं परिशेषं निगदितं च यात्रायाम् ।
बह्वाश्चर्यं जातकमुक्तं करणं च बहुचोद्यम् ॥१४॥

This work contains matters relating to *yātrā* or journey; the work bearing that name gives fuller details that are not mentioned here. I have already written the Bṛhad Jātaka containing very many wonderful materials, also the Karaṇa (astronomical work *Pañcasiddhāntikā*) that contains many arguments (or wonders or inspiring things).

[The author refers to his other works that have already been written by him. They are the यात्रा, बृहज्जातक and पञ्चसिद्धान्तिका. The first two are available in two versions viz. the Bṛhat and Laghu Jātakas, Bṛhad Yātrā and Svalpayātrā. Even the पञ्चसिद्धान्तिका is said to have been abridged by him. The Bṛhad Yātrā or Bṛhad Yogayātrā was also known as Mahāyātrā. From this verse it becomes clear that our author has already composed the three works on journey, horoscopy and astronomy. However, he gives cross references to all his works. For example, in the प. सि. XV.10 he refers to Rāhu-cāra in the बृ. संहिता. This shows that he had planned all the works and their contents at the same time. In some of the editions two concluding verses said to be of Bhaṭṭotpala are given. They are:

आचार्यप्रवरस्य बोधजलधेः पारं तितीर्षुर्जनो
व्यामुह्यन्नभिधेयरत्ननिचयैः काङ्क्षंस्तरीं भ्राम्यति ।
इत्येवंविधमाकलय्य करुणामालम्ब्य भट्टोत्पल-
श्चक्रे तत्कृतिसंहिताविवरणं स्थैर्यं प्लवं कीर्तये ।
यदत्राधिकमूनं वा भ्रान्त्या त्वज्ञानतोऽपि वा ।
विपर्ययेण वा यत् तत्सर्वं संशोध्यतां बुधाः ।।

These are patently forgeries committed by some admirer of the commentator. For, otherwise how could an author refer to himself in the perfect tense, *Cakre* ? Let me too conclude my work of translation and annotation with a verse:

श्रीमत्सिद्धिविनायकस्य कृपया वाराहके संहिता-
ग्रन्थेऽनन्तमहार्घरत्नविभवे व्याख्या मदीया मुदे ।
नूत्ना सिद्धिमगात्सतां भृगुदिने चैत्रे नवम्यां दले
कृष्णे बाणनवाष्टचन्द्रतुलिते शाकाब्दके शोकनुत् ।।]

APPENDIX I (a)

Indian Plants Mentioned in the Bṛhat Saṁhitā

[Sources of modern names: (1) "Glossary of Indian Medicinal Plants". Pub. C. S. I. R. 1956; (2) "Five Hundred Indian Plants" Edn. III Pub. Kanarese Mission Press and Book Depot, Mangalore 1922.]

Sanskrit Names Modern Scientific Names

1. Aguru = Aquilaria agallocha.
2. Agnimantha = Premna spinosca.
3. Aṅkola = Alangium decapetalum. or Alangium salvifolium.
4. Ajakarṇa = Vateria indica [Rāḷa, in Kannaḍa.]
5. Ajamoda = Apium graveolens, *or* Carum copticum [Voma, in Kannaḍa]
6. Ajā = Ocimum americanum, [Rāmatulasi, in Kan.]
7. Añjana = Memecylon umbellatum. [Is it Viṣṇukrāntā = Evolvulus alsinoides ?]
8. Atasī = Linum usitatissimum.
9. Atibalā = Sida rhombifolia.
10. Atimuktaka = Chrysanthemum indicum, [Sevantige, in Kan.]
11. Apāmārga = Achyranthes aspera, [Uttaraṇe, in Kan.]
12. Amṛtā = Eulophia campestris, *or* Tenospora cordifolia, [Amṛtaballi, in Kan.]
13. Ambā = Pongamia glabra, [Hoṅge, in Kan.]
14. Araṇi = Breynia rhamnoides?
15. Ariṣṭa = Xanthium strumarium.
16. Arka = Calotropis gigantea, [Ekke, in Kan.]
17. Arjuna = Terminalia arjuna, [Matti or Biḷimatti, in Kan.]
18. Aśoka = Sarasa indica.
19. Aśmantaka = Bauhinia tomentosa? [Vanasampige, in Kan. ?]
20. Aśvakarṇa = Shorea robusta, [Rāḷadamara, in Kan.]
21. Aśvagandha = Withania somnifera, [Sogade bēru, in Kan.]
22. Aśvattha = Ficus religiosa.
23. Asana = Bridelia montana, [Bēṅga mara, in Kan.]
24. Āmra = Mangifera indica, [Māvina mara, in Kan.]
25. Āmrātaka = Spondias mangifera, [Ambaṭe mara, in Kan.]
26. Ikṣu = Saccharum officinarum, [Kabbu, in Kan.]

27. Iṅguda = Balanites aegyptiaca, [Iṅgalīka mara, in Kan.; Nañjuṇḍa, in Malayālam and Tamil.]
28. Indrataru or Śvetakuṭaja = Wrightia tinctoria, [Kirikodasige, in Kan.]
29. Udumbara = Ficus racemosa, [Atti, in Kan.]
30. Uśīra = Vetiveria zizanioides [Lāvañca, in Kan.]
31. Elā = Elettaria cardamomum.
32. Kakubha = Lagerstroemia speciosa, [Cemmaruta, in Malayalam.]
33. Kaṅgu = Setaria italica, [Navaṇe Akki, in Kan.]
34. Kaṭambharā = Picrorhiza Kurroa, or, Helleborus niger, [Kaṭukarohiṇi, in Kan., Mal. and Tamil.]
35. Kaṭūka = see Kaṭambharā.
36. Kaṇṭakāri = Solanum xanthocarpus, [Nelaguḷḷa, in Kan.]
37. Kataka = Strychnos potatorum (clearing nut tree), [Cilliya mara, in Kan. and Teṭṭāmaram, in Mal.]
38. Kadamba = Anthocephalus indicus.
39. Kadalī = Musa paradisiaca, [Bāḷe, in Kan.]
40. Kapikacchu = Colocasia esculenta. [Kesavu, in Kan. and Śembu, in Mal.]
41. Kapittha = Feronia elephantum, (Wood Apple), [Belada mara, in Kan.]
42. Kamala = Nelumbo nucifera, [Tāvare hū, in Kan. and Tāmara, in Mal.]
43. Kampillaka = Mallotus philippinensio [Honne mara, in Kan.]
44. Karañja = Pongamia pinnata, [Hoṅge, in Kan. and Koṅgu, in Telegu]
45. Karavīra = Nerium indicum, [Kaṇagile, in Kan.]
46. Karīra = Capparis decidua.
47. Karcūra = Hedychium spicatum.
48. Karṇikāra = Pterospermum acerifolium, [Kanaka-campaka, in Kan.]
49. Karpāsa = Gossypium herbaceum, [Hatti, in Kan.]
50. Kalama = Gryza sativa. [A good variety of rice called Kaḷame in Kan.]
51. Kallola = Luffa echinata, [Devadangar (?) in Kan.]
52. Kākodambarikā = Ficus hispida, [Peyatti, in Tam. and Mal.]
53. Kāśmarī = Gmelina arborea, [Kūli mara, in Kan. and Gumuḍuceṭṭu, in Telugu.]
54. Kuṭaja = Holarrhena antidysenterica, [Kodasige, in Kan. and Kodisepala, in Telugu.]
55. Kunda = Jasminum multiflorum, [Duṇḍu mallige, in Kan. and Mogra, in Marathi.]

56. Kundurūka = Boswellia serrata or thurifera, [Mādimara, in Kan. and Paraṅgi Sāmbrāṇi, in Telugu.]
57. Kumārī = Aloe barbadensis, [Loḷīsara, in Kan. and Kattāḷai, in Tam.] Another variety is: Aletris litoralis.
58. Kumuda = Nymphaea stellata.
59. Kuraṇṭa = Striga lutea, [Agiyo, in Guj. and Laghukurandika, in Mara.]
60. Kuravaka = Barleria cristata. [Kariculli in Kan.]
61. Kula = Solanum xanthocarpum, [Kaṇṭakāri or Nelagulla, in Kan.]
62. Kulattha = Dolichos biflorus, [Huruḷi, in Kan.]
63. Kuśa = Desmostachya bipinnata, [Darbhe, in Kan.]
64. Kuṣṭha = Saussurea lappa, [Koṣṭham, in Tam., and Sepuddi in Mal.]
65. Kusumbha = Crocus sativus, [Kuṅkumakesara, in Kan.]
66. Kustumburu = Coriandrum sativum, [Dhaniya, in Hindi; Kottumbari. in Kan.]
67. Kesara (Punnāga) = Calophyllum inophyilum, [Punna, in Mal.]
68. Kodrava = Paspalum scrobiculatum, [Varagu, in Tam. and Kiraruga, in Tel.]
69. Kovidāra = Bauhinia variegata, [Kempu Mandāra, in Kan.; Devakāñcanamu, in Tel.]
70. Kṣīrikā = Alstonia venenata, [Aḍḍasarpa, in Kan.; Pazhamunnipala, in Mal.]
71. Kṣemā = Angelica glauca ? *or* Fagonia Cretica, [Dhamasa, in Māra., Dusparśa (Skt.) ; Ciṭṭigara, in Tel.?]
72. Khadira = Acacia catechu; [Kācu, in Kan.]
73. Kharjūrī = Phoenix sylvestris.
74. Gandhamāṁsī = Nardostachys jatamansi, [Sugandhamuste or Gaṇigalamuste, in Kan.; Namattam. in Tam.]
75. Garuḍavegā = Cocculus hirsutus, [Kāṭṭerkkoḍi, in Tam.]
76. Gāṅgeruka = Canthium parviflorum, [Kāregiḍa, in Kan., Karai, in Tam.; Balusu, in Tel.]
77. Girikarṇikā = Clitoria ternatea, [Śaṅkhapuṣpa, in Kan.; Kākkaṇam, in Tam.]
78. Guggulu = Commiphora roxburghii.
79. Guñjā = Abrus precatorius, [Wild Liquorice—Guluguñji, in Kan.]
80. Guḍūcī = Tinospora cordifolia, [Śīndil, in Tam.; Amṛta, in Kan.] Heart—leaved Moonseed.
81. Guṇḍra = Typha elephantina, [Jambuhullu, in Kan.]
82. Gokṣura = Tribulus terrestris, [Neggilu Mullu, in Kan.]

83. Godhūma = Triticum aestivum, [Godhi, in Kan.]
84. Caṇaka = Cicer arietinum, [Kadale, in Kan.]
85. Candana = Santalum album [Śrīgandha, in Kan.]
86. Campaka = Michelia champaca, [Sampige, in Kan.]
87. Cirabilva = Pongamia pinnata.
or = Elaeocarpus serratus, [Bīgada mara, in Kan.]
88. Coca = Kydia calycina
89. Coraka = Curcuma latifolia *or* Angelica glauca.
90. Jambū = Syzygium jambos, [Jambu neraḷe, in Kan.]
91. Jātī = Jasminum officinale, [Jājimallige, in Kan.]
92. Jātīphala = Myristica fragrans, [Jājikāyi mara in Kan. Nutmeg tree]
93. Jīraka = Cuminum cyminum, [Jīrige, in Kan.]
94. Jīvaka = Bridelia montana, [Vengaimaram, in Tam. and Pantegi, in Tel.]
95. Jīvantī = Desmotrichum fimbriatum, *or* Trema orientalis, [Kiru hāle, in Kan.]
96. Jyotiṣmatī = Cardiospermum halicacabum, Heart seed. [Erumbaḷḷi or Agnibaḷḷi, in Kan.]
97. Tagara = Valeriana wallichii, [Rishawala, in Urdu]
98. Tāla = Borassus flabelliformis, Palmyra palm, [Panemara, in Kan].
99. Tālīsapatra = Flacourtia jangomas, [Tāḷisapatre, in Kan.]
100. Tintiḍī = Tamarindus indica, [Huṇise mara, in Kan.]
101. Tinduka = Diospyros paniculata, [Karunduvari, in Tam.]
102. Timira = It may be turmeric.
103. Tila = Sesamum indicum, [Eḷḷu, in Kan.]
104. Tilaka = Clerodendrum phlomoides, [Takkolamu, in Tel.]
105. Turuṣka = Olibanum tree; Tagetes erecta, [Banti, in Tel.]
106. Trāyamāṇā = Ficus heterophylla, [Koḍiyatti, in Tam., Datir in Mara.]
107. Triphalā = Terminalia chebula, [Aṇile Kāyi, in Kan.]
108. Trivṛtā = Vitis vinifera, [Drākṣe, in Kan.]
109. Tvak = Cassia bark.
110. Danti (Nāgadanti) = Baliospermum montanum, [Niradimuttu, in Tam., Nelajīḍī, in Tel.]
111. Damanaka = Artemisia siversiana.
112. Darbha = Desmostachya bipinnata.
113. Davadagdhaka (Vyāmaka) = Costus speciosus or Arabicus, [Puṣkaramūla, in Kan.]
114. Dāḍima = Punica granatum, [Dāḷimbe, in Kan.]

115. Dūrvā = Cynodon dactylon [Garike hullu, in Kan.]
116. Devadāru = Cedrus deodara.
117. Dhava = Anogeissus latifolia, [Vellaynaga, in Tam., Cirimanu, in Tel.]
118. Dhātrī = Emblica officinalis, [Nellikāyi, in Kan.]
119. Naktamāla = Pongamia pinnata.
120. Nandikāvarta = Tabernaemontana coronaria, [Maddarasa, in Kan.]
121. Nala = Phragmites maxima, [Peddarellu, in Tel.]
122. Nalikā = Hibiscus cannabinus, [Goṅgūra, in Tel.]
123. Navamālikā = Jasminum arborescens.
124. Nāgakesara = Mesua ferrea, [Nāgasampige, in Kan.]
125. Nicula = see Vetasa.
126. Nimba = Azadirachta indica, [Kahibevu, in Kan.]
127. Nirguṇḍī = Vitex negundo, [Biḷe nekki or Karlakki, in Kan.]
128. Niṣpāva = Dolichos lablab, [Avare, in Kan.]
129. Nīpa = Anthocephalus indicus.
130. Nyagrodha = Ficus bengalensis, [Āladamara, in Kan.]
131. Patra = Laurus Cassia, Cinnamomum Zeylanicum, [Lavaṅga-Cakke, in Kan.]
132. Padma – Nelumbo nucifera.
133. Padmaka = Prunus Cerasoides.
134. Panasa = Artocarpus heterophyllus.
135. Parūṣaka = Grewia asiatica, [Palisa, in Tam.]
136. Palāśa = Butea monosperma, [Muttuga in Kan.]
137. Pāṭalā = Stereospermum suaveolens, [Pādari mara, in Kan.]
138. Pāṭhā = Cissampelos pareira *or* Cyclea Burmanni, [Pāḍāvaḷi baḷḷi]
139. Pāṇḍūka = a corn; Sterculia urens?
140. Pārijātā = Erythrina indica.
141. Picumanda = See Nimba.
142. Piṇḍāra = Trewia nudiflora, [Attarasu, in Tam., Eruponaku, in Tel.]
143. Pippalī = Piper longum, [Hippali baḷḷi, in Kan.]
144. Pīlu = Salvadora oleoides, [Varagogu, in Tel.]
145. Punnāga = Calophyllum inophyllum, [Surahonne, in Kan.]
146. Pūgīphala = Areca Catechu, [Aḍike, in Kan.]
147. Pūrṇakośa = ?
148. Priyaka = Anthocephalus indicus.
149. Plakṣa = Ficus arnottiana, [Kāḍa Aśvattha, in Kan.]

150. Bakula = Mimusops elengi [Reñje, in Kan.]
151. Badarī = Zizyphus jujuba, [Bugari in Kan.]
152. Bandhujīva = Pentapetes phoenicea, [Nāgasampige, in Kan.; Nāgapū, in Tam.]
153. Bimba = Coccinia indica, [Toṇḍe, in Kan.]
154. Bilva = Aegle marmelos.
155. Bījapūra = Citrus medica, [Mādaḷa, in Kan.]
156. Bṛhatī = Solanum xanthocarpum, [Kiriguḷḷa, in Kan.]
157. Brāhmī = Centella asiatica, [Vallarai, in Tam.]
158. Bhadrā = Acorus calamus, [Bajegiḍa, in Kan. and Vaṣambu, in Tam.]
159. Bhallātaka = Semecarpus anacardium, Marking Nut tree, [Gerkāyi, in Kan.]
160. Bhāṇḍīra = Indian fig tree.
161. Bhārṅgī = Clerodendrum indicum [Cerutekku, in Mal.; Gaṇṭu bhāreṅgi, in Kan.]
162. Bhūrja = Betula alnoides.
163. Mañjiṣṭhā = Rubia cordifolia, [Tāmravalli, in Tel.; Iṣṭamadhuka, in Kan.]
164. Maṇīvaka = ?
165. Madana = Randia dumetorum, [Karekāyi giḍa, in Kan.]
166. Madayantikā = Arabian jasmine.
167. Madhūka = Cynometra ramiflora *or* Bassia latifolia, [Ippemara, in Kan.]
168. Marica = Piper nigrum. [Oḷḷe meṇasina baḷḷi, in Kan.]
169. Mātṛvṛkṣa = See Ambā.
170. Mālā = Trigonella corniculata, [Piraṅg, in Urdu]
171. Māṣa = Phaseolus radiatus. [Uddu, in Kan.]
172. Māṣaparṇī = Teramnus labialis, [Kattulandu, in Mal.]
173. Mudga = Phaseolus mungo, [Pacce hesaru, in Kan.]
174. Mustā = Cyperus rotundus, [Bhadramuṣṭi or Tuṅge-hullu. in Kan.]
175. Mṛdvīkā = Vitis vinifera [Drākṣe, in Kan.]
176. Maurvī = Sansevieria roxburghiana, [Maruga, in Kan.]
177. Yava = Hordeum vulgare, [Jave-godi, in Kan.]
178. Rasa = Bola = Commiphora myrrha.
179. Rājakośātaka = Luffa cylindrica, [Sore-Kāyi, in Kan.]
180. Reṇukā = Piper aurantiacum, [Shambhaluka buj, in Hindi]
181. Rohītaka = Aphanamixis polystachya, [Cemmaram, in Mal.; Rohada, in Mara.]
182. Lakuca = Artocarpus lakoocha, [Vāṭehuḷi, in Kan.]

183. Lakṣmaṇā = Mandragora officinarum, [Kattai-jāti, in Mal.]
184. Lavaṅga = Syzgium aromaticum.
185. Lavalī = Cicca acida, [Aranelli, in Tam.]
186. Lodhra = Symplocos paniculata.
187. Vacā = Orris root, Acorus Calamus [Baje, in Kan.]
188. Vañjula = See Vetasa.
189. Vaṭa = See Nyagrodha.
190. Vana = Kyllinga mono-cephala, [Nirbishi, in Hindi; Mustu, in Mara.]
191. Varuṇa = Crataeva nurvala, [Hoḷenekki, in Kan.]
192. Vānīra = See Vetasa.
193. Vārāhī = Tacca aspera, [Dukarkanda, in Mara.]
194. Vārida = Cyperus grass.
195. Vālaka = Aporosa lindieyana, [Vittil, in Mal. and Tam.]
196. Vāsikā = Adhatoda vasica, [Āḍusoge, in Kan.; Āḍaloḍakam, in Mal.]
197. Vāsīphala = Gendarussa vulgaris, [Vatankolli, in Mal.; Karunocci, in Tam.]
198. Vikaṅkata = Gymnosporia spinosa, [Kattanji, in Tam.]
199. Viḍaṅga = Embelia ribes,[Vāyuviḷaṅga in Kan., Tam. and Tel.]
200. Vidārikā = Solanum verbascifolium, [Kallaṭe, in Kan.]
201. Vibhītaka = Terminalia belerica, [Śānti mara, in Kan.]
202. Viśveśvarī = Hibiscus mutabilis, [Sūryakānti, in Kan.]
203. Viṣa = Aconitum ferox, [Bish, in Hindi; Vashanavi, in Mal.]
204. Vīraṇa = See Uśīra.
205. Vetasa = Calamus rotang, [Betta, in Kan.]
206. Vyāghranakha = Euphorbia antiquorum,[Vachiram, in Tam. and Chadurakalli, in Mal.]
207. Vyāghrapadā = Gymnosporia spinosa. (See Vikaṅkata)
208. Vyāmaka = Costus speciosus, [Kuravam, in Tam.; Chengalvakoshtu, in Tel.]
209. Śaṇa = Crotalaria juncea, [Saṇabu, in Kan.; Vukku nār, in Mal.]
210. Śatapuṣpā = Pimpinella anisum, [Baḍe sopu, in Kan.; Sonph, in Hindi]
211. Śatāvarī = Asparagus gonocladus, [Halavumakkaḷa tāyi baḷḷi, in Kan.]
212. Śamī = Prosopis spicigera, [Jammi, in Tel.]
213. Śara = Typha elephantina, [Jambu hullu, in Kan.; Jammugaddi, in Tel.]
214. Śallakī = Boswellia serrata, [Gugguḷa mara, in Kan.]

215. Śāka = Tectona grandis, [Tega, in Kan.]
216. Śāla = Shorea robusta, [Kungiliyam, in Tam.; Āsina mara *or* Aśvakarṇa, in Kan.]
217. Śāli = Oryza sativa, common rice, [Nellu, in Kan.]
218. Śālmalī = Morus acedosa, *or* Bombax malabaricum, [Elava, in Kan.]
219. Śirīṣa = Albizzia lebbeck, [Bāge mara, in Kan.]
220. Śivā = Cinnamomum tamala, [Tejput, in Hindi; Talishappattiri, in Tam.]
221. Śiśumārī = a kind of plant.
222. Śiṁśapā = Dalbergia sissoo, [Iruguṇḍi māvu, in Kan.]
223. Śṛṅgavera = Zingiber officinale, [Śuṇṭhi, in Kan.]
224. Śoṇāka [Śyoṇāka] = Groxylum indicum, [Ānemuṅgu, in Kan.; Veḷutta pātiri maram, in Mal.]
225. Śyāmā = Echinochloa frumentacea, [Samul, in Mara.; Chamalu, in Tel.]
226. Śrīparṇī = See Kāśmarī.
227. Śrīvāsa = Turpentine.
228. Śleṣmātaka = Cordia dichotama. [Naruvili, in Tam.; Cinna nakkeru, in Tel.]
229. Ṣaṣṭika = a kind of rice growing in 60 days.
230. Saptaparṇa = Alstonia scholaris, [Hāle mara, in Kan.]
231. Samaṅgā = Rubia cordifolia, [Mañjiṣṭha, in Kan.]
232. Sarja = Shorea robusta.
233. Sarṣapa = Brassica integrifolia, [Sāsive, in Kan.]
234. Sahadevī = Vernonia cinerea,[Karehiṇḍi, in Kan.; Pūvāṅkuruntala, in Mal.]
235. Sahā = Hibiscus tiliaceus, *or* Sida acuta, [Malatanni, in Mal. Nīrparutti, in Tam.]
236. Sārivā = Ichnocarpus frutescens, [Udargoḍi, in Tam.; Pālvalli, in Mal.]
237. Sinduvāra = Vitex negundo.
238. Sindhuka = See 236.
239. Suvarṇataru = Cassia fistula, [Konde mara, in Kan.]
240. Suvarṇapuṣpa = See Campaka
241. Susāra (Sāradru?) = Terminalia tomentosa, [Karuppu marudu, in Tam.; Tempāvu, in Mal.]
242. Sūkaraka = Gironniera reticulata ?
243. Sūkarapādī = Azima tetracantha ?
244. Sūryavallī = Indigofera enneaphylla ? *or* Hibiscus mutabilis ?

245. Somarājī = Centratherum anthelminticum, [Kāṭṭujīrakam in Mal.; Kāḍu jīrige, in Kan.]
246. Somalatā = Sarcostemma brevistigma.
247. Saugandhika = White water lily.
248. Saubhāñjana = Moringa oleifera, Drumstick, [Nugge mara, in Kan.]
249. Spandana = a tree.
250. Syandana = Rathadru = See Tiniśa.
251. Svarṇapuṣpa = Jasminum humile, [Śemmalligai, in Tam.]
252. Haridratara = Coscinium fenestratum, [Doḍḍa maradarasina, in Kan,; Maramañjal, in Mal.]
253. Haridrā = Curcuma longa, [Arasina, in Kan.]
254. Hastikarṇa = Alocasia macrorrhiza, [Marasaṇige *or* Muṇḍigiḍa, in Kan.]
255. Harītakī = Terminalia chebula, [Aṇilekāyi, in Kan.]

APPENDIX I (b)

Fauna Mentioned in the Text.
(Includes Insects and Reptiles also)

1. Abjāda = Lotus-eater, Swan etc.
2. Aja = Chāga = Goat.
3. Ahi = Snake.
4. Ākhu = Mouse.
5. Aṇḍīra = Fish ?
6. Aśva = Horse.
7. Balākā = Crane.
8. Balgulī = Carmacaṭikā = Flying fox or Cockroach ?
9. Bharadvāja = Skylark.
10. Bhāsa = Cock ?
11. Bhaṣaka = Karāyikā = The Blue jay ?
12. Bhujaga = Snake.
13. Biḍāla = Cat.
14. Bileśaya = Burrow-dweller.
15. Cakora = Greek partridge.
16. Cakravāka = Ruddy goose.
17. Carmacaṭikā = See 8 *supra.*
18. Cāṣa = Blue jay.
19. Caṭaka = Sparrow.
20. Cātaka = The Pied crested cuckoo.
21. Chikkara = Civet cat ? (Hindi) Śikra = Accipiter badius ?
22. Chippikā = The Common Indian Nightjar.
23. Chuchu = Musk-rat.
24. Chucchundari = Do.
25. Daṁṣṭrin = Tusked animal.
26. Dardura = Maṇḍūka = Frog.
27. Dhikkara = A Bird whose cry resembles the sound 'Dhik' or a kind of deer?
28. Divyaka = A bird.
29. Duṇḍubha = A Non-poisonous Snake.
30. Dvīpin = Leopard.
31. Dvirepha = Bee.
32. Ekaśapha = Animal with uncloven hoofs.

33. Go = Cow.
34. Godhā = Alligator.
35. Gṛhagodhikā = Lizard.
36. Haṁsa = Swan.
37. Hārīta = A kind of pigeon.
38. Hastin = Gaja = Elephant.
39. Haya = Horse.
40. Ibha = Elephant.
41. Jāhaka = ?
42. Jalebha = Hippopotamus.
43. Jīva = Cakora.
44. Jīvajīva = Do.
45. Jīvaka = ?
46. Kāka = Crow.
47. Kalabha = A young elephant or camel.
48. Kalahakārikā (commentary) = Ralā = A bird.
49. Kaṅka = A heron.
50. Kapiñjala = Osprey.
51. Kapota = A dove.
52. Kāraṇḍava = A kind of duck.
53. Karāya = (Hindi) Kurāya = Screech owl ?
54. Karāyikā = Pūrṇakūṭa = The Blue jay.
55. Karkara = The Demoiselle crane.
56. Karkaṭa = Crab.
57. Kauśika = Owl or Ichneumon.
58. Khadyota = The Glow-worm.
59. Khañjanaka = Khañjarīṭa = Wagtail (of 4 types).
60. Khara = Donkey.
61. Koka = Ruddy goose.
62. Kokila = Cuckoo.
63. Krakara = A kind of partridge.
64. Krauñca = The Curlew.
65. Kṛkalāsa = The Chameleon.
66. Kukkuṭa = Cock.
67. Kulāla-kukkuṭa = Wild fowl.
68. Kuraṅga = Deer.
69. Kurarī—Osprey (Macchlīmār, in Hindi).
70. Kūrma = Tortoise.
71. Kūṭapūrī = The Blue jay.
72. Lāvaka(comm.) = A Quail.
73. Lomāśa = Jackal.

74. Mahiṣa = Bison.
75. Matkuṇa = Bug.
76. Matsya = Fish.
77. Mayūra = Peacock.
78. Mṛga = Antelope.
79. Mūṣaka = Rat.
80. Nakra = Crocodile.
81. Nakula = Mongoose.
82. Naptṛka = A bird.
83. Pārāvata = Pigeon.
84. Pheṇṭa = ?
85. Piṅgala = Crane or owl.
86. Pipīlikā = Ant.
87. Pippīka = ?
88. Pirili = ?
89. Plavaṅga = A kind of bird.
90. Pṛṣata = Spotted antelope.
91. Pṛthuroman = Mīna = Fish.
92. Pūrṇakūṭa = See 52 *Supra.*
93. Rājahaṁsa = Royal Swan or Flamingo.
94. Ralā = See 46 *supra.*
95. Ṛkṣa = Bear.
96. Rohita = A kind of deer.
97. Śalabha = Wasp.
98. Śalya = Porcupine.
99. Sārasa = Crane.
100. Saraṭa = Chameleon.
101. Śaśa = Hare.
102. Śaśaghna = Hawk.
103. Śatapatra = Wood-pecker.
104. Śikhin = Peacock.
105. Siṁha = Lion.
106. Siṁhanāda = A bird.
107. Śivā = Jackal.
108. Śṛgāla = Do.
109. Śrīkaṇṭha = Peacock.
110. Śrīkarṇa = A bird.
111. Śuka = Parrot.
112. Śūkara = Hog·
113. Śvan = Dog.
114. Śvāvidh = Porcupine.

115. Śyāmā = Śāmā (Hindi) = Copsychus malabaricus.
116. Śyena = Hawk.
117. Tarakṣu = Hyena.
118. Timi = Whale.
119. Tittira = Francoline Partridge.
120. Ulūka = Owl.
121. Uṣṭra = Camel.
122. Utkrośa = Osprey.
123. Vānara = Monkey.
124. Vañjula = See 112 *supra*.
125. Varāha = Boar.
126. Vāyasa = Crow.
127. Vesara = Mule.
128. Vṛka = Wolf.
129. Vṛścika = Scorpion.
130. Vyāghra = Tiger.

APPENDIX II

ALBERUNI'S TREATMENT OF THE LAGHUJĀTAKA AND COMETS—A CRITIQUE

Alberuni appears on the Indian horizon as a star of rare brilliance, shedding its light on many a dark page of medieval history. Being an eminent scholar himself, he developed great zeal for a comparative study of the religions, cultufres, philosophies and scientific achievements of other nations. E.C. Sachau, his able translator, says about him: "The Hindus and their world of thought have a paramount fascinating interest for him." Alberuni appreciates scientific statements wherever they are found. In mathematics and architectural constructions he considers the Hindus to have reached a high degree of art, though he ridicules their superstitions and practices.

Though Alberuni's work on astrology is based on corrupt manuscripts and interpretations of Hindu scholars, he has achieved remarkable success in the field of astrology-cum-astronomy, among others. It is known that he has translated into Arabic the Laghujātaka and the Bṛhatsaṁhitā as well as written works on the "Lunar Stations", "Chronology" etc. His translation of these works is likely to open up a vast vista of research possibilities in the field of textual variations.

Alberuni's *India* consisting of 80 chapters deals with Hindu astrology in the last three chapters, quoting many verses in translation from the Laghujātaka and Chapter XI of the Bṛhatsaṁhitā bearing on *comets*. We do not understand why Alberuni considers the comets to have no astronomical significance, as he has relegated this topic to the astrological section rather than to the astronomical one. Actually they do have a scientific, astronomical basis which was visualized by ancient Hindu Sages and which is being proved by modern theories and experiments on meteorites. He states in this connection that his aim in writing this work is to remove the misunderstanding of his own people about the glorified nature of Hindu astrology, and to present to them the real state of affairs as they are. In this paper I shall address myself to the task of examining the performance of

Alberuni in translating and presenting Indian astrological classics such as the Laghujātaka and the Bṛhatsaṁhitā.

In this section he has given very useful tables pertaining to the Karaṇas, Yogas, planets, signs and comets for the benefit of students of astrology. In the tables of planets the author has shown the several months of pregnancy that are presided over by the planets. In a table on page 221 (of Vol. II) he speaks of the aspects exercised by the signs of the zodiac, which is an alien subject to Varāhamihira who knows only planetary aspects. Alberuni does not mention the source of his information. However, the details of this topic must have been supplied to him by local astrologers will-versed in the Horā of Sage Parāśara.[1]

While describing the physical forms of the various Rāśis i.e. signs of the zodiac, he says about Gemini: "The word applies to a man holding a lyre and a club," which is not correct. It ought to be "A man holding a club and a woman a lyre." About the description of Capricorn as *Goat-cum-Crocodile*, he says, it is true only according to Greek astrology. He says the same thing about Kumbha, Aquarius, as it means only a *Pot*, but the figure is that of a human being holding a pot, which answers to the Greek representation of the sign. The name Mīna, Pisces, too means a single fish, not pair of fishes, according to him.

His translation of the verses of the Laghujātaka in many places is more of an explanatory nature than faithful renderings, there being some omissions and additions. In IV-5 of L.J. the author gives a planetary configuration necessary for predicting an illegitimate birth, but Alberuni takes it to indicate short life for the child. In the same verse there is a passage meaning "in case Jupiter does not aspect the ascendant and the Moon", which he translates as, "if the Moon and Jupiter just quit the aspect with the ascendens," (vide p. 232 Vol. II).

In verse 7 the house of confinement is described by Varāhamihira as *Adṛḍha*—not strong or stable—if the Sun be the strongest planet in the chart, but Alberuni construes the word as "will be destroyed". Similarly, the word *Nava*—new—is taken by him in the sense of *beneficent*. The word *Dagdha*-burnt-means, *burning*, according to him. The word *Citra*—colourful or variegated—is taken in the sense of "bow-shaped". He has omitted the meaning of *Manoramam*—charming—corresponding to Venus. Similarly, he has not translated

1. See Chapter IV of Bṛhatpārāśarahorāsāra.

the expression, *Prativeśma sannikṛṣṭaiśca* which means, the house in the vicinity is to be predicted through the planets situated nearby.

While translating verse 8 of chapter IV he interprets the word Bhūmikā meaning storey as *wing*. Another word viz. Viśālam meaning broad or spacious, is translated by him as "having three wings". I should think that his manuscript must have had the reading, *Triśālam*, which is quite correct as contrasted with the following expression, *Dviśālam*.

He has completely omitted verses 10 and 11 of this chapter. He translates verse 12 as follows:— "The number of women who will be present in a house corresponds to the number of stars which are in the signs of the *ascendant* and of the room. Their qualities correspond to the images of these constellations."[1] The correct meaning of this would be—"The number of women (in the lying-in-chamber) should be judged from the number of planets situated between the Ascendant and the Moon." The second half of the verse too is misconstrued by him. For, he uses the expression, *go away*, for *Bāhyāḥ* which means, those that are standing outside, and *Enter it*, for *Abhyantaragāḥ* meaning those that are inside.

Next he takes up the last verse i.e. the 5th, of chapter XIII dealing with the soul's previous place of residence. He takes the word *Tiraścaḥ* to mean *Vṛścikaloka*, whereas it is the world of birds and beasts. The word *Nārakīyāḥ* means, according to him, those hailing from *Bhṛguloka*, whereas it means only those that come from the nether world.

Alberuni does not take the verses in order. It is possible that he thought of giving his readers a succinct and connected account of Hindu astrology, and so changed the sequence of the materials to suit his pattern of writing. While translating XIII-4 dealing with Mokṣa or liberation he omits the expression. *Śeṣair abalaiḥ* (with the rest being weak), which is an important condition. Similarly, he errs in construing the expression, *Janmani maraṇe vā*, as he says:- "If the constellation of the moment of death is the same as that of the moment of birth, in that case the spirit is liberated." It should mean only "at birth or death." He points out that these features are alien to the system prevalent in his country.

While discussing the phenomena called comets he says that the theories and methods of the Hindus are very lengthy and very subtle. First he takes up III-7-12 of the Bṛhatsaṁhitā which describe

1. Page 233, Vol. II

the *Tāmasakīlakas* numbering 33 and their effects.[1] Then he skips over the succeeding seven chapters and treats of the comets in chapter XI. He translates the first seven verses barring the sixth. The second half of the seventh stanza is wrongly coustrued thus: "If the appearance of a comet lasts longer than 1½ months, subtract from it 45 days. The remainder represents the months of its influence." He must have been misguided by the expression, *Pakṣatrayāt paratah̤.* The right meaning of the verse is—"The effects of a comet last for so many months as the number of days it remains visible, and for so many years as the number of months it is visible. These effects will be felt after a month and a half." Here he adds another sentence as "If the appearance lasts longer than two months, ..." which is not warranted by the text. I presume that astrologers whom Alberuni cross-examined gave him this queer explanation. In this connection we cannot but commend the pains the Arab scholar has taken in analysing materials given in this chapter of the Saṁhitā and tabulating the minute details in appropriate columns. He has tabulated the properties etc. of the three categories of the comets described in verses 8 to 41. We shall take up these tables for consideration, later on.

Under verse 42 of this chapter which describes the comet *Dhruvaketu,* Alberuni translates the word *Deśānām* as *empire* instead of *countries.* Varāhamihira means to say that there will be destruction in all the countries where this comet has been sighted on houses, trees or mountains. Similarly, he gives two meanings for the word *Upaskāreṣu,* the second being" sweepings of the house". According to Bhaṭṭotpala it means house-hold utensils and the like such as ladles, winnowing baskets, and brooms. In fact Alberuni has confused *Upaskāra* with *Avaskāra.* Then he jumps to verse 61 Of course he utilizes the ideas of the intervening verses in the tables of comets. Another peculiarity of this scholar is that he takes the word Śikhā or Cūḍā throughout to mean, *tail,* and and not *crest.* This verse too he translates wrongly thus: "If a shooting star falls down opposite to the tail of a comet, health and well-being cease, the rains lose their beneficial effect, and likewise the trees which are holy to Mahādeva and the conditions in the realm of Cola...are troubled." Is it possible that Alberuni had different readings or was his manuscript illegible, which necessitated a strained construction ? Our reading is *Śivaḥ śivataro'tivṛṣṭo yaḥ.* Hence

1. Alberuni follows Varāhamihira in clubbiug together the *Tāmasakīlakas* and the comets mentioned in Ch. XI simply because they have the same generic name, Ketu. Varāhamihira however knew that they were sunspots, solar flares and the like. Hence they are of a different type.

there is no chance of Śiva's tree creeping. It only means *auspicious* and *more auspicious*. No doubt, he has translated the second half of the verse correctly, though he has omitted the word, Avagāṇa (Afghana) from the list of countries affected adversely.

Next he translates verse 62. Here too he goes off at a tangent from the text. For, he says, "Examine the direction of the tail of the comet, it being indifferent whether the tail hangs down or stands erect or is inclined, and examine the lunar station, the edge of which is touched by it. In that case predict destruction...and that its inhabitants will be attacked by armies which *devour them as the peacock devours the snakes*."[1] Here the first line is misinterpreted. It should be— "The quarter where the crest of the comet is bent, where it is projecting..." He has not only omitted the word" Divyaprabhāvanihatān" (destroyed py divine power) but has taken *Garutmān*, meaning Garuḍa, as *peacock*.

Tables of Comets:

Kiraṇas:— These comets number 25. Alberuni calls them "*Children of Kiraṇa*", but actually they are the sons of the Sun. Their effect is *Śikhibhayadāḥ* i.e. creating danger from fire, but he gives *pestilence* as the effect.

The 22 *comets, children of the Earth*:— He omits the adjective *Kiraṇānvitāḥ* (full of rays). For the effect, *Kṣudbhayadāḥ*, he gives "fertility and wealth" which applies to the succeeding set of 3 comets.

Sons of the Moon numbering three: He quotes evil effects as "The world will be turned topsy-turvy". This applies to the next comet called Brahmadaṇḍa, which causes, according to him, wickedness and destruction.

Kanakas: These are 60 comets, children of Saturn. They are omitted by Alberuni.

Taskaras: They are *Nātivyaktāḥ*, not quite clear, but he says, "the eye is dazzled by them" which is wrong. It is possible that he could not find the negative particle *Na* in his manuscript.

Tāmasakīlakas: Alberuni includes them in the tables of comets. Though they are 33, they are given here as 36. Their effect, according to him, is 'fire', while Varāhamihira gives their effects under "The Sun's Transit" in five verses as "famine, trouble to kings, theft, drought etc."[2]

1. P. 239 Vol. II
2. Br. Saṁ. III 12-16.

Viśvarūpas : He gives their effect as 'evil', but it should be "acute danger from fire."

Aruṇas: Children of Wind, numbering 77. Their quality *Vikīrṇa-didhitayaḥ* meaning "possessed of scattered rays" is translated by him as "their rays are united so that these appear as rivulets." About their colour *Śyāmāruṇāḥ*, dark red, he says "reddish or greenish."

Gaṇakas and *Caturaśras* are both children of the Creator, the former being 8 clusters and the latter 204 in number. Alberuni takes Gaṇaka as the name and Caturaśra as its epithet, and gives number as 204. According to Bhaṭṭotpala, Caturaśra is a descriptive name.

Kaṅkas: Alberuni extends their effects viz. *Tīvraphalāḥ*, by bringing in the effects of *Kabandhas* viz. *Puṇḍrābhayapradāḥ*. Even here he has taken the word as *Puṇḍrā bhayapradāḥ*, which gives the contrary meaning, as Bhaya means fear or danger, while Abhaya means protection.

Asthiketu: He reads it as Aṣṭi, and translates *Rūkṣa* as 'less bright.

Śastraketu: It appears in the east, but he says *west*. In its effect he leaves off *Māraka*—mortality.

Raudraketu: It is to be seen in the *Dahanavīthi*, which has been mentioned in connection with the transit of Venus. This Avenue consists of the two stars, Pūrvāṣāḍha and Uttarāṣāḍha, but Alberuni gives the three stars viz. Pūrvāṣāḍha, Pūrvabhādrapada and Revatī. This is against Varāhamihira's rule given in IX. 3. Though the author has told us that its effects are the same as those of Kapālaketu i.e. hunger, mortality, drought and diseases, yet Alberuni gives only "fighting among kings".

Śvetaketu: It is visible in the east at midnight, but according to him in the *south* at the *beginning of the night*. He was misled by the words *Prāk* and *Yāmyāgraḥ*.

Ka: Alberuni omits its form, Yugākṛti, like the yoke. He says that it appears in the *first part of the night*. It should be *midnight*. The adjectives, *Saptadinadṛśyau*—visible for seven days—and *Snigdhau subhikṣaśivadau*—glossy and conducive to good crops and benefits—are applicable to this and the previous comet. He describes Ka as "its flame is like scattered peas." He applies the evil effects of Ka when it is visible for more than a week, to both Ka and Śvetaketu against the textual specific statement. He also gives the effect, viz. destruction of two-thirds of the population, of the following Ketu Śveta (which is omitted by him), as belonging to this pair of comets. Varāhamihira says clearly about the distinctness of Śvetaketu and Śveta. Still Alberuni takes them as identical.

Raśmiketu: It is similar to Śveta in effects, but Alberuni gives a different version of it as "ruining all human affairs and creating revolutions". In reality it is "destruction of two-thirds of humanity".

Dhruvaketu: He does not give the evil effects of this, given in verse 42, which he applies to the entire class of atmospheric comets.

Kumuda: He construes the word *Prākśikha*, meaning, with its crest turned to the east, as "having its tail directed towards the south."

Maṇiketu: He omits its characteristic of being a tiny little star.

Bhavaketu : Here too he omits its glossiness and form of a tiny star.

Padmaketu: He takes the direction of its appearance as South, but it ought to be *Apareṇa*, the West.

Āvarta: It is *Aruṇanibha*, red in colour, but he takes it as 'light gray.'

Saṁvarta : It is described as *Śūlāgrāvasthitaḥ* —situated like the trident—and dreadful. He omits the latter quality and alters the former as "with a tail with a sharp edge."

My above-mentioned criticism of Alberuni is not meant to belittle his yeoman service to the cause of international understanding and of enriching the knowledge of his countrymen, but to show that there is a vast field of research for scholars to prove the veracity and justness of the statements made by the great Arab savant, to whom the world of scholars and lovers of culture owe a deep debt of gratitude.

APPENDIX III

FERTILIZERS IN ANCIENT INDIA

The problem of feeding the population, increasing by leaps and bounds, especially in the developing countries, assumes special importance at this juncture when scientists and technologists are seriously engaged in finding ways and means to increase farm production and reduce wastage by eradicating plant-pests and diseases as well as by devising proper storage methods. It would, therefore, be interesting to all lovers and scholars of Sanskrit hailing from different parts of the world to know something about the efforts made in this direction in ancient India.

Ancient Indian seers had established that plants were also living beings with the difference that their consciousness—Saṁjñā—was internal or dormant.[1] All the same, they have feelings of both pain and pleasure. Sir J.C. Bose had demonstrated this fact to learned assemblies in many parts of the world. Just as preventive and curative medicines are prescribed for human beings, even so are they done for members of the vegetable kingdom. In ancient works on Śilpaśāstra (architecture)[2] and in Kauṭilya's Arthaśāstra[3] as well as in Varāhamihira's Bṛhat Saṁhitā[4] we come across sections dealing with trees or Vṛkṣāyurveda (treatment of plants) in connection with agriculture, gardening and town-planning. In the Atharva Veda too, there are prayers for the sweet and juicy fruits of trees and creepers.[5] Many ancient sages like Kāśyapa, Gārgya, and Parāśara as well as medieval scholars like Cakrapāṇimiśra, Surapāla and King Somadeva III of the Chalukyan dynasty, have written on this subject.

In Sanskrit poems and dramas, we come across the word *Dohada* which, applied to plants, means special treatment or manure or fertilizer. In the Ratnāvalī[6] there is the famous verse, "Uddāmotka-

1. Manu. I. 49
2. Śilpaśāstra of Viśvakarman, LXVII. 3, LXVIII. 8-10, LXX. 7.8.
3. Arthaśāstra, Jolly's Edn. II. 20 p. 30 (Sitādhyakṣa)
4. Bṛ. Saṁ LV.
5. Atharvaveda. I.2.6, III. 6.4.
6. Ratnāvalī II-30.

likām..." which speaks of the wonderful appearance of abundant flowers on the King's jasmine creeper as a result of the application of a Dohada, fertilizer, supplied by a hermit. There is also the case of the Dohadas coming under what are called "Kavisamayas" or poetic conventions.[1]

Rājaśekhara argues that the poetic conventions, fictitious as they may appear, are not to be rejected by poets. For, ancient scholars, well versed in the Vedas and their ancillaries as well as the Śāstras, had roamed over many islands and countries and written these things on the basis of their first-hand knowledge. These things appear strange and untrue at present as a result of vast changes in climatic conditions, times and other circumstances. This is how the poetic conventions originated in days of yore.

These poetic conventions relate to other classes also such as birds and beasts. The Cakora birds drink nectar from the Moon's rays; the Cakravākas get separated from their mates at night; the Cātaka can drink only the water that drops from the clouds. The deer are enraptured by the tunes of hunters and thereby get ensnared. The swan is supposed to possess the capacity to separate milk and water. The bee dies by kissing the Campaka flower, etc. We are not concerned at present with these poetic conventions, but only with the special treatment given to plants for increasing their yield. This subject of fruit and flower culture as well as grafting was practised in ancient India under the aegis of the rulers. This knowledge was also hereditary in some families.

According to poetic conventions the Aśoka tree should bear abundant flowers, if it be kicked by a charming young lady producing jingling sound of her anklets.[2] On the face of it, it would look ridiculous and superstitious, especially to a person of scientific outlook. However, we have to remember that many a scientific discovery owes its inspiration to some so-called superstitions. Though the ancients, who were fond of myths and parables, couched their thoughts not in scientific terms but in figurative language, yet their statements had the value of practical utility and traditional authority. If we analyse these *conventions* with a scientific spirit, I am sure, we may stumble on the truth lying underneath. I think that the jingling anklet subjects the Aśoka tree to sound or music therapy in addition

1. "Aśāstriyaṁ alaukikam ca paramparāyātaṁ yam artham upanibadhnanti kavayaḥ sa kavisamayaḥ," and "Kavimārgānugrāhī katham eṣa doṣaḥ iti Yāyāvariyaḥ." Chapter XIV of Rājaśekhara's Kāvyamīmāṁsā.

2. The verse "Pādāghātād..."

to giving it mild physical vibrations. It is well known that plants need water, light, etc., to prepare their food. Similarly, they depend upon another physical agency viz. sound, which has some influence on their physiology. Music is said to cast a spell on all living beings, as it is 'the food of love'. Experiments were conducted recently by subjecting certain plants and creepers to different tunes in order to find out their effect on their produce. Scientists have come to the conclusion that music does influence, by and large, the life and growth of plants and their yields. In this connection, let us turn to what Dr. T. C. N. Singh, Retired Professor of Botany, Annamalai University, has to say: "If they depend on light, why not on sound?" He discovered under microscope that protoplasm was moving faster in the cell as a result of the sound produced by an electric tuning fork. This discovery led to his conclusion that sound must have some effect on the metabolic activities of the cell. His findings are that the sound of the Vīṇā produces better results than that of the violin. He says further that male voice is healthier to the plant than female voice.[1] Among the Rāgas or tunes, he says, the Cārukeśī is the most helpful in increasing the yield. Originally, it is said, such experiments were conducted in the U.S.A., Canada, Russia, etc. In the West, Bacch Sonnetta (A & B) was found to be very potent. Dr. Singh is of the opinion that the growth and development of forests are largely due to the presence of a large number of birds singing several tunes every day.

As mentioned above, the subject of *Dohada* is often met with in Sanskrit literature. In the Naiṣadhīyacarita of Śrīharṣa (12th century A.D.) who was well versed in many branches of learning, there is the reference to the fertilizer used for the pomegranate: While explaining the word *Dohada-dhūpinī* the commentator Nārāyaṇa says[2] that Dohada is that material by which an extraordinary growth of fruits etc. is achieved. In the particular context the Dohada or fertilizer was fumigation. The editor, Pandit Śivadatta, has quoted from some source three verses which mean : "Dohada is that material evolved by competent persons for producing flowers etc., on trees, bushes, creepers and the like out of season." The next two verses mention the materials used for fumigation: "For increasing the yield of pomegranates the best procedure is to pour on the tree the liquid of mutton and to fumigate it by burning sheep's wool and mutton underneath.

1. Manipal Record, Vol. IV-36. p. 2.
2. Naiṣadha I-82.

If the same tree is smeared with a paste made of fish meal, ghee and Triphalā as well as with the flesh of goats and sheep, and fumigated with the matter, its fruits will be as big as those of the Tāla tree."

The subject of treatment of trees has been ably dealt with by Varāhamihira in the Bṛhat Saṁhitā, Chapter LV, as it forms part of the topic of Gardening. Corresponding to the Green Manure employed in modern agriculture Varāhamihira speaks of the Sesamum Treatment for the soil. According to him if flowers or fruits are destroyed suddenly, the concerned tree or creeper should be watered with milk cooled after being boiled with horsegram, blackgram, greengram, sesamum and barley. Another recipe is the following: Trees, creepers and bushes should be sprinkled daily with a mixture of two Āḍhakas i.e. 128 Palas, of the powder of the dung of goats and sheep, one Āḍhaka of sesamum, one Prastha i.e. 16 Palas, of wheat particles, one Tulā (100 palas) of beef and one Droṇa (256 Palas) of water, kept for seven days.

The *Abhilaṣitārthacintāmaṇi*[1] mentions a few fertilizers: (i) The soil underneath a tree struck by lightning is good for warding off trouble for trees from snowfall. (ii) Fumigation of trees by burning turmeric, Viḍaṅga (Erycibe Paniculata), white mustard, flowers of the Arjuna tree, mixed with fish and the flesh of Rohita (a kind of deer) will not only help the growth of flowers and fruits but will destroy all worms and insects as well as diseases. (iii) Fumigation of a tree by turning Viḍaṅga, asfoetida, Sindūra, pepper, Ativiṣā, Vacā, Bhallātaka and buffalo-horn mixed in equal quantities will destroy all kinds of insects and germs. (iv) Fumigation caused by burning fish, clarified butter, white mustard and banana leaves will cause a bumper crop. (v) To produce fruits out of season, the trees should be watered with a decoction of Aṅkola mixed with ghee and honey and with the fat of parrots and deer. (vi) Milky trees will yield a bumper harvest if they are watered with milk mixed with Viḍaṅga, honey and ghee, and fumigated with the smoke of burnt Naṭa and Kuṣṭha. (vii) The same effect will ensue in case the trees are scratched with thorns and fumigated with cow's ghee, water and fat of parrots and rats. (viii) Vines will bear sweet fruits in abundance when they are manured with the excreta of cocks and the liquid of horse's flesh. (ix) Orange trees manured with any flesh mixed with cow's milk and jaggery will bear plenty of fruits. Similar recipes are given in this work for mango,

1. Abhi. Mys. Introduction xvii-xxiii

banana, wood apple (Kapittha), myrobalan, coconut, jujube, tamarind and such other trees.

Recently there appearad in the South Kanara district and some adjoining areas a peculiar disease of the roots of the banana plant, which has practically destroyed entire plantations. This work mentions a remedy for such a disease: The roots of the banana are to be scratched with a gold needle heated in the fire caused by burning the powder of some article (which is not clear). The Bījapūra (citrons) plant will yield big fruits if it is manured with oil cake, liquor and fish, and then watered. The jasmine which is considered as the queen of flowers in India, will bear flowers when it is burnt with the fire of chaff.

There are some plants that bear flowers having no smell at all. There are fertilizers for making such plants bear sweet-smelling flowers. Such plants are to be manured with the soil taken from the beds of plants bearing fragrant flowers, and watered with a mixture of water, and the powder of Gandhapatra, Mustā (cyperus rotundus), Tagara (tabernaemontana coronaria) and Uśīra (andropogon muricatus).

It is well known that the Āmalaka fruit is astringent, but there are recipes for making it sweet: The tree should be scratched before the appearance of flower with a twig of the Kumāraka (Tamāla according to the Dhanvantari-nighaṇṭu) and the scratched surface besmeared with a paste made of Japā, sesamum and equal quantities of honey and ghee, the mixture appearing like mire. Similarly, the tamarind fruit can be turned sweet, if the tree is watered with a decoction made of the leaves of Jambū, Uśīra and Mustā, or with one made of milk and the flesh and serum of the deer, parrot, antelope and jackal. Creepers besmeared with honey will produce red flowers, whereas with ghee they will bear white flowers. The lotus and lily too will have two flowers on a single stalk, if the plant is smeared with honey and ghee and manured with the powder of Kalāya (a leguminous seed) and mire.

Injections to roots are also prescribed here for specific purposes. A small ball of the flower of Yaṣṭimadhūka, the white Kuṣṭha and honey should be injected into the root of any tree if it does not bear fruit.

There is a recipe for making the fruit ever-green: The branch of the concerned tree should be wound round with cloth in seven rounds, and at the joint of the trunk and branch, it should be well covered with the skins of deer and elephant.

A tree or plant is said to be capable of being transformed into a vine by means of the following fertilizer: The root of the mango plant should be manured with a decoction of Aṅkola, dog's flesh and goat's milk mixed with oil cakes. Such a vine will bear fruit in all seasons.

Cross-breeding of plants which is now practised on a large scale was anticipated by the ancients: When the seed of the Vārtākī (egg plant) mixed with honey and ghee is kept inside a Kuṣmāṇḍa (ash gourd) for a week(?) and then sown, the plant will come to have the leaves of the ash-gourd, but fruits of Vārtākī itself. Similarly, the plantain trunk is supposed to bear a pomegranate when it is watered with the flesh and serum of a boar and decoction of Aṅkola.

The Viśvavallabha of Cakrapāṇimiśra, referred to above, treats of many subjects pertaining to agriculture. In chapter VIII it deals with diseases of trees born of the three humours, and their remedies. A tree suffering from a Vataic disease becomes dry, small, thin, tall, drowsy and lifeless. It also stops bearing flowers and fruits. The remedy for this disease is the following: A sickly tree should be watered with a luke-warm decoction of glossy meat, and sprinkled with the ashes of dried cowdung. It may also be watered with a mixture of the extract of Nirguṇḍi, *cassia fistula*, leaves of Pañcāmra (?) and water, and its roots smeared with a paste of the above materials along with sesamum. Oil cake may be used as a manure for warding off Vataic diseases. Similarly pouring at its root the urine of goats is beneficial. It may also be watered with a decoction prepared with Kulmāṣa, goat's dung, mango bark and Aśvagandha. This work prescribes fumigation of a sickly tree with Nirguṇḍī, Guggulu etc.

This work mentions in Chapter IX some fertilizers for bringing about marvellous effects: Take the dry seed of a ripe Kumuda fruit and smear it daily with dry cowdung powder and buffalo's urine for seven days. Then sow it in a good soil. It will then sprout into a Karavīra creeper. If the same seed be treated with Aṅkola oil for one full day, it would produce a Karela (?) creeper.

We have already seen a recipe for a mango tree to yield in all seasons. In this work a slightly different recipe is prescribed : The seed should be treated 21 times with the blood of hare and tortoise and sprinkled with milk and water. The banana plant will yield fruits looking like mangoes, if its roots are watered with a decoction of hog's blood and fat.

Kuṇapajala: A fertilizing solution called *Kuṇapajala* is mentioned in the *Vṛkṣāyurveda* of Surapāla as well as in the *Upavanavinoda.*

This solution is prepared thus: "Take the flesh, marrow of bones and flesh and fat of the deer, hogs, fish, sheep, goats and Ṣaṅgins, as far as possible, and mix them together and cook the mixture in water. When it is sufficiently cooked, pour the whole thing into a pot and add milk to it. Now add powdered oilcake of sesamum, and honey to it. Mix it with soaked blackgram and ghee. Spread this mixture in a shallow vessel and pour hot water on it. When this is transferred to a pot, the latter should be sealed and buried for a fortnight in the strong room (or granary?). The contents of the pot are now called *Kuṇapajala*, which becomes a tonic for trees."

According to Surapāla's prescription, Mātuluṅga (citron) fruits would become as big as Kuṣmāṇḍas (ash-gourd), if its creeper be watered with a solution of oil-cake, fish-meat, rat-flesh and liquor in water. Bilva and wood-apple trees would bear sweet fruits, if they be watered, before their flowering season, with a solution of honey, ghee, milk, jaggery and its sediment. Similarly, the *Kautuka-cintāmaṇi* gives a prescription for making grapes sweet and to remove sourness of mangoes. The *Agni-purāṇa* has a section dealing with Vṛkṣāyurveda. The *Kṛṣiparāśara,* which is evidently a later compilation, treats of many topics of general interest to agriculturists, such as rainfall in the different months, preservation of seeds, sowing months, etc. "Ghee, oil, butter-milk, lamp and salt should never be kept on seed even by mistake", says the sage. Sage Gārgya too is quoted in this connection.

Just as prenatal care or treatment is necessary for human beings, even so seed treatment is profitable before sowing. All seeds are to be soaked in milk for ten days, taking them out everyday with the hand smeared with ghee. Then they must be rolled many times in cowdung, fumigated with the flesh of deer and hog, and then with flesh and hog's marrow they should be planted. They should be sown in a prepared soil (after the sesamum treatment). Lastly they should be sprinkled with milk and water. Varāhamihira[1] has prescribed in addition some special recipes for the treatment of the seed of Tamarind, Kapittha and Śleṣmātaka. The tamarind seed should be sprinkled with a compound of the fiour of rice, blackgram and sesamum as well as particles of wheat and stale meat and repeatedly fumigated with turmeric powder. The *Abhilaṣitārthacintāmaṇi*[2] gives some recipes for seed treatment on similar lines: Ripe fruits without any blemish ought to be selected and dried in the sun. Then

1. Bṛ. Saṁ. LV. 19-30.
2. Introduction xvii.

they should be coated with cowdung and fumigated with Viḍaṅga and ghee for five days. This is the general recipe for all kinds of seeds. Those of milky trees are treated thus: Soak the seeds for ten nights in cow's milk, dry them in the shade, and mix them with the ashes of Vyāghrī (or Bṛhatī) and of barley and wheat. Lastly give them a coating of cowdung. Seeds kept in the oil of Nṛśaṁsa (?) and Aṅkola for seven days and then sown in a soil wetted with hail-stones will sprout quickly. The pomegranate seed should be wetted 21 times with the blood of Kukura (or Kukkura?) before sowing for a good yield. Any seed soaked in milk mixed with the flesh and serum of fish and boar would be very effective. So would be a tamarind seed kept for seven days in milk mixed with the serum of fish and boar as well as with sesamum oil and then smeared with the ashes of Bṛhatī and Tilakāṇḍa (sesamum plant). To make the fruit unusally big, wet the seed with water mixed with human flesh and serum as well as with the powder of ivory.

Before sowing the seed, the soil should be tested. For fruit cultivation the soil must contain sweet water and be free from pebbles. It must also be glossy and unexposed to frost. If sesamum, blackgram and greengram grow luxuriantly, that soil is ideal for flower and fruit cultivation. The pit for the trees should measure four feet deep and square. The pit too should be treated and manured: It should be filled with plenty of bones and cowdung and burnt. Then remove the ashes and fill the pit with a layer of sand at the bottom and another layer of the flesh and serum of goats over it along with water. After this the seed is to be sown in the pit. Instead of seed a tender plant may also be planted therein. Cooked white rice mixed with curds and rock salt is also thrown into the pits for good results.

The foregoing paragraphs, I am sure, will draw the attention and rouse the curiosity of scholars and scientists, thereby helping them in further researches in the extension of the horizon of human knowledge. It would be excellent, if scientists could analyse some of the ancient fertilizers chemically and throw some light on the genuineness or otherwise of the ancient methods. My aim is just to show that the ancients had evinced sufficient capacity and enthusiasm for analytical thinking and scientific experimentation even in those far-off days when man's activities were guided more by belief than by reason.

INDEX OF VERSES AND PROSE PASSAGES

अ	Ch.	V
अंशुविरोधे	XVII	5
अकलुषांशु	VIII	53
अकारणे क्रोशति	XCII	2
अक्रियमाणक	XCVII	5
अक्षोभः श्रवणं	XC	9
अग्नयः पितरः	XLVIII	69
अग्निप्रकृत्या	LXVIII	110
अग्निभयं च	LXXXVII	31
अग्रतः पृष्ठतो	XXVIII	22
अङ्गारगैरिका	XLVI	78
अङ्गारे स्तेन	LIII	61
अङ्गिरसो	XIII	10
अङ्गुलशतार्धं	L	1
अङ्गुलानि	LXIX	18
अङ्गुष्ठकेन	LIII	101
अङ्गुष्ठनखः	LVIII	20
अङ्गुष्ठमूले	LXX	14
अङ्गुष्टयवै	LXVIII	42
अङ्गुष्ठेन	LI	37
अच्छिन्नः परि	XLVII	23
अच्छिन्नमवनि	XXXV	3
अच्छिन्नरज्जुं	XLIII	58
अजातशाखान्	LV	6
अजोऽव्ययः	XLIII	54
अज्ञातपूर्वाणि	LXXXV	2
अञ्जनभृङ्ग	LXIV	2
अञ्जनमुस्तो	LIV	121
अणुरपटु	XIX	22
अण्डजहा रवि	X	20
अण्डीरकष्टीति	LXXXVIII	26
अतसीकुसुमश्यामं	LXXXI	7
अतसीकुसुमश्यामः	LVIII	32
अतसी वेतस	XXIX	6
अतिकृश	LXVIII	51

	Ch.	V.
अतिमुक्त	XXIX	5
अतिवृद्धिः	XLVI	34
अतिवृष्ट्युल्का	XLII	1
अतीव ह्लेष	XCIII	11
अतृणे सतृणा	LIV	52
अत्यन्तवि	XCVII	12
अत्यम्लति	LXXVI	12
अत्युत्तमोत्त	IX	9
अत्युल्बण	LXXVII	15
अत्र सहस्र	LXXVII	17
अत्राक्रान्ते	IX	17
अत्रारोहेच्छूलि	IX	21
अत्रारोहेद्द्र	IX	19
अत्रैवान्त	CVII	14
अत्रोदित	IX	11
अथ च चतु	LVIII	34
अथ तु भुज	V	6
अथ दक्षिणे	XIV	11
अथ पञ्चमे	LXXXVII	33
अथ पारश	LIII	15
अथ पूर्वं	XIV	5
अथ मधुर	XLV	4
अथवा कृश	CVI	3
अथवाञ्जन	XXIV	16
अथवा समु	XLVIII	12
अथवा स्पृशति	L	10
अथाङ्गान्यू	LI	8
अथातः सां	II	1
अथाप्रश	LXV	10
अधिराज्या	XLVIII	85
अध्यक्षाधि	LIII	9
अध्यर्धहस्त	LXXII	3
अनभिहत	XLVI	62
अनलभय	VIII	17

	Ch.	V.
अनवरत	XXXVIII	5
अनिमित्तभङ्ग	LXVI	8
अनिमित्तसंह्	XCV	8
अनियतचारः	V	5
अनिलभयं	LIII	72
अनिलोऽनिले	XXXII	2
अनुगच्छति	XXIV	32
अनुलोमगे	XXX	19
अनेकवर्णा	XXXVI	5
अनेनैव	XLVIII	87
अन्तःपुरं	XCIII	2
अन्तःस्थे	LI	25
अन्तरङ्ग	LI	27
अन्तरचक्रं	CVII	11
अन्तरमणि	LXXXI	35
अन्तर्धाय	XLVIII	48
अन्तर्वेदी	V	65
अन्तेगुरु	CIII	12
अन्यत्वमूर्ध्वं	LVIII	52
अन्नं जगतः	XXI	1
अन्नैः क्षीर	CV	8
अन्यजन्मा	LXXXVI	5
अन्यप्रतिरु	XC	8
अन्यत्तौं	XLVI	40
अन्यानपि	XI	36
अन्येन	LXXIX	15
अन्येनात्रा	IX	13
अन्येषान्तु	LXXIII	6
अन्येषामुष्ण	LXXIII	5
अन्यैश्च कुम्भै	XXIV	27
अन्योन्य	XCV	43
अपचारेण	XLVI	2
अपरस्यां चल	XI	33
अपरस्यां दिशि	LXXXVII	23
अपरस्यां मणि	XIV	20
अपरस्यां स्वात्या	IX	22
अपरेण	XI	49
अपरे तु	LXXXVII	44
अपरेऽह्नि	XLVIII	23
अपरोऽन्त	LIII	34
अपसर्पणं	XLVI	47
अपसव्यास्तु	LXXXVI	57
अपसव्ये	XXX	4
अपहरति	LXXXI	27
अपि काल	CIV	46
अप्यर्णवस्य	II	17
अप्रतिषिद्धा	LIII	31
अप्रदीपा	II	26
अप्रसिद्धिं	LXXXVI	61
अप्राप्य मक	III	4
अब्जेषु मूर्ध	LXXXVIII	20
अभयाश्च	XCV	9
अभिजिच्छ्रव	XXXII	16
अभिभवति	XXXIII	30
अभिमुख	LXXXV	9
अभिहित	XVI	41
अभ्यन्तरे	LXXXVII	28
अभ्यर्चिज्ञान	XLIV	7
अभ्यर्चितापण	XLIII	26
अभ्यर्च्य	LX	16
अभ्यास	LV	13
अभ्युच्छ्राया	IV	14
अभ्युन्नताभि	LXVIII	68
अभ्युन्नता विय	XIX	8
अमलवपु	III	39
अमृतास्वा	V	1
अम्बरमद्र	XIV	27
अम्बरमध्या	XXXIII	11
अम्बस्पन्द	LXXIX	18
अयं विशेषो	XVII	27
अरभङ्गे	XLIII	22
अरिष्टाशोक	LV	3
अरुणकिरणा	V	55
अर्कग्रहात्तु	V	98
अर्कात्सिते	XL	4
अर्कोदयेऽधि	XXXIX	2
अर्कोदये विजु	XXXVIII	4
अर्चार्थममु	LIX	10
अर्थस्थाने	XL	9
अर्धनिचितं	LIII	105

	Ch.	V.
अर्घपलस्य	LXXXII	8
अर्घपुरुषे	LIV	10
अर्घमतोऽष्टौ	LXXIX	10
अर्घाङ्गुला	LVIII	9
अर्घास्तमया	XLVII	21
अर्घास्तमिता	XXX	1
अर्घेन यदा	XLVI	35
अर्घोदितो	V	28
अर्घोन्नते च	IV	9
अल्पसुत	LIII	73
अवनत्यार्के	V	18
अवमर्दन	V	48
अवाक्प्रदाने	LXXXVIII	46
अविकलपा	LXVIII	19
अविकाजश	LV	17
अविकृतस	V	96
अविदितवैव	II	34
अविरतज	XLIII	59
अव्युच्छिन्ना	IV	15
अशनिः स्वने	XXXIII	4
अशनिजला	LXXIX	3
अशुभनिमि	XLIX	8
अशुभनिरी	CIV	52
अशुभमपि	XLV	15
अशुभाकृति	XXX	21
अश्मक	IX	27
अश्मन्तक	LIV	43
अश्रुपात	LXVI	2
अश्विनीपि	CII	7
अश्विन्यामश्म	XI	54
अश्विन्यामश्व	XV	26
अश्विन्योऽथ	CII	1
अश्वियम	XCVIII	4
अष्टमराशा	XLI	6
अष्टमराशि	XL	3
अष्टशतं	LXVIII	105
अष्टांशाष्टौ	LVIII	19
अष्टाङ्गुलं	LVIII	6
अष्टावंसौ	LVIII	25
अष्टावष्टा	XLVIII	51
अष्टाश्रि	XLIII	43
अष्टाष्टक	LIII	55
अष्टौ च बहि	LIII	56
अष्टौ तु जानु	LVIII	22
अष्टौ सीसक	LVII	8
असनस्पन्द	LXXIX	2
असिकेशं	XI	56
असितघन	XXIV	15
असिते सितेन	XVII	25
असिद्धिसि	LXXXVI	62
असिमुसलं	VI	5
अस्तं याते	XXXIX	4
अस्फुटिता	LXVIII	57
अस्वेदनपीनो	LXVIII	33
अस्वेदनौ	LXVIII	2
अहतक्षौम	XLVIII	50
अहताम्बर	XLIII	24
अहिदेवे	XV	7
अहिराजः	LIV	36
अहिवरुण	X	2
अहुताश	XCVII	10
अहुताशेऽनल	XI	3
अहो धार्ष्ट्य	LXXIV	15
आ		
आकारं	LXXIV	3
आकाररावी	LXXXVIII	33
आगच्छन्तु	XLVIII	20
आगच्छन्त्यो	XCII	3
आग्नेयदि	XCVI	6
आग्नेये कौलि	LXXXVII	20
आग्नेयेऽम्बुद	XXXII	14
आग्नेये यदि	LIV	97
आग्नेये सित	XV	1
आग्नेय्यां दिशि को	XIV	8
आग्नेय्यां दिशि चन्द्र	XXIV	33
आग्नेय्यामनला	XCV	21
आग्नेय्यामपग	V	82
आजानुलम्ब	LVIII	45
आजे तस्कर	XV	23

	Ch.	V.
आज्ञार्थमाना	CIV	34
आज्यं तेजः	XLVIII	52
आताम्रसंहत	LXI	11
आत्मसुतको	XLVI	7
आत्मायमात्मनि	LXXV	4
आत्मा सहैति	LXXV	3
आदावनडुह	XLVIII	43
आदित्यहस्ता	XV	29
आदित्या वस	XLVIII	56
आदित्ये पाञ्चनद	X	6
आदित्ये सत्यौ	XV	5
आदिशेदुभय	XCIV	10
आदौ नेच्छति	LXXVIII	12
आदौ यादृक्सौ	CIV	50
आद्यं द्वितीयं	VIII	34
आद्यं धनिष्ठांश	VIII	27
आद्यः प्लवङ्गो	VIII	43
आद्योऽङ्गिराः	VIII	31
आधूम्रं व्रण	LXXXII	11
आधूम्रया तु	XI	40
आनर्तार्बुद	XVI	31
आपस्तथाप	LIII	49
आपाण्डुपीति	LIV	20
आपाण्डुरस्य	LXXXVIII	13
आपृच्छेद्य	LXXXVIII	43
आपो नामै	LIII	48
आपो हिष्ठाति	XLVIII	72
आप्येऽङ्गवङ्ग	X	14
आप्ये मृदवो	XV	18
आप्ये सलिल	IX	33
आप्योदयर्क्ष	XCVI	5
आब्रह्मकीटान्त	LXXIV	20
आब्रह्मादिवि	I	5
आभीराञ्छब	V	38
आमध्याह्ना	XXXIX	3
आमन्तिन्दुक	LVII	1
आमे वा मृत्पा	LIII	94
आम्रैः क्षेमं	XXIX	11
आयुधज्वल	XLVI	23
आयुधभृन्नर	XXX	23
आयुःश्रीबल	LX	4
आयुष्यं	XLVIII	74
आये रवि	CIII	11
आरक्षक	XVI	20
आरोग्य	LXXXV	5
आरोहणमन्य	XCIII	6
आरोहति क्षिति	XCIII	13
आर्कं पयो	L	25
	LIV	116
आर्द्रं द्रव्यं	XXVIII	2
आर्यम्णं हौत	VII	5
आर्यम्णे मार्द	XV	10
आर्याणामपि	CIV	51
आलभ्य मन्त्रेण	XXIV	8
आवन्तिका जन	V	64
आवन्तोऽथा	XIV	33
आवरणं	V	12
आवर्त्त इति	XI	50
आवर्षात्प्रभ	XLV	16
आवाहितेषु	XLVIII	22
आवाह्यैवं ततः	XLVIII	21
आशाग्रहोप	XXXIII	21
आश्रमतोरण	XLIV	16
आश्लेषार्द्धा	III	1
आश्लेषासु	IX	28
आश्वयुजेऽब्दे	VIII	14
आश्विनवारुण	VII	6
आषाढपर्व	V	77
आषाढीपर्व	XXVII	6
आषाढे जायन्ते	VIII	11
आषा घां पौर्णं	XXVI	15
आषाढ्यां सम	XXVI	1
आसन्नक्रम	XVII	3
आसन्नाः कण्ट	LIII	86
आसन्मघासु	XIII	3
आसीत्तमः	I	6
आसन्नो वल्मी	LIV	24
आस्यं सकेश	LVIII	15
आहिर्बुध्न्ये फल	IX	35
आहिर्बुध्न्ये विप्राः	XV	24

इ	Ch.	V.
इक्षुमतीत्यथ	XVI	4
इक्ष्वाकुरलक	XI	58
इच्छामि प्रष्टु	LI	23
इच्छेद्यदि	LIII	116
इति निगदित	LI	44
इति पिटक	LII	10
इति विबुध	XLVI	17
तीदमुक्तं	LXX	15
इत्येते विंश	LVI	19
इत्येतैश्चान्यै	XLVIII	71
इत्येवमुक्ते	LXXXVIII	45
इदमौशनसं	L	23
इन्दीवरासन्न	XII	10
इन्दोः पयोद	XII	11
इन्द्रतरोर्वल्मी	LIV	69
इन्द्रध्वजनिर्दिष्टा	XLVIII	78
इन्द्रध्वजनीराज	CVII	6
इन्द्राग्निदैवं	VIII	45
इन्द्राग्निदैवते	XV	14
इन्द्रार्कमण्डला	V	2
इमां च विन्द्या	LXXVIII	5
इशिविरुतं	LXXXVIII	39
इष्टद्रव्याकारः	XLIII	31
इष्टस्थाने सौम्या	XLI	12
इष्टानन्दकल	CI	11
इष्टापूर्त्तेन	LVI	2
ई		
ईतिप्राया प्रचुर	VIII	40
ईषत्ताम्रं	LXXX	7
ईषत्प्रभिन्ने	XII	16
ईषद्दन्तुरक	LXIX	20
ईषायोगे	LXXIX	27
ईर्ष्युर्लुब्धो	CI	9
उ		
उकारवर्णे	LXXXIX	15
उक्तं यदुत्तिष्ठ	XLIII	37
उक्तमिदं हय	XCIII	15
उक्तविपरीतरूपो	XI	9
उक्तविपरीतलक्षण	XVII	10

	Ch.	V.
उग्राणि पूर्वं	XCVIII	8
उच्चैःष्ठीवन	LXXVIII	4
उच्चैः स्वराः	LXXXIX	6
उच्चैर्घोरं	XC	15
उच्छ्रायहस्त	LIII	26
उच्छ्रायात्पाद	LVI	13
उच्छ्रायात्सप्त	LIII	27
उत्तमं विंशति	LV	12
उत्तममष्टाभ्य	LIII	4
उत्तरतः कैला	XIV	24
उत्तरतः स्वसु	XVIII	3
उत्तरतश्च करी	LIV	67
उत्तरतश्च मधू	LIV	35
उत्तरदिगादि	XXXIII	15
उत्तरपूर्वे	LIII	112
उत्तरमयन	III	5
उत्तरमार्गे	XLVII	9
उत्तरमार्गो याम्या	IX	6
उत्तरवीथिगता	XLVII	4
उत्तरवीथिषु	IX	8
उत्तरशाला	LIII	37
उत्पतद्भिरिव	XLIV	26
उत्पातगण्ड	LII	9
उत्पातान्गणित	XLVI	99
उत्सर्गान्न शुभ	XCIII	1
उदकार्गल	CVII	7
उदगयने	LX	20
उदगर्जुनस्य	LIV	12
उदगर्घविप्र	LXXXVII	45
उदगादि पुरो	XXXVI	1
उदगादि प्लव	LIII	91
उदगायतो	XI	29
उदगारोग्य	VIII	15
उदङ्मुखःप्राङ्	LXXXV	8
उदङ्मुखश्चा	LXXXIX	5
उदपानयन्त्र	XVI	18
उदयगिरिभद्र	XIV	7
उदयति सततं	XLVII	15
उदयन्नेव सुभि	XI	45
उदयशिखरि	XXVIII	3

	Ch.	V.
उदयसमये यः	XVI	40
उदये च मुने	XII	8
उदयेऽस्ते वा	XLVII	20
उदरं कथय	LXX	25
उदितं यदि	XXIV	31
उदितः पश्चा	XX	8
उद्द्योतिनः	XXX	10
उद्बद्धसङ्ग्र	XCVI	3
उद्बद्धाभ्यां	LXX	17
उद्यानदेवता	XLIII	13
उद्यानसलिल	XVI	29
उद्युक्तान्सह	IV	24
उद्वृन्तदस्यु	XIX	19
उन्नतकुक्षाः	LXVIII	20
उन्नतमीषच्छृङ्गं	IV	8
उन्नतविपुलैः	LXVIII	70
उन्मत्तानां च	XLVI	97
उन्मादः स्वय	LIII	79
उन्मानमान	LXVIII	1
उपचयभवनो	CIV	61
उपचितदेहो	LXVIII	100
उपचितसम	LXIX	13
उपरिचरवसु	XLIII	68
उपरिचरस्या	XLIII	8
उपला विना	XLVI	42
उपहतदाम्भि	XVI	37
उपान्त्यगो	CIV	38
उप्तं च बीजं	LV	26
उभयपार्श्वे	XXX	26
उभयोरपि	LXXXIX	13
उरः कुचं दक्षि	LI	43
उल्कया यदा	IV	28
उल्कया विनिहतः	XII	22
उल्का निपाता	XXIV	25
उल्का पक्षेण	XXXIII	2
उल्काभिताडि	XI	61
उल्का मन्त्रि	V	93
उल्काशनि	XIII	7
उल्का शिरमि	XXXIII	8
उष्णा शीता च	LIV	94
उस्रा क्रीडक	LXXXVII	22

ऊ

	Ch.	V.
ऊरू घनौ करि	LXX	3
ऊरू चाङ्गुलमा	LVIII	17
ऊर्ध्वं सिद्धिः	LXXXVII	7
ऊर्ध्वंकरो दिवस	III	21
ऊर्ध्वमुखाश्चल	XCV	11
ऊर्वोर्द्वाविंशे	L	14
ऊर्वोर्यानाङ्ग	LII	7

ऋ

	Ch.	V.
ऋज्वी हिता	VII	16
ऋज्व्यतिवक्रा	VII	15
ऋतुविपरीता	III	10
ऋतुस्वभावजा	XLVI	96
ऋषिधर्मपितृ	XLVI	10
ऋष्यशिरोरुह	LXV	8

ए

	Ch.	V.
एकं दीप्त्या	XXX	32
एकचरणानु	XIV	31
एकतश्च द्वित	XLVIII	65
एकद्रुमेण धन्यं	LXXIX	38
एकनिभा यत्र	LIV	90
एकर्क्षे चत्वारः	XX	6
एकस्थाने रुवन्	LXXXVI	64
एकस्याः पञ्च	XIV	82
एकादशभाग	LIII	24
एकादशमुद्वंशं	XLIII	47
एकादशे पिङ्गल	VIII	48
एकानंशा कार्या	LVIII	37
एकावली नाम	LXXXI	36
एकाशीतिविभागे	LIII	42
एकेन वर्णेन	LIV	2
एकेनाक्ष्णा	LXXXIX	10
एकेनावाक्	LXXIX	28
एकैकभवैः	LXVIII	81
एकैकाब्देषु	VIII	22
एकैकमेकभागं	LXXVII	18

	Ch.	V.
एकैकस्मिन्नृक्षे	XIII	4
एकैव मूत्रधारा	LXVIII	12
एको दुर्भिक्ष	III	19
एको निशीथे	LXXXVIII	41
एतत्प्रयुज्य	XLVIII	82
एतदनूपे	LIV	89
एतद्गुणयुक्ता	LXXXI	18
एतानि सर्वाणि	LXXXI	30
एता ह्युभेदाश्च	LIV	111
एते दक्षिण	LIII	54
एते द्रुमाः काण्ड	LV	5
एते यदि सुस्निग्धा	LIV	51
एते सर्वे मोक्षा	V	91
एतैः सलिल	LVII	2
एलात्वक्पत्रा	LXXVII	32
एवं देशे देशे	LXXXVIII	10
एवं रवेः क्षेत्र	XCVI	10
एवं विरक्ता	LXXVIII	2
एवमुपराग	V	13
	ऐ	
ऐन्द्रं षडश्रि	LXXX	8
ऐन्द्रं स्तुतकुल	XXXII	18
ऐन्द्रस्य शीत	IV	5
ऐन्द्राग्नाख्ये वैग	X	11
ऐन्द्राग्न्याख्ये वैश्वे	XXIII	8
ऐन्द्रानलदिशो	LXXXVI	29
ऐन्द्रे भूपविरोधः	V	21
ऐन्द्र्यादिदिगव	XCV	19
ऐन्द्र्यां दिशि शान्ता	LXXXVII	1
ऐन्द्र्यान्दिशीन्द्र	LX	11
ऐरावतकुल	LXXXI	20
ऐशानस्यासन्ने	LXXXVII	40
ऐशाने व्रतयुक्ता	LXXXVII	26
ऐशानो यदि	XXVII	9
ऐशान्यां देवगृहं	LII	118
ऐशान्यां देवलको	LXXXVII	16
ऐशान्यां मेरुक	XIV	29
ऐशान्यां सम्प्राप्ति	XCV	24
ऐशान्यादिषु	LIII	83
ऐश्वर्यगम्भी	LXVIII	66

	Ch.	V.
	ओ	
ओजाः प्रदक्षिणं	LXXXVI	43
ओजे तस्कर	XV	23
ओष्ठैः स्फुटित	LXVIII	52
	औ	
औशीनरमपि	XI	55
	क	
ककुभकरीरा	LIV	76
ककुभवटाम्र	LIV	119
कङ्कटकङ्कण	XIV	12
कङ्कप्लवोलूक	LXXI	12
कङ्का नाम वरुण	XI	26
कच्छपकः पुरु	LIV	34
कटिरपि च कृत्ति	CV	2
कटिरष्टादश	LVIII	23
कटुतिक्तरसा	XVI	34
कडिति फला	XCV	55
कण्टकमिश्रे	XCV	37
कण्टकिनो ये च	LXXIX	4
कण्टकमकण्ट	LIV	53
कण्ठाद् द्वादश	LVIII	16
कण्डूयते मद	LIII	59
कथयन्ति पार्थि	XXXVIII	1
कथयाम्यतः	XLVIII	29
कदलीकाण्ड	CV	12
कनकशिला	XXIV	1
कनिष्ठिकामूल	LXX	13
कनिष्ठिका वा तद	LXX	16
कन्यागते दिन	XLII	7
कपित्थवल्ली	LV	22
कपिलः प्रधान	I	7
कपोतकी च	LXXXVIII	5
कमलजविधातृ	XCIX	1
कमलोदरद्युति	LVIII	48
कम्बलमपनीय	XLVIII	54
कम्बुग्रीवो	LXVIII	32
करगौ विरु	XCV	54
करवीरोत्पल	L	21
करिकरसदृशो	LXVIII	35
करिणश्च हस्ति	XXIX	7

	Ch.	V.
करिवृषरथौ	LXVIII	95
करेण कर्म	LXXI	4
करोति कलहं	XCV	51
कर्किणि कोद्रव	XLI	4
कर्किण्यर्के मधु	XLII	5
कर्बूरचोलम	LXXVII	14
कर्णयुग्ममपि	LXX	9
कर्णाटमहाट	XIV	13
कर्णोपान्तः	LVIII	7
कर्तुरनुकूल	LIX	1
कर्पूरस्फटिक	LXXXI	28
कर्बुरकोऽहिः	LIV	42
कर्मप्राप्तिर्दश	CIV	45
कर्मसङ्गमयुद्धे	LXXXVI	47
कर्माङ्गुलं यवा	LXXIX	8
कर्षकपाखण्डि	V	29
कलत्रकलहा	CIV	16
कलशमृणाल	LXVIII	46
कलशेष्वेतान्	XLIV	11
कलशोदकेषु	XLIV	20
कलहः स्वर	LXXXVI	63
कलहो नैर्ऋत	LXXXVII	35
कलास्वभिज्ञः	LXIX	36
कलिङ्गवङ्गान्	V	79
कलुषं कटुकं	LIV	122
कलुषमन्दद्युत	LXXXII	4
कल्माषबभ्रु	XXX	12
कवि सप्तजिह्वं	XLIII	55
कष्टः प्लवङ्गो	VIII	44
का इति काक	XCV	50
काकद्वयस्यापि	XCV	57
काकपदमक्षि	LXXX	15
काकेति विघातः	XCV	53
काकोदुम्बरिका	LIV	19
काञ्चीकलाप	XLVIII	14
काठिन्यं याति	XXI	36
काणेनाख्या	XCVI	12
काणास्तु वर्गाः	XCVI	15
कापोतारुण	V	56
कामं प्रदीपयति	LXXVII	35
कामिनीं प्रथम	LXXIV	18
काम्बोजचीन	V	80
कार्त्तिकेऽश्वयुजि	VII	18
कार्त्तिक्यामन	V	69
कार्मुकमृग	XL	14
कार्मुकरूपे	IV	12
कार्यं तु मूल	XCV	60
कार्यं पौष्टिक	C	5
कार्यस्य व्याघा	XCV	36
कार्या चतुर्भुजा	LVIII	38
कार्या तु केश	LVIII	13
कार्योष्टभुजो	LVIII	31
कालकधुन्धुक	LXXIX	37
कालकसंज्ञं	LXXIX	35
कालोद्भवैः	XII	17
काशियुगन्धर	XXXII	19
काश्मीरकान्	V	70
काश्मीरान्	V	78
किं वातः परमन्य	XXI	4
किञ्चिदध ऊर्ध्वं	XLIII	48
किन्त्वनिलदह	XXXII	7
किमपि किल भूत	LIII	2
किलिकिलिविरु	LXXXVIII	22
किलिकिल्किलि	LXXXVIII	21
किष्किन्धकण्टक	XIV	10
किष्किषिशब्दः	LXXXVIII	16
कीटाखुमक्षि	XCVII	7
कीर्त्तिर्लक्ष्मी	XLVIII	57
कुक्कुटरुतं प्रदो	XLVI	69
कुक्कुटस्त्वृजुतनू	LXIII	1
कुक्कुटी च मृदु	LXXXVI	20
कुक्कुटेभपिरि	LXIII	3
कुक्षिकुचजठ	LI	31
कुजविजिते	XVII	23
कुजेऽभिघातः	CIV	11
कुञ्जर इति	LVI	25
कुट्टकः कुटिल	LXV	9
कुडपमुत्किरति	LXXXIV	9
कुब्जानुजात	LIX	3
कुब्जो नाम्ना	LXI	35

	Ch.	V.
कुमुद इति	XI	43
कुम्भाधस्ताज्ज	LXXIX	30
कुम्भेगुरुर्गवि	XL	7
कुम्भेऽन्तर्गिरिजान्	V	42
कुम्भोऽन्त्यघ्नि	CII	6
कुरुभूमिजाः	XVI	32
कुरुविन्दभवाः	LXXXII	2
कुर्यादहनि	XLIII	51
कुर्याद्गोरो	XLVIII	11
कुर्याद्नवे	C	3
कुर्वन्ति भास्क	CIII	2
कुर्वन्त्येताः	XXXIII	20
कुलजनविना	LXXVIII	10
कुलपांसन	XVI	36
कुवलयवैडूर्या	XXX	20
कुशयुक्ता	LIII	97
कुसुमरसपान	XLVIII	7
कुहकावेश	II	33
कूपेनापस्मारो	LIII	78
कूर्मः प्रथमे	LIV	44
कूर्मवसासृक्	L	22
कृकलासकपि	LXXIX	24
	XCIV	3
कृकलासकाक	L	3
कृकवाकुजीव	XLVIII	6
कृत्वा प्रभूतं	LVI	1
कृत्वा बलिं	LX	17
कृत्वा वरुणस्य	LIV	124
कृत्स्नाङ्गोपाङ्ग	II	24
कृशदीर्घं देमध्नं	LVIII	55
कृषिबीजगृहा	C	4
कृष्टां प्ररूढ	LIII	98
कृष्णचतुर्दश्य	C	2
कृष्णश्वेतक	LXXXI	19
कृष्णाः श्वेताः	LXXXI	4
कृष्णो गलेऽस्य	XLV	3
केकेति पूर्णं	LXXXVIII	25
केचित्तु शकुन	LXXXVI	53
केचिदनन्त	XXXV	2
केचिद्यथाभिवृ	XXIII	4
केचिद्वदन्ति	XXI	5
केतुकुजराहु	XVII	7
केत्वाद्युदय	XXXVIII	8
केन्द्रत्रिकोणे	LXXVIII	25
केवलचन्दन	LXXIX	14
केशघ्नरचिपिट	XIV	26
कैकयवसति	XIV	25
कोटुक्लीति क्षेम्यः	LXXXVIII	17
कोणाच्चतुर्थं	LXXXVII	5
कोशनिगूढं	LXVIII	8
कोशभवनाग्नि	XVI	15
कोशलकलिङ्ग	XVII	22
कोष्ठागारगते	XLVII	5
कौबेरी चात्र	LIV	39
कौबेर्यां दिशि	LXXXVII	25
कौरवचित्रक	IX	30
कौशेयपट्ट	XVI	30
क्रकेति च	LXXXVIII	30
क्रव्यादकौशिक	XLIII	62
क्रव्यादरूपं	LXX	22
क्रियमाणं यदि	XLIX	6
क्रूरग्रहसंयुक्ते	XXI	33
क्रूरष्षष्ठे	XCVI	13
क्रूरोग्रदोष	LXXXVI	68
क्रूरो घनीस्थूल	LXIX	34
क्रोशादूर्ध्वं	XCV	62
क्रोष्टुकोलूक	LXXXVI	21
क्रौञ्चकाञ्ची	LVI	6
क्रौञ्चवद्रिपु	XCIII	7
क्वचित्वृष्टिः	VIII	28
क्वचिदसितसि	XXIV	13
क्वणितं मरणायो	L	5
क्षणतिथ्युडु	LXXXVI	15
क्षतजानला	XI	21
क्षतं क्षितौ क्षपि	XIX	17
क्षमया क्रोध	XLVIII	13
क्षयमिति युग	VIII	52
क्षामा जुगुप्स	III	15
क्षारं पयोऽत्र	LIV	71
क्षारे कदल्या	L	26

	Ch.	V.
	LIV	117
क्षितिकम्प	XXXII	1
क्षिततिनय	I	4
क्षितिरुत्तम	XIX	14
क्षीरं शृतं यः	LXXVI	4
क्षीरघृतं	XLVI	43
क्षीरमृष्ट	XCIV	11
क्षीरेण बस्ता	LXXVI	7
क्षीरेण वा गोक्षु	LXXVI	10
क्षीरे शृते	LV	23
क्षुत्प्रम्लान	III	13
क्षुदनलमृत्यु	XXXIV	15
क्षुन्मारकुद्घट	III	31
क्षेमारोग्य	IV	27
क्षौमं चतुःसूत्र	XXVI	6
क्ष्वेडास्फोटितपु	LXXXVI	39
क्ष्वेडास्फोटितवादि	XXXIII	23
ख		
खं खेतियो	LXXXIX	16
खगनिलय	LIII	120
खञ्जनको नामा	XLV	1
खट्वाङ्गवीणा	LXIX	29
खड्गगदाशर	LVIII	33
खण्डो वक्रः	XLVII	24
खदिरपलाशो	XLIV	12
खप्रकृति	XLVIII	111
खरे खरे पथि	XCV	52
खर्जूरजम्ब्वर्जु	LIV	101
खर्जूरी द्विशिर	LIV	58
खलिनं हयाय	XLIV	22
खसमगध	XIV	6
खुरदेशे यो	LXXIX	31
ग		
गच्छतस्तिष्ठ	LXXXVI	35
गच्छत्यध्वानं	CIV	44
गजदन्तः	LXXIX	19
गतानि वर्षा	VIII	20
गत्वा द्वितीय	XLVIII	75
गन्धर्वदेव	XIII	8
गन्धर्वनगर	XXXVI	4
गन्धर्वपुरं	XCVII	13
गमने कर्ण	XCV	25
गरुडाकृति	LVI	24
गर्ताकुक्कुट	LXXXVIII	8
गर्भः पुष्टः	XXI	35
गर्भयुता जठरे	LI	38
गर्भसमयेऽति	XXI	34
गर्भाणां पुष्टि	XXI	18
गर्भेष्वपि	III	16
गर्भोपघात	XXI	25
गवि वस्त्र	XLI	3
गान्धारयशो	XIV	28
गान्धारसौवीर	IV	23
गार्गीयं शिखि	XI	1
गावो दीनाः	XCII	1
गिरयोऽञ्जन	XXVIII	6
गिरिदुर्ग	XVI	38
गिरिभिः पुरा	XXXII	3
गिरिशिखर	XVI	35
गिरिसलिल	XVI	6
गीतरवतूर्य	XLVI	61
गीतवादित्र	XLVI	91
गुग्गुलुवालक	LXXVII	9
गुञ्जात्रयस्य	LXXXI	12
गुडपूपपायस	XLIII	38
गुरुणा जिते बुधे	XVII	16
गुरुणाजितेऽवनि	XVII	13
गुरुभं गुरुश्चापर	IX	37
गुरुसित	XLVI	11
गुहराजो वृषो	LVI	18
गृहचैत्य	XLVI	70
गृहतरुतो	XXX	6
गृहनगर	LIII	69
गृहपटले	XLV	8
गृहमध्ये हस्त	LIII	92
गोगोष्ठस	XLV	5
गोचरपीडा	XLI	13
गोजिह्वासंस्था	L	7
गोधूमशालि	XIX	6
गोपाः पशवो	V	36

	Ch.	V.
गोपुच्छस्ये	XCV	35
गोपैर्यष्टयाह	CIII	13
गोप्रवेशसमये	XXIV	35
गोमहिषाज	LVII	7
गोमायुगृध्र	XCVII	9
गोलाङ्गुलयोः	XLVI	63
गोशशक्रौञ्च	LXXXVI	22
गोहरणशस्त्र	LXXXVII	39
गौरसितक्षिति	XLIII	16
ग्रन्थतश्चार्थं	II	31
ग्रन्थस्य यत्प्रच	CVI	5
ग्रन्थिप्रचुरा	LIV	81
ग्रन्थोऽन्यथाऽन्यथा	II	15
ग्रसनमिति	V	46
ग्रस्तावुदिता	V	27
ग्रस्ते क्रमान्निमि	V	63
ग्रहणोपगते	V	66
ग्रहशशियोगः	CVII	3
ग्रहसंवर्तसमागम	XX	5
ग्रहांश्च सर्वं	XLVIII	26
ग्रामस्य मध्ये	LXXXIX	18
ग्रामारण्यप्र	LXXXVI	10
ग्रामारण्याम्बु	LXXXVI	6
ग्रामे भषित्वा	LXXXIX	14
ग्रामो मध्यम	LXXXVI	40
ग्राम्यः प्रदीप्तः	XCVI	7
ग्रीवा ज्येष्ठा	CV	4
ग्रीष्मे रक्तो	III	26
घ		
घटमूर्धाध्वा	LXVIII	80
घटवत्सुषिरं	LXXIX	33
घनवालकशैले	LXXVII	13
घृतोशीरतिल	LV	7
घ्राणागण्डे	LII	3
घ्राणाया दक्षिणे	LI	39
घ्राणोद्देशे सवलि	LXI	15
च		
चक्रधनुः	XX	2
चक्रासिपरशु	LXVIII	47
चण्डाघृष्या	LXVIII	92

	Ch.	V.
चतुरङ्गुलं वसिष्ठः	LVIII	8
चतुरङ्गुलविस्ता	XLIX	3
चतुरस्रं धूर्ता	LXVIII	56
चतुरस्रमवनि	LVIII	54
चतुर्णां च माना	II	5
चतुर्थं गृहं	CIV	42
चतुर्थगे स्वजन	CIV	21
चतुर्दशीं पञ्च	IX	36
चतुःषष्टिपदं	LVI	10
चतुष्पदाःस्वयू	XLVI	55
चत्वारिंशत्	VII	13
चत्वारिंशद्द्वियु	LVIII	24
चत्वारिंशद्धीना	LIII	10
चत्वारि मुख्यानि	VIII	26
चत्वार्यर्यम्णा	XXXII	8
चत्वार्येतानि	XLVIII	45
चन्दनकुष्ठसम	XLIV	9
चन्दनतुरुष्क	LXXVII	30
चन्द्रमा यदि	XVIII	2
चन्द्रातपस्फ	LIV	110
चन्द्रोऽग्रस्यः	V	11
चपलाश्चतुरो	CI	3
चम्पककुसुमैः	XXIX	8
चम्पोदुम्बर	XVI	3
चरपुरुषकुहक	XVI	19
चलयति पवनः	XXXII	31
चलिताचल	XXXII	17
चातुर्वर्ण्यव्यासो	LIII	12
चापं मघोनः	XXXV	7
चापगते गृहिणी	XLII	10
चामरदण्ड	CVII	9
चामीकराशोक	XLIII	33
चारवशाद्	CIV	40
चारश्चागस्त्य	CVII	2
चारोदयाः प्रश	VI	12
चाषशिखि	XXXIV	4
चाषस्य काकेन	LXXXVIII	24
चिकित्सितमयै	LV	15
चिक्चिकि	LXXXVIII	29
चितिकेश	LXXXVI	60

	Ch.	V.
चित्रगर्भो	XLVI	95
चित्राम्बरमाल्य	CI	8
चित्राललाट	CV	5
चित्रासु कुरु	XI	57
चित्रास्थे	X	10
चित्रोऽप्यवापि	III	22
चिदिति शब्दः	LXXXVIII	14
चिपिटग्रीवो	LXVIII	31
चिरिल्विरि	LXXXVIII	38
चिह्नंगवा	CVII	8
चिह्नं दर्दुर	LIV	64
चिह्नं ध्वजो	LXXXVI	78
चिह्नमपि	LIV	7
चूर्णीकृतैर्माष	LV	25
चैत्ये भयं	LIII	90
चैत्रसितपक्ष	XXI	12
चैत्रस्य बहुल	CV	6
चैत्रे मन्दा	VIII	8
चैत्र्यां तु	V	74
चौरकवर्णश्चौरा	XCV	7
छ		
छत्रचिति	XCVII	11
छत्रध्वजस्वस्ति	LXXI	13
छत्रध्वजादर्श	XLIII	57
छत्रभङ्ग	XLIII	63
छत्रस्रगम्बर	LIII	113
छागशुभा	LXV	1
छायाः क्रमेण	LXVIII	94
छाया शुभाशुभ	LXVIII	89
छिक्करः कूट	LXXXVI	44
छित्वाग्रे चतु	XLIII	21
छिन्द्यात्प्रभात	XLIII	19
छिन्द्याद्यदि न	LIII	87
छिन्नभिन्न	LI	3
छिन्नाग्रेऽङ्क	XCV	38
छिन्नानुरूप	LXVIII	61
छेदो यद्यवि	LIII	122
ज		
जगति प्रसारित	II	20
जङ्घाग्रे परिणाह	LVIII	21

	Ch.	V.
जङ्घामध्ये	L	15
जनयति च	CIV	27
जनयति शुक्रः	CIV	35
जन्मन्यायास	CIV	5
जम्बूभिस्तिल	XXIX	4
जम्बूवृक्षस्य	LIV	9
जम्बूवेतस	LV	10
जम्बूस्त्रिवृता	LIV	87
जम्ब्वाश्चोद	LIV	8
जयति जगतः	I	1
जये धरित्र्याः	LXXIV	1
जलकेतुरपि	XI	46
जलपरिहीने	LIV	47
जलपरिहीने	LIV	21
जलमध्ये	XXXV	5
जलमांसा	XLVI	19
जलमृत्युरेक	LXVIII	9
जवजाति	LXXXVI	19
जातानि कुत्र	XIX	21
जातीफलपत्री	LXXVII	33
जातीफलमृग	LXXVII	27
जात्यं मनोभव	LXXV	1
जामयो यानि	LXXIV	10
जामित्रकेन्द्र	XL	10
जाया वा स्या	LXXIV	11
जारद्गव्यां	IX	3
जालगवाक्ष	LVI	22
जालश्वचरणौ	LXXXVI	46
जालान्तरगे	LVIII	1
जाहकाहि	LXXXVI	42
जिह्वा ग्रीवा	LI	9
जिह्वा रक्ता	LXVIII	53
जिह्वोपलेढि	V	45
जीमूतध्वनि	LXXVI	59
जीवितराज्य	XLIV	7
जीवे जन्म	CIV	25
जीवेन भवति	LXIX	2
जीवे शुक्राभि	XVII	18
ज्ञेयो विशाल	IV	20
ज्येष्ठाद्यं	IX	18

	Ch.	V.
ज्येष्ठासु न	CI	10
ज्येष्ठासु नृप	X	13
ज्येष्ठे जाति	VIII	10
ज्येष्ठे नरेन्द्र	V	76
ज्यैष्ठसिते	XXII	1
ज्यैष्ठ्यां सम	XXIII	1
ज्योतिःशास्त्रमनेक	I	9
ज्योतिःशास्त्रसमुद्रं	CVI	1
ज्योतिष्मतीं	XLVIII	39
ज्योतिष्मत्यः	LXXXI	5
ज्यौतिषमागम	IX	7
ज्वालाधूम	XLVI	49
त		
तं विष्णुतेजो	XLIII	6
तक्रकाञ्जिक	LIV	114
तक्षकवासुकि	LXXXI	25
तक्षशिलामार्त्तिका	XVI	26
तड्डिद्दमक	XXIV	17
ततो वृषस्य	XLVIII	44
तत्पञ्चमदिशां	LXXXVI	13
तत्परः सकल	VIII	47
तत्र गुणाः	II	3
तत्र ग्रहगणिते	II	4
तत्र देवमुनि	LXXIV	19
तत्र पताकाः	XLIII	27
तत्र षडश्रिर्मे	LVI	20
तत्र सांवत्सरो	II	2
तत्रार्द्धमासाः	XXIV	10
तत्रैव स्वात्याद्ये	XXII	2
तत्सम्पाता	LIII	64
तथैव फाल्गुने	XXV	6
तदनन्तरदिशि	LXXXVII	2
तदनन्तरदिशि नाशः	LXXXVII	30
तदनन्तरे	LXXXVII	36
तदलमति	I	8
तदुपहत	XV	32
तद्धातुमहा	LXIX	4
तनुभूस्पृग्वा	LXI	12
तनूरस्कशिरो	LXXXVI	9
तन्त्रे सुपरि	II	16

	Ch.	V.
तन्मित्रपूजा	LXXXVIII	6
तमोऽधिको	LXIX	9
तरवो वर्ज	LIX	4
तरुणतरु	XLVIII	5
तरुताली	LXXXVI	76
तरुशिखरो	XXVIII	8
तल्लक्षणानि	XXI	2
तल्लक्षणोऽस्थि	XI	30
तस्करविलुप्त	III	14
तस्माद्द्वितायो	VIII	29
तस्माद्राज्ञाधि	II	28
तस्मिन् काले	V	15
तस्मिन्निधि	XIV	12
तस्मिन्मण्डल	XLVIII	24
तस्मिन्सन्ध्या	XLVII	22
तस्य विधानं	XLIII	12
तस्याः कोणेषु	XLVIII	37
तस्याः सगद्गद	XXXII	5
तस्यैव पश्चिमा	LIV	25
ताडयेद्यदि	XXIV	34
तानवलोक्य	XXIV	3
तानि दृष्ट्वा च	LXXXVI	4
तान्यशुचि	LIII	58
तापसे शौण्डि	LI	22
तामसकीलक	III	7
ताम्रः कपिलो	III	23
ताम्रा बलपति	XXX	13
ताम्रैः समेता	LIV	109
ताम्रोष्ठतालु	LXVII	6
तारणं तदनु	VIII	36
ताराग्रह	XXIV	18
ताराग्रहैर्बल	LXIX	1
तारा फल	XXXIII	3
तारापुञ्ज	XI	25
ताराहस्तं	XXXIII	7
तारोल्कापात	XLVI	86
तारोल्कापाता	XXXII	13
तालभूर्जपट	LI	14
तालीपत्रलता	XXVII	3
ताल्वोष्ठदन्त	LXVII	97

	Ch.	V.
तावेव तु यथा	LXXXVI	52
तिथिवाय्वर्क	LXXXVI	58
तिन्तिडीत्यपि	LV	21
तिमिसिताम्बु	XII	6
तिलकाम्रातक	LIV	50
तिलाश्वगन्धा	LXXVI	9
तिस्रस्तिस्रस्तासां	IX	4
तिस्रो रेखाः शत	LXVIII	75
तिस्रो रेखामणि	LXVIII	44
तीक्ष्णं तपत्यदि	XIX	2
तीक्ष्णः प्रकोपः	LXVIII	113
तीव्रदिवाकर	XXI	24
तुम्बवनकार्म	XIV	15
तुरगकरि	XXXIX	5
तुरगतुरगोप	X	3
तुलाधरेऽवन्त्य	V	40
तुल्यैः पत्र	LXXVII	7
तुषसदृशनखाः	LXVIII	41
तृणैरिवाग्नि	LXXV	10
तृतीयगस्त्वौर	CIV	12
ते ग्राम्यसत्त्वै	XCI	2
तै चार्कमण्डल	III	8
तेजो न तद्वत्	LXXV	7
ते रक्तनील	XXXIV	2
तेषां किल जाय	LXXXI	21
तेषां प्रपाण	LXVI	4
तेषामुदये	III	9
तैः संस्तुतः	XLIII	5
तोयं शृतं	LIV	113
तोयानि पद्म	XIX	5
तोयैस्त्वामभि	XLVIII	70
तौलिनि चित्रा	CII	4
तौलिनि तान्तव	XLII	8
त्यजतोऽर्कतलं	IV	3
त्यागो विवास	XLVI	58
त्रयोऽपि योगाः	XXVI	12
त्रस्यन्नेष्टो	XLIV	18
त्रिचतुर्थसप्त	XXXII	32
त्रित्रिद्विद्वि	LIII	19
त्रिदशगुरुः	CIV	29

	Ch.	V.
त्रिपञ्चसप्त	LVI	14
त्रिभिरेव धूम	XCVII	3
त्रिशत्त्र्यधिका	XI	22
त्रिशत्सप्तति	LXXXI	15
त्रिशद्धस्तायामो	LVI	21
त्रिविधस्तस्यो	XLVIII	47
त्रिषु मेषादिषु	XL	13
त्रिषु विपुलो	LXVIII	84
त्रिष्वाद्यवर्षे	VIII	32
त्रीण्युत्तराणि	XCVIII	6
त्रैगर्तपौरवा	XVI	22
त्वक्कुष्ठरेणु	LXXVII	5
त्वक् शुक्रसारः	LXIX	14
त्वगुशीरपत्र	LXXVII	12
त्वाष्ट्रे भूषणमणि	XV	12
त्वाष्ट्रे युगे सर्व	VIII	37
द		
दंष्ट्रामूले	LXXXI	23
दक्षिणकुक्षि	V	84
दक्षिणतो	VI	10
दक्षिणदिक्	XVII	9
दक्षिणपार्श्वेन	IV	6
दक्षिणपार्श्वे पुरु	LXXVIII	24
दक्षिणपार्श्वे मण्ड	LXV	2
दक्षिणभुजेन	LIII	67
दक्षिणविरुतं	XCV	29
दक्षिणविषाण	IV	10
दक्षिणां ककु	XLVII	8
दण्डवधो	LIII	41
दण्डार्घं	LXXIII	3
दण्डी यमो	LVIII	57
दण्डे नरेन्द्र	III	17
दत्वाऽभयं	XLVIII	81
दद्याद्व्रते	CV	7
दधिकुमुद	IX	45
दधितण्डुल	LXXXVII	14
दधिसदृशाग्रो	XXX	18
दन्तभङ्गफल	XCIV	9
दन्तस्य मूल	LXXIX	20;
	XCIV	1

	Ch.	V.
दन्तैर्नागा	XXVI	8
दम्पत्योर्द्वि	C	8
दम्पत्योर्व्युत्क्रमे	LXXIV	12
दर्पण इवैक	V	50
दर्पणवृत्ताकारा	XI	13
दर्शनमस्तमयो	XI	2
दशग्रैवं	LXXXVI	16
दशमगृहगते	CIV	17
दशरथतनयो	LVIII	30
दशसप्तचतु	LXI	3
दाक्षिण्यमेकं	LXXV	5
दाक्षिण्ययुक्त	LXX	7
दान्तः सुखी	CI	4
दारुणनाद	XCV	17
दाहो दिशां	XXXI	1
दिक्पतिसंज्ञा	LIV	4
दिग्देशचेष्टा	XCVI	1
दिङ्मण्डले	LXXXVIII	47
दिनकरकराभि	III	36
दिनकरमुनि	CVI	6
दिनकररथ	XII	7
दिनकरादीनां	II	23
दिनचतुष्टय	XLIII	67
दिनान्तसन्ध्या	LXXXVIII	40
दिवसकर	III	33
दिवसकृतः	III	37;
	XXXVII	3
दिवा प्रस्थान	LXXXVI	48
दिवि भाति	XLVII	11
दिवि भुक्तशुभ	XXXIII	1
दिव्यं ग्रहर्क्ष	XLVI	4
दिव्यमपिशम	XLVI	6
दिव्यस्त्रीभूत	XLVI	90
दिव्यान्तरिक्षा	XLVII	1
दिव्यो धन्वन	LXXXVIII	9
दिशि पश्चिमो	XIV	22
दिशि याम्यायां	LX	1
दिशि शान्तायां	LIII	109
दिशो धूमा	XLVI	93
दीपः संहत	LXXXIV	2

	Ch.	V.
दीप्तमृगविहृ	XXXIV	8
दीप्तमृगाण्डज	XXX	5
दीप्तविहङ्ग	XXX	30
दीप्तोद्विग्नो	XCV	18
दीप्तौजसः प्रच	XXXII	15
दीर्घग्रीवाक्षि	LXVI	1
दीर्घाङ्गुलिरक्त	LXVII	8
दीर्घासंसक्ता	LXIII	69
दीर्घोऽङ्गुलानां	LXIX	28
दुःखशत्रुनिच	LII	5
दुःस्वप्नदुर्वि	II	39
दुर्जनहुताश	CVI	4
दुर्बलिको भाण्डी	LXXXVIII	7
दुर्बलै रपि	LXXXVIII	28
दुर्भिक्षमना	XLVI	38
दुष्टवाक्य	CIV	19
दुष्टस्वभावाः	LXXVIII	16
दूरगो निकट	XXIV	28
दूरस्थचिह्न	III	3
दूर्वाकाण्ड	V	58
दूर्वाकुशकुसु	XXIX	13
दृश्यते न यदि	XXIV	36
दृश्यन्ते च यत	III	20
दृश्योऽमावास्या	XI	31
दृष्टे श्रुतेऽप्य	LI	35
दृष्टेषु यातुधा	XLVI	80
दृष्टोऽनस्तमिते	IX	23
दृष्ट्वार्कमेक	XCV	31
देवकुमार	XLVI	13
देवपत्न्यश्च या	XLVIII	58
देवागारद्वार	LVIII	3
देवानुवाच	XLIII	2
देवैश्चमर्यः	LXXII	1
देशानुरूप	LVIII	29
दैन्यं व्याधि	CIV	9
दैवज्ञेन शुभा	LI	1
दैवतयात्रा	XLVI	9
दैवविदवहित	XXI	3
द्युतिमान्वर्णे	LXVIII	102
द्रविडविदेहा	XVI	11

	Ch.	V.
द्रव्यचतुष्टय	LXXVII	19
द्रुमेभ्योऽन्नरस	XLVI	85
द्रोणः पञ्च	XXI	32
द्वन्द्वरोगा	LXXXVI	25
द्वात्रिंशतानु	LXXXI	33
द्वात्रिंशत्परि	LVIII	14
द्वात्रिंशत्प्रवि	LXXXVII	18
द्वात्रिंशत्प्रविभक्ते	XCV	49
द्वादशदशमै	VI	2
द्वादशदीर्घो	LVIII	18
द्वादश्यामष्टम्यां	XLIV	2
द्वारं च नैर्वा	LIV	120
द्वारं द्वारस्यो	LIII	80
द्वारमानाष्ट	LVI	16
द्वारालिन्दो	LIII	33
द्वारि पुरस्य	XXXIII	22
द्वारे शिरो	LXXXIX	8
द्वारैर्युतश्चतु	LVI	27
द्वावपि मयूख	XVII	11
द्विजनृपतीनुद	V	32
द्विजो यथालाभ	XII	19
द्वित्रिचतुर्घा	LXVIII	11
द्वित्रिचतुश्शाव	XCV	6
द्वित्रीन्द्रियाष्ट	LXXVII	23
द्विपभुजग	LXXXI	1
द्विपवृषभो	LX	9
द्विपहयवनि	LXXX	2
द्विभुजस्य तु	LVIII	35
द्विरदमही	XLIII	36
द्विविधं कथ	XCVI	2
द्वैपायनो यव	XLVIII	67
द्व्यक्षरं चर	XCVI	14
द्व्यङ्गुलतुल्यौ	LVIII	10
द्व्यङ्गुलमितो	LVIII	11
ध		
धनदः	XXXIV	3
धनसुत	CIV	24
धनहानिर्दा रु	LIII	60
धनाप्ति	LII	6
धनिनां क्षुतं	LXVIII	63
धनिनोऽग्र	LXVIII	62
धनुःस्थायी	XLVII	16
धन्विन्यमात्य	V	41
धर्मे स्थिता	CIII	9
धर्म्मं यशस्यं	LIV	1
धात्री घना	XLVIII	17
धात्रीफलानां	LXXVI	6
धान्यगोगुरु	LIII	124
धान्यपरिपूर्ण	LI	18
धान्यहिरण्य	XLVI	41
धारणवर्षण	CVII	4
धिष्ण्या कृशा	XXXIII	6
धीवरशाकुनि	LXXXVII	34
धूपाज्याहुति	XLVIII	32
धूमाकुलीकृता	XXXII	9
धूमाकुलो	LX	13
धूमाभेऽन्ना	VIII	18
धूमावृते	XLIII	65
धूमोऽग्नि	XLVI	21
ध्रुवकेतु	XI	41
ध्रुवनायको	XIII	2
ध्रुवमृदु	LV	31
ध्रुवसौम्येषु	XXXIII	19
ध्वजकुम्भ	XLIII	35
ध्वजचाप	III	32
ध्वजझष	XXXIII	10
ध्वजपरि	XLIII	50
ध्वजशस्त्र	XI	4
ध्वजातपत्र	XXX	27
ध्वनिरुच्चरितो	XIX	13
न		
न कथञ्चिदपि	V	16
नक्षत्रग्रह	XXXIII	17
नक्षत्रजमु	XCVIII	3
नक्षत्रत्रय	XIV	1
नक्षत्राणां तार	XLVII	10
नक्षत्राणि मुहू	XLVIII	59
नक्षत्रेण सहो	VIII	1
नखतगर	LXXVII	26
नगरचतु	XLVI	22

	Ch.	V.
नगरद्वार	II	35
नगरोत्तर	XLIV	3
न ग्राम्यवर्णै	LXXVIII	14
न ग्राम्योऽरण्य	LXXXVI	24
न तत्सहस्रं	II	38
न तथेच्छति	II	40
न तु भाद्रपदे	LXXXVI	27
नदति मही	LIV	54
न दिनत्रयं	LXXVIII	21
न नखदशन	LXXVIII	26
नन्दनोऽथ विज	VIII	38
नन्द्यावर्त	LIII	32
नपुंसकाख्यं	LI	10
न पृथक्फला	III	11
न प्रतिबद्धं	II	14
नभः प्रसन्नं	XXXI	5
नमते यत्र	LIV	93
न मित्रभावे	IX	39
नम्रायतः	XI	62
नरपतिकुमार	XVI	14
नरपतिदेश	XLVI	82
नरपतिपत्नी	XXXIV	21
नरपतिरिम	XII	18
नवकैकाष्ट	XCVII	14
नवगुणसूत्र	LIII	71
नवतिः सैव	LXXIX	9
नवमं नयने	LXX	26
नवमगृहगो	CIV	10
नवमे तु धर्मे	CIV	37
नवाम्बुसिक्ता	LXIX	16
न शतेनापि	LXXIV	14
नष्टचन्द्रार्क	XXVII	8
नष्टात्मजां	CIII	5
न सखीवदनं	CIV	28
न सांवत्सरपाठी	II	30
न स्नातमात्र	XCVIII	13
नाकारणं	L	6
नागगजैरा	IX	1
नागरकाणा	XXXIV	22
नागरकृषि	XVI	13
नागरनृपति	XXXVI	2
नागा तु पवन	IX	2
नाति द्रुतं न	XLIII	61
नातिव्यक्ताः	XI	20
नानाचोद्यप्रश्न	II	13
नानाविचित्रा	XII	12
नानाविधानि	LXXXVIII	35
नानाव्ययैर्द्वा	CIV	18
नाभिस्थे	LXXXVII	19
नाभीस्वरः	LXVIII	85
नामाङ्कितै	XXIV	26
नामानि चाग्न्य	XCVI	16
नार्यः परस्य	XLVI	54
नालेऽब्जयवा	XLVI	33
नासांवत्सरिके	II	29
नासापुटप्रोथ	XCIII	4
नासाललाट	LVIII	5
नासाललाटजंघो	LVIII	46
नासिक्य	XVI	12
नासौष्ठ	L	12
नास्ति लोके	XLVIII	84
निगदितमिदं	LI	29
निगदितरूपै	XXIV	20
निगदितसमये	XCVII	17
निगूढमणि	LXX	11
निचितं तु हंस	LXXIII	1
नित्यमधस्थस्ये	IV	1
निपतति रजनी	XXXVIII	7
निम्नललाटा	LXVIII	72
निर्घातः सुर	V	95
निर्दिशेति गदिते	LI	24
निर्मदाभ्यधिक	LXVII	9
निर्मांसजानु	LXVIII	6
निर्मांसैः कर्णैः	LXVIII	58
निर्मांसौ रोम	LXVIII	34
निशि सुरचापं	XXXV	8
निष्कुटमथ	LXXIX	32
निष्कुटसंज्ञे	LXXIX	36
निष्क्रम्य	XLVIII	18
निष्पत्तिर	XXVI	13

	Ch.	V.
निष्पन्नशाली	VIII	30
निष्पन्नसस्य	XCV	34
निष्पन्नो न च्छेद्यो	L	8
निस्वोऽति	LXVIII	17
निहन्ति शुक्रः	IX	41
नीचेऽरिभे	CIV	53
नीडे प्राक्शा	XCV	3
नीपेऽर्थाप्तिः	CXXXV	6
नीराजने निवृ	XIV	11
नीलोत्पलानि	XXXII	21
नीलो भुजगः	LIV	46
नृतुरगकरि	LXXXIX	1
नृपजयद	XLIII	20
नृपतिरतो	XLVIII	80
नृपतिरपि	XLV	14
नृपभयमत्य	LVIII	50
नृपविपत्ति	XXX	25
नृपसचिवा	LIII	8
नृपसन्दर्शने	LXXXVI	50
नृपसेनापति	LIII	14
नृपाज्ञया	XCVIII	14
नेच्छन्ति	XXVIII	9
नेत्रान्तपाद	LXVIII	87
नेत्रे यस्याः	LXX	19
नेमी भागं	LXXXVII	21
नैकवर्णमणि	XLIV	25
नैम्बं पत्रं	LIV	115
नैर्ऋतकोणे	LIV	98
नैर्ऋतवायव्य	V	86
नैर्ऋती वारुणी	LXXXVI	31
नैर्ऋत्यां दिशि	XIV	17
नैर्ऋत्यां दूताश्व	XCV	22
नैर्ऋत्यां स्त्री	LXXXVII	8
नैव दारुणता	XC	7
नैषामर्घः	LXXXI	22
नोत्पातपरि	VII	1
नो सज्जते	LXX	8
न्यग्रोधपला	LIV	96
न्यग्रोधमधुक	LI	17
न्यग्रोधेन तु	XXXIX	3

	Ch.	V.
प		
पक्षाद्भानोः	XCVII	1
पक्षैश्चतुर्भि	XXXII	30
पक्षौ धुन्वन्न	XLV	10
पङ्क्ते स्वाद्वन्ना	XLV	7
पञ्चग्रहसं	V	17
पञ्चत्रिंशं	LXXXI	11
पञ्चदशाजे	XXIII	9
पञ्चनदरमठ	XIV	21
पञ्चनिमित्तैः	XXI	31
पञ्चभिरायुः	LXVIII	77
पञ्चमं लघु	CIV	57
पञ्चवनस्पति	LXXIV	39
पञ्चशिखो	XLIX	5
पञ्चाङ्गुलानि	LVIII	27
पञ्चापरे	LXIX	31
पञ्चोन्नतिः	LXVII	4
पट्टः शुभदो	XLIX	2
पत्राधिकं	LXXVII	37
पथ्यात्मानं	LXXXVI	11
पदहस्त	LIII	65
पद्मदलाभैः	LXVIII	64
पद्माङ्कितकर	LVIII	44
पनसाशोक	LV	4
परतो न विशेष	L	20
परतोऽपि	LXXXVII	11
परतो वित्त	LXXXVII	38
परदारविवाद	XVI	39
परमाणुर	LVIII	2
परमान्नमोद	LIX	8
परयोनावभि	XLVI	56
परयोनिषु	LXXXVI	66
पराशरः प्राह	LXI	1
परिघ इति	XLVII	19
परिणतदाडिम	LXXXI	8
परिघाविनि	VIII	46
परिभवो घ्नन	CIV	20
परिमण्डलैर्गवा	XLVIII	79
परिमण्डलो	LXVIII	21
परिवेषमण्ड	XXXIV	12

	Ch.	V.		Ch.	V.
परिवेषो रुक्	V	94	पार्श्वायता	LXVIII	23
परिशुष्क	LXVIII	14	पाली प्रागपरा	LIV	118
पर्जन्याद्या	LIII	52	पाशेऽथवा	LXXXIX	25;
पर्यन्तात्पर्यन्तं	LVIII	12		XCVI	6
पर्यन्तेषु गृहीत्वा	V	47	पिक्कापिच्चा	LXXXI	17
पर्यन्तेषु विमलता	V	90	पिचुमन्द	XXIX	12
पर्यन्तेषु सुधा	XXVIII	15	पिण्डमभि	XLIV	19
पर्यन्तेष्वति	V	52	पितरोऽमावा	XCIX	2
पर्वद्वयमङ्गुष्ठः	LVIII	28	पितृपूजा	VIII	6
पलदशभागो	LXXXI	13	पितृवन	LIX	2
पलालधूम	XXX	28	पितृवित्तेन	LXVIII	39
पवनः पवना	XXXIX	1	पित्र्यमैत्र	XLVII	18
पवनघनवृष्टि	XXI	22	पित्र्याद्येऽष्ट	IX	15
पवनसलिल	XXI	37	पित्र्यान्मासः	XCVII	15
पशुहस्ति	LI	19	पित्र्ये धनधा	XV	8
पश्चाच्छिरः	LXXVII	4	पिप्पलीमरिच	LI	15
पश्चात्तु शूद्राः	XXXI	4	पीडयन्ति	XLVII	6
पश्चात्सन्ध्या	XI	51	पीडाः स्युः	CIV	6
पश्चादुदुम्बर	LIV	11	पीडाकरं	V	73
पश्चिमे शर्वं	LXXXVI	49	पीडाकरमति	LIII	81
पश्यन्ग्रस्तं	V	60	पीतो व्याधि	XXXVII	2
पश्वाश्रमिणा	LIII	16	पीनोन्नत	LXXXVI	8
पांशुविलो	V	59	पीलुसमेता	LIV	75
पाको नक्षत्र	LVII	12	पीलोरेव	LIV	65
पाखण्डानां	XLVI	76	पुण्यस्नानौ	LXXVIII	22
पाञ्चालकलिङ्ग	V	35	पुण्याहशंख	XLVIII	73
पातालादूर्ध्वं	LIV	5	पुण्येष्वायतनेषु	XLVIII	15
पादत्र्यंशा	LXXX	13	पुंराशि	XCVI	9
पादाः पञ्चन	LXII	1	पुंस्कोकिल	CV	11
पादाङ्गुष्ठेन	LI	13	पुंस्त्रीनपुं	LI	36
पादे पादे पञ्च	LXII	2	पुत्रमरणं	L	16
पादौ जिघ्रेद्या	LXXXIX	12	पुरपक्षिणो	XLVI	66
पादौ मूलं	CV	1	पुरभवन	LIII	84
पादौ सगुल्फौ	LXX	24	पुरादुदग्यत्	XXIV	6
पापाख्या	VII	12	पुरुषलक्षण	LXIX	40
पापैरुपचय	LX	21	पुरुषश्चटुला	LXXIV	16
पायसेन	XLVI	32	पुरुषार्घे	LIV	30
पारावतक्षौद्र	LIV	108	पुरुषे तु	LIV	32
पार्थिवस्त्वां	XLIII	18	पुरुहूतानल	LIV	3
पार्श्वद्वया	XII	9	पुरोहितो	XLVIII	25

	Ch.	V.		Ch.	V.
पुलहः	XIII	6	पेपीयते	XIX	18
पुष्यस्नानं	XLVIII	3	पौरः पौर	XX	7
पुष्यस्नानविमि	XLVIII	38	पौरन्दरेऽति	XV	16
पुष्याग्नेय	XXXII	12	पौरमहाघन	XVI	24
पुष्ये यवगो	XV	6	पौरेतरघ्न	XXXIII	13
पूजा तस्य	XLIII	11	पौरे पौरेण	XVII	8
पूजितवृक्षे	XLVI	29	पौषाषाढ	VII	17
पूर्णपात्र	XCIII	8	पौषे द्विज	V	71
पूर्णाननः	LXXXVIII	23	पौषे समार्ग	XXI	19
पूर्णाननेऽर्थ	XCV	13	पौष्णाप्यार्द्रा	XXXII	20
पूर्वं चरति	XLVI	98	पौष्णे सलिल	XV	25
पूर्वं पूर्वसमुद्र	XXVII	1	प्रकाश्य	LXXXIX	17
पूर्वं प्रावेशिको	LXXXVI	55	प्रकृत्यापि लघु	CIV	58
पूर्वच्छिन्नं	LXXIX	6	प्रचलत्तिमि	XII	5
पूर्वशिरस्कां	LX	10	प्रचोदयाम्यहं	LXXXVIII	44
पूर्वाचार्य	CVI	2	प्रजापति	XLVIII	68
पूर्वात्रयं	XV	28	प्रतिदिनमर्कं	XXXIV	9
पूर्वादृक्ष	VII	7	प्रतिदिवसमहिम	III	34
पूर्वापरे	LIII	40	प्रतिदिवसमेव	IV	4
पूर्वापरौ प्रीति	VIII	42	प्रतिवाश्य	XCV	30
पूर्वाभिमुखः	XLIV	13	प्रतिषिद्धवृक्ष	LXXIX	5
पूर्वेण पूर्वेण	LXXVII	22	प्रतिसरया	XLIV	5
पूर्वेण पूर्वोत्तर	LIX	13	प्रतिसूर्यकः	XXXVII	1
पूर्वेण प्रग्रहणं	V	87	प्रत्यन्तान्	IV	21
पूर्वेण यदि	LIV	16	प्रत्यर्कसंज्ञः	XXX	33
पूर्वेण सलिल	V	34	प्रत्येकग्रह	II	11
पूर्वे भागे चित्राः	LX	2	प्रथमगृहो	CIV	32
पूर्वे भागे भगवान्	XIII	5	प्रथममुनि	I	2
पूर्वोत्तरदिङ्	LIII	51	प्रथमे पुरुषे	LIV	28
पूर्वोत्तरेण	LIV	63	प्रथमे पुरुषे	LIV	66
पूर्वोत्तरेण वामो	V	83	प्रथमे रविजे	CIV	39
पूर्वोदीच्योः	XC	3	प्रथितनरे	XXXII	28
पूर्वोद्भूताः	XXI	13	प्रद्वेषो यव	XCIII	5
पूर्वोद्भूतैः	XXIV	23	प्रपूरणे चो	XLIII	56
पूषा वितथ	LIII	44	प्रब्रूत सत्यं	LXXIV	6
पृच्छा वृद्ध	LI	20	प्रभूतवस्त्र	LXXI	1
पृच्छासु रूप्य	LXXXVI	80	प्रमथाधिपो	LVIII	58
पृथग्जात्य	LXXXVI	7	प्रमदागर्भ	LXXXVII	32
पृथुबहुल	XXI	15	प्रमदाशिर	XCV	44
पृष्ठं विद्धि	CV	3	प्रलम्बबाहुः	CV	9

	Ch.	V.
प्रविरलतनु	LXVIII	4
प्रविलम्बिनि	LXX	20
प्रविशति यदि	XXVIII	23
प्रविशद्भिः	XCV	46
प्रवेशनं	XCIV	14
प्रव्रजित	LI	5
प्रश्नप्रति	I	11
प्रसवः शुना	XCVII	8
प्रसवविकारे	XLVI	52
प्रस्फुरत्तिमि	XII	4
प्रहरणसदृशेषु	LXXIX	22;
	XCIV	3
प्रहरणसदृशै	III	35
प्रहरहर	XLVI	77
प्राकृतगत्या	VII	14
प्राकृतविमिश्र	VII	8
प्राकृतसंज्ञा	VII	9
प्राक्क्षत्रियाणां	XXXI	3
प्राक्पश्चिमाव	LIII	35
प्राक्प्रग्रहणं	V	88
प्राक्फल्गुनी	XV	9
प्रागर्धरात्र	XI	37
प्रागुत्तरैशाः	LI	6
प्रागुत्तरोन्नते	LIII	115
प्राग्द्वारेषु	XLVII	13
प्राग्भवति	LIII	117
प्राग्वैश्वानर	XI	32
प्राङ्नर्मदा	XVI	1
प्राची तत्क्षण	XXX	31
प्राच्यां चेद्	XLVII	7
प्राच्यादिस्थे	LIII	119
प्राच्यानां दक्षि	XCV	1
प्राजापत्ये शकटे	IX	25
प्राजापत्ये श्रवणे	VI	11
प्राजेशमाषा	XXIV	4
प्राज्ञो वपुष्मान्	LXIX	15
प्रात्यन्तिको	LXIX	23
प्रान्तच्छाया	LV	1
प्राप्तेऽष्टमे	XLIV	8
प्रायेण गोचरो	CIV	2

	Ch.	V.
प्रायेण सूत्रेण	CIV	1
प्रायो ग्रहाणां	XXVIII	20
प्रारब्धमसु	CIV	59
प्रारभ्यमाणेषु	XCVI	11
प्रालेयकुन्द	IV	30
प्रावृट्काले	LXXXIX	7
प्रावृषि शीत	XXVIII	19
प्रासादभवन	XLVI	20
प्रासादलक्षण	LVI	31
प्रासादहर्म्यं	LVII	4
प्राहुः स्थपतय	LVI	30
प्रियभूषणः	CI	1
प्रीतैः कृतानि	XLIII	41
प्रीतो महेन	XLIII	9
प्रेतप्रहरण	XXXIII	9
प्रोक्तस्थाना	IV	16
प्रोक्तस्यैवा	LXXXVII	41
प्रोत्प्लुहंस	XLVIII	9
प्रोत्फुल्लकमल	XLVIII	10
प्लक्षाश्वत्थो	LX	8
फ		
फणिनोऽभि	LXXXVIII	19
फलकुसुम	LIV	56
फलकुसुम	XXIX	1
फलदधि	XLIII	60
फलनाशे	LV	16
फलमास	XC	10
फाल्गुनमासे	XXI	21
फाल्गुनवर्षे	VIII	11
फाल्गुनशुक्ल	XXI	17
फुल्लतीर	LVI	7
फेणगिरि	XIV	18
फेण्टकस्य	LXXXVIII	31
ब		
बदरीरोहि	LIV	72
बन्धं व्याधि	CIV	30
बन्धः सूकर	XCV	47
बन्धघात	LXXXVI	67
बन्धुजीव	LXX	6
बन्धूकपुष्पा	XXX	15

	Ch.	V.
बर्हिपुच्छ	XXXIII	26
बलदेवपट्टनं	XIV	16
बलदेवो हलं	LVIII	36
बवबालव	C	1
बहिर्लोम्ना	LXXIV	13
बहुभुक्पर	CI	2
बहुभृत्यधनो	CI	6
बहुमूल	LXVIII	82
बहुलास्थे	X	4
बहुविहगा	XLIII	14
बहुसंस्थानाः	LXXXI	3
बान्धनशा	XVI	33
बाह्या द्विपदा	LIII	50
बिभ्राणः स्वकर	VIII	47
बिल्वोदुम्बर	LIV	18
बुद्ध्वा देव	XLVI	15
बृहस्पतेरुत्तर	XVIII	4
बृहस्पतौ	IX	42
ब्रह्मणो दुहिता	XXVI	5
ब्रह्मपुरदार्व	XIV	30
ब्रह्मसुत एक	XI	15
ब्रह्मा कमण्डलु	LVIII	41
ब्रह्माणमूचु	XLIII	1
ब्राह्मणाः पाद	LXXIV	8
ब्राह्मणान् पर	XLVI	65
ब्राह्मीं क्षेमा	XLVIII	41
ब्राह्मे द्विजपशु	V	20
ब्रूयादर्घ	XLII	2
भ		
भक्ष्यपान	XCIII	9
भक्ष्यैरन्नैश्च	XLVIII	28
भक्ष्यैर्नाना	LIII	99
भगवति जल	XLIV	1
भगवन्नाम	XXXII	4
भङ्क्त्वा काण्डं	LXXV	2
भचतुष्टय	IX	12
भद्रपदाद्वय	XXI	28
भद्रपदासु भयं	LXXI	7

	Ch.	V.
भद्रस्य वर्णो	LXVII	5
भद्रारिमेद	XIV	2
भद्रासन	XLVIII	46
भयं च शय्या	LXXXIX	20
भरणीपूर्वं	IX	10
भवकेतुरेक	XI	47
भवति धरणिजे	CIV	13
भषकूटपूरि	LXXXVIII	4
भस्मनिभः	IV	29
भस्माङ्गारा	XLVIII	16
भस्मास्थि	XCV	12
भागैश्चतुर्भिः	LXXVII	11
भाग्यादित्य	XXXIII	18
भाग्यार्यमो	VI	6
भाग्ये युगे	VIII	50
भाग्ये रस	X	8
भाग्ये शबर	IX	29
भाद्रपदशुक्ल	XLIII	23
भाद्रपदे वल्ली	VIII	13
भानां यथा	XVIII	1
भानोरलिप्त	XL	2
भानोरुदये	XLVII	26
भानोर्वर्त्म	XII	1
भारद्वाजम	LXXXVI	2
भारवहतक्ष	LXXXVII	24
भारार्धतनुः	LXVIII	106
भार्गवस्य	XVIII	5
भार्ङ्गी त्रिवृता	LIV	48
भिक्षुणिका	LXXVIII	9
भित्वा मघां	VI	9
भिन्दन्गतो	IX	24
भिन्नः सितेन	IV	22
भिन्नभैरव	LXXXVI	36
भीता रुवन्ति	LXXXVIII	34
भीरुक्षुधालु	LXVIII	114
भुक्त्वा सम्यग्	LXIX	19
भुजङ्गमे	LXXI	3

	Ch.	V.
भुनक्ति हंसः	LXIX	26
भूकम्पोल्का	CVII	5
भूच्छायां स्वप्न	V	8
भूजलशिक्य	LXVIII	108
भूतशतपक्ष	XCVIII	2
भूपा न सम्यग्	XIX	9
भूभगणभ्रम	II	12
भूमयो ब्राह्मणा	LVI	9
भूमिः कदम्बक	LIV	78
भूमिकाङ्कलमा	LVI	29
भूयो वराह	XLVII	2
भूरिपुष्पविक	LIII	125
भूस्पृग्वालधि	LXI	18
भृगुःसनत्कुमा	XLVIII	64
भृगुतनये	V	67
भृगुसुतदिवसे	CIV	63
भृङ्गारासन	LXX	10
भृशमवनामिता	LI	28
भेदं यदा	LIV	112
भेदे वृष्टि	XVII	4
भे भेति शिवा	XC	13
भेषजभिषक्	XVI	5
भैरवमुर्ध्वा	XXX	3
भोक्तुं नवाम्बर	LXXI	8
भोगी त्वनिम्न	LXVIII	60
भौमं चरस्थिर	XLVI	5
भौमास्तस्त्वं	LXIX	5
भौमान्तरिक्षं	XLVIII	53
भौमे कुमार	XXXIV	13
भौमेन हते जीवे	XVII	19
भौमेन हते शशिजे	XVII	13
भ्रमरशिखि	LXXXII	5
भ्रूलग्नाभि	LXVIII	78
म		
मकरध्वज	LXVIII	48
मकरे तरुगुल्मा	XLI	7
मगधान्मधुरां	IV	26
मञ्जिष्ठाभं वरुणः	XLIII	44
मञ्जिष्ठाभे भेको	LIII	123
मञ्जिष्ठाया	LXXVII	6
मणिबन्धनै	LXVIII	38
मणिभिश्च	LXVIII	13
मण्डपमध्ये	LX	7
मण्डलकल	LXIX	37
मण्डलपश्चिम	XLVIII	34
मत्स्याङ्कुशा	LXX	2
मथुरायाः	XVI	17
मदिरागन्धे	LXVIII	16
मद्ये वाहन	XLVI	27
मधुगन्धे	LXVIII	15
मधुपर्केण	XLVI	16
मधुररसकुसुम	XVI	7
मध्यं स्त्रिया	LXX	5
मध्यतनुर्वज्रा	IV	19
मध्याङ्गुलि	LXX	12
मध्याह्ने नर	V	30
मध्ये कृशः	LXIX	22
मध्ये तमः	V	51
मध्येन यदि	VI	8
मध्ये पापग्रह	XL	8
मध्ये ब्रह्मा	LIII	46
मध्ये यदि	V	89
मध्वा भवन्ताः	LXVII	1
मनुजानामप	XLVI	3
मन्त्राभिचार	LXIX	30
मन्त्रित्वं	LXVIII	67
मन्त्रिस्थावर	XXXIV	14
मन्त्रैराग्नेयैः	XLVI	24
मन्दपवना	XXX	7
मन्दरसंज्ञो	LXXXI	34
मन्दाकिनी	XVI	10
मन्युं हरेन्न	XXXII	6
मयूरशुक	XXVIII	14
मरणं तु सक्ष	LVIII	51
मरुदेशे भवति	LIV	62
मरुदेशे यच्चिह्नं	LIV	86
मर्त्यसत्त्व	LXVIII	112
मर्मण्यमर्मं	LIII	62
मलिनपरुष	LXVIII	93
महाशान्त्यो	XLVI	81

	Ch.	V.		Ch.	V.
महिषोष्ट्र	XLV	9	मुक्तारजत	XXI	23
महीस्वभाव:	LXVIII	109	मुक्ताशीत्या	LXXXI	16
महेन्द्रार्थमुवा	XLVIII	86	मुक्ते सप्ताहा	V	92
मांसलमृदु	LXVIII	26	मुखपुच्छ	V	3
मांससूकर	LV	20	मुख्यस्थाने	XLVIII	77
माक्षीकधातु	LXXVI	3	मुण्डा: सर्वे	LXV	4
माघसितोत्थ	XXI	10	मुदिता: प्रजा	XLIII	10
मांसानि यस्या	LXXVIII	18	मुनिविरचित	I	3
मांसौदन	XLVIII	30	मुनीनभिजितं	XLVII	12
माघे तु मातृ	V	72	मुहुर्मुहुर्मूत्र	XCIII	14
माघे प्रबलो	XXI	20	मुहूर्ततिथि	II	27
माञ्जिष्ठाभा :	XXX	14	मूर्तो करोति	CIII	1
माण्डव्यगिरं	CIV	3	मूर्धगलकेश	LI	34
मातरं जठरे	LI	26	मूलं मनुजाधि	XLVIII	1
मातृगण: कर्त्तव्य:	LVIII	56	मूलद्वारं	LIII	82
मातृभूघ्न	LXXII	5	मूलमध्यदश	XCIV	8
माथुरकोप	XIV	3	मूलमषाढा	CII	5
मायेन्द्रजाल	XIX	10	मूलशिवशक्र	XCVIII	7
मारुत्यां शस्त्रा	XCV	23	मूलेऽन्नमद्र	XI	59
मार्कण्डेयो	XLVIII	66	मूले भेषज	XV	17
मार्गतरुकोण	LIII	76	मृगघटसंस्थे	XLII	11
मार्गशिर:	XXI	6	मृगपक्षि	XLVI	72
मार्जाराक्षा:	LXI	6	मृगमासादि	XXI	30
मार्जारा भृश	XXVIII	5	मृगशकुनि	XXX	2
मालवान्सभ	LXIX	11	मृगशिरसि वत्स	X	5
मालव्यसेवी	LXIX	33	मृगशिरसि सुर	XV	3
मालव्यो नाग	LXIX	10	मृगशिरसोर्ध्वं	CII	2
माषकचतुष्टयं	LXXXII	9	मृगशीर्षाद्या: केश	CV	14
माषकचतुष्टय	LXXXI	9	मृगशीर्षाद्या गर्भा	XXI	9
माषकदल	LXXXI	10	मृगास्तु ह्रस्वोदर	LXVII	3
माषसूपसहि	LXXVI	8	मृगे तु मूषका	LXXI	2
मासत्रयेण	XLVI	57	मृतपुरुषा	XCV	39
मासनाम	CV	16	मृतविकल	XLV	13
माहिषगोमय	LV	30	मृदङ्गशंख	XLIV	23
मिथुनस्थे	XLII	4	मृदुवर्गो	XCVIII	10
मिथुने प्रवरा	V	37	मृदुसंहत	LXI	10
मिष्टमन्नमपि	LXXI	6	मृद्वी भू:	LV	2
मीने कपाल	XLI	8	मृन्नीलोत्पल	LIV	22
मुक्तप्राप्तौ	LXXXVI	12	मेकलकिरात	XVI	2
मुक्ताफलै	LXXIII	2	मेघा: स्निग्धा:	XXII	8

	Ch.	V.
मेघोद्भवं	LIV	125
मेरुप्रस्तम	XXVII	7
मेरुमन्दर	LVI	17
मेषोपगते	XLII	3
मैत्रे कुलूत	X	12
मैत्रे क्षत्र	IX	32
मैत्रे शौर्य	XV	15
मौनं गता	XC	12
म्लेच्छान्विदिक्	V	33
म्लेच्छा हि	II	32
य		
यः कूष्णाण्डः	LXV	7
यः केवलशि	LXXIX	12
यः पद्मकप	LXXIX	13
यः सर्वः श्री	LXXIX	11
यः सात्त्विक	LXIX	8
यः सार्वजन्यं	LXXV	8
यच्छक्रशुक्र	LXXXVI	1
यच्छब्द	LXXVIII	20
यत्कार्यं	XCIX	3
यत्कालयुक्तं	VIII	49
यत्र च येन	LIII	3
यत्र स्निग्धा	LIV	91
यत्रैते संहिता	II	22
यत्सत्यं सर्वं	XXVI	4
यथा त्वमूर्जे	XLIII	52
यदशुभमव	V	62
यदाग्नेयो	XXVII	2
यदा तु विष्णु	XXII	5
यदा रेणू	XXVII	5
यदा विशाखा	X	19
यदा स्थिता गृह	XXVIII	10
यथा स्थिता जीव	IX	38
यदि कण्टका	LIV	57
यदि कुमुद	IV	32
यदि ताः स्यु	XXII	3
यदि तित्तिर	XXVIII	17
यदि न रिपु	XVI	42
यदि भवति कर्णि	LIV	59
यदि भवति सप्त	LIV	29

	Ch.	V.
यदि मूर्त्तौ	V	4
यदि वाम	XCV	27
यदि वा सुव	LIV	70
यदि वेतसो	LIV	6
यदि शृंखलां	XCV	42
यद्द्रव्यमुप	XCV	15
यद्यद्गात्रं	LXVIII	83
यद्यद्येन विभू	XLIII	49
यद्यमलेऽर्के	XLVI	44
यद्यमोघकि	XXVIII	28
यद्यहिनिलयो	LIV	33
यद्यानीत	XLIV	17
यद्युदयर्क्षा	VI	1
यद्येकस्मिन्	V	26
यद्येको यदि	XI	6
यद्रोहिणी	XXV	1
यद्विस्तरेण	XLVII	28
यन्नक्षत्रमुप	XXI	7
यन्नोक्तमस्मिन्	LIX	14
यन्मात्रमास्यं	LXIX	28
यवग्रीवो यो वा	LXIII	2
यष्टि प्रवेश	XLIII	28
यष्ट्यातपत्रा	LXXII	4
यस्तं बिभर्त्ति	LXXXII	6
यस्तु सम्यग्	II	37
यस्मिन्काले	XXIX	14
यस्मिन् क्षेत्रो	LIV	61
यस्मिन्नुत्सरु	L	9
यस्मिन्नृक्षे	XX	4
यस्मिन्यस्मिन्	III	12
यस्मिन्स्वांशे	XX	3
यस्यान्दिशि दृश्य	XX	1
यस्यान्दिशि धूम	XXXVIII	2
यस्यामूष्मा	LIV	60
यस्याश्चिरं	XXXIII	24
याति चतुर्षु	XXXIV	17
यातूत्तरोष्ठेन	LXX	23
याते द्वितीये	LXXVII	3
यात्रा प्रसिद्धि	LXXII	6
यात्रायां तु	II	19

	Ch.	V.
यात्रायां मद	XLIV	14
यात्राविधाने	LI	7
यात्रासिद्धिः	LXXXVII	6
यादृशेन ग्रहेण	CIV	56
यानं वाह	XLVI	60
यानत्रेरुत्पाता	XLVI	1
यानासनशय्या	LXXXVIII	12
यानि च बुद्बुद	LXXX	16
यानीह भूतानि	LIX	11
यानीह वृक्षे	XLIII	17
यान्तु देवगणाः	XLVIII	79
या मौञ्जिकैः	LIV	103
याम्यां करोत्यवु	V	23
याम्यादिष्वशु	LIII	85
याम्याहीनं	LIII	38
याम्येन कपि	LIV	41
याम्येनाद्ये	LXXXVII	4
याम्ये शिक्ये	XXVI	7
याम्येऽष्टांशे	LXXVII	27
याम्येऽसृक्	XV	27
या रोमाञ्चं	XC	11
यावत एव मुहूर्तान्	XI	48
यावत एव मुहू	XI	52
यावन्त्यहानि	XI	7
यावन्नक्षत्र	CV	13
या व्याख्याता	XLVIII	2
या स्वप्नशीला	LXXVIII	17
या ह्रीत्यग्नि	XC	6
युक्तेन चूर्णेन	LXXVII	36
युगमेव याम्य	IV	13
युग्मासु किल	LXXVIII	23
युद्धं यथा	XVII	1
युद्धं समाग	XVII	12
युद्धानि विजा	XXXIV	16
युद्धाय टाकु	XCV	56
युवराजन्	LXXIII	4
युवराजस्या	XXXIV	20
ये च न दोषा	XLVI	83
ये च पिबन्ति	XVI	27
ये चोद्धरन्ति	LXI	9
यन चाम्बुहर	XII	3
येन धरित्री	XXIII	3
येन सत्येन	XXVI	3
येऽप्यङ्गनानां	LXXIV	5
ये प्रपाण	LXVI	3
ये येषां द्रव्या	XLI	1
ये शस्तास्तान्	XI	53
येषां रथौषार्णं	XLIII	34
येषामुदगच्छति	XVIII	7
ये षु च मेष्वभि	XXIII	5
योगान्तिकेति	VII	11
योगो यथा	XXIV	5
योऽस्तीव दीप्त्या	XXXI	2
यो देवः संस्था	LX	12
यो वा सितैक	LXI	19
यो विस्तारो	LVI	11
योऽसावसुरो	V	14
यौधेयान्सचि	IV	25
(र)		
रक्तं पीतं च	LXXX	11
रक्तं पीनक	LXIX	24
रक्तः श्यामो	XXXIV	23
रक्तपद्मारुणा	XLVI	87
रक्ताक्षमव्यं	VIII	51
रक्ताशोक	XLIII	42
रक्तेऽधिके	LXXVI	1
रक्तैः पुष्पैर्गन्धै	CIV	47
रक्तैराढ्या	LXVIII	10
रक्षःपिशाचगुह्य	XLVI	14
रक्षःपिशाचवा	XIII	11
रजकेन समा	LXXXVII	17
रजतमयी	LX	5
रजनीद्वयं	XXXVIII	6
रज्जूत्सङ्ग	XLIII	66
रज्ज्वस्थि	XCV	40
रतिरम्भसि	LXIX	25
रत्नानि बला	LXXX	3
रत्नानि विभूष	LXXIV	2
रत्नानि सर्वे	XLVIII	42
रत्नेन शुभेन	LXXX	1
रथ्याविद्धं	LIII	77

	Ch.	V.
रवावापदैन्यं	CIV	7
रविकिरण	XXX	16
रविचन्द्रपरी	XXII	7
रविजस्य	XVIII	6
रविजेन बुधे	XVII	17
रविजेन सिते	XVII	24
रविदीप्तो	LIII	106
रविभौमौ	CIV	49
रविरविसुतके	XXIII	10
रविरविसुतभो	XV	31
रविराक्रन्दो	XVII	6
रविवरुण	XLIV	6
राजा कुमारो	LXXXVI	34
	XC	4
राजोपकरण	III	18
राज्ञीविनाशं	XLIII	64
राज्ञीविहार	LXXVIII	11
रात्रौ कृत	LIII	121
राशेर्यस्य	XLI	11
राशेश्चतुर्दशा	XLI	9
राशौ राशौ	XLII	13
राष्ट्रविभेद	XLVI	26
राष्ट्रे यस्यान	XLVI	18
राष्ट्रोत्पातोप	XLVIII	83
राहुद्वयं यदि	V	7
राहुर्नभःस्थल	CIII	10
रिपुगदकोप	CIV	14
रिपुभयकल	CIV	15
रुग्राक्षसांशे	LXXI	11
रुधिरपताका	XLIII	25
रुतकीर्तन	LXXXVI	41
रुदितमदीन	LXVIII	73
रुद्धानि सौम्ये	VII	19
रुधिरनिभो	III	38
रुधिरादि	XXI	26
रुधिरानन	VI	4
रुवन्दिनेशा	LXXXIX	4
रूक्षः श्वेतो	III	25
रूक्षैरल्पै	XXIV	21
रूपायुध	XXXII	11

	Ch.	V.
रेखाः प्रदेशि	LXVIII	50
रेवत्यां राज	X	18
रोगाद्यायुं	LIII	63
रोगान् करोति	XII	20
रोध्रोशीर	LXXVII	29
रोमशकर्णा	LXVIII	59
रोमैकैकं	LXVIII	5
रोहिणीशकटमध्य	XXIV	30
रोहिणीशकटमर्कं	XLVII	14
रोहिण्यां	XV	2
रोहिण्युत्तर	C	7
रोहिण्योऽनल	VIII	19
रोहितमत्स्यो	LIV	15
रोहिताश्वाज	LXXXVI	26
रोहीतकस्य	LIV	68
रौद्रादीनि	VII	3
रौद्रे वध	XV	4
ल		
लक्षणयुक्तं	XLIV	15
लक्ष्मीःशिरीषे	LXXXV	4
लग्नेऽथवेन्दो	XCVI	8
लघुहस्ता	XCVIII	9
लब्धवराः	XLIII	3
लब्धिर्हानि	L	18
लब्धेन युक्तं	VIII	21
लम्बैर्वृषणै	LXI	16
ललाटस्पर्श	LI	30
लाक्षाकुन्दुरु	LVII	5
लाजाक्षतदधि	XLVIII	19
लाजाज्याक्षत	XLVIII	35
लाभहिबुका	XL	6
लाभे तृतीये च	C	6
लिङ्गं वा प्रतिमा	LIX	7
लिङ्गस्य वृत्त	LVIII	53
लिङ्गेऽल्पे धन	LXVIII	7
लिप्ते मषीगो	LXXI	10
लूतापटाङ्ग	XLVII	79
लोमाशिकापि	LXXXVIII	2
लोमाशिकायाः	XC	2
लौहित्यः सिन्धु	XVI	16

	Ch.	V.
लोहे पात्रे	LXXVII	2
व		
वक्ता सुखी	CI	14
वक्त्रं सौम्यं	LXVIII	54
वक्रशिखा	XI	12
वक्रा पादा	LIII	103
वक्रानुवक्रा	I	10
वक्षोऽथकक्षानख	LXVIII	86
वक्षोऽथकक्षावल	LXVII	2
वज्रं न किञ्चि	LXXX	17
वज्रपरीक्षा	CVII	10
वज्राकारा	LXVIII	45
वज्राशनि	XLVI	84
वज्रेन्द्रनील	LXXX	4
वञ्जुलकस्तं	LXXXVIII	11
वञ्जुलो नक्त	LV	11
वडवोष्ट्रकरेणु	L	24
वडवोष्ट्रमहिष	XLVI	53
वधबन्धो रिपु	LIII	75
वनं समाश्रिता	II	25
वनोपान्तनदी	LVI	8
वन्दिजनपौर	XLVIII	49
वन्ये सत्त्वे	XCI	3
वयांसि तेषां	XCVI	17
वरुणेशे	XV	22
वर्गैराग्नेया	XIV	32
वर्णकैर्विवि	XLVIII	27
वर्णन्यूनस्या	LXXXII	10
वर्णप्रसादं	LXXVII	34
वर्णेनं केन	XXXIV	7
वर्णः प्रशस्तै	LXV	11
वर्षत्यपि	XXVIII	24
वर्षाकाले	III	28
वर्षाणि कार्ति	VIII	2
वर्षाप्रश्ने	XXVIII	1
वर्षोपलव	LXXXI	24
वलिमध्यग	LXVIII	22
वल्मीकः स्निग्धो	LIV	37
वल्मीकत्रय	LIV	79
वल्मीकमूर्ध	LIV	77
वल्मीकसंवृतो	LIV	40
वल्मीकस्याण	XCIV	13
वल्मीकानां	LIV	95
वल्मीकेन परि	LIV	84
वल्मीकोप	LIV	14
वल्लीनां गगन	XXVIII	13
वल्लीलतागुल्म	LXXXV	1
वसुभे मानो	XV	21
वस्त्रस्य कोणे	LXXI	9
वस्त्राविक	XLI	2
वातोद्धतश्चरति	XIX	7
वातोद्धताम्बु	XIX	20
वानरभिक्षु	LXXXVII	9
वानरमहिष	LXVIII	104
वापितं करको	LV	28
वापीदेवकुला	LXVIII	49
वामं जिघ्रे ज्जानु	LXXXIX	11
वामः प्रतिलोम	XCV	28
वामदक्षिणगौ	LXXXVI	51
वामसव्यगतो	LXXXVI	72
वामस्तु कुक्षि	V	85
वामावर्त्तर्वामे	LXI	13
वामावर्त्तो	LXXXIV	1
वामेऽथाष्टभुजा	LVIII	39
वामेन हृश्चि	LIV	45
वामे वाशित्वा	XCV	26
वामैश्च पादै	XCIII	10
वायव्यं च यवो	LXXX	10
वायव्याच्च तृतीये	LXXXVII	13
वायव्ये फेनक	LXXXVII	12
वायव्ये भूकम्पे	XXXII	10
वायव्योश्वेषु	XLVI	64
वायव्योत्थै	XLVI	24
वायुग्रस्त	LXXXVII	37
वारुणपौरन्दर	XXXII	29
वारुणमबला	LXXX	9
वारुणमर्णव	XXXII	22
वारुणमवनी	V	22
वारुण्यामर्णव	LXXXVII	10
वार्ता जगत्यपि	XIX	11

	Ch.	V.		Ch.	V.
वाल्लभ्यमाया	LXXV	6	विबुधाग्नि	LIII	47
वासगृहाणि	LIII	70	विभीतको वा	LIV	102
वासराणि	LV	19	विमलकमणि	V	57
वास्तुज्ञान	LIII	1	वियति चरतां	XVII	2
वास्तुनि यो	LIII	11	विरक्तचेष्टा	LXXVIII	7
वाहनलाभो	XCV	48	विरसमुदकं	XXVIII	4
वाहनशस्त्रो	XCV	14	विलम्बिनो	XXX	29
वाहिनीं समु	XLVII	25	विविधैर्वियदु	XIX	15
विंशतिवर्षा	LXVIII	107	विश्वेश्वरे	XV	19
विंशत्याधिक	XI	23	विश्वेश्वरेऽर्क	X	15
विकचानाम	XI	19	विषघातकगो	LXXXVI	32
विकसित	XXIV	14	विषमं कृष्ण	LXXXI	6
विकृतकुसुमं	XLVI	36	विषमवलयो	LXVIII	25
विगतघने	XXIV	22	विषमैर्विषमा	LXVIII	40
विघ्नकरो नवमः	CIV	23	विषमैर्विषमो	LXVIII	30
विचरति	LXV	5	विष्णुः सुरेज्यो	VIII	23
विचरन् भद्रय	VIII	16	विष्णोर्भागवतान्	LX	19
विचरञ्छ्रवण	VII	2	विसर्जयति	LXXXVI	54
विचरन्मघादि	IX	14	विसर्ज्य शकु	LXXXVI	56
विच्छिन्नविषम	XXX	9	विसृक्के स्फोट	LI	32
विच्छिन्नाभि	LXVIII	76	विस्तरशो	XLIX	1
वितथो बृहत्क्षत	LIII	53	विस्तरषोड	LIII	22
वित्ताप्तिरनि	L	19	विस्तारार्ध	LVI	12
विदारिकायाः	LXXVI	5	विस्तीर्णकर्ण	LXVII	7
विदिक्स्थः	LXXXVI	70	विस्तीर्णमांसो	LXX	4
विदिगुद्भूतं	XXXV	4	विहगादिभि	LIII	14
विद्धि भद्रे	LXXXXIII	42	वीथीमार्गानपरे	IX	5
विद्युत्सत्त्व	XXXIII	5	वृक्षं प्रभाते	LIX	12
विधिनानेनै	XL	12	वृक्षस्य स्वच्छाय	V	9
विनिक्षिपन्त्यः	XCV	59	वृक्षस्यैका	LIV	55
विनोपघातेन	XXVIII	7	वृक्षाग्रमध्य	LXXXVI	73
विन्ध्याच्च सिन्धु	XXIX	9	वृक्षोपगे क्रोशति	LXXXIX	19
विपुलविमल	VI	13	वृत्तः समुद्ग	LVI	23
विपुलाः प्रदक्षिण	XXI	17	वृत्तायामाषा	XXVI	14
विपुलामपि	CIV	64	वृत्ते ग्रहे	V	49
विप्रः स्पृष्ट्वा	LIII	100	वृत्ते तु योगे	XXIV	11
विप्रक्षत्रिय	XXXIV	19	वृद्धाकारः	LXIV	38
विप्रमता	LXXI	14	वृश्चिकवृष	XL	1
विप्रयोगमुर	LI	12	वृश्चिकसंस्था	XL	11
विप्रादीनां व्यासा	LIII	25	वृश्चिकसंस्थे	XLII	9

	Ch.	V
वृष एकभूमि	LVI	26
वृषनालिकेर	XIV	9
वृषभोऽप्येवं	LXI	5
वृषस्य वृषदं	XLVIII	76
वृष्टि करोत्य	XXXV	6
वृष्टिः समाद्ये	VIII	25
वृष्टिस्त्र्यहेण	XXXIV	11
वृष्टेऽह्नि भागे	XXV	3
वेणातटे	LXXX	6
वेणीमूले	LI	40
वेणुमती	XIV	23
वेदव्यासे	XLVI	12
वेलाहीने	V	24
वेश्यावट्ट	LXXXVII	15
वैकङ्कतश्री	LXXXV	3
वैडूर्यकान्ति	X	21
वैडूर्यत्विट्	LXIV	3
वैडूर्यमल्लिका	LXI	14
वैडूर्यमुद्गा	LIV	107
वैडूर्यशंख	XIV	14
वैडूर्यसदृश	XLIII	46
वैरमपसव्य	LIII	104
वैशाखमासे	V	75
वैशाखे धर्मे	VIII	9
वैशाखे निरुप	XCV	2
वैश्यानां	LIX	6
वैश्वे युगेशो	VIII	41
वैष्णवश्चर	LXXXVI	33
व्यभ्रे नभसी	XLVI	45
व्याघ्रर्क्ष	LXXXVI	28
व्याप्तं नभः	XIX	4
व्यायामशिखि	LXXXVI	77
व्यालं त्रयोदश	VI	3
व्यालसूकरो	XXXIII	28
व्यासात् षोडश	LIII	23
श		
शकटानलो	VIII	3
शकटेनोन्नत	LXXXVI	74
शकयवन	XIII	9
शकुनसमये	LIII	107
शक्रकुमार्यः	XLIII	39
शक्रचाप	XXVIII	16
शक्रध्वजे	XLVI	74
शक्रायुधपरी-	XLVI	88
शक्रो निरूर्ध्वंति	XCVIII	5
शङ्कूपहता	LX	6
शंखतिमिवेणु	LXXXI	29
शतपत्र	LXXXVI	23
शतपुष्पा	LXXVII	8
शतभिषगा	XXI	29
शतभिषजि	IX	34
शतमभिहित	XI	16
शतमष्टयुतं	LXXXI	32
शतमिदमध्या	CVII	14
शतमेकाधि	XI	5
शतशोऽङ्कोल	LV	27
शनैश्चरे म्लेच्छ	IX	40
शमयोद्गताम	CIV	48
शम्भोः शिरसी	LVIII	43
शरदमल	CV	10
शरदभंगुल्म	XCV	5
शरदि कमलो	III	24
शशरुधिर	III	30
शशशोणित	LXXVII	19
शशिकिरण	XI	14
शशितनये	XVII	20
शशिनि फल	XVIII	8
शशी जन्म	CIV	8
शस्तं वामे	LXXXVIII	18
शस्ता शान्त	XLVII	27
शस्तेऽवनि	LXXXI	26
शस्तौषधि	LIII	88
शस्त्रभयातङ्क	XXX	17
शस्त्रानलप्र	LXXXVII	43
शस्त्रान्तं स्त्री	LXVIII	24
शस्त्रेण वेणी	LXXVIII	1
शस्त्रेण शस्त्र	LIII	102
शकाश्वकर्णा	LIV	105
शाक्योपाध्या	LI	21
शाक्रे युगे	VIII	33

	Ch.	V.
शाखाभङ्गे	XLVI	25
शातकुम्भ	XII	21
शान्तः पञ्चम	LXXXVI	71
शान्तपक्षि	XXIV	12
शान्तात्मा	CI	5
शान्ता स्वब	XC	14
शान्तामैन्द्री	XCV	20
शान्तासु दिक्षु	LXXXVII	29
शान्ति राष्ट्र	XLIV	21
शाम्बस्य गदा	LVIII	40
शार्दूलहंस	LXVIII	115
शालास्त्रिभाग	LIII	20
शालीक्षुमत्यपि	XIX	16
शालेन कलम	XXIX	2
शालेरश्वकर्णे	LXXXV	7
शास्त्रोपनयः	CVII	1
शिखिगल	XXXIV	6
शिखिगुण	XCVIII	1
शिखिदिशि	XCV	4
शिखिपर्जन्य	LIII	43
शिखिभय	IX	44
शिरःसन्धि	LII	4
शिरसि स्पृष्टे	L	11
शिरोललाट	LI	42
शिल्पी भिक्षु	LXXXVI	39
शिवा श्यामा	LXXXVI	37
शिशिरादिषु	XXX	22
शीघ्रमासन्न	LXXXVI	14
शीतवाता	LV	14
शीतानिल	XLVI	92
शीतोष्णविप	XCVII	4
शीतोष्णविपर्या	XLVI	39
शुककपोत	XXVIII	11
शुकवहन	XI	11
शुकवंशपत्र	LXXXIII	1
शुक्तिविशाली	LXVIII	71
शुक्रः सस्यवि	V	61
शुक्रे द्वितीय	CIV	33
शुक्रे बृहस्प	XVII	21
शुक्लः समः	LXXIX	26
शुक्ल:समः	XCIV	7
शुक्लविपुली	XI	28
शुक्लश्चतुर्वि	LVIII	42
शुक्लाः करा	XXX	11
शुक्ला रक्ता	XXXIII	14
शुक्ले पक्षे	IV	31
शुचिर्भूत्वा	LV	8
शुद्धैर्द्वादश	XCVIII	17
शुभं दशापाक	XCV	61
शुभकृज्जगतः	VIII	5
शुभदौ तु शाल	LXXIX	16
शुभमध्येऽलिनि	XL	5
शुष्कविरोहे	XLVI	28
शूर्पाकार	LXVIII	3
शृङ्गेणैके	IV	17
शेषं मङ्गल्य	LVI	15
शेषांस्तु सार्व	XLVIII	33
शैलेयकमांसी	XVI	25
शोणस्य नर्मदा	XVI	9
शोणाकतरो	LIV	23
शोषोऽस्य पाप	LIII	45
श्मशानशून्या	LI	4
श्यामकपुष्प	LXI	8
श्यामास्येन	LXXXVIII	1
श्यामारुणा	XI	24
श्यामेऽर्के कीट	III	29
श्यावाति	LXI	4
श्यावारुण	XXXIII	16
श्येनाः प्ररुदन्तः	XLVI	68
श्रवणानिल	X	1
श्रवणे मघा	XXIII	7
श्रवणे मायाप	XV	20
श्रवणे राजा	X	16
श्रवणोदितस्य	VI	7
श्रान्तस्य यान	LXVIII	116
श्रावणवर्षे	VIII	12
श्रीकर्णरुतं	LXXXVIII	27
श्रीधरनामा	CV	15
श्रीपतिमचिन्त्य	XLIII	4
श्रामाऽऽश्रवणे	CI	12

	Ch.	V.
श्रीवत्सवर्ध	XCIV	2
श्रीवासकरस	LXII	3
श्रीवृक्षवर्धमानच्छत्र	LXXIX	21
	XCIV	2
श्रीवृक्षवर्धमानात्	L	2
श्रीसजंगुड	LXXVII	16
श्रुतं दृष्टं स्पृष्टं	LXXIV	4
श्रेष्ठं चतुर्थ	VIII	35
श्रेष्ठं नन्द्यावर्तं	LIII	36
श्रेष्ठस्वरं	LXXXVIII	32
श्रेष्ठिनः प्रती	XXXIII	25
श्रेष्ठी सुवर्ण	XXIX	10
श्रेष्ठे हयसिते	LXXXVI	45
श्रेष्ठोऽर्जुनोऽज	XLIII	15
श्लक्ष्णां पताका	XXIV	9
श्लेष्मत्यागे	LI	33
श्लेष्मातकस्य	LV	29
श्लेष्मातकाक्ष	XLVIII	4
श्वभिः शृगालाः	XC	1
श्वभिरस्थि	XLVI	71
श्वभ्रमथवा	LIII	93
श्वभ्रोषितं न	LIII	95
श्वानः प्ररुदन्तः	XLVI	68
श्वासं मनुष्येण	LXXVIII	15
श्वेत इति	XI	39
श्वेतां सपूर्ण	XLIV	10
श्वेता कण्टक	LIV	85
श्वेता गोधा	LIV	13
श्वेता दिश्यप	LX	3
श्वेते क्षेमसु	V	53
श्वेते रजो	XXXVIII	3
श्वेतो विश्वम्भ	LIV	26
ष		
षट्सप्तम	XLI	10
षडनागतानि	IV	7
षड्भिः षड्भिर्हीना	LIII	5
षड्भिः षड्भिश्चैवं	LIII	7
षड्भिः सितस्य	XCVII	2
षड्भिर्दन्तैः	LXVI	5
षड्भिर्मासैः	XXXII	23

	Ch.	V.
षड्विंशतिः	LXXXII	7
षण्णवतिः	XI	27
षण्णवतिभेद	XXVII	21
षण्णवतिर	LXIX	7
षण्मासोत्तर	V	19
षष्टिश्चतुश्च	LIII	6
षष्टचन्दयुग	II	6
षष्ठं षण्णक्षत्रं	IX	20
षष्ठाश्रिताः	CIII	6
षष्ठेऽतसी	XLI	5
षष्ठो भृगुः	CIV	36
षोडशकस्य	LXXXI	14
षोडशके कच्छ	LXXVII	25
षोडशके द्रव्य	LXXVII	20
षोडशबाहू	LVIII	26
षोडशभागा	XLIII	40
स		
संवत्सरोऽग्निः	VIII	24
संस्थानविधिः	IV	18
संस्पृशती	XXXIII	12
संहितापारगश्च	II	21
सकरीरा चे	LIV	74
सकलगगना	XXXIV	5
सकिङ्किणीजाल	XLIII	7
सकुशासित	LIV	27
सकृदेकयाम	XI	44
सक्षीरार्जुन	XCV	16
सघृतस्य	XLVIII	36
सङ्कीर्णाः	LXIX	6
सङ्क्षिप्तायां	VII	10
सङ्ख्याविधाना	XII	15
सचिवालये	LIII	89
सतमस्कं	III	6
सत्त्वमहीनं	LXIX	3
सदशांशं	LIII	13
सद्रव्यो बल	LXXXVI	69
सन्तक्ष्य पुन	XLIII	29
सन्ध्याकाले	XXX	8
सन्ध्यानुरक्ते	XXIV	18
सन्ध्याद्वयस्य	XLVI	75

	Ch.	V.
सन्ध्याद्वयेऽपि	XLVI	67
सपलाशा बदरी	LIV	17
सपलाशा यत्र	LIV	83
सपांसुवर्षाः	XXII	6
सपृषतकण्ठ	LXV	6
सप्ततिवर्षो	LXIX	12
सप्त भवन्ति च	LXVIII	96
सप्त मुनीन्	XI	34
सप्तम्यां स्वाति	XXV	5
सप्तरात्रोषितै	LV	18
सप्तर्षयः	XLVIII	63
सप्तर्षीणां	LXXXVI	3
सप्ताष्टावब्य	XCVII	16
सप्ताहं गोमूत्रे	LXXVII	31
समचतुर	LIII	38
सममुत्तरेण	XXV	4
समवक्षसो	LXVIII	29
समशशिनि	IV	11
समागमे	XXVIII	21
समुद्गवद्दक्षिण	XCIII	12
समुद्रोऽन्तः	XII	2
समौ तु संवर्त	XX	9
सम्पत्त्या योजिता	II	36
सम्पाता वंशा	LIII	57
सम्पूर्णाङ्गो वामं	LXIX	32
सम्प्रहृष्ट	XLIV	28
सम्मूर्छिता	XXXIV	1
सरत्नतोयौ	XXIV	7
सरस्सुनलिनी	LVI	4
सरितश्च महा	XLVIII	62
सरो नद्युदपाना	XLVI	89
सर्जरसरसा	LVII	6
सर्जरसश्री	LXXVII	28
सर्जोदुम्बर	XLIV	4
सर्पत्सु तरुषु	XLVI	30
सर्पावासः	LIV	38
सर्वःस्पन्दन	LXXIX	17
सर्वत्र भूवि	XIX	1
सर्वदिगुत्थं	XXXVI	3
सर्वद्रव्या	LXXX	14
सर्वदिक्ष्व	XC	5
सर्वस्य सर्वं	LXXIX	1
सर्वे त्वामभिषि	XLVIII	60
सर्वे दुर्भिक्षकर्ता	LXXXVI	65
सर्वे द्विगुणाया	XLIV	4
सर्वेषां वृक्षाणां	LIV	31
सर्वोपकारान्	LXXV	9
सलिलममर	XII	13
सलिलमये	IV	2
सलिलविकारे	XLVI	51
सलिलोत्पत्ति	XLVI	50
सलिलोद्यान	LVI	3
सवज्रमुक्ता	XLIV	27
सवितरि भ्रष	XLII	12
सवितृसहितः	XLII	14
सविद्युतः	XXII	4
सव्यगते	V	44
सव्यापसव्य	V	43
सव्यासव्यो	LI	41
सव्येन खे	XCV	10
सशर्करातास्त्र	LIV	104
सशिखिचातक	XXIV	19
सशिष्यास्ते	XLVIII	61
सस्ये च दृष्ट्वा	XLVI	37
सस्योपेते	XCV	32
सहां च सह	XLVIII	40
साकेतकङ्क	XIV	4
साचीति यः	LXIX	39
साजमोद	LXXVI	11
साजे शतभिष	X	17
साध्यमनूकं	LXVIII	103
सामयजुभि	XLVIII	31
सामान्यमिदं	LX	22
साम्प्रतमयनं	III	2
सायं प्रातश्च	LV	9
सायाश्रय	LIII	21
सारसकूजित	LXXXVIII	37
सारस्वतेन	LIV	99
सार्पे जलरुह	X	7
सावित्रपौष्णा	XCVIII	16

	Ch.	V.		Ch.	V.
साश्राविल	LXI	2	सुरसं जल	LIV	73
सिंहः सिंहा	LVI	28	सुरास्त्वामभि	XLVIII	55
सिंहकटिर्मनु	LXVIII	18	सुषिरेऽथवा	LXXIX	29
सिंहलकपार	LXXXI	2	सुस्निग्धपत्र	XCV	33
सिंहे पुलिन्द	V	39	सुस्निग्धव्यक्त	LII	2
सिंहे सुवर्ण	XLII	6	सुहृद्युतिश्च	LXXI	5
सिंहोऽथ मघा	CII	3	सूकरनयनं	LXXIX	34
सितकुसुम	LXXIX	7	सूकरिकमाष	LIV	88
सितकुसुमा	XCV	41	सूक्ष्मैलालव	XXVII	4
सितपक्ष	XXI	8	सूत्रच्छेदे	LIII	110
सितरक्तपीत	LII	1	सूत्रे प्रसार्यं	LIII	108
सितरक्तपीत	LIII	96	सूर्यः षट्	CIV	4
सितवर्णः	LXI	17	सूर्यसुते तृतीय	CIV	41
सितवस्त्रो	XLIII	30	सूर्यसुतोऽर्के	CIV	54
सितसर्षपा	LXXX	12	सूर्यस्य विविधं	XXXV	1
सितसितान्त	XXX	24	सूर्याग्निभस्मो	LIV	106
सितसुभग	XVI	8	सूर्याचन्द्रमसो	II	10
सिद्धान्तभेदे	II	8	सूर्यात्सप्तम	V	10
सिद्धार्थमपर	LIII	39	सूर्यादीनां च	II	9
सिन्धुनदपूर्व	XVI	21	सूर्येन्दुपर्जन्य	XLVI	46
सीमागता	XCI	1	सूर्येन्दुभौम	CIII	3
सुखमिच्छन्	CIII	66	सूर्योदयेऽर्का	LXXXIX	2
सुतधनपरि	CIV	43	सूर्योन्मुखः	LXXXIX	3
सुतपीडा	LIII	74	सेनाङ्गेषु	XI	42
सुतलाभः	L	17	सेनापतिनृप	LIII	17
सुदेवा इति	XLVI	73	सेनापतेर्भय	XXXIV	10
सुप्तां सगीत	LX	15	सैकावलीव	XIII	1
सुभगा भव	LXVIII	27	सोमग्रहेनि	V	97
सुभगो विद्या	CI	7	सोमस्तासा	LXXIV	7
सुभ्रूकेशो	LXIX	27	सौगन्धिक	LXXXII	1
सुरगुरुदिवसे	CIV	62	सौगन्धिकगो	LXXX	5
सुरचापपाटित	III	27	सौभाग्यं	CIV	22
सुरचापमन्द्र	XXI	16	सौम्या तु	LVIII	49
सुरदारुचन्दन	LIX	5	सौम्येन पराभू	XVII	26
सुरनिलय	XXIV	2	सौम्येऽब्दे	VIII	4
सुरपतिचाप	XXXIII	29	सौम्यैन्द्रचित्रा	XV	30
सुरपतिहुतवह	LXXXVI	75	सौम्यैशान्यो	XI	17
सुरपितृपिशा-	LIV	9	सौम्योपगतो	IX	26
सुरभिकुसुमा	XVI	28	सौम्योऽस्तोदय	IX	43
सुरभूषणं	LXXXI	31	सौरादीनां	II	7

	Ch.	V.
सौरारजीव	CIII	7
सौरेणारे	XVI	14
सौरे मरुभव	V	68
सौरोऽर्क	CIV	55
सौस्थित्यमवे	CIV	60
स्कन्दः स्वं	XLIII	45
स्कन्धाच्च्युते	LIII	111
स्कन्धावारा	XCV	45
स्कन्धासनां	XCIII	3
स्खलितग	XCIV	12
स्तनवदवल	LXV	3
स्तनहृदयो	L	13
स्तनितं निशि	XXVIII	12
स्तनौ सरोमौ	LXX	21
स्तम्भं विभज्य	LIII	29
स्तम्भकुसूला	XCVII	6
स्तम्भसमं	LIII	30
स्तोतव्या	XXVI	2
स्त्रियः पवित्र	LXXIV	9
स्त्रीणां गुणा	LXXVIII	13
स्त्रीणां विकल्पा	LXXXVI	79
स्त्रीदोषाः	LIII	68
स्त्रीपुरुष	LI	16
स्त्रीमुखमन	LXVIII	55
स्त्रीरत्न	LXXIV	17
स्त्रीरूपे धन	LXXIX	23
	XCIV	4
स्त्रीशूद्रान्	V	31
स्त्रीसंज्ञा	LXXXVI	38
स्थलसलिल	XCV	58
स्थानं पुष्प	LI	2
स्थानकल्प	CIV	31
स्थानभ्रंशात्	CIV	26
स्थानेऽष्टमे	CIII	8
स्थापकदैव	LX	18
स्थालीपाकेन	XLVI	59
स्थिरप्रदेशो	XCVI	4
स्थूलशक्रु	LXI	7
स्थूलाभिर्घन	LXVIII	37
स्थूलास्थि	LXVIII	99

	Ch.	V.
स्थूलोऽभ्युन्नत	XLV	2
स्नातामभुक्त	LX	14
स्निग्धः प्रभा	LXXXII	3
स्निग्धः स्थूलः	XLVII	17
स्निग्धतरूणां	LIV	92
स्निग्धत्वक्का	LXVIII	98
स्निग्धद्विजत्व	LXVIII	90
स्निग्धद्विजस्य	LXXXVII	3
स्निग्धाः प्रभा	XI	18
स्निग्धाः प्रल	LIV	49
स्निग्धा निम्ना	LXVIII	43
स्निग्धायताः	LIV	100
स्निग्धासिता	LXVIII	91
स्निग्धोन्नता	LXX	1
स्निग्धौ सुभि	XI	38
स्नेहं मनोभव	LXXVIII	3
स्नेहः पञ्चसु	LXVIII	101
स्नेहासृङ्	XLVI	48
स्नेहो मृदुत्वं	LXXII	2
स्पृक्कात्वक्त	LXXVII	24
स्पृशभुव	XXIV	29
स्पृष्टे वा वालि	LI	11
स्पृष्टायवा	LXXVIII	8
स्फटिकरजत	LXIV	1
स्फिक्पार्ष्णि	LII	8
स्फुटवाग्	CI	13
स्फुटितो ह्रस्वः	L	4
स्मरणादपि	XII	14
स्रग्गन्ध	XLVI	31
स्रग्गन्ध	LXXVII	1
स्रोतस्तडाग	LXXXVIII	6
स्वकाले	LXXXVI	18
स्वजनविभव	LXXX	18
स्वरूपमेव	XLVII	3
स्वर्तुस्वभाव	XXI	27
स्वल्पवक्त्र	LXVII	10
स्वातावषा	XXVI	11
स्वातौ खग	XV	13
स्वातौ निशांशे	XXV	2
स्वातौ प्रभूत	IX	31

	Ch.	V.
स्वात्याद्यं भवि	IX	16
स्वल्पं पयः	CIII	4
स्वाहावसान	XLIII	32
स्वैरङ्गुलप्रमा	LVIII	4
ह		
हंसकारण्डव	LVI	5
हंसपङ्क्ति	XLIV	24
हनुकुक्षि	V	81
हनुलोचन	LXVIII	88
हन्ति मण्डला	XXXIII	27
हन्त्यैन्द्रो	XXXII	27
हन्यात्कैकय	XI	60
हन्यात्प्रयाग	XI	35
हयनरभुज	LXXXVIII	3
हरार्कवैव	XLIII	52
हरिणाक्षा	LXVIII	65
हरिते रोगो	V	54
हरीतकी	LXXVII	10
हर्म्यपृष्ठमुडु	LXXVI	2
हर्म्यप्रासाद	LXXXVI	17
हलमुसल	LXIX	17
हसितं शुभद	LXVIII	74
हस्तचतुष्के	LIV	80
हस्तत्रयं मृग	XCVIII	12
हस्तद्वात्रिंशा	LIII	18
हस्तविशालं	XXIII	2
हस्ताङ्गुले	LXVIII	36
हस्तादीनि	VII	4

	Ch.	V.
हस्ताप्यसौम्य	XXIII	6
हस्तायतं	IV	24
हस्ते तस्कर	XV	11
हस्ते नापित	X	9
हस्तो मघा	LIV	123
हस्तो मूलं	XCVIII	15
हस्त्यश्वपत्ति	XIX	3
हस्त्यश्वपुरो	XVI	23
हस्त्यारोह	LXXXVII	42
हारमणि	X	10
हारीतस्य तु	LXXXVIII	15
हास्यज्ञदूत	XIX	12
हिमपातानि	XLVI	94
हीनस्य नाशो	XXVI	10
हीनातिरिक्त	V	25
हुं हुं गुग्लु	LXXXVIII	36
हृदयं समुन्नतं	LXVIII	28
हेमकान्ति	VII	20
हेमगिरि	XIV	19
हेमलम्ब	VIII	39
हेमसमीप	XLV	6
हैमी प्रधाना	XXVI	9
होराशास्त्रे	II	18
होतभुजं	XCVIII	11
ह्रदिनीविलासि	XLVIII	8
ह्रस्वतनुः	XI	8
ह्रस्वयाति	LXX	18
ह्लादिमृद्वक्	XXI	14

Total number of verses (including the aphorisms of chapter II) in the Bṛhatsaṁhitā

अ	211	ओ	3	त	123	य	127
आ	95	औ	1	द	137	र	79
इ	26	क	210	ध	35	ल	23
ई	6	ख	14	न	129	व	193
उ	86	ग	75	प	259	श	156
ऊ	7	घ	7	फ	12	ष	23
ऋ	6	च	63	ब	34	स	267
ए	39	छ	16	भ	79	ह	51
ऐ	20	ज	54	म	136	Total	2802

Ch.	V.	Ch.	V.	Ch.	V.	Ch.	V.	Ch.	V.
1	11	23	10	45	16	67	10	89	20
2	40	24	36	46	99	68	116	90	15
3	39	25	6	47	28	69	40	91	3
4	32	26	15	48	87	70	26	92	3
5	98	27	9	49	8	71	14	93	15
6	13	28	24	50	26	72	6	94	14
7	20	29	14	51	44	73	6	95	62
8	53	30	33	52	10	74	20	96	17
9	45	31	5	53	125	75	10	97	17
10	21	32	32	54	125	76	12	98	17
11	62	33	30	55	31	77	37	99	3

12	22	34	23	56	31	78	26	100	8
13	11	35	8	57	8	79	39	101	14
14	33	36	5	58	58	80	18	102	7
15	32	37	3	59	14	81	36	103	13
16	42	38	8	60	22	82	11	104	64
17	27	39	5	61	19	83	1	105	16
18	8	40	14	62	2	84	2	106	6
19	22	41	13	63	3	85	9	107	14
20	9	42	14	64	3	86	80		
21	37	43	68	65	11	87	45	Total –	
22	8	44	28	66	5	88	47		2802

N. B. Out of these verses 10 are repeated once. They are : III. 37, L. 25, 26, LXXIX. 20 to 25, and LXXXVI. 34.

ALPHABETICAL INDEX OF IMPORTANT WORDS OCCURRING IN THE TEXT

[The Roman and Arabic numerals refer to the Chapter and verse respectively]

अंशभागी XLVIII 20
अंशुक LI 14, 17
अंशुमर्दन XVII 3, 4
अंस LVIII 25, LXVIII 34, XCIII 3,
अक्ष II 12, XLVI 9, XLVIII 4
— भङ्ग XLIII 22
— सूत्र LVIII 38, 39
अक्षत XLVIII 19, 35, LIII 99, 101, LXXIX 7
अक्षर XIX 11, XCVI 14
अक्षि LI 9, LVIII 10, XCIII 3, XCVI 12
— कोश LVIII 11
— गत IX 40
— रुक् LI 11
अगम्या LII 8, LXVIII 25, 69
अगस्त्य XII 1, 8, 12, 13, 20
— चार II 23
अगुरु XVI 30, XXVII 9, LXXVII 14, 23, 29 LXXXVII 11
अग्नि XLVIII 69, LIII 49, 71, LIV 3, 106, 112 LXXIV 7, LXXXIX 13 XCVI 16
— उपजीवी X 4
अग्नि—
— कोप XXIV 23, XXVI 13, XXVIII 21, XXIX 13, XXX, 14, XXXV 4,
— ज XI 23
— दैवत LXXI 1
निमित्त LX 12
— प्रकृति LXVIII 110
— प्लुष्ट XCV 36
— भय LIII 61, 102, LXXXVI 1, 31, 40 XC 6, XCV 40, XCVI 6
— मन्थ XLIV 9
— लक्षण LXXXIV 2
— वार्त VI 1, XVII 13
— विकृति LIII 59
— होत्रिक XVI 15
अग्रजात LII 1
— भुक् II 13
— हस्त LVIII 26
अङ्कूर LIV 106
— विकार XLVI 95
अङ्कुश LXXII 4
अङ्कोल LIV 50, LV 27, 29
अङ्ग V 72, 73, IX 10, X 14, XI 56, 60, XVII 26, XXXII 15, LI 8, LIII 58, 59, 105, 107, 109, LIV 1
— द XLV 25
— परिमोटन LI 28
— विनिश्चय I 9
अङ्गना LXXIV 12, 17, XCV 12
— दोष LIII 67, 68
— लाभ LII 7, XCV 44
अङ्गार XLV 12, XLVI 41, 78, XLVIII 16, LI 4, LIII 61, 103 LXXXVI 12
— क XCVII 1
अङ्गिराः XIII 5, 10, XLVIII 63.

अङ्गुल XLIII 21, XLIX 2,3, L 1, 11, 16, LIII 18, 19, 24-26, 65, LIV, 80, LV 26, LVI 29, LVIII 2,4 8, LXVIII 105
अङ्गुलि LI 8, 11, 25, 37, LII 6,8 LVIII 19, 28, LXVIII 36 43, 87, LXX 11, CV 3
— पर्व LXVIII 42
अङ्गुष्ठ LI 8, 13, 25, 37, 40, LII 8, LIII 101, LIV 109, LVIII 18, 19, 28
LXX 14, 16
— यव LXVIII 42
अङ्घ्रि LIII 54, 68
अज IX 1, LV 17, LXV 5, LXXIV 8, LXXXVI 26, LXXXVIII 3, CIV 63b
अजा XLVIII 41
— विक XXIX 7, XLI 6, XLV 8
अजकर्ण XLIII 15
— बन्धक LIV 22
— पाद XCVIII 5
अजमोद LXXVI 11
— विषाण LVII 7
अञ्जन XIV 5, XIX 4, XXI 23, XXIV 16, XXVIII 6, 15 XXX 15, XLIV 9, XLVI 95, XLVIII 30, 35, LIV 11, 50, 107, 110, 121 LXXVII 1, 32, LXXIX 2, LXXXII 1
अट्ट XLV 9
अणिमङ्ग XLIII 22
अण्ड LVI 24, XCV 59
— अवकिरण XCV 6
— उपसङ्क्रान्ति XXVIII 7
— ज XXX 5, XLVI 22, LXXXVI 43
अण्डीरक LXXXVIII 1, 26
अतसी XLIX 6, XLI 5, LVII 3, LVIII 32, LXXXI 7
अतिबला LIV 50
— मर्म LIII 64
— मुक्तक XXIX 5, LV 4, 22, LXXVII 7, LXXXV 5
— राग LXXXII 3
— वक्रा VII 15,16
— वृष्टि XXI 34, XLII 1, XLVI 38, 42
— सार XXXII 18
अत्यम्ल LXXVI 12
अत्रि XIII 5, 10, XIV 14, XLVI 1, XLVIII 63, 66
अथर्वकल्प XLVIII 71
अदिति XLVIII 56, LIII 45, 63, XC-VIII 4
अदृष्ट XXXII 2
अद्भुतदर्शन XLVI 90, 94
अधर LVIII 8 LXVIII 51, 87 LXX 6
अधिकरणिक XXXIX 2
अधिकृत LIII 9
अधिमास II 5, XXVI 11
— राज्य XLVIII 85
— शासन LX 1, 22
अध्यक्ष LIII 9
अध्वा LI 24, LII 7,8
अनड्वान् XLVIII 43, XCV 24
अनन्त XXXV 2
अनय XLVII 6
अनर्घ LXXIX 5
अनलाजीवी LXXXVI 29, XCV 21
— लक्षण XLIV 14
अनवसित CIV 35
अनागत IV 7
अनामयत्व XCV 61
अनामिका LVIII 27
अनावृष्टि XCV 5
अनिमित्त XLVI 8
अनिल LIII 43, 48, 72, LIV 3
अनुरक्तचेष्टा LXXVIII 5
— लेपन XLVIII 27, LV 8
— लोम XXX 19, XXXV 3, XCV 27
— वत्सर VIII 24
— विद्ध XIV 31
अनूक II 14, LXVIII 1, 103

अनूपचर LXXIX 20, XCIV 1
— ज LIV 47, 89, 93, LV 11
अनूराधा LIV 123, XCVIII 10, CI 9, CV 2
अन्त CIII 12
अन्तःपुर LXXVII 4, XCIII 2
अन्तरिक्ष XI 41, LIII 43
अन्तर्द्वीपी XIV 25
अन्तर्वेदी V 65
अन्तविदरण V 81
अन्ध XCVI 12
अन्ध्र XI 59, XIV 8 XVI II XVII 25
अन्न XLVI 6, 35, 46, 59, 65, 85, XLVIII 28, LI 36, LII 3,6, LII 96, LXXXV 6,9 LXXXIX 17, XCV14, 44
अन्यपुष्ट LXXXVIII 3
अपचार XLVI 2, 3
अपरवक्त्र CIV 15
अपराजिता — XLVIII 39
अपरान्त V 70, XIV 20
अपरान्त्य V 40, IX 15,
अपराह्ण LI 6
— वत्स LIII 47, 49, 51
— सर्पण XLVI 47
— सव्य V 43, XVII 3, 5, XVIII 8, XXX 4,9, XXXI, 1, LIII 104, LX 13, LXXIX 27, LXXXVI, 44, 57, LXXXIX 20
— स्मार LIII 78
अपांवत्स XXV 4
अपामार्ग LIV 115, LXXXV 7
अप्सरसः XLVIII 25
अब्ज LXXXII 1
अब्जाद LXXXVI 27
अब्द LI 39, LXXXV 8, XCVII 1, 2, 9, XCVIII 3
— ज्ञ XV 1
अभया XLVIII 39, 81
अभिघात LII 9, XCVIII 7
— चार II 3, XV 4, XVI 19, 24 XLIV 21
— वित् LXIX 37
— जित् XLVII 12, XCVII 15
— भव XLVI 61
— षेक XLVIII 85, XCVIII 9
— सार XIV 29, XXXII 19
अभ्यक्त XCVIII 13
अभ्यञ्जन XLVIII 30
अभ्यन्तरदोषXLVIII 81
अभ्रप्रसूत LXXXI 1, 29
— वृक्ष XXX 2, 18, 19
— सूचीXCVII 3
भ्रमर XLIII 1, LIII 2, 3
— रेज्यलग्न C 6
अमांसभुक् XLV 15
अमात्य XLVIII 18
अमानुषी वाक् XLVI 92
अमावास्या XLII 1, XCIX 2
अमूर्त V 3
अमृता XLIV 9
अमोघ XXX 11, XLVII 20
अम्बकृत LXXIX 17, 18
अम्बर XLI 6, XLVI 22, 31, LIII 113 XCV 23
— रावत XIV 27
अम्बष्ठ IX 19, XIV 7, 17 XVI 22
अम्बु XCVI 16
— चारीXCV 15
— निर्देश XXI 3
— प्रमाण XXIII 2
— यन्त्र II 3
— संशोष XLVI 87
अम्बुद्भव XLI 8
अम्भः LIII 123, LIV 2, 6, 53 64, 74, 75
अम्ल LIII 97
अयन II 4, 27
— नान्त XXVIII 20
अयोघात LII 4
अयोध्या IV 24
अर LXXXVII 18, 21, 23, 25, 28
— भङ्ग XLIII 22
— णि LIII 126

अरव XIV 17
अरिमेद XIV 2
अरिष्ट LIII 87, LIV 105, LV 3, LIX 5
— ष्टिका XLVIII 40
अरुण XI 24, XXX 13, XXXI 1, XXXIII 16, LIII 123
अरुन्धती XIII 6
अर्क XXIX 10, LXXXV 3, LXXXVI 58, XCVI 17
— ग्रह V 8, 98
— ज XCVI 15
— दीप्त XCVI 6
अर्घविशेष XLII 2
— वृद्धि XVII 25, XXIV 33
— हानि XL 11
अर्घा LXXXI 17, 22, 29
अर्चा XLVI 8, LIX 10, XCVII 6
अर्जुन XXIX 11, XLIII 15, LIV 12, 101. 105, LV 10, LIX 5, LXXXV 6
अर्जुनायन IV 29, XI 59, XIV 25, XVI 22, XVII 19
अर्थ LIII 109, 118, LXXXIX 12, XCV XCV 16 29, 27, 29, 41, 44, 47
— आगम LIII 62
अर्थक्षय LIII 67, 86, 117
— सिद्धि L 24
अर्धगुच्छ LXXXI 33
— माणवक LXXXI 33
—हार LXXXI 32
अर्धा LXXXI 17
अर्धोदित V 28
अर्बुद V 68, XVI 31, XXXII 19
अर्यमा LIII 46, 50, 51, XCVIII 4, CI
अर्हन् LI 21, LVIII 45
अलक XI 57
अलङ्कार LVIII 29
अलि XXVIII 15, CII 4
अलिन्द LIII 17, 31 35
अवगाण XI 61, XVI 38
अवग्रह XXX 21
अवट LV 24
अवन्ती V 18, 40, IX 17, 18, 21, XI 35
अवम II 5
— दंन V 43
अवलम्बक II 12
अवस्कर LI 4
अवाङ्मुख LIII 51
अवि LI 19, LV 17
अवृष्टि XXIX 12, XLIII 64, XLVI 38, XLVII 13, LIV 111
अशनि III 33, XIII 7, XXI 25, 33, XXIV 25, XXXIII 1-4, XXXVI 4, XLIII 63, XLVI 84, LXXIX 3, LXXX 18, XCV 36
अशोक XXIX 2, XXXIV 6, XXXVII 2, XLIII 33, LIII 87, LIV 119, LV 3,4, LXXX 10
अश्म XXXIII 4, XLVI 77, LIII 123 LIV 11, 26, 34, 36, 46, 64, 71, 80, 106, 115, LXXXVI 61
— क V 39, 73, 74, 49, 79, IX 18, 27, XI 54, 55, XIV 22, XVI 11, XVII 15, XXXII 15
— न्तक LIV 43
अश्रु LII 2
— मुख VI 2
अश्व XXXII 4, XLVI 95, XLVIII 87, L 24, LIII 107, LIV 118, LXXXVI 26, 73, LXXXVII 20, XCV 48
— उपकरण XCV 22
— कर्ण XXIX 7, LIV 105, LXXXV 7
— वदन XIV 6
अश्वत्थ XIV 3 XXIX 3, XLIV 3, XLIV 12, LIII 85, LIX 5, LX 8, LXXXV 4
अश्विनी LV 31, LXXI 1, XCVII, 14, XCVIII 2, 12, CI 1, CV 1
अश्विनी XLVIII 56, XCVIII 4
अषाढ XCVII 15

अष्टकवर्ग II 18
— भौम LVI 21
— मस्थान CIII 8
अष्टमी CV 6
— मूली LV 22, LXXXVI 41
अष्टाश्रि LVI 18
असन XXIX 5, LXXIX 2, 11, 15, 19
असिक XI 56
असित XI 1
असिनिभ LXXX 11
— मुसल VI 5
— यष्टि L 6
असुर XLIII 1, LIII 44, LIX 8
असृग्वर्ष XLVI 43, 48
अस्त XXVIII 20, XXXIV 9, XLVI 84, XLVII 20, 21, 23, 26
— गिरि XIV 20, XXVIII 18
अस्थि XLVI 40, 71 LI 9, 14, 29, XLVIII 16, LIII 60, 103, 106, 108, LXVIII 96, 99, LXXXVIII 20, LXXXIX 1-b, c, 13, XCV 12, 39, 40
— केतु XI 30
अस्त्र XLI 6
— विद् XIX 10
अहताम्बर XLIII 24, XLIV 15
अहर्व्यास II 12
अहि XXXIII 9, LIII 45, LIV 11, 83, 85, LXXXVI 42, XCV 55
— निलय LIV 33, 35, 43, 88
— राज LIV 36
— व्यवाह XXVIII 7
अहिर्बुध्न्य XCVIII 5
अहोरात्र II 4

आकर XIV, 12, XIX 6, 10
आकरिक XV 1
आक्रन्द XVI 7, XVII 6-8
— न्दासार XXXIV 22
आखु L 25, LXXXVI 23, XCVII 7
आगम XLI 1, XLIII 11, LXI 1
आगामि XCVI 2
आग्निहोत्रिक IX 43
आग्नीध्र XIV 25
आग्नेय XXXII 14, 28, 30, 31, XLVI 24, LIII 118, LIV 97, LX 2, LXVIII 92, LXXXI 8, LXXXVII 20, 31, LXXXVIII 43, XCV 21, XCVI 6
आघातस्थान XLVIII 81
आघ्रात V 43
आचार्य XLIX 1, LXXIX 27
आजि XLIII 2
आज्य XLVIII 35, 52, 53, LI 37 LV 19 LIX 12
आटरूषक LXXXV 7
आटविक II 15, IX 13, XVI 13, XXXVI 3, XCIV 9
आढक XXI 32, XXIII 2 LIII 93 LV 17
आतप LV 14
— त्र XLIV 27, L 2, LXXII 4, LXXIII 3
आत्मज LI 37
— स्वरूप LII 3
आत्मा LXXV 2-4
आदर्श XIV 25, XLIII 57
आदित्य XLVIII 56, XCVIII 11
आधार LXXIX 30
आध्विकयुति XCV 42
आनर्त V 80, XIV 17, 33, XVI 31
आनिल LXXI 4, XCVIII 11
आन्तरिक्ष XLVI 2, 4, XLVIII 53
आन्वीक्षिकी XIX 11
आप: LIII 48, 49, 51
आपण LI 21
आपो हि ष्ठा XLVIII 72
आप्त XLVIII 48
आप्या LXVIII 91, XCVI 5
आभरण LI 19
आभासमात्र LXXV 1
आभीर V 38, 42, IX 19, XIV 12, 18 XVI 31

— नील LIV 110, LXXX 4
पत्नी XCVI 16
— वंशा CIV 18
— वज्र CIV 34
इन्द्रिय LXXV 3
इभ LIV 101, LXXXVI 20
इरावती XVI 27
इष्टकासन्चय LXXXIX 1 (a)
इष्टापूर्त LVI 2
इष्टिकरण C V

ईशणीक LXXXVI 32
ईति V 54, XXIV 33, XLVI 42
ईश LXXIX 27, 31
ईर्षु XLVI 76

उखा XLVI 56
उग्र XXXIII 19, XCVIII 8
— जाति XV 29
उच्चगति II 9
उच्छिष्ट LIII 66
उच्छ्राय LIII 11, 22, 24-27, 113, LVI 11, 13
उच्छ्रुत LIII 16
उज्जयिनी X 15, XI 56, XII 15, LXIX 30
उज्जिहान XIV 2
उञ्छवृत्ति LI 22
उडु-नाश XLVI 21
- पति XCVIII 12
[V 35, XIV 6, XVI 1 XVII 25
फल XIV 7
कुष्ट XXXIII 23, XLVI 49
कोश LXXXVI 2
ंस LVI 7
मधान्य XV 5
र LIV 123, LXXI 3, XCVIII 6
कुर XIV 24
गति II 9, XVIII 1-8
पाण्डय XVI 10
LIII 113, LX 3
मार्ग XLVII 9
— वीथी XLVII 4
— शाला LIII 37
उत्तरापथ IX 41
— यण III 1, 5, LXXXI 20
उत्तरोष्ठ LIII 29, 8, LXX 20, 23
उत्पल L 21, LXXVII 10
— गन्धिक LXXVII 6
उत्पात III 10, 20, V 16, VII 1, XXI 26, 29 XXIV 5, XXXII 23, XLII 1,2 XLVI 1, 2 82, 83, 96, 99 XLVIII 3, 70, 83, 84 LII. 9
उत्सादन XCVIII 8
उदगयन LX 20
उदपान XVI 18
— वृद्धि XLVI 89
उदय XXVIII 20, XLVII 20, 21, 26, XCVI 5, 6, XCVIII 12, 17
— गिरि XIV 7
उदयांश XCVI 1
उदर LI 37, LII 6, LXX 17, 20 25, XCIII 2
— राग्निदीपन LXXVI 11
उदीच्य XVI 21
— वेष LVIII 46
उदुम्बर V 40, XIV 4, XVI 3, XLIII 15 XLIV 4, 12, 20, LI 17, LIII 26, LIV 11, 96, 107, LV 10 LVI 13 LX 8
उद्गता CIV 48
उद्देहिक XIV 3
उद्बन्धमृत XC 8
उद्यान XLV 4, XLVIII 15, LVI 3, 8, LIX 2
उद्वंश XLIII 47
उद्वर्तन XLVI 88
उद्वाह XCVI II 3, CIII 13
उन्मत्तगाथा XLVI 97
उन्माद XXXII 10, LIII 79
उपगीति CIV 49, 50
उपगूहन LXXVIII 6
उपघात XXVIII 7, XLVIII 1, LIII 66

उपचय XLI 10, LX 21
उपज्योतिष XIV 3
उपतुला LIII 30
उपनन्द XLIII 39
उपयाचित II 17
उपराग V 12
उपरिचर XLIII 8, 68
उपरिदंष्ट्री XCV 57
उपलरत्न LXXX 2
— वैचित्र्य LXXX 3
उपवङ्ग XIV 8
उपवास CV 6
उपवाह्यतुरङ्गम XCIII 6
उपश्रुति II 15
उपसर्ग XXIV 29, XLVI 2, XLVIII 83
उपस्कर XI 42, XLVI 63
उपाध्याय LI 21
उपानत् LXXXIX 1 (b) (C), 12, XCV 14
उपेन्द्रवज्रा CIV 11
उभयचारी LXXXVI 6
उर: LI 9, 12, 30, 43, LII 4, LIII 51, 52, 100 LXVIII 85 LXX 5 CV 2
उरग LXXXVIII 20 XCVII 7
उरस्य LXX 5
उलूक LXX 22, LXXI 12, LXXIX 24 LXXXVI 21, 49, LXXXVIII 2, 36
— चेटी LXXXVIII 4
उलूखल LXXXIX 1 (a)
उल्का III 33, IV 28, V 93, XII 22, XIII 7, XV 31, XVI 40, XXI 25, XXIV 25, 63, XXX 32, XXXII 13, 24, XXXIII 1-3, 8, 13, 14, 18, 21, 23, XLII 1, XLIII 63, XLVI 4, 86, 94
उल्मुक LXXXIX 1 (c)
उल्लेख XVII 3, 4
उल्लोपिका LIX 8
— उशीनर IV 22, XI 55, XVI 26
उशीर LIV 100, 121, LV 7, LXXVII 12, 13, 29
उष्ट्र XXIV 21, XLV 9, XLVI 43, L 24, LIV 106, 109, LXXI 12, LXXXVI 26, LXXXVII 44, LXXXVIII 3, XCV 47 CIV 63 (b)
उष्णघ्न LXXIII 5
— वक्त्र VI 1
उष्णीष XLIII 30, XLIV 27
उष्ट्रा LXXXVII 22 LXXXVIII 9

ऊरु LI 8, 41, 43, LII 7, LIII 53, 100, LVII 17, LXVIII 4, LXX 3, 24 LXXXIX 11, CV 1
ऊर्ज LXXVII 35
ऊर्ध्वकण्ठ XIV 8
— तरण XLVI 89
ऊर्मिमाला CIV 45
ऊर्व XLVIII 66
ऊषर XLVIII 16, LI 4
ऊष्मा LIV 60

ऋक् XLVIII 31, 74, 77
ऋक्ष III 36, LXXXVI 21, 28, 4: LXXXVIII 3, XCVI 1, 5, LII 13
ऋजुगति VII 15, 16
ऋतु II 4, 27, III 10, XXI 18, 27, : XXX 22, XXXIV 7, XXXV: 1, XLVI 39, 40, 82, 83, 9: XLVIII 35
— समय LXXVIII 26
ऋषभ XIV 15, LXXXVI 1, 40
ऋषिक XIV 15
ऋषिकृत LXXXVI 7
— पुत्र XLVI 83
ऋष्य LXV 2, 8

एकत XLVLII 65

— पद XIV 7, 31
— पुलक LXXXVIII 6
— भूमिशृङ्ग LVI 26
— मणि LXV 3
— विलोचन XIV 23
— वृषण LXVIII 9
— शफ LXXXVI 23
एकानंशा LVIII 37
— वली XIII 1, LXXXI 36
— शीतिविभाग LIII 42
एला XXVII 4, LXXVII 32, 33
एष्यत्सूर्य LXXXVI 12

ऐन्दव XCVIII 10
ऐन्द्र XXXII 16, 18, 27, 29-31, LX 11 LXXX 8, LXXXI 7, LXXXVII 1, 29, XCV 19, 20
ऐरावत IX 1, XXX 8, XLVII 20, LXXXI 20
ऐशान्य LIII 43, 48, 83, 118, LIV 27, 74, LXXXVII 15, 26
ऐश्वर्य L 19, LI 23
— सम्पन्न XV 2

ओङ्कार LXXXVIII 32
ओज LXXXVI 43
ओदन LI 30, LIX 8
ओषधि X 13, XVI 7, XIX 12, XXXII 10, XLI 2, XLVIII 41, 42, LIII 88, LX 8, LXXVIII 22
ओष्ठ LI 8, 31, 33, LII 3, LXVIII 52, 97, LXX 25, LXXVIII 6

औडूक V 73
औपच्छन्दसिक CIV 60
औपयिक LIII 122
और्वीछाया V 10
औशनस L 23
औषध XCVIII 9, C 5, CIV 63 (a)

क XI 37, 38
ककुद LXI 4, 11, LXVI 2
ककुद्मान् LXI 18
ककुभ XLIV 4, LIV 76, 119, LXXXV 3
कक्कोल LXXVII 37
कक्ष LI 8 LII 4, LXVIII 43, 86
कक्ष्या II 11, LVIII 24, XCIV 13
कङ्क XI 26, XIV 4, L, 3, XLIII 62, LXX 22, LXXI 12, LXXXVIII 11, XCV 46
कङ्कट XIV 12
कङ्कण XIV 12
कङ्गु VIII 10, XXIX 4
कच LI 8, 14 3
कच्छ IV 28, XIV 16
कच्छप V 40, XXVIII 14, LIV 34
कच्छपुट LXXVII 25, 29
कच्छार XIV 27
कञ्चुकी XLIII 23, LIII 8
कटम्भरा XLIV 10
कटाक्ष LXXVIII 3
कटि LI 8, 43, LVI 11, LVIII 23, 37, LXVI 2, LXVIII 18 LXX 24, CV 2
कटु XLVIII 4, LIII 97, LXXVI 12
कटुका LI 32, LIV 122, LXXVII 7, 30
कणभुक् I 7
कण्टक LIV 85
— स्थल XIV 10
कण्टकारिका LIV 57
कण्टकी XLIII 13, XLVIII 4, LI 3, LIII 86, LIV 53, LXXIX 4 LXXXVI 60, LXXXIX 1 (b) XCV 2, 37 40, XCVI 6, 7
कण्ठ LVIII 16
— धान XIV 26
कण्व XLVIII 65
कतक LIV 121
कदम्ब LIV 38, 78, 119, LV 10, LXXIX 16 LXXXV 5
कदली XXIX 7, XLI 4, XLIII 57, L 26, LV 4, LXXX 8

कद्रू XLVIII 57
कनक XI 18, XXIX 8, XLI 2, XLIV 12 XLVI 6, XLVIII 46, L 22, LI 17, LIII 101, LIV 39, LXXXVI 80, LXXXVII 2, 3, 30, XCV 15, XCVII 17
कनकलश XIV 21
कनिष्ठिका LVIII 27, LXX 13, 16
कन्दमूल XV 7, XLI 4, XLII 9, 12
कन्धरा LXX 25
कन्या LI 40, 41, LXXXVI 45, CII 3
— पिता LXVIII 13
कपाट XLVI 74, LIV 120
कपाल XLI 8, LI 4, LIII 60, LXXXVI 60
— केतु XI 31
कपि XXXIII 9, LXXIX 24 LXXXVI 38, LXXXVIII 1, 22,
— कच्छु LXXVI 4, 9
कपिञ्जल XLVIII 6, LXXXVI 22
कपित्थ XXIX 12, LV 22, 23, LVII 1, 5, 7
कपिल I 7, XIV 17, XXX 12, LIII 123, LIV 15, 104, 107
कपिष्ठल LXXXVI 1
कपोत XXVIII 11, XLIII 62, XLVI 68, LIV 22, LXXI 13, LXXXVI 21 LXXXVIII 1, 5, 12, 13
— पालि LVI 30
कबन्ध III 8, 17, XI 27, L 3, LXXIX 25
कमलभव LIII 1 V 2, XCVIII 4, C 1
कम्प (मही XVII 17, XXI 25, XXIV 25 XLVI 75, 88
कम्पिल्लक LIV 21
कम्बल XLII 8, XLVIII 50, 54
कम्बुनिचित LXX 5
कर LI 5, 38, LIV 11, 53, 68, 74, LVIII 26, LXVIII 39, 40, 87, 97, LXIX 22, LXX 11, LXXI 4, CV 3
करका IX 42, XXI 33, 35, LV 28, 30
करञ्ज LIV 33, LXXXV 4
करट LXI 2, 6
करण I 10, II 15, V 18, XVII 1, XXIV 5, XLIII 12 XCVI 1, XCIX 3, CIII 13
करभ XXXIII 9, XLII 7, LIV 62
करवीर L 7, 21, LXXXV 6
— क LVIII 13
करायिका LXXXVIII 4, 16, XCV 1
करी XXIX 7
करीर LIV 67, 74, 76, 106
करीष LV 30
करेणु L 24
कर्कटक III 4, XLVIII 16, CII 2
कर्केतर LXXX 4
कर्बूर LXXVII 14
कर्ण LI 34, 38, 40, 42, LVIII 5-8, LXVIII 58, 59, LXX 9, 21, XCV 25, C 6
— कण्डूयन LXXVIII 4
— धार XV 25
— पाली LI 9
— प्रावेय LIV 18
कर्णाट XIV 13
कर्णिकार LIV 59, LXXX 9
कर्दम LXXI 10
कर्पट LI 12
कर्पास XV 9, 14, XXIX 5, XLI 3
कर्पूर LXXVII 13, 15, 16, 33, LXXXI 28
— बोध LXXVII 11, 12, 26, 27
कर्म I 7, III 15
कर्माङ्गुल LXXIX 8
कर्मान्ताध्यक्ष LIII 9
कर्मिवध LIII 111
कर्वट XIV 5, XVI 13
कर्षक XV 2, XVI 8, 13
कर्षत्रय LXXXII 7
कलमशालि XXIX 2
कलविङ्कनेत्र LXVII 6
कलश XLVIII 37, 50, 51, LIII 125
कलह LIII 119, LXXIX 5, LXXXVI 60, 63, LXXXVII 30, LXXX-

दिनकृत् XCVIII 4
दिवस XCVIII 3
दिविष्ट XIV 31
दिव्य XI 41, XLVI 2, 4-6, 90 XLVIII 53, 58
दिव्यक LXXXVIII 9,18
दिव्यदृक् LV 31
दीक्षा XCVIII 16
दीक्षित XLIV 15
दीप LXXXIV 1, 2
— वर्ति LIII 94
— शिखा LXXXII 5
दीप्त III 10, XXX 3, 4, 30, XXXIV 8, XXXVI 4, XXXIX 1, XLV 16, XLVI 67, 68, LXXXVI 12, 57-61, 64, 70, 71, LXXXVII LXXXVII 29, 34, ·42, LXX-XVIII 11, 14, 15, 17, 25, 26, 31-33 35,36, 38, 47, XCI 1, XC III 2, 10, XCV 18, XCVI 8, 10
दीर्घकेश XIV 23
— ग्रीव XIV 23
— तपा: XLVIII 66
दीर्घास्य XIV 23
दुःखविनाश LII 5
दुग्ध L 24
दुग्धभावित LV 19
दुण्डुभ LIV 17
दुन्दुभि VIII 50
दुर्ग II 15, XVI 13, 38
दुर्दिन XXVIII 24, XCV 16
दुर्बलिक LXXXVIII 7, 28
दुर्भिक्ष IV 21, XI 36, XXIX 11, XXX-III 12, XLVI 27, 38, XLVII 13, LXXXVI 65, XCV 7
दुर्मति VIII 48
दुर्मुख VIII 38
दुर्वासा XLVIII 65
दुर्विनीत XLVIII 65
दुश्शीलता LII 2
दुष्टलाङ्गूल IV 10
दुष्टाङ्गना LXXVIII 9
दुहितृशोक LI 11
दूत X 10, XVI 19, XIX 12, XXXI 3, LIII 9, LXXXVI 34, LXXXVII 8, XCV 22
दूत्य: LXXVIII 9, 10
दूर्वा XXIX 13, XLI 4, LIII 97, LIV 37, 47
दृग्गणित II 8
देवकुल LIII 89, 118, 120, LVI 1, 2, 9, 10, LVII 3
— गुरु XLVIII 73
— च्छन्द LXXXI 32
— ताविद्ध LIII 78
— सान्निध्य LVI 3
देवदारु LXXIX 2 15
— दीप्त LXXXVI 15
— पत्न्य: XLVIII 58
— मातर: XLVIII 58
देवर: LXX 20
— राज XLVIII 67
देवल VII 15, XI 1, LXXXVI 1
देवविकार XLVI 15, 17
देवा: कपोत XLVI 72
देविका XI 35
देश XCVI 1, 6
— नाश XXX 5
भ्रंश XLVI 25
— संक्षय XLVI 52, 76, 82
देहस्पन्दन II 15
दैत्य LXXX 3
दैत्येन्द्रपूज्य XCVIII 17
दैर्घ्य LIII 4-7, 10, 11, 13
दैव LXXX 1
दैवज्ञ XLIII 12, 23, XLIV 13, XLVIII 18, 78, 80, LI 1, LIII 10, LIX 1, LX 14, 18
दैवतभाग LXXI 11, 12
दैवतयात्रा XLVI 9
दोधक CIV 23
दौकूल्य LXXIII 1
दौर्भाग्य LII 2, C 5, CIII 4

काश्मीर V 70, 77, 78, IX 18, X 12, XI, 57, XIV 29
काश्यप XXI 2, XXIV 2
काष्ठ XLVI 77, LIII 102, LXXVII 34, LXXIX 39, LXXXVI 60, LXXXVIII 20, LXXXIX 1 (b) XCV 18, 40
काष्ठमातृका XLIII 58, 66
काष्ठा XLVIII 59
कास XXXII 10
किंशुक XXIV 14
किंस्तुघ्न C 2, 5
किङ्किणी XLIII 7
किञ्जल्क XXX 20
कितव X 6, LI 5
किम्पुरुष XLVIII 62
किरण XI 10, XXX 2, 8,11, 20, 31, XXXIV, XLVII 8
किरात V 35, 80, IX, 17, 35, XI 54, 60, XIV 18, 30, XVI 2, XXXII 19, 22
किरीट LVIII 32
किष्किन्ध XIV 10
कीचक LXXXVI 80
कीट XV 7, LIV 93, LXXIX 37, XCVII 7
कीनाश XV 23
कीर IV 23, XIV 29, XXXII 19
कीर्ति XLVIII 57
कील LIII 58, 110
कीलक III 17, LIV, 124, XCVII 2
कुकुर V 71, XIV 4, XXXII 22
कुक्कुट XLVI 69, LXXXVI 20, 48, LXIII 1, LXXXVII 6, LXXXVIII 1,7
कुक्कुर XXVIII 9, 10, LXII 2
कुक्षा LXVIII 19, 20
कुक्षि V 81, LI 31, LXVI 2, CV 2,
कुक्ष्य LXXIX 10
कुङ्कुम X 11, XLII 10, L 21
कुच LI 31, 43, LII 4
कुचिक XIV 30
कुंज XCVI 15, C 7
कुजात्मज XI 21
कुञ्जर LVI 17, 25
— दरी XIV 19
कुटज XXIX 12
कुटिल LXV 9
कुटुम्ब LI 18, 23
कुट्टक LXV 9
कुठार LVIII 58, LIX 12
कुडव CIV 46
कुड्य LIII 32, LVII 4, LXXXIX 9
— मत्स्य LXXXVIII 8
कुण्डक XXIII 2
कुण्डल IV 15, XLIV 25, LVIII 32, 36, 47
कुतुप XLI 2
कुनट XIV 30
कुन्त LXXII 4
कुन्तल XVI II
कुन्तिभोज X 15
कुन्द XXIX 5, L 21
कुन्दुरुक LVII 3, 5, LXXVII 8, 24
कुबेर LVIII 57
— हृद XLVIII 71
कुब्ज LIX 3, LXVII 10, LXIX 31, 35, XCVI 12
कुमार LXXXVI 34, XCVI 16
कुमारी LXX 1, LXXVIII 9
कुमुद IV 30, XI 43, XXIX 10, LIV 20 23
कुम्भ LI 18, LIII 111, LXXI 13, LXXIX 23, 29, 30, LXXXI 21, CII 6
कुरङ्ग LXXXVI 23, 26, 48, LXXXVIII 3, 33
कुरण्ट XLIII 33
कुररXLVIII 9
कुरवक XXIX 8, LIV 119, LXXXVIII 4
कुरु V 38, IX 29, 34, XIV 4, XVI 32, XXXII 11

— क्षेत्र V 78, XI 57
कुलविन्द LIV 28, LXXXII 1, 2
कुल LIV 100
कुलटा LXX 16, CIII 10, 12
कुलत्थ XXIX 5, XLI 5 LIV 36, 114, LV 16, LXXXVII 22, XCV 21
कुलनाशा XLVI 52, LIII 78-80, LXXII 5, 36, XCIV 10
कुलपांसन XVI 36
कुलाल LXXXIX 1 (b)
— कुक्कुट LXXXVIII 1, 8, 22
कुलूत IV 22, X 12, XIV 22, 29, XΛII 18
कुलोपसर्ग LIII 111
कुवलय XXX 20
कुश XXIX 13, XLIV 4, 8, LIII 97, LIV 27, 37, 77, 100, 103, LX 7, 8
कुशलकर्म XLVII 12
कुष्ठ XVI 25, XLIV 5, 9, LI 15, LXXVII 5-7, 32
कुसुम XLI 2,7, XLVI 36, 41, LIII 95, 99, 101, LIV 124, LV 20, LIX 8, LXXIX 7
कुसुमदन्त LIII 44
— नग XIV 14
— विकार LIV 56
कुसुम्भ XXIX 8
कुसूला XCVII 6
कुस्तुम्बुरु LXXVII 7
कुहक II 15, XVI 19, XIX 10
— ज्ञ LXXXVI 32
— प्रयोग LXXV 15
कुहू XLVIII 57
कूजित LXXXVIII 37
कूटपूरी LXXXVI 20, 44, LXXXVIII 4
कूप LIII 78, LIV 77, 97, 98, 121, 123, LVII 4, LXVIII 5, LXX 19
कूर्म L 22 LIV 44, LXIV 1, 3
कृकलास XXVIII 8, L 3, LXXIX 24
कृकवाकु II 23 XXVIII 6, XLVIII 6, LXXIII 1, LXXXVIII 7
कृकाटी LI 9, LXVIII 86
कृतयुग IX 45
कृत्तिका LXV 5, CI 2 CV 2
कृत्याहृत LXXIV 10
कृत्रिम XV 7
कृमि LI 3, LXXXVIII 23
कृश LI 10
कृषि C 4
कृषीवल XV 28, XVI 5, 13, XXXIII 21, XXXIV 12, LXXXVII 23, LXXXIX 4, CIV 63 (a)
कृष्ण XIV 14, LII 1 LIII 96, LVIII, 37, LX 2, LXXXI 19
कृष्णल LXXXI 11
केकर LXX 19
केतु III 7, 11, XI 2, 3, 5, 16, 26, 28, 53, XVII 7, XXI 25, XXIII, 10 XXXIV 15, 18, XLIII 2, 59, 60, 62, 64, XLVI 9, 20, 74, 82, XLVIII 83
केन्द्र XXVIII 1, XL 2, LX 20, LXXVIII 25, XCVIII 17, CIV 61 (b)
केयूर XLIII 44, 45
केरल XIV 12, XVI 11
केश XLVI 22, XLVIII 16, LI 34, LIII 60, LVIII 15, LXVIII 5, 81, 87, 90, LXXVII 23, LXXVIII 3, LXXX 15, LXXXVI 60, LXXXVIII 20, XCV 12
— धर XIV 26
— रेखा LVIII 13
केशव XLIII 2, CV 8, 16
केसर LIX 6, LXXVII 5, 30
कैकय IV 22, V 67, XI 60, XIV 25, XVI 26, XVII 18
कैलावत XIV 26
कैलास XIV 24, LVI 17, 21
कैवर्त XVI 33, LI, 21 LXXXVII 7
कोक LXXXVI 21
कोकिल XLVI 69, XLVII 28, LXXXVI 23, 26
कोङ्कण XIV 12, XVI 11

कोटिवर्ष IX II
कोटिहोम XLVI 6
कोण XLVIII 37, LIII 45, 48, 49, 55, 56, 83, 84, 112, LIV 5, 98, LXXI, 9, LXXXVI 77, LXXXVII 3, 5, 9, 31
कोद्रव XXIX 6, XLI 4, LXXXII 2
कोपच्छद LXXVII 11
कोलाक्ष LXXIX 32, 33, 36
कोल्लगिरि XIV 13
कोविदार XXIX 13, LIV 27
कोश XVI 15, XVIII 3, 5, XX 5, 7, 9 XXVI 10, XXXIV 19, XLVI 7, L 5, 10, LIII 9, 14, LIV 120, XCIII 2
कोशधान्य VIII 8
कोशाध्यक्ष LXXXVI 29
कोष्ठ LIII 42
कोष्ठागार X 7, XV 8, XVII I4, XLVII 5
कोसल V 69, 70, IX 26, X 4, 13, XIV 7, 8 XVI 6, XVII 22
कोहल XIV 27
कौङ्कुम XI 21
कौणिन्द XIV 30, 33
कौबेर LIV 39, 54, LXXXI 2, 6, LXXXVII 25
कौरव IV 24, 25, IX 30
कौलव C 1, 3
—कौलिक LXXXVII 20
कौलिन्द IV 24
कौलूत X 11
कौशाम्बी XVI 3
कौशिक XLIII 62, XLVI 68, XLVIII 4
कौशिकी XVI 16
कौशेय XVI 30, LI 19
— कौष्माण्ड XLVIII 71
कौसलक X 9 14
कौसुम्भ X 11
कौस्तुभ XLIII 3, LVIII 31
क्रकर XLVIII 6
क्रतु XIII 6, 11, XV 24, XVII 15, XIX 6
— दीक्षा XCVIII 14
क्रव्याद XIV 18, XV 8, XLIII 62, L 3, LI 33, LXX 22, LXXI 12
क्रियादीप्त LXXXVI 15, 51
क्रीडावापी LXIV 3
क्रूर XCVI 13
— ग्रह XXI 33
क्रेता XLII 7
क्रोड LXXXVI 42, LXXXVIII 9
क्रोश XCV 62
क्रोष्टुक XLVI 63, LXXXVI 21, XC 15
क्रौञ्च XIV 24, LVI 5, 6 LXXXVI 22, 27, XCIII 7
— द्वीप X 18, XIV 13
क्रौडपिशित LV 19
क्लीब XV 21
क्वणित L 5
क्वाथ XLVI 49
क्षण XLVIII 59, XCVI 5, XCVIII 12
क्षत LI 10
क्षतजकारी XCV 30
क्षति LII 7
क्षत्र LIII 13, LIX 5
क्षत्रियाद्य LXXXVI 34
क्षार L 22, 26, LIV 22, 66, 68, 71, 75, 104, 115
— शाक LXXVI 12
क्षितितनयदिन LXI (c)
क्षिप्र XXXIII 19
क्षीर XXXIV 4, XLVI 43, XLVIII 28, LV 7, 15, 20, 23, LXXVI 4, 7, 10, CV 8
— वृक्ष XLVI 24, XLVIII 37, 46, LIII 86, 120, LIV 101 106
क्षीरस्राव XLVI 26
क्षीरिक XLVI 2
क्षीरोद XIV 6, XLIII 2, 3
क्षुत LI 29, LIII 104, LVIII 63, LXXXVIII 35, XCV 60

क्षुद्रय XLVI 45, XLVII 4, 16, LIII 80 XCV 8, 11
क्षुद्र X 3, XI 45
— धान्य XXXIV 12
— मीन XIV 24
क्षुप XCIV 13
क्षुरार्पण XIV 20
क्षेत्र II 4, XLVIII 7, LI 13, LXXV 2, XCV 32, XCVI 10
क्षेम XXIX 11, XXXVIII 5, XLVII 4, LXXXV 3, LXXXIX 10, XC 15, XCV 25, 47
— धूर्त XIV 28
क्षेमा XLVIII 41
क्षोभ XC 10
क्षौद्र XLIII 60, XLVI 43, LIV 108,
LV 7, LXXVI 6
क्षौम XLVIII 50, LIV 108,
क्षौर XCVIII 12-14
क्ष्वेड XXVIII 23, LXXXVI 39

ख XLVIII 69, LXXXI 24
खगनिलय LIII 120
खचर XIV 28
खञ्जनक XLV 1, 3, 6, 10, 11, 15 LXXXVIII 1, 20
खड्ग L 3, 5, 9, LIII 123, LVIII 33
खण्ड XIV 18, XLVII 24, LXXXII 4
खदिर XXVI 9, XXIX 11, XLIV 12, LIX 5, 6, LXXXV 6, LXXXVI 80
— चञ्चु LXXXVIII 5
खद्योत XXVIII 23
खनि LXXX 10
खपुर XXI 25, XXXVI 1
खप्रकृति LXVIII 111
खर XXXIII 9, XLII 7, LIV 106, 109 LXI 2, LXXI 12 LXXXVI 44, LXXXVIII 1, XCV 47
— चर्म LXXIV 13
खररोम LVII 7
खर्जूरी LIV 58, 101
खल LXXXVI 46
खलिन XLIV 22, XCIII 9
खस X 12, XIV 6, 30, LXIX 26
खस्थ XIV 22
खात XLVI 50
खानक LXXXIX 9
खिक्खिमिनी LXXVIII 18
खुर LXXIX 31
खेटक LVIII 33, 40

गङ्गा XVI 16
— यमुनान्तराल LXIX 26
गज IX 1, XXXIII 4, LI 18, 34, LXXXVI 73, LXXXVIII 20
— दन्त LXXIX 19
— पृष्ठ LVI 25
— मद L 21
— मुख LVIII 58
गजाध्यक्ष LXXXVI 34
गण X 13
गणक XI 25
गणनायक XV 15, 17, XVII 24
— राज्य XIV 14
गणिका XLIII 25, LI 20, LXXXVII 39
गणित XV 12, XIX 10, XLVI 99
गण्ड LI 8, 33, 42, LII 3, 9, LXVIII 60, LXX 19
गति LXVIII 115
गदा LVIII 33, 34, 40
गन्ध XLII 5, XLIII 24, 36, XLIV 15, XLVI 31, 50, XLVIII 27, 31, 32, 35, 42, L 21, LIII 96, 125, LIV 124, LIX 8, LXXVII 1, 4 7, 17, 19, 21, 26, 30, 36, XCII 18
गन्धमांसी LI 15
— युक्ति XV 12, XVI 18
गन्धर्व XIII 8, XXX 2, 21, XXXVI 4, XLVI 4, XLVII 26, XLVIII 25,
LIII 44, LXXIV 7, LXXXVII 33
— पुर XCVII 13

गन्धार्णव LXXVII 14
गन्धोदक LXXVII 31, 32
गर C 4
गरुड LVI 17, 24
— वेगा LIV 87
गरुत्मान् XI 62, LXXXVI 1
गर्ग XI 1, XXI 2, 5, XXIII 4, XXIV 2 XLVI 1, 53, 57, 80, XLVIII 38, L 15, LVI 31, LXV 8, LXXXVI 3
गर्ता LIII 90
— कुक्कुट LXXXVIII 8
— श्रय XVI 36
गर्दभ XLV 9, LXXXVIII 5, 32
— राव LIII 108
गर्भ XXI 3, 6, 7, 9, 10, 12, 18, 23, 25, 22, 31, 33, 35, LI 37, 38 LVI 12, LXXV 1, LXXVIII 20, LXXX-IX 5
— दिवस XXI 5
— निपतन LI 35
— भय XXXIV 15, LXXXVII 32
— गर्भिणी XVII 17, LI 35
गल LI 8, 34, 42, LII 3
— ग्रह XXXII 18
गवल XIX 4
गवाक्ष XLIII 57, LVI 22
गव्य XIV 28, LVII 7
गात्रसंस्पर्श LI 44
— स्फोटन LXXVIII 4
गाथा CIV 54
गान्धर्व XIV 31, XV 3, 9, 12, XVI 18, XIX 10, XXXII 11, XCV 21
गान्धार IV 23, V 77, 78, IX 21, X 7, XIV 28, XVI 26, XVII 18, 26, LXXXVI 40
गाम्भीरिका XVI 16
गिरिश्वर LXXIX 20, XCIV 1
गिरिनगर XIV 11
गिरिव्रज X 14
गीत XXXIII 23, XLIV 7, XLVI 17 61, 91, LX 14, LXXXVI 22, 39 XCVIII 10
गीतक CIV 52
गुग्गुलु LVII 3, 5, LXXVII 9, 11
गुच्छ LXXXI 33
गुञ्जा LXXXI 8, 11, 12
गुड X 8, XIV 3, XLI 4, XLIII 38, LXXVII 8, 8, 10, 15, 16, 26, 30, LXXXIX 1 (a), XCV 20, CV 8
गुडूची LIV 115
गुण्ड्र LIV 100
गुद LI 8, LII 6, LXVI 2
गुरु LIII 124, XCVIII 16
— भ LV 31, XCVIII 12
—सुत XI 39
गुलुहा XIV 22
गुल्फ LII 7, LXI 4, LXX 1, 24
गुल्म XLI 7, LIV 90, 100, 101, 105, LV 18, XCIV 13, XCV 5, 35
गुहराज LVI 18, 25
गुह्य LXX 3, 17, LXXX 9, CV 1
गुह्यक XLVI 14
गृध्र XLVIII 4, LXXIX 24, LXXXVIII 1, 11, XCV 46, XCVII 9
गृह LIII 69, 83, 100, 105, 125, XCV 18, 19, C 4
गृहगोधिका LIV 16, LXXXVI 37, LXXXVIII 47
गृहचुल्ली LIII 40, 41
— गृहधूम LVII 5
— ग्रहपटल XLV 8, XCV 24
गृहभर्ता LIII 58, 59, 66, 98, 105, 109, 110
गृहाङ्ग XCVI 13
गेयज्ञ X 3, XLIII 26
गैरिक XLVI 78
गो IX 1, 2, XVII 18, 19, XIX 2, 5, 14, XXIV 35, XXVI 8, XXVIII 7, 8 XXIX 7, XXX 13, XXXII 29, XL 6, XLV 5 XLVI 6, 46, 73, 85, 95, XLVII 16, XLVIII 68,

LI 18,34, LIII 98, 124, LVII 7 LXI 2, LXXIV 8, LXXXVI 22 27 45, 77, 80 LXXXVII 39, LXXXVIII 3, 9, 35, LXXXIX 1 (b) 5, 9, 10, XCII 1,3, XCV 55, XCVII 17, C 5
गोक्षुर LIV 100, LXXVI 10
—चर XLI 13, CIV 2
गोच्चा LVIII 9
— जिह्वा L 7
गोदावरी XVI 9
गोदोह XLVI 6
गोधा XXXIII 9, LI 35, LIII 122, LIV 13, 69, LXXXVI 42, LXXXVIII 3, 8
गोधूम XV 6, XVI 7, XIX 6, XXIX 4, XLI 2, 3,5,
गोनर्द IX 13, XIV 12, XXXII 22
गोप LXXXVI 30 LXXXVII 45
गोपीती XLV 3
गोपुच्छस्थ XCV 35
— पुर LXXXIX 19
गोमती XVI 12
गोमनन्त V 68, IX 13, XVI 17
गोमय LV 6, 7, 19, 30, LXXI 10, LXXXIX (a), XCV 38
गोमांस LV 17
गोमायु XXVIII 24, LXXI 12, XCVII 9
गोभक्ष XVI 35
गोमी XXXII 22
गोमूत्र L 21, LIV 115 LXXVII 31
गोमेदक LXXX 5
गोरजः CIII 13
गोरस LIV 20
गोरोचना XLVIII 35
गोलक्षण LXI 1
गोलाङ्गूल XVI 3
गोविन्द CV 14
गोशीर्ष IX 2
गोष्ठ XLVIII 11, LXXXIX 9, XCII 3
गोस्वामी LXXXVI 32
गौड XIV 7
गौरग्रीव XIV 3
ग्रन्थ CVI 5
ग्रन्थि LIV 81, LXXIX 29, 31, 37
ग्रसन V 43
ग्रस्त V 7, 27
ग्रह XLVI 90, XLVIII 26
— घात XXXIII 21
ग्रहण XXXII 24, XLII 1, XLVI 82, LXXXI 20
ग्रहभक्ति XVII 27
— माला XX 3
— यज्ञ XLIV 14, XLVIII 29
— युद्ध V 95, XVI 40, XXI 25, XLVIII 83
— शान्ति XLIII 37
ग्राम LIII 69, 84, LIV 97, LXXXVI 6, 40, LXXXIX, 14, 18, XCV 8, XCVII 8
ग्राम घात XXX 3, LXXXVI 64
ग्रामीण LXXXVII 45
ग्राम्य XCVI 7
— सत्त्व XCI 2
— स्थिरभ XCVIII 17
ग्रास V 18, XCIII 7
ग्राह XCIV 14
ग्रीवा LI 9, 30, LII 4, LVIII 5, 15, LXVIII 31, 86, LXX 5, 18, XCIII 7, CV 4
ग्रीष्म III 23, 26, XXVII 7, XL 1, 3, XLII 3, XLVI 87
ग्रैवेयक XLIII 46
ग्रैष्मिक IX 43, XXV 2, XL 2, 13

घट LIII 29, LVI 15, 18, 26, LIX 2,
— कार XV 1
— कुट्टन XCV 44
घटोदर LXVIII 18
घटोपवहन XCV 44
घण्टा XLIII 7, LXXXVI 23, LXXXVII 26

घन LXXVII 10, 13,
— विनाश XLVII 12
घर्मांशु LV 9
घाण्टिक X 6, 12
घास LII 4
— क LXXXVI 46
घृत XVI 20, XLII 5, XLIII 60, XLVI 32, 43, XLVIII 36, 77, L 21, LIII 96, LIV 108, LV 7, 15, LXXVI 3 9, XCV 24, CV, 7, 8
घृतकम्बल II 23
— वर्षण XCVII 10
घोर VII 8, 11
घोष XIV 2, 30, LXXXVI 78
घोषिक X 6
घोणा LI 39, LII 3, LXI 15

चकोर XLVIII 9
चक्र XX 2, XLIV 4, XLVI 9, 60, LVIII 33, 34
— चर X 12
चक्रवाक LVI 5, LXXXVIII 1
चञ्चूक XIV 18
चटक LXXVI 7, LXXXVIII 1, 9
चणक XV 14, 34
चण्डवृष्टिप्रयात CIV 61 (d)
चण्डाल XV 30
चतुरस्र LVI 28
चतुरानन XCVI 16
चतुर्थ CIII 4
चतुर्द्वार LVI 27
चतुर्मुखत्व LXXIV 20
चतुष्कोण LVI 18
चतुष्टय LXIX 1
चतुष्पथ LI 4, LIII 89
चतुष्पद LI 16, C 2, 5
चतुष्षष्टिपद LVI 10
चन्दन XVI 30, XLIV 9, LIX 5, LXXVIII 30, LXXIX 2, 12, 14, 18, LXXXVII 11
चन्द्र XCVI 12, 17
— पुर XIV 5
— भागा XVI 27
— योग II 18
— शाला LVI 25, 27
चन्द्रातप LIV 110
चमरी LXXII 1
— चमूप X 4, XVI 8, XLVI 12, LI 21, LXVIII 41, 47, 58
चम्पक XXIX 8, L 21, LXXVII 6, 7
चम्पा XVI 3
चम्बूक XIV 18
चर X 10, LXXXVI 34, XCVI 2, 4
चरक LXXXVI 33
चरकर्म XCVIII 11, C 2
चरकी LIII 83
चरगृह XCVI 14
चरण LXVIII 2, 3, 97 LXX 2
चरदल II 12
चराचर XLVIII 68
चरु XLVI 36, 37
चर्म XLII 6, XLVIII 43-46, 75, LI 3 LIII 103, LVII 7, LXXXVI 76, LXXXVII 8, 35
चर्मद्वीप XIV 9
चर्मरङ्ग XIV 23
चलकेतु XI 33
चाक्रिक X 9
चाटुकार LXXXI 35
चातक XXIV 19, XXVIII 14, LXXXVI 27
चातुर्वर्ण्य LIII 12, 14
चान्द्र II 5
— पुर XIV 5
चाप LXXII 4
चामर XVI 24, XLII 7, XLIV 24, XLV 5, LXXII, 41, LXXIX 21, LXXXIX 1 (a)
चामीकर XLIII 33
चार XLVII 1
चारण XLIII 66, LXXIV 19, LXXXVII 6

चारानुकूल C 8
चारुदेवि IX 18
चाष XXVIII 14, XXXIV 4, XLIII 62, XLVIII 6, LXXXVI 23, 41, 43, 48, LXXXVIII 1, 23-25
चिकित्सा LV 15
चिति XLIII 13, LXXXVI 60, XCVII 11
चित्र XLI 7
— कर IX 30, LXXXVII 15, 40
— कर्म LVIII 14
— कूट XIV 13, XVI 17
— गर्भ XLVI 95
— ज्ञ X 10
— भाण्ड X 10
चित्रा IX 30, X 10, XI 57, LXXI 4, XCVIII 10, C 6, CI 8, CV 5
चिन्ता LII 2
चिपिट LXXX 16, LXXXI 28
चिपिटनासिक XIV 26 LXVIII 61
— विषाण LXI 2
चिबुक LI 42, LII 3, LVIII 5
चिरबिल्व XXIX 5
चिह्न LIV 7, 17, 28, 29, 47, 86, LXXXVI 78, XCVI 13
चीन V 77, 78, 80, X 7, 11, XI 61, XIV 30, XVI 1, 38
चीर XLIV 8
— निवासी XIV 31
चुम्बन LXXVIII 4, 6
चुल्ली LIII 38
चूचुक LXVIII 27, 51
चूत LXXXVI 80
चूर्ण LV 25, LXXVI 10, 11, LXXVII 12, 31, 36, LXXXI 17
चेदि XIV 8, XVI 3, XXXII 22, XLIII 8
चेर्यार्यक XIV 15
चेष्टा II 18, 1, LI LXXXVI 53, 58, XCV 57, XCVI 1, 7
चैत्य XLVI 70, LIII 90, LIX 2, LXXIX 3
— तरु XXXIII 21
चैत्र XXI 12, XXV 6, C 8, CV 6
चैद्य XI 59, XIV 8, XVI 3
चोक्ष LXXXVII 43
चोच XVI 30, XLI 4
चोरक XVI 25, XCV 7
चोल V 40, XI 61, XIX 13, XVI 10, 38, LXXVII 14
चौर LI 21, 24, 26, 28, LII 6, LXXIV 15, LXXXVII 10, 31, LXXXIX 3, 13, XCV 7, 19, CIV 63 (b)
— स्वामी LXIX 27
च्यवन XLVIII 66

छत्र XXXIII 27, XLIII 7, 57, 63, XLV 5, XLVIII 9, 73, LIII 113, LIV 101, LXXI 13, LXXIII 6, LXXIX 21, LXXXVI 74, LXXXIX 1 (a), XCVII 11
— च्छाया XCV 14
छन्दोविचिति CIV 64
छर्दि XXXII 18
छाग LXV 1, 7, 8
छादन XXIV 34
छाया II 3, 8, III 3, III 3, XXXI 2, XLVI 44, LI 2, LV 1, 29, LXVIII 89-91, 94, LXXXVI 74
छिक्कर LXXXVI 20, 44
छिद्र LXXIX 32, 33, 35
— पत्र LIV 105
छिप्पिका LXXXVIII 2, 35
छुच्छु LXXXVI 37
— न्दरी LXXXVIII 5, 47
छेद XLII 5, 6, LIII 122, LXXI 12, 13, LXXIX 21, 26, XCIV 2

जघनचपला CIV 3
जघन्य LXIX 31, 33, 34
जङ्घा LI 9, 25, 34, 43, LII 7, LIII 53, LVIII 17, 21, LXI, 13, LXVIII 4, 86, LXX 2, 17, 24, LXXIX 30, CV 1

जटाधर XIV 13
जटासुर XIV 30
जटिल LXV 9
जठर LI 31, 38, 43
जठराङ्ग XIV 8
जड XCVI 12
जतु LI 9, LXVIII 30, LXX 25
जनवाद XCVII 10
जनित्री LXXIV 11
जन्मकाल XCVI 13
जन्मर्क्ष XXXIV 11
जन्माधिप XXXIV 11
जन्मान्तर LXXXVI 5
जप XLVI 51, 58
जपाकुसुम XXVIII 14
जम्बुक XLVI 68
जम्बू XXIX 4, LI 17, LIV 8, 9, 86, 87, 101, 119, LV 4, 10 LXXXII 1, LXXXV 7
जय XLIX 6, LI 24, LIII 48
जयन्त LIII 43, 54, 63
जयविजये XLIII 40
जरण V 81, 88
जरद्गव IX 1
जरन्निव LXXVI 12
जरान्वित LXXVI 3
जल XLVIII 69, LIV 11, 13, 14, 16, 17, 39, 41, 45, 47, 49, 54, 55, 63, 67, 73, 77-79, 90, 92, 96, 106 LV 24, XCVI 5
— केतु XI 46
— खग XLVIII 8
— आजीव XI 55
— मार्ग XV 18
— मृत्यु LXVIII 9
— यन्त्र II 8
जलाशय XXVIII 4, 12, 17, 19
— धिदैवत LXXI 5, CI 11
— क्षय LV 1
जल्पित XCVII 6
जागरण LX 14, LXXVIII 11
जाङ्गल IX 29, LIV 86, 89, 93
जाति LXXXVI 7
जाती LXXXV 4
— फल XVI 30, LI 17, LXXVII 7, 26 27, 33
जानु LI 9, 31, 43, LII 7 LIII 22 LXVI 2, LXVIII 6, LXX 2, 24, LXXXIX 11, CV 1
— कपिच्छा LVIII 17
जाबालि XLVIII 64
जामि LXXIV 10
जामित्र XL 10
जाया LXXIV 11
जारद्गवी IX 1, 3
जाल LVI 22, LVIII 1, 2, LXXXVI 46
जाहक LXXXVI 42
— जिघ्रण LXXXIX 13
जित XVII 9
जिन LX 19
जिह्वा LI 9 32, LXVIII 53, 87, 97, 101
जीमूत XLVIII 69, LXXXVI 59
जीरक LI 15
जीव XLVIII 6, XCVI 15, 17, XCVII 1, XCXIII 4
जीवक XVI 19, XLVIII 6, LIX 6
जीववर्ग LX 20
जीवा XLVII 39
जुङ्ग XIV 21
जृम्भण LXXVIII 4
जैगीषव्य XLVIII 64
ज्ञ XCVI 17
ज्ञाति LII 8
ज्ञान LII 3
ज्या XLVII 16
ज्येष्ठा IV 7, LIV 125, CI 10, CV 4
ज्यैष्ठ XXII 1, XXIII 1
ज्योतिश्शास्त्र CVI 1
ज्योतिष्मती XLVIII 39, LIV 87
ज्योतीरस LXXX 5
ज्वर XXXII 10, 14, XCV 35, XCVIII 3

ज्वलन XLVI 19, 28, 86, L 5, XCIII 1-4, XCVII 10
ज्वाला XLVI 29, 49, XLVII 10, XC 6, 7

झष XXXIII 10, CII 6
— पित्त L 24

डमर II 29, XVI 41, XLII, 2. LXXXVI 56
डामर XIV 30
डोम्ब LXXXVII 33

तक्र LIV 114, LXXVI 11
तक्षक LXXXI 25
तक्षशिला X 8, XIV 26, XVI 26
तक्षा XLIII 29, LXXXVII 20, 24
तगर XVI 25, LI 15, LXXVII 5, 7, 13, 24, 26
तङ्गण IX 7, X 12, XIV 29, XVI 6, XVII 25, XXXII 15
तडागभेदी LXXXVIII 6
तडित् XXX 8, 31, 32, XXXII 21, XXXIV 8, XLVI 20
तण्डुल LXXX 12, LXXXVII 14
तनयलाभ LII 4, 6
तनुकम्बल LXI 12
तन्तुवाय XV 12
तन्त्र I, 9
तमः XLVI 21
तमाल XXI 23, XXIV 17
तमोऽधिक LXIX 9
तमोऽन्त्य V 43
तरलक LXXXI 35
तरला LXXVI 11
तरु XLI 6, XLVIII 67, LIII 85, 87, LIV 92, LV 8, 13, LIX 4, 8, LXXXV 3, LXXXVI 76, LXXXVIII 40, XCV 3, 17, XCVIII 6
तर्कुक LXVIII 41
तस्कर XI 20, XIV 11, 23, XVI 4, 34, XXII 3, XLIII 63, XLVII 4, LIII 102, LXXXVI 31, LXXXVII 36, XCII 1, XCV 40
ताडन XXIV 34
तान्तव XLII 8
तापस XIV 15, XV 13, XVII 15, XIX 2, LI 22, LIX 2, LXXXVI 29
तापी XVI 12
तामसकीलक III 7, XI 22, XXI 25
ताम्बूल XII 9, LXXVII 35
ताम्र XXX 23, XLVIII 46, LIV 71, 104, 109, LX 5, LXXXI 19
— चूड LXXXVIII 34
— पर्णी XIV, LXXXI 2, 3
— लिप्ती X 14, XIV 7
तारकामान XCVIII 2, 3
तारक्षिति XIV 21
तारा XXXII 13, XXXIII 1-3, 7, XLVI 86, 90, 94, XLVII 10, 21, LVIII 11
— ग्रह I 10, XX 1, XXXIV 18, LXIX 1
— प्रमाण XCVIII 2
ताल XIV 22, LI 14 LIV 119
— गर्भ L 24
तालाशत LV 23
तालिकट XIV 11
तालीपत्र XXVII 3
तालु LI 9, LXVIII 53, 87, 97
तिक्त XVI 20 XLVIII 4, LI 33, LXXVI 12
तित्तिर XXVIII 17, LXXXVIII 21
तिथि II 19, 27, LXXXVI 58, XCIV 10, XCVI 9, XCIX 3, C 8, CIII 13
— पतप XCIX 1
तिन्तिडी LV 21
तिन्दुक XXIX 3, LI 17, LIV 50, 112, 115, LVII 1, 5, LIX 6, LXXIX 2, 11, 15
तिमि LXXXI 1, 23, 29,
तिमिङ्गिलाशन XIV 16
तिमिर LX 11

तिर्यक्स्वभाव LXVIII 108, 114

तिल XV 14, XVI 37, XXV 2, XXIX 4, XLI 6, XLVI 35, XLVIII 30, 35, 77, LI 33, LIV 115, LX 2, 7, 16, 17, 21, 25, LXXVI 9

तिलक XXIX 6, L 9, LII 10, LIV 37, 50, LV 11, LXXXVII 24

तिष्य XCVIII 16

तीक्ष्ण VII 8, 10, XCVIII 7

— विषाण V 12

तीर्थ XLVIII 15, LX 9

तुम्बवन XIV 15

तुरग XLI 6, XCIII 9, 14, XCV 23

— क्षय LIX 13

— भिषक् XLIV 13

— गानन XIV 25, XVI 35

तुरुष्क LXXVII 7-9, 23, 26, 30

तुला LIII 30, LV 17

— भिमन्त्रण XXVI 1, 5, 9, 10

तुष XLVIII 16, LI 4, 14, 29, LIII 62, LXXIX 8, LXXXVIII 20

— धान्य XV 4, 7, 11, 27, XVI 4, XLI 4

तुषार XIV 22, XVI 6, XLVI 92

तूर्यनाद XXXII 26, XLIII 24, XLIV 7, XLVI 61, 62, XLVIII 49, 26, LX 10, 16, LXXXVI 39, XCVII 9

तृण LI 4, LIII 102, LIV 52, 90, LXXV 10, LXXXVIII 20, LXXXIX 6, XCV 18, 36

तृतीय CIII 3

तैतिल C 1, 3

तैल XV 9, XVI 20, 32, XXXIV 4, XLII 5, XLVI 35, L 25, LV 27, LXXVII 6, XCV 22

— वर्षण XCVII 10

तैलिक X 5

तोटक CIV 39

तोय LIV 6, 7, 9, 10, 13-18, 27, 29, 31, 34-36, 51, 60, 65, 103, 107-109, 113, XCVIII 5

— स्वभाव LXVIII 109

तोरण XXX 6, XXXVI 2, 5, XLIII 25, XLIV 3, 8, XLVI 20, 70, 74, LIII 125, LX 1, LXXI 13, XCVII 8, 11

तौली CII 4

त्याग XLVI 58

त्रयी XIX 11

त्रायमाणा XLIV 10, XLVIII 39

त्रास XCV 54

त्रिशाश II 18

त्रिक LI 9

त्रिकालदर्शी XXI 4, XLVI 99

त्रिकोण LXXVIII 25

त्रिगर्त IV 24, IX 19, XIV 25, X 11, XVI 22, XVII 16,

त्रित XLVIII 65

त्रिनेत्र XIV 31, XLVIII 77

त्रिपुर V 39, XIV 9

त्रिफल XVI 29

त्रिमधुर XLVIII 31

त्रिवलि LXX 5

त्रिवृता LIV 48, 87

त्रिस्थान LXI 5

त्रुटि II 4

त्वक् XLI 4, XLVI 41, LIV 115, LXVIII 87, 90, 96, LXXVII 5, 6, 7, 12, 24, 28, 32, LXXXV 2

त्वष्टा III 6, XCVIII 4

त्वाष्ट्र XCVII 2, XCVIII 16

त्सरु L 8

दंष्ट्रा LXVIII 52, LXXXI 23

दंष्ट्री XIX 1. XXXIII 9, LXXXVI 44, XCV 40

दकार्गल LIV 1, 99, 125

दक्ष XLVIII 64

दक्षिण LII 9, LVIII 34, 38, XCV 26, 27, 29, 30, XCVI 12

दक्षिणपूर्व LIII 43

दक्षिणभुज LIII 67

— मार्ग XLVII 4
दक्षिणा XLIII 38, XLVI 17, 32, 46, 59, 65, 72, 73, LX 11
— पथ IX 40, XLVII 8
— यन III 1
— वर्त LXI 13
दक्षिणीय XLVIII 80
दण्ड III 17, V 95, XX 2, XXIV 9, XXVIII 12, XXX 2, 8, 16, 30, XXXIII 24 XLVII 19, LIII 39, 41, LXXII 23, LXXIII 2, 4, 6, LXXIX 23
दण्डक XI 56, XIV 16, XVI 11
— नायक LXXIII 4
— नीति XIX 11
— पिङ्गलक XIV 27
दद्रू XXXII 14
दधि XXX 18, XLIII 60, XLVI 43, XLV 6, XLVIII 19, 35, LIII 99, 101, LIX 8, LXXIX 7, LXXXI 5, LXXXVI 45, LXXXVII 14, XCIII 8, XCV 22
— भक्त XCV 51
दधीचि LXXX 3
दनु XLVIII 57
दन्त XXVI 8, LIII 103, LXVIII 97, 101, LXX 21, LXXIX 20, LXXXVII 9, LXXXIX 17, XCIV 1, 7, 9
दन्तकल्पन XCIII 15
— काष्ठ LXXVII 31, LXXXV 1, 2
— भङ्ग XCIV 7, 9-11
दन्ती LIV 48, XCIII 15
दन्तुरक XIV 6
दम्पती LXXIV 12, XCV 43
दरण XLVI 75, 88
दरद V 42, 79, XIII 9, XIV 29
दरी LXXXVI 78
दर्दुर XIV 11, XXIV 19, LIV 31, 32, 64
दर्पण IV 2
दर्भ XLVIII 34, XCV 5
दर्वी XLVI 63
दशन LI 8, LXVIII 32, 87
दशपुर XIV 12
दशभौम LVI 21
— रथतनय LVIII 30
दशान्त LXXI 9
दशापाक XCV 61
दशार्ण V 40, 15, XIV 10, XVI 26, XXXII 11
दशाह्निका XCVII 9
दस्यु XIX 19, XXXVII 2
— भय LII 79, 81
दहन IX 1, 3, XCVIII 4, 8
दाक्षिण्य LXXV 5
दाडिम LV 4, 10, LXXXI 8, LXXXV 7
दान XLVI 58
दानव XLVIII 30
दामोदर CV 15
दाम्भिक XVI 37
दार XLVI 7, XLVIII 61, 63
दारातिक्रमण LXXIV 13
दारु XLIV 3, LIII 23, 60, 86, 122, LX 4, LXXIX 6, 27, 35, 37
दारुण XXXIII 19, C 5
दार्व XIV 30
दाशेरक V 67, XIV 26
दासमेय XIV 28
दासी LI 13, 21, 25, LXXVIII 9
दाह LIV 97
दिक् XLVIII 69, XCVI 1, 5, 9, XCVII 13
दिक्चक्र LXXXVI 76, LXXXVII 18, LXXXVIII 46, XCV 49
— पति LIV 4, LXXXVI 75
दिग्गज XXXII 1
दिग्दाह III 10, XXI 25, XXIV 25, XXXI 1, 5, XXXII 13, 24; XCVII 4
दिग्बल II 18
दिति XLVIII 68, LIII 45, 49
— तनय XLVIII 30

दौवारिक LIII 44
द्युति LXIX 4
द्यूत IX 34, LI 20
द्रव LXXVII 10
द्रविड IX 15, 19, XIV 19, XVI 2, 11, XXXII 15
द्रविडाधिप IV 23
द्रव्य I 7, XXIX 1, XLI 1, 12, XLVIII 38, LXXVII 18-20, 25, 29, LXXIX 36, LXXXV 5, LXXXVI 69, LXXXVII 1, 5, XCIII 8, XCV 15, 18
द्रव्यवर्धन LXXXVI 2
द्राक्षा LV 4
द्राविड LVIII 4
द्रुतपद CIV 20
द्रुम LIV 105, LV 5, LIX 7, LX 1, LXXIX 38 XCV 38
— पतन LXVIII 50
द्रेष्काण II 18
द्रोण XXI 32, 34, XXIII 6, 7, 9, LV 17, LVII 2
द्वन्द्व LXXXVI 25
द्वादशभौम LVI 20
द्वादशांश II 18
द्वार LI 39, LIII 24, 31-35, 71, 76, 77, 80, 113, LIV 120, LVI 10, 12, 16, 20, LVIII 3, LXXXIX 8, XCI 3
द्विगुणाश्रि LXXX 15
द्विग्रहयोग II 18
द्विज XLVIII 20, LXX 6, LXXXVI 34, XCVII 17, C 3, 5, CV
द्वित XLVIII 65
द्वितीय CI 14, CIII 2
द्वितीयवेदी XLVIII 75
द्विदैवत LXXI 4
द्विप LIV 118, LXXX 2, LXXXI 1
द्विपद LI 16
द्विमूर्ति XCVI 14
द्विरदवर XLIV 15
द्विवज्रक LIII 28
द्वीप XIV 14, XVI 6
द्वीपी LXXXVI 28, LXXXVIII 3
द्वैपायन XLVIII 67

धन LI 17-19, LII 2, 4, 6, LIV 52, 53, LXXII 5, XCV 34, 38, 51
— वान् LXXXVI 32
— हानि L 16, LII 8, LIII 60, 74
धनिष्ठा III 1 VII 2, IX 3, X 16, XV 21, LIV 123, CI 12, CV 3
धनुः XX 2, XXXIII 6
धनुष्मान् XIV 24, CII 5
धन्य LII 9 LXVIII 116
धन्वन LVII 1, LXXXVIII 9
धरण LXXXI 13, 15, 18
धरातनय XI 13
धर्म XLVI 10, XCVIII 6, C 3, CIII 9
— पट्टन XIV 14
धर्मारण्य XIV 3
धर्मेश XCIX 1
धव XLIII 15, LIII 120, LIV 105, LV 22
धाता XLVI 12, 59
धातु LXIX 4, LXXX 15, LXXXII 2, 4, XCV 21, CIV 91 (d)
धातृभवन LXXIV 18, 19
धात्री LI 37, LV 22, LXXVI 5, LXXVIII 9
धान्य XLI 3, 6, XLII 4, 8, 11, XLVI 41, 46, LI 16, 18, LII 6, LIII 16, 118, 124, LXXVII 14, 15, LXXXI 6, LXXXIX 9, XCV 5, 11, 22
धान्यकूट XLV 6
धारण (गर्भ) XXII 2 ,4
धार्मिक LXXXVI 30, LXXXVII 21
धिक्कर LXXXVI 38
धिक्कार LXXXVIII 7
धिष्ण्य XXIV 5, XXXIII 1, 2, 6, XCVIII 15, CV 6, 8
धीवर LXXXVII 34

धुन्धुक LXXIX 32, 35, 37
धूप XLIII 24, XLIV 15, XLVI 31, XLVIII 31, 32, LIII 99, 113, 125, LIV 124, LIX 8, LXXVII 1, 4, 10
धूम XXX 13, 21, XXXII 25, XXXIII 9, XXXVI 3, XXXVIII 2, XLIII 65, XLVI 21, 22, 29, 49, 75, 84, 86, 93, XLVII 10, LIV 60, LX 13, XCIII 3, 5, XCVII 13
धूमकेतु XI 9, XCVII 3
धूमिनी LXXXVI 12
— धूम्र LIV 36, LXXXII 11
धूर्तगृह LIII 89
धूसर LIV 13, 44
धृति XLVIII 57
ध्रुव XI 34 XIII 2, XXXIII 19, XLVII 12, XLVIII 63, XCVIII 6, C 2, 4
ध्रुवकेतु XI 41
ध्रुवम LV 31
ध्रुवावर्त LXVI 4
ध्वंस XLVII 10
ध्वज III 32, XVI 24, XXXVI 5, XLIII 5, 6, 7, 10, 18, 57, XLIV 4, XLV 5, XLVII 7, XLVIII 73 L 2, LXXI 13 LXXII 4, LXXIX 21, LXXXVI 78, LXXXIX 1 (a), XCVII 13
ध्वजिनी XLVII 26
ध्वाङ्क्ष III 8, 17, XXIV 21, LXXIX 24, LXXXVIII 1, XCV 38, 46

नकुल LIV 32, 71, LXXXVI 41, 43, LXXXVIII 3, XCVII 12
नक्तमाल LIV 101, LV 11
नक्र XXVIII 14 XXXIII 9
नक्षत्र II 27,XLVIII 59, XCVII 14, 16, XCVIII 3, XCIX 3
— पुरुष CV 5
— माला LXXXI 34, CV 13
— सूचक II 9, 16
नख LI 8, LVIII 20, 28, LXVIII 41, 86, 90, 101, LXXVII 8, 9, 14, 16, 24, 26, CV 3
— विक्षत XLVIII 8
नगर LIII 69, XCVIII 6
नग्न LI 5, LIII 124, LX 19
नग्नजित् LVIII 4, 15
नग्नशवर XIV 10
नट X 10, XV 9, XVI 20, XLIII 26
नत LXXVII 29
नन्द XLIII 39
नन्दन VIII 38, LVI 17, 22
नन्दा XCIX 2
नन्दिकावर्त XXIX 8, LIII 32, 36, LXXIX 22
नन्दिवर्धन LVI 17, 24
नपुंसक LI 10, 36, LXXVIII 24, LXXXVI 9
नप्तृक LXXXVI 49
नभस्तल CIII 10
— नयन LXX 26
— वाल्लभ्य LIII 72
नर्कुटक CIV 52
नर्तक X 3, XVI 20, XLIII 26
नर्दन XLVI 92
नर्मदा V 64, XVI 1, 9
— नरेन्द्रधूप LXXVII 11
नल LIV 100
नलिका LIV 100, LXXVII 5
नलिनी LVI 4
नवकोष्ठकाधिप LII 46
नवनीतनिभ LXXXI 4
नवम (अहः) XCVIII 13
नवमालिका LIV 48
नवांश II 18, XCVI 10
नवाम्बर LXXI 8
नष्टराज्य XIV 29
नाक्षत्र II 5, XI 53, XIV 1, XXI 7, XXXIV 18, XLIII 12, XLVI

90, XLVII 10, 13, XLVIII 26
नाग IX 1, 2, XLVI 14, XLVIII 20, 25, 31, 62, C 5, LIV 101, 111, LXXXVII 24
— कुसुम XLIV 10
— केसर XXIX 12
— दन्त LIII 62
— दन्ती XLIV 9
— पुष्प LXXVII 14, 32
— फल LVII 5
नागर XXXVI 2
नागवीथी XLVII 17
नागसम्भूत LXXXI 26
नाटक CIV 61 (d)
नापित X 9, XV 1, LI 5, LXXVIII 9
नाभस XLVI 5
— योग II 18
नाभि LI 9, 25, LII 6, LVIII 16, 24, LXVI 2, LXVIII 21, 23, 85, LXX 4, 24, LXXVIII 3, LXXXVII 18, 21, 28, 45
नाम XCVI 14, 16
— नायकचिव्रित XLVI 78
नारद XXIV 2
नारायण XLVIII 77, CV 14
नारिकेलद्वीप XIV 9
नारी LII 9
नारीमुख XIV 17, XVI 12
नाल XLVI 33, LIV 115
नालक LI 42
नाविक IV 9, IX 31, XVII 17
नासा LI 8, LVIII 5, 10, LXVIII 60-62, 86, 88, LXX 7, XCIII 4, CV 4
नासिक्य XIV 13, XVI 12
नास्तिक XLVI 76, LXIX 35
निकष L 8
निगड LXXXVI 77
निगम LI 21
निगर LXXXI 17
निचुल XXIX 12, XLVIII 12, LIV 119, LVI 5
नितम्ब LXX 4
नित्यगति XLVIII 77
निमित्त II 14, XLIII 30, XLVIII 78, XLIX 8, LI 7, 21, 33, LIII 59, 105, LIV 5, 89, LIX 1
निम्ब LIII 129, LIV 115, LVII 5 7 LXXXI 6
नियुद्धकुशल XV 23
निर्ऋति LIV 3, XCVIII 5
निरोध V 43
निर्गुण्डी LIV 14
निर्ग्रन्थ LXXXVII 34
निर्ग्रंथी LI 21
निर्घात III 10, V 95, XVI 40, XXI 25 XXIV 25, XXXII 23, 24, XXXIX 1, XLVI 4, 84, XCVII 6
निर्विन्ध्या XVI 9
निर्हार LXXXVI 62
निवसन LI 19
निवेश XLIII 47
निशाचर XVI 8
निषाद V 76
— राष्ट्र XIV 10
निषेक II 14,
निष्कसमा LXXIV 7
निष्कुट LXXIX 32, 33, 36
निष्ठीवित LIII 104
निष्पाव XVI 34, XLI 5, LXXIX 33
निस्त्रिंशभृत् L 10
नीचगति II 9
नीड XCV 2
नातिवृत्ति X 17
नीप XIV 2, LIV 101, 119, LXXXV 6
नीराजन XLIV 1, 2, XLV 11
नील XXX 18, XXXIII 16, XXXIV 2, XXXV 4, LIII 123
नीलोत्पल XXI 23, XXIX 9, XLIII 33, L 7, LIV 22

नीहार XXX 21
नूपुर LXXVIII 1
नृत्य LX 14
नृपगृह LIII 14, 17, 24, 31
— सुता LXXXVIII 5
नृपाज्ञा XCVIII 14
नृशंस XVI 13
नृसिंहवन XIV 22
नेता LXXXVI 34
नेत्र LII 2, LVIII 8, 11, LXVIII 87, 97 101, XCIII 4, CV 4
नेत्ररोग LXXI 6
नेपाल IV 22, V 65
नेमि XLIII 22, LXXXVII 21
नैकृतिक V 28, X 3
नैधनगृह XCVIII 17
नैमिष XI 60
नैर्ऋत LIII 48, 118, LIV 98, LXXI 5, LXXXVI 31, LXXXVII 8, 22, 35, XCV 4, 22, XCVI 7
नैर्वाहिकद्वार LIV 120
नैस्व्य LIII 75, 119
नौ LXXXVI 73
न्यग्रोध XXIX 3, LI 17, LIV 96, LXXXVI 80

पक्वेष्टका LIII 23
पक्ष II 41, XLVIII 59, XCVII 1, 9, 11
— क्षय XXVIII 20
— घ्न LIII 38
पक्षावसान XCVI 5
पङ्क L 21, LV 15
पङ्कज XXVIII 14, XXIX 10, LI 19
पङ्क्तिपावन II 13
पञ्चगव्य LX 9
— ग्रहसंयोग V 17
— नद X 6, XI 60, XIV 21
निमित्त XXI 31, 37
— मस्य CIII 5
पञ्चर्च XLVI 64
— वनस्पति LXXIX 39
पट LI 14
— वास LXXVII 12
पटह XLIII 59
पटोल XIV 30
पट्ट XLIX 1-6, 8
पण्य X 17, XCVIII 9
— पण्यस्त्री X 8
पतङ्ग LXXXVIII 23
पताका XXIV 9, XXXVI 5, XLIII 25, 27, 64, XLVIII 33, LX 2
पतिवध XCV 12
पत्र XVI 30, XLI 4, XLVI 95, XLIX 6, LIII 82, LV 8, LVI 15, LXXVII 5, 7, 23, 29, 32, 33, 36, 37, XCV 12
पत्रोर्ण XVI 30
पथिकागम XCV 52
पथ्या LXXVI 3, LXXVII 29, CIV 55
पद LIII 64, 65
पद्म XIV 5, LIII 29, LIV 100, LVI 23
— क LXXIX 2, 13
— केतु XI 49
— नाभ CV 15
राग LXXX 4, LXXXII 1, 7, 11
पनस LIII 87 LV 4, 11
पन्नग LXXXI 25
पय: LI 31
पयोऽनुपान LXXVI 4
पयोष्णी XVI 10
परचक्र III 15, XX 3, XXXIII 12, 16, XXXVIII 6, XL 7, XLVI 20, 34, 48
— दार XV 4, XVI 39, CI 2
— पुष्टा LXXXVI 37
— भूमि XLVI 54, 55
— माणु LVIII 1, 2
— मान्न XLVI 65, LIX 8, VCV 23
— योनि XLVI 56, LXXXVI 66
— रन्ध्रवित् LXIX 21
परशु XLIII 19
परस्वहृत् XV 16

पराभव VIII 42
पराशर XI 1, XVII 3, XXI 2, XXIII 4, XXIV 2, XLVIII, 66 LXI 1
परिघ XXI 26, XXVIII 16, XXX 2, 25, 30, 31, 33, XLVII 19, 23, LXXXVI 51
परिघात C 4
परिघावी VIII 46
परिधि XXX 2, 8, 26, 33, XLII 1, XLIII 50, XLVII 19, LVIII 23
— माण LXVIII 105, LXIX 25
परिवत्सर VIII 24
— वेष III, 34, V 94, XXI 19-22, XXII 7, XXVIII 6, 16, XXX 2, 8, 31, 33, XXXII 26, XXXIV 1, 4, 12, 16, 22, XLII 1, XLVI 4, 84, 88, XCVII 3
परिव्राड् LI 20
परुष LIII 104, 106
परूषक LIV 50
पर्जन्य LIII 43, 49, 52
पर्णशबर XIV 10
पर्यङ्क LXXIX 11, 13, 14
पर्याण LXXXIX 1 (a), XCIII 6
पर्व III 6, L 1, LVIII 27, 28 LXVIII 87, LXXII 5, LXXIII 2, LXXIX 34
— काल V 2
पर्वत XLVIII 67, LXXXVI 78
पर्वेश V 10
पल LIII 93, LXIX 25, LXXXI 13, LXXXII 7
पलल LIX 8
— भोज्य XCV 22
पलालधूम XXX 28
पलाश XXIX 6, XXX 7, XLIV 12, LIV 17, 59, 83, 112, LV 22, XCIII 4
पलितान्विता LXXVIII 17
पल्लव V 38, XLVIII 37, LX 1
पवन XXX2, 4, 6, 7, 14, 31, XXXIX 1, XLVI 4, XCVIII 4
पशु XXXIII 4, XLVI 59, XLVIII 81, LI 19, LIII 16, 60
— निर्वाप XLVI 36
— पाल XIV 29, LI 22
— भय XCV 19
पह्लव XIV 17, XVI 38, XVIII 6
पांसु XXII 6, XXX 21, 31, XLVI 41, LIV 120, XCVII 13
पाक XLVI 7, 14, 30, LXXXVI 5, XCVII 1, 6, 14-16
पांखण्डी XV 10, 24, XXXI 4, XLVI 76
पाञ्चाल IV 22, V 35, 38, 41, IX 29, 34, X 4, 13, XIV 3, 32
पाटल XXIX 7, XXXV 4
पाठा XLVIII 39
पाणिग्रह C 7
— तल LI 7 LXX 10
पाण्डु XIV 3
— पत्रता LV 14
पाण्डुर XXXIV 2, LIV 104, 109
— रोग XXXII 14
पाण्डूक XXIX 2
पाण्ड्य IV 10, VI 8, XI 56, LXXXI 2
— वाट LXXXI 6
पाताल LIV 5
पाद LI 8, 25, 40, 43, LII 8, LVIII 17, 18, LXVIII 87, LXIX 22, LXX 1, 10, 24, LXXIV 8, XCIII 3, 10, CV 1
— तोरण XLIII 58
पादप LIV 100, LV 31, LXXV 2, XCIV 11
पादाङ्गुष्ठ LI 11, 13, 25, 40
पादुका LXXI 9
पान XLVIII 28, LI 36, LII 6, XCIII 9
पाप VII 8, 12
— यक्ष्मा LIII 45
पायस XLIII 38, XLIV 11, XLVI 32, XLVIII 36
पायु V 81, LI, 43, LXVIII 97, XCIII 2

पारत X 5, 7, XIII 9, XIV 21, XVI 4, 13, 22
पारद LXXVI 3
पारलौकिक LXXXI 2, 4
पारशव XIV 18, LIII 15, LXXXI 2, 5
पारा XVI 10
पारावत XLVIII 6, L 25, LIV 10, 28, 30, 32, 108
पारिकर्मा LXXXVII 20
परिजात XXVII 9, LXXVII 27, 37
पारियात्र V 68, VI 10, X 15, XIV 4, LXIX 11
पार्थिव VIII 36
पार्वतीय XVII 16, 23, XVIII 2
पार्श्व LI 9, 43, LII 4 LIII 53, LXVIII 19, 26, CV 2
— शायी IV 13
पार्ष्णि LI 9, 40, LII 8
पाली LIV 118
— वत LV 4
पाश LXXIX 25
पाशान्त LXXI 9
पाशिक XV 22, CIV 63 (b)
पाषाण LIV 7, 10, 20, 44, 56, 73, 118, XCV 42
पिक्का LXXXI 17
पिङ्गल VIII 48, LXXXVI 21, 37, 49, LXXXVIII 2, 4, 38
पिचुमन्द XXIX 12
पिच्चा LXXXI 17
पिटक XLIII 7, 41, 50, 57, 61, 64, LII 1, 9, 10
पिण्ड XLIV 19, LXXVII 9, 16, 19
पिण्डार LIV 50
पिण्डिका LI 9, LVI 16, LVIII 3, 54, LX 17, LXX 17
पितरः XLVI 10, XLVIII 25, 30, 69, LIII 44, 54, 63, LIX 9, LXXIV 19, XCVIII 4, XCIX 2, C 5
पितामह XXXII 3, 5, LXXXVIII 40
पितृकार्य LXXXIII 1
— वन LIX 2
पित्त XIX 9, CIV 55
पित्र्य XCVIII 8, CI 6
पिनाक LVIII 43
पिपीलिका XXVIII 7, LXXXVIII 23, XCV 59
पिप्पल LIV 96
पिप्पली XVI 30, LI 15, LXXVI 11
पिप्पीक LXXXVI 38
पिरिली LXXXVI 20, 44
पिशाच XXXIX 4, XLVI 14, XLVIII 30, LIX 9, LXVIII 108, 113
पिशिक XIV 14
पीडा LIII 58
— स्थान XLI 11
पीत XXX 13, 18, 22, XXXI 1, XXXIV 7, XXXV 4, XLII 8, LII 1, LIII 96, 122, LIV 7, LX 3, LXXX 11, LXXXI 19, LXXXVII 25, XCV 15
पीताम्बर LVIII 32
पीलु XXIX 11 LIV 63, 65, 75
पुंराशिलग्न XCVI 9
पुंस्कोकिल XLVIII 7
पुंस्त्री LXXIV 20, LXXXVI 6
पुच्छ XCIII 2
पुञ्जन्मयोग LXXVIII 25
पुटभेदक LIV 7
पुटा CIV 43
पुण्ड्र V 70, IX 15, X 14, XI 27, 58, XIV 7, XVI 3
पुण्यायतन XLVIII 67
पुण्याह XLIII 26, XLIV 7, 16, XLVIII 49, 73, LX 10, LXXXVI 23, 39
पुत्र LI 25, 40
पुनर्भू XXXI 3
पुनर्वसु VII 10, LXXI 2, XCVIII 12, 15, CI 4, CV 3
पुन्नाग XXVII 9, LIII 87, LV 3, LXXXVIII 24

पुमान् LII 9, LXXXVI 8, 37
पुर XX 2, LIII 84, LIV 97, LXXXIX 18, 19, XC 12, XCI, 3
पुरन्दरभक्त XV 14
पुरप्रभेद X 19
— रोध XXXIV 20
पुराकृत III 15
पुरिक XIV 10
पुरीष LI 18
पुरुष XXXIII 8, LI 17, LIII 51, LIV 6-20, 23-38, 41, 44-48, 55-61, 63-68, 74, 75, 93
पुरुषाद IV 22, XIV 6
पुरोहित III 21, X 13, 16, XV 1, XVI 23, XXIX 10, XXXIII 27, XXXIV 13, 17, XXXVI 1, XLIII 30, 63, XLIV 14, 19, 22 XLVI 7, 59, XLVIII 19, 21, 24, 48, 50, 54, 77, 78, 80, LIII 10, LXXIX 9, XCIV 9
पुलक LXXX 4
पुलस्त्य XIII 5, 11, XLVIII 63
पुलह् XIII 6 11, XLVIII 63
पुलिन XLVIII 8, LVI 7, XCV I6
पुलिन्द IV 22, V 39, 77, 78, IX 17, 29, 40, XVI 2, 33
पुष्कर V 68, XVI 31, LXVII 7-9
पुष्करारण्य XI 35
पुष्कलावत XIV 26, XVI 26
पुष्टि XLIV 5, C 5
पुष्प XLIII 60, XLVIII 54, LI 36
पुष्पराग LXXX 5
पुष्पिताग्र CIV 17
पुष्य VI 7, X 6, XV 6, LIV 123, LXXXI 21, XCVIII 9, 15, C 6, CI 5, CV 4
पुष्यस्नान XLVIII 3, 38, 54, 88, 86, LXXVIII 22
पुस्तक LVIII 38, LXXXVII 11 37
पूगफल LXXVII 36, 37, LXXXVII 2
पूजा XLVIII 20-22, 29, 33, 36, 50 73, LII 8, LIII 99, 112, 121, LV 8, LIX 4, 9, 10, LXXXVII 1, XCV 14, CV 8
पूतना LIII 83
पूतिमांस LV 21
पूप XLIII 38
पूर्ण LXXXVIII 11, 14-16, 26, 33, 36, XC 1. 2, XCIX 2
— कुम्भ LXXIX 7, XCV 44
— कूट LXXXVIII 1, 4, 25
— कोशा XLIV 10, XLVIII 40
— पात्र XCIII 8
पूर्वदेश XIV 5
पूर्वशास्त्र III 1
पूर्वा VII 7, XV 9, 28, XCVIII 8
पूर्वाचार्य LXXXII 11, CVI 2
पूर्वाह्ण LI 6
पूषा LIII 44, XCVIII 5, 12
पृथुलोमा LXXXVI 65
पृथ्वीधर LIII 47
पृषत XLVIII 76, LIV 109, LXXXVIII 3, 33
पृष्ठ LI 9, LII 5, LXVIII 32, 86, LXXIV 8 CV 3
पेचिका LXXXVIII 4
पैतामह II 4
पोत X 10
पौण्ड्र V 73, 80, LXXX 7
पौर XVII 6-8, 14, XVIII 3, 6, 7, XX 6, 7, XXXIII 17, XXXIV 22, XLIII 64 XLVIII 48, 49
पौरव XIV 27, 31, XVI 22, XXXII 19
पौर्णमासी XLII 1
पौलिश II 4
पौष XXI 9, 19, C 8
पौषीशान्ति XLVIII 82
पौष्टिक II 3, XVI 23, XLVI 20, C 3, 5
पौष्ण LXXI 7, XCVIII 10, 16, C 6, CI 14
प्रकीर्णक LXXX 10
प्रकृति LXIX 4, CVI 3

प्रजल्पित XLVI 49
प्रजा XLVIII 81, XLIX 6
— क्षय LIII 86
— तरु XLVIII 1
प्रजापति VIII 24, XLVIII 68
— सुत XI 25
प्रजेश्वर LXXI 1
प्रतिघात XLVI 3, 57, 80
प्रतिमा XXXIII 20, XLVI 15, LVI 16, LVII 4, LVIII 3, 29, 49, 52, LIX 7, LX 4-7, 14
प्रतिलोम XLVI 69
— सर XLIV 4, XLVIII 33
— सूर्य III 37, XXI 16, XXVIII 16, XXX 31-33, XXXVII 1-3, XLVII 19
प्रतीहार LVI 14
प्रत्यन्त IV 21, V 30, 31 IX 17, 21, X 6, XVI 38
प्रथमकर्म LV 2
प्रदक्षिण LIII 104, 112, 121, LXXIX 27, LXXXIV 2, LXXXVI 34
— णाम्भः XLVIII 15
णावर्त XXX 10, LXX 4
— प्रदीप्त XCVI 5, 7, 9
प्रदेशिनी LIII 101, LVIII 18, 27, LXVIII 50, LXX 13, 16
प्रदोष XLVI 69
प्रद्युम्न LVIII 40
प्रधान I 7
— प्रपाणLXVI 3, 4
प्रबन्धवर्ष XLVI 40
प्रबाहु LVIII 25
प्रभव VIII 28
प्रभास XVI 32
प्रथम LIII 82, LVI 15
प्रमदा LXXXVI 31
प्रमाण LVIII 1, 4, 23
प्रमथी VIII 33
प्रमादी VIII 45
प्रमिताक्षरा CIV 37
प्रमेह LXVIII 7
प्रमोद VIII 29
प्रयाग XI 35
प्रलय XXXIV 17, XLVII 11
प्रलीनक LIII 28
प्रवाल XLII 10, LI 37
प्रवास LIII 81
प्रव्रजित LI 5, LXXVIII 9, LXXXVII 7
प्रव्रज्या LII 2
प्रशस्ताद्रि XIV 20
प्रष्टा LI 1, 6, 7
प्रसभ CIV 13
प्रसव XXI 7, 10, 24, 32, 37
— विकार XLVI 52, XCVII 4
प्रसादपट्ट LXXIII 5
प्रस्थ LV 17
प्रस्थल XVI 26
प्रस्फोटन LIV 113
प्रहर LXXVII 3
प्रहरण LXXIX 22
प्रहर्षणीय CIV 22
प्राकार XLV 9
प्राकृत VII 8, 9, 13, 14, LXXXVI 3
प्रागीश IV 25
प्राग्ज्योतिष XIV 7, XV II
प्रागद्वार XLVII 13
प्राची LIII 46, 119, LIV 3, LXXXVI 45
प्राच्य XLVII 7, XCV 27
प्राजापत्य XLVI 59
प्राण II 4
प्राकृत XCV 62
प्रात्यन्तिक LXIX 23
प्राप्तार्क LXXXVI 12
प्रारब्ध CIV 59
प्रावृट् XXI 1, XXVI 1', XXVIII 1, 19, XXX 21
प्रावेशिक LXXXVI 55
प्रास XX 2
प्रासाद XLV 4, XLVI 20, LVI 19, 31, LVII 4, LXXXIX 6, XCV 5, 34

प्रास्थानिक XLIII 12, LIX 1, LXXXVI 55
प्रियक XLIII 15
प्रियङ्गु XLIV 9, LV 3, LXXVII 8, 23, 29, LXXXV 7
प्रियाप्ति LII 4
प्रेत XXVII 4, XXXIII 9, XLVI 78
प्रेष्य LI 25
प्रोष LXVI 2, XCIII 4
प्रोषित LI 22, LXXVIII 6, XC 15
प्लक्ष LI 17, LIII 85, LIV 119, LXXXV 4
प्लव X 10, XLVI 89, XLVIII 15, LIII 91, LXXI 12
प्लवङ्ग VIII 43, 44

फण LXXXI 25
फणिकार XIV 12
फणी LXXXVIII 19, XCVIII 4, C 2
फल XLI 4, 7, XLII 3, 9, 12, XLIII 60, XLVI 36, 41, XLVIII 28, 35, 37, LI 1, 36, LIII 82, 101, LV 13, 27, 28, 30, LXXXVII 7, 9, XCIII 8, XCV 23, XCVII 4
— नाश LV 16
— पुष्पसमृद्धि LV 16, 18
फली LIII 86
फल्गुलुका XIV 23
फाणित XLII 5
फाल्गुन XXI 21, XXV 6
फाल्गुनी CI 7, CV 1
फेणगिरि XIV 18
फेप्ट LXXXVIII 1, 26, 31
फेन LIV 36

बकुल LIII 87, LIV 119, LXXVII 7
बदर LI 17, LIV 114
बदरी XXIX 5, LIV 16, 17, 43, 72, 74, 75, LXXXV 5
बन्ध L 16, LI 5, 14, LII 7, 8, LIII 102, XCIII 3, 10, XCV 19, 37, 42, 53, XCVIII 7, 8
बन्धकी X 9 XXIX 13, XLIII 65, LXX 19, LXXXVII 16, LXXIX 8
बन्धनमोक्ष XLVIII 81, XCVIII 14
बन्धु LI 24
— जीव XXIX 8, LXX 6
बन्धूक XXX 15
बभ्रु XXX 12, 14
बम्भारव XCII 3
बर्बर V 42, XIV 18
बर्हिकेतु LVIII 41
— चित्रक XLVII 2
बर्हीं LXXXVI 41
बल LXXX 3
वलदेव LVIII 36, 37
— पट्टन XIV 16
— मत LIV 125
बलपति XXIX 10, XXX 13, LIII 24, LXXIX 9
— विद्रव XLVII 25
बलि XLIV 11, XLVI 16, 81, XLVIII 18, 33, 50, LIII 121, 125, LIV 124, LVIII 30, LIX 4, 10, LX 16
— भुक् XCV 31
बव C 1, 3
बस्त L 24, LXXVI 7
बहुगिरि XVI 26
बहुधान्य VIII 33
बहुलपक्ष CV 6
बादर XIV 19
बादरायण XL 1
बालक्षय LIV 98
बालव C 1, 3
बाल्य XCVI 17
बाहु LI 5, LVIII 25, 26, LXVIII 35, 88
— ल्य LIII 26, LVI 13
बाहूपधान LXXLIII 15
बाह्य LI 25
बाह्लीक V 37, 80, IX 10, X 7, XVI 1, XVII 13, 25, XVIII 6, XXXII 15

बिडाल LXXXVI 22, LXXXVIII 3, 35
बिलेशय LXXXVI 28, 44
बिल्व XLVIII 42, LIV 18, 50, 76, 105, LVII 3, 5, LIX 5, LXXXV 5
बीज XVI 20, XXIV 8, 11, XXVI 1, XLVIII 41, LIII 98, LV 19, 26, 27, 29, LXXV 2, XCVII 11 C 4
— पूर LV 4, 10
बुद्ध LVIII 44
बुद्बुद LXXX 16
— देक्षण LXI 14
बुध XCVII 1, XCVIII 16
— ज XI 20
बृंहित XCIV 13
बृहती LXXXV 5
बृहत्क्षत LIII 44, 53
बृहद्रथ LXI 1
बृहस्पति XXIV 2, XLVIII 77, 86
बोध LXXVII 16
ब्रह्मघ्न LXVIII 3
— तीर्थ LXVIII 48
— दण्ड XI 15
— पुर XIV 30
— मणि LXXX 5
— लोक II 30
— वादी XXVI 4
— सुत XI 15
ब्रह्मा I 5, XLIII 1, XLVI 10, XLVIII 55, LIII 46, 54, 66, 78, LVIII 41, XCVIII 5
ब्रह्मायतन XXXIII 22
ब्राह्मण LIII 98, LXXIV 8, XCV 54
— संमत XCVIII 14
ब्राह्मी XLVIII 41

भ LV 31, LXXXVI 58, XCIV 10, XCVI 11
भक्तिदेश XVIII 7
भक्ष्य XLIV 11, XLVI 16, XLVIII 28, LIII 99, LIX 8, LXXXIX 13, XCIII 9, XCV 43
भग VIII 23, LXXI 3
भगण II 5, V 4, 6, LIV 123
भगन्दर XLVIII 64
भगिनी LI 25
भग्न LI 10
भद्र XIV 2, 7, 16, XVII 18, XLV 2, LXVII 1, 4, 5, LXIX 2, 7, 13, 19, LXXXI 20
— दारु LXXXV 7
— पदा LXXI 7, CI 13, CV 2
भद्रा XLVIII 40. XCIX 2
भद्राश्व IX 11
— सन XLVIII 46, LX 7
भरणी X 1, XV 30, LXXI 1, XCVIII 8, CI 1, CV 5
भरत XVI 21
भरुकच्छ XIV 11, XVI 6, LXIX 11
भल्ल XIV 30
भल्लाट LIII 45
भल्लातक XXIX 11, XLIV 5, LIV 50, LVII 3
भवकेतु XI 47
भवनप्रवेश XCVIII 17
भषक LXXXVI 38, LXXXVIII 4
भस्म XXX 14, XLV 9, XLVIII 16, LI 4, 14, LIII 61, 102, LIV 106, 109, LV 24, LXXXVI 60, LXXXVIII 20, LXXXIX 13, XCV 12
भागवत LX 19, LXXXVII 25
भागुरि XLVIII 2, LXXXVI 1
भाग्य CI 6
भाजन LXXXI 26
भाण्ड XLII 8, 11, 12, LIII 58, XCV 13
भाण्डीक LXXXVIII 7
भाण्डीर LXXXV 6
भाण्डोपस्कर LIII 118
भाद्रपद XXI 10, 11, XXVII 8, XLIII 23, LXXXVI 27

भानामीश्वरा: XCVIII 5
भानु XCVII 1, CIV 61 (a)
भार LXVIII 106, LXIX 18,
भारतवर्ष XIV 1
भारतुला LIII 30
— द्वाज LXXXVI 2, 41, LXXXVIII 1, 15
— सह LXI 9, 14, 16
भार्ङ्गी LIV 48
भार्या LI 25
भाव LXXVIII 3, 12
भास LXXXVI 38
भासापर XVI 11
भिक्षांदेहि LXXIV 13
भिक्षाटन LII 4
भिक्षुक X 8, LXXXVI 30, LXXXVII 3, 9, 25
भिक्षुणिका LXXVIII 9
भित्ति LIII 23, LVI 12
भिषक् IX 32, X 9, 16, 17, XV 7, 17, XVI 5, XLVIII 56 LIII 10
भीमरथा XVI 9
भुज LI 8, LIII 52. LXXVIII 3, XCIII 3, CV 3
भुजग LIII 45, LIV 28, 46, 66, 70, LIX 8, LXXI 3, LXXIX 24, LXXXI 1 29, LXXXII 5, LXXXVIII 3, XCV 40, XCVIII 7, XCIX 11
भुजङ्गप्रयात CIV 42
— विजृम्भित CIV 47
भुवोविदरण XCVII 9
भू C I
भूकम्प III 10, XXXII 2, 10, 23, 24, 27, 32, XXXIII 12, XLVI 84, XCVII 5
भूच्छाया V 8
भूत XLVI 90, LIII 2, LIX 10
— तन्त्र XVI 19
— पुर XIV 27
— शब्द XCVII 12
भूमि LIII 22, 96
— का LVI 23
भूर्ज LI 14
भूषण LII 3 5, LVIII 29, LXXXI 36, XCVIII 9, 10
भूस्वभाव LXXX 3
भृगु XLVIII 64, LXXXVI 43, C 7
— भांश XCVI 8
— सुतदिवस CIV 63 (a)
भृङ्ग LIV 107, 109
— राज LIII 44, 63
भृङ्गार LXXIX 23, LXXXVIII 6
भृङ्गि IV 22
भृश LIII 43, 63
भेक LIII 123
भेद V 81-86, XVII 3, 4, LIV 112
— सम्बन्ध XCVIII 7
भेरी XLIII 59
भेषज XV 17, XVI 5, XIX 1
भोगप्रस्थ XIV 25
— वर्धन XVI 12
— वृद्धि LXXI 11
भोजन LXXVI 12
भोज्य XLVI 81
भौजङ्ग LXXXI 27, CI 5
भौम XI 41, XLVI 2, 5, XLVIII 53, LIV 125, XCVI 17
— क्षंलग्न XCVI 7
भ्रमर LXXXII 1, 5,
— विलसित CIV 25
भ्रुकुटी LXXVIII 7
भ्रू LI 8, 33, 37, LII 2, LVIII 7, 12, 13, LXVIII 68, 69, LXX 8, 26, LXXVIII 3
मकर III 4, CII 5
मक्षिका LXXX 15, XCII 2, XCV 58, XCVII 7
मक्षीक LXVI 5
मग LX 19
मगध IV 22, 26, V 69, 79, X 10, 14, 16, XI 55, XIV 6, 32, XVI 1, XXXII 11

मघवान् XLVIII 70
मघा VI 8, 9, 12, IX 14, XXI 29, LIV 123, LXXI 3, CV 4
मङ्गल XLVIII 42, 49, 84, LIII 82, XCVIII 10
— ल्यविहग LVI 15
— सिद्धि C 5
मज्जा LXVIII 96, 98, LXIX 21
मञ्जिष्ठा LVII 5, LXXVII 6
मणि XLII 6, 7, XLIV 25, LIII 101, LX 4, LXIV 3, LXV 3, 11, LXVIII 10, 12, 13, LXX 3, LXXXI 36, LXXXII 3, 6, 7, LXXXVI 1, XCV 12
मणिगुणनिकर CIV 27
— बन्धन LII 5, LXVIII 38, 44, LXX 11, 12
मणिमान् XIV 20
— शृङ्ग LXI 7
— सुत XI 44
— सोपान LXXXI 35
मण्डप LV 26, LX 1, 7
मण्डल III 3, IX 22, XXIII 4, XXVIII 20, XXXII 23, 26, XXXIII 27, XXXIV 17, XLVI 67, 69, XLVIII 34, L 7, LIII 122, LXXXIX 16
मण्डलक LXIX 31, 37
— क्रम LX 19
— वृष्टि XCV 4
मण्डूक XXVII 6, XXVIII 4, LIV 7, 8, 18, 30, 67
मतङ्गज LXXX 7
मत्कुण LXVII 10
मत्तमयूर CIV 26
— वारण LXXIX 7
मत्स्य IV 24, V 37, IX 18, 38, XIV 2, XVI 22, XVII, 22, XXI 33, XXX 8, XXXII 11 XLI 8, XLIV 4, LI 35, LIV 10, 15, 22, 94, LV 25, 26, LXXXI 23
मथित L 26
मथुरा IV 26, XIV 3, XVI 17, 21
मदनक LXXVII 14
— फल LVII 5
— वागुरा LXXVI 2
—क्षय LXXIV 14
मदयन्तिका LIV 102
मदवृद्धि XLVI 85, XCIV 13
मद्य XLVI 27, XLVIII 30, LIX 8, LIII 96, LXXVI 11, LXXXVII 23
मद्र IV 22, V 40, X 4, XI 59, XIV 22, 27, 33, XXXII 19
मधु III 23, XLII 5, XLIII 63, XLIV 11, XLV 14, XLVI 27, 32, 70, 85, XLVIII 35, LI 37, LV 24, LIX 12, LXXVI 3, LXXVII 11, 27, 32, XCV 58
— निलय XCVII 8
— पर्क XLVI 16
— मधुररस LI 31, LIII 97
— सूदन CV 14
मधूक XXIX 4, LI 17, LIV 35, 119, LVII 5, LIX 5, LXXXV 3
— धूच्छिष्ट XVI 25
मध्य LVIII 27. LXX 5, XCIV 11, XCVI 17
— तमः V 43
— देश V 78, X 5, XI 35, XIV 4, XVII 19, 20, 22, XVIII 4, XLVII 7
मध्यम LXXXVI 40
मध्ययोगी IV 7
— मध्यविदरण V 81
मध्याङ्गुलि LIII 101
मनश्शिला XLIV 9
मनस्ताप LIII 117
मनु XIX 11, XLIII 39, 51, XLVIII 61, LVI 31, LXXIV 6
मनुष्यभाग LXXI 11
मनोज्ञवृक्ष XCV 33
मन्त्र XLIII 16, 51, 56, XLVI 16, 24,

51, XLVIII 19, 51, 54, LX 11, LXXVIII 22, LXXXVI 77, LXXXVIII 41, XCVIII 7, C 5
मन्त्रिषिक XVI 11
मन्त्री LIII 9, LXXIX 9
मन्त्रौषध LXXV 5
मन्द LXVII 2, 4, 5
— गति II 9
मन्दर LVI 17, 21, LXXXI 34, CVI 1
मन्दाकिनी XVI 10
मन्दाक्रान्त LIV 9
— ग्नि LXXVI 10
मन्मथ VIII 38, XCIX 1
मय XXIV 2, LVI 29, LVII 8
मयूर XXVIII 14, LXXIII 1
मरकत LIV 46, LXXXIII 1 LXXX 4
मरण XCV 58
मरिच LI 15, LXXVII 32
मरीचि XIII 5, 8, XLVIII 63
मरु IV 22, V 40, 68, XIV 2, XVI 38, LIV 62, 86, 89
— कुच्छ XIV 23
मरुचीपट्टन XIV 15
मरुत: XLIII 52
मर्म LIII 57, 61, 62, 64
मलय XIV II, XVI 10, XXVII 2, LXXVII 7, 8, 14, 24
— ज LI 19
मर्त्यसत्त्व LXVIII 112
मल्ल V 38, 41, XV 19
मल्लिकाक्षी LXII 2
मशक LII 10
मषी LXXI 10
मसूर XLI 2, XLIII 43
महाग्रीव XIV 9
— टवि XIV 13
— नदी XIV 10
— नस LIII 118
— नील LXXX 5
— भूत LXIX 4
— मात्र IX 28, XV 11, 19, XVI 27
— राष्ट्र X 8
महारौहिण XLVIII 71
महार्घ XLI 11
— र्णव XIV 19, XVI 6
— व्रत XXIV 8
— शान्ति XLVI 81
— शिरा LIV 4, 61
महिष IX 10, XVII 26, XLI 3, XLV, 9, XLVI 53, LI 19, 34, LVII 7, LXXXVI 28, LXXXVII 6, XCV 35
महिषी XLIII 63, XLIX 2, 5, LXXVIII 1, XCII 3, CIV 63 (b)
मही LIII 88, 97, LIV 28, 52, 54, 104, LXVIII 90, 109, XCIII 10
— दान XLVI 9
महेन्द्र XIV 11, XVI 10, LVIII 42
मांस XLVI 40, 48, XLVIII 30, LI 33, 34, LV 20, LXVIII 96, 100, LXXXVI 45, LXXXIX 13, XCV 22, 41
— जल LV 26
मांसी XVI 25, LXXVII 9, 24
माक्षिक XV 9, LXXVI 3
मागधी CIV 54
माघ XXI 10, 20, XXV 5
माञ्जिष्ठ X II, XII 20, XXX 12, 14, XLIII 43, LIII 123
माणवक LXXXI 33
माणहल XIV 27
माण्डलिक XLVI 11, XLVIII 47, LXIX 23
माण्डव्य XIV 2. 22, 27, CIV 3
मातङ्ग LXXXVI 30
मातर: XLVIII 26, LI 26, 37, LVIII 56, LX 19
माथुरक XIV 3
माधव XLVI 85, CV 14
माध्यमिक XIV 2
माध्वीकविक्रय LI 5
मान LIII 15

मानव LIV 99
मानोन्मान LXVIII 107
माया XV 20, XIX 10
मारीमृत LXXXVII 33
मारुत C 2
मारुती LIII 118, XCV 23
मार्कण्डेय XLVIII 66
मार्ग XLVII 1
— पिशित LV 19
मार्गर XIV 18
— शिरः XXI 6, 9, 19
मार्जार XXVIII 5, LXXXVI 65, XCVII 12
मार्जाराक्ष LXI 6
मार्त्तिकावत XVI 26
मालती XVI 10, CIV 14
मालव IV 24, XIV 27, XVI 26, XXXII 19, LXIX 11
मालव्य LXIX 2, 7, 10, 12
मालाकार X 9, LXXVIII 9, LXXXVI 32
मालिनी CIV 24
मालिन्य XIV 11
माल्य XLVIII 27, 31, 32
माल्यवान् XIV 5
माष XV 14, XVI 37, XXV 2, XXIX 4, XLI 5, LI 31, LV 16, 21, 25, LXXVI 4, LXXIX 33, LXXX-VII 22, XCV 21
माषक LXXXI 9, 10, LXXXII 8, 9
माषपर्णी LIV 88
— सूप LXXVI 8
मास II 4, LI 39, XCVII 2-4, 6, 7, 10-16, CV 15, 16
मासिक XCVII 1
माहिष LV 30
माहेन्द्री XLVI 81, LIV 36
मित्र V 22, LI 20, LIII 47, XCV 50, XCVIII 4, C 1, 3
— भ LXXI 5
वैर LIII 117
मित्राप्ति XCV 20
मित्रार्थ XCVIII 10
मिथिला X 14, XIV 6
मिथुन LVI 15, CII 2
मीन XXVIII 14, LXXXVII 7
मुकुट XLIV 25
मुक्ताफल LXXIII 2, LXXX 5, LXXXI 1, 13, 16, 21, 25, 30
— कं LXXXVI 12
मुख LIII 51, LVIII 4, CV 4
— चपल CIV 2
मुख्य LIII 45, 63
मुञ्जाद्रि XIV 31
मुण्ड LXV 4, 11
मुद्ग XV 14, XXV 2, XXIX 5, XLI 5, LIII 123, LIV 107 LV 16
मुनि XXI 2, 3, XLI 1, XLIII 47, XLVI 63, 71, 99, XLVII 12, 28, XLVIII 19, 23, 25, 51, 60, LIII 1, LIV 99, 125, VXXIV 19
— प्रवाद X 21, LIV 110
— मत LXIX 40
मुष्क LXVI 2, LXX 24
मुस्ता LIV 121, LXXVII 9-11, 24, 29
मुहूर्त II 4, 19, 27, XLIII 12, XLVIII 45, 59, XCVI 1, 6, XCIX 3
मूत्र LI 27, LXVIII 10-12, XC 11, XCIII 14
मूर्ति CIII 1
मूर्धज LXX 9
— राग LXXVII 1
मूर्धा LI 26, 34, LII 2, 10, LIII 51, LXXXII 5
मूल VI 11, 12, VII 6, 11, IX 32, X 2, XV 17, XLI 6, XLII 3, XLVIII 28, LV 7, 13, 22, 31, XCIV 8, XCVIII 7, 15, C 5, CI 10, CV 1, 6
— च्छेद LV 5
— द्वार LIII 82
— परिधि LXXIX 20, XCIV 1
— शकुन XCV 60

मूल्य LXXX 12, 16, LXXXI 9, 11-13, 15, 18, LXXXII 8-11
मूषक XLVIII 16, LIII 123, LIV 20, LXXI 2, LXXXVI 65, XCV 4, 12
— नयना LXI 2
मृग IX 1, 3, XXX 2-5, 7, 30, 31, XXXIII 9, XXXIV 8, XLVI 67, 72, 95, L 24, LI 34, LIII 44, LXVII 3-5, LXXI 2, LXXVII 12, 26, 27, LXXXVI 23, 26, 43, LXXXVIII 3, 33, LXXXIX 18, XCI 2, XCVII 7, CI 3
मृगशिरा: X 5, XV 3, XCVIII 12, 15, CV 4
मृजा LXVIII 1
मृत् LIV 7-8, 10, 13, 15, 20, 22, 32, 44, 46, 64, 73, 83, 103, LV 25, 28, 30, LX 9
मृतसूतक XCVIII 14
मृत्पात्र LIII 94
मृत्यु XLVI 22, 61, 71, XLVII 4, L 19, LIII 60, 110, 111, 117, LXXI 3, 11, LXXII 5, LXXXVI 56, LXXXIX 1 (c), 3, 6, 16, XCI 3, XCII 1, XCV 7, 39, 52, CIII 3, 8, 10
— सुत XI 12
मृदङ्ग XLIII 59, XLIV 23, XLVIII 49
मृदुतीक्ष्ण XCVIII 11
— भ LV 31
— वर्ग XCVIII 10
मृद्वीका LV 10
— भू: LV 2
मृन्मयी LX 4
मृष्टपय: LIV 104
मृष्टाश्न LXXXV 9, LXXXIX 10
मेकल V 39, 73, XIV 7, XVI 2
मेखला LVI 6, XCVIII 16
मेघतरु XLVIII 23
मेघवान् XIV 20
मेघोद्भव LIV 125, LXXXI 24
मेचक XXXIV 3, LIV 107
मेढ्र LII 6, LIII 54, LVIII 16, LXVIII, 7, LXX 24, XCIII 2
मेद: L 21, LXVIII 96, 98
मेध्य LXXIV 8
मेरु XIV 24, 29, XXVII 7, LVI 17, 20
मेष LI 34, LXXXVI 80, CII 1, 7
मेषोदर LXI 15
मेहन LI 9
मैत्र XCVIII 16
मैथुन XLV 12, LXXXVI 66
मोक्ष V 91
मोक्षकभस्म LIV 113
मोदक LIX 8, LXXXIX 1 (a)
मौक्तिक XVI 7, XXI 23, XXIV 16, XXIX 6, 9, XLII 6, 10, XLIV 27, LIII 101, LIV 110
मौञ्जिक LIV 103
मौर्वी LIV 87
मौलिकIX 32
म्लेच्छ II 14, V 29, 33, 54, 79, IX 13, 40, XIV 21, XVI 11, 35, XVII 14, 16, 20

यक्ष XIII 8, XLVI 92, XLVIII 25, LIV 111
यजमान X 5
यजु: XLVIII 31
यज्ञ XV 6, XVI 8, XIX 13, XLIII 37, XLV 5, LXXXVI 78
यज्ञोपवीत XLVIII 33
यति LI 5
यन्त्र XVI 18
यन्त्रार्गल XLIII 58
यम V 19, LIII 44, 53, LIV 3, LVIII 57, LXXXI 7, XCVIII 4, XCIX 1, C 1
यमर्क्ष XCVI 6
यमल XLVI 33, 53
यमसूर्य LIII 39, 40

यमुना XVI 2
यव XV 6, XVI 7, XIX 6, XXIX 3, 4, XLI 2, 3, 5, XLVI 33, LV 16, 25, LVIII 2, LXVIII 42, LXXX 10, LXXXVII 4
यवक्रीत XLVIII 67
— ग्रीव LXIII 2
यवन II 14, IV 22, V 78, 80, IX 21, 35, X 6, 15, 18, XIII 9, XIV 18, XVI 1, XVIII 6
यवस XCIII 5
यवागू LI 31
यशोधर्म LVI 1
यशोवति XIV 28
यष्टि XLIII 8, 21, 24, 28, 29, LXXII 4, LXXXI 36
याग XLVI 46, CIII 13
याजक X 5, XLVIII 18
यात LXXXVI 6
याता LXXXVI 54, 56, LXXXVII 5, LXXXVIII 19, 22, 32, 35, LXXXIX 1 (a) (d), XCV 25, 26, 32, 41, 48
यातुधान XLVI 80
यात्रा I 10, II 15, XLIII 31, 37, XLIV 14, 18, XLVIII 22, LI 7, LXXII 6, LXXXVI 10, 62, LXXXVII 5, 6, 27, 28, LXXXIX 12, 14, XCIII 11, 13, XCIV 13, XCV 25
— कार LXXXVI 3
यान XLVI 60, LII 7, XCV 60, XCVIII 9
— यान्तु देवगणाः XLVIII 79
याम II 4
यामुन XIV 2, 25, XVI 2
याम्य IV 5, LIV 44, 48, 65, 118, LX 1, 2, LXXX 8, LXXXVI 21, LXXXVII 4, 6, 27, XC 8, 10 XCV 3, 21
याम्यगति II 9, XVIII 1, 7
यायी V 33, IX 35, XVI 5, XVII 6-8, 13, 17, 21, XVIII 2, 5, XX 6, 7, XXX 19, XXXIII 13, XXXIV 14, 22, XXXV 2, XXXIX 5, LXXXIX 1 (b), XCV 27, 51, 52
यावक XLIV 11, LI 30
युग II 4, 6, VIII, 26, XLVI 9
युगन्धर XXXII 19
युगान्त XI 15
युगेश XIII 23
युधिष्ठिर XIII 3
युद्ध II 10, 18, XVII 1, 3, 5, 12, XVIII 8, XIX 3, XXXIV 16, XLVII 1, LXXXVI 47, XCV 46, 56
युवति LI 18, LII 6, XCV 21
युवराज XLIX 2, 5, LIII 7-9, LXXIII 4
यूक LVIII 2
यूथ XLVI 55 LXI 6, 7, 17
यूप XCVII 11
योग XXIV 5, 9, 11, 29, XXV 1, 4-6, XXVI 10-12, XXVII 2, 3, LIV 121, LVII 8
— तारा XXIV 34
— युक्त XV 2
योगान्त VII 8, 11
योजन II 11, XXX 32, 33, XXXII 31
योध LI 21
— वृष XLVIII 44
योनि XCVIII 4
यौधेय IV 25, V 40, 67, 75, IX 11, XI 59, XIV 28, XVI 22, XVII 19
यौवन XCVI 17

रक्त XXXIV 2, 23, XLVI 84, LII 1, LIII 96, LIV, 103, 106, LXVIII 96, LXXVIII 2, 20, LXXIX 25, LXXX 11, LXXXVII 35, XCV 18
— सार LXVIII 97
रक्ताक्ष VIII 51

— शोक XLIII 42
रक्तोत्पल XXIX 8
रक्षः XLVI 14, 92, LXVIII 108
रक्षोपजीव्य IX 43
रजः XXX 2, 15, 30, XXXII 24, XXXVIII 1, 3, 6-8, XLVI 21, 84, LVIII, 1, 2, LXIX 8, LXXIV 9
रजक X 5, XV 22, LXXVIII 9, LXXXVII 17, 41
रजत XXI 23, XXVI 9, XXIX 6, XXXIII 10, XXXIV 4, XLII 6, XLIV 12, XLVIII 46, LI 19, LIII 61, 101, LX 5, LXXXI 26, CV 8
रजताकर XVI 27
— नी XLIV 9
रज्जु XLIII 58, 66, LI 14, XCV 40
रण XCVIII 13
— विमर्द IX 27
रणोद्योग XLVI 25
रति LIII 9, 14, 16, XCVIII 9
रत्न XLI 7, 8, XLII 9, 12, XLIV 25, XLVIII 32, 38, 42, LI 37, LX 10, LXXXIV 1, 2, 4, LXXIX 7, 14, LXXX 1-3, LXXXVII 1, 10, XCV 22, XCVII 17, CIV 1, CV 7
रत्नपोत XLVIII 12
रथा XVI 16
रथिक LXXXVI 73
रथोद्धत CIV 31
रद LI 42
— कोश LXXXI 21
रमठ X 5, XIV 21, XVI 21
रला LXXXVI 37, LXXXVIII 6
रवक LXXXI 17
रवि LVIII 46, XCVI 10
— दीप्त LIII 106
रशना XLIII 42
रश्मिकलाप LXXXI 32
— केतु XI 40
रस XVI 25, XLI 4, XLII 4, XLVI 50, 85, XLVIII 41, LIV 2, LVII 3, 6, 7, LXXXVIII 5, 6, 23, 28
रसन XLVI 88
— विक्रयी X 8
— वैकृत्य XCVII 13
— स्रुति LV 14
रसायन XVI 20 34, LXXVI 1
राक्षस VIII 47, XVI 37, LIX 9
राक्षसी LIII 83
— सांश LXXI 11
राग LXXVII 36, LXXVIII, 15
राजकोशातक LIV 121
— धान्य XV 12
राजन्य LXXX 11
— पुरुष LIII 8, 14, XCV 19
— भय LIII 102, XCV 19
— मणि LXXX 4
— महिषी LIII 6
— यक्ष्मा LIII 47
योग II 18
राजा LXXXVI 34
— धिकृत X 16
राज्य L 19, C 5
— विनाश XLIX 7
रात्रि LI 6
राम LVIII 30
राल XLI 2
राशि II 18, XCVI 13, XCVIII, 17, C 6
राष्ट्र LIV 111, LXXXII 6
— भय XXXIII 23, 27, XLVI 39, 60, XLVIII 83
राहु V, 4, 7, 13, 14, 32, XI 22, XVII 7, XX 6, XXI 26, XXXIV 15, XLVIII 83
रिक्त XLV 3, LI 28
रिक्ता XCVIII 13, XCIX 2, C 8
रिपुभय LIII 119

रिष्यमूक XIV 13
रीतिका LVII 8
रुग्मय XXIV 36
रुचक LIII 28, 35, 36, LXIX 2, 7, 28, 30
रुचिरा CIV 21
रुत LXXXVI 6, 42, 52, LXXVIII 22, 25-27, 34, 35, 37, 45, LXXXIX 15 XC 8, 10, 12, 14, XCV 29, 50, 51, 54, 55, 57, 62, XCVII 7
रुतज्ञ XCVI 1
रुदित XLVI 49, LI 29, LXVIII 73, XCVII 6
रुद्र XLVI 10, XLVIII 26, 55, 56, 71, LIII 48
— जप XLVI 31
रुद्रायतन XLVI 6
रुधिरक LXXX 4
— हेतु XCV 30
रुधिरानन VI 4
— रोद्गारी VIII 50
रुरु XLVIII 76, LXXXVI 38, 48
रूक्ष LI 10, LIV 49, 105, LXXIX 25
रूप LXIX 4, XCVI 13, CV 5
रूपक LXXXI 11-14
रूप्य LI 17, LXXXVI 80, XCV 15
रेखा LIII 100, LXVIII 43, 44, 47, 50, 75, LXIX 22, LXX 13, 14
रेणु LXXVII 5
रेवती VII 6, X 18, CV 2
रेवन्त LVIII 56
रेवा XII 7
रैवतक XIV 19 XVI 31
रोग LIII 45, 60, 63, 74, 110, LV 14, LX 6, LXXII, 5 LXXVII 35, LXXVIII 11, LXXIX 36, LXXXII 6, LXXXVI 25, 56, LXXXIX 8, XCII 1, XCV 5
रोदसी LIII 2
रोघ XCV 8
—कृत् VIII 43
रोध्र XVI 30, LI 15, LXXVII 29, LXXXVI 80
रोपितद्रुम LV 9
रोम LXVIII 5, 90
रोमक II 4, XVI 6
रोमत्यक् XCIII 11
रोमन्थ XLVIII 11
रोमाञ्च XC 11
रोहिणी VI 9, 10 X 4, LIV 123, XCVIII 6, CI 2, CV 1
— शकट XXIV 30, XLVII 14
रोहित XLVII 20, LIV 15, 72, LXXXVI 26
रोहीतक LIV 68, 79
रौद्र VIII 49, XI 32, 51, LXXXVI 16
रौद्रर्क्ष CI 3

लकुच LV 4, 10
लक्ष्म LII 10
लक्ष्मणा LIV 48
लक्ष्मी XLVIII 57, LXXIV 4, XCIII 12, CIV 36
लग्न XXVIII 1, XXXIV 9, XLV 16, LX 20, LXXVIII 25, XCIV 10, XCVI 6-13, XCVIII 17, C 6, 8, CIII 13, CIV 61 (a)
लघु XCVIII 9
लङ्का XIV 11
लता LIII 88, LV 18
— गुल्म XLVIII 5, LXXXV 1
ललाट LI 10, 30, 41, 42, LII 3, LVIII 5, 6, LXVIII 70, 72, 75, 85, LXX 3, 8, 20, 26, XCIII 3, CV 5
ललितपदा CIV 29
ललिता CIV 41
लव XLVIII 59
लवङ्ग XXVII 4
लवण X 8, XV 9, 25, XVI 7, XXVIII 4, XLI 6, LIV 104, 122, LXXVI 11
लवली XXVII 4

— फल LXXVII 37
लाक्षा X 11, LVII 5, LXXVII 9, LXXVIII 19
लाङ्गल IV 9, XLVI 63
लाङ्गूल LXII 1, LXXII 1
लाज XLIII 36, 60, XLVIII 19, 35
लाट LXIX 11
लाभ XLII 3-13, LI 23
लालास्वभाव XC 7
लावण्य CV 8
लिक्षा LVIII 2
लिङ्ग LVII 4, LVIII 53, 55, LIX 7, LX 5, LXVIII 7, 86
लूतापट XLVI 79
लेखक X 10, XXXIV 14
— हार XV 3
लेखा II 8, LXXXII 4, LXXXVII 8
लेख्य XV 12, XVI 18, XIX 10
लेह V 43, XXVIII 5, XLI 6, 7, XLII 11, LI 17, LIII 60, 102, LIV 8, 39, LXXVII 3, LXXXVII 3
लोक LIV 2
— पाल XLIII 58, XLVI 10 XLVIII 26
लोचन LXVIII 88
लोमाश LXXXVI 22, LXXXVIII 2, XC 2
लोष्ट LXXIX 22, XCVII 7
लोहचूर्ण LXXVI 3, LXXVII 2
लौहित्य XIV 6, XVI 16

वंक्षण LXI 16, 18
वंश XLIV 4, L 3, 4, LIII 57, 65 ·
—गुल्म XXXIII 27
— पत्र L 7, LXXXIII 1
वंशपत्रपतित CIV 40
वक्त्र LI 9, 32, LVIII 9, LXVIII 54, XCIII 2, 13, XCIV 13, CIV, 56
वक्र XLVII 13, 24 XCVII 1
वक्रा VII 15, 16
वक्षः LIII 100, LXVIII 29, 86, XCIII 3
वङ्ग V 72, 79, IX 10, IX 14, XIV 8 XIV 1, XVII 18, 22, XXXII 15
वचा XVI 30, XLIV 9, LVII 1
वज्र XX 2, XXI 2, XXIX 8, XXXIII 10, XLI 8, XLIV 27, XLVI 84, LIII 28 LIX 3, LXXX 2, 4, 6, 14, 17, 18
— तल LVII 7
— लेप LVII 3, 6
— सङ्घात LVII 8
वञ्जुल XLVIII 6, LIV 50, LV 11, LXXXVI 20, 48, LXXXVIII 1, 5, 11, XCV 15
वट LIII 85, LIV 96, 119, 124, LX 8, LXXXV 3
वटु LXXXVII 14
वडवा XLVI 53, L 24
— मुख XIV 17
वणिक् LI 21, C 4
वणिज C 1, 4
वत्स X 5, XIV 2, 8, XVII 18, 22
वत्सनाभ LXXIX 32, 34, 36
वदन LXVIII 85
वदनरोग XXXII 18
वध XCV 31 36, 47, XCVIII 7
— बन्ध LIII 75
वध्य LI 21
वध्र XLV 8
वन LXXVII 29
— माला XLIII 25
— राज्य XIV 30
— राष्ट्र XIV 29
— वासी IX 15, XIV 12, XVI 6
वनसम्प्रवेश LIX 1 14
वनस्पति LV 18
वनिता LXXX 2
— भय LIV 98

वनौघ XIV 20
वन्दाक XLIII 13
वन्दिग्रहा XCI 2
वन्दिजन XLVIII 49
वन्ध्या CIII 9
वन्य XCI 1, XCV 57, XCVII 8
वयः XCVI 17
वरत्रा LXXXIX 1 (d), XCV 42
वराह XXVIII 14
— मिहिर XLVII 2, LIV 125, LXX-XVI 4, CIV 64
वरुण V 19, XI 26, XII 14, XXXIV 2, LIII 44, LIV 3, 50 124, LVIII 57, LXXXI 7, XCVIII 5
वर्ग XCVI 15
वर्ण LII 1, LIII 69, 94, LIV 2, LXVIII 102, LXIX 4, 5, XCVI 15, 16
वर्णक XLVIII 27
— दण्डक CIV 62
वर्ति LXXXIV 1
वर्धकी XLIII 22
वर्धमान XIV 7, XVI 3, L 2, LIII 33, 36, 64 LXXI 13, LXXIX 21
वर्म XLII 6
वर्ष XCV 52. 54 XCVII 1, 2
वर्षाः III 23, 26, 28, XXVIII 1, XLVI 89, LV 6, 9, LXXXIX 6
वर्षोपल LXXXI 24
वलन V 18
वलभी LVI, 25, LVII 4
वलि LI 8, LXVIII 22, 24, 25
वल्कल LI 14
वल्गुली LXXXVIII 2
वल्मीक XLIII 13. XLIII 16, LIII 90, LIV 9, 12, 14, 16, 18, 24, 25, 27, 29, 37, 40, 45, 51, 63, 65, 69, 72, 77-79, 81, 82, 84, 88, 90, 94, 95, LIX 2, XCIV 13, XCV 35, XCVII 9
वल्लकी LXXVI 2
वल्लपुष्प LXXX 7
— भत्व XLI 12
वल्लरी LV 21
वल्ली XLVIII 5, 67, LIV 101, 105, LV 18, 22, 26, LVI 15, LIX 2, LXXIX 3, LXXXV 1, LXXXIX 1 (d), XCV 5, 23, 37, 42, XCVI 6
वसन LI 15, LII 3
वसन्त XXVII 1, LXXXVI 26
— तिलक CIV 33
वसा XLVI 40, L 22, XCVII 10
— केतु XI 29
वसाति XIV 25, XVII 19
वसिष्ठ XIII 5, 6, 9, XXII 3, XXIII 4, LVIII 8
— गोत्र V 72
वसु XLVIII 56, XCVIII 5, XCIX 1
— धन XIV 31
वसुन्धरा VLIII 40
— मान् XIV 24
वस्ति LI 34, LII 6, LXVI 2, LXVIII 14
वस्त्र XLI 2, 3, XLVI 15, XLVIII 33, LI 7, LXXI 9, LXXVIII 3 XCV 15, 54, XCVIII 10, CV 7, 8
वह्न LIII 29
वह्निकृत् XCV 18
— गृह LIII 16
वाक् LXVIII 101
वागीश LXXXVI 1
वाजिरक्षक LXXXVI 33
वाजी XXIX 7, XLII 7, LXVI 1, LXXX-VIII 20, XC 11, 12, XCIII 5-7
वाटक LXXXI 2, 6
वाटधान XIV 26, XVI 22
वात XXXII 24, LIII 39, 41, 63
वातल XVI 34
— रोगी LXXXVII 11
— वृष्टि XXXII 25, XXXIV 12
वातापि XII 1

वातोद्भ्राम XCV 10
वादक X 3
वादनैपुष्य CIV 16 (d)
वादित XXXIII 23
वादित्र XLIV 16, XLVI 91, LXXXVI 22
वानर LXXXVI 28, 42, 48, LXXXVII 9
वानीर LV 10
वाम XXXVI 4, LII 9 LXXXVI 43, XCV 36
— कर LVIII 33, 34
— किरीटी LVIII 57
वामन LXV 9, LXVII 10, LXIX 31, 32, CV 14
— क LXIX 31
वा मनो XLVI 73
वामपार्श्व LIII 54, 67, XCV 26-29
वामावर्त LXI 13, LXX 17, LXXIX 34, LXXXIV 1
वायव्य XLVI 64, LXXX I0, LXXXI 8
— मण्डल XXXII 8, 10, 27, 28, 30, 31
वायु LXXXVI 58
— ज 24
— धारणा XXII 1
— स्कन्ध LXXXI 24
—स्वभाव LXVIII 110
वारण LXXXI 29
वाराह LXXXI 23, 29
वाराही LIV 87
वारिद LI 15
— मार्ग LIV 120
वारुण XXXII 20, 22, 27, 29-31, XLVI 51, LIV 37, 46, LXXX 9, LXXX-VI 31, LXXXVII 10, 36, XCV 22
वार्ता XIX 11
बाल LXXVII 7, XCIII 11
बालक LXXVII 5, 9, 13, 28
— धि LXI 12, 15, 18
हेतु LXXII 1
वालाग्र LVIII 2
वालुका LIV 91
वालेय LXXXVI 26, LXXXVIII 5
वाल्मीक XXXV 5, XLVI 70, LX 9
वासर XCVI 1
वासव LXXI 6
वासिका LV 22
वासिष्ठ II 4
वासीफल LXXX 16
वासुकि LXXXI 25
वास्तु LIII 11, 15, 20, 31, 37, LIX 14, LXXXVII 18
— कर्म LVI 9
श्वान LIII 1
— नर LIII 3, 67
वाहन XCV 14, 48
वाहिनी XLVII 25
विकङ्कत XLVIII 42, LXXXV 3
विकच XI 19
विकत्थन LXXV 7
विकला VII 15, 16
विकारि VIII 39
विकृत VIII 37
विक्रम VIII 33
विक्रेता XLII 4, 6, 7
विचर्चिका XXXII 14
विजय VIII 38
— च्छन्द LXXXI 31
विजया XLIII 40, XLVIII 39, XCIX 2
विजिगीषु XV 16
विटक XVI 2
विडङ्ग LV 7, 15
विडम्बना LXXVII 37
वितथ LIII 44, 53, 63
वितस्ता XVI 27
वितस्ति XXVI 9
वितान LXXII 4, CIV 46
वित्त LII 3, LIII 119
विदरण V 81, 89, 90, IX 13, 21
विदर्भ IX 27, XIV 8
विदारी XIII 83, LXXVI 5, 9, 10
विदिक् XCVI 8
विदिशा XVI 32

विदूरथ XLVIII 66, LXXVIII 1
विदेह V 41, 71, XVI 11, 16, XXXII 22
विद्याधर IX 27, 38, XII 7, XIII 8
विद्युत् XXV 5, XXXIII 1-3, 5, XLVI 88, L 22
विद्रुम XXIX 8
विधवा CIII 1, 6, 10
विधाता LIII 3, XCIX 1
विनता XLVIII 57
विनायक XLVI 12, LIX 9
विनाश LII 4
विन्ध्य XII 1, 7, XIV 9, XVI 3, 10, 12, LXIX 30
विपद् XCVI 11
विपाशा XVI 21
विपुला CIV 64
विप्र XXIX 10, XXXIII 15, 18, 22, XXXIV 19, XXXVI 1, XLIII 23, 38, 59, XLIV 21, XLVI 10, XLVIII 49, 73, LII 1, LIII 13, 25, 69, 70, 91, 96, 100, LXXXVI 45, XCIII 8, CV 8
— मत LXXI 14
— योग LI 12
विभीतक LIII 120, LIV 24, 102
विभूषण LXXVIII 3
विमर्द II 10
विमलक LXXX 4
विमान XLVI 90
— च्छन्द LVI 17, 22
विमिश्र VII 8, 9, 14
वियद्ग LVIII 47
विरक्तचेष्टा LXXVIII 7
विराट् XVI 12
विरुद्धस्नेह XCVII 12
विरोधी VIII 37
विरोपण LV 7
विलम्बितगति CIV 16
विलास CIV 53
विलासिनी XLVIII 8, 10, CIV 32
विलोचन LXVIII 64, 65
विवस्त्रा स्त्री LXXXVI 30
विवस्वान् LIII 46, 53
विवासन XLVI 58
विवाह LXXI 8, 14
— काल XLIII 37, XCVIII 14
विशाख XLVI 11, XLVIII 26
विशाखा IV 6, VI 9, IX 3, X 19, LV 31, XCVIII 11, CI 9, CV 3
विशोधन LV I5
विश्वकर्मा XLIII 42, XLVI 12, LVI 29, LXXIX 10
विश्वदेव XLIV 6, XCVIII 5, XCIX 1
— मातरः XLVIII 68
— म्भरक LIV 26
— रूप XI 23
विश्वावसु VIII 41
विश्वेश्वरी XLVIII 39
विष LI 29, LXXXII 6, XCVIII 8
— घातक LXXXVI 32
— प्रदिग्ध LXXVIII 1
— भय LXXX 18
विषम LXXXI 19, 28
विषाण LVII 7, LXVII 9
विष्कम्भ LIII 24, 25, LXXIX 10
विष्टि XCVI 6, XCVII 13, C 1, 4, 8
विष्ठाकरण XCV 14
विष्णु VIII 23, XLVIII 26, 55, LVIII 31, 35, LX 19 XCVI 16, CV 6, 14
विसर्पिका XXXII 14
विसूचिका LXXXVII 44
विसृक्क LI 32
विस्तार LIII 11, 22, LVI 11, 12
विस्फुलिङ्ग LX 13
वीथी IX 1, 5, 8, 9, LIII 20
वीरण XXX 24, LIV 47
वीरुधि LIV 87
वृक LXX 22, LXXXVI 27, LXVXVIII 3
वृक्ष LV 2, 12, LXXXVI 73, XCV 2
वृत्त LIII 28, LIV 99, 110, LVI 18, 23, 26, LXXXI 28, CIV 2, 58

— परिधि LVIII 53
वृद्ध XCVI 17
— गर्ग XIII 2, XLVIII 2
— श्रावक LI 20
वृद्धि XLIX 6, 8, L 18, 22, LIII 119, LVIII 29
वृश्चिक L 3, LIV 73
वृष VIII 34, XIV 9, XLVIII 76, LVI 18, 26, C 2
वृषण LI 8, LII 6, LXI 5, 16
वृषदंश XLVIII 76
— द्वीप XIV 9
वृषभ IX 1, LXI 5, 7, 8, LXXXVII 22, XCII 2
— चरित CIV 10
— ध्वज XIV 5
वृष्टि LXXXIX 6, 7, XCII 2, XCV 3, 16, 17, 58, 59, XCVI 5
— नाश XLVII 12
— निमित्त XXVIII 7, 18
वेणा IV 26, XIV 12, XVI 9, LXXX 6
वेणी LXXVIII 1
— मूल LI 40
वेणु XLIII 8, LXXXI 1, 28, 29
— मती XIV 23
वेतस XXIX 6, LIV 6, 89, 101, 119, 124, LV 10, 22
वेताल XCVIII 7
वेतालकर्म XV 4
वेत्र LXXII 4
— वती XVI 9
वेद XVI 32, XLIII 26, XLVIII 60
— निर्घोष LX 10
— व्यास XLVI 12
—शिर: XLVI 73
वेदि XLIV 8, 14, XLVIII 34, 36, 45
वेध III 3, LVIII 23, LXXXI 22
वेध्य C 6
— वेपन LXXXIV 1
वेल्लूर XIV 14
वेश्या XXXIX 3, LIII 8, LXXXVII 14,
वेष LVIII 29
वेसर XVI 20, LXXXVI 66
वैकङ्कत LXXXV 3
वैकृत XXI 26, XXXII 24, XLVI 4, 10, 12, 13, 23, 24, 30, 32, 88
वैखानस XLVIII 62
वैडूर्य XXVIII 3, XXIX 8, XXX 20, XXXVII 1, XLIII 33, 46, L 22, LIV 107, LXI 14, LXIV 3, LXXX 4, LXXXIV 2, LXX-XVII 10
वैतालीय CIV 54, 59
वैदर्भ IX 27
वैद्य XV 26
— वैधव्य CIII 7
वैधृति C 8
वैमानिक XLVIII 61
वैयाघ्रचर्म XLIV 13
वैरोचनि LVIII 30
वैशाख XXI 22, XXV 6, XCV 2
वैश्य X 7, XIV 21, XXXI 3, XXXIX 3, LIII 13, 100, LIX 6, LXXX 11
वैश्व CI 11
— देव LXXI 6
— देवी CIV 44
वैष्णव LXXI 6, LXXX 8, LXXXI 7, LXXXVI 33
— मन्त्र XLIII 30, XLIV 6
वैहायस XLVIII 62
वोक्काण XIV 20, XVI 35

व्यक्ति LXXXVI 7
व्यतिपात C 8
व्यय VIII 36
व्यसन LXXVIII 11
व्याघ्र XLVIII 76, LI 19, LXXXVI 28, LXXXVIII 3
— नख LXXVII 6, 13
— पदा LIV 88
— मुख XIV 5
व्याघ्राक्षि LXXX 9

व्यात्त LVIII 9
व्याघ्र LXXXVII 10
व्याधि XXIX 12, XXXVII 2, XLVI 25, LI 14, LXXIX 5, 29, XCVIII 3
व्याम LXXVII 7
व्याल VI 3, XLIII 65
— ग्रीव XIV 9
व्यास LIII 12, 17, 23-25, 65
व्याहृति LI 1
व्यूढोरस्क LXI 11
व्यूह VI 7
व्योम LXXXVI 6
व्रण XLIX 7, L 1-3, 9, 10, 14, 16, LII, 10, LXXXII 11, XCVI 13
व्रत XVI 20, 23, 33, XCVI 17, XCVIII 16
व्रात्य LXXXVII 39
व्रीहि LV 21

शक V 38, 75, IX 21, XIII 9, XVI 1, XVII 26, XVIII 6
— काल XIII 3
शकट IX 25, XXXIV 5, XLIII 21, XLV 7, LXXXVI 74
शकुन LIII 107, LIX 1, LXXXVI 5, 25, 35, 52, 56, 57, 61, 70, LXXXVII 1, LXXXLIII 10, XCV 62 XCVI 9, 10
— द्वार LXXXVI 52, 53
शकुनि XXX 2, C 2, 5
शकृत् LI 27, LV 17, XC 11, XCIII 14, XCIV 12
शक्र XLVIII 77, LIII 54, LXXXVI 1, XCVI 16, XCVIII 5, 7, XCIX 1
— कुमारी XLIII 39, 58, 65
— केतु XLIII 14, 37
— जनित्री XLIII 40
शक्राग्नी XCVIII 4
शङ्कर LIV 3
शङ्कु LX 6
शङ्ख XXIX 6, XXXIII 10, XLII 10, XLIII 24, 59, XLIV 7, 16, 23, XLVIII 49, 73, LI 8, 34, LII 2, LVIII 6, 33-35, LXVI 2, LXVIII 70, LXXVII 10, LXXX 5, LXXXI 1, 28, 29, LXXXVI 23, 39
शण XXIX 6
शतद्रु XVI 21
— पत्र XLVIII 6, LIV 101, LXXXVI 23
— पुष्पा LI 15, LXXVII 8, 30
शतभिषक् IX 3, 34, X 17, XXI 29, LIV 123, CI 13, CV 4
शतावरी XLVIII 40
शत्रु LII 5, 7, XCV 9
शनिकुजार्कतिथि XCVIII 13
शनैश्चर XCVI 17, XCVII 2
— सुत XI 18
शपथ LXXXVIII 41
शफरी LVI 6
शबर V 38, IX 15, 29, X 15, 18, XVI 1, 33, XXXII 15, LXXXVII 10
शबल XXX 12, 14, XXXIV 2 LXXXII 2
शमी XXIX 11, LIII 87, LIV 81, 83, 85, LIX 5, LXXXV 6
शम्भु LVIII 43, LX 19
शय LVI 23
शय्या XLVI 22, LXXI 6, LXXIV 1, LXXVIII 4, LXXIX 1, 5, 8, 18, 26, LXXXIX 1 (a), (b), 20, XCV 12
शर CIII 97, LVIII 33, XCV 5
— क्षार LIV 113
शरत् III 24, XII 9, XXV 2, XXVII 1, XL 1, 12, 14, XLIII 6, XLVI 91, LXXXVI 27, XCV 3
— सस्य X 18, XV 15
शरस्थान XIV 26
शराव XLVIII 36
शर्करा XLV 9, LIV 15, 103, 104, LXXVII 9, LXXXII 4
शर्वरी VIII 39

शलभ LXXXIV 1
शल्य LIII 58, 59, 62, 108, LXXXVI 23
शल्लकी LVII 1
शव XLVI 71, LXXXVI 45
शश LI 34, LXIX 2, 7, 20-23, 39, LXXXVI 22, 26, 42, LXXXVIII 2, 21
शशघ्न LXXXVIII 1
— शोणित LXXVIII 19
शशाङ्क LXXVIII 25, XCVIII 4 XCIX 1
शशिकान्त LXXX 4
— सुत XI 14
शष्कुलिका LXXVI 9
शस्त्र XVI 13, XVII 20, 24, LI 44, LII 7, LIII 60, 102, LV 15, LXXXVI 46, 59, XCV 14, 23, 40
— केतु XI 30
— घात XCVIII 8
— पात L 23, 25
— प्रकोप XI 38, 52, XXX 17, 21, XXXI 2, XXXIV 10, XXXV 4, 5, XXXVII 2, XXXVIII 3, XLIII 27, XLVI 63, LXXXVII 30, 32, 35
— भय LXXIX 36
— मृत्यु LIII 102, LXVIII 29
— व्याहार XLVI 71
शाक LIV 105, LXXIX 2, 13, 16
शाकटिक X 5, XV 2
शाकुन LI 33
— सङ्ग्रह LXXXVI 4
— सूक्त XLVI 73
शाकुनिक XV 22, XVI 33, LIII 106, 109, LXXXVI 31, LXXXVII 34
शाक्य LI 21, LX 19
— भिक्षु XVI 15
शाखा LIII 26, LV 6, 28, LVI 13, 14, LXXXVIII 46, XCV 3
— भङ्ग XLVI 25
— शोष LV 14
शाङ्कर LXXI 2
शाठ्य XV 4 XCVIII 8
शाद्वल XLV 7, LI 2
शान्त XXX 4, 7, XXXVI 2, XLV 16, XLVII 27, LIII 109, LXXXV 9, LXXXVI 12, 16, 36, 53, 61, 71, LXXXVII 1, 29, LXXXVIII 21, XC 3 14, XCV 20, 32, XCVI 5
शान्ति LVIII 33, 34, XCVII 17, XCVIII 6
शान्तिक II 3, XIV 20, XLIV 20, XLVI 3, 5, 17, 24, 36, 46, 50, 53, 54, 80, XLVII 9, XLVIII 2, 21, XLIX 8
— सप्त XLIV 4-6
शाम्ब LVIII 40
शारद XCV 4
— वल्ली XLI 3
शार्दूलवत् CIV 4
शाल LIII 87, LIX 6, LXXIX 2, 13, 16, LXXXV 7
शाला LIII 17, 18, 20, 32, 37, 38-40
शालाक्य XV 12
शालि XV 6, XVI 7, XIX 6, 16, XLI 3, XLIV 5, LI 30
शालिनी CIV 30
शालूक XLI 3
शालेक LIII 11
शाल्मली LVII 1
शाल्यन्न XCV 20
शास्त्र XV 10, XXI 4, XLII 6, L 10, LVIII 39, LXXIV 12, LXXVIII 1, 21, LXXIX 1, LXXXI 29, LXXXVIII 10, CIV 1, CVI 1, 2, 6
शास्त्रकार LIII 16, 21
शिंशपा LIV 105, LXXIX 2, 12, 15
शिक्य XXVI 6
शिखर LVI 21, 27
शिखरिणी CIV 8
शिखा XLIX 5

शिखिकण्ठ LXXXII 5
शिखी XI 1, 4, 14, 27, 61, 62, XII 22, XX 6, XXIV 19, XXXIV 4, XLIII 65, XLVII 12, 14, 15, XLVIII 6, LIII 43, 51, 119, LXXXVI 20, 38, LXXXVII 6, LXXXVIII 1
शिबि IV 24, V 67, XI 59, XIV 12, XVI 26, XVII 19
— कागम LXXXVI 73
शिबिरगिरि XIV 6
शिर: LI 10, 42, LII 2, 4, LIII 5, 67, 100, LVIII 14, LXVIII 79, 80, LXX 9, 26, CV 5
— स्नान LXXVII 4, 5
शिरा LIII 65, LIV 1, 4-6, 8, 11, 19, 21-26, 30, 33, 34, 36, 37, 39, 40, 42, 46, 52, 54, 56, 60-63, 66, 69, 71, 73, 74, 80, 96, 100, 124, LXI 5
शिरीष XXIX 4, LIV 50, LX 8, LXXX 6, 11, LXXXIII 1, LXXXV 4
शिरोघात LI 11
— रुक् LIII 111
— रुह CV 5
शिला LIII 112, LIV 107, 111-114, 120
शिलाजतु LXXVI 3
— विघात L 25
शिल्प XCVIII 9
शिल्पी XV 5, 9, 17, XVI 18, XXXI 3, XXXII 11, LXXXVI 30
शिव XCVIII 7
— लिङ्ग L 2
शिवा XXX 30, XLVIII 40, LIV 87, 111, LXXXVI 37, XC 3, 5, 11-13
शिशिर III 23, XIX 2, XXX 22, XXXVIII 8, XLVI 95, LV 6, LXXXVI 26, XC 1
— किरणवासर CIV 61 (b)
शिशुभाषित XLVI 97
शिशुमारी LIV 87
शीतक XIV 27
— काल LV 9
— रश्मि XCVI 15
— वात LV 14
— शीतोष्णविपर्यास XCVII 4
शीर्षणी LXXIX 31
शीर्षोपधान LX 7
शुक XXVIII 11, 14, XLVIII 6, LXXXIII 1, LXXXVIII 1, 11
शुक्ताम्लकेश LXXVII 2
शुक्ति IV 24, LXXVII 6, 30, LXXXI 1
शुक्र LXVIII 14-16, 96, 99, LXIX 33, LXXVI 1, 12, LXXXVI 1, XCVI 15, 17, XCVIII 16
— सुत XI 17
शुक्ल XXXIV 2
— शिरोरुह LXXVII 1
शुण्ठि LI 15
शुन:शेफ XLVIII 66
शुभकृत् VIII 41
— तारा XCVIII 12
शुष्क LI 33, LXXIX 3, XCV 2, 38
शुष्कविरोहण XLVI 88
शूक LI 30
शूकर LI 34
शूद्र IX 40, XIV 18, XVI 31, 35, XVII 16, XXXI 4, XXXIV 19, LIII 13, 100, LIX 6, LXXX 11, XCV 54
शून्यायतन LI 4
शूरसेन V 35, 69, IX 11, 17, XI 54, XIV 3, XVII 13, 22, LXIX 26
शूर्प XLVI 63
— कर्ण XIV 5
शूर्पाद्रि XIV 14
शूल XI 32, XLIV 21, L 7, LXIX 23
— भृत् XCVIII 4
शूलिक IX 15, 21, X 7, XIV 23, XVI 35
शृगाल LIII 108, LXXXVIII 3, XC 1
शृङ्खला LXXXIX 1 (d), XCV 42
शृङ्ग LVI 23
— बेर LXXVI 11

शृङ्गाटक II 23, XX 2, XXXIV 5, LXXX 9
शृङ्गी XVI 8
शृतशीत LV 16
शैलक LXXVII 10
शैली LX 5
शैलेय XVI 25, LXXVI 3, LXXVII 11, 13, 23
शोक LII 2, 4, 6, LIII 77
शोण V 65, XVI 1, 9, XXX 22
शोणाक LIV 23
शोणितशुक्रसाम्य LXXVI 1
शोष XLVI 47, LIII 45, 63, XCVII 5
शौच LXXIV 7
शौण्डिक IX 34, X 17, XV 22, LI 22, LXXXVI 31
शौलिक XIV 8
श्मशान XLV 9, LI 4, LIII 120, LXXIX 3, LXXXIX 1 (b), 14
श्मश्रु LXVIII 57
— धर XIV 9
श्यामा XXIX 13, LIV 87, LV 22, LXX-XV 6, LXXXVI 37, LXXXVIII 1, 5, 14
श्यामाक XIV 28
श्याव XXXIII 16, LXXIX 25
श्येन XLIII 62, XLVI 68, 9?, LXXIX 24, LXXXVI 38, LXXXVIII 1, 11
श्रमण LXXXVII 9, 36
श्रवण VI 7, 11, VII 2, IX 3, X 1, 16, XV 20, LI 8 LV 31, LXXXI 20, XCVII 16, XCVIII 11, 12, 15, CI 12, CV 4
— व्याधि IX 33
श्रावण XXI 9, 10, XXII 2, XXIV 26, LXXXVI 27
श्री: XLVIII 57, LXXVII 11, 16, 24
श्रीक XLVIII 6
श्रीकण्ठ LXXXVI 38
— कर्ण LXXXVI 38, LXXXVIII 1, 27
— धर CV 14
— पर्णी LIV 105, LXXIX 11, 15
— पर्वत XVI 3
— वत्स XLIII 3, LVIII 31, 45
— वासक LVII 3, LXXVII 28
श्रीवृक्ष XXXIII 10, L 2, LVI 15, LXXI 13, LXXIX 21, LXXXV 3
श्रुतयुक्त XV 11
श्रुति XLIII 59
श्रेणी VIII 10, X 13, XXXIV 19
श्रेष्ठी XXIX 10, XXXIII 25, LXXXVI 34
श्रोणी LVI 7, LXX 3
श्रोत्र LII 3, LIII 52
— हीन XCVI 12
श्रोत्रिय XLVIII 80, LXVIII 5
श्लेष्म LI 27, 33
श्लेष्मातक XLVIII 4, LV 27, 29
श्लोक XLVI 53, 57, 83, XLVIII 23, LX V8, LXXXVI 7, CIV 57
श्वपच LI 5, LIII 84
श्वभ्र XLVIII 16, LIII 90, 92-95, LX 6
श्वमुख XIV 25
श्वयथु XXXII 10
श्वशुर LXX 20
श्वा LI 18, LIII 107, 108, LXII 1, LXXXVI 27, 46, LXXXVII 36, LXXXVIII 9, LXXXIX 1 (a) 3, 8, 14, 16, 18, XC 1, XCV 57, XCVII 8
श्वावित् XLVIII 16, LXXXVIII 3
श्वासकास IX 44, LXXVIII 15
श्वेत XCVII 3
— केतु XI 37, 39
श्वेता XLIV 10, LX 3, LXXXI 19
षड्श्रि LVI 20, LXXX 8
षड्ज LXXXVI 40
षड्भौम LVI 22
षड्वक्त्र XCIX 1
षण्ढ LXVII 10, LXXXVI 46, XCVI 6

षष्टिक XXIX 3, LI 30, LXXVI 8, 9
षष्टपञ्च VIII 27
षष्ठाश्रित CIII 6
षाड्गुण्य II 19
षोडशाण्ड LVI 22
— श्रि LVI 18
ष्ठीवन LXXVIII 4

संयम LII 5
संयोग LI 23
संवत्सर VIII 24, XIX 3, 6, 9, XLVIII 59
संवर्त XI 51, XX 5, 6, 9
— क XLVIII 66
संस्कार XCVIII 16
संस्कृत LXXXVI 3
संस्थान II 12
सक्तु XLVI 64, LV 17, 21
सखी LXXVIII 9
सङ्कुरी XVI 11
सङ्कीर्ण LXVII 3, 5
सङ्केतहेतु LXXVIII 11
सङ्क्षय XLVII 14
सङ्क्षिप्त VII 8, 10, 14
सङ्ख्यात XIV 2
सङ्गम LXXXVI 47
सङ्ग्रह XL 14, XLII 3, 4
सङ्घात LXVIII 100
सचिववेश्म LIII 6, 8
सञ्च्छर्दन V 81, 87
सत्य LIII 43, 52
सत्प्रव LXVIII 44
सत्त्व LXVIII 85, 108, LXIX 3-5
— युद्ध XLIII 28
सद्म LIII 23
सद्यःफला XCVII 14, 15
सनक XLVIII 64
सनत्कुमार XLCIII 64
सनन्दन XLVIII 64
सनातन XLVIII 64
सन्दंश LXVI 5
सन्धि LI 8, LII 4
सन्ध्या III 34, 35, XXI 8, 16, 19, XXIV 18, XXVIII 14, XXX 1, 4, 8, 15, 20, 22, 29, 31, 32, XXXII 26, XXXIV 8, XLVI 67, 75, 79, 84, 87, XLVII 21, 22, 27, LI 6, LXXXVI 59, LXXXVII 40, XCIII 10, XCVII 3, XCVIII 13
सन्निपात XX 5, 8, 9
— सप्तजिह्व LXXIV 16
सप्तपर्ण XXIX 4, LIV 29
सप्तभौम LVI 24
सप्तमराशि CIII 7
सप्तमरीचि XLIII 37
— मुनयः XI 34, XIII 1, 3, XLVIII 62, LXXXVI 3
समज्ञा XLIV 9, XLVIII 39
समतट XIV 6
— मण्डल II 8
— समर्थ XL 13
समागम II 10, 23, XVII 11, 12, XX, 5, 8, 9, XXVIII 20, 21, XLVII 1
समाज XX 5, 7, 9
समित् XLIV 12, XLVIII 77
समुद्ग LVI 17, 23, XCIII 12
समुद्रदण्डक CIV 63 (d)
समृद्धि स्रक् XLVIII 71
सम्पद् L 16, XCVI 11
सम्पर्यासन XLVI 9
सम्पूर्ण XLV 2
सम्भार XLVIII 34, 36
— सम्मूत्रण LXXXIX 1 (a), (b)
सम्मोह XX 5, 6
सरः LVI 4
सरट LIII 123, LXXXVI 41
सरयू V 65, XVI 16
सरस्वती XVI 31, XLVI 98, XLVIII 56
सरित् XLVIII 62
— सङ्गम LIX 2
सरीसृप XXVIII 13, LXX 22
सर्ज XLIV 4, LIV 105, LVII 3, 6, LIX 5, LXXVII 11, 16, 28

सर्प XXV 3, LIII 123, LXXI 12, LXXVI 65
सर्पास्यरूप LXXX 8
सर्पि: XLVI 24, XLVIII 50, LXXVI 4, 8
सर्वतोभद्र LIII 31, LVI 18, 27, LXXVII 26
सर्षप XXIX 5, XLI 5, XLVI 24, LXXVII 4
सलिल LIV 122, LVI 1
— लाशय XLVI 50
— लोपजीवी V 42, XV 6
सविता LIII 46, 52, LX 19, XCIX 1
सवितृसुतदिवस CIV 63 (b)
सव्य V 43, 44, XXX 4, 24, XXXVI 4
सस्फुलिङ्ग LXXXIV 1
सस्य XXXIX 4, XL 1, 3, 8-10, 12, LI 2, LIV 61, 95, XCV 32, 34
सस्यक LXXX 5
— विकृति XLVI 34, 37, 42
सस्यसम्पत्ति XXIV 33, 36, XXV 2, XXVI 15, XXVII 1, 5, 6, 9, XXIX 1, 3, XL 6, 7, 11, 12
सहकार LXXVII 27
सहदेवी XLIV 10, XLVIII 40
सहा XLVIII 40
सह्यगिरि LXIX 30
सांवत्सर II 2, XII 16, XLIII 30, LIII 1, 98
साकेत XIV 4
सागर XLVIII 61
साची LXIX 31, 39
सात्त्विक LXIX 8
सादन XLVI 9
सादभङ्ग XLVI 60
साधारण VIII 43, XXXIII 19
साधु LXXXVI 45
साध्य XLVIII 55
साम XLVIII 31
सामन्त LIII 8
सामर्थ्य XLI 12
सामुद्रवित् LXVIII 1
सायाश्रय LIII 21
सार LXVIII 96, LXIX 21, LXXIV 1, 17
सारदारु LIV 118
— धान्य XV 24
— मेय LXXXIX 2, 12, XCII 2
सारस XLVIII 9, LXXIII 1, LXXXVIII 3, 37
सारस्वत XIV 2, XVI 22, LIV 99
सारिका LXXXVIII 30
सारिवा LIV 87
सार्थवाह LXXXVII 14
सार्वभौमवध XI 58
साश्व V 76, XIV 2, XVI 21, XVII 13, 18
सावन II 5
सावष्टम्भ LIII 21
सावित्र LIII 48, 52, LX 22, XCVIII 16
सिंह XLVIII 76, LVI 18, 28, LXXXVIII 3, CII 3, 7
—नाद LXXXVI 20
सिंहपुरक V 42
सिंहल XI 60, XIV 15, LXXXI 2, 3
— स्कन्ध LXI 12
सिकता LIV 13, 15, 44, LX 7
सिक्थक XXVI 8, LXXXI 17
सित XXX 22, LII 1, LIII 96, LXXX 11, XCVII 2
— सर्षप LXXX 12
— हूण XI 61, XVI 38
सिता LXXVII 11
सिद्ध XIII 8, XLVIII 25, 55
सिद्धान्त II 8
सिद्धार्थ XLIV 5, XLVIII 35, LIII 39, 40
सिद्धि XLVIII 56, LI 10
सिनीवाली XLVIII 57
सिन्दुवार XXIX 9, LIV 101
सिन्धु IV 23, V 66, 80, IX 19, X 6, XIV 17, 19, 33, XVI 16, 21, XVIII 6, LXIX 11
सिन्धुक LIX 6
सिप्रा XVI 9

सीसक LVII 8
सुकुमारक LVIII 7
सुक्षेत्र LIII 37
सुख LIII 66, 68
सुगन्ध LX 10
— केश LXXVIII 15
सुगन्धि LXXIX 26
सुग्रीव LIII 44, 63
सुतमरण LIII 68, 115, 119
सुदेवा XLVI 73
सुधाम्बु LIV 112
सुभग XV 9, CIII 3, 6, 10, CV 12
सुभिक्ष IV 9, XI 8, 14, 29, 38, 43, 45, 46, 48, 49, XVIII 3, 4, XXIV 20, XXIX 12, XXX 30, XXXII 28, XXXIII 10, XXXIV 4, XXXVII 1, XLVII 4, LXXXIX 10, XCV 2, 4, 6
सुर XLVIII 25, 26, 52, 55, 61, LIII 49, 124, LIX 9, LXVIII 108, 111, LXXXIII 1
— गुरु XCVIII 17
— गुरुदिवस CIV 62
— चाप III 27, V 95
सुरतविधि XCVIII 10
— दारु LIX 5, LXXIX 2
सुरद्विट् XCVII 2
— भितनय XLI 3, XLVI 56
— भूषण LXXXI 31
सुरसा XLVIII 57
सुरा XLVIII 28, LIV 114
सुरालयज LIX 2, XCVI 4
सुराष्ट्र IV 22, V 79, X 6, XIV 19, XXXII 19, LXIX 11
सुलेखा LI 8
सुवदना CIV 6
सुवर्ण XLI 7, XLII 6, LIII 61, LX 10, XCV 20, CV 8
— तरु LIV 70
— पुष्प XXIX 10, XLIV 9
— भू XIV 31
सुवीर V 79
सुवृत्ता CIV 7
सुव्रत XV 2
सुषिर LXXIX 29, 33
सुसार LXXXVII 23
सुस्थित LIII 21
सुहित LI 29
सुहृद् LI 18
सुह्म V 37, XIV 5, XVI 1
सूकर LXXXI 1, LXXXVI 27, XCV 47
सूकरक XXIX 2, LXXXVIII 3
— नयन LXXIX 32, 34, 36
— पादी LIV 48
— वसा LV 20
— रिका LIV 68
सूकरी LXXXVI 37, LXXXVIII 9
सूक्ष्मैला LXXVII 12
सूचक XVI 19
सूचिक X 9
सूत X 10, LXXXVII 20
सूतिका LI 20, LXXXVI 31
सूत्र XXVI 6, XLVIII 37, LIII 108, 110, CIV 2
— धार XLIII 12
सूर्य LIII 43, LIV 106, 109, XCVI 10, 12, 16
— ग्रहण XCVII 2
— दिवस LXXXI 20
— वल्ली LV 22
— सिद्धान्त XVII 1
सृक्विणी LXXXIX 17
सेतु XV 18, XVI 17, XIX 12, XXVIII 5
सेनाङ्ग XI 42
— नेता XV 16, 26 XXXIV 10, XXXV 7, XLIX 3, 5, LIII 14, 17, LXIX 20, LXXIII 4
— पतिसख LIII 5
सेनाप्रवाद II 19
— वास XLVIII 17
सैंहिकेय V 3
सैक्य XLI 6, 7

सैन्धव V 71, XVI 25, LI 32
सैन्य LXXXVI 11, XC 12, XCV 46
— क्षोभ XXXIV 20, XXXVIII 7
— घात XXX 3
सैरिन्ध्र XIV 29
सोम LIII 45, LXXIV 7, XCVII 1
— ग्रह V 97
— पीथी XV 3, XVI 7
— राजी XLIV 10
— वल्ली LIV 108
सोष्णीष LIII 20
सौकरिक XV 22, XVI 33
सौगन्धिक XXIX 10, LXXX 5, LXXXII 1
सौनिक LI 5
सौभाग्य LII 2, 6, LXXVII 35, C 3
सौम्य XXXIII 19, LXXXVI 16, XCVI 15
सौम्याह: CIV 61 (d)
सौर II.4, 5, CIV 55
सौराष्ट्र IX 19, XVI 17, V 68, XVI 31, XXXII 11, LXXX 6, LXXXI 2, 4
सौरिकीर्ण XIV 11
सौपरिक LXXX 6
सौवर्णी LX 4
सौवीर IV 23, IX 19, X 6, XIV 17, 33, XVI 21
स्कन्द XLIII 45, XLVI 11, XLVIII 26, LVIII 41
स्कन्ध I 9, LI 42, LII 4, LIII, 111, LV 5-7, XCIII 3
स्कन्धक CIV 54
स्कन्धावार XCV 45
स्तन LI 8, 39, LIII 51, LVIII 24, LX-VIII 88, LXX 21, 25, LXXVIII 3, 6, 15
— पान XCVI 17
स्तम्भ LIII 27, 29, 30, 58, •78, 112, XCVII 6
स्तेन LIII 61
स्त्री LXXIV 1, 4, 7-9, 15,17, 19, LXXV 2, LXXVI 1, 4, LXXVIII 10, 13, 21, LXXXVI 9, LXXXVII 40, LXXXIX 11
— जनन LIII 72
— दोष LIII 75, 78, 119
— द्विट् XV 8
— द्वेष्य XV 21
— निर्जित LXVIII 6
— राज्य XIV 22, XVI 6, XVII 26
— रूप LXXIX 23
— लक्षण LXXVIII 18
— लाभ XCV 43, 55
स्थण्डिल LX 7
स्थपति LIII 99, 105, LVI 30, LX 18
स्थान II 18, LXXXVI 58, 62, 63
स्थापक LX 14, 18
स्थालीपाक XLVI 16, 59
— स्थावर XXXIV 12, 14, C 5
स्थिर XCVI 2-4, 14, XCVII 4, C3 CIV 38
स्थूलपक्ष्मा LXI 14
स्नात XCV 16
स्नान XLVIII 36, LV 8
स्नेह XLI 8 XLVI 27, 48, 85, LXVIII 101, LXIX 5, LXXVIII 3, LXXXIV 1
स्पन्दन LXXIX 2, 17, 18
स्पृक्का LXXVII 5, 13, 24
स्फटिक LIV 110, LXVIII 89, 93, LXX-III 2, LXXX 4, LXXXI 28, LXXXII, 1, 2
स्फिक् LI 8, 43, LII 8, LIII 53, LXVIII 17, LXIX 23, LXX 20
स्फुटित XLIX 7
स्फुलिङ्ग XXXII 25, XXXIII 28, XLVI 22, XLVII 10
स्फोट XLVI 86
स्मरोद्दीपन LXXVII 7
स्मृति XVI 32
— लोप LIII 110, LX 13
स्यन्दन LIX 6

स्रक् LIII 113
स्रग्धरा CIV 5
स्रुक् XLIV 12
स्रुघ्न XVI 21
स्रोतः LXXX 10
स्रोतोऽन्यत्व XCVII 5
— भेदी LXXXVIII 6
स्वगुप्ता XLIV 10
स्वजन LI 25
स्वजाति पिशिताशी LXXXVI 65
स्वन LXXXVI 36
स्वप्न XLVIII 22
स्वभाव I 7, XXI 27
स्वर LXVIII 85, 95, LXIX 5, XCVI 1, 7, 15
— दीप्त LXXXVI 63, XC 3
स्वस्तिक XXXIII 10, L 2, LIII 24, 36, LVI 15, LXVIII 46, LXXI 13, LXXXVIII 23
स्वागत CIV 19
स्वाति IX 16, 31, X 10, XIV 19, XV 13, XXI 29, XXII 1, CI 8, CV 4
स्वाहा XLIII 32, XLVIII 56
स्वेद XCIII 5, XCVII 6

हंस XXXIII 10, XLIV 24, XLXIII 9 LVI 4, 5, 7, 18, 26, LXI 17, LXIX 2, 7, 24, 26, LXXXVI 22, LXXXVIII 3
— पक्ष LXXIII 1
हक्का LXXXVIII 4
हनु V 81, LI 34, 42, LII 3, LVIII 5, LXVI 2, LXVIII 88
हय LXXX 2, LXXXVI 44, LXXXVIII 3, XCIII 1, 15, CII 7
हयप IX 35
हरण C 5
हरवग्ध LXXVIII 14
हरि XCVIII 5 XCIX 1, C 6
हरिणप्लुत CIV 28
हरित XXX 12, 13, XXXIV 2
हरिताल XLIV 9, LIV 30, 110, LXXXI 7
हरिद्रतरु LIV 45, LXXIX 2, 16
हरिद्रा LV 21, LXVII 5
हरिश्चन्द्रपुर XXXII 24
हरीतकी LXXVI 11, LXXVII 10
हर्म्य XLV 4, LVII 4, LXXVI 2 LXXXVI 17, XCV 34
हल XIV 22, XVI 6, XXXII 19, LVIII 36, LXXXVI 46
हलड XIV 22
हविः L 23
हसित LXVIII 74, LXXVIII 4, CV 4
हस्त XXXIII 6, 7, XLIV 3, XLVIII 47, LI 8, 13, 40, 42, LIII 4, 16, 22, 26, 52, 65, 92 LIV 6, 8, 12, 18, 21, 22, 25, 51, 53, 65, 66, 70, 72, 75, 76, 78, 123, LV 12, 19, 24, 31, LVI 20, 21, LXX 22, XCVIII 9, 12, 15, CI, 7, CV 3
हस्तिकर्ण XXIX 7
हस्तिनपुर XIV 4
हस्तिनी XLVI 53
हस्ती XLVIII 87, L 17, LI 19, LIII 107, LIX 3, LXXXVI 27, LXXXVII 17, 42
हार LXXXI 32
— फलक LXXXI 34
हारहौर XIV 33
हारीत XLVIII 6, LXXXVI 21, LXXXVIII 1, 15
हास्यज्ञ XVI 19, XIX 12
हिंस्र LXXXVI 31
हिङ्गु LXXVII 7
हिङ्गुलुक LIV 110, LXXVII 30
हिमवान् XIV 24, XVI 17, LXXII 1 LXXX 7
हिमागम LV 6
हिरण्य XXIX 10, XLVI 41, XLVIII 42 48
हिरण्यनाभ LIII 37

— वर्णा XLVIII 72
— विकृति XCVII 13
— शकल LX 17
हीन LIII 12
हुडु विषाण L 25
हुतभुज XXXII 12, 27, LIII 48, LXXX 8, XCVIII 12
XLVI 47, XLVIII 8
हुताश LIII 63, 124, XCVII 11
— भक्त XV 14
— सुत XI 11
हूण XIV 27
हृदय LI 9, 43, LII 4, LIII 54, LVIII 16, LXVI 2, LXVIII 28, LXX 25, LXXV 4, LXXXV 8
हृषीकेश CV 15
हेम LI 37, LIV 110, LXXXIV 2
— कुड्य XIV 9
— गिरि XIV 19
— ताल XIV 28
हेमन्त III 24, 26, XLVI 69, 93, LXXXVI 28
हेम XXVI 9, LXXXI 2, 5,
हैरण्यक LXXXVII 32
हैहय XIV 20
होता LX 13
होम XLVI 31, 51. 58, 65, 73
होरा I 9, II 3, 6, 18, XXXIV 11, XCVI 1
ह्रस्वकेशी LXXVIII 11
ह्लेषित XCIII 7

INDEX

A

Abandoned
  Animal to be : 386.
Abdomen : 606.
Abhicāra : 659.
Abhidhānacintāmaṇi : 169.
Abhijit : 134, 398, 864, 875.
Abhilaṣitārthacintāmaṇi : 529.
Ābhīras : 52, 54, 104, 180, 200.
Abhisāra 182.
Ablution:
  Royal—: 405-423.
Abortion : 48, 442.
Abroad
  To die—: 603.
Abu, Mt. : 200.
Ācārya : 600.
—s : 329, 736.
Actions, Cause of universe : 4.
Actors : 112, 114, 116, 786.
Ādarśa : 180.
Addicted to forbidden women : 609, 614, 623, 625, 626, 628, 653.
Āḍhaka : 245, 485, 532.
Adhikamāsa : 9.
Adhivāsana
—ceremony : 568-571.
—Maṇḍapa : 568.
Ādityadāsa, author's father : 937.
Adulterers : 185, 202.
Adulteress : 810.
Advaitins : 695.
Advice to young men : 702.
Aerial Cities : 863.
Aerial City
  Effects of—: 324, 325, 401.
Affection, winning of—: 693-698.
Afflicted : 190.
Afghans : 143, 202.
Āgama
  Knowledge of—: 710.
Āgamas : 572.
Agastya : 152, 154-160.
Agate : 738.
Age of measurement : 642.
Ages of persons : 859.
Agnideśa : 119.
Agnipurāṇa : 104, 177, 178, 183, 926.
Agriculture : 221.
Agriculturists : 96, 194.
  Danger to—: 809.
— will suffer : 35, 50.
Ahicchatra : 117.
Ailments
  Bilious—: 220.
— of wind : 111.
Airāvata : 287, 292, 400.
Airy nature : 643.
Aitareya Brāhmaṇa : 141, 166, 179.
Ākranda : 208, 209.
Akṣaragaṇas with presiding Deities : 898.
Akṣara-Kośa of Yavaneśvara : 848, 859.
Alakā
  Chief of— : 141.
Alaṁkāra-śāstra : 722.
Al-beruni : 115, 157, 166, 173, 175, 177, 650.
—On Comets : 121, 124, 136, 143.
Alexander's time : 140.
Alkali : 703.
Allahabad Praśasti
  Samudragupta's—: 169, 177.
Allies : 842.
Alligator : 497.
Alliteration : 112, 153, 154, 158, 219, 345, 352, 638, 664, 717, 750, 828, 888.
Alliterative verse : 677.
All planets in 7th House at marriage are harmful : 894.
All planets in 11th House at marriage are good : 895.
Almanac : 15, 22.
Altar : 421.
  Western—: 414.
Amarakośa : 362, 509, 513, 534, 611, 624, 633, 639, 685, 702, 737, 768, 800.
Amarasiṁha : 708, 709.
Amazonian Kingdom : 178.
Ambarāvata : 180.
Ambaṣṭha, according to Manu : 168.
Ambaṣṭhas : 104, 198.
Ambrosia
  Churning the milky ocean for— : 935.
Amethyst : 738.
Amnesty to prisoners : 422.
Amogha : 400.
— rays of the Sun : 279.
Amorous
— ardour : 718.
— talk : 723.
Ānarta country : 63, 184.
Anavasitā : 913.
Ancient
— Discipline : 757.
— Persia : 572.
— Writers : 23.
Andhra : 213.
  King of— : 142.
Aṅga country : 61, 102, 104, 117, 118, 141, 193, 213, 300.

Aṅgaviniścaya : 5.
Aṅgiras : 163.
Anglers : 188.
Animals
—— at town gate : 818.
—— living on grass : 50.
—— Three classes of—: 642.
—— With uncloven hoofs : 63.
Aquatic— : 51, 108, 115, 213, 842.
Destruction of ,, — : 33.
Inauspicious—: 679.
Ankle-joints : 601, 660, 673.
Antarvedi country : 60.
Anthill : 502-508, 511-515, 517, 518, 570, 825, 836.
Anubandhas : 11.
Anurādhā : 243, 400.
Rulership of— : 187.
— with Kaulava : 877.
Anuṣṭubh : 222, 273, 436, 527, 921.
Apāmārga : 756.
Aparājitapṛcchā of Bhuvanadeva : 450
Aparānta : 53.
Aparavaktra : 31, 113, 255, 741, 905.
Apasavya : 206, 207.
Aphorisms : 7.
Aphrodisiacs : 199.
Apiary : 434.
Apogee : 10.
Aquarius : 54.
—— as ascendant : 873.
Aquatic products : 788.
Arabs : 177.
Arage : 122.
Arbuda mountain : 60.
Architect : 489, 544.
celestial—: 450.
Architecture : 450-498.
Architrave : 460.
Ardhā : 745.
Ardhasamavṛtta : 399, 755, 801, 802, 905, 906, 918.
—— of Mātrāsamaka : 799.
Ardhavirāṭ : 687.
Ārdrā : 237.
Rulership of—: 185.
Areca-nut : 718.
Arghā : 745.
Aries : 636.
Arimeda : 165.
Ariṣṭapura : 142.
Ārjikiya : 198.
Arjuna 722, 755.
—— tree, Good for rain : 284, 521, 525.
Arjunāyanas : 40, 142, 180, 198, 212.
Arka
—— Dīpta : 763, 775.
—— plant : 284.
Armed Conflict : 64, 76, 114.
Armies
Commanders of— : 614, 624, 626.
Armoury : 434.
Arm-pits : 612, 657.
Raised— : 633.
Arms : 636.
Kings— : 613.
Long— : 633.
Army
—— Chiefs : 50.
—— Commanders : 114.
—— on the march : 51.
—— revolt : 48, 66, 101.
—— Subdivisions of— : 685.
—— To be destroyed : 349.
Trouble from alien— : 29.
Artha : 2.
—— Śāstra : 178.
—— ,, of Kauṭilya on rain : 248.
Arthāntaranyāsa : 7, 402, 672, 725.
Arthāpatti : 679.
Artisans : 119, 722, 767.
Artists : 50, 107.
Arundhatī : 162, 163.
Āryā : 1, 442, 520, 898, 899, 918-920, 929.
Āryabhaṭa : 32.
Āryabhaṭiya : 9, 11, 208.
Āryans
Observant— : 55.
Āryaśūra : 173.
Āryāvarta : 60, 167, 180.
Āṣāḍhas - 16, 262, 265, 270.
Asafoetida : 115, 176.
Ascendant : 5, 11, 14, 372, 844-847, 852,
Benefic— : 826.
Fiery— : 845.
Natal— : 636, 873.
Asceticism : 636.
Ascetics : 433, 636, 757, 768, 781, 864.
Asikas
Chief of— : 141.
Asita : 121, 230.
Āśleṣā : 237, 398, 864.
Place of—triad : 169.
Rulership of— : 186.
—— with Nāga or Śakuni : 877.
Aśmaka
King of— : 140.
People of— : 53, 62, 63, 104, 106, 177, 178, 211.
Trouble to— : 300.
Aṣṭabandha : 546.
Aṣṭakavargas : 14.
Aṣṭaśrī : 541.
Asterisms : 114, 372, 374, 419, 479, 636, 844, 846, 863.
Auspicious— : 346.
Common rulership of— & lunar days : 875-877.
Common rulership of — & Muhūrtas : 878.
—— devoid of qualities : 677.
Effects of birth in— : 884-889.
——for masculine sacraments : 872.
—— for shave : 869-872.
Functions & properties of— : 866-873.

—— of 6 categories : 311.
Swift— : 868.
Temporary— : 869.
Tender— : 868.
,, dreadful— : 869.
unhurt— : 564.
Asthma
—— Result of Earthquake : 299.
Asthmatic complaints : 95, 112.
Astrologer : 7, 8, 11, 12, 15, 18-21, 48, 410, 411, 416, 422, 428, 432, 442, 453, 488, 564, 571.
Astrologers
—as observers of Quarters : 17.
Canons for— : 7, 13, 17.
Quack— : 20, 21.
Royal—: 406.
—— uncontaminated by sin : 19.
Unique position of— : 22.
Virtues of— : 8.
Astrological
—— lore : 935.
—— works : 646.
Astrology : 1, 3, 5, 11, 13, 14, 20, 719, 931.
Ascetics' interest in— : 18.
—— as social Science : 18.
Belief in— : 842.
—does not teach fatalism : 757.
Electional— : 677, 894.
Horary— : 781.
Knowledge of— : 2.
Mundane— : 139, 190.
Political— : 344.
Astronomers : 107, 162.
Astronomical
—— Calculations : 8, 12.
—— Science : 12, 21.
—— Works : 208.
Āśvalāyana-sūtra : 900.
Aśvamedha : 405.
Aśvattha : 166, 282, 755.
Āśvina : 233, 243, 361, 362, 829.
Aśvinī : 636, 864.
Rulership of— : 189.
Atharvaveda : 141, 166, 168, 419.
Atheist : 658.
Atkinson : 178.
Atom : 549.
Atomic theory : 4.
Atonement for bad deeds : 21.
Atri : 163, 373.
Attendants
Kings'— : 657.
Attitude
Scientific— : 121.
Auguries : 14, 434, 489, 564.
—— for clouds : 254.
—— of fire : 421.
Augury : 207, 586, 730.
Aupacchandasika : 52, 95, 155, 222, 431, 671, 691, 811, 844, 922.
Authority
unnamed— : 602, 606, 660.
Author's
—— humility : 936.
—— literary art : 255.
Autumn : 155, 157, 392.
Autumnal
Crops : 112, 187, 829.
grains : 63, 66.
Āvāhana : 410.
Avanti : 53, 103, 104, 134, 184.
Āvantika : 1, 59, 62.
Avenues
—— of Venus : 97-102.
Conflicting opinions re— : 101.
Directions of— : 98
Northern— : 395, 397.
Aversion of the opposite sex : 696.
Ayodhyā-King : 39.
Āyurveda : 75, 186, 640, 699.

B

Back : 612.
Short— : 633.
Back-bone : 595.
Badakshan : 141.
Bādarāyaṇa : 7, 230, 333-335.
Bagchi, P. C. 170.
Baghelkhand : 142.
Bāhlikas : 116, 211, 213, 300.
Bāhulaka : 723.
Baladeva : 499, 526.
Balance : 267.
Bali : 556.
Balkh : 52, 116.
Baluchistan : 115.
Bamboo
Pearls from— : 747.
Bāṇa, poet : 181, 691, 696, 718, 719.
Banavāsi : 172.
Baneful year : 93.
Bankers : 118.
Banner
Trees good for— : 347.
Banyan tree: 282.
Barbara : 54.
Barbarians : 111.
Barbers : 116, 433, 722.
Bards : 786.
Barley : 92.
Bath
Royal— : 406.
Bathing : 14, 16.
Battles
Bloody— : 48.
Baudhāyana-sūtra : 900.
Bearers
of burdens : 54.
Beds
Dimensions of— : 730.
Beef : 532.
Bee-hive : 862.
Before eclipse
Mercury's effects— : 861.

Belching aloud : 441.
Bell
—— makers : 117.
—— ringers : 115.
Belly : 595, 636.
Folds on— : 609.
Pot-like—: 607, 669.
Benares
Edition : 526.
People of — : 61.
Bengal : 142.
People of— : 61-63.
Benzoin : 198, 709.
Beryl : 521, 577, 583, 738, 753.
Bestial nature : 644.
Betel : 717.
—— Chewing : 718.
Bhadra : 165, 646, 651, 652, 657, 746.
Bhadrā : 826, 874.
Bhadrabāhu : 110.
Bhādrapada : 233, 243, 273, 829.
Bhadrāśva : 102.
Bhadravirāṭ : 801
Bhagavadgītā : 307, 649, 693, 694.
Bhāguri : 405, 758.
Bhānubhaṭṭa : 106.
Bhāra equals 200 Palas : 642.
Bhāradvāja : 481, 757, 758.
Bharaṇi : 846.
Rulership of— : 189.
—— with Viṣṭi : 877.
Bharata (on triangular buildings): 472.
——'s rules : 555.
Bhāratavarṣa : 165.
Bhāravi : 110, 687.
Bhartṛhari : 692, 717.
Bhāsa, poet : 155, 353.
——'s Svapnavāsavadatta : 724.
Bhaṭṭasvāmin : 178.
Bhaṭṭotpala : 1, 3, 83, 95, 106, 110, 115, 117, 124, 141, 185, 186, 203, 206, 216, 217, 242, 386, 393, 535, 538, 544, 576, 579, 595, 607, 623, 629, 637, 659, 690, 699, 779, 782, 788, 822, 872, 911, 929, 941, 942.
Bhavabhūti : 2.
Bhaviṣyapurāṇa : 572.
Bhīṣma's departure -: 162.
Bhoja : 402.
Bhoṭa tribe : 180.
Bhramara-kīṭanyāya : 693, 695.
—— vilasita : 909.
Bhṛgu : 772.
Bhṛṅgis : 39.
Bhujaṅgaprayāta : 255, 915.
—— vijṛmbhita : 917.
Bhūmaka : 177.
Bhūrjakaṇṭaka : 455.
Bhūtas : 659.
Bile, Vitiated— : 920.
Vitiation of— : 102.
Biliousness : 904.
Bilva : 521.
—— & fig joined together : 503.
Birch-bark : 436.
Birds : 107.
Aquatic— : 407.
Auspicious— : 539.
Carnivorous— : 401.
„ — : sitting on banner : 359.
Destruction of— : 120.
Inauspicious— : 407.
Trouble to— : 58.
Birth
of Sons : 730.
—Star of next issue : 445.
Bitches bringing forth young ones in forest: 862.
Black
grains : 111.
—— magic.
Expert in—— „ : 659.
Blanket : 417.
Blaze in quarters : 16.
Blind : 847.
Blood
—— a vital substance : 640.
Flow of— : 802.
Excess of woman's—leads to female birth : 699.
—— stone : 738.
Blue jay : 772.
—— fighting with Crow : 801.
Boars : 111
Pearls from— : 746.
Bodha : 710, 711, 714.
Bodhāyana : 419.
Bolt : 400, 412.
Bone fractured : 837.
Bones
Strong— : 635, 640.
Books
One will get— : 787.
Border
People living in— : 50.
Boring earlobes
Planetary positions and Stars for—:881.
Bosoms : 663.
Bow-makers : 62.
Brahmacārin : 860.
Brahmagupta : 107, 161.
Brahman : 2, 3, 12, 42, 481, 558, 630-632, 804.
—— of Vedāntins : 692.
—— to be guarded : 475.
World of— : 19.
Brāhmaṇa period : 142, 398.
Brahmāṇḍa : 630.
Brāhmapurāṇa : 630.
Brahmaputra : 168.
——Valley : 143.
Brahma siddhānta : 32, 34, 44, 45.
Brāhmasphuṭa siddhānta : 11, 106, 107.

Brahmin astrologer : 20.
—— murder : 106.
Brahmins : 39, 111, 112, 118, 154, 159, 164, 189, 194, 212, 284, 377, 378, 381, 382, 385-388, 398, 404, 416, 433, 454, 465, 488, 560, 570, 571, 575, 677, 679, 682, 685, 689, 699, 764, 794, 931, 933.
Trouble to— : 58, 61, 62, 96, 103.
Brahmoktaviśvakarmaprakāśikā : 450.
Braying is 'Burning' : 803.
Break of Chin : 64.
Breast
Broad— : 633.
Muscular— : 651.
Breath
Sweet— : 643.
Bredichin, Professor : 145.
Brewers : 118.
Bṛhadratha : 574.
Bṛhadyātrā : 6 .
Bṛhajjātaka : 1, 2, 6, 17, 110, 194, 312, 637, 647, 728, 848, 850, 884, 890, 918, 919, 942.
Bṛhaspati : 249, 322, 451, 485, 757, 758.
—— taught Indra : 423.
Bricks
Burnt— : 457, 466, 524.
Bride
Suitable— : 660.
Bridges : 197, 221.
Construction of— : 188.
Broach : 650.
Brows : 625.
Arched— : 665.
unconnected— : 625.
Well-knit— : 651.
Buddha : 559, 572
—— era : 162.
Time of— : 141.
Buddhism : 722.
Buddhist monk : 786, 792, 925.
Buffalo : 370, 612, 786, 824, 836.
Buildings
Varieties of— : 464, 466.
—— in neighbourhood : 484, 485.
Bull-fighting : 416.
Bulls : 574; 576-578.
Burdwan : 192.
Burgled
Danger of being— : 810.
Burial ground : 370.
'Burning' direction
Animals in——: 818
Burning organ
woman with— : 726.
Butchers : 433.
Butter-milk : 523.
Buttocks : 607, 654.

C

Caitra : 233, 392.
Cakravāka : 155.
Cakṣu (Oxus) : 116.
Calamities : 862.
Sixfold— : 94.
Calendar : 232.
Cālukyas : 104.
Camara deer
Tails of— : 681.
Camels : 58.
Campā : 141, 193.
Campakamālā : 583.
Camphor: 710, 711, 715, 716.
Campūrāmāyaṇa : 402.
Cāṇakya : 13.
Cancer : 23, 24, 52.
Caṇḍavṛṣṭiprayāta : 926.
Cannibals : 39.
Canopus : 16, 152, 154, 155, 159.
Setting of— : 160.
Capalā : 929.
Capital
Destruction of : 29.
—— to be stormed : 119.
Capricorn : 23, 24, 54.
Caraka : 7, 718.
—— Saṁhitā : 5.
Carakhaṇḍas : 11.
Cardamom : 199.
Cargo of gems : 408.
Carmaraṅgas : 177.
Carpenters : 118.
Carriage-makers : 118.
Cartmen : 82, 114.
Cārudevī river : 104.
Castes
—— assigned to parts of sky : 50.
Suffering of— : 27.
Categories : 4.
Cats : 111, 765.
sight of— : 803.
Cattle : 438.
Arrival of— : 260.
Death of— : 51, 144.
—— owners : 52, 102, 103, 605, 608.
Rich in — : 628.
—— to be destroyed : 112, 212.
—— to progress : 221, 222.
Trouble to— : 35, 75, 79, 94, 159.
Caurapañcāśikā : 686.
(of Bilhaṇa)
Cave-men : 103, 104, 115.
Cawing of Crows : 16.
Cedi : 142.
Central regions
— to be troubled : 56, 63, 66, 95.
Cereals : 186, 187.
Chameleon in front : 771.
Characteristics
Natural— : 643.
—— of blessed men : 645.
Charcoal : 371, 372.
Charioteers : 116.
Charitably disposed : 659.

Charlatans
Condemnation of— : 12, 21.
Charms and herbs :
Skilled in— : 54.
Cheeks : 622, 653.
—— with dimples : 670.
Chemists : 197.
Chenab : 200.
Chest : 636.
Even — : 611.
Raised — : 633.
Chidambara Iyer : 249.
Children : 640, 668.
Bereft of— : 626
Father of many — : 606.
Few — : 603.
—— in the womb suffer : 63.
Chin : 619.
Chinese : 62, 63, 143, 202.
Cholera : 403.
Chowries : 733 , 787.
Crystal handle of— : 681,684.
Signs of —: 681.
Cīnaraṭṭha : 183.
Cīnas : 116, 117, 192.
Circle of quarters : 805, 806, 839.
Circular worship : 572.
Circumference : 561.
—— of head : 552.
—— Waist : 554.
Citrā : 400.
Rulership of — : 187.
Clark W. F. : 11.
Clash of arms : 24, 27, 48, 75, 82, 290, 792.
Clashing of rays : 205, 207.
Classes
Four— : 120.
Clay for making images : 564.
Cleaving
Effect of — : 211.
Clitoris : 661, 739.
Clothes : 676-678.
Constellations for wearing new—: 676.
Effects of cuts in — : 678.
Location of gods, men and devils in— : 677.
Stains on — : 677, 678.
Cloud formations : 16.
— tree : 289.
Clouds : 419, 861.
Mars afflicting— : 240.
Pearls from — : 746.
Ruin of — : 211.
Shapes of — : 291.
Tree-shaped — : 401.
Types of — : 241.
Clove : 199.
Coastal people : 103.
Cobbler : 483, 722, 786, 792.
Cobwebs : 390.
Cocks : 16, 581, 582, 786.
—— Crowing in the evening : 389.
Cohabitation with forbidden women: 601.
Coitus : 693, 726.
Cokṣa : 794.
Cola : 53, 119, 143, 202.
Colebrook : 157.
Colic : 654.
Collar-bone : 611.
Collyrium : 414, 521, 522, 583, 706.
Colours
Sun's——in the seasons : 28, 29.
Symbolism of— : 27.
Colt : 593.
Combat
Single— : 189.
Combustion : 6.
Comet : 153, 398, 399, 423.
—— afflicting king's star : 140.
—— Bennet: 122.
Brahmadaṇḍa — : 127.
——Causing mortality : 126, 132.
Disastrous effects of Kiraṇa — : 126.
Donati's— : 145.
—— Encke : 122.
Portentous — : 125.
—— Striking Agastya : 160.
Comets
Analysis of — : 121.
— born of Death : 123.
Charts of — : 146-148, 150, 151.
Composition of — : 144.
Duration of effects of — : 124.
Good effects of — : 125, 127, 136-138, 143.
How—are recognized : 123.
—— known as *Tāmasakīlakas* : 24, 25, 147, 149.
Three kinds of — : 122.
Commandants : 188, 189, 194.
Commanders of elephants : 107.
Commentary
Two other schools of — : 783.
Commentator : 91, 93, 115, 116, 118, 125, 126, 142, 153, 160, 205, 208, 214, 222, 232, 233, 240, 243, 245, 251, 252, 369, 370, 379, 382, 387, 392, 400, 407, 412, 421, 428, 429, 432, 433 436, 460, 463, 467, 470, 478, 482, 489, 492, 497, 498, 503, 509, 512, 519, 520, 524, 526, 528, 529, 532, 536, 538, 542, 545, 549, 551-553, 558, 561, 570, 575, 580, 585, 587, 591, 595, 596, 598, 599, 601, 603, 608, 614, 638, 639, 643, 647, 648, 650, 652, 656, 657, 660, 666, 677, 681-683, 692, 695, 697, 700, 704, 708-711, 713, 714, 717, 718, 723, 725, 734, 736, 738, 740, 741, 743, 747, 749, 754, 758 760, 767, 770-772, 774, 776-779, 784, 787-789, 793, 794, 797, 799-801, 810-813, 818, 820, 822, 826, 831-834, 839-841, 845, 846, 848, 851, 853, 858, 860-862, 869, 871, 888, 892, 894, 900, 912, 913, 922, 923, 929, 942.

Complexion : 641.
Compound perfume : 709, 715.
Conch : 594, 616.
—— figure : 635, 636, 652.
Pearls from——shell : 747.
Concubinage
Addicted to—— : 604.
Concubines
Prosperity of—: 284.
Conflict with southern enemies : 64.
Conjugal happiness : 635, 664.
——marred : 696.
Conjunction
Moon's— : 214-216.
—— of Jupiter & Saturn : 119.
—— with eclipsed disc : 59, 60.
Conjunctions : 10, 14, 16.
Connoisseurs
—— of gems : 737.
—— of wares : 187.
Consonants assigned to planets : 849, 859.
Constellations : 11, 14.
Fined, Dreadful, Fierce etc.—: 867, 868.
Number of stars constituting— : 866.
Presiding Deities of— : 866.
Conversion of shadow into time : 11.
Corals : 195, 443, 738.
Cordiality :
——among the people : 83.
—— ,, rulers : 34.
Corn : 39.
Abundance of— : 214, 215.
Corporations
Heads of— : 187, 200, 213.
Corpulent : 654.
— body : 644.
Cosmic forces
Release of— : 406, 415.
Cot : 731, 732.
Cross-beams of— : 735.
Cotton
Destruction of— : 62.
Couch : 571, 677, 678, 686.
Couches & Seats
Signs of— : 729-736.
Cough : 112.
Countries : 829.
—— allotted to stars : 16.
Conquest of— : 143.
Destruction of— : 29, 402, 777.
Eastern— : 40, 112.
—— in the South : 404.
—— in the West to suffer : 396.
—— lying between Ganges & Jumna : 655.
North-Eastern— : 182.
Northern —— : 179.
North-Western — : 177.
Trouble to prosperous — : 55.
Country will be denuded : 830.
Courage
Deep— : 633.
Couriers : 116.
Courtesan : 116, 788.
Attributes of— : 12.
Courtyard : 476.
Cowherds : 60, 767, 794.
Cowpen : 408.
Cows : 16, 488, 570, 597, 764, 765.
—— bring fortune to owner : 819.
Dung of — : 438.
Features of— : 416, 574-579.
Intention of — : 819.
lowing of— : 782.
—— lowing without reason : 819.
Milch— : 389.
——obstructed by dogs indicate rain: 819
—— with tail touching the ground : 577, 578.
—— with tears in eyes indicate owner's death : 819.
—— with white feet : 579.
Crafty : 608.
Cranes : 804.
Creation : 3.
Creator's boon : 42, 46.
Creatures
Diurnal & nocturnal— : 795.
ugly — : 383.
Creepers
Produce of— : 85.
Cries
—— of birds & beasts : 795-806.
—— of crows : 829.
Science of— : 844.
—— that are full, burning, auspicious : 798.
Criminal
Condemned— : 438.
Crops : 94, 95, 106, 132, 222, 244, 257, 273.
Abundant— : 24, 34, 37, 38, 47, 62, 78, 84, 85, 93, 104.
Autumnal— : 118.
Danger to— : 29, 48, 53, 57, 58, 62, 64, 83, 86, 102, 103, 220.
Destruction of— : 299, 334.
Growth of— : 336-339, 381.
—— prosper : 333, 334.
Summer— : 112.
Crow : 402.
—— attacking people : 831.
—— building nest : 829, 830.
—— striking a vehicle : 832.
—— with two or more fledgelings : 830.
Crown : 16.
Crowns : 424, 425.
Crests of— : 424.
Crown-work : 544.
Crows
Different sounds of— : 840.
—— flying at night : 831.
Cruel men : 189.
Cry
Burning— : 801-803.

Full— : 801, 803, 804.
Malignant — : 797.
Crystal : 41.
Cubits
Small — : 681.
Three kinds of — : 464, 465.
Cuckoo : 402, 664.
Cūlikas : 104.
Cunningham
——on Bhadra : 176, 196.
—— on Brahmaputra : 183.
Cupid
Activities of— : 93.
Cupid's snare : 699.
Cūrṇa : 745.
Cutch : 39.
Cycle of sixty years : 9, 89, 96.

D

Dacoits : 96.
Dahana Vīthī : 133.
Dakṣa's Sacrifice : 123.
Dāmaras : 183.
Damayantī : 170.
Daṁdānī : 797.
Damsel : 692, 719, 721, 723, 726, 741
Charming— : 686.
Damsels
young— : 834, 838, 908, 919.
Dancers : 62, 84, 786.
Daṇḍa : 287-289, 539.
Daṇḍaka : 807, 923, 926, 927.
Chief of — : 141.
Surāma — : 155.
Daṇḍin : 12, 168, 170, 696.
Danger
—— to life : 635.
—— to people : 30, 93.
—— to world : 79.
Daradas : 54, 63, 119, 164, 182.
Darbhanga : 104.
Darkness : 3.
Dark Shafts : 24.
—— Causing sufferings : 26, 129.
Colours of — : 27.
shapes of — : 26.
Darśa : 119.
Dārva : 183.
Daśānta : 677.
Daśārṇa : 53, 118.
Daśarūpaka : 687.
Daśās of planets : 14.
Dāśeraka : 60.
David Brunt : 241.
Dawn : 285.
—— to be disastrous : 287.
Day : 9.
Death : 37, 47, 403.
—— at the hands of a woman : 623.
—— by hanging : 815.
Danger of — : 812.
News of — : 815.
—— of commander : 27.
—— of king : 31, 67, 389.
—— of Pāṇḍya King : 35.
—— of queen : 65.
Owner's— : 379, 381, 481.
—— through hunger : 29.
Decanate : 13.
Decay of vehicles : 816.
Decoction : 569.
Decorative motifs : 482.
Deer : 16, 803, 812.
Defeat
Signs of— : 208, 209.
——of Mars and other planets : 211-213.
Defeatist mentality : 688.
Deformed body : 659.
Deities (8) of houses : 479, 480.
Demon : 778.
Demoniac nature : 644.
Demonology : 197.
Demons : 152.
Deodar : 756.
Depression at the Corners of eyes : 552.
Destiny : 21.
Destroys enemies : 755.
Destruction
—— of countries : 23, 287, 795.
—— of enemies : 683.
—— of fighters : 40.
—— of King's enemies : 590.
—— of landed property : 437.
—— of owner : 561.
—— of people : 31, 35.
—— of traders : 36.
Determination of strength : 13.
Devala : 43, 78, 97-99, 119, 121, 127, 225, 230, 246, 293, 499, 758.
Devikā river : 134.
Devilish nature : 644.
Devoted to elders & Brahmins : 656, 659.
Dey : 180, 199.
Dhaniṣṭhā
Rulership of — : 188.
Dhanvantarinighaṇṭu : 514, 523, 524.
Dharaṇa : 744.
Dharmaśāstra : 10, 497, 598, 690, 699, 719, 727, 934.
Dharmāraṇya : 166, 167.
Dhasan river : 118.
Dhātus : 640.
Dhīralalitā : 915.
Dhūmaketu : 861.
Dhūpa : 709, 710.
Dhvani : 156.
Diagram
Circular— : 411, 412.
Planets in the— : 412.
Diameter of Day-Circle : 11.
Diamonds : 170, 737, 739-741.
Deities of — : 738.
Diction

Graceful — : 157, 158.
Dictionary
Apte's — : 770.
Diet
Regulated — : 920.
Digestion
Weak — : 702.
Digit : 796.
Own — : 550.
Practical—: 730
——varies from person to person : 642.
Digs at grammarians etc. : 21.
Dīkṣit S. B. : 89.
Diminutive month : 9.
Dimple : 551.
Dinacaryādhyāya in Āyurveda : 754.
Dīpta : 797.
Direction
—— afflicted with famine : 226.
—— of rainfall : 233.
Tranquil — : 806.
Directions
Determination of — : 252.
— for worship-room : etc. 495.
Disaffection
Indications of — : 721.
Disasters : 101.
Discord between king & army : 105, 207
Disease : 40, 58, 69, 74, 76, 78, 86, 93 94, 96, 103, 105, 110, 132.
Freedom from — : 92.
—— of anus : 65.
—— of bile : 112.
—— of ear 108.
Outbreak of — : 334.
Diseases : 144, 159, 207, 403, 437.
Fatal — : 138.
Dissolution of the world : 398.
Distillers of liquor : 108, 188, 768.
Distinguishing sex of creatures : 759.
Divine
—— Mothers : 561.
—— Nature : 644.
—— visitation : 381.
Divyaka, good to the left : 799.
Dodhaka : 41, 120, 215, 280, 292, 396 443, 644, 677, 802.
Dog :
—— Barking in cemetary : 811.
—— Coming towards traveller: 808.
—— in a village : 812.
—— sporting with Cows : 810.
—— urinating on cow-dung : 807.
Dogs : 16, 580.
—— barking before rain : 277.
—— bringing bones into house : 389.
—— in tracing criminals : 276.
Domestic animals : 833.
Donkeys : 111.
—— standing still : 802.
To wear —— hide : 690.
Door : 477-479, 481, 482, 539.
—— being pierced : 481.
Side-frames of— : 458.
Doubt about conflict and Conjunction : 210, 211.
Dove on vehicle : 798.
Downpour
Torrential — : 255.
Dragon's Head : 42.
Dramatics : 719.
Drāviḍa kings : 39.
Draviḍas : 103, 104, 119, 176, 192, 300,
Dravyas : 4.
Dreams
Future thro'— : 14, 411.
Dress and ornaments : 555.
Droṇa : 532.
Drought : 29, 36, 47, 58, 59, 69, 70, 72, 74, 79, 83, 85, 86, 92, 107, 108, 112, 114, 132, 144, 159, 290, 403, 830, 842.
Druggists
Harm to— : 108.
Drunkards : 108, 118.
Drutapada : 907.
Drutavilambita: 153, 255, 277, 291, 360, 659.
Dubin
Maurice — : 122.
Dumb-bells : 616.
Dūrvā : 508, 514.
Dust-storms : 16, 31, 112, 224.
—— after eclipse : 67.
Duṣyanta : 181.
Dvādaśāṁśa : 13.
Dvādaśī for worship of Lord Viṣṇu: 934.
Dwellers on river-banks : 118.
Dyers : 115.

E

Ears : 622, 658, 665.
Earth
Orbit of — : 122.
—— to be submerged : 105.
Earthquake : 16, 36, 46, 67, 862.
Extent of — : 306.
Fruition of — : 303.
Reason for -- : 296, 298.
Earth's prayer to Brahman : 297.
Earthy nature : 643.
East
—— Coast : 60.
Countries in the — : 168.
Eclipse : 216, 319.
—— Commencing when the luminary is half-risen : 50.
Recurrence of — : 59.
Ten varieties of — : 54.
Total — : 49.
Eclipsed luminaries rising or setting : 49.
Eclipses
Cause of — : 44, 45.

Commencement of—in Different directions : 51.
—— Compared : 45.
Effects of — : 48, 50, 57, 58, 60-63, 257.
End of— beneficial to countries : 50, 65.
Liberations of— : 66.
Miscarriage arising from — : 65.
—— Occurring in Aries etc. : 52-54.
—— ,, ,, the Solstices : 51.
—— of the Sun & Moon : 10, 42, 46, 48.
Popular belief about — : 46.
Rituals at — : 68.
Ten kinds of ending of — : 63, 64.
Ecliptic : 9, 25.
Economic ruin : 78.
Edge of Cloth
Stain on — is bad : 678.
Effulgence
Physical — : 637.
Eighth house with the Sun or Saturn good for marriage : 894.
Ekānaṁśā : 557.
Electional astrology : 14, 15, 144.
Element ether is generous : 638.
Elements : 4, 600, 638, 647.
Presiding Deities of — : 639.
Elephant-Catchers : 116.
—— driver : 788, 793.
Elephants : 187, 198, 213, 733.
Attitude of — : 825-828.
—— breaking anthills : 827.
Colour of — : 596.
Commanders of — : 826.
Effects of — tusk breaking : 826.
Features of — : 16.
Four types of — : 595, 596.
Heights of — : 596.
Impotent — : 598.
Palate of — : 597.
Pearls from — : 746.
Pregnant — : 598.
Rug on — back : 908.
Signs of — : 595—598.
—— suffer : 60, 61, 101, 111.
Tail of — : 596.
—— to die : 51.
—— tusk, abode of Gods etc. : 825.
Value of — : 267.
Elixirs : 925.
Emblem of Śiva : 21.
Embrace of the beloved : 687, 692.
Embryo : 241.
Retention of — : 243.
Emerald : 738, 752.
Emigration resulting from Dark Shafts : 26.
Eminent personage
Arrival of an — : 847.
Emperor : 642.
Death of an — : 141.
Employment of Spies etc. : 14.
Encirclement of cities : 109.
Encyclopaedia
This work, a veritable — : 935.
Enemies 403.
Deadly — becoming friends : 863.
—— Increase : 831.
Subjugation of — : 842.
Enemy
——attack : 334.
——'s country : 598.
Engineer : 635.
Enjoyer
—— of many women : 609.
—— of pleasures : 607, 611, 620, 621, 622, 624, 636.
—— of wealth : 605.
Enterprise
Scientific — : 704.
Epic poetry : 686.
Epidemics : 58, 83, 95.
Epigraphic records : 182.
Epilepsy : 481.
Equator : 9.
Erotic
—— bliss : 691.
—— experience : 692.
—— pleasures : 693.
—— Recipes : 699-703.
Erotics : 719.
Esoteric Science : 415.
Ether
Characteristics of — : 644.
Eunuchs : 188, 200, 212, 221, 728, 759, 847.
Exchequer
Lord of— : 767.
Exit from the world : 14.
Expiatory rites : 374, 378, 380, 382, 384, 385, 422, 425, 865.
Extent of outstretched arms : 648, 650, 651.
Eye
—— balls : 653.
—— disease : 111, 435, 676.
Eyes : 624, 664.
—— like Kuberākṣī : 652.
Long — : 633.
Red corner of — : 633.
Squint — : 624.
—— with extremely black pupils : 624.
Eye-sight
Loss of — : 702.

F

Face : 621.
Raised — : 633.
Faces of Mars : 69.
Facial disease : 64, 70.
Fa-hian : 173, 742.

False fire : 67.
Family
Destruction of — : 601.
Famine : 24, 27, 36, 37, 49, 58, 59, 61, 67, 79, 94, 103, 105, 112, 114, 120, 127, 132, 159, 160, 207, 380, 398, 402, 403 829, 830.
Fancies : 368.
Farmers : 61.
Trouble to — : 34.
Fast runner : 634.
Fatalism
Philosophy of — : 374.
Fat and marrow, cause of handsome body : 641.
Fate and Free will : 757.
Fate
Cruel — : 865.
Father of many sons : 609.
Fauna and flora : 347.
Favourite of all : 756.
Fear : 104.
of death : 802.
Feast : 19, 20, 755.
Sumptuous — : 676, 812.
Feet
King's — : 601.
Red — : 633.
Feminine
—— excellence : 686.
—— features : 634.
—— treachery : 719.
Fertilizers : 16.
—— In Ancient India : 531.
Festivities : 93, 844, 862.
Fever disappears : 866.
Fiery disposition : 643.
Fifth house at marriage :893.
Fig : 501.
Fighting
Panic caused by — : 56.
Figures of speech : 154.
Fine Arts : 52, 635.
Learned in — : 658.
Finger
knuckles : 633.
Fingers : 615, 658, 667.
Little— : 636.
Three vertical lines on — : 636.
Long — : 613.
Six types of — : 614.
Thin— : 633.
Fire
accident : 904.
Danger from — : 33, 58, 86, 94, 830.
—— circle of earthquake : 300, 306.
Destruction by — : 112.
Destructive — : 403.
—— God : 570.
—— oblations : 350.
Outbreak of — : 92, 95, 102.
Fire-workers : 60, 211.
Harmful to — : 69, 82.
First house at marriage : 892.
Fishermen : 140, 188, 200.
Fishes : 54, 120.
Fish-tail : 616.
Fitting of frame of Cot : 734.
Flag method for finding direction : 251.
Flags :
Breaking of — : 863.
Flames : 379, 863.
Fleet : 172, 180, 181.
Flesh-strong : 641.
Flock : 575, 576, 586.
Luck to — : 578.
Floods : 31, 51, 55, 94, 109, 114, 144.
Florists : 116.
Flower experiment : 486.
Flowers : 82, 115.
—— and fruits out of season : 380, 381.
Atasī — : 120.
Bāṇa — : 120.
Freakish — or fruits : 382.
yellow — : 119.
Foetus
Development of — : 693.
Growth of — : 237.
miscarriage of — : 236, 237, 239.
Months of formation : 238.
Release of — : 232.
Food : 755, 756.
Abundant — : 256.
Blessed with — : 635.
Cannot digest — : 734.
Destruction of — : 380, 791.
—— grains : 52, 63, 64, 70, 86, 101, 102, 207, 830.
—— in plenty : 85, 92,159, 829, 830, 838.
—— of barley : 441.
Rājasa type of — : 702.
—— to be costly : 84.
Foot : 636.
Fore-head : 626, 627, 665.
Broad — : 633.
Foreign lands
Dwells in — : 887.
Foresters : 103.
Lord of — : 654.
Forests
Denizens of — : 53, 54, 61.
Destruction of — : 33.
Entering — : 564-567.
Fortnight : 8.
Sun's effects within a — : 861.
Fortresses
Time for capturing — : 15.
Fortunate : 610, 623, 624, 641.
Fortune
—— ensured. 755.
Good —— : 636, 645.
—— line : 635.
Makes — abroad : 636.
Fourth house at marriage : 893.
Freak birth : 14, 385.

Frequentative : 652.
Friday good for painting, clothes etc. : 927
Friends
Estrangement of — : 103, 111, 117.
Frog :
Green — : 505.
—— near tree : 506.
yellow — : 512.
Fruition
Time of — : 861.
Fruit-tree, beneficial : 732.
Fumigation : 714.
'Fundamentals of Astrology' : 346, 728, 901.
Funeral pyre
Women enter their husband's — : 691.

G

Gāhā : 577.
Gait
of elephants : 827.
Impeded — : 906.
—— of men : 600, 644, 645, 653.
Gamblers : 108, 115, 434.
Gambling : 438, 636.
Gaṇa -devatās
Sacrifice for — : 919.
Gaṇas
Relationship of — : 898.
Gāndhāra : 39, 62, 63, 104, 116, 212, 655.
—— Note : 771.
Gandhārṇava perfume : 710.
Gandharvadeśa : 181.
Gandhayukti of Īśvara : 710.
Gaṇeśa : 1, 377, 563, 566.
Ganges : 117.
Gaolers : 200.
Gardens : 527.
Brindavan — in Mysore : 527.
Garga : 3, 5, 24, 29, 34, 48, 70, 73, 78, 81, 83-86, 98-101, 110, 111, 114, 116, 120, 121, 123-132, 134, 139, 157, 159, 204, 205, 206, 209, 210, 217, 230, 231-233, 237, 238, 245, 246, 248, 249, 253, 256, 290, 298-304, 307, 317, 318, 322, 330, 331, 345, 349, 354, 358, 360, 373-376, 379, 380, 385, 387, 389, 391, 396-399, 401, 414, 422, 423, 429, 430, 450, 456, 457, 460, 461, 465, 479, 481, 486, 487, 490, 491, 499, 535, 545, 566, 580, 581, 584-587, 599-601, 630-633, 636, 639, 644, 660, 663, 664, 666, 673, 678, 684, 757-759, 808, 811, 840, 863, 875, 880, 924-929, 931.
—— Sāmudrika : 619.
Garuḍa : 143, 541, 758.
Gate
—— leading to court : 476.
Temple—in cardinal directions : 538.
Gāthā : 313, 799, 802, 920.
Gatidīpta : 763.
Gauhati : 169.
Gauragrīva : 166.
Gavyūti : 819.
Gāyatrī mantra : 793.
Gedrosia : 177.
Gem : 427.
Gemini : 52.
Gems : 17, 152, 153, 443.
—— born of Dadhīci : 737.
Examination of — : 737-741, 752.
Flaws of — : 749.
—— have spiritual powers : 752.
—— of inestimable value : 750.
—— on the hoods of serpents : 750.
Qualities of — 749.
Genital organ : 603, 604, 652, 669.
—— Like Aśvattha leaf : 661.
Short — : 633.
Gentle people : 62.
Geographical units : 39.
—— relating to constellations : 54.
Geography
Knowledge of — : 154.
Ghaṇṭaśāla : 170.
Ghaṭa : 541.
Ghazni : 115.
Ghee and honey become dear : 58.
Ghee, dispeller of Sin : 417.
Ghoṣa : 166.
Ghosts
Danger from — : 734.
Gifts
—— of Ghee : 931.
—— of Gold, gems and Cows : 865.
Girivraja : 117, 143, 179.
Girls
Father of — : 605.
Girnar inscription : 172.
Gītā : 692, 802, 933.
Gītaka : 919.
Gīti : 918, 920, 929.
Globe
Division of the — : 165.
Gloss in five things : 641.
Glow-worms : 281.
Glue
Adamantine — : 546-548.
—— named Vajrasaṁghāta : 547.
—— ,, Vajratala : 547.
Glutton : 612.
Gluttonous : 608, 623, 643, 726.
Gnomon
for finding Ayana : 23.
Shadow of — : 10, 12
Goats
Features of — : 16, 585.
—— testes : 701.
—— without horns : 585, 587.
Go-betweens
are the cause of ruin : 722.
God
of Death : 561, 639.
of Love : 223.
of Rain : 111.

Goddess of Wealth
Arrival of — : 753.
Sons of — : 587.
Godhūli period ideal for marriage : 896.
Godowns : 116.
Gods : 112, 752, 764.
—— of quarters : 500.
Visitations of — : 8.
Where — dwell : 537, 538.
Worship of — : 8.
Gold : 11, 118, 443, 571, 832, 833.
Dealers in — : 62.
Discolouration of — : 863.
—— in foundation : 474.
Weighing — : 267.
Golden Age : 40.
Blessings of — : 92.
Golden Egg : 3.
Golden precept : 697.
Goldsmiths : 50, 834.
Gonarda : 103.
Good & bad men contrasted : 936.
Good speaker : 889.
Gorakhpur : 104.
Gorocana : 414.
Governor of a Province : 654.
Govindarāja : 630.
Grafting : 527-529.
Season for — : 529.
Grahagaṇita : 14.
Graha-yajña : 365, 917.
Grains dear : 38.
Grammar : 737.
Expert in — : 644.
Grammarians : 198.
Grammatical expression : 223.
Granaries : 211, 862.
Grazing : 205, 207.
Great Bear under attack : 163.
Great Men
Signs of five— : 646-659.
—— do not boast : 697.
Greek
—— Astrology : 20.
—— Horoscopy : 217.
—— settlers : 104.
—— writers : 181, 200.
Green gram : 62.
Grief : 110.
Ground
—— plan of 81 squares : 467.
—— sloping towards north etc. : 485.
Gruel
Sour — : 706.
Guḍa : 166.
Guest at Śrāddha : 19.
Guharāja : 541.
Guild of Silk Weavers : 173.
Gulf of Cambay : 742.
Guluhas : 177.
Guñjā : 745.

H

Haihayas : 176.
Hail-stones to fall : 112, 239.
Hair : 552, 651, 659, 665.
—— becomes black : 707.
—— dyes : 706.
Man of grey — : 706.
Single — in a pore : 602, 629.
Thick — : 610.
Thin — : 633.
Hair-oils
Perfumed — : 707, 708.
Hairy circle : 449, 577, 593, 610.
Hala : 194.
Haladas : 177.
Halas : 177.
Halāyudha : 669, 670, 673.
Halos : 315, 316, 374, 392, 400, 861.
Assassination of Kings due to — : 317.
Planets inside — : 318, 319.
Hamlets : 115.
Hampi ruins : 171.
Haṁsa : 348, 541, 646, 658.
—— has reddish face : 654.
Handle
Colours of — : 682.
Hand of Peace : 557.
Hands
of the rich : 613.
Red — : 633.
Severance of — : 614.
Hanumān : 555, 599.
Happiness : 37, 40, 41, 47, 55, 56, 58, 61, 78, 83, 86.
Enjoys — : 642.
Haragauri-sāmudrika : 618, 668.
Hārahaura : 184.
Hardness of men : 600.
Hare is auspicious : 800.
Harems : 16, 50.
Hariṇapluta : 910.
Hariṇī : 96, 204, 275, 441, 904.
Harivaṁśa : 171.
Harlots : 116, 119.
Harṣacarita : 719.
Harvest : 268.
Bumper — : 215.
Hasta
Rulership of — : 187.
Hastināpura : 166.
Haze : 328, 329.
Head : 636, 665.
—— bath : 707.
circumference of — : 634.
Double — : 629.
—— line : 636.
Round — : 628.
Health : 83, 86, 842.
Heart
—— line : 668.
Raised — : 610.

I

Description of — : 549-563.
Dress and ornaments of — : 555.
— of Gods in Indonesia : 555.
Parts of — : 550.
Ikṣumatī river : 192, 193.
Ikṣvākus : 62, 103, 141.
Ill health : 635.
Illustrious : 629.
Images Flaws, in — : 560.
—made of metals : 568.
—— of Gods : 378, 546, 556-561, 569, 571, 862.
—— of Jupiter etc. : 377.
Imbecile : 847.
Importance of Bhaṭṭotpala's commentary: 499.
Impotent : 614.
Imprisonment : 448, 626, 638, 802, 837-839, 844, 910.
Incense : 707.
History of— : 708.
Indian culture : 842.
Indra : 117, 405, 558, 750, 757, 906, 912.
— Sūkta : 298.
Indra's Banner : 158, 313, 344-360, 494, 496, 567, 570, 862.
Worship of — : 346.
Indra's circle : 301, 305, 306.
,, Daughters : 354, 360.
Indravajrā : 62, 80, 156, 158, 215, 250, 294, 304, 313, 352, 357, 358, 360, 381, 382, 434, 522, 525, 534, 587, 595, 603, 637, 643, 644, 654, 657, 658, 668, 678, 681, 688, 696, 707, 725, 748, 755, 783, 795, 803, 809, 814, 820, 844, 859, 872, 881, 912.
Indravaṁśā : 156, 352, 756, 906.
Indus : 115.
Banks of the — : 60, 63.
Infanticides : 195.
Infant mortality : 519.
Infirm : 52.
Inherent properties : 4.
Inscription
Nāgārjunakoṇḍa — : 193.
Inscriptions : 104.
Installation
of Images : 568-573, 927.
Planet at — : 573.
—— of Sacred Fire : 874, 875.
Solstice good for — : 572.
Instinctive power of scenting coming events : 798.
Instrumental music : 765.
Instruments
Musical — : 114.
Intelligent : 608.
Intercalary month : 9.
Invasion by a foreign army : 381, 385.
Irascible : 643.
—— born of Fire : 638.
Irritable : 887.
Iṣāyoga : 734.
Issue : 636.
Issuless : 603, 621, 702.
Ītibādhās : 57, 92.
Ivory for cots : 732-734.
Iyer, Chidambara : 121, 402.

J

Jackals : 863.
'Burning' — : 815.
—— Causing horripilation : 816.
Cries of — : 814-817.
Flaming — : 815.
No rain, if — howl : 281.
Jagannātha, Paṇḍitarāja : 692.
Jaggery : 75, 116, 195.
Jaghanacapalā : 900.
Jaghanya : 658.
Jahravar : 115.
Jālandhara : 180.
Jamadagni : 419.
Jambūdvipa : 167.
Janamejaya : 405.
Jaraṇa : 66.
Jar filled with water : 584.
Jasmine : 41.
Jātakas : 142, 173.
Jāti : 520, 898.
Jaṭila : 586, 587.
Jaundice : 112.
—— resulting from earth-quake : 300
Jaws
Long — : 633.
Jayā : 826, 874.
Jesters : 221.
Jetuttara : 142.
Jewellers : 187.
Jewels : 194.
—— ensure good luck : 737.
Jhelum : 115, 200.
Jina : 559, 572.
Joints : 661.
Even number of —: 754.
Strong — : 641.
Journey : 758, 759, 777, 786, 790.
—— forbidden : 840.
Initial omens at — : 842.
—— in the direction of Venus : 111.
Judges to suffer : 85.
Jugglers : 188, 197.
Jugglery : 221.
Juices
Dealers in — : 116.
Destruction of — : 106.
Jumna banks : 52.
Jupiter : 554.
—— and Saturn : 119.
—— ,, Venus opposite to each other: 110.
—— Cutting lunar disc : 39.

Cycle of — : 90.
—— represented by sword : 636.
Rulership of — : 198.
Transit of — : 909-911.
Voice derived from — : 647.
Jupiter's
aspect on eclipsed disc : 59.
—— beneficial movement : 86. 96.
—— Colours : 86.
—— years : 81, 82.
Good effects of — years : 222.
Justice
Administration of — : 221.
Jyeṣṭhā : 398, 400.
Rulership of — : 188.
—— triad : 176.
—— with Bava or Gara : 877.

K

Kabul Valley : 104, 116.
Kāca : 594.
Kacchapa region : 53.
Kaikayas : 212.
Kailāsa : 541.
Kakṣyāsūtra : 266.
Kalacuris : 170.
Kālakoṭi : 166.
Kalamā rice :
Prosperity of —: 282.
Kālapuruṣa : 13, 930.
Kali Age : 1, 89, 92.
Kālidāsa : 2, 7, 31, 111, 118, 141, 143, 155, 168, 170, 171, 173, 174, 176, 181, 195, 197, 230, 252, 255, 275, 298, 323, 348, 351, 361, 367, 368, 402, 407-409, 537, 538, 559, 609, 611, 661, 663, 666, 672, 686, 694, 695, 720, 725, 742, 798, 912, 932.
——'s words : 935, 936.
Kaliṅgas : 52, 61-63, 102, 106, 118, 140, 184, 192, 211, 212, 739.
Trouble to — : 300.
Kaliyuga
Commencement of — : 162.
Kalmāṣas : 60.
Kalpa : 933.
Kalyāṇavarman : 648, 657.
Kāmandaka : 719.
Kāmandaki : 719.
Kāma sūtra : 175, 720.
Kāmbojas : 52, 63, 141, 164, 192.
Kāmpilya : 117.
Kaṁsa : 698.
Kaṇāda : 4.
Kanaka : 177.
Kanakagiri : 175.
Kaṅgu grain : 85.
Kaṅka : 166.
Kaṇṭakāri : 510.
Kaṇvāśrama : 167.
Kānyakubja : 142.
Kāpāla vow : 106.
Kapila : 4.
Kapiṣṭhala : 166, 758.
Karaṇa : 14, 346, 347, 844, 874, 877.
Lords of — : 879.
Qualities of — : 879-883.
Works to be done under — : 880.
Karṇāṭa : 119.
Karṣa : 750.
Kārṣāpaṇa : 740, 750.
Kārtavīryārjuna : 142, 180.
Kārttika : 233, 243, 361, 362.
Kārus : 722.
Kāśi : 61, 104, 114, 142, 301.
King of — : 719.
Kashmir : 61-63, 103, 117, 141.
Kashmirians : 117.
Kāśikā : 180.
Kaśyapa : 42, 48-51, 57, 64-66, 74-77, 81, 82, 87, 97, 100, 108, 109, 123, 135, 163, 191, 193, 194, 196-198, 200-202, 205, 206, 292, 295, 296, 305, 306, 309, 311, 314, 316, 319, 325, 327, 332, 337-340, 343, 362, 363, 369, 371, 372, 375, 418, 720, 722.
Kāśyapa : 217, 226, 228, 230, 231, 235, 243, 246, 249, 425, 427, 451, 452-454, 499, 527-532, 536, 538, 540-545, 555, 562 565, 569, 721, 723, 726, 815, 839, 843.
Kathiawad peninsula : 115.
Kaṭhopaniṣad : 694, 695.
Kātyāyana : 118, 171, 600, 630.
Kauravas : 698.
Kauśika : 6.
Kauṭilya : 266.
Kaveri banks : 59.
Kāvyaliṅga : 695.
Kāvyānuśāsana : 166.
Kedārabhaṭṭa : 396.
Kekayas : 39, 60, 62, 142.
Kerala : 195.
Kern H : 17, 107, 166, 173, 175-178, 183, 192, 206, 207, 217, 351, 450.
Ketu
is represented by Flag. : 636.
Rulership of — : 202.
Khadga rulers : 169.
Khadira tree for fame : 284.
Khakkas : 168.
Khasas : 117, 655.
Khasthas : 177.
Killer of tigers : 607.
Killing : 189.
King :
Ideal — : 39.
Trouble from — : 833.
—— will be destroyed : 827.
—— ,, ,, victorious : 827.
—— ,, never suffer from poison : 750.
Kingdom
Consists of food and damsel : 691.

Hereditary — : 842.
Kings : 116, 609, 610, 612-615, 628, 629, 635, 729.
Brings victory to — : 684.
Favourite of — : 659.
Interview with — : 774.
—— suffer : 60, 95, 112, 117.
To become — : 645, 648.
—— To be free from enmity : 83.
Twelve — : 208, 209.
King's army to be mobilized : 39.
Danger to—— son : 64.
—— death : 29, 40, 55, 56, 58, 62, 86, 95.
—— duty to astrologers : 18, 19, 21.
—— exit : 399.
Increase of——wealth : 38.
—— murder by minister : 30.
—— patronage : 636.
—— preceptor suffering : 117.
—— running away : 37.
—— tyranny : 35, 84.
Kingship : 627, 636.
Kiraṇākhyatantra : 451, 454, 457-460, 463, 495.
Kirātas: 63, 103, 108, 115, 116, 140, 142, 301.
Knees : 603, 661.
Knuckles : 667.
Far-removed — : 614.
Kosala : 60, 61, 104, 106, 114, 116, 117, 738.
Koṭivarṣa : 102.
Kratu sage : 163.
Krauñcadvīpa : 118.
Krauṣṭuki : 6.
Kṛtayuga to prevail : 113.
Kṛttikā : 398, 399, 846.
Rulership of — : 185.
Kṛtyā : 659.
Kṣatrapa : 104.
Kṣatriya Chiefs : 39.
Kṣatriyas : 103, 211, 398, 404, 565, 700.
Affliction of — : 61, 62.
Destruction of — : 58.
Hostility among — : 108.
Kṣīrasvāmin : 115, 320, 512, 513, 525, 611, 624, 685, 703, 707, 709, 717, 768.
Kṣudrakas : 168.
Kubera : 561.
Kubja : 598, 658.
Kuḍava : 917.
Kukṣya : 731.
Kukundura : 932.
Kukuras : 61, 166.
Kulinda : 39.
Kullūka : 453.
Kulūta : 212.
Kulūtakas : 39, 117, 177.
Kumāradvīpa : 166.
Kumārasambhava : 7, 298, 661, 663.
Kuṇḍa : 37.
Kuṇinda : 184.
Kuñjara : 541.
Kuntibhojas : 118.
Kūrcaghara : 119.
Kūrmacakra : 166.
Kūrmavibhāga
Historical meaning of— : 17.
Kuru : 39, 40, 52, 107, 108, 166.
—— Kṣetra : 63, 141.
Kuśa & Lava : 170.
Kūṣmāṇḍa Homa : 419.
Kusumavicitrā : 256, 257.
Kuṭaka : 440, 919.
Kuṭila : 586, 587.
Kuṭṭaka : 586, 587.

L

Labourers to suffer : 51, 107.
Lac : 117, 126.
Lagna : 372.
Lakes to dry : 224.
Lakṣmaṇasena of Bengal : 673.
Lakṣmī : 913.
Lalitā : 915.
Lalitapadā : 910
Lambert : 122.
Lamp :
—— experiment on site : 486.
—— forebodes evil : 753.
—— with pure oil : 753.
Lampākas : 192.
Lamps : 17.
Signs of — : 753.
Landlord : 635.
Lāṅgala : 34.
Language
Elegant — : 694.
Vulgar — : 725.
Lapis lazuli : 120.
Lāṭas : 650.
Latitude of place : 11.
Laughter : 627.
Auspicious — : 627.
Lauhitya river : 168, 169.
Laukāyatikas : 4
Lavalī fruit : 718.
Law, B. C. 179, 183.
Leader
—— of armies : 653.
—— of Gang of thieves : 656.
Leaders : 84.
Left palm stands for wife : 635.
Leg of cots with 5 parts : 735.
Leo : 53.
Letters : 849-851.
—— derived from rising Navāṁśas : 853-858.
Levi, S. : 115, 176, 181.
Lexicon : 602, 704, 756.
Libra : 53.

Licentious : 635, 636.
Life : 635, 636, 668.
Lightning : 378.
 Death by— : 837.
 Risk from — : 58, 112.
Limbs : 629, 630.
 Gender of—: 435.
 Science of — : 432-445.
Line
 Male — : 635.
 Partner's — : 635.
Lines
 are the writing of creator : 634.
 —— on the palm : 615.
Linseed : 283.
Lip
 Lower — : 597, 619, 663, 664.
 Red ,, — : 633.
 Upper — : 619.
Liquor : 606.
Lives 100 years : 604, 616, 627.
Lizard
 House — : 806.
Locks : 636.
 —— scented : 726.
Locusts : 29.
Logic
 Science of — : 221.
Longevity
 —— from lines on forehead : 628.
 —— of Great men : 650, 652.
Lords of half-yearly periods : 47.
Loss of bodily fluids : 906.
Lovers
 Passionate — : 728.
Low-class people : 54, 60, 85.
Luminaries : 3, 647.
Lunacy : 299.
Lunar days
 Benefic — : 826.
 Functions and Properties of — : 374.
 Increase and decrease of — : 9.
 Lords of — : 874.
Lunar eclipse
 following Solar one : 68.
Lunar mansions : 21.
Lunar system of measurement : 9.
Lunatics : 393.
Lustration Ceremony : 361-368.
Lustre, born of Elements : 600.
Lustrum : 93-95.
 Years of —: 88, 90.
Luxurious living : 887.
Luxury goods : 704.
Lying on a side : 36.

M

Madana trees : 154.
Madder : 117, 159, 415.
Madhuparka : 377.
Mādhyamika : 166.
Madra : 39, 53, 114, 142, 177, 184, 212.
Mādrī : 142.
Maga : 572.
Magadha : 39, 40, 60, 63, 117, 140, 168, 184, 192.
 King of— : 118.
 —— measure : 245.
Magadhadvija
 Author called — : 758.
Māgadhī : 920.
Maghā 237, 400, 864.
 —— occupied by Seven Sages : 161.
Māgha : 110, 233, 235.
Magician : 768.
Mahābhārata : 1, 167, 168, 170, 173, 174, 178, 192, 201, 346, 537, 585, 685, 688, 693, 820, 900.
 —— period : 142, 143.
 —— War : 162.
Mahābhāṣya : 180.
Mahākāvyas : 31.
Mahāmāyūrī : 177, 180.
Mahārāṣṭra : 116, 178.
Mahāsthāna 739.
Mahāvrata : 251, 265.
Mahāyuga : 89.
Mahendranagara : 119.
Mahiṣa : 102.
Mahiṣakas : 213.
Maidens : 119.
 Characteristics of — : 660-675.
Maināka : 152.
Major period of a planet : 636, 648.
Mālatī : 905.
Mālava : 39, 181, 650.
Mālavikāgnimitra : 2.
Mālavya : 646, 650, 658.
Male - birth : 781.
Mālinī : 73, 112, 158, 216, 225, 242, 275, 378, 445, 449, 583, 796, 827, 842, 908, 915.
Mallikākṣa : 578.
Mallinātha : 742.
Man
 Physical part of — : 634.
Mānasa lake : 155.
Mandākrāntā : 94, 440, 447, 753, 843, 903.
Maṇḍala : 102-105, 280.
Maṇḍalaka : 659.
Mandara : 541.
Mandasor : 173.
Māṇḍavya : 165, 177, 900, 926.
Manes : 90, 94, 376, 412, 419, 692, 752, 927.
 Food offered to — : 19.
 Propitiation of — : 875.
 Worship of —83.
Mango juice : 715.
Maṇi : 605.
Maniguṇanikara : 910.
Maṇis : 584, 585, 587.
Mankind : 162.

Mansions : 546, 547, 686, 764.
Pleasure — : 454.
Mantras : 2.
Power of —: 575.
Mantra-Śāstra : 416.
Mantreśvara : 656.
Manu : 4, 221, 266, 320, 354, 455, 499, 520, 521, 545, 688-691, 696.
—— dharmāḥ : 765.
—— Smṛti : 3, 106.
Mārgaśira : 231, 233, 234.
Mārgaśīrṣa
Importance of — : 933.
Marici Sage : 123, 163.
Marine products : 787.
Marital
Alliance : 779.
Pure in——relations : 609.
Mārkaṇḍeya-purāṇa : 166, 173, 175, 180.
Marks :
circular — : 635.
—— of three kinds on body : 634.
Planetary — : 636.
Marriage : 14, 677, 679.
—— a sacred link : 660.
Ascendant for — : 882.
Asterisms of — : 866, 882.
Planetary positions at — : 892-897.
Mars : 3, 5.
Accelerated motion of — : 403.
Bad effects of—year : 220.
—— bad for kings : 71.
—— Causing joy : 72.
—— Cutting lunar disc : 39.
—— destroying clouds : 72.
Faces of — : 69, 70.
—— joining with eclipsed disc : 59.
Paths of — : 73.
—— represented by Triangle : 636.
Retrogression of — : 69, 403.
Rivers under — : 196.
Rulership of — : 195.
Stars affected by — : 72.
Three worlds troubled by — : 71.
Transit of — : 904-906.
Valour derived from — : 647.
Marrow : 654.
Maru region : 53, 60, 62.
Marwar : 165.
Marwaris : 39.
Māsa : 750.
Maśakāvatī : 140.
Massacre of men : 836.
Massaga town : 178.
Material Cause : 4.
Mathematicians : 187.
Mathematics : 712.
Mathurā : 40, 140, 166, 181.
Matkuṇa : 598.
Mātrās
Upper — : 851.
Matsyapurāṇa : 68, 104, 116, 162, 171.
Matsyas : 52, 104, 166, 198, 212.
Mattā : 402.
Mattamayūra : 909.
Maya : 20, 249, 466, 544, 546-548.
Mayūracitraka : 322, 395-404.
Measure : 549.
measurements of limbs : 556.
Measures of halls and verandah : 456.
Mechanics : 197.
Medicines : 188, 366, 415.
Megasthenes : 195.
Meghadūta : 118, 171, 195, 197, 323.
Meghavisphūrjita : 903.
Meghavitāna : 917.
Mekala : 53, 62, 192.
Memory :
Loss of — : 570.
Men
Features of — : 16.
Menial work : 103.
Menses
Prohibition during — : 727.
—— remove women's blemishes : 689.
Menstrual blood : 726, 727.
Merchants : 50, 53, 213, 787.
Threat to — : 107.
Mercury : 5.
Beneficial Colour of — : 80.
—— causes fluctuations in prices :74.
Conjunction of — with Venus : 280.
Courses of — : 76.
—— cutting the lunar orb : 40.
Duration of visibility etc. of — : 77.
Good effects —'s year : 221.
Reason for ——'s different motions: 78
—— represented by Arrow : 636.
Rulership of — : 197.
—— Transiting asterisms : 74-76.
Transit of — : 907, 908.
—— troubling physicians etc. : 75.
Weight & growth from — : 647.
Meritorious acts : 637, 651, 688.
Meru : 165, 179, 541.
—— Summit : 249.
Messengers in trouble : 107.
Metals : 564.
Metaphor : 156, 407, 538, 935, 936.
Meteor :
Fall of — : 67.
Meteorology : 230.
Mateors : 40, 307-311, 374.
—— falling on images : 312.
Fruition of effects of — : 308.
Varieties of — : 307.
Metre
Fine — : 157.
Mettle : 647.
Inner — : 644.
Mica : 371.
Middle country : 115, 134.
Mihira : 630.
Military
—— expedients : 14.
—— Expeditions : 14, 15.

Milk
—— in abundance : 305.
Scarcity of — : 212.
Mind, birth-place of Love : 725.
Minerals : 60.
—— & Metals : 653.
Mines of beryl : 172.
Ministers : 40, 50, 52-54, 60, 107, 114, 622, 624.
Minor lapses of women : 691.
Mirashi, Dr. : 758.
Miscarriage : 67.
Miser : 621, 622, 626, 888.
Miserable : 602, 612, 621, 629, 636.
Mist indicating disease : 67.
Misty circles around Sun & Moon : 16, 67.
Mithilā : 117.
Mixed
nature : 649.
—— types : 648, 657.
Mixing of timber : 732.
Mlecchas : 50, 103, 115, 177, 211, 212.
Destruction of — : 58, 63.
Mobilization of armies : 35.
Mock-Sun : 31, 326, 327, 400.
Mole on woman's face : 427.
Monarchs : 621, 629, 639, 650, 657.
Monday,
—— good for ornaments, pearls, silver etc. : 924.
—with Mūla for worship of Viṣṇu etc.: 931.
Mongoose : 772.
Monier Williams :175.
Monks
Buddhist — : 195, 438.
Monsoon : 16.
Importance of — : 230.
Month : 8.
Moon's effect within a — : 861.
Moon : 9, 280, 399, 400, 479.
—— is represented by a Square : 636.
Natal — : 901.
Physical lustre from —: 647.
Transit of — : 903.
Moon's Appellation : 415.
—brightness : 32. 41.
—— Colours : 40, 41.
—— conjunction with monsoon stars: 16.
—— conjunction with stars : 33, 34.
Good effects of — year : 219.
—— horns : 399.
—— Nodes : 46.
—— phases : 32, 33.
—— rulership : 194.
—— Shapes : 34-37, 40.
—— Transit : 33.
—— unusual appearances : 34.
—— ,, form leading to death: 37.
—— waxing properly : 41.
Mortality : 72.
Morung : 143, 180.
Motions of planets : 5, 10.
Mountain
Climbing — : 774.
—— infested with snakes : 903.
Rising — : 168.
Mountains : 39.
People living on — : 54.
Moustachis : 621.
Mouth : 621
Broad — : 633.
Mṛgaśirṣa
Rulership of — : 185.
Mṛjā : 600.
Mṛtasañjivinī : 670.
Mudrālaṁkāra : 908.
Mudrārākṣasa : 178, 687.
Muhūrta : 8, 14, 347, 416, 763, 844, 869, 870, 874.
Mukhacapalā : 899.
Mūla
Rulership of — : 188.
Multan : 115.
Mundane astrology : 190.
Murder of Brahmins : 601.
Murderous persons : 189.
Murders
Element Air causes — : 638.
Mushrooms : 520.
Music
Fond of —: 888.
Musical instruments : 387, 416, 570, 787.
Musicians : 53, 62, 114, 116, 834.
Mūṣikanagara : 141.
Musk : 710, 711, 715.
—— rat : 806.
Mutual contradiction of omens : 775.
Mystic circle : 414.

N

Nāḍī : 8.
Nāgas : 412.
Nāgavīthī for happiness : 400.
Nagnajit : 550, 552.
Nail marks forbidden at impregnation : 728.
Nails : 614, 635, 653.
Convex — : 597.
Glossy — : 660.
Raised — : 633.
Red — : 601, 633.
Naimiṣa forest : 142, 143.
Naiṣadha of Śrīharṣa : 361.
Naked monks : 791.
Name
Letters in the — : 849-851.
Names
Auspicious — : 416, 419, 433.
Mention of — auspicious, but not sight : 771.
—— of months : 933.
Synonyms of — : 859.

Nandā : 826, 874.
Nandana : 541.
Nandin : 80, 322, 478, 539, 630, 923.
Nandivardhana : 541.
Nārada : 123, 249, 630, 631.
Narkaṭa ka : 31.
Narkuṭaka : 919.
Narmadā : 59, 154, 192.
Nāsadīya Sūkta of Ṛgveda : 4.
Nasik : 104.
Natal
  asterism affected : 29.
  —— chart : 643.
Navāṁśa : 13.
Navel : 662.
  Deep — : 633.
  Round — : 608.
Navigation : 188.
Neck : 636, 656.
  Conch-like — : 612.
  Flat — : 612.
  Girth of — : 634.
  Raised nape of — : 633.
  Short — : 633, 670.
  — with three lines : 663.
Neminātha : 175.
Nepalese : 39, 60.
Neptune
  Orbit of — : 122.
New Moon : 9.
Newton : 145.
Nidarśanā : 12.
Nigara : 745.
Ninth day of arrival bad for departure : 871.
Ninth House at marriage, bad with Rāhu, Saturn or Moon : 894.
Nipa : 165.
Nipples : 610.
Nirukta : 157.
Noble men : 54.
Non-Aryan : 80.
Non-luminous planets : 5.
Non-recovery of stolen articles : 440.
North
  People living in the — : 60.
Northern country : 112.
Nose : 6́6́4.
—— like parrots' beak : 623.
  Long — : 633.
  Lovely — : 651.
  Raised — : 633.

O

Objects
  Auspicious — : 679.
Oblations to Soma : 382.
Observation
  by ancients : 38.
  Telescopic — : 122.
Obstacles : 808, 842.
Occultation : 107, 205, 207.
Oceans : 54.
Octogenarian becoming young : 700.
Odd no. of joints, good : 682.
Officers
  King's — : 118.
Oilmongers : 115-117, 119, 200.
Oil on water : 46.
Old age : 701.
Old and infirm : 54.
Omens : 14, 46, 374.
  Auspicious — for journey : 564.
  Belief in — no superstition : 799.
  Blasted — : 790, 846, 847.
—— blasted by action : 763, 774.
—— blasted by divine agency : 763.
—— blasted by lunar days : 763, 775.
—— blasted by lunar mansions : 763.
—— called Parigha : 774.
—— caused by various creatures : 758.
—— causing famine : 777.
—— ,, rain : 845.
  Cries of—beyond a Krośa, ineffective : 843.
  Diurnal and nocturnal — : 796.
  —— for imprisonment : 778.
  Fructifying time and place of — : 781, 782.
  Further — : 844-860.
—— Gate : 774.
  General principles of — : 784.
  Good — on maturing of Daśā: 842.
  Inauspicious — : 425, 491.
—— in 'Burning' inter-quarter : 779.
—— in quarters : 778.
—— in reverse order : 773.
—— in seasons : 766, 767.
  Musical notes as — : 771.
  Ocean of — : 860.
  —— on funeral pyres : 776.
  —— on tree : 780.
  —— on two sides : 770.
  —— relating to women : 782.
  Rural — : 846.
  Science of — : 797.
  Stable and unstable — : 844, 845.
  —standing between two : 780.
  —— to be ignored : 766.
  Tranquil — of 10 kinds: 764, 785, 788, 790.
  —— through birds and beasts : 757-784.
  —— ,, horses and elephants: 366.
"On Architecture in Ancient India' : 486.
Ophthalmic Surgeons : 187.
Orator has a thin tongue : 635.
Orgasm : 606.
Orion : 398.
Orissa : 52, 62, 104.
Ornaments
  Ac uisition of — : 447.

—— made of pearls : 747.
—— offered by Gods to Banner: 355
Outcasts : 190.
Ovum is soil : 699.
Owls
Cries of — : 804.
Owner
in peril : 813.
—— will be imprisoned : 818.
—— ,, meet with his end : 831.
Oxus : 104.
—— valley : 178.

P

Paddy : 92.
—— fields : 53.
Padma : 541.
Painters : 62, 116, 793.
Paitāmaha : 9.
Pāla : 485.
Palace
Dimensions of — : 451.
Varieties of — : 451.
Palate
Red — : 633.
Pallavas : 52.
Palm : 666, 667.
—— red like lac : 614.
Sunken — : 614.
Palmistry : 634.
Modern — : 614, 668.
Pamir : 141.
Paṇa : 740.
Pañcāla country : 52, 108, 117, 184.
Pañcālas : 39, 53, 107, 114.
Pañcāṅga : 22.
Pañcarātra system : 931, 932.
Pañcasiddhāntikā: 5, 6, 10, 32, 37, 47, 157, 160, 205, 217, 218, 232, 250, 942.
Pāṇḍu : 142.
—— guḍa : 166.
Pāṇḍya
Country : 119.
—— King : 71, 141.
Panic : 48, 67, 70, 71, 74, 76, 79, 85, 105, 110.
Pāṇini : 142, 180, 181, 602, 640, 768, 823.
——'s grammar : 869.
Paṅkti : 40, 396, 399.
Paps
Long space between — : 633.
Parāśara : 6, 20, 24, 30, 30, 31, 70, 71, 7 7, 79, 87, 98, 99, 101, 105, 109, 110, 113, 118-121, 123, 129, 132-139, 144, 160, 167, 169, 174, 176-178, 181, 184, 205, 206, 209, 217, 230, 231, 234, 235, 237, 239, 245, 256, 280, 288, 292, 298-302, 305, 306, 430-445, 470, 486, 527, 574-576, 579, 590, 593-597, 599, 646, 648, 660, 670, 679, 757, 762, 767, 770, 781, 808, 838, 841, 867-69, 871, 875, 877, 878, 884-889.
——'s statement : 623.
—— Tantra : 76.
Pārata country : 115, 116, 164, 177, 198.
Parents :
Devoted to — : 61.
Murderer of — : 628.
Pargiter : 162, 168, 180.
Paridhi : 287, 292, 400.
Parigha : 278.
Pariveṣa : 278, 287.
Pāriyātra mountain : 60, 72, 118, 650.
Parthians : 174.
Parvan : 42.
Pārvatī : 41, 663, 665, 692.
Pāśānta : 677.
Past deeds
Intention of — : 757.
Pāśupata system : 932.
Pāṭaliputra : 196.
Patañjali : 4, 12, 173.
Pathetic fallacy : 156.
Pathyā : 920, 929.
Paṭola : 183.
Patrimony : 614.
Pauliśa : 9.
Pauṇḍra : 739.
Pauras : 208, 209.
Pauravas : 181, 301.
Pauṣa month : 233, 235.
Pauṣa year of Jupiter
Good effects of — : 83.
Peace and plenty : 40, 144.
Pea-cocks : 684, 786.
Pearl -necklaces of 17 types : 748.
Pearls : 54, 189, 194, 738, 742-744.
Sources of — : 742.
Pedestal : 561, 571.
Penis : 635.
Penniless: 607, 610-612, 614, 621, 624, 629, 670.
Penurious : 602, 607, 619.
Penury : 636.
Perfidy : 690.
Perfumers : 221, 793.
Perfumes : 189, 707, 804.
Bakula — : 716.
Bathing — : 715.
—— for mouth : 715.
—— for royal personages : 704.
Preparation of — : 704-718.
Perigee : 10.
Peril
from wind : 776.
—— to town : 818.
Period of retrogression
Effects of Mars during — : 861.
Periplus : 140, 175, 180.
Perpetrator of dreadful deeds : 779.

Persia : 175.
Persons one will meet : 847.
Peshawar : 104.
Passimism : 757.
Pestilence : 40, 49, 132, 160, 403.
Pests : 57, 83.
  Increase of — : 862.
Phaladīpikā : 12, 646, 650, 652, 653, 655, 728, 902, 914.
Phalaśruti : 159.
Phalgukas : 177.
Phālguna : 233, 235.
Phālguna year
  Bad effects of — : 84.
Philanthropist : 614.
Philologists : 198.
Phlegm
  spits — : 440, 441, 717.
Phlegmatic ailments : 92, 102.
Phosphoric lights : 123.
Physical lustre of 5 kinds : 637, 638.
Physicians : 53, 63, 108, 112, 114, 116, 118, 119, 186, 189.
  Royal — : 453.
Physiognomy : 634, 641.
  Feminine — : 660.
  —— of men : 599-645.
  Thirteen items of — : 599.
Piccā : 745.
Pikkā : 745.
Pillar
Parts of — : 459.
Pillars : 862.
Pimples : 17, 446-449.
Piṅgala : 287, 323, 396, 651, 673, 795, 802, 823, 900.
  —— cchandaḥ : 912, 915.
  —— ,, Śāstra : 929.
Pisces : 54.
Pitāmaha : 123.
Pit experiment on site : 485.
Place
  Inauspicious — : 433.
  —— of Royal Bath : 406-409.
Planetary
  Colours : 737.
  — Combination : 227.
  —— ,, for male birth : 728.
  —— Configuration : 226.
  —— triangle : 17, 226.
  —— War : 67, 113, 423.
Planets :
  Aspects of — : 14, 849.
  Castes of — : 13.
  Conjunction of — : 227.
  Dimensions of — : 11.
  Marching — : 208.
  Movements of — : 5, 16.
  Orbit of — : 11, 16.
  Origin of — : 6.
Positions of — : 8 23.
Pṛṣṭhodaya — : 851.
  Rising and setting of — : 280.
  Śirṣodaya — : 851.
  —— Striking Moon's horn : 38.
  Worship of — : 917.
Pleasure of royalty : 707.
Plough
  Evil — : 35.
  Holder of — in the north : 773.
Poesy of astronomer : 41.
Poetic
  —— fancy : 41, 156.
  —— Gifts : 154.
  —— talents : 219, 222.
Poets : 53, 119, 406.
  Destruction of — : 114, 118.
Poison : 741, 792, 794.
  Anklet smeared with — : 719.
  Danger from — : 676.
Pole-Star : 134, 161, 398.
Political expedients : 687.
Politicians : 118, 119, 198.
Politics
  Knowledge of — : 15.
Ponds
  Construction of — : 524.
Popularity : 636.
Population
  Annihilation of — : 381, 397.
Portentous phenomena : 373-394.
Portents : 16, 27, 46, 113, 360, 373, 406, 423, 758, 820.
  Aerial — : 387.
  —— at eclipse : 59.
  Auspicious —— : 391-393.
  —— due to comets on the Sun : 25.
  Evil effects of — : 380, 385.
  —— of animals and birds : 388.
  —— of birth : 384.
  —— of Cooking utensils : 387.
  —— of Crops : 381.
  —— of quadrupeds : 385.
  —— of rainfall : 382, 383.
  —— of trees : 380.
  —— of water : 383.
  —— of wind : 386.
  —— relating to asterisms : 863.
  Terrestrial — : 374.
  —— through fire : 378.
  —— ,, Idols : 376.
  —— ,, Indra's Banner : 389.
Pots, as Rain-Gauge : 257.
  Holy — : 417, 438.
Potters : 116, 117.
Poverty : 614, 636.
  —— stricken : 639.
Prabhava year : 91.
Pracita : 926.
Pradhāna : 4.
Praharṣiṇī : 265, 276, 277, 394, 397, 820, 908.
Prahlāda (Physiognomist) : 599, 601-604, 606, 607, 609, 610, 612, 614, 615,

617, 620, 622, 623, 625, 626, 628, 630, 634, 660, 662, 663, 665, 666, 670, 671, 673.
Praise of good astrologer : 12, 13, 15.
Prakṛti : 4.
Pramāṇikā : 291, 395, 677, 802, 804, 914.
Pramitākṣarā : 913.
Prāṇa : 8.
Prāṇāyāma : 843.
Prasabha : 905.
Prasādapaṭṭa : 685.
Prastha : 532.
Prattling
Given to — : 644.
Pratyanta : 115.
Prayāga banks : 134.
Preceptor of men : 609.
Predictive astrology : 12-14.
Pregnancy : 443.
—— of clouds : 231.
Pregnant women to suffer : 211.
Preservative work : 83.
Presiding Deity : 759.
Previous birth
to be read from face : 642.
Price-fluctuations : 16, 340-343.
Price of corals : 283.
—— diamonds : 283, 740.
—— elephants : 283.
—— horses : 283.
—— pearls : 283, 744.
Prices
Fair — : 50, 144.
—— of oils to rise : 75.
—— to increase : 83, 213.
Pride produces repulsion : 696.
Priest : 27, 118, 570, 571.
Prime meridian : 172.
Princes
Trouble to — : 64.
Printers
Danger to — : 792.
Priyaṁvadā : 399.
Procession : 571.
Professional direction : 767.
Profits
Good — : 341-343.
Prognosis through
elephants : 14.
—— fire : 14, 351.
—— flowers and creepers : 282.
Prognostics : 394.
Progressive purpose : 752.
Propitiation of evil planets : 737, 757, 781.
Propitiatory rites : 864, 865, 917.
Prosody
Knowledge of — : 864.
Prākṛta — : 670.
Science of — : 929
Prospects for Kings : 283.
Prosperity : 34, 37, 41, 56, 58, 61, 70, 83, 94, 101.
Prostitute
Sinful — : 669 .
Proteges of Kings : 118.
Pṛthvi : 278, 398, 667, 906.
Psychological
background : 798.
—— implications : 726.
—— problem : 693.
Ptolemy : 115, 140, 168, 177, 179, 182, 183.
——'s Lariki : 650.
Public health : 756.
Pukkasa : 483.
Pulaha : 163.
Pulastya : 163.
Pulindas : 39, 62, 63, 103, 107, 111, 192, 200.
Puliśācārya : 210.
Pulses to thrive : 84.
Pun : 156, 641, 899, 903.
Punarvasu
Rulership of — : 186.
Puṇḍra : 61-63, 103, 117, 131, 141, 142, 169.
Pungent Substances : 200.
Punjab : 115, 142.
Puṇyāha : 350, 363, 366, 421, 570.
Purali : 742, 743.
Purāṇa : 485.
Purāṇas : 6, 42, 104, 143, 154, 170, 935.
Purandaradāsa : 936
Puranic
Story : 152, 692.
—— verses : 738.
Pūrṇā : 826, 874.
Purohita for Grahayajña : 365.
Puruṣa : 500, 509, 510, 514.
Pūrvābhadra : 237.
Rulership of — : 189.
Pūrvaphālgunī
Rulership of — : 186.
Pūrvāṣāḍhā : 231, 237, 245, 247.
Rulership of — : 188.
Puṣkalāvata : 180.
Puṣkalāvatī : 104.
Puṣkara : 60.
—— forests : 134.
Puṣpitāgrā : 41, 59, 157, 204, 248, 254, 314, 353, 372, 602, 651, 652 728, 800, 865, 906.
Puṣya : 406.
—— asterism : 422.
Rulership of — : 186.
—— Snāna : 423, 926.
Puṭā : 915.

Q

Quadrupeds : 102.
Quarrels : 846.
—— with women : 811.

Quarrelsome : 887.
Quarter
Burning — : 833.
Tranquil — : 490, 779, 834.
Quarters
Burning, Charcoal, Smoking, Tranquil— : 760, 761.
Circle of — : 785, 794.
Lords of — : 781.
Owners of — : 768.
Signs of — : 782, 784.
Smoking — : 814.
Substances indicated by — : 783, 784.
Tranquil — : 814.
Queen : 119.
—— of timber : 732.
Woman becomes — : 667.
Queens, agents of foreign powers : 719.
Querent
touching limbs : 428.
Queries : 14.
—— of rain : 274.
Querist : 435, 436, 438-443, 781.
Query : 435, 443, 858.
Name of person arriving at a — : 858.
Object of — : 848.
Place of — : 433, 434.
Time of — : 432.
Quintuplets : 444.

R

Rack and ruin : 390.
Raghu : 408, 559.
Raghu's expedition : 352.
Raghuvaṁśa : 155, 168, 169, 687, 743.
Rāhu : 6.
—— becoming a planet : 42.
Criticism of ancient views on — : 43.
—— in III house at marriage causes death : 893.
—— represented by Bow : 636.
Rulership of — : 201.
——'s sons : 24.
Rain : 27, 29, 31, 35, 37, 56, 58, 61, 62, 64, 65, 67, 78, 83, 84, 86, 91, 92, 94, 95, 102, 106-108, 110, 112, 143, 144, 245, 246, 260, 287, 401, 809, 810, 812, 833.
Absence of — : 247.
Indications of immediate — : 274-76.
Plentiful — : 257, 829, 840.
Quantity of — : 247.
Query regarding — : 274.
Rainbow : 278, 321-323, 401, 861, 862.
—— boding evil to ruler : 29.
Rainfall : 16, 231.
Copious — : 239.
Duration of — : 238.
Extent of — : 238.
Measures of — : 239.
Scanty — : 61, 62, 114.
Scientific explanation of — : 240.
Rain-gauge : 245.
Rains
Failure of — : 207.
Rainy season : 91, 280, 833, 842.
Rajas,
belongs to Mercury and Venus : 648, 649.
Rājaśekhara : 166.
Rājataraṅgiṇī : 178.
Rājayoga : 14.
Rāmagaṅgā river : 183.
Ramaṭha country : 115, 198.
Rāmāyaṇa : 141, 142, 159, 173, 175, 298, 599, 820.
Randhra : 593.
Rapti river : 104.
Rashness is not valour : 696.
Rāta : 900, 926.
Rathoddhatā : 93, 95, 214, 215, 254, 258-260, 368, 380, 381, 396, 397, 399, 401, 433, 436, 437, 439, 440, 498, 533, 581, 582, 591, 664, 677, 681, 692, 700, 701, 802, 810, 822, 826, 858, 911, 934.
Ravaka : 745.
Rāvaṇa : 698.
Rawalpindi : 104.
Real love
Signs of — : 719, 720.
Recipes for kings : 700.
Recluses : 189.
Harmful to — : 112.
Regulus : 107.
Release of animals : 422.
Religious
——Practices : 84
—— rites : 14.
—— students : 102.
Remedial,
—— ceremony : 367.
—— measure : 374.
—— purpose : 752.
Reptiles
Appearance of — : 137.
Results of year etc. : 225.
Retention
Days of — : 244.
Retrograde motion of Mars : 861.
Revanta : 561.
Revatī
Rulership of — : 189.
—— triad : 182.
Revolts : 120.
Ṛgveda Saṁhitā: 5, 142, 168, 198, 934.
Ṛgvedic time : 298.
Rhapsodists : 116.
Rhetoricians : 7.
Rheumatism
One suffers from — : 787.
Rhys Davids J. W. : 178.
Rice : 223.
Ṣaṣṭika — : 441, 701.
Rich
Immensely — : 642.

Richter
Nicholas — : 122.
Riktā : 826, 874.
Rising periods : 11.
Rivers
Change their course : 862.
In charge of — : 119.
Robbers : 27, 50, 55, 58, 70, 76, 84, 95, 96, 112, 119, 192, 220, 224.
Trouble from — : 830.
Robbery : 40, 904.
Rod : 400.
Rogue : 608, 635, 653.
—— with a round face : 621.
Rohiṇī : 16, 237.
Rulership of — : 185.
Wain of — : 105, 259, 399.
—— with Bālava or catuṣpāt : 877.
—— yoga : 249, 258.
Rohita : 278, 400.
Romaka : 9.
Romans : 20, 194.
Roots and fruits
Destruction of — : 108.
Those who live on — : 62.
Rose-apple : 282.
Rotation of Earth : 11.
Rough and tough : 53.
Royal
patronage : 117.
perfume, named *Kopacchada* : 710.
protege : 635.
Splendour : 636.
Ṛṣabha : 757.
Ṛṣika : 141.
Ṛṣiputra : 49, 81, 110, 206, 214, 230, 231, 238, 253, 322, 391, 394, 600, 763
Ṛṣya : 585, 587.
Ruby : 738, 751.
—— born of black salt : 749.
Price of —: 750.
Rucaka : 646, 659.
—— dies by weapons or fire : 657.
—— has fine brows and hair : 656.
Rucirā : 907.
Rudradāman : 172-174.
Rudrādhyāya : 381.
Ruin of
family : 730, 736.
town : 561.
Rukmavatī : 397.
Rulers : 53.
Change of — : 830.
Despotic — : 59.
Trouble to — : 64.
Rulership
Change of — : 26, 29, 30.
Rūpaka : 407.

S

Śabaras : 52, 103, 107, 118, 192, 200,
Śabdaśaktimūla-dhvani : 236.
Sācin : 657.
Sacred
hymns : 185.
Studies : 61.
Sacrifice
—— for planets : 14.
of form : 931.
Performance of — : 144.
Performer of — : 606, 616.
Sacrificers : 616.
Destruction of — : 112, 115.
Sacrifices : 219, 927.
Sacrificial
altars : 414, 364, 863.
Learned in——lore : 194.
—— materials : 364.
Safe period : 727.
Safflower : 117.
Saffron : 117.
Sages : 2, 5, 13, 18, 42, 110, 678, 757, 798.
—— on Rāhu : 43.
Opinions of — : 659.
Sagittarius : 53.
Sāhityadarpaṇa : 555, 627, 721.
Sahya mountain : 53, 657.
Sailors : 107, 116, 119, 189, 211.
Śaka Era
Commencement of — : 161.
Śaka kāla : 162.
Śakas : 52, 62, 104, 164, 177, 192.
Sāketa : 166.
Śākhā : 5.
Śakra : 465.
Śaktibhadra : 687.
Śākuntala : 252.
Śākyas : 572.
Sāla trees : 282, 756.
Śālihotra : 578, 588.
Śālinī : 41, 257, 284, 293, 304, 360, 390, 397, 435, 442-44, 524, 580, 584, 603, 638, 657, 658, 670, 671, 694, 707, 755, 799, 810, 817-19, 911.
Śālivāhana era : 88, 89, 161.
Salt : 116, 189, 194.
Sālva : 165, 166, 198, 211, 212.
Sālvas : 62.
Samādhi : 401.
Samānikā : 313, 644, 670, 802, 804.
Samāsasaṁhitā : 28, 33, 37, 38, 40, 51, 54, 63, 67, 74, 77, 90, 91, 96, 100, 105, 125, 152, 158, 183, 202, 218, 219, 221-224, 227, 228, 236, 238, 242, 245, 247, 256, 260, 265, 274, 279, 303, 307, 308, 311, 314, 317, 319, 331, 373, 375, 481, 923-928.
Saṁhitā : 6, 8, 15, 21, 48, 157, 432.
Contents of — : 16, 17.
Definition of — : 5.
Śamī-class : 85.
Saṁkarācārya : 18, 687.

Saṁkhyāta : 165.
Samuccayālaṁkāra : 899, 903.
Samudga : 541.
Samudra : 599-605, 660, 661, 664, 666.
Samudra-daṇḍaka : 928.
Sāmudrika : 630, 632.
—— Śāstra : 7.
Saṁvatsara-puruṣa : 87.
Sanctum Sanctorum : 539, 544, 571.
Sandals : 677, 678.
  Damages to — : 679.
Sandalwood : 199, 732.
Sanitation : 756.
Saṅkāśya : 193.
Sāṅkhya philosophy : 4.
Śaṅku : 492.
Sanskrit
  learning : 712.
  literature : 208, 757, 827, 930.
Sapphire : 522, 738.
Saptaśatī : 356.
Sārālaṁkāra : 686.
Sārasvata : 499-507, 509, 512, 513, 515-520.
Sārasvatas : 167, 198.
Sarasvatī : 166.
Sārāvalī : 17, 646, 647, 651, 653,-655.
Sarayū
  Banks of — : 60.
Śārdūlavikrīḍita : 5, 38, 39, 54, 61, 63, 87, 152, 260, 264, 270, 272, 273, 278, 293, 401, 432, 525, 572, 580, 602, 603, 653, 655, 666, 687, 708, 721, 753, 795, 822, 873, 881, 901, 932.
Sarvatobhadra : 541, 715.
Śaśa : 646, 653, 654, 659.
Sāsanavaṁsa
  Pāli — : 183.
Śastras : 102.
  Other — : 298, 472.
Śāstri, V. S. and M. R. Bhat : 412.
Śatabhiṣaj : 237.
  Rulership of — : 188.
  —— triad : 179.
Śatapatha : 398.
Satire on carping criticism : 936.
Sattva : 644, 651.
  derived from Sun and Mars : 60, 647.
Saturday, good for she-buffaloes, slaves, hunters : 928.
Saturn : 5, 639, 846.
  Colours of — : 120.
  Complexion, derived from — : 647.
  —— cutting lunar disc : 40.
  Evil effects of — 's year : 224.
  —— represented by a Pentagon : 636.
  Rulership of — : 200.
  Transit of — : 114-120, 914-916.
Saura : 9.
Saurāṣṭra : 60, 63, 104, 115, 650.
Saurpāra : 738.
Sauvīra : 39, 63, 104, 115, 198.
  —— Añjana : 175.
Sāvana : 9.
Sāvitra-Śāstra : 573.
Savya
  Explanation of — : 206, 207.
Scent
  Bakula — : 708.
  Campaka — : 708.
  Good — : 709.
  Jasmine — : 708.
  Lotus — : 708.
  Smaroddīpana — : 708.
Schoff : 180.
Scholars : 54.
  —— Come to grief : 60, 101.
Schwabe : 149.
Science : 20.
  —— of Omens : 757.
Scorpio : 53.
Scribes : 53.
Sculptors : 561, 571, 794.
Sculpture
  Experts in — : 553.
Scythians : 104, 213, 215.
Sea-faring people. Trouble to — : 34.
Search for lost article : 773.
Sea-shore : 408.
Seat of Skins : 421.
Seats : 677, 678.
Second-house with Moon, Mercury, Jupiter or Venus, at marriage : 893.
Seeds : 415, 568, 699.
  Destruction of — : 33, 51.
  Methods of sowing —: 533-535.
  Treatment of — : 532, 533.
  —— weighed in balance : 265.
Self-realization : 18.
Semen : 606.
  Copious and thick — : 641, 655, 658.
Ṣaṣkulī increases — : 701.
Seminaries : 117.
Sensuality among bulls and birds
  Increased — : 392.
Serpents : 111.
  Danger from — : 837.
  Pearls from — : 746.
Sesamum : 62, 119, 382, 414, 532.
—— treatment for soil : 527, 528.
Seven Classes of human beings : 190
Seven Sages : 134, 161, 398, 758.
Seven Seers
  Course of — : 161.
Sex of Child to be born : 443.
Sexual
  Act : 723.
  —— activities : 692, 700.
  —— Congress : 606, 725.
  —— craving does not subside : 690.
  Enjoyment of — pleasures : 810.
  Fond of — „ : 653, 701.
  —— guilt : 690.
  —— instinct of animals : 767.

—— union of human beings with sub-human species : 777.
—— union on even nights for male-birth : 727.
Sexual desire
Tokens of— : 720, 721.
Sexual relations to be shunned : 726.
Shanks : 602, 661, 669.
Short — : 633.
Shastri A. M. : 172.
Shave
When — is forbidden : 870.
Shaving
Exception in the case of— : 677.
She-buffaloes : 111.
Shepherds : 52, 103.
Shoulders
Hairy — : 613.
Śibi : 39, 60, 142, 212.
Siddhāntas : 9, 10.
Siddhāntaśiromaṇi : 12, 208.
Siddhasena : 230, 231.
Side-beams of cots : 735.
Sidereal : 9.
Sides
Fleshy — : 608.
Tender — : 610.
Siege
of a city : 159.
—— to be lifted : 80.
Sign
Natal — : 914.
—— of birth : 636.
Signs
Length of— : 852.
Rural — : 873.
Śikhariṇi : 152, 271, 272, 399, 435, 447, 448, 582, 688, 903.
Silver : 832.
Siṁha : 541.
Simhala : 119, 142.
Siṁhapura : 54.
Siṁhikā : 42.
Simile : 7, 18, 33, 143, 345, 368, 407, 409, 637, 638, 664, 698, 903, 917.
Homeric — : 878.
Sindhu : 39.
—— regions : 61, 104, 115, 215, 650.
—— Sauvira : 184.
Sinful activities : 635, 644.
Sinner : 20.
Sins
Committing — : 636.
Śirā : 475.
Śiśupāla : 142.
Śiśupālavadha : 110, 320.
Śiva, Lord : 41, 416, 599, 656, 692, 725.
Emblem of— : 561.
Śiva's Hosts : 539, 563, 566.
Six months
Rāhu's effects within — : 861.
Venus's ,, ,, — : 861.
Sixth house with Moon or Venus at marriage, bad : 894.
Skanda : 412.
Skandha : 1, 5.
Skandhaka : 920.
Skin : 633.
Glossy —: 640.
Thin — belongs to scholars : 640.
Slaves : 104, 610.
Sleeping above cows, elders forbidden : 497.
Śleṣa : 143, 154.
Slits of garments
Omens from — : 676-680.
Śloka : 18, 244, 436, 440, 441, 444, 448, 534, 536, 545, 677, 781, 814, 891, 921.
Sluice built of stones : 525.
Slump in market : 72.
Smiths : 51, 114, 352.
Smoke-wick : 718.
Smoky directions : 372.
Smṛti texts : 727.
Snake : 836.
—— moving towards traveller : 795.
Snake-Charmers : 101.
Snakes : 213, 220.
—— Causing trouble : 106.
—— Climbing down trees : 279.
Destruction of— : 115.
Sneezing : 842.
—— of the wealthy : 623.
Snigdhā : 651.
Snobbery : 925.
Social order being confused : 103.
Ṣoḍaśāśri : 541.
Soil suited to four classes : 487.
Solar disc.
Dark streak across — : 30.
Meteor striking — : 30.
Solar eclipse
—— following a lunar one : 68.
Magnitude and direction of— : 46.
Peculiarity of— : 44.
Solar flare : 26, 129.
Solar system : 10, 122.
Solar years in a Mahāyuga : 89.
Soldiers : 212.
Soles : 601, 660, 661, 666, 667.
Vertical lines on — : 654.
Solstice : 8, 10.
Correct method for fiinding — : 23.
Soma : 20, 521, 689.
—— sacrificers : 61.
Śoṇa river : 60.
Songs and ornaments
Fond of— : 644.
Sons : 640, 641.
—— and daughters : 616.
Son will be born : 831.
Soppu Koragas : 171.
Sorcerers : 186.
Sorcery : 20.

Soul
—— goes with mind : 694.
—— is reborn like a seed : 693.
Mystic seat of — : 695.
—— to be realized : 695.
Sound
Burning — : 814.
Full — : 814.
South
Countries in the — : 171.
South-East
Countries in the — : 169.
Southern country : 111.
Southward
Passing — : 205.
South-West
Countries in the — : 174.
Sovereignty
Bestows — : 800.
Space : 4.
Span of life : 14, 642, 643, 668.

Sparrows : 597, 701.
Speech full of courtesy : 664.
Sperm : 727.
Excess of — leads to male-birth : 699.
Loses — : 702.
Spies : 116, 201.
Spiritual
discipline : 221.
—— glory : 636.
—— light of Soul : 637.
—— peace undermined : 697.
—— vibrations : 416.
Spleen
Enemy of — : 513.
Spy : 768.
Śrāddha : 172.
One who eats at — : 788.
Sragdharā : 272, 447, 591, 594, 650, 827, 892, 901, 933.
Śravaṇa : 353, 864.
Rulership of — : 188.
—— with Vaṇik : 877.
Śrāvaṇa : 233, 243, 252.
Śrī : 323.
Śrīdravyavardhana : 757, 758.
Śrīkṛṣṇa : 162, 651.
Śrīparvata : 193.
Śrīpatipaddhati : 218.
Śrī Rāma : 555, 556, 687, 698, 700.
Śrī Rāma's body
Description of — : 607, 611, 625, 630.
Śṛṅgāra, most pleasing sentiment : 686.
Śṛṅgāraśataka of Bhartṛhari : 686.
Srughnas : 198.
Stages of life to be read from feet upwards : 673.
Star-gazer : 20.
Star of birth : 636.
Starry firmament : 54.
Stars
Disappearance of — : 379.
Sighting of — in the daytime : 392.
unfavourable — : 679.
Starvation : 792.
Danger from — : 383.
Stealing nature : 636.
Stein : 178, 182.
Stellar Circle of 4 divisions : 299.
Stellar Deity
Form of—with stars for limbs : 930.
Procedure for worshipping limbs of—: 931.
Worship of — : 930-934.
Sthālipāka : 377.
Sthira : 914.
Sticks have esoteric powers : 755.
Stomach
Raised — : 608.
—— trouble : 56.
Stone
for making images : 564, 749.
Stones
Methods for breaking — : 523, 524.
Precious — : 676, 737.
Storm : 31, 92.
Troubles from — : 809.
Stormy rains : 94.
Strength : 640.
Strirājya : 178, 194.
Subhadrikā : 905.
Subhāṣita : 645, 696, 697.
Substances : 4, 13.
Signs ruling over — : 332.
Śuddhavirāt : 40, 53.
Sudhākara Dvivedi : 572.
Śūdraka, King : 718.
Śūdras : 96, 103, 111, 404, 565, 841.
—— suffer from diseases : 58.
Suffering of the beautiful : 84.
Sugarcane : 92, 223.
Śukanāsopadeśa : 697.
Śukra : 6, 757, 758.
Śukti : 39.
Sukumāraka : 551.
Śūlikas : 103, 104, 116.
Sumha : 52, 168, 192.
Sun
becoming Ākranda : 208.
becoming Paura : 208.
becoming yāyin : 208.
—— Conferring blessings : 31.
Heated by the — : 489.
—— is represented by a circle : 636.
Misty ring around — : 30.
—— passing thro' Ārdrā : 280.
Rulership of — : 191.
—— Screened by clouds : 291.
Southerly and Northerly courses of—: 23.
The Divine — : 937.
Transit of — : 901, 902.
Sunday, good for gold, copper etc. : 923.
Sun-God : 1, 20, 22, 572.
Sun's

Bad effects of — year : 218.
—— natural colours in the seasons : 27.
—— rays leading to war and drought : 287.
Sun's halo : 293.
Sun-spots : 25, 129, 149.
Superstitions : 757.
Śūrasena : 166.
Śūrasenas : 52, 61, 102, 103, 118, 140, 211, 212, 655.
Surāṣṭra : 738.
Surat : 39, 115.
Surgeons : 63.
Sūryadeva Somasut : 351.
Sūryasiddhānta : 9, 11, 32, 33, 45, 107, 205, 208.
Sutee custom : 691.
Suttanipāta : 173.
Suvadanā : 902.
Suvarṇa : 745, 926.
Suvarṇabhū : 183.
Suvṛttā : 903.
Svāgatā : 80, 96, 153, 160, 360, 400, 448, 497, 523, 598, 650, 652, 907.
Svastika figures: 539, 616, 626, 679, 800.
Svāti : 16, 237, 243, 262-264.
Rulership of — : 187.
—— with Kiṁstughna : 877.
Śvetaketu : 861.
Swords : 16, 426-431.
Dents on— : 426.
—— drinks : 430.
Shapes of— : 427.
unguent for — : 431.
Śyāmākas : 181.
Symbolism
Ṛgvedic — : 156.
Symmetrical body : 889.
Symposium, "On the History of Sciences of India" : 486.
Symptoms of conception of clouds : 234, 235.

T

Table of contents of this Śāstra : 938-942.
Tail of cow : 836.
Tailors : 116.
Takṣaka and Vāsuki,
Lineage of — : 746.
Takṣaśilā : 104, 116, 180.
Tālas : 177.
Tale-bearer and poet : 658.
Talk of troops as omen : 14.
Tāmarasa : 276, 804, 910.
Tāmasakīlaka
Effects of — : 24, 25, 237, 861.
Tamas, belongs to Mars and Saturn : 648, 649.
Tāmbūla : 718.
Tāmralipti : 117.
Taṅgaṇas : 103, 117, 182, 194, 213, 300
Tank : 527, 536.
Rectangular — for water : 524, 525.
Tantra : 5, 687.
Tantrāntara : 466, 467, 498, 544, 871.
Tantrasamuccaya of Kerala : 486.
Tārāgrahas : 10.
Tartary
Highland of — : 179.
Tastes being spoiled : 69.
Tattvabodhinī : 116.
Taurus : 52.
Tearing of shoes and clothes : 17.
Teeth : 653, 664.
Antya — : 594
Auspicious — : 619.
Central — : 594
Incisor — : 594
——, sign of horse's age : 593.
Small — : 635.
Thin — 633.
Temple-architecture : 16.
Temples : 626, 651, 830.
Construction of — : 546, 547.
Description of — : 537-545.
Dimensions of — : 538.
Door-keepers of — : 539.
Door of — : 539
——for different communities : 538.
Gardens near — : 537.
Height of — to be double the width: 539.
Site of—to be of 64 squares : 538.
Twenty types of — : 539, 541.
Walls of — : 539 :
Worship in — : 572.
Tenth house, with Mercury, Jupiter and Venus, good at marriage : 895.
Territories
Destruction of — : 144.
Testicle : 604, 636.
Theft : 792.
—— of cattle : 792.
Prediction of — : 440.
Thief
Crying "Thief ! Stop !" : 691.
Thieves : 40, 54, 57, 59, 103, 115, 116, 128, 403, 438, 439, 621, 623, 624, 787, 809, 844, 905.
Thighs : 448, 658, 661.
Thomas Heath : 144.
Three horizontal lines on the fore-head : 627.
Throat-disease : 112.
Throbbing of limbs : 14, 449.
Throne of gold : 416.
Thumb
Lines at the root of — : 616, 636, 668.
Root of—like altar : 616.
— with yava : 614.
Thunder : 46.
Portentous — : 862.

Thunder-bolt : 904, 912.
Thursday, good for gold, silver, horses, herbs etc. : 927.
Tīkṣṇamaṇḍala : 105.
Tilak, B. G. 398.
Tilottamā : 692.
Timber : 497, 524, 730, 732-734, 736.
Excellent — : 362, 684.
Time : 4, 432.
measurement of — : 9, 10.
—— of birth : 636.
—— of impregnation and birth : 14.
Tirade against quacks : 12.
Tithi : 9, 14.
Tithis
Nandā and other — : 346.
—— of Venus's rising and setting : 109.
Tobacco : 718.
Tocharians : 194.
Toddy-seller : 438.
Toe : 553.
Big — : 435, 440, 449.
Little — not touching the ground : 669.
Toes : 635, 660.
Toilet powder : 710.
Tongue
Reddish — : 620, 633.
Tonics for increasing sperm : 699.
Tooth
—— decay : 716, 717.
Powder : 716.
—— sticks : 716, 717, 754-756.
—— troubles : 754.
Tortoises
Back of — : 597, 601. 661.
Features of — : 16, 583, 584.
Toṭaka : 153, 157, 255, 279, 398, 576, 880, 914.
Tourists 187, 629.
Toxins : 717.
Trade : 653.
—— guilds : 85.
Traders : 107, 112, 116, 118, 189.
—— luck : 284.
Tradition
Indian — : 833, 865.
Traditional sources : 759.
Traducers needed : 936.
Tragic end
To meet with — : 622.
Tranquil
direction : 756.
movements : 774.
Sound : 800.
Transit effects.
Time of fruition of — : 918.
Transmigration of Soul : 758.
Transplantation : 527.
Travellers : 108, 786.
Death of — : 775.
—— will have danger : 831.
Traveller's ear : 835, 836.
Travels : 907.
Treacherous : 621.
Treasure : 371, 509.
Treasury : 195, 454, 455.
Tree
Arjuna — : 833.
Asterism for planting — : 535.
Banyan — : 519.
Bilva — : 616, 666, 679, 733.
Celestial — : 450.
Date — with two tops : 510, 520.
Desert — : 516.
Holy Fig — : 519.
Jujube — : 502, 813, 823.
Mokṣaka — : 523.
Rotang — : 500.
Śami — : 515, 516.
Thorny — : 829, 837, 846.
Worship of — : 566.
Trees : 564, 565, 677, 784.
Direction of — : 565.
Distance between — : 530.
—— for beds : 729.
—— for house-construction : 496.
—— for images : 565.
Forbidden — : 484, 564, 729.
—— growing on moist soil : 530.
Milky — : 826, 833.
Symptoms of diseases of — : 531.
Treatment of — : 527-535.
—— uprooted by winds : 111.
—— with red flowers : 95.
Worship—before grafting : 530.
Triads of stars
Nine — : 184.
Tribal chiefs : 39.
Tribes : 60.
Trigarta : 39, 104, 117, 180, 198, 211.
Triṁśāṁśa : 13.
Trinity : 1.
Triple Śāstra : 1.
Tripura : 53.
Triṣṭubh : 314, 402.
Troops
Marching — : 108.
Trouble to people : 27.
Trumpeting like thunder : 597.
Trunk
Round — : 597.
Trunks of elephants : 613, 661.
Truṭi : 8.
Tuesday, good for gold, mines, corals etc.: 925.
Tumult : 40.
Turmeric : 415.
Turpentine : 711, 714.
Turret : 370.
Tuṣāras : 177.
Tusked animals
Trouble from — : 70, 96.
Tusks : 733, 734.
Glossy — : 597.

Tvaṣṭā : 24, 861.
Twelfth house with Mercury, Jupiter and Venus at marriage, good : 895.
Twelfth lunar day : 353.
Twigs
  unknown — : 754.
Twilights : 16, 285, 289, 290, 392, 400, 402, 776, 861.
Twin flower or fruit : 381.
Twins : 728.
Tyranny of kings : 55.

U

Uddālaka : 123.
Uddehika : 166, 167.
Udgatā : 918.
Uḍra : 213.
Uḍudīpta : 763, 776.
Udumbara : 53, 166.
Ujjain : 657.
Ujjayinī : 118, 141, 157.
Ujjihāna : 165.
Ulcers : 449.
—— in the limb : 847.
Umbrellas : 616, 733, 780, 863.
  Cylindrical rod of — : 685.
  Diameter of — : 684.
  Height of — of ordinary citizens : 685.
  Height of — of state officials : 685.
  Signs of — : 684, 685.
Unfortunate : 621, 888.
Unguents : 524, 571, 591, 594.
Union of man and woman : 719-728.
  —— as a spiritual act : 726.
Universal love : 697.
Universe
  born of union of male and female : 692.
  Material cause of — : 4.
Unnamed source : 607-611.
Unrest : 119.
Upagīti : 918.
Upajāti : 6, 39, 61-63, 88, 94, 95, 155, 159, 190, 214, 215, 250, 267, 276, 293, 345, 352, 358, 360, 395, 399, 431, 435, 500, 521, 522, 534, 566, 574, 595, 634, 643, 644, 649, 652, 654-656, 658, 659, 662, 665, 672, 678, 681, 686, 696, 699, 706, 720, 747, 754, 782, 801, 809, 814, 818, 820, 828, 841, 844, 859, 872, 899, 905, 932.
Upajyotiṣa : 166.
Upamā : 154.
Upaniṣads : 230.
Uparandhra : 593.
Uparicaravasu : 346.
Upasthitā : 402.
Upendravajrā : 53, 119, 213, 295, 587, 668, 700, 819, 820, 841, 844, 859, 904.
Upper cloth : 678.
Upstarts : 697.
Ūrdhvadaṇḍa : 105.
Urinate noisily : 605.
Urine : 605.
Ūrmimālā : 916.
Ursa Major : 16.
Uśīnara : 39.
Uśīnaras
  King of — : 140.
Uṣṇik : 40.
Utpala : 115, 123, 143, 159, 180, 190, 199, 204, 207, 210, 218, 315, 379, 383, 388, 400, 432, 447, 450, 451, 453-455, 459, 464, 465, 472, 485, 491, 499, 512, 523, 534, 535, 540, 543-545, 547, 550, 551, 561, 566, 570, 573, 575, 577, 578, 583, 599, 602, 605, 608, 610, 611, 624, 633, 640, 643, 667, 681, 682, 684, 690, 697, 698, 701-703, 707, 708, 726, 728, 731, 733, 738, 755, 758, 768, 770, 778, 780, 797, 815, 819, 826, 827, 831, 835, 848, 853, 859, 871, 872, 888, 938, 941.
——'s mother tongue : 913.
Utprekṣā : 155.
Utsavasaṅketas : 192.
Uttarābhādrapada : 237.
  Rulership of — : 189.
Uttarakālāmṛta : 194.
Uttaraṇe : 524.
Uttaraphalguni
  Rulership of — : 187.
  —— with Taitila : 877.
Uttarāṣāḍhā
  Rulership of — : 188.
  —— triad : 177.

V

Vāhika country : 142, 178.
Vāhlikas : 63, 102.
Vaidhṛti : 882.
Vaidyaka Text : 707.
Vaikhānasa system : 932.
Vaiśākha : 234, 235, 392, 829.
Vaiśeṣika system : 4.
Vaiśvadevī : 916.
Vaiśvānara : 105.
Vaiśyas : 96, 116, 404, 565.
  Harm to — : 58.
Vaitālīya : 40, 52, 191, 204, 215, 277, 306, 360, 371, 372, 399, 573, 597, 816, 822, 920, 922.
Vajra : 205, 230, 616.
Vaktra : 921.
Vālmīki : 409, 537, 538, 611, 625, 674, 691, 694, 700, 921.
  —— Rāmāyaṇa : 630.
  ——'s verse : 345.
Value of π : 480.
Vāmana : 587, 598.
Vāmanaka : 657.
Vaṁśa : 473.

Vaṁśapatrapatita : 915.
Vaṁśastha : 110, 156, 251, 325, 368, 433, 652, 710, 812, 823, 906.
Vāṇa flower : 154.
Vane
Mechanical — : 251.
Vaṅga : 102, 117, 212, 300.
Vaprakrīḍā : 827.
Varāhamihira : 1, 5, 98, 99, 105, 119, 162, 166, 174, 176, 181, 183, 198, 217, 390, 395, 405, 432, 464, 466, 479, 498, 517, 520, 523, 528, 572, 576, 580, 600, 659, 672, 691, 720, 725, 736, 757, 758, 860, 923, 929, 941.
——'s catholicity : 20.
—— 's Scientific attitude : 23, 42, 45, 48.
Vārāṇaseya Edition: 199, 442, 563, 679, 691, 788, 797, 885.
Vārāṇasī : 406.
Vararuci : 588, 591, 592, 594, 630, 632.
Vardhamāna : 679, 733.
Vargas : 13.
—— of seven Sages : 163.
Varṇas
Rulership of — : 190.
Vārttika : 118.
Varuṇa : 561, 845.
——'s circle : 302, 305.
Vasantatilakā : 13, 39, 41, 53, 54, 61-63, 120, 143, 156-158, 159, 218, 352, 359, 360, 395, 402, 427, 431, 522, 526, 545, 597, 600, 634, 637-639, 657, 661, 693, 700, 717, 720, 750, 784, 800, 824, 842, 845, 870, 880, 892, 912, 936.
Vasātis : 180, 212.
Vasiṣṭha : 9, 20, 43, 163, 231, 244, 297, 551, 937.
Vāsiṣṭha
Lineage of — : 61.
Vāstuvidyā of Bhaṭṭotpala : 473.
Vāstuviśvakarmaprakāśa : 465, 475.
Vāsudeva, Lord
Devoted to — : 657.
Vātadhāna : 180, 198.
Vātadīpta : 763, 775.
Vātamaṇḍala : 105.
Vātāpi : 152.
Vātormī : 400, 755, 916.
Vatsa : 115, 166, 212.
Vātsyāyana : 178.
Vāyupurāṇa : 171.
Vedas : 3, 230, 419, 497.
Ancillary of — : 22.
Vedasmṛti : 200.
Vedha : 710, 714, 901.
Vedic
Authority : 690.
Chants : 2, 219, 222.
hymns : 350, 357, 358, 362, 366, 570, 766, 782.
literature : 387.
Mantras : 416.
period : 398.
recitation : 865.
scholars : 62, 187, 422, 602.
Studies : 221.
texts : 5, 12.
Vedic lore
Rich heritage of — : 638.
Vegetable kingdom : 708.
Vehicles : 39, 112, 380.
Vein
Great — : 500.
Veins : 603, 604, 635, 644.
Full of — : 610, 612, 622, 626.
Venā river : 40.
Veṇumatī river : 177.
Venus : 5, 280, 846.
Circles of — : 102.
—— Conferring blessings : 113.
—— cutting the lunar orb : 39.
Glossiness, derived from — : 647.
Good effects of —'s year : 223.
Planets ahead of — : 111.
——represented by a Quadrilateral : 636.
Rulership of — : 199.
Transit of — : 911-913.
Verandah
Sarvatobhadra — : 460.
Verse
Musical — : 651.
Vessels
Painted — : 116.
Vetāla : 659.
Victory
—— of kings : 36.
Signs of — : 208, 209.
Vidarbha : 106.
Videha : 53, 61, 103, 104.
Vidiśā : 118.
Vidūratha, King
Murder of — : 719.
Vidyādharas : 106, 111, 164.
Vidyunmālā : 401, 656.
Vikaṭa : 598.
Vikrama era : 162, 181.
Vikramorvaśīya : 688.
Vikṣepa : 214.
Vilambitagati : 906.
Vilāsa : 919.
Vilāsinī : 912.
Village to be destroyed : 777.
Vimānacchanda : 541.
Vindhya Range : 118, 152, 153.
Vindhyavāsin : 6, 892.
Vinegar : 706.
Vipulā : 920, 929.
Vīrabhadra : 43.
Virāṭa : 39, 52.
Virgins : 116.
Virgo : 53.
Virodhābhāsa : 154.
Virtues and physical features : 7.

Vi:tues attain eminence : 698.
Virtuous men : 52, 53, 187.
Viśākhā : 243, 400.
Rulership of — : 187.
Viṣamavṛtta : 919.
Viṣṇu : 20, 42, 143, 188, 377, 412, 571, 599, 768, 790.
Viṣṇucandra, Ācārya : 216.
Viṣṇugupta : 13.
Viṣṇuloka : 933.
Viṣṇupada
Glory of — : 934.
Viṣṇupurāṇa : 199.
Viṣṇu's worship : 572.
Viṣṭi karaṇa : 846.
Viśvakarman : 377, 464, 465, 478, 481, 497, 544, 730, 731, 736.
Viśvakarmavāstuśāstra : 450.
Viśvanātha : 723, 724.
Viśvavallabha of Cakrapāṇimiśra : 531.
Vitality : 651.
Vital substances : 640.
Vīthis : 98-101, 228.
Vitiation of Dhātus : 75.
Vivāhapaṭala : 6, 892-895.
Vivṛti : 1, 929.
Viyoginī : 22, 52, 259, 276, 634, 655, 675, 800.
Voice
Agreeable — : 717.
Deep — : 633.
—— Similar to sound of elephants : 639.
Sweet — : 655.
Vowels assigned to the Sun : 859.
Vṛddhagarga : 6, 28-30, 35-38, 46, 49, 50, 67, 69, 74, 76, 77, 79, 86, 124, 133, 161-164, 206, 214, 139, 297, 405, 406, 409, 411, 417, 759.
Vṛṣa : 541.
Vṛṣabhacarita : 904.
Vṛtra : 157, 738.
Vṛtta : 520, 541, 898, 899.
Vṛttaratnākara : 155, 315, 323, 699, 807, 903, 905, 906, 910-912, 914, 916, 917, 919, 921.
Vulnerable
—— parts : 475.
—— points : 473.
Vultures : 838, 863.
Vyālamārga : 105.
Vyāsa : 405, 587, 697, 725, 871.
Vyatīpāta : 882.
Vyatirekālaṁkāra : 686.

W

Wagtails : 16, 369-372.
Colours, names and effects of — : 369.
Wain of Rohiṇī being cut by Venus : 105
Waist -607.
—— girth : 634, 656.
Slender — : 654.
—— with three folds : 663.
Wakhan : 115, 176.
Wanderers : 629.
War : 159, 403.
Conditions for — : 286.
Dangerous — : 401.
Devastating — : 379.
—— of planets : 6, 10, 16, 205, 206.
—— presaged : 29, 30, 36.
—— veterans : 117.
Warding off evil caused by eclipse : 67.
War-mongers : 39, 119.
Warriors : 52, 60, 188, 211.
Wars : 58, 78, 86, 92, 95, 111, 112, 120, 132, 135, 139, 207, 839.
Washermen : 115, 119, 188, 722.
Watch : 8.
Watches of the day : 759.
Water : 507-509, 515, 519.
—— appliances : 10, 12.
Brackish — : 504.
Directions of — : 496.
—— first creation : 3.
—— in desert areas : 511, 516.
Inexhaustible — : 522.
Jambū, indicator of — : 501, 520.
Plenty of — : 55.
—— products : 54.
Proof against — : 525.
Purification methods of — : 525, 526.
Scarcity of — : 404.
Rain — : 499.
Sources of — : 499.
Sweet — : 521.
Tastes of — : 500.
Teachers of Science of — : 499.
Trouble to — : 116.
Water-divination : 16, 499-526.
Water-sport
Haṁsa loves — : 655.
Water veins : 499, 500, 504, 505, 507-509, 511, 513.
Watery
—— asterism : 845.
—— grave : 604.
—— nature : 643, 650.
—— Signs : 274, 845.
Weaknesses
Śaśa knows others' — : 654.
Wealth : 104, 640, 641.
Abundant — : 835, 836.
—— amassed : 688.
Immense — : 661, 663, 664.
Lords of — : 119.
Loss of — : 638.
Wealthy : 658.
Weapons : 834, 837.
Poisoned — : 53.
Risk from — : 70, 94.
To meet one's end by — : 611-613.
Wielders of — : 54.
Wearer

Disease or Death to — : 678.
Weather conditions
Change of — : 382.
Weavers : 187, 722.
Wednesday, good for drama, gems, perfumes etc : 925.
Weekday : 3, 14.
Weeping
Auspicious — : 626.
Weight : 642.
—— of Haṁsa : 655.
—— of men : 600.
Weights
Table of — : 740.
Weights and measures : 266, 532.
Persons in charge of — : 119.
Welfare of people
to be moderate : 85.
Wells : 547.
Asterism for sinking — : 526.
—— bad in S. E., S. W., & N. W. : 519.
Destruction of — : 62.
Sinking of — : 107.
West
Countries in the — : 176.
Western border : 61.
Western country : 112.
Whales : 153.
Pearls from — : 746.
Wheels : 652.
—— on finger-tips : 636.
Whirlwind : 831.
Wicked : 114.
Widows : 119, 201, 547.
Wife :
Amiable and jolly — : 887.
generous — : 888.
Wild animals
Behaviour of — : 818.
Wilson, Alexander : 149, 199.
Wind-circle : 270, 299, 306.
Winds : 16.
Layers of — : 746.
Wine : 380.
Winnowing basket : 601.
Winter
—— jackals get passion for mating in — : 814.
—— Solstice : 745.
Witch-craft : 689.
Wives
Many — : 640.
Wolf, Rudolf, Dr. : 149.
Woman :
—— breathing in unison with man : 726.
—— is a gem : 688.
—— of phlegmatic and rheumatic constitution is bad : 726.
—— of wicked nature : 726.
—— with abiding love : 726.
—— with squint eyes is wicked : 670.
Womb
Foetus on the right side of — : 728.
Women : 60, 118.
—— are like pure gold : 689.
—— are to be guarded : 723.
Cynical — : 688.
Excellences of — : 724.
Features of — : 16, 669.
Flaws of — : 688.
Gems of — : 724.
—— Goddesses of Fortune : 688.
Miserable — : 669.
Moon etc. gave — purity etc. : 689.
—— of high class : 52, 62.
Praise of — : 686-692.
—— traduced by men : 688.
Vanquished by — : 658.
Wood
Blemishes of — : 735.
—— for making images : 564.
Wooden affliction : 474.
Works on journey, horoscopy and astronomy : 942.
World to perish : 399.
Worship
—— of Agastya : 158.
—— of Deities : 158.
—— of Mahendra and Indrāṇi : 391.
—— of tree, abode of Piṅgalā : 804.
Worshipper of Deity : 788.
Wrestlers : 52, 53, 112, 188.
Wrists : 614.
—— joints : 667.
Lines going up from — : 616.
Writers : 62, 116, 197.
Writing materials : 781.

Y

Yājñavalkya : 793.
Yakṣas : 377, 393, 413, 659.
Worship of — : 14.
Yama : 482, 778.
Śaśa goes to ——'s abode : 654.
Yamaka : 153.
Yamunā : 166.
Yāska : 141, 157, 174, 241.
Yathāsaṁkhya : 345.
Yātrā : 14, 15, 351, 365, 411, 413, 830, 942.
—— of Siddhārtha : 922, 923.
Ṭikaṇikā — : 351.
Yaudheyas : 40, 53, 60, 62, 102, 181, 198, 212.
Yavakṣāra : 703.
Yavanas : 20, 39, 63, 104, 108, 115, 118, 164, 192, 215, 217.
Yavaneśvara : 218-224, 848, 873, 902, 904, 906, 908, 911, 914, 916, 919, 923-928.
Yāyin : 208, 209.
Year : 8, 9.
Body of — : 87.

Commencement of — : 28.
Jupiter's effects within a — : 861.
Lord of — : 16.
Rāhu's effects within a — : 861.
Saturn's effect within a — : 861.
Years
Effects of — : 217.
Yellow objects : 112.
Yellow orpiment : 522.
Yield
Increasing — : 532.
Yoga : 2, 13, 14, 650.
Lunar — : 14.
Mahāpuruṣa — : 647.
Nābhasa — : 14.
Proficiency in — : 636.
Yogatārā : 248, 351, 365, 871.
Yogic Slumber of Viṣṇu : 361.
Yogins : 22, 694.
Yojanas
Motion of planets in — : 11.
Yoke : 36.
Yuan Chwang : 181, 183.
Yudhiṣṭhira : 161, 698.
Yuga : 8-10, 92, 95.
Lords of — : 90.
Yugandhara : 301.

Z

Zodiac
Division of — into Signs : 890, 891.
Signs of — : 2, 5, 11, 13, 14, 403.
Zodiacal Signs
Lords of — : 647.